AMERICA'S
Quarter Horses

Also by the author

THE THIRSTY PONY

MUSTANG ROUNDUP

AMERICA'S
Quarter Horses

PAUL LAUNE

Illustrated with photographs
and with drawings by the author

1973

DOUBLEDAY & COMPANY, INC.
GARDEN CITY, NEW YORK

To my wife Irene and son Paul,
who waited patiently at the gate
while I rounded up these horses.

ISBN: 0-385-04404-6
Library of Congress Catalog Number 72-89327
Copyright © 1973 by Paul Laune
All Rights Reserved
Printed in the United States of America
9 8 7 6 5 4 3 2

Contents

1. The Horse the West Made	1
The Coronado and De Soto Horses	2
Horse Before the Motor Age	3
Horse Census	12
2. Backtracking the Quarter Horse	14
The Hot-bloods	16
The Cold-bloods	19
Building the British Breeds	20
The Spanish Horse in North America	24
The First Quarter Horses	31
Patriarchs of the Quarter Horse Breed	34
Janus (1746–79)	37
The Horse Experimenters	44
The Cowhorse	48
3. Founding Families	54
PRINTER I	56
COPPERBOTTOM	56
SHILOH	57
STEEL DUST	58
OLD BILLY	62
COLD DECK	63
ROAN DICK	65
LOCK'S RONDO	66
TRAVELER	67
SYKES RONDO	69
OLD FRED	69
PETER MCCUE	71
THE BLAKE HORSES	76
JOE BAILEY	77
LITTLE JOE	78
ZANTANON	79
OLD SORREL	81
DELLA MOORE	84
The Foundation Sires of the AQHA	86
KING P–234	101
POCO BUENO P–3044	103
MAJOR KING	104
The Seven-Eighths Thoroughbred	107
4. In Search of Your Own Quarter Horse	109
Horse Prices	114
Other Costs	115
A Gelding, a Mare, or a Stallion	115
Age	116
Size	118
Color	119
Buing a Grade Horse	121
Buying a Registered Horse	122
A Bargain Horse	124
What a Judge Looks for in a Quarter Horse	126
Conformation	126
Blemishes	128
Auctions	129
How to Be Introduced to a Horse	130

Temperament	131	**7. Feeding and Grooming**	178
		Feeding	178
5. Stables and Corrals	135	Hay	178
Layout	136	Alfalfa Pellets	180
Floor Plan	136	Grain	181
Box Stalls	138	Cane Molasses	182
Tie Stalls	139	Creep Feeding	182
Construction	139	Feeding for Trophies	182
Mangers and Feed Buckets	141	Carrots, Apples, and Turnips	183
Brackets and Hooks	142	Water	183
Flooring	143	Feed Bags	183
Feed Room	143	Poisonous Plants	184
Tack Room	145	Starving Horses	185
Grooming Area	146	Grooming	185
Medicine Cabinet	147	Blankets and Clipping	190
Doors, Locks, and Latches	147		
Water	148	**8. Feet and Shoeing**	192
Lights and Electric Outlets	149	Shoes and Shoeing	192
The Corral	151	Navicular Disease and Shoeing	195
The Manure Pile	152	Contracted Heels	197
Bedding	154	Corns	197
Rubber Mats	154	Founder and Laminitis	198
Straw	155	Grain Founder	198
Dried Sugar Cane and		Water Founder	198
Peanut Hulls	155	Road Founder	200
Wood Shavings and Sawdust	155	First Aid	200
Peat Moss	155	Treatment	200
Insect and Pest Control	155	Seedy Toe	201
Brands and Silks	158	Ringbone	201
Barn Dogs and Cats	159	Faults of Movement	202
		Forging	202
6. The Nature of the Beast	160	Speed Cutting, Scalping,	
Temperament	162	and Crossfiring	203
Intelligence and Reasoning	163	Brushing	204
The Eye	164	Paddling	204
Ears and Hearing	166	Toeing-in	204
The Heart	167	Cracked Hoof	204
Muscles and Skin	167	Shoes for Performance Horses	205
Sense of Smell	169		
Stomach and Digestive System	170	**9. Ailments, Their Symptoms,**	
Feet	171	**Causes, and Treatment**	208
Teeth	171	When to Call the Veterinarian	210
Life-span	174	First Aid for Injuries	210

Digestive Ailments	212	Broken Wind	227
Azoturia	212	Choke	227
Colic	213	Coughs and Colds	227
Founder	213	Equine Influenza	227
Impaction	214	Pneumonia	227
Eye Injuries and Disease	214	Heaves	227
Injuries—Abrasions, Cuts, Lacerations, Punctures, and Bruises	214	Skin Eruptions	228
		Hives	228
		Teeth	228
Capped Elbow or Shoe Boil	215	Floating	228
Galls	216	Wolf Teeth	229
Selfast	216	Methods of Treatment and the Medicine Cabinet	229
Mutilation	216		
Fistulas and Tumors	216	Bandaging	230
Contagious and Infectious Diseases	218	Blistering	230
		Cold Packs and Cold Water	230
Strangles (Distemper) and Glanders	218	Drenching	230
		Enemas	231
Encephalomy Elitis (Sleeping Sickness)	218	Liniments	231
		Pills	231
Swamp Fever (Malaria)	219	Pinfiring	231
Tetanus	219	Massage	231
Internal Parasites	220	Treating Wounds	231
Environmental Ailments	222	Twitch	231
Heatstroke or Sunstroke	222		
Shipping Fever	222	**10. Horse and Riding Equipment**	**234**
Legs, Feet, and Lameness	223		
Bog Spavin	223	Equipment for Training	235
Bone Spavin	223	Clothing for the Horse	235
Bowed Tendons	223	Saddles—English	235
Bursitis	224	Saddles—Western	238
Chapped Heels	224	The Horn and Western Riding	244
Curb	224	Stirrups	245
Fracture	224	Tapaderos	245
Sidebone	225	Cinches and Girths	246
Splints	225	Breast Straps	246
Stringhalt	225	Spurs	247
Thoroughpin	225	Bits	249
Thrush	226	Snaffle	250
Windgall	226	Curb	251
Wounds		Pelham	251
Lungs, Throat, and Respiratory Ailments	226	The Hackamore	251

Martingales	255	Tying	304
The Standing Martingale	255	LungeTraining	305
The Running Martingale	256	Driving with Long Reins	306
Draw Reins	256	Hackamore Training	307
Whips, Bats, Quirts, Romals	258	Head Setting	307
Hobbles	260	Saddling and Riding the	
Ropes	261	Green Horse	308
Care of Tack	264	Backing Up	311
Riding Clothes and Accessories	264	The Sliding Stop, Pivot, Spin,	
English Style	264	and Roll Over the Hocks	311
Western Style	266	Training the Quarter Horse	
11. Riding and		Jumper	315
** Horsemanship**	270	The Saddle	318
Saddling and Bridling	270	The Bridle	318
Mounting the English Saddle	272	Riding the Jumper	325
Mounting the Stock Saddle	274	Crop and Spurs	326
Riding the Forward Seat	276	The Show or Open Jumper	327
Riding Western Style	277	The Working Hunter	329
Reins and Bits and Ways of		Training the Cutting Horse	331
Using Them	279	Training the Roping Horse	335
Riding with Slack Reins	281	Riding and Training the	
Flat Saddle Riding and		Barrel Horse	342
Reining	283	Training for Pole Bending	
The Gaits	284	and Stake Racing	342
The Walk	284	Training for the Reining and	
The Jog Trot	284	Working Cowhorse	
The Fox Trot	285	Contest	343
The Single-foot	285	Training for the Western	
The Rack	285	Pleasure and the Trail	
The Trot	285	Horse Class	344
The Canter	286	To Show or Not to Show—	
Changing Leads at the		A Summary of Training	346
Canter or Lope	287	Traveling with Your Horse	347
The Flat Saddle Rider	287	**13. Bad Habits and Vices**	
Collection	289	** and Their Corection**	350
Cold Weather Riding	290	Barn Sour	350
Safe Ways of Handling		Biting	351
Your Horse	292	Bolting or Running Away	353
How to Say "No"	297	Carrying Head Too High	354
12. Training Methods	299	Cribbing	355
Training the Colt	302	Gulping Down Feed	356
Handling the Feet	304		

Jiggling, Head Tossing, and Tail Wringing	356
Kicking	358
Moving When Mounting	360
Pulling Back on the Lead	362
Rearing	364
Refusing the Bit, Hard to Bridle	366
Shying and Head Shyness	367
Tail Rubbing	368
Weaving	368
Orneriness in General	369

14. Racing Quarter Horses 371
Grading and Qualification Standard	372
Among the Winners	375
Breeding for Speed	388
Reunion of Runners	390
Three Bars (1940–68)	390
Leo (1940–)	395
AQHA World Record Holders	400

15. Shows and Contests 402
Register of Merit	404
AQHA Champions	405
AQHA Supreme Champions	407
The Point System	408
Horse Show Judges	415
Classes and Contests	415
Halter Classes	415
Working Cowhorse Contest	418
Reining Contest	420
Trail Horse Class	423
Western Riding Horse Contest	425
AQHA English Pleasure Class	426
Western Pleasure Class	427
AQHA Jumping Class	427
Working Hunter Class	429
Calf Roping	430
Team Tying and Dally Team Roping	432
Barrel Racing Contest	432
Pole Bending	434
AQHA Polo Pony Class	434
Quarter Horse Polo Ponies	431
Broom Polo	440
Training the Polo Pony	440
Small Shows	440

16. Partners in Big Business 442
All-Time Rodeo Greats	444
Roping	445
Steer Roping	446
Calf Roping	446
Team Roping	449
Famous Roping Quarter Horses	450
Steer Wrestling	454
Cutting Horse Contests	460
Great Cutting Horses	463
Bronc Riding	466
Saddle Bronc Riding	469
Bareback Bronc Riding	474
The Broncs	476
Bull Riding	478
The Clowns	481
Girls Rodeo Association	482

17. Youth in the Saddle 485
Youth Activities Programs	485
Youth AQHA Champion	489
Showmanship at Halter	490
The Stake Race	490
4-H Clubs and Other Riding Clubs	491
National High School Rodeo Association	494
National Intercollegiate Rodeo Association	495
Vaulting and Drill Teams	497

18. **Trail Rides**	500	**D.** Spanish and Mexican Color Terms for Horses	542
19. **Roundup**	510	**E.** Spanish and Mexican Horse, Ranch, and Southwestern Terms	543
Appendix A. Genealogical Charts	517		
B. Early Western Studs	527		
C. Contributors to the Quarter Horse Branch of the Thoroughbreds	529	**Glossary**	545

AMERICA'S
Quarter Horses

1

The Horse the West Made

This book is not only for those who have to ask, "Just what is a Quarter Horse?" but also for those who love to ride and train and care for horses, and who want to know more about America's most versatile breed of saddle horse—a breed whose genes, blended from many horse tribes, have produced in the last thirty years well over 700,000 pedigreed American Quarter Horses, more than the registered horses of all other American breeds combined.

In this book I parade the horses of the world in order to draw attention to those that turned into the side paths that led, after many wanderings, into a peculiarly American breed, the Quarter Horse.

"What is the Quarter Horse?" Well, it all depends. To paraphrase the late Stanley Walker, the native Texan editor of the New York *Journal,* when asked about his home state, a truthful answer would be, "He's whatever you had in mind."

The American Quarter Horse Association came into being in 1940, and its first registry was opened in 1941 with 105 stallions (the first 19 of which to be given numbers were designated its foundation sires) and 451 mares, a total of 556 horses which had been chosen during 1940 to become the charter members of a new breed. In selecting 556 individuals, a singular parallel in Southwestern history was made. It so happened that exactly 400 years earlier, in 1540, the muster rolls of the Coronado Expedition showed precisely that number of horses, 556, the first horses (since the glacial age) to put a hoofprint above the Rio Grande.

Although none of the animals in the earlier group remained north of the Rio Grande to contribute to the later breed, many of their Mexican descendants eventually returned to do so.

The Coronado and De Soto Horses

Contrary to the romancing about the origins of wild horses of the West, none were descended from the Coronado or De Soto expeditions. All the Coronado horses except those that died or were killed by Indians returned to Mexico. Coronado's brown stallion, his favorite among the seven in his own string, was still going strong when Coronado rode him back into Mexico City at the head of a column of rather dejected horsemen whose exploration and fruitless search for gold had lasted almost three years. Nor were there any horse survivors of the De Soto wanderings in Florida, Georgia, Alabama, Mississippi, Arkansas, and Oklahoma. The forebears of our Quarter Horses came from other sources, which we'll get to.

But in my boyhood and youth in Woodward, Oklahoma, I rode the same plains that Coronado and his knights are supposed to have crossed, often imagining I was riding in their very tracks. In a way I have been working subconsciously on this book ever since those impressionable years when horses were such an important part of our daily lives, when they weren't primarily for pleasure or for show but were used from morning till night. Ranchers, cowboys, sheriffs, doctors, lawyers, judges, merchants, newspaper editors, bankers, school children and the teachers, in fact almost everyone was on a horse or being pulled by horses daily. The general concern with horses was comparable to the then growing preoccupation with cars. Models and types and sizes of horses were discussed and studied. Speed, power, and general performance were tested and compared. But there was a world of difference between the handling of a hay burner and a gasoline burner. Transcending the mechanics of transportation was an awareness, in the case of horses, of dealing with living, breathing personalities that could arouse in the owner and trainer the full range of emotions from affection and admiration to frustration, quick anger, and even deep antipathy. A vast body of information, misinformation, and lore of horses was bound to accumulate. Anticipating Freud, we all indulged our bent for analysis by practicing on horses—a much better pastime, it seems to me, than practicing on friends.

My own judgment about horses and what constitutes the ideal size, conformation, breeding, and best methods of schooling may have changed through the years, but love of the beasts and my interest in them as creatures with a unique relationship with people have remained constant.

Horses Before the Motor Age

Horses, simply by being there and sharing in almost everything we did, presented a drama of action with a kind of beauty of its own. It was a compelling, unforgettable association with superathletes who lent us speed and prowess and an extra set of muscles at the touch of a spur or the flip of a rein.

Horses, hitched along Main Street, received salutations from passersby who knew them and identified them with their owners. The horses were personalities. Stories about their behavior during actions that ranged from high comedy to sheer heroics were well enough known to rate this or that horse an extra pat or glance as he stood at the hitch rail swishing flies.

My mother's own buggy mare Dixie was more or less accepted as an eccentric. Many times she was seen sedately walking up Main Street with the only occupant of the ridiculous, narrow, high-seated rig she was pulling, one called a stanhope, being our little terrier Brush. Mother had a habit of failing to hitch Dixie. And Dixie, although unfailingly docile and agreeable, would on occasion grow impatient and return home without waiting for her. Brush was fond enough of members of our family, but his real devotion was for Dixie and he went wherever she went. If Dixie were alive today (she lived to be twenty-nine years old), she would be considered a Quarter Horse, having had a Sprinting Thoroughbred father and a range mother. As a quick starter under saddle, she possessed the prime Quarter Horse characteristic.

Occasionally tragedy struck our horse world, as it did when a young boy named Hudson mounted a rough-edged, half-broken bronc to head some steers back to the Tandy Bar Z corrals south of town. He was thrown and kicked to death when his foot hung in a stirrup. The whole town mourned his loss. The Hudson home, shadowed under a clump of large cottonwood trees, never failed after that to cast a spell of sadness over us as we young boys rode by it on the way to pasture with the neighbor's milk cows.

Horses were mixed up in everything, including hunting accidents. A visiting lawyer, out quail hunting with my father and some other friends, lost his bearings in the sagebrush, and when he came up over a ridge, his apparently overeager blast at a flushing covey spattered the hind ends of our buggy team with bird shot. The horses raced across the pasture until stopped by a fence corner. We were up half the night picking lead pellets out of their rumps by lantern light.

Another equine character of the time was one called the *drunk* horse, because of his noticeable listing from side to side as he wended his way out of town trying to stay under his rider, who had taken a snootful at the old Race Track saloon. The usually genial owner of this big black horse, when under the influence, was metamorphosed into a creature of supersensitive dignity with a nervous trigger finger; a combination that proved fatal on two separate occasions to men slower on the draw.

Improbable as it may seem, I had an opportunity to ride the drunk horse when I was six or seven years old. I was visiting a young friend in the country when it occurred to us to reconnoiter the watermelon situation at the nearby home of the owner of the drunk horse.

If anyone had been at home when we skirted the house, I am sure things would have turned out differently. We might have been invited to come in and eat our fill of melon that had been cooled in the springhouse. But all was deserted, and we proceeded to the melon patch, which offered a wide choice. Where watermelon-stealing ethics were concerned, juvenile delinquency had rather blurred edges at the time. Melons were so plentiful and brought so little on the market they were thought of somewhat as public domain, like free range for cattle. Anyway, we had pulled from the vines a fine rattlesnake-stripped watermelon and two large cantelopes when the owner came riding up on his big black horse, and with a steely glance nailed us to our barefooted tracks. I recall only the gist of the lecture that ensued—but I do clearly remember the ending. ". . . and how in hell did you two think you were going to get those melons home, anyway?" My eyes were fixed unwaveringly on the heavy six-shooter that sagged the big rancher's holster (he was the only man we knew, except the sheriff, who carried one), and both of us must have wondered if it was going to leap out to end our lives of crime. Instead, the rancher dismounted and walked toward the barn, and before we had come out of our trance, he was back with a gunny sack. Into it went the watermelon and the cantelopes, and when he had it tied he slung it across the saddlebow. Then the no longer irate nemesis grabbed me and tossed me into the saddle and threw my friend up behind me, and with a slap on the rump, he ordered his faithful black horse to take us home. "And when you get there, tie the reins on the horn and send my horse home," was his final admonition. There wasn't a weave or stagger in the drunk horse's gait as he carried boys and melons home.

I recall the Fourth of July picnics as gay and colorful affairs full of ready horseplay and sudden challenges. Under the sheltering cottonwoods along a creek, a bunting-draped hamburger stand and a cold-drink and ice-cream counter became the center of a collection of ponies, saddle horses, buggies, carriages, wagons, buckboards, and a few Buicks, Reos, Brushes, and Fords. Women sat on spread blankets and stirred the hot dry air around themselves and infants with palm leaf fans. Dogs and children yelped and shouted and an occasional bombardment of firecrackers sent men scurrying to secure their frightened horses. Foot races for all ages and a baseball game were usually followed by some pony and horse races. Distances of 220 to 440 yards were paced off and a judge or two was selected for the starting and finishing lines. Men and boys and tomboys, as the girl riders were called, all rode bareback. Bud Starkey, well known on the Diamond Tail and Rocking Chair ranches in the Panhandle of Texas, and known to my mother's family when they lived in that vicinity, once carried weight reduction to an extreme. He won a quarter-mile race wearing nothing but his striped long-John underwear. The gray, rather sway-backed mare he rode later beat the famous stallion Rocky Mountain Tom in a race at Childress, Texas.

At these picnic races, the horses were lined up and sent away from a standing start with a shouted "go" and a down-swing of a big hat. Sometimes a pistol report was the starting signal and sometimes a startled pony squatted and went sideways until convinced he hadn't been shot.

Big turnip watches were hauled out of vest pockets and the time of each race was announced simultaneously by several men—with discrepancies of only three or four seconds, which seemed accurate enough. Whatever the time, it can be taken as a certainty that among these hard-worked cowhorses there were some really talented sprinters.

Bucking bronc riding was another welcome divertissement, whether at picnics or other public gatherings or performed impromptu in a pasture or in the middle of the street in front of a livery stable. After the County Fair was established, local ranch talent, both men and horses, was rounded up to put on informal rodeos. Later Woodward was to establish the Annual Elks Rodeo, which continues to rank with the very best in the country.

Most of the performers were well known to us all, and they seemed to do their stuff with an aplomb and zest somehow lost in today's professionalism.

There was Mr. Jim Selman, a rancher from north of town who

Luther Minks coming off Amos at an early rodeo near Woodward. Standing in the background are Jim Selman and Hal Cooper. Ralph Chappel is on the fence. *Courtesy Harvey La Fon.*

considered gray striped trousers, white shirt, black tie, and a dark vest a suitable costume in which to rope, throw, and tie steers in front of the grandstand. The horses he and the others rode were breedy and trim—very much like today's Quarter Horses.

Professional horse racing with the accent on sprint races was another memorable feature of our County Fair. As a small boy, I saw horses raced which none of us ever dreamed would find mention some day in the annals of a new breed. One such horse was Badger, a blue stallion—lighter and grayer in color than a grulla (pronounced gru-ya and meaning crane colored or slate gray), who was brought to the Woodward races by his farmer-owner Roy Cochran of Cordell, Oklahoma. According to Nelson Nye, the noted Western writer and authoritative Quarter Horse historian, Badger found no match races in Woodward—his reputation for speed had gotten there ahead of him—but he did run in some purse races. These were either 220- or 440-yard sprints. It made no difference to Badger—he was always first off the score and first home.

Badger was the son of Peter McCue, one of the greatest sires of sprinting horses in the early years of this century. Peter McCue had reached the peak of his fame while owned and managed by Milo Burlingame of Cheyenne, Oklahoma—a long day's ride (on horseback, that is) south of Woodward.

Although Badger's racing career was a short one and his entire breeding career consisted of two foals, his place in Quarter Horse annals was assured by his remarkable son Midnight, to whom he passed on the rare Peter McCue qualities of speed, good conformation, and agreeable disposition. Midnight, who oddly enough was a flea-bitten gray, raced on the brush tracks of western Oklahoma and Texas and for many years was used to sire fast cowhorses on the huge Waggoner Ranch near Vernon, Texas, and on the JA Ranch in the Texas Panhandle, while maintaining his professional standing as an all-around cowhorse. He lived until 1933 and in his old age, when he was somewhat over at the knees, he sired his greatest son, Midnight Jr., who became a charter member of the Quarter Horse breed, holding permanent pedigree P-210. His blood flows in the veins of such record holders as Bob's Folly and Jet Deck.

Then there was a mare named Cut Throat who ran away from everything in organized sprint races. When as a small boy I saw her race I wondered how she could breathe past the barbed-wire gash in her neck, let alone win races. But win she did, and with such consistency that her owner, Tom Moore of Laverne, Oklahoma, northwest of Woodward, finding it impossible to match her in races, resorted to racing her as a Thoroughbred after somehow getting papers for her in the name of May Matteson. Her sire was the well known Thoroughbred Bonnie Joe, whereas her dam, we are told, was a Quarter running mare Big Em, by Rocky Mountain Tom, who traced directly to Steel Dust. When Cut Throat left the track, Tom had her bred to Dennis Reed, a Thoroughbred stallion then in southwestern Kansas. The resulting foal was a deep bay colt with a nice fat star in his forehead. Tom named him Oklahoma Star.

Tom Moore started training him for short racing at the age of two. In his first race, Oklahoma Star was confidently matched against the local best and his greased lightning start enabled him to present a rear-end view to the favored Slip Shoulder.

For about ten years Tom Moore raced him against all comers, often riding him himself—for fear the jockeys might sell him out—and thus adding considerable burden since Tom weighed about 150 pounds.

Tommy Moore stands behind Cutthroat's foal Oklahoma Star. The man holding Cutthroat is unidentified. *Courtesy Robert M. Denhardt.*

Oklahoma Star lived until 1942 and was among the first chosen to found the Quarter Horse breed, being given permanent pedigree number P-6 in the first Quarter Horse Stud Book.

Years later I was to learn more about Oklahoma Star when after a chat with Monsoor Moore, a noted QH breeder and horse-show judge, on his ranch east of Dewey, Oklahoma, I was directed across his rolling pastures to the Nowata, Oklahoma, ranch of Ronald Mason. It was Ronald Mason who had owned Oklahoma Star the last half of his life and who had increased the great horse's fame as a sire of sprint racers.

Beyond a large stone residence I walked to the brow of the hill to be met by Mr. Mason coming toward me waving a machete in a mock threatening manner. He had just finished cutting down the weeds, he told me, on the graves of Oklahoma Star and Beggar Boy. These two stallions had headed up the long list of famous Mason horses.

In Ronald's study the talk that afternoon was largely about horses, and not altogether about Quarter Horses because Beggar Boy was a Thoroughbred, as were many of the superb polo ponies developed on the Mason ranch. However, the talk always got back to Quarter Horses because most of the renowned progeny of Beggar Boy took their places in the ranks of the Quarter Horses.

It is quixotic to expect any man to speak ill of the horses of his youth —but, in truth, it must be said that the Badgers, Cut Throats, Oklahoma Stars, Peter McCues, and Midnights were notable exceptions to the general run of horses in our part of Oklahoma at that time. The average cowpony was only a generation or so removed from his mustang and Indian pony forebears. The best cowhorses were Thoroughbred-cross horses—usually the get of sprinting Thoroughbred stallions on range mares who more often than not showed relationship to the Spanish mustangs. We did not call even the best of them Quarter Horses. When we used that term it meant a quarter-mile sprinter. All cowponies, as I recall, looked a little rougher and harder used than ranch horses do today. They were a good match for the tough men and the raw land.

Roping and·branding and cutting were more demanding jobs then. Squeeze chutes and handy corrals were scarce. More cattle had to be roped and thrown in open pastures for branding and doctoring for screwworms. The cowpony was under a heavy man and saddle for longer hours in all kinds of weather. Only the larger, more prosperous ranches had sufficient saddle stock to allow for frequent changes of mounts. After work the pony served as mere transportation to and from far pastures. In some districts the cowhorse was an errand runner, carrying his man to town over roads that only an agile-footed horse could negotiate. Then, after all his work, the cowpony was often called upon for some rodeo action on a Sunday afternoon just for fun.

It was a rough, unprosperous country then, buffeted by an erratic economy and a seemingly perverse and capricious climate. Even so, few people indulged in complaints. It took a lot of dry months, gaunt stock, burned up grass and crops before even the least stoical would let fly with a few critical opinions. And for those who did, there were always defenders ready with a rebuttal. Once when a cowman burst out with "B'God, I'm sick and tired of riding in a hot sand-blasting wind that tries to tear my stetson off, head and all!" a calmer voice pointed out, "At least the wind nearly always dies down in the evening to a soft breeze." The poetic local editor had once likened it to "a sigh of the prairie night."

My Oklahoma-booster father, who had come to Woodward fresh out of law school at Ann Arbor, Michigan, making the "run" when the Cherokee Strip was opened for settlement, would, under the stress of severe drought, admit that it didn't rain nearly enough. He once casually told a group that "schoolteachers go out occasionally and throw bird shot on the roof to teach the children what rain sounds like."

Stories of hardihood were the rule. Cowboys especially were rawhide tough and saw no point in concealing the fact. In conversation with a whang leather top hand—I was pretty youthful at the time—I asked if he had been thrown by many broncs. "Naw," he answered, "most of these here ponies ain't too rank. They don't bother me none."

"But you must have been on outlaws that gave you a bad time," I pressed. Of course, this was asking for it.

"Well, now," the cowboy drawled, as his beady eyes hidden in squint wrinkles came to bear on me, his expression as unreadable as a Cheyenne's, "there *was* a time I tangled with a very unusual animal. He was loco, I think. Always catched me off guard, never bucked when I expected him to. One day riding along as quiet as you please—me treating him as kindly as if I knew his folks—the son-of-a-bitch ups and bucks me higher'n a kite and I land astraddle of a bob-wire fence. Split me clean up to my belt buckle"—a pause long enough for me to come out with "Well, that must have kept you off a horse for a while."

"Yes, it sure nuff did," and he slowly added, "until I could let my stirrups down."

With the coming of tractors, trucks, and cars, a lot of horses were freed of much stupefying, killing drudgery. But the cowhorse with his specialized work of roping and cutting remained unsupplanted. While the numbers of harness horses and run-of-the-mill saddle horses dwindled, the status, if not the numbers, of the cowhorses of special breeding and training rose. They were no longer seen on the roads or standing at hitch rails in the towns. They were back at the ranch where they were needed for expert work, not for transportation.

To the general public it seemed in the twenties and early thirties as if the whole tribe of Western saddle horses was doomed. This assumption, however, failed to take into consideration one of the West's anomalous characteristics—a bulldog tenacity in clinging to traditional ways in some things while at the same time welcoming changes in others.

Change, in plenty of course, came to the West. Comparing the Oklahoma I knew as a youth to the Oklahoma of today makes it seem in some ways like a different country. Now roads are good—some are superhighways. Stores, offices, motels, restaurants, filling stations, public buildings, churches, recreation parks, etc., all bespeak the forward look. The finding of oil and gas moved things along, of course. Throughout the countryside, there is a neater appearance. Fences are straighter and stronger and more often than not contain registered livestock.

At the breeding farm of Monte Reger near Woodward, I once saw horse after horse led across the lawn while Monte and his son, Buddy, filled me in on each one's breeding. The breeding program that produced these fine horses had been in operation ever since the Quarter Horse breed was founded. In the Reger home, loaded with trophies and photos, Monte's lifetime in the horse and rodeo world can be reviewed.

Once he toured the country with a specialty act—riding a hurdle-jumping longhorn steer. Those longhorns were an ever present danger. Being clipped by them, Monte said, was like being knocked on the head.

On the Hal Cooper Ranch northwest of Woodward, fine saddle horses have been raised for over forty years, and, as at Monte's, Quarter Horses have been raised exclusively ever since the founding of the breed. From this ranch came the roping horse of Don McLaughlin, World Champion Calf Roper for four consecutive years, and the mare that produced Miss Doby, whose daughter Miss Tequila was an AAA runner of note.

On the Selman Ranch north of town, Bob Selman, son of Jim, the founder of the ranch, raises equally highly bred Quarter Horses. Some of his trace to Old Sorrel, the founding father of the King Ranch horses, and to Traveler through Zantanon, King, and Poco Bueno.

F.L. Lady Bug, bred by W. A. Yeager of Woodward, is a Quarter Horse mare the home town can be proud of. On a memorable day in 1968, this great mare's progeny ran second, third, fourth in America's richest race—the All American Futurity at Ruidoso Downs, New Mexico —to win $135,000. The winner, Three Oh's, received $160,372 of this record purse, a sum greater than the entire purses of the Kentucky Derby, Belmont Stakes, or Preakness. To date F.L. Lady Bug's produce has won over a half-million dollars, and many of her sons and daughters are still on the track, increasing their winnings and their own value.

Marvin Barnes, of Ada, Oklahoma, who kept close watch on F.L. Lady Bug and her foals, owned and sold her twice and then had the shrewd judgment to buy her a third time.

Near the Antelope Hills southwest of Woodward lies the Merrick 14 Ranch—and off to the east at Perry, Oklahoma, is the Bud Warren Breeding Farm, whose horses are among the greatest of all Running Quarter Horses. These ranches will be referred to again.

The few Quarter Horse breeders of just one part of Oklahoma who have been mentioned are good examples of the horsemen throughout the United States and in thirty-eight foreign countries, whose devotion to the American horse that can do so many things so well has created the world's largest breed of saddle horses.

In 1959, the last year the United States Department of Agriculture took a horse census, the horse population had dwindled to four and a half million. Nearly all were saddle horses. The use of draft animals on farms is almost a thing of the past. Mechanization has enabled the average American farmer to plow forty acres a day as compared to the world average of less than one acre a day.

Since the 1959 census the horse population has almost doubled. In 1970 it was estimated to be close to eight million, with Quarter Horses outnumbering all other breeds. The U. S. Department of Agriculture has predicted that the horse population will reach ten million by 1975, with eighty-two million Americans riding horses.

All breeds are on the increase, with the possible exception of the small pony breeds, which may be lagging due to the fact that young children are learning to ride and care for larger horses.

Horse Census

The amazing growth of America's registered saddle horse population is shown in the following listing of the well-known breeds. The figures were supplied by the various breed associations.

	Registry established	1970 Registrations	Total Registrations
AMERICAN QUARTER HORSE	1941	90,878	704,159
THOROUGHBRED	1894	24,596	533,583
APPALOOSA	1938	28,700	143,612
TENNESSEE WALKING HORSE	1935	8,700	140,421
AMERICAN SADDLE HORSE	1891	3,942	136,620
ARABIAN (N. American Registry)	1908	8,629	74,500
MORGAN	1894	2,378	42,119
AMERICAN PAINT HORSE	1962	2,152	16,000
PINTO HORSE	1956	2,500	15,800
PONY OF THE AMERICAS	1954	900	13,000
PALOMINO	1936	150	8,000

The following are some of the smaller, more recently founded breed associations that are preserving, improving, and popularizing the less well-known types of saddle horses. All information came direct from the breed associations.

	Registry established	1970 Registrations	Total Registrations
MISSOURI FOX TROTTING HORSE	1958	619	6,128
STANDARD QUARTER HORSE	1963	491	4,500
ALBINO	1937	181	2,650
GALICENO	1959	123	1,816
AMERICAN PASO FINO	1964	400	1,500
AMERICAN INDIAN HORSE	1961	100	550
SPANISH MUSTANG	1957	8	318
PERUVIAN PASO HORSE	1970	150	205
ANDALUSIAN HORSE	1969	less than →	100
NATIONAL QUARTER HORSE	1956	not available	
ORIGINAL HALF QUARTER HORSE		not available	

As I write this I can look out the window and see seven- and ten-year-old Lisa and Tara Bird, with their blond hair flying as they scramble from one of their four horses to another to give them their daily workout in the corral. Both ride bareback and change mounts without touching the ground. The horses handled by these little girls are representative of the amiability of Western-trained horses. Yet when ridden by grown-ups, they come very much alive and show high spirits.

Horse shows, which were once the preserve of society people, are now welcoming more horses owned and shown by horse lovers who never wore a white tie. Low-cost community stables, backyard corrals, and 4-H Club training—the Little League in horsedom—where lessons in riding and caring for horses can be had at a very modest cost, have all contributed to the breakdown of exclusiveness. In all this flourishing equine universe, the World of the Quarter Horse has made the most startling growth. The versatility of the Quarter Horse, his beauty, his amiable disposition coupled with blazing bursts of speed, and the fact that he is "a horse that can do something," have made him popular with enough people so that now the training, outfitting, transportation, care, and showing of this animal, once the lowly cowhorse, represents the largest segment of a twelve-billion-dollar-a-year horse industry.

2

Backtracking the Quarter Horse

The origins of all horses are lost in the mists of prehistory. The origins of the Quarter Horse, when traced back, lead to the Spanish and English horses. Whatever conditioned the hotbloods of Africa, the chargers of Spain, and the racers of England left its mark on the Quarter Horse of today.

The fact that there were no horses in the Americas until they were brought by the Spaniards in the wake of Columbus presents a zoological mystery because the Southwestern part of North America had seen the very beginning of the horse species. Over a span of sixty million years—give or take a few million—a creature no bigger than a fox, called the eohippus (dawn horse), evolved into the equus, the progenitor of the modern horse. The little eohippus had four toes and a vestigial splint on each forefoot and three toes and two splints on each hind foot. The toes of the equus had amalgamated into solid hoofs.

Man and horse ran a somewhat parallel course in that they had attained full physical development before the glacial advances and retreats, when so much water—and there is just so much of it in the world—got banked up in mountains of snow and ice. The oceans, being thus depleted, sank to lower levels. Land, formerly submerged, was revealed. Shifting of weight to the polar areas forced other areas of the earth's surface to rise. Isthmuses joined all the large land masses except Australia. The Isthmus of Panama joined North and South America. A land bridge appeared at Bering Strait, making land travel possible for men and animals between Asia and North America. England was joined to the continent of Europe.

With these new outlets the equus ranged far afield. He went south across the Panama Isthmus and northwest across the land bridge to Asia. Starting out as an equus, he was not to stop until, as a horse, he circled the earth. When the sixteen head of horses that came with the army of Cortés were set ashore in Mexico in 1519, the horse had come back to the continent of his origin.

It was after the coming of the Indians to the Americas, presumably over the land bridge that joined Alaska to Asia, that all the equus in both North and South America disappeared. It is certain that the Indians hunted the equus for food. But is it likely that the Indians were such avid hunters as to bring the equus race to extinction in the Western Hemisphere? A form of tsetse fly or some epidemic has been suggested as their destroyer. Theories have also been forwarded that a sudden glacial advance might have done them in, or that forests so supplanted the grazing lands as to starve them out. All theories falter in the face of the fact that buffalo and pronghorn antelope and musk ox managed to survive. Why the equus disappeared from the Western world remains to date an unsolved mystery.

What happened to the equus in Asia, Africa, and Europe is only vaguely understood, but we do have an accurate glimpse of the wild horses of Western Europe as they looked twenty to twenty-five thousand years ago. We see them today through the eyes of the remarkable cave artists who drew pictures of them on the walls and ceilings of caves along the Dordogne River in France, and in the caves of Altamira in Northern Spain. These horses, which the cave men hunted for food, were a species of wild horses thought to be the forerunner of the tarpan, from which came the pony stock of Europe and Asia.

The wild tarpans survived to modern times in the forest of Bialowieza in Eastern Poland, where the last were captured in 1812, and in the Ukraine, where the last survivors were killed in 1851. Tarpan stock seems to have contributed most to the domesticated horse of Central Europe. Another species of primitive horse is the Przewalski horse, specimens of which were captured alive in Mongolia in 1942 and 1945.

When horses were first domesticated is not known. It is generally supposed that somewhere in the vast tablelands of Central Asia men first captured and domesticated horses. Then other Neolithic people on the borders of the Black and Caspian Seas mastered and spread the new development. Undoubtedly it began with the purpose of controlling the meat, milk, and leather supply, somewhat in the manner that yaks are still used in parts of Tibet where the animal is a walking manufactory.

Assuming that domesticated horses of prehistoric times served in similar multiple ways, it is certain that their eventual value as pullers of chariots saved them from the dismal destiny of the yaks.

When horses entered the dawn of history, about 2000 B.C., they were already racing with the chariots of the Hurrians, a people who lived between the Caucasus Mountains and Lake Van. From them the Hyksos learned the new art of horse and chariot warfare, and with it conquered Egypt in 1580 B.C. Then for a while, the Mitanni, whose capital was in the vicinity of present-day Ankara, Turkey, became the dominant horse people. They also credited their victories over the armies of Egypt to their swift horses and chariots.

A Mitanni horseman wrote an elaborate treatise on the care and training of chariot horses in 1360 B.C. It exists in the form of cuneiform tablets, called the Kikkuli text. A Mitanni princess who married Pharaoh Ikhnaton is perhaps the best-known of the Egyptian queens, Queen Nefertiti, whose lovely sculptured likeness can be seen in many museums.

Many horse authorities believe that all horses derive from three categories: the *Flemish,* the source of all cold-blood large-footed draft horses; the *Mongolian,* the source of the pony stock of Europe and Asia; and the *Libyan,* the source of all hot-blood horses. The most controversial opinions center around the origin of the last, the hot-blood horses.

As strange as it may seem, the combined efforts of the historians, archaeologists, zoologists, and paleontologists have failed to come up with satisfying answers to the origin of the Arab and Barb horses, the progenitors of all of today's hot-blood horses, including the American Quarter Horse.

The Hot-bloods

Whatever their origin, it is agreed that hot-blood horses evolved on the open plains and deserts. Fleetness of escape was their main protection from predators, animal and human. Alertness, bursts of speed, austere living in the more arid places of the earth developed trim bodies, slender and sinewy legs free of long hair, hard teeth, hoofs and bones, high spirits and intelligence. Those that maintain they are of African origin point out that purebred Arabs and Barbs differ from other equine species in that, like the wild African ass and zebra, they had but small callosities or chestnuts on the front legs, and only very small ones, or none at all, on the hind legs. Furthermore, Arabs and Barbs, and even their descendants the Spanish mustangs in America, have but 17 sets of ribs, 5 lumbar and 16 tail vertebrae. The indigenous strains of Europe and Asia have 19 sets of ribs, 6 lumbar and 18 tail vertebrae.

Any clues the ancient historians give us as to where the hot-blood horses evolved are meager and tantalizing.

The finest representations of ancient horses are the spirited ponies that slow-canter and prance in the processional that once ornamented the Parthenon in Athens, Greece. They antedate the Arab horses. General Carter, the horse historian, states flatly that Phidias, the master sculptor, used as his models Asian cold-bloods. John L. Hervey, historian of the light-horse breeds, says they were the forerunners of the Arabs. Others, including myself, who studied them in the Elgin marbles in the British Museum, think they resemble Barbs. Certainly they are reminiscent of the Barb horses I saw in Morocco, which were surprisingly Arab-like except for lower sprung tails and shorter coupled bodies.

All we really know is that in the Mediterranean world and the Near East there eventually developed a marked distinction between the common horse of Asia and Europe, known as the cold-bloods, and a superior, more spirited desert breed, known as the hot-bloods represented by only two strains, the Arabs and Barbs.

At about the time of Christ, the tribesmen of Arabia got into the horse business in a big way. The horse culture they carried on was done with fanatical devotion because to them horses were a war machine. Blood stock was guarded with all the resolution that is now expended on modern weaponry. As it turned out, their horses so excelled in battle they brought their owners very close to mastery of the world.

The Arabian horses were literally hand raised, often sharing the tents of their masters. Foals got as much attention as did newborn babies. Mares were watched over during pregnancy and after giving birth had their bellies bandaged to help them regain their attractive figures. The Arabs' devotion to horses is expressed in their saying that Allah created the horse out of the wind, and Adam out of mud.

The challenge, interest, and hope of gaining wealth and prestige by the excellence and speed of their adored horses had the beneficial results of bettering the breed, just as those same motives do today. In fact a horse caste system developed. At the top of the social scale were the nobles. They were of bloodlines pure and ancient. A noble mare lived out her life foalless if she could not be mated with a noble sire. A rank below the nobles were the animals of ancient blood, but whose ancestors somewhere in the past had sullied it by a vulgar relationship outside the better families. The third and lowest class was made up of the common horses—Arabs, of course—but with no family background to speak of.

Five Arabian strains seem to have derived from a single mare named Keheilet Ajus. Keheilan is supposedly the most aristocratic strain and is named for her. They are the fastest of all and are mostly bays. The Darley Arabian was said to have been of this family, although his immediate family name was Mannicka.

Lady Wentworth in her *Horses of Britain* writes: "The English Thoroughbred originated from the Arabic Keheilan of which 'Thoroughbred' is a literal translation—meaning pure bred all through."

The largest family went by the name of Kohls—kohl being the black antimony used by Arabian women to paint their eyebrows and lashes—because of the blue-black skin of the Arab horse, regardless of hair color. Although the skin of the Arab was always black, the color of the coat varied. They were, and are, blacks, bays, chestnuts, grays, and whites, but never any mixed colors such as paints, piebalds, or skewbalds. Nor are there any duns. Throwbacks to duns, skewballs, or line-striped horses are a definite indication of Asian or cold-blood somewhere in the past. In North Africa, where the Arabian and Barb horses met with various incursions of horses from Europe, spotted horses and duns are commonplace. The Algerians and Moroccans have a very poetic name for paint horses. They call them Hejar-el-wad, which means stones-in-the-river.

The Mohammedans first invaded North Africa, where their Arab horses upgraded the Barbs. Then when they entered Spain in A.D. 711 with their Arab-Barb horses, they started a conflict that was to rage for almost eight hundred years. The horse culture that centered in Andalusia throughout these centuries brought to perfection what came to be known as the Andalusian horse or Cordoba horse, or simply the Spanish horse. Perhaps no other breed of horse was ever under the saddle for such a long period of time during which the demands on him were so unrelenting. By the time Ferdinand and Isabella brought the Moorish war to a close in 1492, the Spanish Horse was without a peer in Europe. Throughout many centuries this hot-blood strain had been free of cold-blood outcrossings. It was this Arab-Barb horse that was taken to the New World, whose discovery fantastically coincided with the end of the Moorish conflict in Spain.

These were the hot-blood horses ridden by the conquistadors whose descendants—the Spanish mustangs—contributed to the cowhorse strains and eventually to the American Quarter Horse.

Since so many references have been made to hot-blood horses, it may be well to take a brief look at the cold-bloods. They also contributed to the horse strains in the Western United States.

The Cold-bloods

The cold-blooded horses lived in marshy swamps and river valleys and thrived on the succulent herbage rich in nutritive salts. Such a diet combined with miry footing and cold winters caused them to become massive, hairy, heavy-coated, big-footed, powerful animals. They were seldom molested by such wild beasts as preyed on the smaller horses of the plains. Thus they were not subjected to trials of speed for survival. This circumstance alone tended to make them heavy and phlegmatic. The Black Flemish horse and the New Forest horse of England were the ancient forebears of the heavy war horses of the knights, and from them came the draft breeds of today.

The cold-blood's day of glory came in Europe and England when the armorers' art had reached such perfection as to allow a man to move with fighting ability inside of thirty to seventy pounds of metal. This was roughly from the thirteenth to the seventeenth centuries. Counting the weight of the man himself with his body armor, sword, lance, dagger, mace, and shield, plus the saddle, bridle, and elaborate horse armor, the war horse of that time had to be able to carry four hundred pounds or more and be fairly active about it. The knight on his massive horse was the tank of the time. After the day of the large war horses, the cold-blood strains were used mostly for heavy farm work and as pack carriers. It was only after the improvement of roads that the draft breeds were developed and perfected for shoulder haulage.

The sorrel Belgians, the English Shires, the Suffolk Punch, and the Clydesdales, the pride of Scotland, are all enormous horses that attain heights of 17.3 hands and weights of well over a ton. These horses, however, did not feature in the stock that left England for the early American colonies. None were fixed breeds until the last century. The Clydesdale's upgrading dates from only about 1850, as does the Percheron's.

The dapple-gray Percheron, most widely dispersed of all draft horses, is known to everyone who ever saw a circus. Despite their bulk, Percherons can maintain good even action, such as a slow canter, making their broad backs ideal moving platforms for performing equestrians in the ring, where they earned the name of rosinbacks. The breed was perfected in the French district known as Le Perche. Because the Percheron is so active for his size—16.1 to 16.3 hands high with weights of 1600 to 2100 pounds—with legs only moderately hairy and with trim feet, the breed is presumed to have been crossbred somewhere along the line with horses of Arab or Barb background: "Activated," to use a current word, with some hot-blood. Beginning around 1875, Percherons got a strong foothold in the United States. Many were shipped to the northwestern part of the country to add weight and bone to the horses there, a blood legacy that was passed on to some strains of Quarter Horses.

Building the British Breeds

While Spanish horses were being developed with great stamina and maneuverability, the horse breeders of Britain were also bringing to a high state of perfection their various strains.

The country itself was, and is, a veritable horse heaven with nutritious grass and a mild climate. With many indigenous types of horses to draw on, and with imports that found their way to England over the centuries, there emerged distinctive families ideally suited for various uses—from pack and draft ponies to heavy war horses, road travelers, and racers. England, more than most nations, enjoyed long periods of prosperity and security—at least for the sports-loving landed gentry and the nobility—which gave continuity to the horse-breeding programs that produced for Britain the foundation stock for the world's greatest turf breeds. But these horses, which were to contribute eventually to the English Thoroughbred, the American Thoroughbred, and many other racing breeds including the American Quarter Horse breed, did not burst upon the scene with the dramatic suddenness that seems so often implied in the recounting of the arrival in England of three famous Oriental sires in the seventeenth and eighteenth centuries. The efforts to improve speed and stamina had in fact ebbed and flowed for many centuries.

It is possible that the earliest hot-blood horses to join the native stock of England took place around 1000 B.C., when the blunt-prowed ships of the Phoenicians nosed into St. Michaels Mount off southwestern Britain to trade horses for Cornish tin. In Cornwall today a few tin mines are still being worked and among the gorse and briar are many scars of ancient diggings to strengthen the belief in a thriving prehistory trade. If horses did come down the ramps of the Phoenician ships, were they Barbs from Africa? Were they from Asia Minor? Or horses from Spain?

Julius Caesar, who landed in Britain in the year 55 B.C., gave no clue to their origin, but he did mention the "fast chariots drawn by the Britons' horses." He also commented on the daredevil way in which the island warriors ran out on the chariot poles between the horses in order to get a better whack at his legionnaires.

A hundred years after Caesar's five-week visit to Britain the Romans made themselves masters of a large part of the island. Among other innovations, they set up well-organized breeding farms for the raising of cavalry mounts. After the Roman withdrawal in A.D. 407 the breeding of horses fell back into a haphazard state.

After the Moorish invasion of Europe a large breeding stock of Arab-Barb horses developed in France and Spain, which was to affect the English breeds. In A.D. 1066, when William the Conqueror crossed the Channel to England with his Norman knights, these improved horses came with them. William himself is supposed to have ridden a Castilian stallion of the race of "Rinfaz, Horse of the Night," a gift from a "King of Spain."

Much pictorial evidence relating to the Norman horses is to be found in the tapestries of the time, which teem with mounted knights. The most remarkable one is the Bayeux Tapestry, a strip of brown linen 20 inches wide and 231 feet long. It contains 1512 embroidered figures, 200 of which are horses. Although the horses, like the men, boats, weapons, and the rest, are highly stylized, enough aspects of reality are evident to narrow the gap between that time and this. The Barb horses are depicted with uniformity, and since they carry no concealing armor their conformation is revealed. They have straight noses, trim legs without hairy fetlocks, and muscular necks and hind quarters.

Many English historians, instead of decrying the Norman invasion, have expounded on the advantages that accrued from it. Certainly the incoming Norman horses improved the native stock of England. Among the first actions of William the Conqueror was the establishment of stud farms, with the result that Norman horse strains of his time are perpetuated today in English breeds.

Later the comings and goings of men and armies to and from the continent made the importation of more Arab-Barb horses not only possible but inevitable. Their blood upgraded most of the breeds of the British Isles. Remote as they are, even the Connemara horses of Ireland carry their quota of hot-blood. Some interbreeding, it has been said, resulted from the horses saved from the wreck of the Spanish Armada in 1588. Be that as it may, it is more than likely that Arab-Barb blood stock came to Ireland much earlier, since the merchants of Galway had for centuries traded regularly with Spain.

Of all established English breeds, the Cleveland Bay is the oldest.

This bay horse of great stamina, quick action, and good appearance with clean legs, had forebears that were related, it is thought, to the Norman chargers or other hot-blood strains. The Cleveland Bay's forerunners featured prominently in the magnificent cavalry that carried Cromwell's Ironsides to victory in the English Civil War. Since then Cleveland Bays have been beneficial contributors to light draft and coaching strains and in recent times have been used for crossbreeding with Thoroughbreds to obtain hunters of quality, up to weight, and with good conformation.

Cromwell's time merged closely with the beginning years of the founding families of the Thoroughbred breed. Cromwell himself had a stud farm under the management of a man named Place, whose name was given to one of the farm's greatest stallions, Place's White Turk. To this sire and others of the Yorkshire strain and to a few imported Arabian stallions all great turf horse bloodlines trace.

The mysterious alchemy of the blood of the desert horse—the hot-blood—that had high-mettled the English horse stock, reached its greatest potency and was given permanency by better record keeping when three immortals—three Oriental stallions—were brought to England following the Restoration. To the English, all Arab-Barb horses from the countries around the Eastern Mediterranean were called Oriental horses.

The first of the immortals was the Byerly Turk, a charger ridden by Captain Byerly in King William's War of 1689 and then brought to England, where he stood at stud as late as 1698. It will be noticed in the genealogy chart in Appendix A that he was the great great grandfather of Diomed, who was brought to Virginia in 1798, where he became one of the founding fathers of the American Thoroughbred and American Quarter Horse breeds.

Schoolteacher Justin Morgan's horse (known for many years as Figure and later as "Justin Morgan the Horse"), founder of the Morgan breed, traced directly to the Byerly Turk, according to the breed's records. King Herod—a name that looms large in Thoroughbred genealogy—was a grandson of the Byerly Turk.

The second of the immortal three to arrive in England was the Darley Arabian. This bay stallion was born in the Palmyra district in Syria in 1700, where he was purchased and shipped to Yorkshireman Darley by his merchant brother, who had become established in Aleppo, Syria. He was a clean bred horse, being from the family Mannicka—pure Arabian—and was well set up, being 15 hands high and with weight estimated at around 1100 pounds. His near forefoot was white, as were both hind feet, and he had a prominent blaze down his face. Toward the end of the Darley Arabian's life—around 1717 (some say 1715)— he sired Bulle Rock, who was the first blood horse to be brought to America (in 1730). His greatest son was Flying Childers, also sired during the last year or so of his life. Flying Childers was used on a mail route and raced at Newmarket. Locally he was called the "fastest horse that ever lived." When he was eighteen years old, Flying Childers sired the famous Blaze, a chestnut with a white snip down his nose and four white feet, who was foaled in 1733 and lived till 1753. Blaze is credited with being the supreme progenitor—so many traced to him—of all race horses regardless of nationality, whether in harness or under the saddle. His daughters were prominent in founding the Russian trotters, the Orloff breed. His greatest son, Old Shales, became Number 1 in the *Hackney Stud Book* and contributed along with others of his progeny in establishing the Norfolk trotters, whose blood in turn contributed to the most prominent racing and show breeds that were imported to America.

The third famous Oriental stallion was the Godolphin Arabian—sometimes called Barb—who was thought to have been foaled about 1724 and is known to have lived until 1753. Unless one accepts highly romanticized versions of his beginnings, there is little actually known about him until he came into the possession of the young sportsman Lord Godolphin.

It was the Godolphin Arabian's son Lath—next to Flying Childers the best horse to race at Newmarket—and his son Old Cade and grandson Matchem who established the bloodline. His stock, crossbred with that of the two other prepotent Oriental sires, produced the English Thoroughbred, the American Thoroughbred, the Standardbred, the American Saddlebred, the Tennessee and the American Walking Horse, the Morgans, and the American Quarter Horse. The portrait of him, painted for Lord Godolphin when he was Chancellor of the Exchequer, still hangs at 11 Downing Street in London.

The genealogy charts in Appendix A are an attempt to show in a greatly abbreviated form the main bloodlines that flowed into the present day Quarter Horse families. Anything like a complete list of even the most outstanding sires and dams would require volumes. The intention here is to concentrate on strains that came to America and became influential in producing the Quarter Horse.

One fortunate aspect of horse culture in America was that the only outcrossings available for the English horses and the comparatively few

French and Dutch horses that were brought in were with horses that carried the potent regenerative blood of the Arab-Barb. These were already well established in the Hispanic settlements.

The Spanish Horse in North America

The first horses to arrive in the Western Hemisphere were twenty stallions and mares, survivors of the thirty-four that Columbus started out with on his 1493 voyage to colonize Española. Within a few years ranching was a booming business in the West Indies. More and more horses, hobbled and lashed to the decks of the westward-bound caravels, arrived to spearhead the exploration and conquest of the newly found lands. Of the original settlers, far more became wealthy from livestock raising than from seeking gold. Diego Velásquez, the first Governor of Cuba, did well with a horse farm at Payamo that specialized in pintos. Even with the pressing need to mount more men and to replace horses worn out or killed on the many probing expeditions into the mainland of the unknown Americas, the island supply soon caught up with the demand. Before 1550 the expensive, hazardous shipment of horses from Spain had practically ceased. Horse ranches sprang up in each newly conquered land. In Mexico, Cortés founded a large horse ranch at Tlaltizapán, one of several that he owned. Viceroy Mendoza purchased from Juan Coronel, a conquistador, the pueblo and entire valley of Ulizava to be used exclusively as a horse-breeding ranch. He is said to have presented as gifts to his chivalrous friends over three hundred head of trained Andalusian horses. Cristóbal de Oñate and many other men of power and wealth also set up stud farms.

By the end of the sixteenth century, horses, cattle, mules, and sheep were numerous and cheap. When Juan de Oñate, son of Cristóbal, moved north in 1598 to assume the governorship of New Mexico, his caravan was trailed by seven thousand head of livestock. Only those who have ridden with sizable droves can possibly visualize such a large herd.

From the present towns of Socorro to Taos, mission settlements and ranches were established in New Mexico. In 1610 Santa Fe was made the capital of the province. Years of intermittent strife with the Indians followed. The Pueblo Indians on whom the Spaniards depended for labor and much of their field crops gradually resigned themselves to their fate of being a conquered people. Many of them became Mission

Because outbreeding was rare, the horses ridden by today's Mexican vaqueros, like these in the State of Morelos, are direct descendants of the Andalusian horses of the conquistadors, even though size and quality have not been maintained. *Photo by the author.*

Indians, that is to say they became devoted converts and followers of their Jesuit instructors and masters. Unlike the Plains Indians the Pueblo Indians had permanent, hereditary homes. They were held in place by their way of life as cultivators of fields, land that they would not consider abandoning.

And there were times when the Pueblos saw an advantage in having the Spaniards there. They welcomed their help in fighting off their traditional enemies, the Navajos, and when the Apaches and Comanches showed up annually to barter furs and tasajo (buffalo jerky meat) for knives, corn, and pottery—and often confused trade with raid.

As in New Spain, far away to the south, there was a law which prohibited Indians from riding horseback, but since the Pueblo Indians were useful as vaqueros and horse handlers, the law was never rigidly enforced. As for the Apaches and Comanches, the horses they could hunt down in the outlying pastures were mainly killed for food. However, it is to be supposed that a few of the adventurous young hunters managed to steal some sufficiently tame horses, on which they learned to ride.

Although living in the midst of an exploited and resentful people, the Spaniards of New Mexico fell into a monotonous routine which after three generations passed for security.

But there came a year of famine and distress which intensified the unrest of a people smarting under the harsh rule of their Spanish overlords. For five years a medicine man named Popé of pueblo San Juan had been preaching revolt. Assuming the role of chief, he and Chief Antonio Bolsas, the first known horse-riding Indian leaders in America, rode from pueblo to pueblo and to the camps of the Plains Indians who came to Taos to trade, fanning the smoldering embers of revolt. The Comanches and Apaches needed little urging to join in a fight against the palefaces. The prospect of getting much loot—particularly horses—was lure enough.

When Franciscan churchmen in Santa Fe brutally punished several tribal leaders for taking part in their pueblo's nature worship ceremonies, Popé had only to set the day for the fire of revolt to burst into flames. Only a few Mission Indians remained loyal to the Spaniards. One of them, Chief Juan de Ye, tried to give warning of the impending uprising, but his warning was not taken seriously.

Legend says that Popé murdered his own son-in-law, fearing he might betray his plans. Whatever desperate measures were taken to assure secrecy, they were effective, because the Spaniards were utterly unprepared for the concerted Indian attacks that erupted in every district of the province on that fateful day in August 1680.

Many Spanish people and Mission Indians were killed and most of the livestock was run off. To the Comanches and Apaches went practically all of the horses. The Pueblo Indians had no real use for them. During the revolt Governor Otermin with the largest party of survivors —about 2000 including 317 Indians—fought their way down the Rio Grande to find refuge below El Paso del Norte. Fourteen years elapsed before the Spaniards returned with an army to reconquer New Mexico. Missions were re-established in New Mexico and new ones were set up in Texas and Arizona by men with a pioneering spirit to match their religious fervor and vision. The indefatigable Father Kino pushed into Sonora's unknown country. Trained by the Jesuits as a topographer, he mapped vast areas and set up mission churches, schools, and settlements. He saw that each one was liberally stocked. In the late 1600s he moved a herd of 1400 head of livestock consisting of cattle, sheep, mules, and hundreds of Spanish horses north from his Sonora headquarters of Nuestra Señora de los Dolores into what is now Arizona. Father Francisco Tomás Garcé's, a Franciscan, rode thousands of miles in Arizona and Southern California while discovering hundreds of isolated Indian villages. It was he who named the Colorado River. Father Junípero Serra, another Franciscan, opened up California, founding nine missions before his death in 1784. In California the Indians were generally peaceful, but in the rest of the Southwest—now that mounted Indians had to be contended with—the problem of protecting the settlements and their herds was one that was to plague the Spaniards for generations to come.

Before that moment in history in 1680, American Indians had never had the help of any domesticated animal except the dog. Now the Plains Indians, mounted on horses—"big dogs," as they first called them —entered a radically new phase of their culture.

Horses with their high value as trade items bolstered the Indian purchasing power, and with the great aid to hunting and added mobility in warfare horses enabled the Plains Indians to slow down, if not to stand off, the encroaching white civilization until the latter part of the nineteenth century.

With a booming horse-trading operation going for them, the Comanches and Apaches were ever on the hunt to replenish their supply. Horses they had taken in the revolt of 1680 found buyers at the French posts on the Arkansas and Red Rivers before the decade was out. Soon after this time the Chickasaws were riding horses from the Hispanic Southwest. Among the Pawnees along the Arkansas River the French explorer Claude Charles du Tesne counted three hundred horses in 1719.

One of the more successful entrepreneurs in the Western horse trade was the personable French Canadian Louis Juchereau de St. Denis, who pressed his trade up the Red River, beyond his Natchitoches post in Indian country and on into the Spanish province of Texas. It was a risky business because Spain had a closed-door policy.

St. Denis preferred horses acquired directly from the Spaniards to those that had passed through the hands of the Indians. Contrary to the voluminous romance dealing with the subject, Indians generally were seldom good or even adequate horse raisers. Even the Chickasaw horses were at their best from 1700 to 1740 when fresh from the western plains. Although they bettered any horses this tribe may have gotten from the miasmic swamps of Florida, all soon lost stature. During the years 1751–62 a French lieutenant Jean Bossu traveled extensively in the Choctaw nation—allies of the French—on the fringes of the Chickasaw domains. In letters he mentioned the excellence of the Chickasaw riders. But he was no horseman. He made no comment about the horses. Another traveler, an Anglicized Dutchman, Bernard Romans, visited seventy-four Chickasaw towns—allies of the English—in 1771–72, and he was greatly impressed by the superiority of the intrepid Chickasaw warriors and their horses. Unfortunately for us, he also was no horseman, so he gave no detailed description of the latter.

William Bartram, an early American botanist, after a trip to the Chickasaw country a year later described the horses as "the most beautiful and sprightly species [of horses] anywhere to be seen . . . a small breed and as delicately formed as the American roe buck."

John Adair, a trader among the Indians for thirty-five years, had high praise for the Chickasaw ponies and their riders. He noted that the latter always mounted from the right side. It appears that from earliest times and in all parts of the world right-hand mounting was customary until near-side mounting was introduced by the Romans, who carried their swords on their left, which barred off-side mounting.

When Atlantic seaboard colonials mentioned Spanish or Indian horses, it was nearly always the Chickasaw ponies they referred to. Governor Patrick Henry of Virginia was aware that they came from farther west. In 1779 he made an effort to get a sampling of this strain of Spanish horses by writing to his friend, George Rogers Clark, who was then in the Northwest Territory near the Mississippi River. He asked him to buy "Two Horses" and "Eight Mars" without sparing "the cost of the horses or the expense of sending them in" and not to "loose a moment in agreeing for them, for vast numbers of people are about to go out after them from here and will soon pick them all up and raise the price very high." He wanted "Blood bays as large as possible, fine delicate heads, long Necks, Ears small and pricked and near at Ends. Deep shoulders and chests, Large Arm, well Legg'd, upright pasterns, Clear of Long Hair. Bodys good, Loins round and very wide, Out Hock'd, Haunches Straight and go Wide behind. [If the horse] stands on Small Blazes, with either Hind foot white, so much the better. But there is something so striking and inexpressibly beautiful in a fine Horse that it is hard to describe [what I want]."

Clark had his hands full fighting the British along the Wabash, but he found time to answer, saying, "you have conceived a greater opinion of the horses in this country than I have." He went on to say that it was true that he himself had an excellent stallion that came from New Mexico, and if it were not for the flooded lands of the Wabash he would send him along to his friend. The Pawnees, six hundred miles to the west, he had heard had superior horses. He would inquire about the chances of getting some of them. As for the Illinois mares, he had seen some good ones, but hard usage from their barbarous horse masters had ruined them. There the matter dropped.

Nineteen years later, Thomas Jefferson tried to learn more about the Spanish horses rumored to be running wild by the thousands on the plains of Texas. He wrote to Philip Nolan of Natchez, who was reputed to have journeyed into prohibited Texas to bring out hundreds of Spanish horses and mules for sale to planters east of the Mississippi River.

Jefferson wrote, "You will render to natural history a very acceptable service if you will enable our Philosophical Society to add so interesting a chapter to the history of this animal."

Nolan was a daring young man about whom romance and legend thrived. He was the protégé—perhaps the foster son—and mysterious agent of the equally mysterious General James Wilkinson, whose alleged conspiracy with Aaron Burr and intrigue with the Spanish governor of Louisiana, Garondelet, have never been fully explained. At the time Jefferson's letter arrived, Nolan was again in Texas. Some months later, Jefferson learned that Nolan had been killed by Mexican dragoons in Texas—near present day Waco—where he and his party had built a corral in which to trap mustangs.

The interest of such men as Jefferson and Patrick Henry in Spanish stock points up the fact that the short horse was still in favor—at least in some parts of Virginia—long after the beginning of the trend toward four-mile races and the importation of English blood horses for that purpose.

Between 1700 and 1740 almost all Plains Indians, including the ones that ranged into Canada, had come into possession of horses through trade, stealth, or open warfare. By 1730 the lush pastures of the Nez Percé, Walla Walla, Umatilla, and Cayuse were dotted with horses. Cayuse became synonymous with horse when, later, Northwestern cowboys called any saddle horse a cayuse.

Many of the horses that got to the various tribes had passed through the hands of the Apaches, Comanches, and Kiowas, who lived closer to the source of supply, the Mexican and New Mexican ranches.

Most Indians preferred stealing horses to raising them. One old

Comanche chief, when asked why they didn't run their greatly outnumbered enemies, the Spaniards, out of the Southwest, answered, "We allow them to live here so they can raise and break horses for us." Certainly Indians were still stealing ready broken stock from the Southwest a hundred and fifty years after they first came into possession of horses. The horses that Lewis and Clark purchased from the Shoshones in 1805 carried Spanish brands. And farther to the west in the Nez Percé country, both horses and mules were similarly branded. As to the quality of the horses, Lewis and Clark, both Virginians and knowledgeable horsemen, praised them highly. Lewis wrote in his journal, ". . . Many of them would make a figure on the south side of the James River, or the land of fine horses." One herd was estimated by them at over four hundred head. Comanche and Apache raids in the Southwest and deep into Mexico continued until the end of the Indian wars in the late 1870s. Little effort was made by them to keep the best stallions for breeding purposes. It was a regular practice of the Comanche and Kiowa horsemen to hobble their mares and turn them out in wild horse country surrounding the Wichita Mountains in order to get a crop of foals from fine stallions they were unable or unwilling to capture. In this district in 1833, Colonel H. C. Brish, U.S. Cavalry, saw a large body of mounted Comanches. He later reported that he thought the Spanish horses he saw were "superior to any other on the face of the earth for cavalry purposes."

Around 1800 the Osages in western Missouri, eastern Kansas, and northeastern Oklahoma came into possession of some Chickasaw ponies rumored to have been upgraded with some Virginia Quarter Horse blood. When Washington Irving was visiting the Osages in the late 1820s and when George Catlin was with them in the early 1830s, Chief Clermont—whose portrait Catlin painted—took great pride in showing them his splendid horses. Among them were some line striped duns. Years later in this district—Claremore, Oklahoma, is where Chief Clermont's village stood—many duns, called Coyote Duns, were raised and were rated by more than a few cowmen as the best all-around cowhorses.

Spanish horses gradually fell into three main groupings: the ones on the Mexican ranches; the ones that became Indian ponies; and the ownerless ones, the feral mustangs. Each group suffered a change in environment and usage that affected size, speed, and conformation. On the open plains the mustangs and the Indian ponies fended for themselves. They were sometimes attacked by predatory animals. They never tasted grain. Living unsheltered through the bitter winters, they had to scrape their hoofs in the snow crust to find cured grass beneath. Failing that, they gnawed on the bark of cottonwood trees. Lean and gaunt each spring, they quickly fattened on the lush June grass.

As for the horses on the Mexican ranches, nearly all, except for the ones that were kept up and grained to run in the local races, were allowed to deteriorate because of the lack of a market and lack of competition. But no matter what group he was in, there was one quality the Spanish horse never lost. It was his amazing stamina. Vaqueros demanded endurance in their mounts. Men of early Texas and California reported that riders often kept their horses at a lope for hours on end. No matter what happened to them, the Spanish ponies still carried the genes of an ancient, well-set breed. It was not until the coming of the settlers from the East, with their cold-blood strains, that the true Spanish horse of the Western states became mongrelized.

The First Quarter Horses

To learn that the Quarter Horse is the oldest breed of horses (sans stud book, we must quickly add) in the United States often comes as startling news. To prove this assertion, those who would backtrack the Quarter Horse to his origins must of necessity go back over many crisscrossed paths on which the tracks of the Quarter Horse have been all but obliterated by the passage of generations of horses of all kinds. But regardless of how faint and meandering, all Quarter Horse trails in this country lead back eventually to Colonial Virginia at the time Englishmen were getting their first foothold in America.

There in Jamestown in 1610, six mares and one horse arrived with the "third supply" in one of Captain Newport's ships. However, the distinction of establishing the first equine family of Virginia was not to be theirs. Unfortunately, all seven were eaten during the following winter. The F.F.V. honors were reserved for seventeen sea-weary horses and mares that were helped off the ships of Thomas Dale in the spring of 1611. More horses were added three years later when Samuel Argall brought in several head from his sack of French Port Royal in Nova Scotia. There is little doubt that these horses were of the Spanish breed, having previously been captured by the French in the West Indies. Their arrival gave an early opportunity for the hot-blood of the Spanish horses to warm the colder although not predominantly cold-blood of the English horses.

Short racing had been legalized in Jamestown and the other colonies that were soon after established, when all were still struggling for a firm foothold in America. The sport was all the more appreciated because horses were hard to come by. Costs of shipping, possible injuries, or loss from storms and shipwreck, piracy or enemy attack kept the colonies in short supply for many years.

Certainly a remarkable interest in horse breeding occurred at an early period in the Virginia Colony. In 1649 the horse census there showed but 200 head all told. By 1671 there were close to 10,000 head. In a report of that date Governor Berkeley stated that 8,000 head were suitable for militia cavalry.

Among the group who, more than 300 years later, promoted and organized the American Quarter Horse Association was a scholarly young history professor named Robert Moorman Denhardt. Toward the end of the 1930s he was associated with the late Jack Hutchins, manager of the Shanghai Pierce Estate Ranch near Wharton, Texas, and the Johnny Ferguson Ranch nearby, in their horse-breeding programs. With the encouragement of his employers and many others, including Dan D. Casement and his son Jack Casement, Jim Minnick, R. Lee Underwood, Mrs. M. G. Micheals, Robert Kleberg, Dr. Northway, J. Ernest Browning, W. B. Warren, and others who shared an interest in preserving and improving the old Quarter Horse blood, Bob Denhardt with crusaderlike zeal went to work to research horses and breeders and to lay the foundation for the association. Helen Michaelis of Eagle Pass, Texas, horsewoman extraordinary, who with her husband carried on livestock operations in both Texas and New Mexico, also made invaluable research in the backgrounds of the Quarter Horse families which were to become the founders of the breed. The result of their combined studies convinced them that the Quarter Horse was practically set as a breed of sprint racers and all-around-using horse as early as 1665.

Whatever the exact time, but certainly long before 1700, the Virginia sprinters or short-horses were reproducing their kind with consistency. This is to say that the quarter-mile running horse—the Quarter Horse —predated the English blood-horse, whose General Stud Book was first published in 1793, with the resulting English Thoroughbred stud book making its appearance in 1827.

There can be little doubt that the grand "can do" Quarter Horse was in one sense the oldest and in another, America's youngest breed.

In predating the American Thoroughbred, the Quarter Horse contributed to that breed. Unfortunately, the records of the early breeders of Quarter Horses were haphazard, misleading, or nonexistent. Thus nearly all proof relating to Quarter Horse bloodlines, prior to the founding of the American Quarter Horse Association Registry in 1941, comes from the early American Stud Books that helped establish the Thoroughbreds. Few of these early books concerned themselves with the sprint horse branch of America's racing strains after they started their trek west. Subsequently, the Jockey Club of New York acquired the American Stud Book and henceforth closed it to all except distance-running Thoroughbreds.

Horses who rated a costly trip from England were of good stock, but it was not until 1730 that the first so-called blood horses, that is, ones of Oriental or Arabian breeding, were imported to America. Outcrossings before this time along the Atlantic seaboard had largely been with Spanish stock. These animals were captured in forays on the Spanish colonies in Florida and their mission settlements among the Guale Indians of present Georgia and the Temuca and Apalachee tribes of western Florida.

Although these sporadic acquisitions of hot-blood horses may have revivified the colonial strains, I have found no evidence of a lively trade in Spanish horses before 1700. It was about this time that the Chickasaw and Choctaw tribes came into possession of horses from west of the Mississippi River. At this time the English established an alliance with the Chickasaws which was to be unbroken for almost a hundred years, and during that time the Chickasaw Pony was a source of outcrosses for the colonial short-horse.

The Spanish horse came to the Chickasaws by a devious route. As mentioned previously, following the Indian Revolt of 1680 in New Mexico, all Spaniards were driven out of the province. Many of the horses looted from the Spanish missions and ranches fell into the hands of the Comanche and Kiowa-Apache Indians. To Indians, ever on the move, hunting game and raiding encroaching tribes, horses offered a miracle of mobility. News of them spread rapidly from tribe to tribe and in a remarkably short time they were trade item number one.

Just seven years after the 1680 New Mexican revolt, horses were for sale on the gulf coast of Texas. There La Salle, with his lost and disgruntled exploring party, was able to barter some hatchet heads and some glass beads for five horses. All wore Spanish brands. A few days later the French hope of getting a toehold in the Texas region died with the murder of La Salle by his mutinous men. But farther to the north on the Red and Arkansas Rivers, French trading posts were soon bartering guns, powder, lead, knives, hatchets, rum, beads, face color, ribbons, cloth, cooking pots, needles, looking glasses, candy, and many other items for furs and horses.

The horses went to the French traders at Natchez and on to the French post on Mobile Bay after it was established in 1702 by the "Canadian Cid," a sobriquet bestowed on Iberville. From Natchez and Mobile Bay the horses were sold to the Choctaws in present Mississippi and from them—no doubt after some hard fighting—their neighbors to the north, the Chickasaws, came into possession of Spanish horses from the American Southwest.

The extent of the use of Indian horses (Spanish horses) in cross breeding with the early American Quarter Horse is still a matter of speculation. Dr. George H. Conn thinks it was extensive. In his book *The Arabian Horse in America* he writes:

"The native American horses in Virginia and surrounding states at the time of the importation of English blood horses were chiefly of Chickasaw breeding." And he adds, "There was a marked improvement both in size and speed of these horses after the Chickasaw mares were cross-bred with English stallions."

Patriarchs of the Quarter Horse Breed

From Baltimore to Charleston in the late 1700s every schoolboy knew the initials C.A.Q.R.H. meant Celebrated American Quarter-mile Running Horse and that by changing the last letter to an M a mare was designated.

There were many good reasons for the popularity of short racing in the Southern colonies. For one thing the climate was warm and owners didn't want to punish their horses with grueling three- and four-mile races run in heats, particularly since most horses were used in other ways besides racing and couldn't take the necessary time to cool out and rest up. There were no central gathering places, as in England, with permanent long race courses laid out (even straight stretches along ordinary roads seldom exceeded one-fourth of a mile). But perhaps the most compelling reason for short racing was due to the unique society that developed in these English colonies. Although the Southern colonies were predominant in the sport, horse racing was popular in all the colonies.

In England—and all of Europe for that matter—horse racing was the exclusive sport of the wealthy landowning class and the noblemen.

Only they were able to maintain elaborate breeding establishments where horses could be raised for racing—and for nothing else. But in the burgeoning democracy of America, racing was a sport open to anyone who happened to have a fast horse, and most everyone owned horses. Rich or poor, they took pride in owning good ones. And to many men a good horse was synonymous with a speedy one. Most horses were *using* horses, that is, they served for transportation, for stock handling and other work, as well as for pleasure riding, cross-country hunting, and occasional racing.

In an age with few forms of entertainment, horse racing was the number one sport. Every village tavern, in its small way, was a racing club. The tracks were simply straight stretches found on the meandering country roads. If the smoothest and straightest bit was near the local tavern, all the better.

Here was the gathering place for neighbors to admire or fault each other's mounts and get in the proper mood to back their judgment. Generally the wagers were sizable enough to make the owning of a quarter-mile runner very worth while.

The prime requirement for short racing was that the horse break away fast from a standing start. He must have early speed, as they say, or quick burn. What men of those days wanted was much the same as is required of Quarter Horses today.

The Quarter Horse was, and is, a "big little horse," one whose balance, because of a generous sized head and muscular neck and breast, is farther forward than that of the more slender Thoroughbred. If you could pick him up with a pair of tongs, you would also find his center of gravity relatively low to the ground and forward of center. Thus his line of thrust is less elevated at take-off than a Thoroughbred's. Like a projectile with great power behind it, he requires less trajectory, moving off in a straight line closer to the ground.

His short coupled muscular body is held in a four-square stance by comparatively short legs set well under. The knees and hocks are low in proportion to the length of the legs. The compact body seems to be always poised, without agitation, ready for a sudden take-off in any direction. Forearms, thighs, stifles, and gaskins bulge with power. Sinewy, trim cannon bones join with strong articulated ankles and medium-length, medium-sloped pasterns. The feet are trim with flint-hard hoofs and well-padded heels.

The day in the life of a Quarter Horse of old Virginia might have gone something like this: while carrying his master on his plantation rounds he was turned aside perhaps to follow some hunting hounds across country where fences or downed logs or narrow creeks must be jumped (contrary to general opinion, riding after hounds cross-country originated in America rather than in England, where later the liveried, organized hunt was formalized). In the afternoon he might be seen waiting at a hitch rail, drowsing in the sun, when awakened by a rising drone of tavern talk which becomes excited and is climaxed with a rush of men from the tavern door. Then the pin ears prick forward and the bright eyes become alert to the men who swarm about him and another horse hitched nearby. Our Quarter Horse surmises that he has been matched in a hoss race.

Then with his master, or a boy he knows, up on his back, he quietly walks, then jogs, then canters a quarter mile or so down the road and, becoming more excited, is quite aware of his opponent, who moves along not far away. After jockeying and crowding the other horse for position behind a mark drawn across the dirt road with a stick, and after a few false starts, the jockeying ends with the drop of the hat—the race is on, bullet quick, from a standing start—and it is all over in less than twenty-five seconds.

Some starts were scored: that is, they were running starts beginning some distance behind the mark, and if the horses were lapped (the head of the horse behind overlapping the rear of the horse in front) when they crossed the line the starter yelled "go." Another way of starting was the *ask* and *answer* method. After the shinplasters were bet (paper money or promissory notes), someone spit on a chip of wood or a stone and threw it into the air and the contestants called out *wet* or *dry*. The winner got the choice of path—the right or left side. The toss was repeated for the *word*. That is, who was to *ask* and who was to *answer*.

Whether it was a standing or scored start one rider after jockeying for position would ask if the other was ready. If the answer was "yes," the race was off to a start. Two men usually judged the start and two judged the outcome. Not infrequently in the more rural areas the judges couldn't agree, which brought on a general fight. Then before too much damage was done the fight stopped and everybody got drunk.

While his boss pays off or collects, our Quarter Horse gets walked around for a little while to cool out. Then he carries his man home, where later on he may be ridden by a boy to bring in the cows from pasture for the evening milking.

The importation of English blood-horse stallions, the first being Bulle Rock, son of the Darley Arabian (according to many published reports but not in the general stud book), who arrived in 1730, did of course continue to benefit both the distance runners and the sprint horses of America.

A year later a Spanish—or Barb—stallion and several Spanish mares came from Spain to the Belair Stud, which had been established near Annapolis by Samuel Ogle, Lieutenant Governor of Maryland. Ogle sent one of his mares to Virginia to be bred to Gist's Bulle Rock. The results of this mating must have encouraged an interest in further cross breeding, because around 1742 the Belair Stud farm acquired three English imports, a stallion named Spark and a mare, Queen Mab, who had a filly by her side named Moll Brazen. Thus a cross of English and Spanish horses became the foundation stock for the Belair Stud. It continued until 1761.

When longer races—three- and four-mile heats—became popular in England, the racing gentry in Virginia soon followed the trend. As early as 1737, at a big picnic given by William Byrd II on St. Andrew's Day, the entertainment included a fiddling contest, foot races and wrestling, and a three-mile horse race run in heats.

Not long after this the center of horse breeding in Virginia shifted from the Quarter Horse country along the Rappahannock to the James River valley, where English distance runners (of Oriental breeding) were to set a course that would lead to the branching of the road of the long and short horses while at the same time contributing mightily to the latter breed and ensuring its recognition later on.

JANUS (1746–79)

Janus was brought to Virginia by Mordecai Booth, a well-to-do shipper and plantation owner, in 1752 say some, or in 1755, according to the late John Hervey, respected historian of the light horse breeds. This stocky stallion was named Janus and he was sired by Old or English Janus by the Godolphin Arabian. He stood about fourteen and a half hands high, was very muscular, had one white hind foot, a narrow blaze in his forehead, and a speckled rump. He had been foaled in England in 1746 and there had won some four-mile races before being retired by a pulled tendon, as some have conjectured. Perhaps because he had not been at stud long enough when sold to Mr. Booth for his stock to prove itself on the track, or for some other unknown reason, he was never listed in the English General Stud Book.

In America the leg injury, if that was what had taken him from the track, apparently healed, for he had a chance to prove his speed in fast

This imaginary portrait of Janus is based on descriptions of him made by men who had seen him.

James River company. He once beat a William Byrd horse in a race run in four mile heats. After that, little more is heard of him on the Virginia turf, but, standing at stud, he became known as a sire of amazing prepotency. Most of his distance running get were mares, however, and as more renown clings to stallions than to mares, his worth as a sire of distance horses was recognized only at a later date.

Somehow or other the sprint breeders south of the James River and in North Carolina obtained him. There quarter racing continued to be more popular than in the more settled and fashionable districts along the James and north of it. The American Revolution slowed up racing but never brought it to a halt. Although many good horses were dispersed and destroyed in Virginia and Maryland, the loss was not nearly so severe as it was in New England, New York, New Jersey, Pennsylvania, and parts of the Carolinas. In Chowan, Halifax, and Bertie Counties, North Carolina, and other more rural sections, Janus was taken from place to place to cover quarter-running mares of reputed Chickasaw breeding. His blood being largely Arab-Barb nicked so naturally with theirs that his sons and daughters were endowed with a heritage of startling speed. Through them their old sire's name was saved from oblivion.

Senator John Goode of Mecklenburg County, Virginia, a dominant figure among the horse-racing gentry, was one who had never lost sight of the old prepotent stud, as evidenced by the fact that he bred and owned two of Janus' famous sons, Babram and Twigg. The latter foaled after Janus went to North Carolina. Babram was foaled in 1766 and was considered the best race horse of his day. At the age of twenty-two when he was ahead of Old Jupiter in a race on the Lewis paths, he fell and broke his neck. C.A.Q.R.H. Twigg was foaled in 1778 when Janus was in his thirty-second year. He was a beautiful bright bay horse, heavily made, with a blaze face and two white hind feet. Standing at 14.1, he was one inch shorter than his dad, which strengthens the belief that his dam was of Chickasaw breeding. Patrick Nisbett Edgar says in *The American Race Turf Register* that "It was impossible for any horse in existence to beat him unless he was made to carry heavy weights, or run a distance beyond one quarter of a mile." He beat Polly Williams eight out of nine races and Paddy Whack eleven out of twelve races. The two times he was beaten, he was carrying twenty pounds more than his rival. One can imagine that the number of tons of tobacco wagered on these races was considerable.

Senator Goode decided that it was no credit to his state or to himself as a racer of Janus stock to have the old campaigner die away from his first American home. So for 150 pounds, Virginia currency, Senator Goode purchased Janus, and late in the fall the old horse started the road trip north. He was nearing his thirty-fourth year, extremely aged for a horse, and he never made it. He became ill on the road and was given care and shelter in a stable on the plantation of Colonel Haynes in Warren County, North Carolina. There he died either late in 1779 or early in 1780.

It was many years after his death that Janus was given the accolade of the printed word that was to fix his worth and fame beyond the vagaries of horsemen's lore. *The Gentlemen's New Pocket Farrier*, published in Richmond, Virginia, by Richard Mason in 1814, gave his pedigree thus:

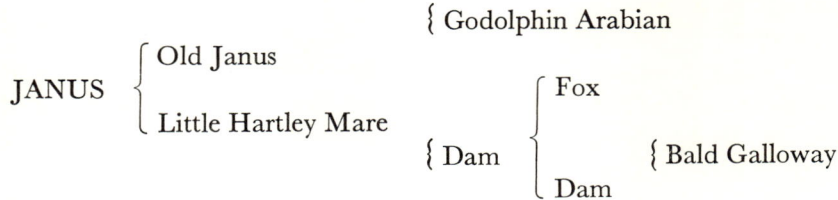

stating that it was "probably genuine" although not in the stud book (English). *The American Farmer,* published by John Stuart Skinner, the leading stock journal of the 1820s, stated that "although Janus partook of every cross in his pedigree calculated for the distance turf horse, yet his stock were more remarkable for speed than bottom. Janus from his shoulder back was considered the most perfectly formed horse ever seen in Virginia by the most skillful connoisseurs; he was remarkable for roundness of contour, strength of articulation, and indicating great power in his whole conformation. His stock partook of these qualities in an eminent degree, and for 30 or 40 years they were considered as a 'peculiar stock,' as they invariably exhibited even in the third and fourth generation from the old horse, the same compactness of form, strength and power. The Janus stock have exceeded all others in the United States for speed, durability and general uniformity of good form."

This opinion is well backed by *The American Race Turf Register,* which lists dozens of Janus mares. In her book *Matriarchy of the American Turf,* Mrs. Marguerite Farlee Bayliss points out the considerable contributions Janus made to the American Thoroughbred. One of his daughters was the queen mother of the Maria West strain. Regret, the only filly ever to win the Kentucky Derby, traced to the Maria Wests.

In Volume I of *The American Race Turf Register,* John Randolph is quoted as saying that the belief that the Janus stock lacked bottom was a "vulgar error" which "arose from his getting the speediest quarter horses out of ordinary mares," but, "whenever he had blood-mares he got horses that ran any distance."

John Randolph, described by a man who knew him as having "as much assumed self-consequence as any two-footed animal I ever saw," was the founder of the famous Roanoke Stud. During its thirty-eight-year existence (1795–1833) it produced many horses known to the tracks from Baltimore to Charleston. Quarter Horses were always featured among the lot, which shows that even the exaggeratedly aristocratic nurtured in their hearts a deep affection and regard for the hardy, compact sprint horses.

In recalling his early twenties, Randolph said he spent most of his time "riding from one race field to another," and he mentioned Pride's Old Field, Gilles Field, Ravenscroft, Newmarket near Petersburg, Nicholson's in Mecklenburg County, the Lewis Paths near Alexandria, and others. Once he rode a horse named Koulikhan, who, like Steel Dust sixty-five years later, was not raised as a race horse and was over ten years old when he ran his first race. Randolph brought him in a winner over the favored Quarter Horse Bajazet.

This "old lover of the smack of the whip," as Randolph once referred to himself, rode in many match races, usually on his own horses, many of which were of Janus breeding, where "owners up" was often made a requirement. Late in life he wrote, "The need to 'plumb the track' as I have heard old racers say, conjure visions of that earliest form of Virginia horse sport which had its origins in the mists of Saxon England."

Babram, Celer, Twigg, Peacock, Janus Jr., the sire of Printer I, and many other sons and daughters of Janus were given biographies in Patrick Nisbett Edgar's *Sportsmans Herald and General Stud Book*, published in New York in 1831. Celer, bred by Mr. Meade of Virginia, sometimes referred to as Meade's Celer, was foaled in 1774, and in the opinion of Richard Mason, founder and first editor of *Mason's Farrier*, propagated a stock superior to that of his sire. Which reminds us that it is the difference of opinion that makes horse races.

The Janus family did much to broaden the base of Quarter Horse stock that was to branch away from the long Thoroughbred. These two paths, representing the long and the short of the same breed, would become widely separated at times but never so far that they did not converge on occasions. In any event, it appears certain, regardless of meager and careless records, that more than half of the founding families of the Quarter Horse breed which came along over a hundred and fifty years later traced to Janus.

In New England the Pilgrims had brought no horses to their original settlements, but in 1629, nine years after their first landing, the founders of the Bay Colony brought in thirteen head. Before the century was out the canny New England merchants had opened a lively trade with the West Indies in which horses featured not so much in the sport of racing, although that too was indulged, but as counters in a three-way money-making go-around. From the West Indies, where horse raising had been given up to make way for the more profitable sugar crop, Spanish horses were taken in trade for Yankee goods. Then when the West Indian planters, who no longer raised them, were in the market for horses, the New Englanders traded horses for molasses. The molasses made into rum was the medium of exchange for slaves purchased in Africa. By the year 1700 the islands of the Caribbean were visited regularly by the Yankee "Jockey Ships," as they were called.

Horse racing came into popularity after Governor Richard Nicolls captured New York from the Dutch. In 1665 he had a two-mile oval track laid out at Hempstead Heath on Long Island. New York State was also the first important center for trotting races, first under the saddle and then in harness.

In Rhode Island the family of horses known as Narragansett Pacers was founded, according to reports, by a Spanish Barb horse that was found on Judith Point. It was assumed that he swam ashore from the wreck of a ship. He was named Old Snip. Governor Robinson of Rhode Island bred him to mares reputed to have been Irish Pacing Hobbies and Scotch Galloways or a cross of the two. Even French coach horses and Canadian Pacers were considered as contributing to the Narragansett Pacers. The strain survived for many generations in the locality where it originated, and some were taken into South Carolina and Virginia.

Following the arrival of Janus in Virginia in the mid-1700s many English blood-horses were brought to this country. In addition to the Belair Stud in Maryland previously mentioned and the Roanoke Stud of John Randolph in Virginia, there were noted breeding establishments in most of the colonies. Edward Fenwick's John Island Stud off the coast of Charleston, South Carolina, imported many stallions that carried the blood of the Godolphin Barb, which he crossed on Chickasaw mares. Narragansett Pacers had also added their blood to the John Island horses prior to 1700. Spanish and Arabian horses were imported to the Carolinas until about 1804.

New York received twenty English race mares between 1765 and 1829. North Carolina, New Hampshire, Vermont, Pennsylvania, Connecticut, and Massachusetts all improved their horses with imported stock. One in Massachusetts that gained popularity was a beautiful black stallion shipped from Arabia via England to Timothy Ruggles, a well-known politician in the state.

In Vermont, Justin Morgan's horse (as previously mentioned) so proved his ability as a worker, racer, and sire that a breed was built on his progeny. The breed of Morgan horses still adds luster to Vermont.

Bellsize, an English blood-horse, upgraded the horses around Philadelphia shortly before the Revolutionary War. But it was Virginia that stood out as the supreme horse-breeding area. Here, on its rolling pastures, were raised the predominant number of America's founding families of light horse stock.

Following Janus, another blood-horse imported from England contributed much to both the sprint and distance runners of Virginia. He was named Diomed, and he was a great-great grandson of the Byerly Turk and the Darley Arabian, and related as well to the other great Oriental sire, the Godolphin Barb. He was in direct line from the never beaten race horse King Herod.

It seems that Diomed and his grooms didn't hit it off too well and some of his foals were considered intractable. Whatever the causes—besides, of course, the fact that he was also getting a little long in the tooth—he was sold at the age of twenty-one to a Virginian for $250. The sea voyage that followed in 1798, and his new environment near the James River, apparently gave Diomed a new lease on life. From that time on until his death in 1808 at the advanced age of thirty-one, when owned by Colonel Holmes, he sired some of the best known turf horses of the time. Among them were Truxton, Andrew Jackson's famed race horse, and Duroc, the father of the celebrated American Eclipse. When he was twenty-nine years old he sired the magnificent Sir Archy, who was to rank close to Janus as a founding father of the Quarter Horse tribe (See genealogical charts in Appendix A).

Sir Archy was commandingly beautiful, a bay with the only white on him being his off hind foot. He stood 16 hands high and weighed—in good flesh—1400 pounds. He was out of imported Castianira, who was taken in 1804 by her owners, Colonel Taylor and Colonel Randolph, to be served by Diomed, then standing at Colonel Seldon's farm a few miles south of Richmond. Many years later, when Sir Archy's breeding was questioned, Seldon's son stated that he had witnessed the mating of Castianira and Diomed. Sir Archy was foaled in 1805 on the plantation of Ben Lomond near Rock Castle, Virginia. Strangely—because Sir Archy himself was a long horse, a four-miler, as were most of his sons—it was his grandsons and granddaughters who produced sprint horses.

Ten years after his death in 1833, Sir Archy was rated by *The American Race Turf Register* as the "supreme American horse" on the turf and in the stud. Like his ancestor King Herod, he never lost a race. General William R. Johnson, who had paid $5,000 for him as a colt, retired him to stud at the age of five because he could no longer find anyone who would wager against him in a race.

No less than 160 of his daughters are in the American Stud Book and almost that many sons. Through his son Bertrand came the numerous tribe of Bertrand horses in Kentucky, and through another son, Wilke's Wonder, his blood flows in the Tennessee Walking Horse breed. Copperbottom, Sir Solomon, Timoleon, Director, Henry, Sir William, Jenny Bertrand, Betsy, and Vanity are just a few of Sir Archy's famed sons and daughters who live in American turf history.

Printer I, a grandson of Janus by Janus II, was foaled in 1800 and lived until 1828. From Virginia he was taken to Fairfield County, Ohio, where pioneering conditions favored the versatile sprint racer and using horse just as they had in early day Virginia.

Settlers who migrated west from the tidewater country treasured with nostalgic fervor the good horse blood they brought with them to be the foundation stock in a new land. My own ancestor, Colonel George West I, having served in the Virginia Light Dragoons in the American Revolution, settled along with Captain (naval) Clark, his father-in-law, and family near Clarksville, Tennessee, in 1784. If when leaving his home in Bertie County, North Carolina, the stamping grounds of Janus, his entourage included no kin of Janus, it would seem strange. All we really know, however, is that he spoke lovingly of his horses in the will he made shortly before his death in 1810. In it he mentioned "the Halequin [sic] Filly" and "my young stud Snap Dragon." We can only suspect that they were Quarter Horses, considering the time and his place of origin. It is known that Imported Dragon by Woodpecker first stood in North Carolina and then in Tennessee, where he died in 1812, and that he sired Cage's Dragon of Tennessee, whose first dam was by Truxton and second dam by Barey's Grey Medley.

Before 1850, Copperbottom, the son of Sir Archy and Shiloh, who traced directly to him, and Steel Dust, who traced to both Sir Archy and Janus, had extended the branching trail of the Quarter Horse to Texas. There they were soon joined by horses of Printer I breeding (from Janus). It was from this heritage, followed by various experiments in outcrossings, that a numerous progeny of cowponies came to spread throughout the West while riding herd on a vast cattle industry.

The Horse Experimenters

Horses were so badly needed in the winning and settling of the West that horse breeders experimented in the hope of developing a type especially suited to the needs of the time and the region.

When Missouri, Kansas, and Nebraska were first settled, horses for cattle ranching were not the main concern. The prime need was for light draft, coach stock, and saddle travelers. To supply this need, Morgans, Thoroughbreds, and the coaching strains of Cleveland Bays or crossbreeds of all three, called "American" horses, were further crossed on range mares, with widely varying results.

Over the Western trails to California and Nevada, the Oregon Trail and the Santa Fe Trail and all the offshoots traveled horses of every description. Things were moving so fast few horse breeds could become well set. Each new thrust into the West plumbed the very bottom of horse endurance. For instance, the 400 head of horses quickly purchased for the pony express in 1859–60 were made up of both Spanish and American horses. The HORSES WANTED ad that appeared in a St. Joseph newspaper asked for ". . . 200 grey mares from 4 to 7 years old —not over 15 hands high—well broke to saddle—with black hoofs . . ." How many were obtained that met these exact specifications is not known. But shortly after the ad ran in the paper, Ben Ficklin, the general superintendent of the pony express, was in the vicinity of Santa Fe, New Mexico, buying top grade Spanish horses. In Utah, Doc Faust supplied rough broken wiry mustangs from his Rush Valley ranch. For the California and Nevada relay stations, W. W. Finney and Bolivar Roberts gathered together a bunch of durable broncs from California ranches.

The boom of a starting cannon sent Johnny Frey and his nervous Thoroughbred mare Sylph plunging out of a cheering crowd in St. Joseph, Missouri, on that memorable April evening in 1860, to make the first run for the pony express. After crossing on the ferry to the Kansas side, Sylph settled down to the serious business of getting someplace else. According to Ralph Moody in his *Riders of the Pony Express,* she raced her lap of about twenty-two miles in approximately one hour and forty-five minutes, and most of it in pitch darkness. Changing at relay points to three other mounts, Johnny covered eighty miles that night in six hours and twenty-five minutes. In his pocket he carried a quarter given to him by Ben Ficklin just before the start. "What's this for?" Johnny had asked. "To buy a rope to hang yourself with, in case you fail to ride into Seneca tonight on scheduled time," was Ben's blustering reply.

The initial run was a foretaste of the killing demands on the horses —not to mention the men. Later schedules called for runs of from twelve to fifteen miles for the horses and sixty to eighty miles for the men, regardless of obstacles that most of them were to encounter at one time or another, such as rivers to be crossed, hostile Indians to be outraced, buffalo herds and wolf packs to be avoided, storms, frozen trails, snowbanks, and gallops under a blistering sun.

It wasn't long until the pony express had to replace many of the American horses with hardy Spanish stock. However, for other uses the situation was reversed. Spanish horses were poorly suited to shoulder pulling and where they served as wagon and stagecoach teams they were supplanted by American horses as soon as the latter were available. For cavalry use the troopers wanted the taller American horses that gave them the upper hand in horse-to-horse and hand-to-hand conflict.

In the northwestern part of the United States and in Canada quite a different type of horse was developed. In that region the Indian ponies of the same Arab-Barb heritage, of course, but grown heavier and larger on the very nutritive northern pasturage and in a bracing climate, were not only crossed with the American horses and moderately sized cold-blood draft stock but were also interbred with the really large Percherons and the feather-footed Clydesdales. These outcrossings produced pack and saddle animals as well as draft stock with bones and leg joints heavy enough to reduce incidents of lameness on the stony mountain trails. Their added bulk, which won them the name of *chunks,* served as padding against the bitter winter cold. The bigger-footed hairy-fetlocked types were given the nickname of *puddin' foots.*

Although the chunks at various periods predominated in the Northwest, there remained plenty of pasture room for breeders of a more refined type. Montana had legalized racing almost from its beginning, which gave the Thoroughbred tradition an early start. Beginning in the 1880s Tom McAllister became one of the largest operators in the range horse industry. Thousands of his horses ranged from the Mizpah and Rosebud creeks of southern Montana to the Milk River near the Canadian border. He is reputed to have imported Thoroughbred stallions by the carload, to be turned loose on his Montana range to improve his stock. Other ranchers emulated him in lesser degrees. In 1884, according to Government statistics, 7000 head of American horses were taken west to improve the range horse strains. By 1900 Montana had more range horses than any other state. Miles City became the nation's largest horse market, supplying the major proportion of the 45,000 head that the United States exported to foreign countries each year, a number that didn't begin to deplete Northwestern horse herds.

When the prices for horses slumped during the money panic of the early 1890s, ranchers all over the West saw some dark days. As William Anson, owner of the Head of the River Ranch—it was on the Concho

River near San Angelo, Texas—put it, "money panic followed drought, cheap horses followed the money panic; cattle began to increase in value; what was the good of breeding horses which would not pay when you could make good money out of cattle; sell 'em, give 'em away; make room for cattle; and this went on for several years until it was arrested by large purchases of the British government during the Boer War."

In 1902 the number of horses sent abroad jumped to 103,000. This time the Southwest supplied the greater number of them. This was partly because it was thought that the trimmer horses from the warm Southwest would do better in Africa, where they were to be used, than the heavier chunks and other types from the Northwest. And it was due also to a large extent because William Anson of Texas, the younger son of a British nobleman, was given free rein as the horse-purchasing agent for the British Government. Anson was well known as a booster of Texas horses and had promoted them as polo mounts. When visiting in London he always took a Texas horse along to ride in Rotten Row.

Following the Boer War the price of horses took another header. Only in the pastures of the most dedicated breeders were the individuals preserved who represented the best bloodlines of the Quarter Horses.

In the Northwest the pastures were alive with horses. With no active market for them the ranchers no longer went to the trouble and expense of branding. Wild herds increased alarmingly. More and more ranch lands were cut up into farms, and the wild herds became such a menace to the young stock and crops the Forestry Department in Washington sent out orders for rangers to kill all wild horses on government domain. Then came World War I, and with it a fresh demand for horses. Wranglers leaped into their saddles with a shout of joy and started on the biggest horse roundup the West had ever seen. From 1914 to 1918 over a million head of horses found buyers in Grand Island, Nebraska, which for that period was the largest horse market of all time.

In military markets, the chunk, somewhat refined with outcrosses of Thoroughbred or Morgan blood, was called the American Artillery Horse and was considered the world's best.

Following the war the horse population in the United States again declined rapidly. Military and civilian mechanization, motorized transportation, hard-top roads, engine-powered farm machinery—all contributed. A small upsurge in the demand for horses did occur for a short time in the depression years of the early 1930s, when small farmers found machinery and the gas to run it too costly. To supply them, some old-time mustang roundups took place.

Being all-around hard workers under the saddle and in harness, the chunks have survived all adversity. They are still numerous. In almost any stable that rents out saddle horses to inexperienced and uncritical riders, whether it be east, west, north or south, the chunks are to be seen. They are the least expensive to buy and the easiest to keep. To most everyone except Westerners they still represent the *Western* horse. The term is so encompassing that it often precludes the very thought that the West is also the home of a large proportion of America's most highly bred horses, which includes the Quarter Horses.

Not all chunks were the bench-legged, hairy, rawboned beasts that so many of us can call to mind. Some of the more refined ones of Spanish, Thoroughbred, Quarter Horse, and Percheron crosses became very fast, heavily muscled cowhorses. A distinctive strain of these horses was good enough to be labeled Bulldog horses, a term usually reserved for chunks crossed with the old Steel Dust strains. They had so many things going for them, such as early speed, very sturdy legs, and constitutions to withstand hard work and rigorous winters, that any deficiencies they had were often overlooked. Some of these families of horses accepted as Quarter Horses had such exaggeratedly low withers, so rounded and fat, that they merged with a thick neck leaving little to which the saddletree could cling. In fact, to minimize slipping, special saddles were finally made for use on the mutton-withered kangaroo horses, as they were called in some horse circles. These horses did much to discredit Quarter Horses in certain districts.

Before dismissing the chunks the rather specialized field in which they really excelled should be mentioned. When rodeos found widespread popularity, the chunks moved into the spotlight. It was from their ranks that the bucking stock was recruited. This mongrelized strain with its heterogeneous breeding which commingled hot-blood, cold-blood and sometimes pony blood, often from the very best families, seemed to produce individuals simply loaded with TNT. They get further mention in the chapter dealing with rodeos.

Although many chunks and mixed breed horses are still around, their days are numbered. They are rapidly being supplanted by more refined saddle stock in which registered animals predominate.

The Cowhorse

When the first Anglo-American stockmen arrived in the Southwest, they found two natural resources that were a phenomenon of the time and place: Spanish horses and longhorn cattle roaming the country in a feral state. Both had been conditioned and acclimatized by almost two centuries in the limestone hills, prickly pear and mesquite valleys, and high plains, during which time they had populated a wide area. The longhorns, hiding in the brush, were there for the taking by men hardy enough and smart enough to round them up and find a market for them. The first problem for the ambitious longhorn gatherers was to get astride cowponies with savvy and guts to match their own. Just such animals were found in three main groupings into which Spanish horses had fallen; in wild mustang bands, on Mexican ranches, and in Indian pony herds.

All were ideally equipped for the role of pointing up the vast beef industry which was so soon to follow on their heels. They met a need at a time when neither the country nor the economy was ready for more refined stock. Both the longhorns and the mustangs that jumped them into line had inherited from their desert-bred ancestors flint-hard hoofs and bones which kept them going on the long hoof-wearing drives to markets at distant army posts, railhead towns in Kansas, and grazing ranges farther to the north, often over trails with meager forage and infrequent watering places, and the longhorns whose heads sprouted lances were more than a match for marauding lobos.

The wind and endurance of the mustangs were simply phenomenal, as I discovered on many occasions in my youth. At various times my father had purchased carloads of mustangs—about forty to the car— shipped in via the Santa Fe Railway from Roswell, New Mexico. The mention of them to Roy Davis, editor of the *Quarter Horse Journal,* started us checking on dates, and Roy came to the conclusion that his own father may have been the one who rounded up these very same ponies in the vicinity of the Santa Rosa Indian Reservation.

Boldness and courage were other admirable qualities the Spanish mustangs inherited from their war-horse ancestors. A mustang would fight for his life, whether trapped, caught in quicksand, or just plain sick, with more tenacity than any other kind of horse I know of, and his clever foot action made him a joy to ride, easy on one's seat at all gaits and for long hours. All in all, the mustang was a sure-footed willing worker, spunky and wise in the ways of cattle. The very expression "cow savvy" was inspired by him, a trait, I must say, that is now claimed for most ranch-bred saddle horses including the Morgans, American Saddle Bred, and all Quarter Horses, even though the last might be as much as fifteen-sixteenths Thoroughbred.

One well-known book on horsemanship written from the Eastern viewpoint dismissed all Western horses as being "mean natured." Apparently, the author had never had the pleasure of meeting a Quarter Horse. The good nature and amiable disposition of this breed is so well known as to be taken for granted. By *Western* horses, the author was probably taking a slap at the chunk—not the mustang—because few Eastern people ever saw a real Spanish mustang and fewer still ever rode one. My friend Bob Brislawn, who founded the *Spanish Mustang Registry,* informs me there are but one hundred and thirty alive today in the United States. The pure Españoles when well broken were as dependable and gentle as any horse on earth. It was a practice with me as with many others who rode them over treeless plains under a hot sun to sometimes dismount and take a rest or even a nap in the shade of one's horse. Mustang shade, I found, was as safe as any. In my book *Mustang Roundup* (1964) I tell of my experiences with these intriguing animals.

Today it is *de rigueur,* particularly among breeders of racing Quarter Horses, to minimize any contribution made by the Spanish horse of the Southwest—even to the early cowhorse strains of the Quarter Horse. One breeder told me that he never saw a mustang or Indian pony that was worth a bowl of jailhouse chili. It is an opinion held by many. However, there are a few who have taken a longer and kindlier look at the truly remarkable heritage of the Spanish horse as he was before being mongrelized by heterogeneous outbreeding with various types of cold-bloods brought to the West by settlers from east of the Mississippi and widely dispersed by the Indians. That Spanish horses contributed to the Quarter Horse breed is incontrovertible.

Dan Casement, one of America's notable stock raisers, who had ranches in Kansas and Colorado (and whose son Jack Casement carries on the family devotion to the breeding of fine horses), was one of the major influences in getting the American Quarter Horse Association established, and he was outspoken in his praise of the Spanish cowhorses. He stressed their amazing aptitude at handling cattle, their versatility, maneuverability, endurance, and absolute trustworthiness. A man whose opinion he highly regarded and who had sold him his first notable Quarter Horse stallion, Concho Colonel, was William Anson, previously mentioned as a horse buyer for the British Government.

William Anson came to Texas in 1893, where he established the Head of the River Ranch southwest of San Angelo. He is credited with being the first Texas horse breeder to make a studious effort to trace the bloodlines of the Quarter Horse. In a 1907 article he wrote: "The original ancestors [of the Quarter Horse] were brought to Texas by the first settlers who came mostly from Tennessee . . . and who . . . brought their race horses with them. The Mexicans thought they had the fastest short distance horses in the world, and were prepared to back their opinions, but the American ponies, or rather horses, invariably won the races that were matched, and by this means a good many of the Mexican ponies passed into the hands of the Americans and were bred to the Tennessee stallions."

Since William Anson used the word "pony" and then corrected himself so as not to be misunderstood by the sticklers for the rule book, perhaps this is as good a place as any to mention that the word "pony" can have an entirely different connotation in the West than it has in the East. According to the American Horse Shows Association you are correct in calling any horse under 14.2 hands a pony. But in being arbitrary about it you should remember that the word "pony" will include many breeds such as Arabians, Morgans, Palominos, Hackneys, Quarter Horses, Appaloosas, Spanish mustangs, and Galiceños. In the West "pony" is often used as a term of affectionate regard. "My ole pony" could well be a reference to a horse sixteen hands high. Indian ponies were of all sizes. In the northwest districts Indian ponies of the better mounted tribes averaged close to fifteen hands in the heyday of the horse Indians.

In an article on "Genetic Trends in the Quarter Horse Breed," written by Dr. A. O. Rhoad at the invitation of the AQHA and published in the *Quarter Horse Journal,* he stated that only 38 per cent of the 556 horses that were accepted for tentative registration by the American Quarter Horse Association in 1940–41 traced to the old established bloodlines, that is, to the fourteen Quarter Horse families researched by Robert Denhardt and the late Helen Michaelis and included in the Quarter Horse Stud Book. While the 556 horses were the source of future breeding operations, they were not the only source. As Dr. Rhoad points out, they were "not even the major source."

In looking at the chart of the founding families of the Quarter Horse breed in the Appendix, it seems that all bases are covered, that few places are open for horses of unknown origin. However, many bloodlines if traced back a few generations peter out into blank spaces—usually on the bottom line, the dam's side.

From the original 556—105 stallions and 451 mares—Dr. Rhoad took 100 at random, traced each back to the fourth generation, and found that the average progenitor had 15.5 per cent Quarter Horse blood, 14.9 per cent Thoroughbred blood, and 69.6 per cent of unknown blood. Of the original 556, more than a fourth had Spanish names.

Following the Civil War, which interrupted the cattle business just as it was getting started, the industry boomed throughout the West. Soldiers on the frontier, Indians forced to live on reservations, an increasing urban population swelled by millions of immigrants who poured into the country from Europe to man the burgeoning industrial plants, all created a demand for more meat and hides. The new manufacturing machinery required enormous quantities of leather belting to transmit power to the whirling pulleys and shafts. This item alone accounted for the tough thick hides of untold thousands of longhorns and buffalo. It was a demand that brought them to the brink of extinction.

Within the life span of a good old cowpony the grazing lands of most of Western North America were stocked with Texas cattle. And the most important factor in their handling—next to the cowboys—was the horses they rode. Man and horse shared the closest of teamwork, some of it explosive and dangerous. Almost every man who ever helped head a trail herd north could tell of river crossings, rope work, storms, and stampedes, when his life depended on the intelligence, agility, or speed of his horse.

When one considers that the pioneer cattlemen and cowboys spent a good part of their lives on the backs of horses shufflefooting the grass lands from the Rio Grande to the far reaches of Western Canada, the interest they had in developing a cowhorse as near as possible to the heart's desire becomes understandable. It followed that the upgrading of the cowhorse began almost with the arrival of the first cowman.

With all his virtues, the Spanish horse of the time and place, whether mustang or Indian pony (except for the treasured racers on the haciendas), fell far short of the ideal. For one thing he lacked stature and muscles for weight carrying. Nor did he have the blazing take-off speed for roping that was needed to put his man in throwing position without running the steer or calf all over hell's half acre. Moreover, the Spanish range ponies lacked grace of neck and style. Only the exception could be called a beautiful animal. Caballeros, cavaliers, charros, chivalry, chevaliers, cavalrymen, and cowmen—horsemen the world over, whether of the "c" fraternities or not—are all proud men. Whatever the action, they want the horse under them to do a specialist's job, and they want him to look good while he is doing it. What the cowmen and the working cowboys wanted was *muy caballo,* truly a dream horse. One that could do the fast hard work of a cowhorse, turning abrupt speed on and off without getting nervous about it; one that could carry a big man and a heavy stock saddle for hours on end on workdays and still have enough *go* left in him to win sprint races on Sunday; one with cow savvy so he could outguess cattle and dominate them; with brains enough to learn tricky jobs and know when to perform them without constant direction; one that could forage and thrive, if need be, on stinted rations; and it went without saying that he should have easy riding gaits, a pliant nature, good wind, and willingness galore.

What resulted after years of experimental breeding was remarkably close to this demanding ideal, a type of horse which was to become in 1940 the American Quarter Horse.

3

Founding Families

For simplification the ancestors of the American Quarter Horses are listed in three main groups: the Patriarchs; the sprinting sires of the nineteenth and early twentieth centuries who established dominant Quarter Horse families; and the Forerunners of a New Breed, horses who contributed greatly to the Quarter Horse breed but who came along too early to be registered in it. For brevity only three stallions and one mare are mentioned in this group. They are Little Joe, Zantanon, Old Sorrel, and Della Moore. Many others whose stock won recognition are mentioned later on.

From 1850 to 1911 fourteen dominant Quarter Horse families emerged. All were established by champion sprint race stallions. Helen Michaelis, at the time of the founding of the AQHA, listed them:

			Family established	
1.	PRINTER I	1800–28	1804	Pennsylvania and Ohio
2.	COPPERBOTTOM	1828–60	1832	Pennsylvania and Texas
3.	SHILOH	1844–69 (foaled in Illinois)	1848	Texas
4.	STEEL DUST	1845–74 (foaled in Illinois)	1849	Texas
5.	OLD BILLY	1862–86	1866	Texas
6.	COLD DECK	1868–90	1872	Missouri and Oklahoma
7.	ROAN DICK	1879–1901	1883	Illinois
8.	LOCK'S RONDO	1880–97	1884	Texas
9.	TRAVELER	1885–1910	1889	Texas
10.	SYKES RONDO	1887–1907	1891	Texas
11.	OLD FRED	1893–1915 (foaled in Missouri)	1897	Colorado
12.	PETER MCCUE	1895–1923 (foaled in Illinois)	1899	Illinois, Texas, Oklahoma, Colorac
13.	BLAKE FAMILY	c. 1900	1900	Oklahoma
14.	JOE BAILEY	1907–34	1911	Texas

Not included in this list is the family founded by Little Joe, the most notable son of Traveler. Although he was foaled in 1905 and sired many sprint racers, the most famous being Zantanon, the Little Joe family had to wait for the amazingly prepotent King P-234, the son of Zantanon, to bring it widespread recognition.

Without resorting to a labyrinthine recitation of the "begats," Don Marquis' term for the biblical Patriarchs, a few of the more important individuals should be mentioned to clarify their position on the main genealogical chart.

There will always be some element of doubt as to the exact breeding of some of the early Quarter Horses. All early stud books were, because of the nature of racing, the money involved, and the nature of the men who "plumbed the track," works of considerable fiction. No turfman was inclined to darken his animal's past by mentioning misalliances. How could a gentleman editor of the British Jockey Club's *General Stud Book* question the bald statement of a gentleman of noble blood and avoid swords or pistols at dawn? American compilers of race-horse pedigrees faced the same problem. What could one do when his host, perhaps a prominent hard-drinking turfman, insisted on some questionable point in a pedigree, if he had no positive proof to refute it? Spit in his eye? Sir Archy, Copperbottom, Shiloh, Steel Dust, Cold Deck, Mary Cook, and others have had their accepted pedigrees questioned. The diligent and most trustworthy research made by William Anson, Robert M. Denhardt, Helen Michaelis, Nelson Nye, and others has been greatly beneficial to the AQHA in charting bloodlines in the founding families. There remain, however, points of controversy. Errors are proliferated by writers who have done no independent research, who repeat the errors of others.

Often confusion is caused by the use of similar names. There were three Januses, half a dozen or more Brimmers, two Printers, three Tigers, three Cold Decks, two Rondos, two famous Kings (not to mention lesser ones), and perhaps hundreds of other duplications. A good example of the confusion of names occurred in an early bloodline chart issued by the AQHA itself. In it Printer II (1872–92) was listed as being the sire of Mary Cook. This mare had to have been sired in the 1820s by Printer I (1800–28) if by any Printer, because she was shown as being the great-grandam of Mittie Stephens, foaled in 1869. Naturally, the whole genealogical sequence that followed was thrown completely out of kilter.

The following short biographies of the founding fathers of the dominant horse families that contributed to the Quarter Horse breed are based on old stud books previously mentioned, the opinions of many modern writers on the subject, and from conversations with many horse raisers. The genealogy of the more important individuals, both sires and dams, can be followed on the charts in the Appendix. (After experimentation with many forms of charts the method used by Darrell B. Sprott for charts prepared for the AQHA some years ago was adopted, and to him I acknowledge my indebtedness. At first glance it may appear as a hopeless maze, but experiments showed it to be the most quickly comprehended form when so many individuals are related.)

PRINTER I (1800–28)
This horse by Janus II by Janus was one of the early horses whose status is well authenticated. He is listed in Colonel Sanders D. Bruce's *American Stud Book*—Volume VII, where it simply states, "He was a quarter horse." Taken from Virginia to Pennsylvania and finally to Fairfield County, Ohio, he sired many sprint horses who ran on the pioneer tracks of the new territories.

His stock contributed to almost every prominent Quarter Horse family. Peter McCue traced directly to him through his grandam Butt Cut; Joe Bailey through his daughter Mary Cook. Cold Deck's dam Maudy, the Missouri race mare, was, I believe, although I have no documentary proof, by Bay Cold Deck, a grandson of Printer. Printer II, a descendant, also became well known.

COPPERBOTTOM (1828–60)
The first Quarter Horse to achieve Texas fame was Copperbottom, a beautiful son of the superb Sir Archy. He was foaled in 1828 on the Lancaster, Pennsylvania, farm of Edward Parker. He had gained a local reputation as a short-horse racer and sire when, at the age of eleven, he was purchased by General Sam Houston, then President of the Lone Star Republic of Texas.

After being shipped to Galveston, Texas, Copperbottom was taken to Houston's home at Sabine City. In the same year, 1839, while on a trip to Alabama, Houston purchased seven blooded horses for which he paid six thousand dollars in "Sabine City Scrip." Later, when the general moved to Huntsville, Texas, Copperbottom pranced along in the procession that followed the big yellow family coach. In his new home in Hopkins County, the aging stud ran many races and set some local records, but because of poor record keeping only one of his descendants got listed in the *American Stud Book*: a brown mare foaled up along the Red River near Hopkins County was credited with tracing to Copperbottom. The old campaigner died in Hopkins County in 1860.

General Sam Houston's youngest son, Temple Houston, and my father, Sidney Benton Laune, were young lawyers when they arrived in Woodward, Oklahoma, on the day the Cherokee Strip was opened for settlement. They made "the run" on a train that brought them, and over two hundred and fifty others, from Higgins, Texas. Our family and the Temple Houston family became close friends and we heard many stories of the Houston men, both father and son. One I recall, and recently found revived in essential details in Sue Flanagan's book, *Sam Houston's Texas* (1964). The story stresses Sam Houston's impatience with anything less than a real good horse under him. Houston, who had been converted to religion late in life, was riding with a fellow Baptist when he was suddenly shaken in the saddle. The new convert blurted out, "God damn a stumbling horse!" When his friend reproached him for his blasphemous language, Houston dismounted, knelt down in the path, and prayed for forgiveness. Then as he swung his six foot four inches back into the saddle he remarked, so the story goes, "And that, my friend, was a damn good prayer."

SHILOH (1844—died between 1869 and '74)

After Copperbottom the next great short-horse sire to arrive on the Texas scene was Shiloh, generally called Old Shiloh. He was a dark bay or brown horse that had been foaled in Maury County, Tennessee, in 1844 and brought to Texas in 1849. His owner was Jack Batchler, a big husky ex-blacksmith turned farmer and race horseman. From Rusk County, where he first settled, Batchler moved farther west in 1855 to the richer soil of Ellis County, Texas. There on Ten Mile Creek he met Middleton Perry and Jones Green, the sons-in-law of Thomas McKee Ellis and the joint owners of Steel Dust, the inevitable rival of Shiloh, although it appears that their respective owners remained on friendly terms.

Shiloh, according to his accepted pedigree, traced directly to Sir Archy and transmitted the genes of that illustrious sire to such well-known Quarter Horse strains as the Billys, Baileys, Cold Decks, and the Rondos. That he was somewhat overshadowed by his contemporary Steel Dust is due to the fact that the true worth of his stock was not known until later when proved by his excellent daughters and granddaughters.

He was a speedy short-distance horse and was matched with the best in his part of the country. According to Wayne Gard in his article in the *Western Horseman* of August 1949, Shiloh's most important race was to be one against Steel Dust. But as it turned out, the two never raced against each other because of an accident which is described in detail in the account of Steel Dust, which follows.

That the respective owners had high regard for the other's horse is evident. Each bred mares to the other's stallion. Henry Batchler, the son of Jack Batchler, became a well-known race-horse man himself. He raised Tom Driver, who was by Steel Dust and out of a Shiloh mare named Mammoth. Henry Batchler recalled Shiloh as the most beautiful horse he ever saw. He said the old stallion was nearing thirty years of age when fatally injured in a fight with another stud, the classic ending for the supermale.

STEEL DUST (1845–74)

The name Steel Dust, to many old cowmen, is synonymous with Quarter Horse. He is better known to most people than Janus or Sir Archy, the George Washingtons of the breed. Yet there is an element of vagueness and legend about him. For instance, there is no detailed description of him and his biography is thought by many writers to be largely conjectural. Much study and hot debate have centered about the family tree he had been given, because so much was based on hearsay. Hearsay evidence has always been suspect. But in certain instances it should not be ruled out completely. After all, there were many old cowmen—and not race-horse men with an ax to grind—who cherished the accuracy of bloodlines and who were walking encyclopedias on horse families. Their firsthand information was often passed on, it is true, by word of mouth, but much of it with an accuracy equal to that of the written word. Many great horses, especially the ones in pioneering countries, never got their bloodlines committed to paper. Nor did J. S. Skinner's *American Stud Book,* first published in Baltimore in 1848— the logical source for bloodline accuracy—record the birth, three years earlier in 1845, of a colt named Steel Dust. Nor is such an omission surprising when one considers that Steel Dust was long gone from that country when this stud book was published. Steel Dust was only a yearling when he arrived in Lancaster, Texas, in 1846 in the Cavalcade of Middleton Perry and his brother-in-law, Jones Green. Both had married daughters of Thomas McKee Eliss and were young farmers and stockmen who loved good, fast horses. They didn't think of themselves as professional race-horse men, so there had been no incentive to keep breeding records.

Somewhere in the thicket of memories among the descendants of the

Perrys, Greens, Ellises, and Batchlers (all of whom once knew and handled Steel Dust), Wayne Gard and Robert Denhardt, his best-known researchers, have found what must be close to the basic truth about this almost phantom steed. From them we learn that Steel Dust was foaled in Kentucky in 1845, sired by Harry Bluff by Short Whip, who traced to Janus and thus to the "immortal three" Oriental sires who were the predominant founders of the English Thoroughbred. Harry Bluff's dam was Big Nance, a daughter of Timoleon by Sir Archy.

The breeding of Steel Dust's dam, like almost everything relating to him, has been questioned. The *AQHA Stud Book* says she was "a cold-blooded mare." Regardless of his parentage, it is certain that Steel Dust exemplified the Western attitude; it is not what your folks *were* but what *you are* that counts. And there has never been a question about the fact that a horse named Steel Dust made a lasting name for himself throughout the cattle country long before the writers of history got interested in him.

Before he was weaned Steel Dust changed owners twice. First he went to Bill Green of Greene County, Illinois; then to Middleton Perry and Jones Green, who lived nearby.

Years after his death old-time horsemen pointed out Steel Dust horses who had the general appearance of very compact Thoroughbreds, only being a little closer to the ground, and with big jaws, heavily muscled forearms and gaskins and withers. If they were blood-bay, about fifteen hands high, and weighing around 1200 pounds, they said they were the spittin' image of the old boy himself. As for the big jaws, they must have been a telling characteristic, because the Steel Dust horses were often called the "Big Jaws." They are still a noticeable feature in many Quarter Horse families of today.

After migrating from Illinois the Perry and Green families settled southeast of Dallas on Ten Mile Creek. There, as Steel Dust attained his growth, his owners realized they had a bundle of speed on their hands, and it can be assumed that he was matched in a race occasionally.

But it was not until he was twelve years old that Steel Dust's big chance came. At this time, Jack Batchler, the owner of Shiloh, moved to the vicinity of Ten Mile Creek and became acquainted with Mid Perry and Jones Green. Batchler was a shrewd judge of horses and after seeing Steel Dust's powerful driving muscles propel him from a starting chute with astonishing speed, he rated him as a quarter runner that would be hard to beat. He was in need of just such a horse. Recently he had lost a fine sorrel mare, Belton's Queen, whom he had wagered in a race against Alfred Bailes's racing stallion Brown Dick, and he wanted to even the score. For what reason he didn't race his own horse, Shiloh, is not known. At any rate, he wanted to borrow Steel Dust. Perry and Green hesitated. They didn't want to get involved in a horse race against Alfred Bailes, knowing he was a fiery devotee of racing, and besides, he had recently married the third Ellis daughter, making him a brother-in-law. All had seen bad blood stirred up over race rivalry and they wanted to avoid it in their families if they could without hurting Steel Dust's track career.

Finally taking the calculated risk, Steel Dust's owners handed him over to Jack Batchler to be put in training for the race against Brown Dick. When the race was run on a track just west of Lancaster, Texas, Batchler's judgment paid off. Brown Dick ate the dust of defeat. We can assume it called for the utmost tact of the sisters, Mrs. Perry, Mrs. Green, and Mrs. Bailes, to keep family relations on an even keel.

The race definitely put Steel Dust in the big time. So it wasn't long before a challenge came from adjoining Collins County, where Harrison Stiff, a prominent businessman, lived in the county seat town of McKinney. He had great confidence in his race horse, Monmouth, a Thoroughbred he had brought in from Kentucky. The challenge was accepted and a date was set. Thirteen-year-old Henry Ellis, who may have ridden him before in a casual race or two, began breezing Steel Dust every morning to condition him. The boy was so light he had to wear a money belt loaded with buckshot in order to make the weight requirement. Then an unexpected calamity fell. Henry Ellis's Baptist mother heard that the race was to be run on a Sunday and she put her foot down. Henry was refused permission to ride. Nothing he could say or do would dissuade her, and he had to stand back and watch Tom McKnight, a Negro boy, get tossed aboard as the jockey. One of Wayne Gard's informants said that the boy rode without a saddle but that he took the precaution of smearing some blackstrap molasses on Steel Dust's back to help him stick on when the horse came charging out of the chute.

It was agreed that the race would be run on a track outside McKinney, and on the day of the race the little town was jam-packed with people from miles around. All of them seemed to have strong opinions about the upcoming race and were eager to lay wagers on it.

When the Lancaster delegation arrived with Steel Dust, it was noted that the crowds that tried to get close to the horse were warded off by burley Jack Batchler and Mid Perry and their friends who formed a bodyguard about him. Excitement, greed, ribald or good-natured or brawling challenge grew in intensity until it peaked during a moment in the afternoon that lasted not much more than one third of a minute. Steel Dust won. With one concerted gasp the Monmouth backers were deflated, and before the stupefied town came to its senses Steel Dust and his entourage were well down the road headed for home.

Whether or not this race was the deciding factor, it had long been in the cards—and was soon announced—that Steel Dust and Shiloh would try their speed against each other in a matched race. Details of date, place, wagers to be put up, and manner of starting were settled. It was agreed that starting chutes would be used.

Like so many race horses, Steel Dust, though docile at other times, was highly excitable during the tense moments at the start of a race. Before the race against Shiloh he threw his weight around in such a frantic effort to leave the chute that he lunged into a side board and shattered it. A large splintered piece of wood entered his shoulder muscles.

The race was called off. Batchler claimed the forfeit he was entitled to and got it. Steel Dust never raced again, and it is said the injury caused him to go blind. Wayne Gard in his book *The Fabulous Quarter Horse, Steel Dust* suggests that the horse already might have been handicapped by failing eyesight, which could account for some of his nervousness and his banging into the chute.

With the question of which of these two great horses was the faster forever unanswered, both passed into legend and history undiminished.

From this time until his death, blind Steel Dust stood at stud. His fame had spread far and many mares of speed breeding as well as many mustang mares were brought to him. Before the Civil War came on to curtail this activity, his sons and daughters were increasing his reputation and spreading his prepotent genes. At the close of the war it is presumed he had a period of great productivity. It was the heyday of the big cattle drives north across the Indian Nations to the Kansas shipping points, and riders sought the very best horses "to ride the rivers with."

Strange as it may seem, more is definitely known about the last days of Old Janus than about those of Steel Dust, who came along so much later. Lon, the son of Jones Green, said his father died in 1864 and that his widowed mother sold Steel Dust for one thousand dollars to a man in Hillsboro, Texas, where the great stud lived on to the age of twenty-eight or twenty-nine. Another story has it that he was sold for five hundred dollars to Bill Raburn, who after several years sold him to Jim Brown, who took him to southern Texas, where he died at the age of thirty-two.

Steel Dust was the first widely publicized Quarter Horse in the West. His fame was carried by riders on all the cattle trails that fanned out from Texas. Cowmen, cowboys, horse breeders, race-horse men, all could spot his big-jawed, short-backed, muscular stock at a glance. The name was one that stayed in the memory. It had a fire-breathing sound. Sitting about the evening fires in cow camps that sprinkled the grass lands from the Rio Grande to Canada, saddle men were seldom caught short when asked about the parentage of their favorite mount. Steel Dust was the best-known name and was used the oftenest. Undoubtedly, many an old beloved cowpony was given, on the spur of the moment, a complimentary relationship to Steel Dust. But without this added following, his definitely recognized sons and daughters were numerous enough to contribute to every Quarter Horse family of note, even to the more recent families that carry as much as fifteen-sixteenths Thoroughbred blood.

OLD BILLY (1862–86)

To go back to Alfred Bailes for a moment, and to the mare Belton's Queen, whom he won from Jack Batchler in a race against Brown Dick, we find that Belton's Queen and Brown Dick were mated, and in due time a beautifully formed seal-brown filly was born. She was named Paisana. The firm of Oliver and Bailes, then in Guadalupe County, Texas, sold her to W. B. Fleming at the close of the Civil War.

Before joining the Confederate Army, William (Billy) Fleming had come to Texas from Georgia and had learned over a period of several years with the Texas Rangers how important fast horses can be while fighting Comanche Indians. Now, on his return from the war, a scarred and wounded veteran, raising fast horses became his main interest. He was a bachelor and remained so throughout his long life. First, he started out to find a good mate for his newly acquired racing filly, Paisana. The horse he found was a five-year-old pile of bones chained to a tree, where he had been most of the time his original owner was away fighting the war. The chain had rubbed the dark brown hair off his neck and it never grew back again. His hoofs were so grown out they had to be cut off with a saw. It can be assumed that Fleming knew something about the animal's breeding, because he bought him and showed further confidence in him by giving him his own name, Billy. In time, the horse was known as Old Billy, as was his owner, when Fleming's long blond mustache and flowing beard turned to silver.

Billy the horse was sired by Shiloh and his dam was Ram Cat by Steel

Dust. It was just about all the short-horse breeding one could ask for at that time. With the recurrence of those well-known names, the close-knit society of both horses and horse people in early Texas is emphasized.

The single transaction that brought Old Billy and Paisana together created a family of over a dozen full brothers and sisters who all won recognition in their own right. Paisana was truly a matriarch of the breed, just as Old Billy was a patriarch. Old Billy's genes not only nicked with hers but with other mares' as well, and with such prepotency that Billy horses soon meant the speediest on the brush tracks and among roping horses with the fastest getaway.

Little can be said with certainty about Old Billy's early years except that since he had been foaled in 1860, his racing career must have been delayed by the Civil War. Before he was weaned, South Carolina had seceded, and Sam Houston was stumping the state of Texas trying unsuccessfully to keep it from doing the same. Shortly thereafter, horses were combed from the pastures, rough-broken, and sent on their way as cavalry mounts. Others were lost or scattered in raids and counter raids. Ranch workers and horse trainers left for the army. The wonder is that any good blood stock survived. And perhaps only the very best did survive.

There is little doubt that the clearing out of second-rate stock was beneficial when at the close of the war those breeders with a nucleus of quality breeding stock were able to supply sprinting horses for the short tracks and top cowhorses to gallop into the booming cattle business.

Old Billy supplied more than his share of these fast horses. With sons like Anthony, Whalebone, Pancho, Little Brown Dick, John Crowder, Joe Collins, Billy McCoy, Cold Deck, and many others, his line was well established. Through his progeny the blood of Old Billy flows like a strong current in the veins of nearly all the families that founded the Quarter Horse breed.

And if the Southern Texans had had their way, the horses of the new breed would have been called "Billys." Opposing it was Dan Casement, who held out for "Steel Dusts" as his choice of a name. Bob Denhardt favored the name "Quarter Horse." He later remarked that, while it did not at the time completely satisfy him, it turned out to be the best compromise name suggested.

COLD DECK (1868–92)

It was a rough-and-tumble time when young Cold Deck made his debut on the small town tracks of Missouri, Indian Territory, and Arkansas. At the time Jesse James and the Younger and Dalton gangs were abroad in the district, commuting by horseback to their various appointments. All were said to be knowledgeable horsemen, whose profession required the best, and they were avid followers of horse racing. No pari-mutuel regulated the odds in betting, nor were track stewards around to check out every animal's pedigree. So some chicanery and off-track skulduggery were more or less customary. Race-horse men often illuminated or beclouded horse relationships to serve some immediate purpose. Because Cold Deck was in the hands of such men a good part of his life, it is not surprising that there is some vagueness about his origin. One story has it that while Old Billy or Steel Dust—whichever name carried more weight with the audience of the moment—was stabled at some unnamed track, strict orders were given to his groom that he was not to be bred under any circumstances while his owner was away. This contretemps was, however, circumvented by a wily turfman whose fervid wish was that his speedy mare, Maudy, then in heat, be mated with the great racing sire. This was accomplished by getting the stallion's groom into a poker game, during which, to abate any undue risk, a new deck of cards—a cold deck—was introduced. After taking all the groom's money, the service of the stallion was accepted as a wager.

The entire story, which smacks of fiction, becomes even more suspect when one recalls that the name Cold Deck had been used several times before; a grandson of the first Printer, for instance, was named Bay Cold Deck.

In order to account for the name Cold Deck it is reasonable to suppose that an informed breeder would consider some illustrious name from the animal's ancestry. Maudy, as all agree, was a race mare from Missouri. Near Lineville, Iowa, William Summers and Sons raised a Maude who some said traced to Printer I through Hamburg Dick and Bay Cold Deck. A few years later the Summers Farm produced a whole tribe of Maudes and Maudys. Two of them well known on the tracks and registered in the *American Stud Book* were Maudy Miles, dam unknown, and Decoy Maid, who was out of a mare named Maude. What would be better than to distinguish a colt by making evident its ties to Bay Cold Deck and thus to his highly regarded grandfather, Printer I?

The late Helen Michaelis stated with assurance that Cold Deck was bred by Tom Martin of Kyle, Texas; that in 1867 he took his Missouri-bred racing mare Maudy to Old Billy at Fleming's place near Belmont, Texas, not forty miles away, and that in 1868 she gave birth to a sorrel colt that he named Cold Deck. No deceptive antics are attributed to Tom Martin.

In any case, Cold Deck grew to be a dark sorrel a scant fifteen hands high and weighing in good condition about 1175 pounds. First he was sold to Tom Stodgen, who took him to Carthage, Missouri, and started him on his racing career as a quarter-mile racer. Next, Foss Barker, a race-horse man known to every track in the Southwest, came into possession of Cold Deck. Under his astute management, Cold Deck ran on all kinds of tracks for any kind of a wager he could promote. Over his stall Barker hung a sign that stated, "Cold Deck Against the World," and claimed his stud was "the fastest animal on earth." It was Foss Barker, says Robert Denhardt, quoting Coke Blake, who spread the romantic story of the Cold Deck name.

Cold Deck produced a large family of fast, sought-after sons and daughters. Four founded Quarter Horse families that became prominent. His son, Printer II (1872–92) founded the Printer family of Missouri. Another son, Barney Owens, sired Dan Tucker, the sire of Peter McCue. A third son, Berry's Cold Deck, was the father of Tubal Cain, the founder of the Blake family of horses in northeastern Oklahoma. And his son, Diamond Deck, was the great-grandsire of Joe Bailey of Gonzales, the holder of Pedigree Number Four (P-4) among the founding fathers of the Quarter Horse breed. Just as Sam Bass, the Texas bandit, owned and raced the Denton mare, the fastest quarter runner in his district, romance has it that Jesse James rode a Cold Deck horse and that Cole Younger and other members of his gang rode race horses, something difficult to prove or disprove. Homer Croy, whom I knew when he lived in New York in the 1930s, came from the same district in Missouri as did Jesse James, and in his biography of Jesse, he had more hard, cold facts than I've seen in any other book about him. Homer referred to Jesse's very fast race horse named Red Fox, but made no assumption that the horse was of Cold Deck breeding. Anyway, since Cold Deck was a dark sorrel, the Red Fox name seems to fit. Fast horses were the souped-up getaway machines of the time.

Fictionists might do better in trying to link Belle Starr's favorite mount to Cold Deck. This notorious hawk-faced woman whose first love was bandit Cole Younger and who consorted, it seems, with the entire outlaw brotherhood of Missouri, Indian Territory, and Texas, was photographed in her bedraggled finery, plumed hat and all, sitting sidesaddle on a dark sorrel that does look breedy. So who knows?

ROAN DICK (1879–1901)

Roan Dick was by Black Nick by Stewart's Telegraph and was out of a mare by Greenstreet's Boanerges, a grandson of Printer I. His reputation seems to have been based more on his turf record than on the number or distinction of his immediate stock. Some credit him with being the sire of Bob Wade, the horse that was clocked at 21.25 seconds for the 440 at Butte, Montana, in 1890 from a scored start.

LOCK'S RONDO (1880–97)

Lock's Rondo, as indicated by the many lines that fan out from him on the chart, established a large family that in turn contributed greatly to the short-horse stock of the West. He was a grandson of Old Billy and Paisana. His father was Whalebone by Old Billy and his dam was the granddaughter of old Shiloh. His pioneer ancestors had done so well that he was born an aristocrat. He was bred by Charles Haley at Sweetwater, Texas, and was foaled in 1880. From his very colthood he showed a talent for early speed. Soon he was burning up the brush tracks—a form of arson that made him a wanted horse. So badly wanted, in fact, that he changed hands several times. His turf days had ended when he was seven years old and in the hands of Tom Martin of Kyle, Texas, the breeder of Cold Deck. At this time he was sold to another consummate race-horse man, W. W. "Bill" Lock, who had set up his LO Ranch near the same town. For the next ten years Rondo was Bill Lock's number one stallion. His son, Blue Jacket, a grullo, was his fastest offspring and did much to spread Rondo's reputation as a breeder of speed, making it increasingly difficult for Lock to find anyone who would match racers with him.

In the years that followed, Rondo's stock was brought into even more prominence when W. T. Waggoner, owner of the immense triple reverse D Ranch near Vernon, Texas, got Rondo's grandson, Yellow Jacket. Waggoner was always on the lookout for horses that could wave good-by to anything his neighbor, Tom Burnett, owned. With the acquisition of Yellow Jacket Waggoner knew he had found what he wanted—a horse that could breed speed. Yellow Jacket was by Little Rondo by Rondo and out of a mare named the Barbee Dun, whose dun-colored mother had been brought from Mexico by Jim Barbee. From Rondo through his grandson, Yellow Jacket, came three founding fathers of the Quarter Horse breed. Cowboy P-12 was bred by Ed Thompson of Folsom, New Mexico. The brood mare, Roan Lady, that bore him was line-bred to Peter McCue. Another founding father, son of Yellow Jacket, was Yellow Boy P-18, whose dam was also from the Peter McCue line. Yellow Jacket's daughter, Nettie Jacket, was the dam of Waggoner's Rainy Day P-13, another founding father.

Yellow Jacket. *Courtesy AQHA.*

TRAVELER (1885–1910)

Finding Traveler, the foundation sire of the Traveler strain of horses, was comparable to picking up a fabulous diamond on a dusty road. The story goes that John Cooper, a saloonkeeper in the town of Granbury in West Texas, was driving a span of mules to a buggy when he came across a mule skinner with a mismated team—a mule and a gaunt chestnut horse. With a fresno scraper the man was hauling earth to mound up a railway roadbed. While the sweating team was given a chance to blow, some swapping talk got going. The teamster said he had won the horse in a crap game. After a while when Cooper drove on he was the one with a mismated team—a gaunt chestnut and a mule.

Back in town Cooper got his partner, Brown Seay, to take a ride behind the new horse. Seay remarked on the willing action of the chestnut, saying he was a good traveler, and Traveler became his name.

Traveler. *Courtesy AQHA.*

Although his origin was unknown, the story got around that Traveler had come to Texas in a carload of Kentucky horses. It is said that he must have been a Thoroughbred. More than likely he was.

Traveler was a lightly built horse about 15 hands high, and when in good condition probably never weighed more than 1,000 pounds. His distinguishing marks were a narrow blaze streak down the face and a white stocking on the near hind foot. As for age, it was estimated he had been foaled about 1885.

His speed was evident as soon as he was out of heavy harness and under a saddle, and as soon as he could be conditioned he was matched in races. Since he won most of them, his reputation spread beyond the San Angelo area, where he had been discovered.

Among the famous sons of Traveler were Booger Red, Bulger, Chulo

Munde, Texas Chief, Little Joe, and King Cardwell (Possum). King Cardwell (see Sykes Rondo) had a son named Little King, who sired Joe Bailey P-4, among the earliest chosen to be a founding father of the new Quarter Horse breed.

Texas Chief's grandson, Old Jim P-10, was also a low-numbered founding father. But of all his sons, it was Little Joe who founded the largest and most important Quarter Horse family of the Traveler line.

SYKES RONDO (1887–1907)

Columbus Sykes, who raised Billy horses in North Texas, was related by marriage to Joe Mangum. Mangum had some mares of Tiger breeding, the best of which was May Mangum. From the union of McCoy Billy and May Mangum came Sykes Rondo. Although Joe Mangum bred him, this horse headed up the Sykes as well as the Mangum strain of horses and was always called Sykes Rondo. There seems to be no direct relationship to account for the Rondo part of the name.

The Sykes and Mangum horses soon found favor outside their own locality. One named Blue Eyes went to the Palo Hueco Ranch, owned by Dow and Will Shely, near Alfred, Texas. And it was later, on this ranch, that Sykes Rondo's odyssey ended after covering mares in several districts of Texas.

Sykes Rondo's inclusion in the annals of the breed is due principally to two daughters who carried on his fusion of the Billy and Tiger lines. One was Jenny, the dam of King (Possum) Cardwell by Traveler. Possum was famed in Texas as King and in Arizona as Possum. His son, Brown Possum, was made a founding father with pedigree number P-15. He was bred by John Rhoades of Sombrero Butte, Arizona, and was later owned by the Santa Mariana Ranch of Tucson. Jenny was also the dam of Little Joe, a full brother of Possum, an amazingly prepotent individual whose stock came to prominence too late to be among the founding fathers, but who headed up large families of registered horses later on.

The other mare by Sykes Rondo to produce a noted line was Babe Ruth out of May Mangum, who was the dam of Paul El, by Hickory Bill. He was a famous turf horse who transmitted his speed to Spokane and others.

OLD FRED (1893–1915)

Coke Robards, who had Peter McCue the last years of his life, had another large stallion who added to his reputation as a breeder of Quarter

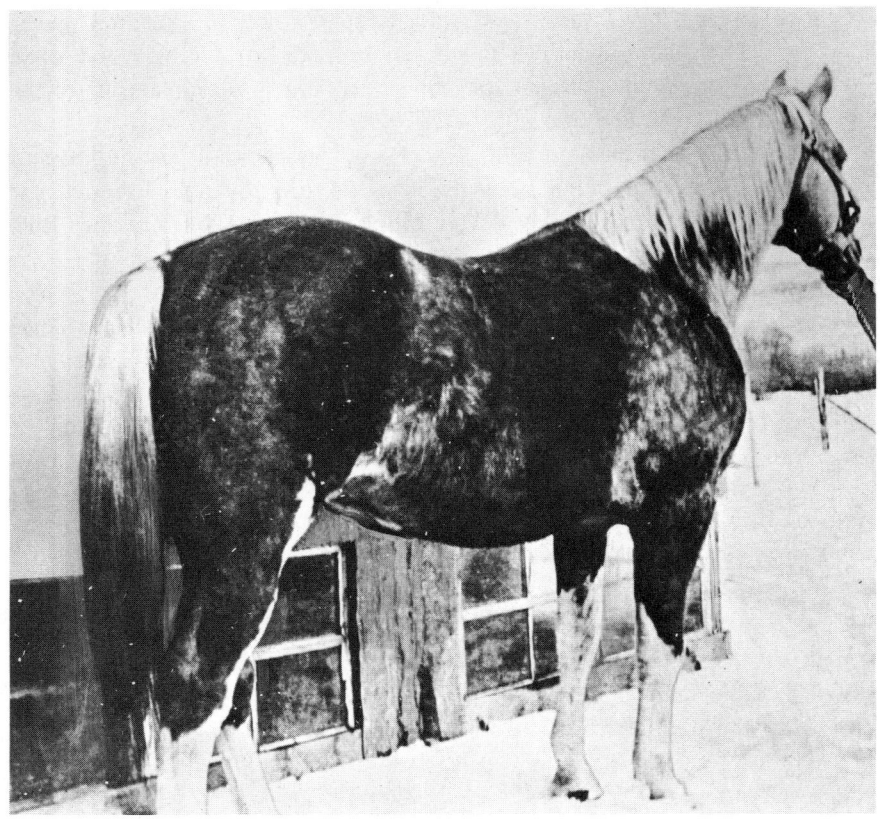

Old Fred. *Courtesy AQHA.*

Horses. This one was Old Fred, a golden, dappled Palomino with flaxen mane and tail. He and his full sister who resembled him had pulled a freight wagon all the way to Colorado from the Freeman Farm in Missouri, where they had been foaled. Old Fred had been foaled in 1893, so he was an aged horse wearing harness when the keen horseman's eye of Coke Robards spotted him in 1910. A photo taken in Pueblo, Colorado, of the team in harness shows them both to be in good flesh. It is said that Coke Robards started trading for Old Fred as soon as he could stop his own team and crawl out of his buggy, and that he bought him then and there.

On Coke Robards' ranch at Hayden, Colorado, the handsome stallion proved to be all and more than Coke Robards hoped for. His stock was fast—especially his daughters. From one daughter, Pet Dawson, came

Sheik P-11 by Peter McCue. From Stockings, another daughter, came Buck Thomas, an outstanding race-horse who ended up on the Three D Waggoner ranch at Vernon, Texas, where he sired a whole herd of excellent brood mares.

PETER McCUE (1895–1923)

Before the serious horse historians got to work on Peter McCue's biography, many conflicting statements about him had been circulated. The first *AQHA Stud Book* listed him as a Thoroughbred—a logical assumption since he was registered as such in the *American Stud Book*. Twenty mares sired by him were also registered as Thoroughbreds, and his sire was listed as Duke of the Highlands, a Thoroughbred.

Subsequent *AQHA Stud Books* listed Peter McCue as a Quarter Horse stating that his sire was Dan Tucker, a grandson of Cold Deck. There was never any question that his dam was Nora M, a Thoroughbred. The switch to the belief in his Quarter Horse breeding was based on an affidavit signed by William Cassidy stating that Dan Tucker was the sire of Peter McCue. The controversy over the grand old stallion's past was quieted when William (Bill) Welch of Missouri and Colorado, a breeder of fine Quarter Horses, obtained from Walter Watkins, the son of Samuel Watkins, the breeder of Peter McCue, an affidavit attesting to the pedigree shown here:

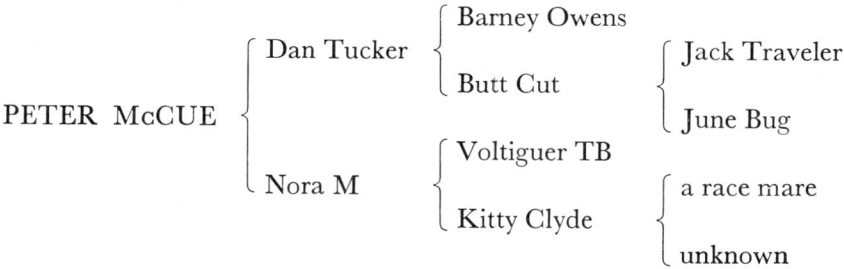

Statements were also obtained from other people who had known his equine majesty, including one from Dick Hornback, the man who had broken him. Following this, Wayne Dinsmore, then secretary of the Horse and Mule Association of America and a respected authority on all breeds, was commissioned by the AQHA to ferret out the facts on Peter McCue's racing record.

His research generally confirmed what had been published by William Welch. In addition, Dinsmore produced Peter McCue's race record as it appeared in Godwin's Turf Guide. All of his findings were published in the November 1951 issue of the *Quarter Horse Journal.*

Based upon such research, and on data gleaned from other sources, including conversations with men who knew the big stud in Oklahoma, the biography of Peter McCue shapes up like this:

He was foaled during February 1895 on the Little Grove Stock Farm of Samuel Watkins near Petersburg, Illinois. For many years Watkins had been assembling some highly prized foundation stock. One mare named June Bug traced through her mother, Munch Meg, to Printer I and thus to Janus. Munch Meg was by Harry Bluff (see Puss B.—S. D. Bruce's *American Stud Book,* Vol. 7, p. 1230); therefore a half sister of Steel Dust, if one accepts the pedigree given him. June Rug was mated with Jack Traveler, the son of Steel Dust (but called an unknown in the *American Stud Book*). The result of this union was a beautiful filly with heavily muscled hams. In her maiden race she became excited and waved her rump into a starting chute and was badly cut. The incident gave her the name of Butt Cut. After being bred to Barney Owen, a son of Cold Deck, Butt Cut dropped a colt that Samuel Watkins named Dan Tucker, from the old song his children often sang. Dan Tucker was a big Quarter Horse and a mighty fast one, and in spite of failing eyesight that shortened his racing career, he shared top honors at the Little Grove Stock Farm with a Thoroughbred stallion named Duke of the Highlands. It was the mating of Dan Tucker with Watkins' mare, Nora M, mostly Thoroughbred, that brought into being Peter McCue.

The colt was named for Mr. McCue, a trainer who worked for Samuel Watkins. Later he was turned over to young Dick Hornback, who worked for Charles Watkins, a nephew of Samuel, to be readied for the track. Years later Dick Hornback told Bill Welch, "Peter McCue was the fastest horse I ever rode or ever saw." When it came time to put the large, long-barreled colt on the regulation tracks, which were open only to Thoroughbreds, he was registered as a Thoroughbred and as having been sired by Duke of the Highlands. Charles Watkins, the nephew, and Thomas Watkins, another of his uncles, contracted to race the promising colt. The deception in his registry was a rather usual procedure at the time. It was often practiced by race-horse men to get around the ruling which limited racing to Thoroughbreds. It is maintained that a gentleman's agreement prevailed whereby the buyer of such a horse whose racing pedigree was fictitious would be told of his true breeding. Thus after Peter McCue left the track it was generally known by breeders that his sire was Quarter Horse Dan Tucker and not Thoroughbred Duke of

This rare photograph of Peter McCue was given to Bob Denhardt by Milo Burlingame, who owned this remarkable prepotent stud, and who is holding the bridle reins. *Courtesy Robert M. Denhardt.*

the Highlands, as appeared in the Jockey Club's *American Stud Book*. Those who knew the horse have stated that he had a striking resemblance to Dan Tucker and none at all to Duke of the Highlands.

As a two-year-old, the big colt—now getting on to sixteen hands high —ran two races in Forsythe, Indiana, two races in St. Louis, Missouri, three races in Joliet, Illinois, four in Detroit, Michigan, and five in Windsor, Canada. His showing was brilliant. He won eight of the sixteen races and placed in three others. Distances ranged from 3½ furlongs to 5½ furlongs. In the race of 3½ furlongs—the shortest race he ever ran on a recognized track—his win was in 42 seconds. There is no record of his time for the first quarter mile, but the entire distance was covered at the rate of 24 seconds per quarter mile, an amazing speed, as any clocker will agree.

As a three-year-old, Peter McCue started in 13 races at distances of 4 to 5½ furlongs. It was in this year that little Milo Burlingame, who later owned him, recalled having ridden him to victory against April

Fool, Geraldine, and Dora Mae, all of whom were track favorites. The records show, however, that out of the thirteen races he won only two and placed in five. As a four-year-old, his final year of racing, the best he could do was come in with one second and one third. Obviously, he had been raced too hard and too often. Records show that he never won a race of over a half mile and that many he started in were more than that. It was obvious that he was a sprint racer, a quarter horse, and not a distance runner. He broke down after his last race on October 7, 1899. One report is that he broke or badly injured his right foreleg at the pastern. It was at this time that Thomas Watkins, being very displeased over the way his nephew was overracing and mishandling the horse and his winnings, resorted to legal action to recover Peter McCue. The horse had now attained his full height of a shade over 16 hands and had put on a weight of 1430 pounds.

For the next seven years Peter McCue stood at stud on the farm of a Mr. Michaels in Logan County, Illinois. In 1907 John Wilkins, a onetime resident of Cheyenne, Oklahoma, purchased Peter McCue, and took him to the vicinity of San Antonio, Texas.

Stories persist that Peter McCue was frequently matched and consistently won sprint races all over the Southwest. Many published accounts tell of men who reported having clocked him (unofficially) in the quarter mile at twenty-one seconds flat—and from a standing start.

Milo Burlingame, ex-jockey who ran a saloon in Cheyenne, Oklahoma Territory, prior to statehood in 1907, held a vivid memory of the big boy's blazing speed and of races in St. Louis in which he had ridden him to victory. When he had an opportunity in 1911 to purchase Peter McCue from John Wilkins, his onetime townsman, he jumped at the chance.

Nelson Nye of Tucson, Arizona, who has known more Quarter Horses and their breeders and written more about Quarter Horses than any other writer I know of, reported Milo Burlingame as saying that he bought Peter McCue knowing that he was registered as a Thoroughbred and that his intention was to raise registered Thoroughbred horses. With this in mind he bought five top mares. One he got from Dr. Comas, and another mare named Waldorf Belle was purchased from Hix & Harper. Soon afterward Waldorf Belle won the Derby at nearby Elk City, Oklahoma. Milo was the owner of many race horses, of which Sleepy Dick was perhaps his fastest, with Scar Face, Hay Seed, Nellie Miller, and Gray Rabbit not far behind, and he rode in many races as his own jockey.

Paul Burlingame, Milo's son, also a jockey, rode Peter McCue and several of his speedy offspring. He said that the old stud was never unruly or hard to handle. Milo himself never left anyone in doubt as to his opinion of the horse, stating simply that he thought Peter McCue was the greatest short-horse in the history of the world—and the finest breeder. He would add that the horse had a twenty-seven-foot stride and was the fastest at leaving a barrier of any he had ever seen. Plenty of commentators on the breed have shared Milo's opinion.

For the next four years, while in Milo Burlingame's ownership, Peter McCue served the best brood mares in western Oklahoma and the Panhandle of Texas. Claude Stinson, who lived just fifteen miles east of Cheyenne, brought his sprightly mare, Little Annie, to Peter McCue and got a colt he named Chief, who became Quarter Horse founding father number P-5. Chief was a bargain. Tom Caudill, who helped handle Peter McCue in 1911, said his stud fee was only twenty-five dollars. Through Peter McCue's son Badger and Badger's son Midnight, a large family of Peter McCue horses upgraded ranch saddle stock wherever they went.

Milo Burlingame sold Peter McCue when he was twenty years old to Si Dawson, a well-known horse breeder of eastern Oklahoma, who also had a ranch near Hayden, Colorado. Shortly afterward, Si took over the management of a large ranch in Brazil and turned Peter McCue over to his friend and neighbor Coke Robards, an Oklahoman who had also moved to Hayden to set up a ranch. Si died in São Paulo, Brazil, in 1919. Under the astute management of Coke Robards, Peter McCue's reputation grew, and by the time of his death in 1923, the blood of the renowned stallion and his stock had been intermingled with almost every well-known strain of Quarter Horse. From his son, Hickory Bill, came two famous hierarchies. One derived from Paul El, who contributed to the basic stock of Johnny Ferguson's race horses at his ranch southwest of Wharton, Texas. The other son of Hickory Bill to found a large family was Old Sorrel, the fabulous working cowhorse to whom the many generations of King Ranch Quarter Horses are line bred.

The extent to which Peter McCue stamped his trademark on the Quarter Horse breed is quickly seen in the genealogy chart. Ten out of the nineteen stallions who were designated as the founders of the Quarter Horse breed were line bred to Peter McCue. Two were sons. Two were grandsons. Three were great-grandsons. Two were great-great-grandsons. And one, Waggoner's Rainy Day P-13, was a great-great-great-grandson.

THE BLAKE HORSES (c. 1900)

When C. S. (Coke) Blake of Pryor, Oklahoma, saw Cold Deck at the track at Van Buren, Arkansas, when the famous stud was ten years old, he realized that his ideal of what a Quarter Horse should be was right there before him in the flesh. Then and there he planned to become the possessor of a Cold Deck son. The quest led him to Joe Berry of Mount Vernon, Missouri, only to learn that Berry's Cold Deck had been sold into Tennessee. So it was in Wendell, Tennessee, that Blake found and purchased Berry's Cold Deck. He soon changed his name to Young Cold Deck.

The close relationship of Quarter Horses of the latter part of the nineteenth century is again stressed if one goes along with the *AQHA Stud Book* and accepts Dolly Croker, by Lock's Rondo, by Old Billy, as Young Cold Deck's dam. This would made him a Billy on both upper and lower lines.

While in Tennessee Coke Blake became acquainted with the Bertrands and Brimmers, who represented the Sir Archy and Janus lines. Based on this stock, a strain called the White Lightnings had been developed on the Alsup Farm. Here Blake purchased a mare named Lucy Maxwell by Alsup's Red Buck. As far as I know, no one has stated just who Lucy's dam was, but when she was mated with Young Cold Deck and produced a colt who was named Tubal Cain, we are given a strong clue.

On the William Summers and Sons farm in Iowa, where there were so many Maudes and Maudys, the top stallion was Imp. Tubal Cain. He was the sire in the late 1880s and early 1890s of Maudy Miles, Decoy Maid, Walter Howard, and Larosa. All were well-known turf horses. The last three were full brothers and sisters out of a mare named Maude. As stated in the case of old Cold Deck, breeders reach into the bloodlines of their stock to find names. They seldom just pull them out of a hat. Only if Lucy Maxwell (or her sire Red Buck) was out of a mare by Imp. Tubal Cain does Blake's choice of the name Tubal Cain seem logical.

Tubal Cain grew into a large Quarter Horse, standing 15.2 and weighing 1440 pounds, and was the founding father of the Blake horses, which were widely known among ranchers, rodeo performers, and officers of the U. S. Cavalry Remount Service. Tramp, a son of Tubal Cain, was presented to the Remount Service at El Reno, Oklahoma. I like to imagine I saw some of his colts when as a young man I used to drive across the Cheyenne and Arapaho Reservations and on by El Reno on my way to Oklahoma City. It was always a temptation to stop a moment and look at the horses there in the large pastures. As I recall they were well up to height, fifteen hands and over, and of all colors, although bays and sorrels seemed to predominate.

In the twenty-nine years of its existence—from 1920 to 1949—the Remount Service, according to Colonel E. J. Purfeld, accounted for 200,000 head of horses. The service insisted that only Thoroughbred stallions be used. But in placing such horses with independent breeders mistakes were made, says Colonel Purfeld in an article in the *Western Horseman* in 1949. "Some of the tall slim stallions should never have been put out or at least not anyplace except where they were to be bred to short legged heavy mares . . . some were getting too much Thoroughbred blood in their horses and gradually losing substance." Colonel Grove, who was in command at El Reno Station, recognized in the Blake horse Tramp and in other well-bred Quarter Horses their valuable qualities, knowing that they carried almost as much Thoroughbred blood in their veins as the regulations called for, plus being consistently well muscled with sturdy legs.

Another son of Tubal Cain was Red Man, whose son out of a mare of Cold Deck and Printer breeding was Red Buck (named for his grandfather), who was number P-9 in the *AQHA Stud Book,* being one of the first nineteen stallions designated as founding fathers of the Quarter Horse breed.

JOE BAILEY of Weatherford (1907–34)

Old Joe Bailey was an aristocrat who traced to Sir Archy on both the upper and lower lines; through his sire Eureka he traced several times to Shiloh and through his dam Susie McQuirter he traced to Steel Dust, Old Billy, and Rondo.

This slender bay horse was bred by Dick Baker of Weatherford, Texas, and was owned by A. E. Whiteside of Sipe Springs, Texas, when he died in 1934. His small number of exceptional offspring include the dam of Stranger, Mike Hasting's great bulldogging horse. His son Yellow Wolf sired Topsy, the dam of One Eyed Waggoner and King Joe. Another son, Dan, sired Jimmy Allred (owned by Helen Michaelis), who sired Blondie and other sprint horses of note. Still another son, Fred Bailey, sired Buckskin Joe.

Four more horses who lived just prior to the founding of the AQHA are so important to the breed that any saddle-sprung elder could recite their names instantly even if aroused from a sound sleep.

Two, Little Joe and Zantanon, came from the Traveler family. Old

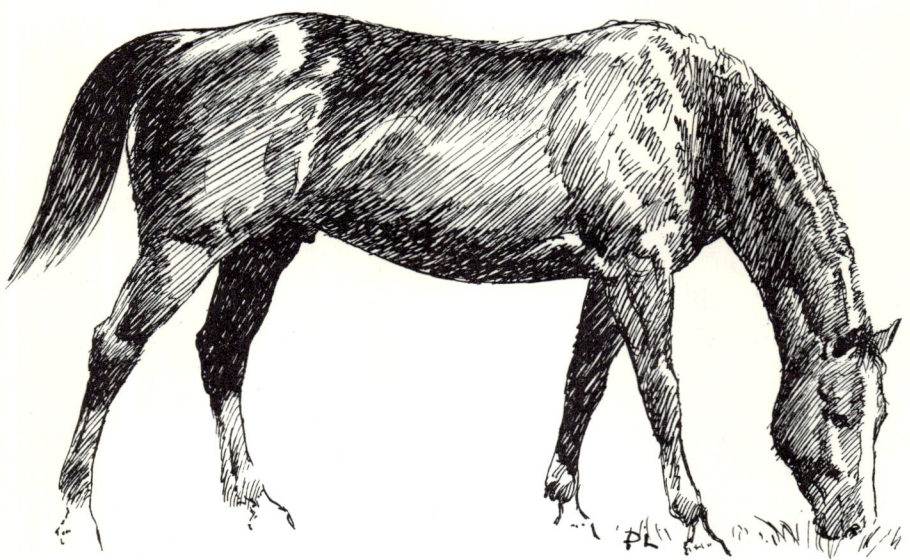

Old Joe Bailey.

Sorrel, from the Peter McCue family, was to transmit his great qualities to the King Ranch strain of distinctive horses. The fourth, the mare Della Moore, although not descended from any of the fourteen founding families, made such a name for herself on the brush tracks the yellowed papers of her little-known forebears were later carefully thumbed through.

LITTLE JOE (1904–29)

Little Joe, Traveler's greatest son, was bred by Will and Dow Shely of Alfred, Texas. He was out of a Sykes Rondo mare whose dam traced to Tiger. When sold to George Clegg in 1907 he was undersized and appeared to be a slow developer. Then with good care he suddenly blossomed out, though never a large horse, and when he was four years old in 1908 he nosed out Carrie Nation, a daughter of the great Peter McCue, in a race at the San Antonio Fair. The next track celebrity of the time to see Little Joe whiz past was Katy M; he was the first and only horse that ever beat her. One man who saw him run said he had "blinding speed" for the quarter mile "and you could not beat him shorter" than that.

At the age of eight Little Joe passed into the hands of Ott Adams, one of the truly dedicated breeders of Quarter Horses. For almost eighty of his ninety-five years this slightly built man raised running horses. He

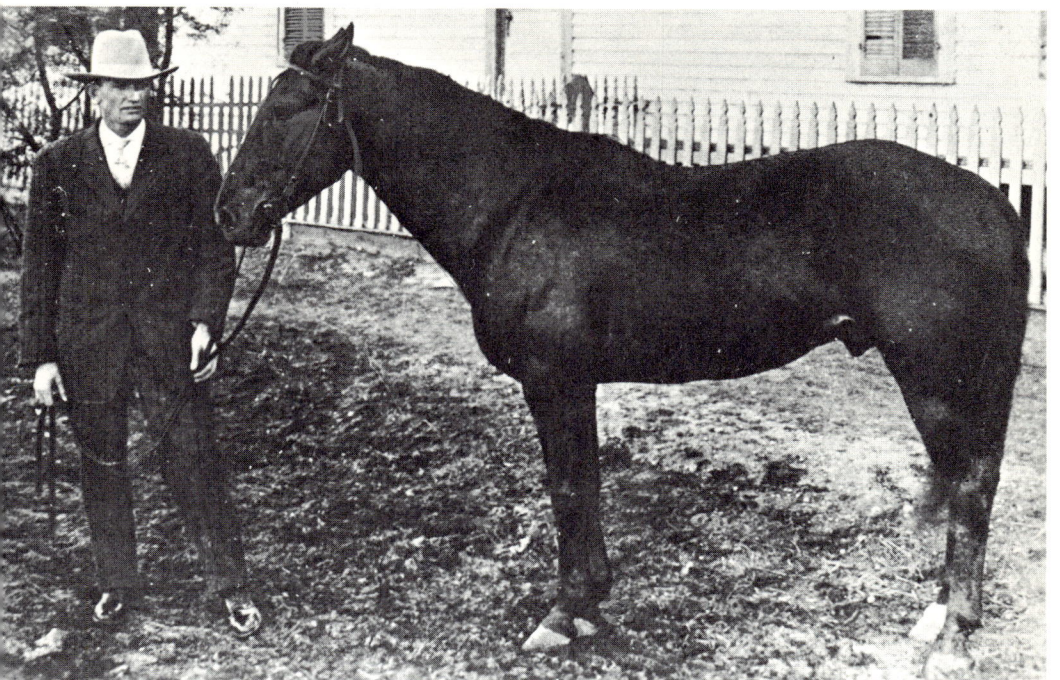

Little Joe at the peak of his racing career. *Photo McCormick Co. Courtesy Quarter Horse Journal.*

never raced them. He was content to allow that risk and thrill and honor to go to others. George Clegg was his neighbor and mentor, and it was from him that he got his basic stock. Many of the brood mares he obtained were of Billy breeding. Since speed was what he bred for, he wanted it on both the upper and lower lines. So when Della Moore, a consistent winner, was retired from the quarter-mile tracks, he bought her. When bred to Little Joe she produced Joe Moore and Grano de Oro and thereby started a whole new line of turf champions.

Other famous sons of Little Joe included Zantanon, San Simeon, Dutch, Cotton Eyed Joe, Old Poco Bueno, Poncho Villa, and Balmy Days. It was Zantanon who was to do more than any of his sons to enlarge the reputation of South Texas horses.

ZANTANON (1917–41)

Zantanon by Little Joe was out of Jeanette, one of Ott Adams' mares that was of Old Billy and Sykes Rondo breeding. A sorrel with a sock

Zantanon was called the Mexican Man O' War by the racing fans along the Rio Grande. *Courtesy Robert M. Denhardt.*

on his right hind foot, he resembled his grandfather Traveler, and beginning with Erasmo Flores, the first to buy him, he made money for a series of owners on both sides of the Rio Grande.

Garford Wilkinson's article in the *Quarter Horse Journal,* August 1962, told of the Laredo ranchman Benevides Volpe, who bought the old campaigner when he was fourteen years old and brought him back to the Texas side of the Rio Grande. Zantanon had survived hard usage that might have broken down a lesser spirit. He was so emaciated he could hardly walk. Volpe learned of the years when Zantanon, although dubbed the Mexican Man O' War, was underfed and overraced, walked or jogged miles over hard streets to get to a track for a workout, then taken back over the same hard streets and without any cooling out tied under a tree to remain there through the heat of the day. Toward evening the trip to the track was repeated and there he invariably won the race. Once he ran the 300 yards in 15.4 seconds. It is said that at night he was fed some oats and corn with cornstalks and shucks for roughage.

Benevides Volpe was one of the dedicated breeders of Quarter Horses of the time. With compassion and expert care he soon had Zantanon in good condition. Two years later, Zantanon sired on Volpe's mare Jabelina the greatest Quarter Horse of the era—King P-234.

OLD SORREL (1915–45) and the King Ranch Horses

Old Sorrel, the son of Hickory Bill by Peter McCue, was bred by George Clegg of Alice, Texas, and sold when six months old to Caesar Kleberg, then general manager of the King Ranch. The suggestion that this grandson of Peter McCue be acquired for a breeding program to improve the King Ranch using horses came from Robert J. Kleberg, Jr., a cousin of Caesar and grandson of the founder, Richard King, who later became the managing executive of the huge ranch. He particularly

Old Sorrel. *Courtesy the King Ranch.*

wanted to concentrate on dark sorrel horses, partly because that coat color doesn't fade under a hot sun, but mainly because it is a recessive color and with it white can be more easily eliminated and white is where sand burns appear.

After careful training, Sorrel—later Old Sorrel—became the best cowhorse on the King Ranch. He won many roping contests and short races. He seemed to have everything that could add quality to stock that would wear the famous running W brand of the King Ranch. He had good conformation, unusually keen cow sense, and, to top it off, a gentle disposition.

Based on his own extensive study of genetics and helpfully advised by A. O. Rhoad, geneticist, and Dr. J. K. Northway, the noted King Ranch veterinarian, Robert Kleberg, Jr., had already established a breeding program that engendered America's first distinct breed of cattle—the Santa Gertrudis. Applying the same general principles, he had Old Sorrel bred

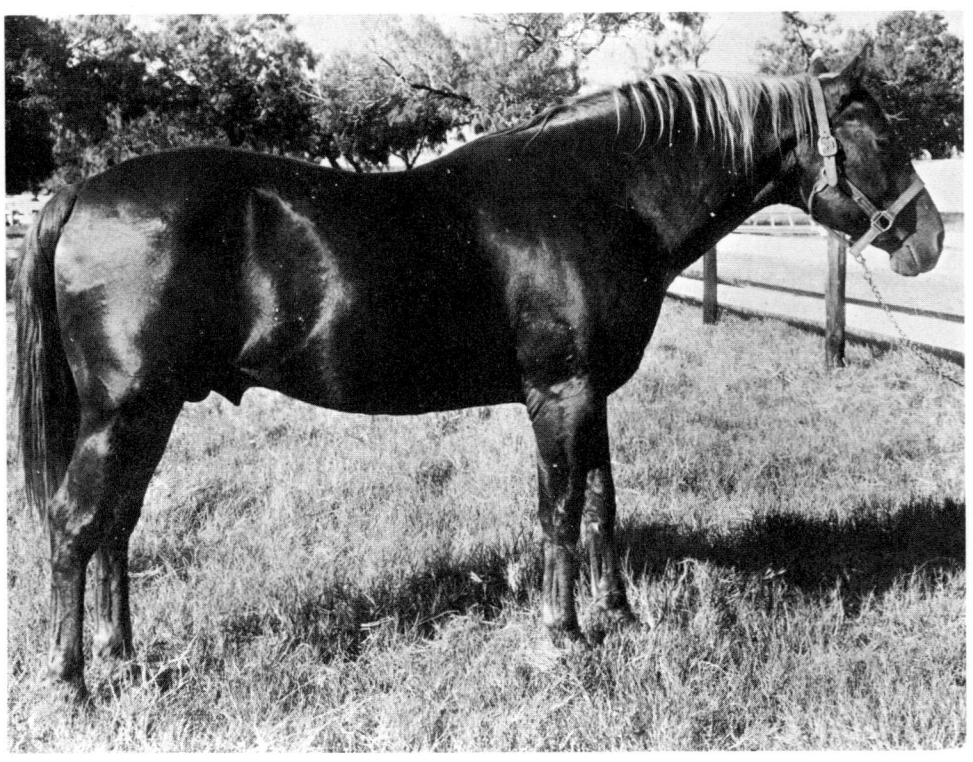

Hired Hand is considered the greatest son of Old Sorrel. *Courtesy the King Ranch.*

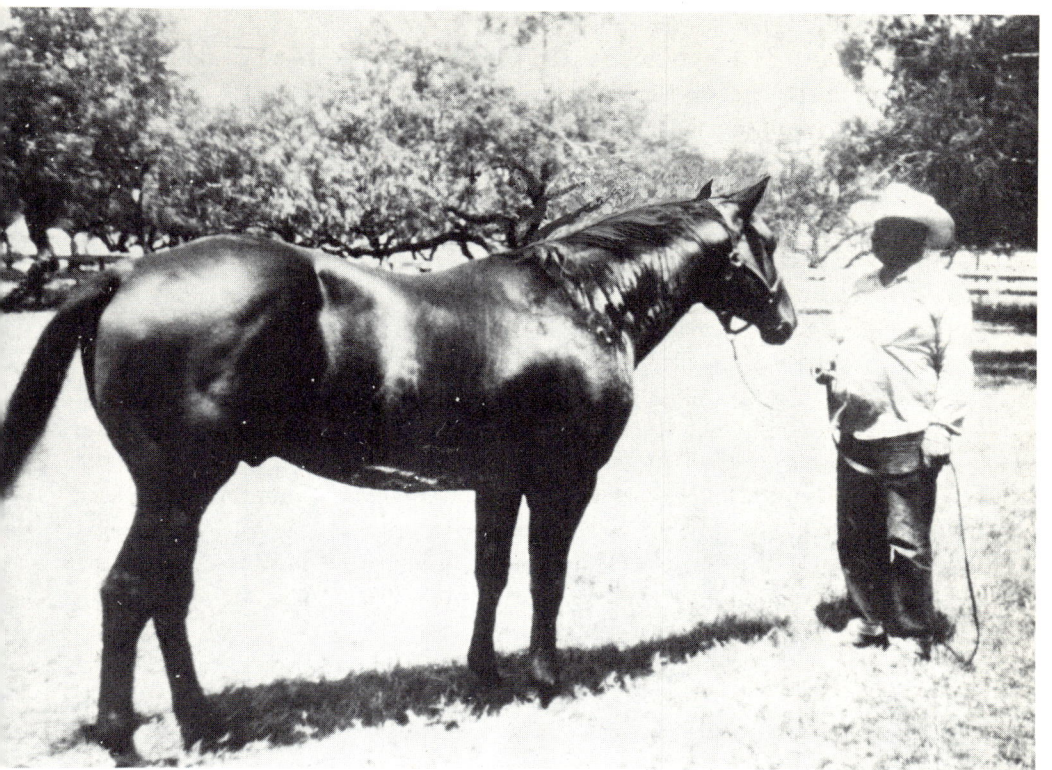

Hired Hand's Cardinale with Senor Maldonado of the King Ranch. *Photo by the author.*

to the best brood mares on the ranch. Then through succeeding generations a system of inbreeding and line breeding multiplied Old Sorrel's superb characteristics with the consistency of peas in a pod. Only rarely does an individual have a balance of genetic qualities that will stand the test of inbreeding. Through this period a drastic policy of culling the King Ranch horses was maintained. At one time in the mid 1940s the King Ranch vaqueros drove 1200 mares across the Rio Grande to be given away in Mexico.

Three horses of the Old Sorrel family became foundation sires of the Quarter Horse breed. Little Richard P-17 and Tomate Laureles P-19 were sons of Old Sorrel, and Wimpy P-1, a grandson, heads the list of the foundation sires.

DELLA MOORE (1909–28)

Della Moore came from an obscure background to win recognition, first on the track, and then like Paisana, the matriarch of the Billy horses, she became famous as the mother of champions.

She was bred by a Louisiana farmer named Ludovic Stemmans, who fancied horse racing. From a mare who moved pretty fast he got a filly sired by a local turf celebrity named Sam Rock. The filly given the name of Belle nosed out enough local talent to make it difficult to match her, so she was taken from the track and bred to Dedier, a rather well-known race horse of the district. His name had been simplified by the non-Cajun patois of the place to D.J. The filly this union produced was Della Moore. Boyd Simar, a Louisiana short-horse specialist, recognizing that her speed potential deserved a wider field, got her to the Texas tracks where she pounded out an impressive list of wins. For some reason—it is said without Simar's knowledge—she was bred to the popular Thoroughbred racer Joe Blair. Although it put her out of the running for about a year, it was fortunate for the Quarter Horse breed because she produced Joe Reed P-3, a foundation sire. His son, Joe Reed II P-985, was the sire of Leo, whose progeny today are legion.

When she left the track, Della Moore had the good fortune to join the select society of the Ott Adams running horses of South Texas. There, when she was ten years old, she was bred to Ott Adams' pride and joy, Little Joe. The colt that resulted was Joe Moore. Strangely, Ott Adams misjudged him. With such distinguished parentage, perhaps he expected to see a paragon of perfection. But Joe Moore, like his daddy, was a sleeper and slow to prove his quality. He was sold to be used as a cowhorse and part-time stud. It was not until Adams saw Joe Moore's foals hit the ground practically running that he hurriedly bought him back. Joe Moore never raced. He didn't have to. His get did it all for him—and with distinction. His son, Joe Less, was the sire of No Butt, the 1962 World Champion Quarter Running Horse, Mare and Aged Mare. Four of the seven AQHA Supreme Champions trace to Della Moore.

Many other superior horses came along a few years too early to be registered in the books of the new Quarter Horse breed.

Among the well-remembered ones are: Carrie Nation (King); Possum; Balleymooney, and Joe Hancock.

Della Moore. *Courtesy Nelson Nye.*

Joe Moore. *Courtesy Nelson Nye.*

THE FOUNDATION SIRES OF THE AQHA

The first nineteen horses who were given permanent pedigree numbers in the *AQHA Stud Book* were designated as foundation sires of the new breed. They were chosen for their superiority of conformation, disposition, and ability as well as for their proven ability to pass on their good qualities to their get.

Carrie Nation was the best-known daughter of Peter McCue and was the dam of Billy Sunday, the great sprinter who sired Rialto P-2. Carrie Nation, the mare, was a track celebrity at the time Carrie Nation, the woman for whom she was named, was busily smashing saloon mirrors and campaigning for prohibition. Both were raised southeast of Woodward, Oklahoma. *Courtesy AQHA.*

OPPOSITE:
(King) Possum, 1904–25, was by Traveler. Like his full brother Little Joe he was a great money-maker at the quarter tracks. J. J. Kennedy took him to Arizona, renamed him Possum because he already had a King, and saw him become the most famous sire in the state. Two of his well-known sons were Guinea Pig and Red Cloud. *Courtesy AQHA.*

Joe Hancock, a large brown horse by John Wilkins by Peter McCue, was bred by Walter E. Hancock at Perryton, Texas. He had a brilliant racing career, and his many offspring performed with distinction on the tracks, in the rodeo arenas, and in ranch work. *Photo McCormick Co. Courtesy AQHA.*

WIMPY P-1 by Solis by Old Sorrel, who headed up the King Ranch strain of Quarter Horses, won the championship at the Southwestern Exposition and Fat Stock Show at Fort Worth, Texas, in 1941, the year the stud book registry of the AQHA was opened, and, as had been agreed by the board of directors, the winner of this show was to be honored by receiving the first pedigree issued to foundation sires.

As might be expected, his progeny have contributed mightily to the breed in the West, but they have also, largely through his son Bill Cody, a grand champion in twenty-four classes, infiltrated all parts of the country.

Strange as it may seem to Westerners, the oldest ranch in the United States is not in the West, but on Long Island near the famous Montauk Lighthouse on its eastern tip. For many years it has been called the Deep Hollow guest ranch, where for the last decade or more the genial Dickinsons, Jack and Joan and their son Dale, have greeted and cared for a multitude of sojourners. Here Western riding is enjoyed. And here on adjoining land was where Phin Dickinson, a brother of Jack, developed and trained the 1959–60 champion Joe Cody, who was later acquired by the Willow Brook Farms at Catasauqua, Pennsylvania, where Easter Cody, another grandson of Wimpy, became the top reining horse of the nation in 1965 and top working cowhorse of 1966–67.

Wimpy is number one in the *AQHA Stud Book. Photo by Dodd, Kingsville, Texas. Courtesy the King Ranch.*

Rialto P-2. *Courtesy Robert M. Denhardt.*

RIALTO P-2 (1923–44) was a chestnut by Billy Sunday, by Horace H (TB) out of Dora Du Mar by Little Joe, by Traveler. Through his dam he also traced to Old Billy. He was bred by the grand old horseman of South Texas Ott Adams of Alice. Rialto—the name means High River in Spanish—had such quality there was general agreement when he was chosen as number two horse on which to found a breed. Adams sold him to Tom and Jasper Singleton, Negro brothers who were excellent horsemen, the latter an ex-jockey. Jasper was going to leg Rialto up for the tracks, but other work prevented it. So Rialto never proved himself as a sprinter. His offspring did it for him. He passed into the ownership to John H. Taylor of Kendleton, Texas, and then into that of O. C. Quinn of Houston, Texas. The registered get of Rialto came along late in his life, but they amounted to forty-one.

JOE REED P-3 (1921–47) was by Joe Blair (TB) and out of Della Moore, the most acclaimed racing mare of her time. From his son and daughter came Leo, the sire of the largest family of performance and racing Quarter Horses. Joe Reed also sired Firebrand Reed, the father of Fire One, the Quarter Horse that made a name for himself in international jumping.

Joe Reed P-3. *Courtesy* Quarter Horse Journal.

Bred by Henry Lindsay of Granger, Texas, Joe Reed P-3 was owned for many years by J. J. Slankard of Elk City, Oklahoma. His registered get were forty-six horses and ninety-two mares.

Joe Bailey P-4 (1919–47) referred to usually as being from Gonzales, to distinguish him from Joe Bailey of Weatherford, was a dark sorrel fifteen hands high who weighed 1150 pounds. The blaze on his face ran down into his mouth. He was by Possum (King Cardwell) by Traveler. He was out of the Brown Nixon Mare, whose grandfather was Joe Bailey of Weatherford. Robert M. Denhardt, who with Jim Minnick inspected him as a possibility for the prospective AQHA Stud Book, rode the horse in 1938, when he was nineteen years old. He wrote, "I doubt if I have ever ridden a faster horse."

Dr. Nixon, who bred Joe Bailey, sold him to a Negro horseman named Thomas, who sold him to C. E. Dickinson and J. B. Ellis of Gonzales. His progeny in the stud book were not numerous, but his tribe of grandsons and granddaughters is a large one. Little Joe Jr. was his greatest son.

Joe Bailey P-4. *Courtesy Robert M. Denhardt.*

Chief P-5. *Courtesy Robert M. Denhardt.*

CHIEF P-5 (1917–46), a brown horse bred and owned by W. Claud Stinson of Hammond, Oklahoma, was by Peter McCue and out of Little Annie. Stinson kept him throughout his life. There are sixty-six mares and twenty-seven horses sired by him in the AQHA registry.

Oklahoma Star P-6. *Courtesy* Quarter Horse Journal.

OKLAHOMA STAR P-6 (1915–1942) by Dennis Reed (TB) and out of Cutthroat was a blood bay with a large star on his forehead. Mention of him and his get appears in many places in this book, so we will not repeat it here, other than to say he was bred by Tommy Moore of Laverne, Oklahoma, raced by him, and then sold at the age of eleven to Ronald Mason of Nowata, Oklahoma, where he remained the rest of his life. Sixty mares and nineteen horses represent him in the AQHA Stud Book. Many of his line became famous in rodeo.

COLUMBUS P-7 (1922–42) was purchased by M. G. Michaelis and his wife Helen, the first secretary of the AQHA, from his breeder, Frank Auerback, of Columbus, Texas, and he died on their place at Eagle Pass, Texas. All of his fifteen registered get were mares, most of whom produced superior cowhorses for Texas ranchers. He was by Ben Bolt by Aguinaldo, a grandson of Lock's Rondo.

COLONEL P-8 (1925–47) was one of the four sorrel horses among the elite nineteen. He was a beautiful horse with a large star between his

Colonel P-8.

eyes and with stockings on both hind legs. His breeder was C. S. Springer of Cimarron, New Mexico, and he was by Springer's Little Joe, a grandson of Harmon Baker. His dam also was from the Peter McCue line. He was owned by Allen Whitworth of Wewoka, Oklahoma. His registered get were forty-four mares and two horses.

OLD RED BUCK P-9 (1924–c. 45) brought to the breed the blood of Cold Deck and Tubal Cain, the progenitor of the Oklahoma Blake horses, being by the latter's son Red Man. From his dam, Pet Dawson, he perpetuated the Printer strain. Bred by John Dawson of Oklahoma, he later was owned by rodeo celebrity King Merritt, on whose place at Federal, Wyoming, he died.

OLD JIM P-10 (c. 1920–50) was a Traveler on both sides—top and bottom. His sire was Little Tex by Texas Chief by Traveler, and his dam was Baby King by (King) Possum by Traveler. Bred by Jim Harkey, he passed to the ownership of Foster Conger, both of Texas. Old Jim was a handsome, well-proportioned horse and was an excellent roping

Old Red Buck P-9.

Old Jim P-10.

horse. Before his death on the Conger ranch near Sterling, Texas, he had put thirty-nine fillies and eleven colts in the AQHA registry.

SHEIK P-11 (1918–c. 46) was the only grulla horse among the select nineteen. He had a large blaze that came down to give him a white upper lip, and his mane and tail were dull flaxen. His sire was Peter McCue, but his odd coloring came from his dam, Pet by Old Fred, a slightly spotted Palomino, and whoever Pet's dam was. He was bred by Coke Robards of Hayden, Colorado, and sold to the Diamond 2 Cattle Company and Cort Carter of Kirkland, Arizona, where he sired forty-two fillies and thirteen colts that were registered.

COWBOY P-12 (1922–46) was a powerful horse with well-muscled shoulders and hind quarters. He was bred by Ed Thompson of Folsom, New Mexico. His breeding has been questioned—unreasonably so, judging by the things I have read—but now it is well accepted that his sire was the Waggoner ranch Yellow Jacket by Little Rondo by Lock's Rondo. His dam was Roan Lady by Stalks by John Wilkins by Peter

Cowboy P-12. *Courtesy Robert M. Denhardt.*

Waggoner's Rainy Day P-13. *Courtesy AQHA.*

McCue. His eighty-nine registered offspring—sixty-seven were mares—appear in the pedigrees of today's Quarter Horses the country over.

WAGGONER'S RAINY DAY P-13 (1925–c. 46) represented two major families, Rondo and Peter McCue. He was by Ben Hur by Rainy Day and out of a mare by Little Ace. Aside from many ranch workers he sired 125 registered get before he died at Stillwater, Oklahoma, while owned by J. A. (Art) Beall. He was dun with no white marking.

OLD RED BIRD P-14 (1924–45) was bred by Coke Robards of Hayden, Colorado, and was later owned by Morris S. Clark of Wichita Falls, Texas. He was sired by Buck Thomas, a half brother of Sheik, and was out of a Peter McCue mare. Twenty-nine of his get were registered.

BROWN POSSUM P-15 (c. 1925–45) was by (King) Possum by Traveler. He was the only brown horse among the nineteen foundation sires. Bred by John Roades, well known in rodeo, of Sombrero Butte, Arizona, and last owned by the Santa Mariana Ranch at Tucson. His get were largely used as ranch horses and performance horses in rodeo.

Old Red Bird P-14.

Brown Possum P-15.

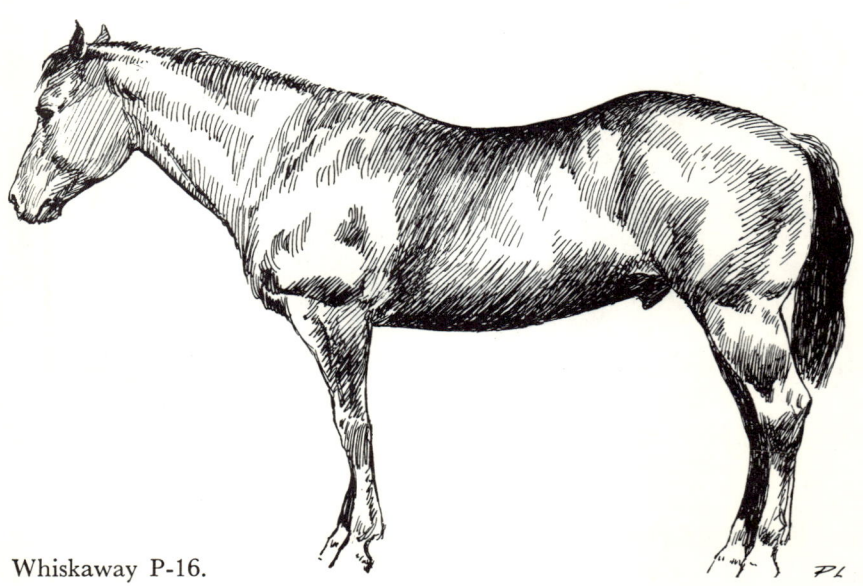

Whiskaway P-16.

Little Richard P-17.

WHISKAWAY P-16 (1924–c. 46) was by A. D. Reed by Peter McCue and his dam was Snip by Speedy Bull. He was bred by E. A. Meek of Foss, Oklahoma, and his last owner was L. E. Chafin of Tucumcari, New Mexico. Most of his stock was used for ranch work, but three colts and fifteen fillies were registered.

LITTLE RICHARD P-17 (1922–50) was by the King Ranch's Old Sorrel. At the time of his death he was owned by Guy Troutman of Tucumcari, New Mexico, the second of the foundation sires to go to that district of good horses.

YELLOW BOY P-18 (1927–c. 50) was the second dun horse to get in the registry. He was a three-quarter brother of Cowboy P-12, being by Yellow Jacket and out of Bonnie Wilkins by John Wilkins by Peter McCue. Bred by Oscar Blivins of Amarillo, he spent his life in the Panhandle of Texas, where he sired many unregistered ranch horses for the JA (John Adair) Ranch, plus sixty-six fillies and fifteen colts that are in the registry. His last owner was John T. Sims of Pampa.

Yellow Boy P-18.

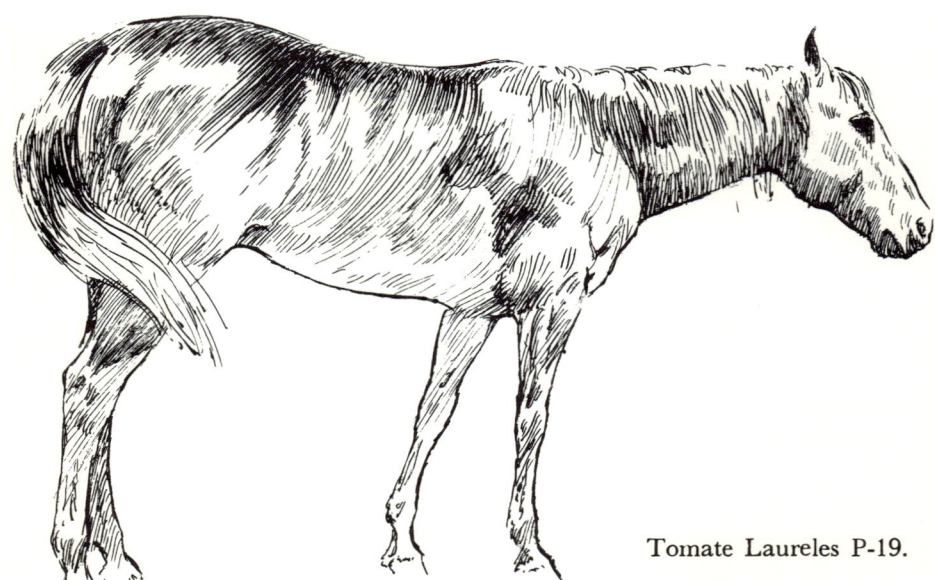

Tomate Laureles P-19.

TOMATE LAURALES P-19 (1927–61), the last of the designated foundation sires, was a son of Old Sorrel and out of a Dock Lawrence mare by Tom Thumb. Forty-two of his get—thirty were mares—got into the registry. He lived out his long life, thirty-four years, on the King Ranch, where he was foaled.

Old Sorrel, a grandson of Peter McCue, had two sons and a grandson selected as foundation sires. In addition, two of Peter McCue's sons and five other horses who were of his breeding were made foundation sires. Thus eleven out of nineteen horses were of Peter McCue breeding.

Although only four traced to Traveler, the get of his son Little Joe and Little Joe's son Zantanon were soon challenging the preponderance of the Peter McCue line.

As destiny would have it, the first great prepotent sire of the Quarter Horse breed was not one of the nineteen foundation sires, or even one of the 105 stallions first chosen for the registry. He was:

KING P-234 (1936–58)

King was a Quarter Horse who came along before the running Quarter Horse strains became predominantly of Thoroughbred breeding. He was the son of Zantanon by Little Joe by Traveler. His dam was Jabelina, a mare who traced to Lock's Rondo through Strait Horse and Yellow Jacket. As previously stated, King was bred on the ranch of Benevides Volpe near Laredo, Texas. Volpe raced him twice—winning both times—before selling him as a two-year-old to Byrne James, who trained him as a roping horse. His next owner, Wynn Duboise of Uvalde, Texas, continued his training and with Johnny Stevens got him to some of the best rodeos in the Southwest where he won praise from men who knew a good roping horse when they saw one.

Jess Hankins, a successful businessman and rancher of Rocksprings, Texas, was looking for a good stallion to mate with a fine racing mare he owned, when one of the cowboys told him about the stud named King. "The minute I saw him I knew he was the best stallion I had ever seen," Jess told me when I met him in Amarillo, Texas, at the time he was president of the AQHA.

He paid eight hundred dollars for King, and this amazing horse proceeded to repay his cost a thousandfold. Jess Hankins made King famous—and vice versa. Heading up the family of carefully selected mares acquired by the Hankins brothers, Jess, J.O., and Lowell, and serving superior brood mares that were trailered to him from all over

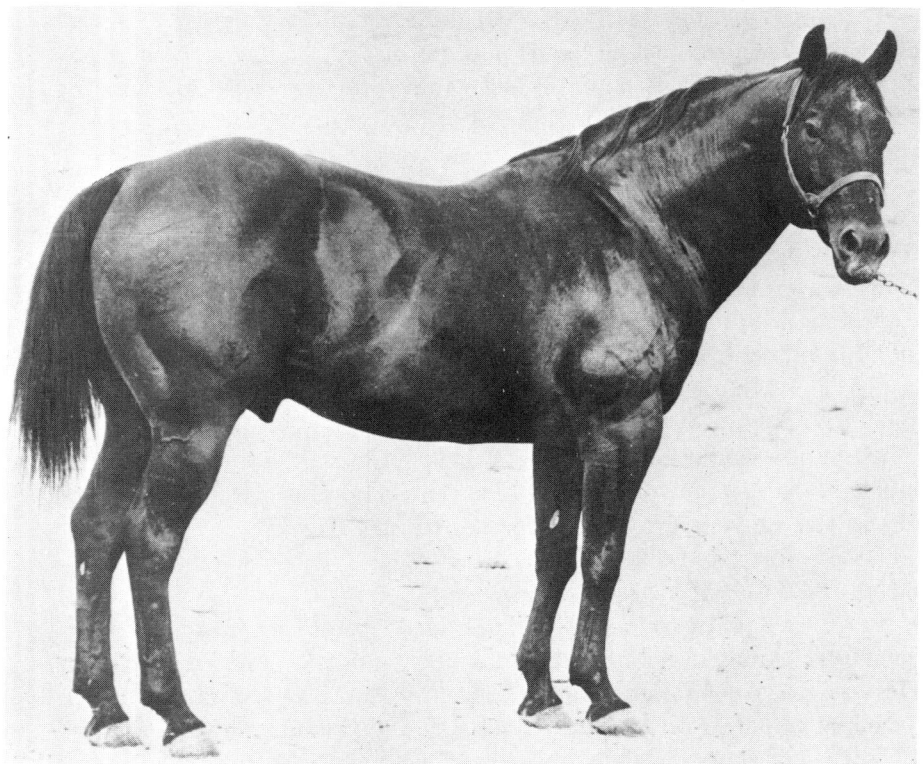

King P-234. *Courtesy AQHA.*

the country, he fathered the largest hierarchy within the breed. He put 275 registered sons and 336 registered daughters on the ground. Eighteen became AQHA champions. His stock featured in every way champion Quarter Horses can: as racers, cutting horses, in reining, as roping horses, Western pleasure and barrel racing horses, and in halter classes, and, very importantly, as brood mares.

Every state in the Union, Canada, Mexico, Australia, and several other countries have large numbers of King's progeny, which if computerized, would prove to be in the thousands.

One of King's daughters, Squaw H, developed by J. O. Hankins, beat every Quarter Horse of her day on the tracks and further publicized her dad by winning at halter and producing highly successful turf horses. I had the good fortune of getting within touching distance of one of King's great sons, Poco Bueno, when I stopped at his home near Vernon, Texas.

Poco Bueno P-3044. *Photo by the author.*

POCO BUENO P-3044 (1944–69)

Poco Bueno, one of the big assets of the 510,000-acre Waggoner Ranch near Vernon, Texas, was shown to me by Fagan Miller, his handler, and the manager of the three reverse D's Quarter Horse breeding establishment. The late E. Paul Waggoner, the owner, who was there at the time, assured me old Pokey, as he affectionately called the nineteen-year-old stallion, was still breeding with the zest of a young horse. He was a friendly horse, and came right over to the arena fence to see us. "He looks at you just like a man," Fagan remarked.

Poco Bueno—pronounced *Poco Wayno* and meaning *Pretty Good*—had the most modest name imaginable when one considers he has been horse royalty almost from birth. His sire was King P-234 and his dam was Miss Taylor by Old Poco Bueno. E. Paul Waggoner paid Jess Hankins, his breeder, $7,600 for him as a yearling, a sum that seems paltry in retrospect when the horse showed that he excelled at everything. As a cutting horse, he was superb, winning close to $200,000. Like his father, his prepotency was remarkable. He has passed on his inherited virtues to sons and daughters that have sold for well over one million dollars. At one sale in 1960 thirty-six of his get brought $293,725.

His pedigree is impressive:

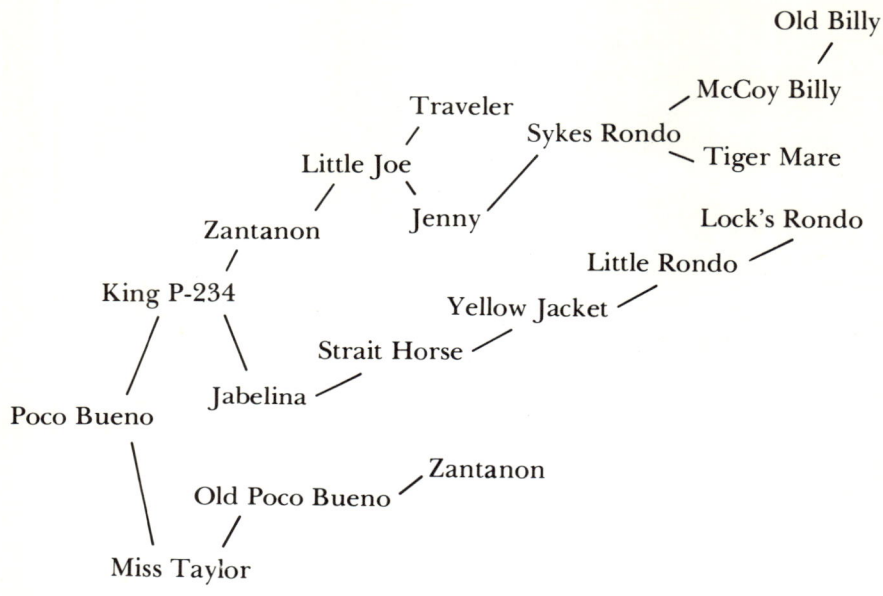

MAJOR KING (1946–)

Major King is the pride and joy of the M&M Ranch near Milford, Texas. The M&M stands for Mike and Millie Leonard, a husband and wife team who started raising quality stock horses before the Quarter Horse breed was founded. Both are ranch-bred Texans. Mike was once a Texas Ranger along the Rio Grande. During the years when Mike was a busy executive in Dallas, much of the management of the ranch was assumed by Millie, a charming lady whom one might expect to be more at home as the hostess of some charity ball than overseeing a large horse-breeding establishment.

In 1945, Millie, whose knowledge of bloodlines is encyclopedic, bought the mare Moon Harris, a consistent winner in halter classes, whose sire was the famous roping and running horse Billy the Kid by Thoroughbred Elmendorf. At the time, Moon Harris was in foal by Royal King P-2392, a half brother of Poco Bueno.

The colt that came along in August 1946 was Major King. He grew into a beautiful deep-chested, short-coupled sorrel with a blaze face and three white stockings. In the coming years, the plans and hopes the M&M Ranch had for him unreeled as if Major King had written the script himself.

He became one of the best cutting horses of the time. His performance record and wins at halter are too numerous to mention, as are those of his get. One son, Major Thunder, a noted roping horse, won four grand championships and four reserve championships.

After seeing a movie of Major King in action, I better understood the remark made by Melvin Hall, the foreman of the M&M Ranch, after riding him in a cutting contest. "When Major King gets all four feet on one side, I have trouble staying on."

This rare photo of Poco Bueno, cutting with Pine Johnson riding, shows the concentration and determined action that set the young stallion on the road to fame. *Courtesy the Waggoner Estates.*

The great stud was seventeen years old when Millie brought him out into a paddock and introduced us. I was impressed by his alert, youthful appearance. He seemed the picture of grace and refinement. For an active stud it was surprising to see that he was as gentle as a family riding horse. In fact Millie said she often rode him to some outlying pasture to catch up some mare that was ready to be bred and would lead her back to the barns behind Major King.

Later, without the benefit of roads, Millie maneuvered her white Cadillac through pasture after pasture, inspecting and showing me the bands of brood mares and the frolicking progeny of Major King. Curious and alert, they came running to cluster about the car.

The M&M horses are on pasture the year round. The grasses are the result of much experimentation and are so nutritious few supplements are needed other than mineral salt and sulphur blocks. The horses are closely watched and frequently handled. Feet are trimmed periodically; any accidental cuts or bruises are attended to, and worming is done when necessary. Their horses are prime examples of Quarter Horses that are bred not only for good conformation, early speed, and top arena performance, but also for that all-important quality of the Quarter Horse —a good disposition.

There were, of course, a great many horses worthy of note in many parts of the country which excelled in racing, performance, and as sires, and which contributed to the rapid growth of the breed in its first two decades. Many are mentioned in the following chapters on racing, shows, and rodeos.

Throughout the early years of the AQHA, breeders naturally bred for what they believed was the ideal Quarter Horse. The race-horse breeders put the accent on speed and crossbred with suitable Thoroughbreds, trusting that conformation and other Quarter Horse characteristics could be retained if the Thoroughbreds they used were well chosen. Men who had identified with ranch horses, rodeo competition, and performance horses were inclined to be purists, maintaining that the bloodlines of the old Quarter Horse stock must be perpetuated with a minimum of outcrossing with the Thoroughbred.

Almost from the beginning of the AQHA, there were predictions that it was bound to split into separate associations—one to represent the racing Quarter Horses, and one to represent the breed of performance Quarter Horses. Schisms did occur. Dan Casement, who had been influential in forming the AQHA, sided with the latter group and with-

Major King with Millie Leonard at halter. *Photo by the author.*

drew in protest at the too frequent use of Thoroughbred sires. Others threatened withdrawal if a limitation of their use was made. A large faction did make an effort in the early 1960s to get a date set after which no outside blood—meaning of course the Thoroughbred—could be used. This effort was defeated.

THE SEVEN-EIGHTHS THOROUGHBRED

As for outbreeding, the establishment rule now allows a foal to be eligible for registration as a Quarter Horse if one of its parents is a Quarter Horse. Thus many strains of running Quarter Horses today are as much as seven-eighths Thoroughbred. Only when one sees the individual and notices the Quarter Horse conformation does one understand the care that had been taken in the selection of the TB forebears— muscular, wide-chested types that blended so well with the traditional Southwestern Quarter Horses.

```
                       TB
  QH foal                       TB
  ⅞ TB     QH mare                       TB
            ¾ TB     QH mare
                      ½ TB     QH mare
```

The breeders of racing Quarter Horses, with all their concern for speed, try to hold to the tenuous Quarter Horse characteristics of tractability and conformation, knowing that a high percentage of their horses will never make it to the tracks and therefore must be sold to compete with performance and show horses or, in the majority of cases, serve as well-mannered pleasure horses.

The breeders of show and performance horses can see many advantages in working along with the breeders of running horses. First and foremost, all Quarter Horses should have all the early speed that can be bred into them, and Quarter Track celebrity blood can give that little extra hustle that is so important in all competitive events. Moreover, most like the added arch to the neck and more refined head.

With some, the main point of disapproval of the seven-eighths Thoroughbred Quarter Horses is that they are more difficult to quiet down after exertion. If once raced, more time is consumed in retraining them for show and performance than is required with the old line-bred Quarter Horses. Others maintain it is all in the careful selection of the Quarter-type Thoroughbreds used for cross breeding and the methods of training. They have the greatest examples to point to: the AQHA supreme champions, who are not only race horses with a high percentage of Thoroughbred blood but also performance horses with cowpony dispositions.

With all the inner stresses and strains, the American Quarter Horse Association with its active and adroit management emerged as beneficial to most factions. There are, however, besides the Racing Quarter Horse Breeders Association, three small Quarter Horse Associations that carry on independently: the National Quarter Horse Registry, Inc., of Raywood, Texas; the Standard Quarter Horse Association of Denver, Colorado; and the Original Half Quarter Horse Registry of Hubbard, Oregon. The last three associations mentioned are devoted to preserving the best characteristics of Quarter Horses of the old established bloodlines before outbreeding became such a widespread practice. Each stresses its own way of improving registry requirements, showing, judging, and the system by which points and awards are handled.

4

In Search of Your Own Quarter Horse

Aside from professional uses of horses for breeding, racing, ranching, and rodeo, the reasons for wanting a horse of one's own are many and varied.

The primary reason for most of us is that we love to be with horses, to care for them and train them and to enjoy the wonderful feeling of creating a subtle understanding that brings a response from another, but very different, living being. Then, too, there is the sharing of the exhilaration of action in the big outdoors, which always looks bigger from the upper deck of a horse.

I don't believe many people deliberately go out and buy a horse just because riding is good exercise. Yet we all know it is one of the best and most enjoyable ways to exercise. When riding, the muscles from head to toes are put into movement. And a glance at people who ride often and consistently tells us there is no better way to reduce the hips and abdomen.

A horse in the family usually does something nice for family relations. Whether as a topic for family talk or because of the co-operation between the members of the family that a horse demands, he somehow pulls everyone a little closer. Boys and girls who take on the responsibility of a horse seem to grow in added stature and importance in the eyes of parents. They know that the mastery of anything—and certainly a horse and the art of riding him—requires thought and effort and will power. Taking the responsibility of a living creature many times their own size is a test welcomed by most young people, while they regard the joy and freedom and the exhilarating action it involves as pure bonus.

Before any decision as to what kind of a horse to buy is made, prospective horse owners begin by asking themselves some questions. "Why do I want to ride? For what purpose will I keep a horse?" And if parents are in on the decision making they will no doubt ask, "Why do we want

"Just for the fun of it" is one of the good reasons for owning a horse. *Courtesy AQHA.*

our boy or girl to ride? Is it to bring an active and happy change in his or her life—one that could result in a lifelong fondness for horses and the out-of-doors? Is it to give our teenagers the chance to be alone, away from the family oftener so they can work out their own way of growing up? Is it to place them in a better social group and foster a taste for competition? Does the vision ahead include trophies and ribbons won in the show ring or in performance events and contests?"

When these questions have been considered and answered, the type of horse and his training and even his price range and the equipment needed will be answered. The search for the right adviser as well as the right horse can start. Sensibly enough, most people start on a modest scale and work up. It will certainly pay the beginner to start by investing in some riding lessons. It can be your first step toward owning a horse.

If your aim is to gain horse knowledge and confidence in riding without having your enthusiasm drilled out of you, try to find an instructor of a local group of riders who have the most fun. This is assuming, of course, that the instructor is capable and that his place is well run with reasonably good horses.

Is your preference for stock-saddle or flat-saddle riding? If for the flat saddle, don't rule out the Quarter Horse simply because you think of him as a Western horse. The Quarter Horse works equally well under either type of saddle.

If your intention is eventually to own a beautiful horse, one that will win ribbons in shows, whether in the AHSA (American Horse Shows Association) or in the AQHA, find an instructor who trains winners for these shows. And if you are interested in equitation classes such as the Maclay and Medal classes, try to get an instructor whose pupils consistently win in these events.

For the young beginners and for those who want to stick to a low budget, there are many Pony Club branches and 4-H Clubs, depending on the locality, where lessons can be had at moderate costs. Also more and more civic-minded horsemen are sponsoring riding clubs in various parts of the country.

Sometimes good riders have the opportunity of riding excellent horses belonging to others. My daughter, Sidney, when in her teens, rode some top performance horses in Madison Square Garden to exercise them on days when there were no matinees of the World's Champion Rodeo. Mike Hastings, my long time friend, several times world champion bulldogger, vouched for her. But even so, it was a compliment to a young rider's ability, since an unsure hand on the reins or unbalanced seat can

In this flag race the action really flows. *Photo by Guy Kassal.*

in a few minutes disturb the precisely tuned reflexes of a highly trained arena horse.

As pointed out by Mr. Mackay-Smith, editor of *The Chronicle of the Horse,* "two of the best riders in the world, Kathy Kusner of the U.S. Equestrian Jumping Team, and Michael Page of the U.S. Equestrian Three-Day Team, have never owned a horse." It is also true that Crompton (Tommy) Smith, Jr., didn't own Jay Trump when he teamed up with that long-shot horse to be the first American pair ever to win the Grand National Steeplechase at Aintree, England, in 1965.

However, if one has the time to devote to a horse, but less dedicatedly, of course, than the three just mentioned, riding horses that belong to others will never approach the pleasure of riding one's own horse.

After you have become a pretty good rider is time enough to start looking the field over for a horse of your own. Knowing you and your riding ability, your instructor can now advise you. As for the horse you buy, age, size, and temperament must be considered. If the buyer happens to be a girl, she is no longer at a disadvantage. Sellers of horses have learned never to underestimate the frailer sex when it comes to riding, training, and judging horses. Actually, girls outnumber boys in most horse show and Pony Club events. I think every young girl I ever talked with wanted to have a horse. Certainly it seems more girls than boys become enamored of horses and will make the effort to own them and do the necessary work of caring for them. One father with four daughters said that the minute each one of his girls reached adolescence she became horse crazy. "It's love—the mother instinct," he said. "A horse becomes the embodiment of their love and attention." Ellin Roberts, editor of this book, put it another way: "Few young girls have been able to dominate anything or anybody, certainly nothing as big as a horse. To do so satisfies the ego." A Long Island woman whose menage includes boys, girls, dogs, and horses, gave as her opinion: "Boys want to show off their own physical prowess. Girls want to show off their horse."

Whether boy, girl, man, or woman, the first bit of advice for the horse buyer is to assume that the horse you want can be found. All horse books, including this one, stress all the ailments, blemishes, and bad habits that horses are heir to. It is done, of course, in order to be helpful, to sharpen your judgment, and to put you on guard against your own sentiments. Try to put such dire warnings firmly in the back of your mind, however. Above all, your quest for a horse should be a happy one. Remember, all the unpleasant possibilities, all the don'ts and bewares that you will read and hear about apply to only a small percentage of horses. The best assurance is, of course, to deal with people who guard their good reputations by selling thoroughly inspected and sound stock.

Horse Prices

To generalize on the price of horses is never helpful because the price range is so wide. It starts at nothing—not infrequently horses are given away in order to get them into a good home—and it has been known to reach more than a million dollars for a famous racing stallion.

For the beginner who wants a nice, sound, well-mannered horse, the price depends on whether it is a grade or unregistered horse, its age, conformation, disposition, location, sex, show or arena background, the time of year, and how badly the seller needs the money. I don't think a full or quarter-moon has anything to do with it.

In the spring, with months of enjoyable riding ahead, the price is higher. In the late fall, with the prospect of wintering a little-used horse, the price is lower. In the South and Southwest, where the seasons vary less, the price fluctuations are less.

In general, expect to pay from $250 to $1,000 for your first horse. If you want a highly trained horse or one that can win at halter or any sponsored show event, expect to pay more.

A lady in Florida told me of buying a nice-handling, good-looking saddle mare for $150. Unbeknown to either her or the seller, the mare was with foal. The colt that came along was a good one, so she couldn't resist gloating over buying two horses for the price of one.

People who can train as well as ride horses have a great advantage. They can buy green horses, horses that are rough-broken but have no finished training. While enjoying riding they can increase the value of their horse many times his purchase price by perfecting his training. It can be in reining, Western pleasure, or even in the more specialized show events such as jumping, roping, cutting, barrel racing, etc. Horses that are given this training are almost without exception registered horses. The reason is obvious. Only AQHA registered horses can enter AQHA sponsored shows. A grade Quarter Horse even with specialized training for ranch work or for small unsponsored shows will always carry a lower price tag. The basic rule is: Grade horses cost less than registered horses.

One man who buys and sells saddle horses, when asked to generalize on price, said, "Pay $250 for the horse and $750 for his training."

Other Costs

Depending on the location, boarding a horse out will cost from $600 to $800 per year. After adding the cost of such extra items as tack, grooming equipment, and about eight sets of shoes a year, plus probable occasional veterinarian fees, the hobby will amount to an expenditure of around $100 per month.

Owners with their own stable and paddock who feed and care for their own horse can do so for about $50 or $60 per month. As mentioned in the chapter on feeding, it can be done for less if there is natural pasturage.

Traveling to shows or other activities will incur vanning fees or necessitate the purchase of a horse trailer. If the trailer is used on roads too rough for a car, a pickup truck would be required to pull it. Other costs at shows are entry fees, stall fees, badges, passes for grounds, etc. And, of course, your own appropriate clothing.

A Gelding, a Mare, or a Stallion

I have known and ridden with many men who preferred to ride stallions, and who did so with firm command. The majority of great Quarter Horse sires distinguished themselves in performance events and on the track before they were retired to stud.

However, unless you are an experienced horseman and can have a registered stallion, it is better to have a good performance gelding. Stallions whose offspring have not won distinction sell for less than geldings that excel in arena events.

Statistics show that too many small breeders still keep horses for sires that should have been gelded. As stallions, many horses cannot pass the rigid inspection for registration, whereas the same animals, if gelded, can be registered. A slight imperfection in conformation in a gelding may not bar him from registration. A stallion, who can pass deficiencies along to potentially numerous foals, is harmful to the breed and will not be sanctioned for registration. Consequently an unregistered stallion is a liability. Neither he nor his progeny can compete in approved AQHA shows or contests.

The largest body of horsemen, the pleasure riders, will always be happier and safer if they avoid the responsibility of owning and handling

Lisa and Tara Bird and Joyce Armstrong of Scottsdale, Arizona, exercise their horses every day. *Photo by Irene Laune.*

breeding stock. The ideal horse for any riding **purpose is the gelding.** He is stronger and usually less temperamental than a mare, and he is far more tractable than a stallion.

If a mare is chosen, it is preferable that she be registered. The day may come when she is given time off to have a foal. Then if the colt or filly is a good one it would be shortsighted indeed to have it barred from entering shows.

Age

"Well, I was looking for a younger horse" is a familiar phrase to horse sellers and one that could just as well be skipped. Don't pass up a horse that has just reached his peak of training. If "young" means three or four years old, the prospective buyer is asking for a horse still in training, which he must be capable of continuing. Race horses are not part of this discussion. They are usually off the track before they are five.

Top polo, roping, cutting, reining, and other performance horses are often at their best around fifteen years of age. Many keep turning on and off bursts of speed and doing smart expert work until they hit the twenty mark or more. One of the best cutting horses I ever rode was over twenty-five years old. His forelegs were beginning to go over at the knees, but if allowed to blow a bit and take his time re-entering the herd he would work his steer with zest and bring him out, sometimes with his teeth nipping at the root of the steer's tail to scoot him into the cut-out herd. This, of course, was in pasture, not arena, cutting.

Certainly for those just learning to ride or those just entering competitive events there is great advantage in getting a horse with good training and experience, even if he is ten to fifteen years old. This is to assume, of course, that the horse is sound and shows no signs of wear and tear beyond the usual little bumps and superficial scars. At this age the price may also be a little more to your liking.

Really old horses are sometimes worth the extra care they need. General Schuyler's horse, who carried him through the American War of Independence, was retired to pasture at the age of twenty-three. Because his teeth were going, he soon became skin and bones. Seeing this pure-bred, once magnificent animal in such condition disturbed Prime, the slave of the Marquise de la Tour du Pin, who lived on the vast lands of the Van Rensselaers in the Mohawk Valley of New York State. Prime asked his mistress to ask General Schuyler for the old horse, which she did. The general was glad to see his old charger get better care and readily complied with the request. Prime fed the horse carrots, boiled grain, and fine-cut hay. To everyone's surprise he became a grand-looking animal again. For several years thereafter he carried the marquise on his frequent trips to and from Albany.

An aged horse is not necessarily a less active horse or one that tires quickly, although a considerate rider will allow for his age and see that he is not overworked. Nor is an aged horse a lazy horse.

Even if you are not the most confident horseman, think twice before buying a lazy horse. A lazy slowpoke horse is that way because a lot of things combined to make him that way, and you will not have time to cope with all the reasons and make a new horse out of him. He will tire quickly and have very short periods of concentration, which means he'll be a slow learner. A lazy horse is likely to barn sour (hate to leave the barn) or be sullen if pressed for more exertion, and may put his ears back or switch his tail to show irritation. Just pass him by and look some more.

Teeth are the best gauge for judging age. Perhaps the most usual expression concerning the age of horses is, "He's getting long in the tooth." If a horse's teeth protrude at an angle, that is, are getting longer, most horsemen can make a fairly accurate guess as to his age. More expert horsemen look at the cups of teeth for wear and change. Charts showing the changes in the teeth at different ages are in Chapter 5.

Geldings seldom have a full mouth (all their permanent teeth) until the age of five, whereas fillies usually get all their permanent teeth a year sooner. At the age of ten all the cups in the incisor teeth, both upper and lower, are worn down so that they do not show, making the horse a smooth-mouth or aged horse. The term aged means mature, not senile. The usual argument for not buying a horse over twelve years of age is that his years of usefulness are limited. Reasoned another way, it can be assumed that riders in their early teens will find that a horse of twelve or even fourteen years will serve them well for the four or five years before they are off to college.

Also, a beginner can learn from a wise old horse. Being sensible and familiar with tack and the many things about a stable and fences and highways, he can be counted on to avoid a lot of trouble that a younger horse might get involved in.

But when it comes to buying an older horse, he should be judged just as critically as a young one. He should be a horse you like, one whose looks and gaits and good nature appeal to you. And remember, any bad habits or faults he may have are pretty well set and will take much longer to correct, if it is at all possible to correct them, than if he were a younger animal.

Size

Measure the height of your own chin, then when you stand close to a horse's withers you can impress others with your accuracy in judging the animal's height. The height to the withers is based on so many hands (a hand being four inches). A horse fourteen hands two inches (14.2), for example, is fifty-eighty inches high at the withers.

The horse you buy should be of a size that goes well with your own.

A little guy or gal looks definitely mismatched when perched on a horse seventeen hands high. And the getting on and off problem such height poses is something to consider. The two-hundred-pounder looks just as ill-matched astraddle a 13.2-hand pony. A lot depends on the way a horse is muscled. The Quarter Horse, being more heavily muscled, carries more weight per hand high than horses of any other saddle breed. A Quarter Horse of 14.2 hands can carry well over two hundred pounds and work with bursts of speed for hours on end. Whereas a 16-hand, light-muscled, long-legged, narrow-chested horse carrying the same weight might in his constant struggle for balance tire sooner.

Although the trend may be toward slightly taller Quarter Horses, there will remain a wide range of heights to choose from, so that pleasure riders can get what they want anywhere between 14.2 and 15.2 hands high. The generally accepted height and weight limits for mature Quarter Horses are: 14.3 to 15.1 hands and 1100 to 1300 pounds.

Color

Quarter Horses come in solid colors—quite a range of them—with head and leg markings similar to those of other breeds. They have no excessive white or unusual markings or spots that would indicate Pinto, Appaloosa, or Albino breeding.

The old cliché "there is no bad color on a good horse" got by for a long time with horsemen, but the AQHA draws the line on registering Pintos, Skewbalds, and Piebalds. Pinto and Skewbald describe vari-colored spotted horses. Piebald limits it to black and white spotted horses.

Registered Quarter Horses must have a solid colored coat, with the exception of various blazes, stars, stripes, and snips on the face and socks and stockings on the pasterns and legs.

The official handbook of the AQHA lists the colors that are acceptable for horses that are considered for registration. They are:

Bay: ranging from tan through red to reddish brown; mane and tail black; usually black on lower legs.

Black: true black without light areas; mane and tail black.

Blue Roan: more or less uniform mixture of white and black hairs, usually with a few red hairs (some are bluish black).

Brown: brown or black with light areas at muzzle, eyes, flank, and inside upper legs; mane and tail black, usually black on lower legs.

The seven face markings as designated by the AQHA are: 1. Blaze. 2. Stripe. 3. Star, strip and snip. 4. Star and strip. 5. Star. 6. Bald. 7. Snip.

The five leg markings are: 1. Sock. 2. Pastern. 3. Stocking. 4. Coronet. 5. Half pastern.

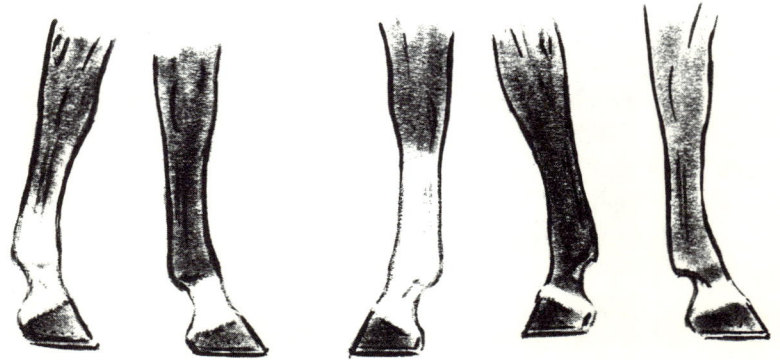

Buckskin: a form of dun, yellowish or gold; mane and tail black; usually black on lower legs.

Chestnut: (in the first years of the AQHA this color was not accepted—being used only as chestnut-sorrel) dark red or reddish brown; mane and tail usually same color as body, but may be flaxen.

Dun: yellowish or gold; mane and tail may be black, brown, red, yellow, white, or mixed; often has dorsal stripe, zebra stripes on legs, and traverse stripe over the withers.

Gray: mixture of white and black hairs; usually born solid-colored or almost solid-colored and gets lighter with age.

Grulla: smoky or mouse-colored (not a mixture of black and white hairs but with each hair mouse (colored); mane and tail black; usually black on lower legs.

Palomino: golden yellow; mane and tail white (flaxen).

Red Dun: a form of dun with body color yellowish or flesh-colored; mane and tail red.

Red Roan: uniform mixture of white and red hairs.

Sorrel: reddish or copper red; mane and tail usually same color as body, but may be flaxen.

It will be noticed that, no matter how orange-colored or how bright the red, a horse is considered a bay if he has a black mane and tail. And no matter how dark the red, a horse is considered a sorrel if the mane and tail are body-colored.

Buying a Grade Horse

If you buy a grade horse—that means an unregistered one—you may get just what you want for a pleasure horse. He doesn't have to be a rare beauty or an athlete of record-breaking performance. What most pleasure riders want and get is a well-built, healthy animal that is well mannered and not too excitable. One that they feel at ease with when they walk, jog, trot, canter, and gallop over the paths and local trails. One they can trailer to more scenic or open places for long trail rides with friends, or ride in open show classes and unsponsored arena games. Of all the Quarter Horses—registered or not—put on the market each year, the ones that are sold for pleasure riding outnumber all the racing, cutting, roping, and rodeo prospects put together. Without registration papers the price of a horse is generally lower when you buy him—and when you sell him.

For all you know, the unregistered horse you get may be a member of a distinguished Quarter Horse family. But to prove it would be difficult. Each season the top breeders of the country get rid of their second-best horses. These animals go to dealers to be widely dispersed —often through several dealers before they find a home as someone's pleasure horse. Vagueness about their origin is easily understood. If their origin was known, the reputation and value of their brothers and sisters would suffer. It follows that in buying unregistered stock, unless directly from the breeder, one knows only that part of the animal's breeding that the dealer or seller wishes to tell.

In the racing strains of Quarter Horses a higher percentage of Thoroughbred blood is present. In the performance strains of the cowhorse, Quarter Horse blood is retained. The more Thoroughblood blood there is in the horse the more likely he is to have a longer, arched neck and a more excitable nature. The more old-line Quarter Horse blood in the horse the more likely he is to have a shorter, more muscular neck and a more tractable disposition with easily controllable bursts of speed.

As recently as 1967, B. F. Phillips of Frisco, Texas, a large-scale breeder, trainer, and prominent horse judge, whose own horses carried as much as fifteen-sixteenths Thoroughbred blood, had this to say: "For every horse that gets off the track and then makes good in the arena performance, there are a hundred nuts." So, in choosing a pleasure horse, if you are not an experienced horseman, shy clear, if you can, from the ex-race horse and ex-polo pony. Time and again I have heard this advice from breeders of racing Quarter Horses.

All Thoroughbreds that get to the tracks are given a lip tattoo. It is not a requirement for Quarter Horse racers, but some are lip-tattooed. Therefore, any horse with a lip tattoo was intended for racing whether he ever did or not.

All registered Quarter Horses and Thoroughbreds come from racing stock. But not all breeders raise horses for racing. Many put the accent on performance and pleasure horses.

Buying a Registered Horse

In buying a registered Quarter Horse a transfer report should be received from the seller. Be sure that the last name on the Registration

Certificate is the same as the name of the seller. Don't confuse an application with the registration itself.

If purchased through an auction company, be sure the name of the person who consigned the horse to the auction is the same as the last recorded owner on the Registration Certificate. It is forbidden by the AQHA to transfer animals to any other person than the actual purchaser. The seller must send a transfer report signed by both seller and buyer along with a five-dollar fee to the AQHA.

The purchaser must give his name to the auction company or individual selling the horse exactly the way he wants the horse's ownership recorded. If the seller authorizes someone other than himself to sign a transfer, he must so notify the AQHA.

Be cautious of sellers who promise to deliver a Registration Certificate at a later date—except of course, when the horse is bought on a time payment plan. If an official transfer form is not available (they can be obtained from the AQHA without cost), a bill of sale is prepared for the buyer with the registered name and number of the animal. In buying a horse with a pedigree, you are assured of his bloodlines. Information about sires and dams can be obtained from the AQHA.

The kind of registered horse you select will depend on the events in which you want to compete. And the opportunities of competing are almost limitless. In the United States and Canada, not to mention other countries, there are well over a thousand shows a year. Nearly all of them include youth activity events and classes. Age classifications for exhibitors and contestants and their horses give a wide range for stalking trophies, ribbons, and prizes. Operating in co-operation with the AQHA are other sponsored shows and competitions such as the NCHA (National Cutting Horse Association) and NBRA (National Barrel Racing Association). Then there are AHSA (American Horse Shows Association) events and others.

While the Quarter Horse is abundantly versatile, special breeding as well as specialized training is necessary for horses to be consistent winners in the various events. For instance, it takes a very fast reining horse to win in barrel racing or pole bending, whereas a horse that is only moderately fast might be a consistent winner in the Reining, or Working Cowhorse Class. And an even slower horse might do well in the Western Pleasure Class. A beautifully built winner at halter might not be able to win at all in skilled performance events.

There are other motives that enter in when selecting a horse. The breeder who shows a stallion or mare at halter finds winning itself a sufficient reward, without a money prize, because it publicizes his stock. The one-horse owner showing a gelding at halter can win only a trophy or ribbon. The only financial gain whatever is the increased value it might give his horse. If one owns a mare that can produce registered foals, that is a different story. There are seldom any money prizes for halter classes.

Those who want to make money in arena competition go in for the events that call for much training and skill in both man and horse, such as roping and cutting and steer wrestling. In these events great profits sometimes accrue also to the breeders of the horses that win distinction.

A Bargain Horse

Unless you are a gambler it is advisable to get a veterinarian's opinion before buying any horse that is "damaged goods." If, however, the injury, blemish, or defect is examined and understood, you may find that the horse will serve well as a pleasurable and dependable saddle horse. Don't be disturbed by minor blemishes such as healed-over scars (some covered by white hairs) that resulted from cuts and scratches, cinch galls, back sores, and the like. They seldom detract from the horse's worth or ability. Even blindness in one eye does not keep an animal from halter shows.

Bumps, puffiness, and blemishes from the hocks and knees down are the ones that should be considered carefully, as they can be indications of lameness or of injuries that will result in lameness when the legs are subjected to exertion.

One of the most publicized examples of a bargain horse was the beat-up, gaunt, dirty old horse who was on his way to the slaughterhouse to be killed for dog meat when Harry De Leyer's keen judgment and sympathy tipped the scale and caused him to buy the pitiful animal. At his stable on Long Island De Leyer named the aged white horse Snow-Man, brought him back to flesh and vigor with good care, and when he discovered an unexpected talent for jumping, he fostered it and with expert training saw that Snow-Man reached stardom in the open jumping classes in the National Horse Show at Madison Square Garden in New York.

Ike Rude's famous rope horse, Baldy, had scars from his foot to his head, caused by near-fatal burns when the trailer he was in caught fire, and he went on to become one of the greatest roping horses the rodeo arena has ever seen. Steel Dust, Lexington, Dan Tucker, and a lot of other horses that were blind were bargains regardless of the price paid for them. Nearly all old horsemen recall riding excellent working and pleasure horses that were blind in one eye. Cutthroat, mentioned earlier, had an unsightly scarred gash in her neck, but daylighted almost every horse that was run against her and she added to her worth by producing Oklahoma Star, a foundation sire of the Quarter Horse breed.

The most serious kind of injury to watch for in a horse is the kind that may have damaged his spirit. Bad training, slipshod handling, poor care, or cruelty can make a horse so sour, so distrustful, so unwilling that only someone with unlimited time and patience can hope to retrain him into a worth-while animal.

The gentle disposition of the Quarter Horse was well demonstrated when Roy Davis, long-time editor of the *Quarter Horse Journal*, walked up to his young stallion General Ray in open pasture and, without the need of a rope or halter, petted him and examined his legs. *Photo by the author.*

A well-built horse, one with good conformation that stands erect and alert, is usually healthy and sound. This is so because any serious faults in structure or health soon affect his posture and appearance.

At the end of every season, guest ranches, summer camps, and schools have horses to be sold. At sale barns or auctions an experienced horseman can pick up some real horse bargains. A very reasonable purchase price allows for the wintering costs. Horses such as these, even though they have seen hard usage as hacks, in most cases can be built up with rest and good care to show action when properly handled.

While some people are concerned with finding a good pleasure horse, others are worrying about how to find a good home for a horse that circumstances force them to part with. Classified ads in newspapers or horse journals bring many such people together.

And try not to fall in love with a horse until he has been tried out, received the okay of a veterinarian, and the details of price, delivery date, and so forth have been settled.

Just remember that every horse purchase is a compromise. So look for his good qualities as well as his faults. Judge him by what he can do as well as what he can't do. No horse is a bargain unless he is sound where it matters—in legs, heart, wind, and disposition.

What a Judge Looks for in a Quarter Horse

Although judges have opinions, which vary in subtle ways, as to what the ideal Quarter Horse should be, there are basic standards that are accepted by most of them. But rest assured that few judges will see your horse exactly as you see him. Remember the skeptical judge who said, "He's a fine horse—at least on this side!"

Conformation. The head should be refined, with a straight nose and rather wide between the eyes. Eyes that are soft, clear, sparkling brown, that are alert without being agitated—kindly eyes—are liked by judges. They should be generous in size and not set too low in the head.

The muzzle is small, the mouth somewhat shallow and firm. The ears are short, wide apart, and active. The jaws are well developed, showing strength, but no longer exaggeratedly so as in the old Steel Dust horses. The lower edges of the jawbones are wide apart, which enables the horse to work with his head drawn in without restricting his breathing.

In this respect it is interesting to note that nature adjusts to special requirements. For instance, the English bulldog, through selective breeding, had his nose brought far back behind protruding teeth so that he could hang on and still breathe while his teeth were clamped into a bull's neck.

The introduction of more Thoroughbred blood has given more arch to the Quarter Horse neck and reduced the abrupt angle at which it joins the head. The neck is muscular and should have depth from the withers to the point where it joins the chest.

The shoulder line that slopes at an angle of thirty-five to forty-five degrees, generally following the same slope as the pasterns, is considered favorable, as it gives spring to the gallop and acts as a shock absorber. Pasterns that are too long or with too much slope can cause bowed tendons.

The girth through the heart is rated for its generous depth. The withers should be slightly higher than the rump. No longer do Quarter Horses with low, ill-defined withers find approval.

The chest is wide, with forelegs tied in well above the bottom line, to give strong balance, allowing for feet that are well separated to support legs that are angled slightly inward. The muscling on the inside of the forearms is pronounced.

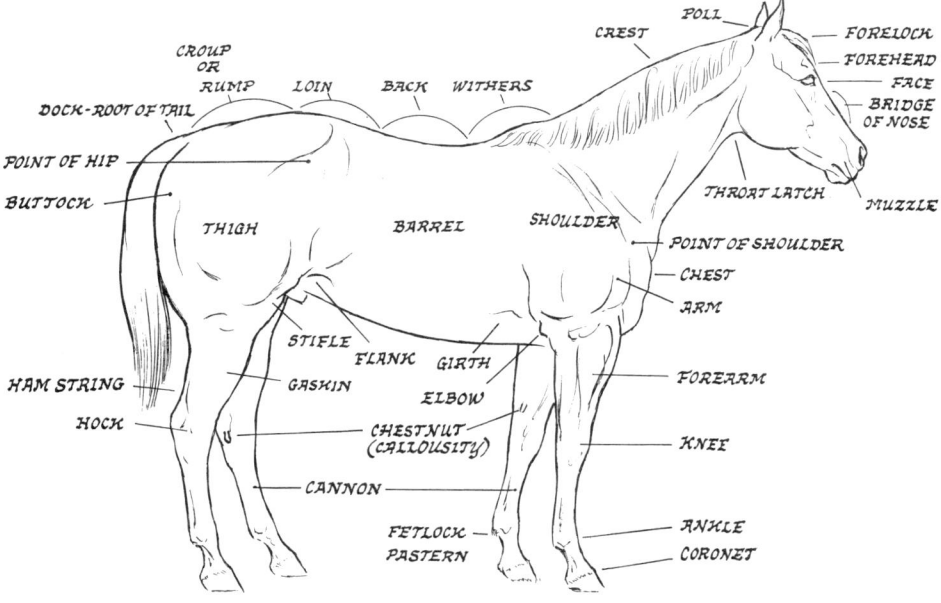

Conformation—the salient points.

Muscles should be long and tapering into ligaments that tie to the bones without lumpiness. They should be well developed and rounded out in the forearms, stifles, and on both inside and outside of the gaskins.

The lower line or belly should be long without going up too high into the flank, and the top line should be short. The back should be full and powerful across the loins, with a deep barrel with well-sprung ribs. From withers to coupling should be short, and from the point of hip to the buttock or point of rump should be long to give power to the hind legs.

The cannon bones are short with the knees and hocks close to the ground. The principle is that of a derrick. The cables above the joint exert great power over the shorter length below the joint. In circumference the cannon bones should be generous in proportion to the leg and, from the side, should appear broad and well separated from the tendons.

A front cannon bone carries all the weight at intervals in the gallop, and the rear cannon bones take much weight when stopping and pivoting.

The rear quarters are broad, deep, and heavy—let down, some say—when viewed from either side or rear, and are muscled so they are full through the thigh, stifle, gaskin, and down to the hock. The croup should be long and slope gently from the hip to the tail set. The loin blends into the croup.

The well-built horse is symmetrical and smooth. Each component part blends into other parts to give over-all balance, style, and beauty. *In motion* the grace and ease with which the horse handles himself are closely watched by judges. *Disposition* and attitudes are critically observed. The horse with a kindly, willing nature shows it in the ease with which he is handled. Bored or tired-looking or irritable and unruly horses will certainly lose points.

With colts and fillies, a certain amount of friskiness and cutting up is expected, and the judges are generally tolerant—even pleased to see—a little exuberant action if it doesn't get out of hand and become a time-consuming nuisance.

Blemishes. Judges are not usually concerned with minor blemishes such as scratches or scars which do not render the animal unserviceable. They are, however, quick to note any abnormality in structure or function which may cause unsoundness, or any defect that is **inherited**.

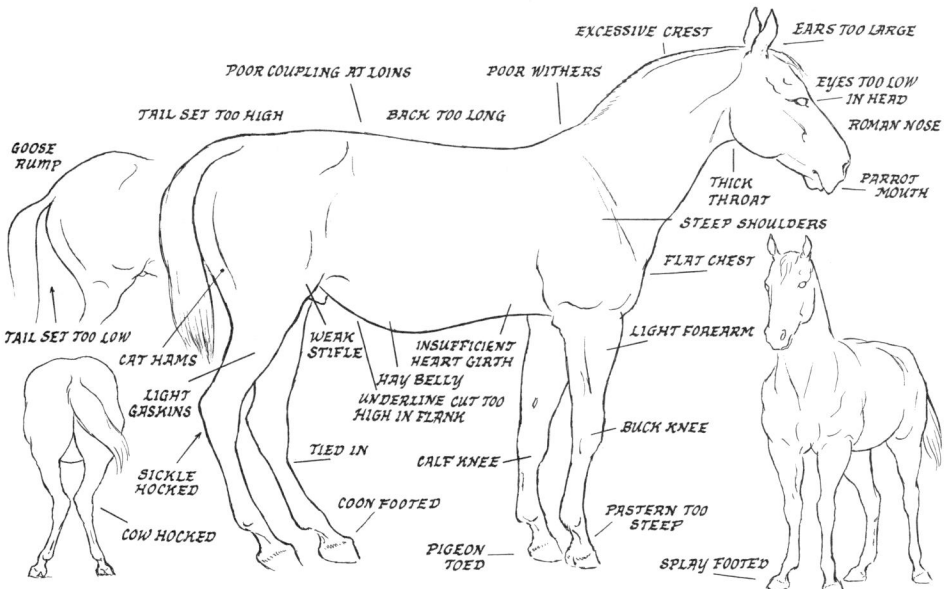

Conformation defects.

Auctions

When buying at an auction listen for the announcement or look for a notice that tells you whether the auction is "without reserve" or "with reserve." If the latter, it means the seller reserves the right to refuse to sell his consigned horse if the price is not to his liking. Many auctions are assumed, and legally so, to be "with reserve" unless otherwise announced.

If the auction is "without reserve," the horse must be sold to the highest bidder. There is little recourse if the owner or a friend or agent bids and buys back his own horse, although the practice is frowned on, and in some states laws forbid it. But the only effective deterrent seems to be the bad publicity such an operator gets. It is a different matter if an owner openly announces that he will enter the bidding if he thinks the horse is going at too low a price. Such frank honesty deserves respect.

An auctioneer works fast and is quick to pick up various movements or signs that indicate a bid. At an auction I witnessed a woman reach up and scratch her head. The auctioneer pointed at her and started to say "sold" when she realized what she had done, let out a squeal, and shouted, "No bid was meant!"

On meeting this young horse for the first time I politely said "Hello," and then turned away.

Buyers arrange to look over the stock before the sale begins. They keep a list of the numbers—one is pasted on each animal's rump in order to identify him when he comes into the sales ring.

As each animal is brought up for sale, its age, training, general breeding, soundness or lack of it are customarily stated by the auctioneer or the owner of the stock.

How to be Introduced to a Horse

When you meet a horse for the first time, try and be on your best horse manners by acknowledging the introduction with quiet reserve. Do not pat him in the face. He does not like it. Treat him as you would

A moment later the horse made a friendly overture by nibbling my shoulder.
Photos by Irene Laune.

a child. Don't rush things. When you first approach him, look him in the eyes and then turn away from him but stay close to him. Pay no more attention to him. Do not touch him. In a few moments he will get curious about you, and when he does he will turn his head in your direction. This is the moment you should speak to him and pat him on the neck or shoulder. Now that he has shared in the ritual of getting acquainted, he is more likely to accept you as his friend.

Temperament

Temperament is the catalyst that will meld a rider and a horse into a team or defeat all efforts to do so. I have heard that in the Mounted

Police Service of New York City an imperturbable, deliberate man is teamed with a spirited, mercurial horse; while a nervous, restless, quick-moving man is always assigned a composed, hard-to-fluster horse. Whether this is strictly true or not, it is certain that the interplay of muscular reactions and tensions are communicable and that a good balance of temperament is needed if rider and horse are to get on well together.

Perhaps the temperament of the Quarter Horse is the hardest to judge by appearances. A Quarter Horse can be standing in a droop-headed slouch, practically in a doze, and just a split second later be in a back-humping run. A roping horse that comes out of the box like a streak of lightning can, after he has held his calf and the job is done, be a quiet, easygoing horse. This kind of temperament is the result of centuries of selective breeding of Barb and Spanish horses that had to work with on-and-off bursts of speed. All who are familiar with Quarter Horses have seen them brought in lathered and excited, yet so self-controlled that they will accept a child on their back and walk calmly about the yard as they cool down.

Maneuverability, abrupt stops, and the ability to regain calmness quickly are not required of race horses. Yet many Quarter Horses that have run in AAA time have proved to be, after careful training, easily controlled as performance and pleasure horses.

It is difficult to imagine a polo player jerking the bridle from his mount and continuing the game without any head control. Yet a fast-moving Quarter Horse, a son of Oklahoma Star named Nichels, bred by Ronald Mason of Nowata, Oklahoma, had his bridle stripped from his head by his trainer and owner Chalk Dyer during a jackpot roping contest, just to show off what his horse could do. Chalk rode him into the box and turned him facing out and as he played out his loop the way he wanted it, Nichels, although keyed up and dancing, waited for the calf to burst from the adjoining chute and the tape to snap across before he tore out after it. Then putting his man in good throwing position, the instant the calf was snagged and he felt Chalk's weight going out of the saddle, on his own initiative he "sat down and bedded it" and held steady while Chalk wrapped it up.

Another instance of the initiative and composure of the Quarter Horse was demonstrated at Fort Worth in 1950 by Philip Williams and his cutting horse Skeeter, who was then Reserve World's Champion Cutting Horse, and who took top spot as World's Champion Cutting Horse in both 1950 and 1951.

On the night of the finals at Fort Worth, with two go-arounds already won, Phil suddenly decided to demonstrate supreme confidence in Skeeter —regardless of possible loss of points—by slipping the bridle from Skeeter's head. Skeeter moved slowly into the herd, and when he spotted his cow, threw the switch and went into precise action. Although points were not allowed for performing in this unorthodox manner, the crowd gave the team an ovation.

No one, whether old hand or novice, wants to ride a horse with such excitability that he won't quit fighting his head and quiet down. Recently on an all-day ride into the mountains, I rode a beautiful horse that nervously jigged and danced if asked to walk. I had never ridden the horse before and was very pleased with his easy gaits, good mouth, and easy response—except that he would not walk! It was a long day in the saddle. The nervousness the horse showed was perhaps the result of always having been ridden as a lead horse or used in fast competitive events. If ridden for a while by the same rider the horse could, no doubt, be taught to relax and walk. The thing that can't be changed is the natural temperament of an animal.

Buying a horse is a very personal thing. You, as well as the horse, will be judged. Your size, temperament and riding ability will be considered. It is natural to want a good-looking showy horse—but be sure before buying him that such a horse is well trained and not beyond your ability to handle. Only when one is in command can a worry-free ride be enjoyed.

More accidents happen to adult riders than to younger ones, possibly because adults are more persuasive in their demands for showy, active mounts. People are inclined to overestimate their horsemanship. As a consequence, they rent or buy horses that are too much for them. This can lead to embarrassing and possibly dangerous situations.

Don't buy any horse until you have tried him out and know you are really sold on him—and that you can handle him without a fight. Keep in mind that the more temperamental the horse, the more time you should plan to work with him and exercise him. The nervous, jittery horse is the type that will barn-sour the soonest. No one wants a horse that is lazy—this was mentioned earlier—or one that is quiet to the point of insipidity. But the potential buyer should think twice before overmatching himself with a horse whose nervous energy and vigor exceed his own.

Whether rhythm is more a thing of temperament or physical reaction is a moot point, but in riding it is important that the rider be in rhythm

The Laune family ready to start out on a desert ride.

with the movements of a horse. Some riders on some horses seem never to be dancing to the same music. Short, choppy strides will suit one rider and annoy another. If you find a horse whose beat in his gaits is in tune with your timing, it may be the beginning of a long friendship.

When at last you have found the horse you like, he will quickly become a member of your family. If he is registered, his name—particularly if his original name used the full quota of sixteen letters allowed by the AQHA—may have to be worked into an easy-to-say nickname. Because a horse's name is used a lot when he is being handled and trained, it shouldn't be too much of a mouthful. Incidentally, to change the name of a registered Quarter Horse after he is eighteen months old costs one hundred dollars.

When you have found a horse that meets most of your requirements, he is perhaps the one you should buy. You may never find one that meets your ideal in every single detail.

5
Stables and Corrals

Arrangements for keeping a horse should, of course, be made before the search for the horse begins, although I know of many horses that were staked out on open lots or kept in the backyard by the garage while the proud owner scurried around building a shelter and a small corral. Westerners generally use the word corral, or pen if it is small, while paddock and training ring are words favored by others.

Many surburban districts are zoned so that horses can be kept on one's home property. This usually calls for a small stable and a neat board or rail fence corral. The more severe the winters are, the more substantial the stable should be.

To start at the top, the ideal way to own and care for saddle horses is to live in the country and have good limestone-based pastures through which a stream of clear pure water meanders, large stables with snug box stalls, white board corrals, and fences that divide the pastures, and farm workers, grooms, and trainers to see that the horses have the best of food and care. Such establishments can be seen in every part of the country.

The next best arrangement—certainly the least time-consuming—for those without acreage or a big horse establishment is to board the horse or horses at a stable that specializes in keeping saddle horses. Depending on the location and extra services, such as exercising, training, etc., the basic cost for boarding a horse in a well-managed commercial stable will range from $50 to $150 per month. And of course, there will be additional charges for veterinarian and farrier services.

The least costly way to maintain a horse, if you don't already have such facilities yourself, is to make arrangements with someone who has an extra stall in his barn and a pasture or field where your horse can run free and get to water in a stream or tank. The cost will be less if the owner goes out daily to feed, groom the horse, and clean out his stall. Some young horse owners can arrange to do enough chores for the owner of the place to pay for their horse's keep.

Layout

If you own a Quarter Horse you should certainly give him a good home. Old garages or tool sheds have been converted into usable stables and may serve your purpose, but where possible it is better to start from scratch and build a new one. To make it convenient and practical, there are a number of things that should be carefully planned.

Select the best-drained ground—the highest you have—for the stable. And the next best and most level for the corral. The more level it is, the better it is for the horse's feet. If necessary, to avoid dampness, or too much slope, have an elevation bulldozed for the barn and corral area. Check on the zoning laws. Most of them require the stable—even in areas zoned for horses—to be from fifty to eighty feet from the adjoining property. And there are restrictions as to how close the stable can be to any habitation including your own.

The access road should have room enough for a turn-around for a horse trailer. Backing one with ease or accuracy is something not so easily mastered. Those who bring feed and hay and haul away manure will also welcome a convenient roadway.

The manure pile should also be on well-drained ground—away from the barn because it draws flies, and near the road for easy loading.

The corral can be as small as thirty by thirty feet, but it should be larger if the ground and more money for fencing can be spared. If there are no trees for natural shade, a shed roof is advisable for shelter from sun and rain. But if the stall opens directly into the corral so that the horse can go in and out at will, there is no need for an additional shelter. Horses should be out of doors every day the weather will permit.

If there is a choice, consider the direction in which the stable will face. Prevailing breezes, sunshine in stall windows, convenience to house and driveway, and nearness to electric and water lines are some of the things that will influence your decisions. Various features of the stable and corral plans shown here may be helpful.

Floor Plan. The essentials for a stable are: stalls for the horses, a room for riding equipment, a place for hay and feed, and an open space or passageway where horses can be groomed and saddled. Beyond these basic needs there is no limit to the conveniences and luxuries that can be added. As in everything else today, timesaving methods must be

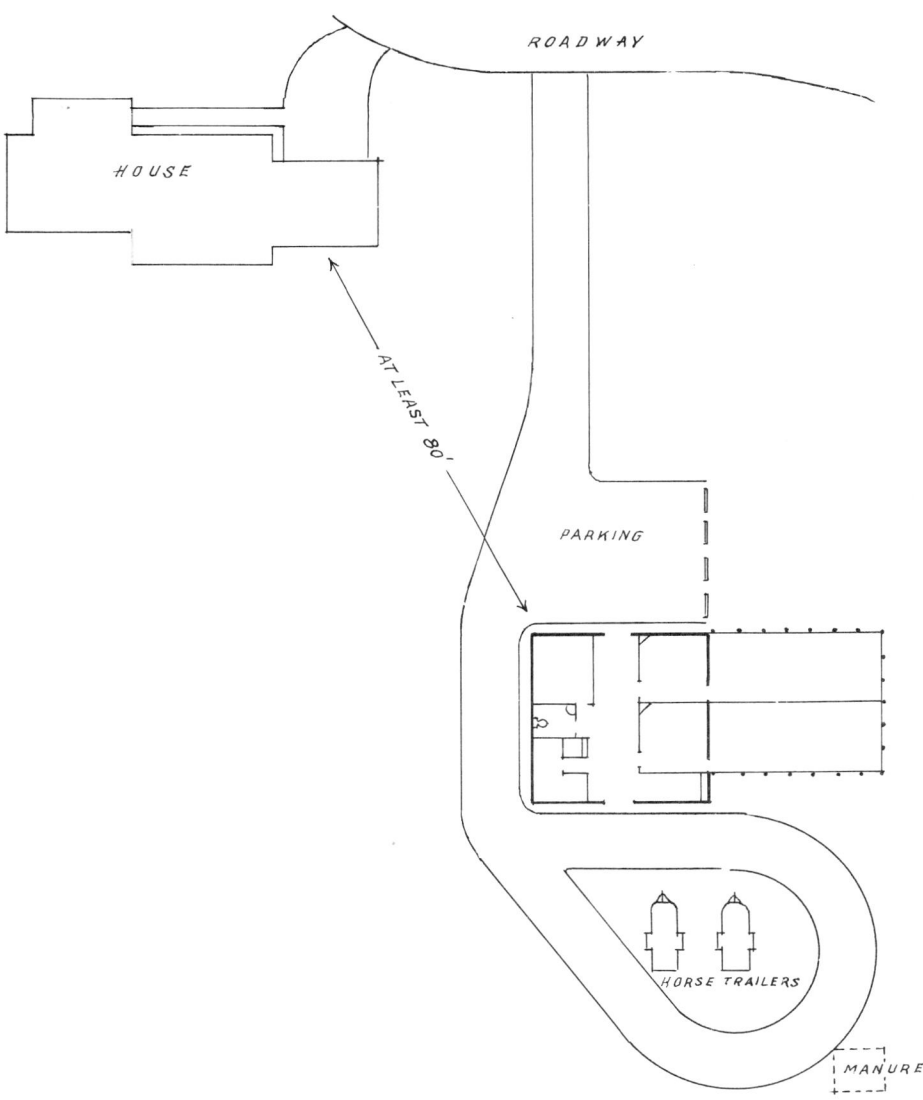

This layout shows the main requirements for maintaining a stable near one's home. The better the arrangements are for access for feed deliveries, trailers, cars, and the removal of manure, the more time one can enjoy riding.

sought in order to make stable management less of an arduous chore so that more time can be devoted to riding and training and pleasurable excursions with one's horse. The first thing to be considered is the stalls —the kind and the size. They are for the horse, and the basic reason for the stable. The rest of the barn is for you, and the way you place the feed room, tack room, hay storage room, and the doors to them will determine the convenience or lack of it in your part of the stable.

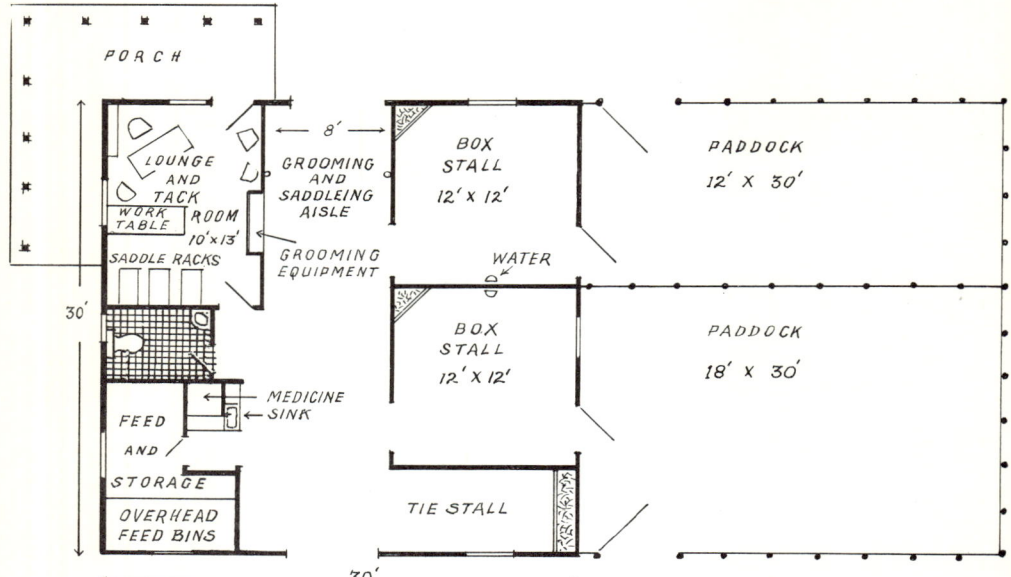

This barn incorporates the features generally wanted but not often obtained by the one- and two-horse owner. With this arrangement, horses have their own drinking fountains and can go out to the paddock at will. The feed room cannot be entered by a horse if the door should be left open. The grooming tools and equipment are on recessed shelves, which eliminates an obstruction that can cause bumps and scrapes. The tie stall is a handy place to put a horse while his box stall is being cleaned. It is also a place to keep the manure cart out of the way. The sink and other conveniences make the life of the horseman easier.

Box Stalls that are twelve by twelve feet are considered sufficiently roomy. Since there is always the possibility that you might someday have more than one horse, it is well to plan a stable with an extra box stall or two. In the meantime, the extra room will be handy for hay or other storage, for a paying horse guest, or for shifting a horse while his own stall is being cleaned or worked on. Box stalls give a horse more freedom, thereby reducing the boredom that can lead to vices. The bedding is comfortable because it is not confined to the exact place where the horse stands, and thins it out, as in a straight or tie stall. In cold weather the horse can move about to keep up body heat and can seek the best place to avoid drafts. Horses that are ridden and groomed the year round are deprived of their natural winter coat, so must be well housed. A box stall is the most satisfactory place in which to doctor horses, and about the only place in a stable a horse can be treated if he gets down or, to use horsy talk, "gets cast." The only disadvantage of box stalls is the initial cost of their construction, the larger building required, the considerable amount of bedding that must be used in them, and the chore of keeping them clean. Another thing that might be considered a disadvantage is the difficulty, without having two doors, of arranging for the horse to go at will from his stall to an adjoining pen or corral.

Tie Stalls. The disadvantages of a tie stall are many. It is very restricting for the horse during cold weather when he must stand tied by the head day after day. This close confinement can barn-sour some horses, regardless of the weather, making them sullen and listless. The bedding cannot be kept deep and springy because the horse wears it thin where he must stand in it. He will require more grooming because his rear quarters are likely to get soiled, since he must lie down where the bedding is soiled.

Tie stalls, being open at the back, are more vulnerable to cold drafts of air than are box stalls. Some owners stretch canvas across the rear of the stall to block such drafts.

Tie stalls take up the minimum amount of barn room. They are convenient for use when box stalls are being cleaned, or as temporary feeding places for visitors' horses.

Construction

Regardless of size, the stable should have proper insulation to keep out excessive summer heat and to retain what heat there is in the wintertime.

In the dry Southwest, where dampness is not much of a problem, hollow block construction—cinder, cement, or pumice block—is considered ideal, although it is not the least inexpensive to build. Such buildings are sturdy, hold the paint well, furnish their own insulation against heat and cold, and reduce the fire hazard.

In colder country, outside walls made of hollow blocks are inclined to sweat and cause dampness. If used they should be insulated and lined with tongue-and-groove boards or heavy duty plywood attached to furring strips. For inside partition walls, hollow blocks serve without added work as excellent fireguards between the stalls and the tack room. In dry climates where the winters are mild the usual construction in residential districts zoned for horses is a simple frame made with two-by-fours and covered with exterior type plywood panels, clapboards, or vertical boards with batten strips. The only insulation is under the roof. These little structures give protection for tack and feed and serve as a windbreak on one side where a shed roof extends far enough out to shelter the horse from the sun and rain. Where space is too limited for storing hay the bales are stacked on a low board platform a few inches off the ground to keep them dry. A plastic sheet tied down securely keeps off the rain. With this arrangement the horses live out of doors almost entirely. There are no stalls to muck out and no bedding required. Hay is thrown directly on the ground. Feed is set out in hard rubber buckets. Scooping up the droppings in the corral every day is the only considerable housekeeping chore. I have seen highly bred horses of all kinds—Quarter Horses, Arabians, Thoroughbreds, American Saddlebreds, etc.—handled in this manner and they appear healthy, active, and well groomed.

In planning your stable, keep in mind that horses are powerful animals and that everything built to hold and contain them must be of stout materials. Stall doors, tie rings, fences, all must be able to withstand more than people-pressure. The partitions between box stalls should be made of heavy planking (2 inch) about five feet high and extended up another three feet with strong mesh fencing or window mesh. This will keep the horses from reaching over and biting one another, yet they do not feel so isolated as long as they can see another animal. If the wire mesh is doubled by being attached to both sides of the partition it will prevent any gnawing of the wood along the top.

Local contractors or building supply companies can recommend the most suitable and economical building material for your district. In some places aluminum or steel buildings are practical. They require a special type of insulation. Without it they can get insufferably hot.

Mangers and Feed Buckets

If a hay manger is used in either a box stall or a tie stall, it should not be over three feet high. A horse feeds more naturally if his head is down below the level of his chest rather than above it.

Some owners—perhaps the majority—prefer to throw the hay directly on the floor of the stall or on the ground if the horse is in a corral. The disadvantage of doing this is that it is an invitation to some horses to nibble at and get in the habit of eating their bedding. In a corral, of course, this is no problem because there is no bedding. If a manger for hay can be made of metal pipes or any form of metal, it will present no temptation to the horse that relieves his boredom by gnawing the wood rail of his manger. Whatever material is used should have no spaces or openings along the front that are large enough for a horse to get his foot caught. A place by the side of or within the manger should be made to hold the hard rubber or plastic feed bowl. The bowl should be secure so it can't be easily knocked out and trampled but should be removable so it can be cleaned frequently.

The water fountain, or bucket if one is used, in the box stall should be across from the manger. Some owners put a salt block in the corner of the manger, knowing that if a horse wants salt he will soon learn to eat the hay or push it aside to get at it. Some prefer to have the salt block on a corner shelf—with ledge to keep it secure—near the water.

A metal feed bin attached to the corral fence with snaps can be easily removed for cleaning. *Photo by Irene Laune.*

LEFT

A popular plastic feed bin that fits in the corner of stall or corral. Cribbers can't chew it as they do wood or rubber feeders. *Photo by Irene Laune.*

RIGHT

A plastic feed bucket can be hooked into a stall corner, an arrangement that allows it to be used also as a water bucket. *Photo by Irene Laune.*

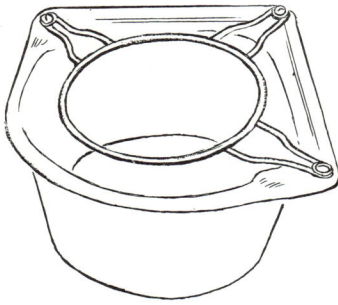

A feed saver ring like this one keeps a horse from crowding grain or pellets over the rim and wasting feed.

Brackets and Hooks

Having a bracket or hook or shelf for everything that is used regularly is the only way to keep a stable tidy and workable. The halter should have a handy place near the stall door. If easily reached it will encourage the habit of returning it where it belongs. All brackets and hooks should be out of the way so that a horse cannot get raked by them.

Sketches accompanying the text show ways to plan a stable so that things can be hung in recesses where horses can't bump them; ways of making effective but inexpensive saddle and bridle racks and supports for saddle blankets that will allow them to dry out faster.

Flooring

Flooring for the tack room, feed room, and the isle or passageway is best if made of concrete, which is easy to clean, cannot be gnawed through by rodents, and is not subject to decay caused by manure or frequent washing.

Dirt floors for stalls are generally too damp unless the soil used has a considerable amount of clay in it or is somewhat chalky, like the caleche soil in the Southwest.

Asphalt floors are favored by some, while others prefer cork composition blocks. Both are satisfactorily resilient and are easy to keep clean. The cork blocks retain more odor, perhaps, than does the asphalt.

Wood plank flooring is sometimes used but it is slippery, retains dampness and odors, and can sometimes rot and splinter before the weakness is detected.

Whatever material is used, a slight slope toward a drain is practical. The drain, of course, must be planned before the foundation of the stable is laid.

Feed Room

It should be difficult or impossible for a horse to enter the feed room, even if the door to it has been carelessly left open (see plans). Unlike a mule, a horse has no restraint where his appetite is concerned. If free to eat his fill he will seldom stop until he has foundered himself. The security of feed should be given high priority.

As with the rest of the stable the feed room should be as free of dampness as possible. Grain as well as hay can get moldy. Metal bins will keep mice and rats out of the feed if lids are tight fitting, but the best way to defeat these rodents is to get rid of them. There are commercial preparations that will exterminate them rather quickly. Whichever one is used, be sure to follow directions carefully, taking every precaution

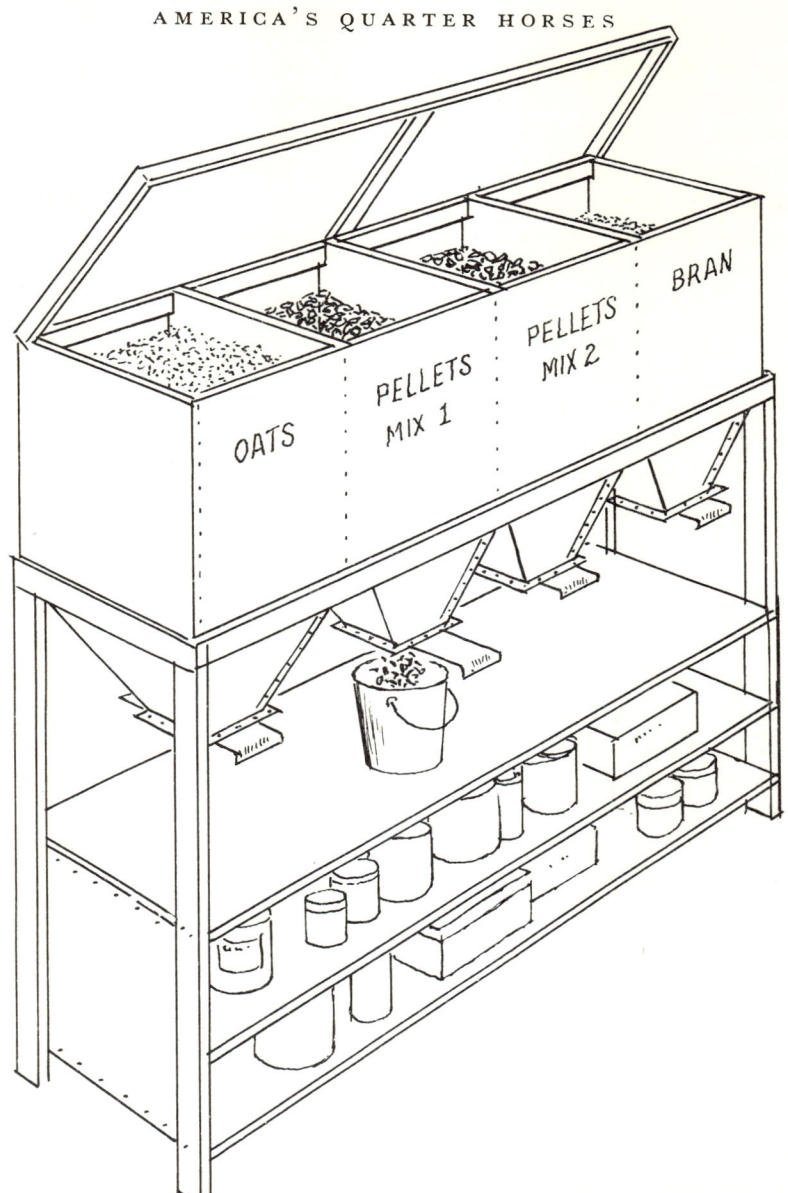

For the horseman who does his own barn chores and who wants convenience, efficiency, and vermin-proof feed storage, a sheet-metal bin built on a frame made with two-by-four-inch lumber and three-quarter-inch plywood ends and dividers is the answer. The openings through which the feed pours and the cut-off gate can be made in several ways, depending on the ingenuity of the builder. There are also some on the market.

for your dog or cat. Keep poisons, sprays, soaps, liniments, and medicines in a special room or cabinet where they can be locked up and where they are well away from the feed.

The most readily available containers for feed are metal garbage cans. The lids fit snugly, keeping out mice and rats, and they are clean. But the most efficient way to store feed, and ration it out, is to have built-in metal-lined bins with dispenser gates at the bottom. The feed supplier opens the sacks and pours the feed into the top of the compartment designated. If plans are made before the stable is built—with drawings furnished the builder that show dimensions, placement, etc.—these super feed bins may not cost as much as might be expected. Getting the feed containers up off the floor keeps the barn free of clutter. The floor can be swept without having to move heavy cans, and the feed measuring and mixing done on a counter top are easier and faster.

Tack Room

Where saddles, bridles, chaps, saddlebags, leather repair tools, and the medicine cabinet, etc., are kept can be simple or elaborate depending on one's wants and resources. The main purpose is to have a place for things so they will be better kept and not strewn about.

Leather articles should be kept from dampness and put where they won't be creased or warped. With proper racks to support them, saddles and bridles will keep their shape. A chest along the wall to hold things can serve as a seat.

There are times when one must wait at the stable for the delivery of feed, or for the veterinarian or the farrier or someone during cold weather, so to be comfortable the tack room must be heated in some way. Whatever equipment is used, every precaution should be made to reduce the fire hazard. A fire extinguisher on the wall is one precaution that can be taken.

A desk and a chair or two can add to the comfort of the place and will encourage better record keeping. A shelf of horse books and journals will add a touch of authority—and can resolve or intensify differences of opinions held by one's horse-loving friends. A calendar of horse shows and other events tacked on the wall may keep one from missing out on some of the local horse fun.

Both doorways—the one between the stall section of the barn and the outside door of the tack room—should have screen doors as well as solid wooden doors that can be locked.

For those who find the scent of Corral No. 5 somewhat pervading, a light partition that separates the sweaty horse gear—pads, blankets, etc.—from the lounging part of the tack room may be considered.

Far exceeding these more or less basic suggestions are tack rooms that are large and as finished in appearance as a room in one's home, with attractive furnishings, and with built-in places for displays of trophies and ribbons.

Grooming Area

In the passageway used for grooming and saddling, it is convenient and safe to have ropes—some use small chains—attached to tie rings in the side walls opposite each other to which the halter ring can be snapped. Cross-tied in this manner, the horse can't move around or swing his head.

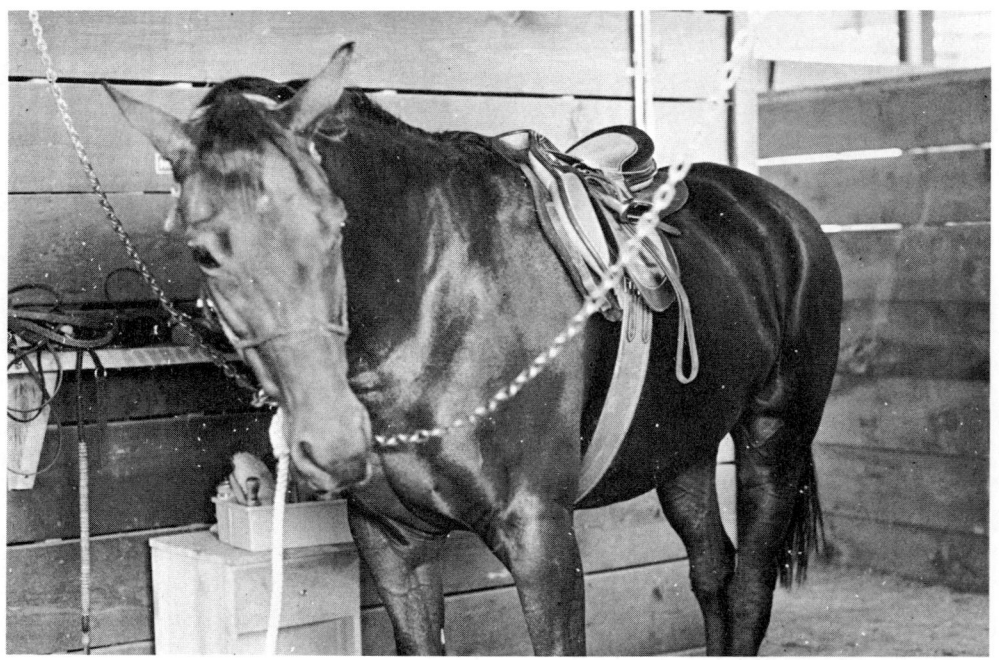

Cross-ties should be strong and securely fastened to the walls. Placed high up, they are out of the way for grooming and saddling. The weight of chains makes the horse think he is tied tighter than he is. *Photo by the author.*

Medicine Cabinet

In a stable the medicine cabinet is no tiny bathroom type affair. There seem to be more items and in larger quantities, so it is advisable to have plenty of shelf space. There should also be a counter even if it is a small one. Nothing is more exasperating than to have one's hands full and find there is no place to put anything down.

If children are in and out of the stable, the medicines should be kept in a cabinet or small closet that can be locked. In fact, for general security they should always be under lock and key. If the tack room is locked except when the owner is in the stable, it may be the most convenient place to store the medicines, sprays, soaps, hoof dressing, liniments, etc. And where they are kept is perhaps the best place to have a wash-up sink.

Doors, Locks, and Latches

Sliding doors for the box stalls and for the large entrance doors to the passageway are the ones I would recommend. They are out of the way when open, which reduces the chances of accidents. They are more easily secured and there is no banging and swinging in the wind. A large variety of hardware fittings for rails and rollers and fastening devices are on the market. The entrance doors to the passageway should be wide enough and high enough for a pickup truck to drive through so feed and hay can be delivered and unloaded out of the weather.

Many people favor Dutch doors so the cooped-up horse can look out and dispel his boredom by enjoying the sights and sounds of the outdoors. This requires a hinged swinging door in two parts. To my way of thinking a sliding window unrelated to the door better serves the purpose. With it a horse is not encouraged to crowd against a hinged door and the latch that holds it. With the one- or two-horse owner, the horses are more likely to have the freedom of going out into the corral when the weather permits, rather than longingly gazing out. All doorways should be smooth-faced and free of any projecting hooks or latches, another argument for sliding doors, and they should be about four feet wide and eight feet high.

Think of the frequent trips you will make to the feed room and the tack room and the hay room and try and plan the direction in which the doors swing or slide so they will better suit your traffic pattern.

Latches should be sophisticated enough to baffle a smart horse. A lock for the medicine room or cabinet is essential. Some find that a combination type padlock is more convenient than a lock with a key, because they can remember the combination more readily than they can remember where they put the key. This is a one-man setup, however, making it impossible for someone else to get at the medicines even in an emergency But there is this advantage: if you are reached on the telephone you can give the combination—and a key is something you can't give over the telephone. If the tack room contains the medicine cabinet and is locked at all times except when the owner is on hand, the one lock serves both. A handy arrangement that requires but one lock for the entire stable is to secure both large passageway doors with a stout timber that fits a bracket on the inside, then go out through the tack-room door and lock it.

Many owners keep a strong chain and lock on the corral gates. Had I done so one weekend when I was away, a good mare might not have been stolen. She was found three miles away the next Monday morning on the edge of a neighbor's pasture. Sweat marks still showed the outline of a saddle pad. I suppose it would be expecting too much of a thief to have properly cooled the mare out and washed her back.

The most notable horse theft I know of took place one night when the first foal, a recently weaned filly, of the great race mare Leola was stolen from Ed Honnen's Quincy Farm near Denver, Colorado. She was never heard of again. Leola was bred by Bud Warren of Perry, Oklahoma, and she was by his famous stallion Leo out of a mare that was line bred to Traveler. The stolen filly was by Three Bars. Such breeding made her potentially very valuable. Not knowing the circumstances, there is a question whether locks of any kind would have prevented this theft, but their use seems to be a precaution many horse owners take.

Water

Aside from having a brook that runs through the corral, the simplest arrangement for watering a horse is to fill the horse tank or bucket or whatever is used from a long garden hose. But since this won't work where there is freezing weather, the practical horse owner plans for a more convenient way before the stable is built by having water piped in as an extension of the system that supplies the house. Some way of heating the area in the stable where the faucet and perhaps a wash-up sink and a toilet are placed must be made to avoid frozen pipes. And, of course, if a sink and a toilet are installed, a connection with a sewer or cesspool must be made.

An added luxury for both the owner and his horse is to have automatic water fountains in each box stall, or where weather is always mild, in the corral. These devices have a metal flange or trip which, when pressed by the horse's nose, opens a valve and replenishes the water in the bowl of the fountain. Horses learn quickly how to use them. The only disadvantages in their use that I have heard of, aside from the initial

A water fountain that serves equally well in the box stall or the paddock. *Photo by the author.*

cost, is that on rare occasions a horse will play with the trip mechanism and cause the fountain to overflow, making a mess of the floor of his stall.

The ultimate luxury is to have hot as well as cold water piped into the stable. For washing the horse and one's self, for general cleaning up, and for bran mashes, the hot water from a tap eliminates having to wait for water to heat on an electric plate.

Lights and Electric Outlets

In the days before many Oklahoma barns had electric lights, a lot of us maneuvered about in the dark, depending on the braille system. Once I entered a dark barn and walked right into the north end of a horse facing south. Unknown to me someone had brought this unbroken horse in from pasture and tied him in a straight stall near the door. Had I jumped back, the startled animal would have undoubtedly kicked and he could hardly have missed. Instead I threw both arms around the quivering horse with my hands flat against the points of his hips. This action and my weight against him caused him to squat down rather than kick, which gave me the precious split second it took to ooze over to the side.

Stables should be well lighted, although it is noticeable that even the good ones seldom are. The wiring must be done by an expert so that it will pass building codes and fire insurance specifications.

The placement of lights is important. They should be where they are effective but never where a horse can rear into or bump against them. Recessed lights or lights with sturdy metal cage guards reduce the fire hazard. A light should be over each stall, but high up and in a cage. Since feed is usually kept in a secluded out-of-the-way place, a light is required for measuring it and additives, and for detecting evidences of mice or rats or spilled liniment, or anything that could contaminate the feed. In the tack room, a light by a workbench is helpful and an outlet for some kind of water heater and a coffee maker is a welcome convenience.

Outlets where extension cord lights—also in wire cages—can be plugged in are very helpful for close examination of the horse, or for hunting things dropped or lost in the dark corners.

In the aisle area where the grooming and saddling are done there should be an outlet for electric hair clippers. In all cases the outlets should be placed so that they will not require long cords that can get tangled around the horse's legs. Head-high outlets on the walls will help to keep cords off the floor. Some handymen rig lightweight springs or pulleys to support the cords.

An outside floodlight that lights the area between the house and the stable is always advisable, with the switch, of course, in the house. Such a light serves as a security measure, as an aid in parking vehicles at night, and is greatly appreciated when sudden nocturnal visits to the stable must be made.

When the wiring is being done, and assuming there is still some stretch in the budget, consider adding the convenience of an intercom that links the tack room with the house. With a stable about a hundred yards from the house I found such a system a real timesaver, making unnecessary much running back and forth and shouting.

The Corral

Good safe fences can be made of wood posts with boards or rails, aluminum, steel, galvanized pipes or steel mesh, but never barbed wire. Fences are as strong as the posts that support them. Posts of any kind of metal usually need to be set in concrete. Wooden posts approximately six by six inches, set two feet deep and well tamped, will in most soils be sufficiently firm. The slender steel posts that are driven into the ground are too easily bent to be suitable for corral fences.

For effective training use, a corral must be at least forty by fifty feet, but for a runway and outdoor home for a horse a smaller one, say, thirty by thirty feet, will serve. For training, a board corral about five feet high is generally preferred, with the boards attached to the inside of the posts.

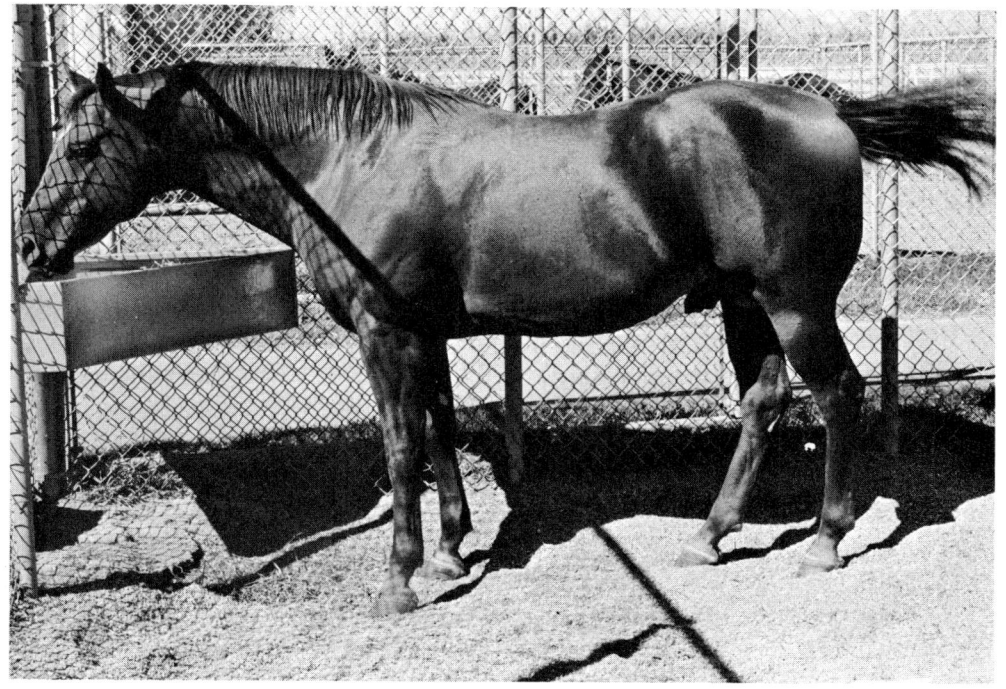

Pipe and steel mesh fencing for corrals offers a maximum of security with a minimum of opportunity of injury to the horses. This is Vanny Bar at Charles Mickle's Valley View Ranch in Scottsdale, Arizona. *Photo by the author.*

This gives a smooth inside to the corral so that the horse, or the rider's legs, cannot bump into the posts.

Fences made of boards painted white are attractive and the least expensive. Steel mesh fences are safe and sound if the metal posts are set in concrete and the top has a metal rail to keep it from sagging. They are also expensive—as are steel rail and aluminum rail fences. But they are enduring and strong and have no rough places to snag a horse. The meshes should be small enough so that a horse's hoof cannot get in them.

Gates should be at least four feet wide, firmly braced and strongly hinged.

The Manure Pile

The soiled bedding from the stalls and the droppings from the corral can be wheeled in a barrow to the manure pile, which should be far enough from the stable so that the flies it draws will be away from the horses. In sunny weather, spread the manure so that the pile is shallow and will dry quickly. In rainy weather reduce the area of the pile and make it higher. Lime can be sprinkled over the pile to control flies and reduce odor without affecting the value of the manure as a fertilizer. But some fly sprays will make it unsuitable and valueless. If it is to be sold as fertilizer, the type of spray used should be checked out beforehand—especially if it is to be sold to mushroom growers, who require large quantities of horse manure. The type of bedding used will also determine whether or not the manure has commercial value.

A cement floor for the manure pile, with low retaining walls on three sides, improves the appearance of the barn areas, gives better drainage, and makes loading for hauling away much easier.

There is an insecticidal paint that is lethal to ants, flies, spiders, wasps, roaches, moths, silverfish, mosquitoes, claim the manufacturers, if the areas are completely covered by a solid coat. There are fly killers that hang like jack-o'-lanterns and others that are electric that can be set to turn on and off at intervals during the day or night. Some of these devices require frequent cleaning.

To prevent flies from breeding on manure piles, the method that is used mostly in England is said to kill 90 per cent of the fly larvae. The construction is rather expensive to build, but after the initial cost there is no expense for maintenance.

In a concrete tank with walls only six inches high (see drawing) water is kept at about four to five inches deep. A platform is built to

Large stables find that manure dump buckets on overhead rails cut labor costs. *Photo by Irene Laune.*

stand in the tank on legs that holds it up about one foot above the water. Manure is thrown on the platform, covering it clear to the edge. The manure pile is where most of the flies breed and lay their eggs. When the larvae grow and start to migrate, they fall off the edge of the platform and drown in the water. A sump pump with a screen collects the maggots. The pool should be pumped out about once a week. It is assumed fresh manure is to be thrown regularly on the pile. Flies will not lay eggs in manure that is over ten days old.

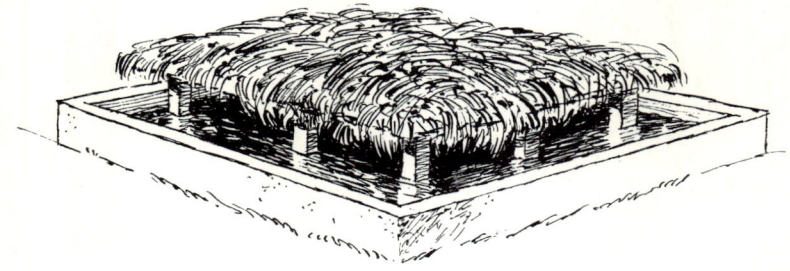

A concrete structure with a shallow pool is a good method to prevent the breeding of flies.

Bedding

The snug barn may be ready with feed and hay on hand for the new horse, but if the bedding has been forgotten, the poor horse will have to sleep on expensive hay. This situation is not a rarity.

Even the bedding calls for more decisions to be made, there being several kind to choose from. And it doesn't quite end there because you will have to decide whether to have salable manure or the kind you will have to pay someone to haul away.

Rubber Mats. Some owners use durable rubber composition mats instead of loose bedding. They are advertised to be soft enough to prevent scuffed knees and fairly easy to keep clean with a daily sweeping and a weekly hosing down. With their use the manure pile that accumulates is much smaller. The disadvantage to their use, I am told, is that they add little comfort on wintry nights; not comparable at least to the old tried and true deep straw bed that makes a cozy nest and blocks the drafts.

Straw. Wheat straw is generally the most readily available, the least expensive type of bedding, and is used by the majority of horsemen. It makes a springy bed. It is clean and easy to handle, starts off with a pleasant odor, absorbs moisture well, and winds up making a very good grade of salable manure.

Because it retains bad odors it must be changed rather frequently. The other disadvantage to its use is that it is just palatable enough to cause horses to nibble at it, which can foster the bad habit of eating their bedding.

Dried Sugar Cane and Peanut Hulls are not inexpensive except perhaps in the immediate district where they are produced, but they are easy to handle and are clean and dry. They do not tempt horses to eat them. As mentioned in relation to various sprays that might affect the manure, the kind of bedding used will also determine whether it is salable or not, therefore the type of bedding should be discussed with whoever hauls it away—or, better yet, purchases it from you.

Wood Shavings and Sawdust make soft bedding if used plentifully. It is usually clean and fragrant but should be examined when spread for splinters and wads of resin. It does not retain an excessive amount of odor although it is absorbent. In certain districts it is cheaper than straw. Horses are not tempted to eat it. Disadvantages are that it is messy to handle, will clog up drains, sometimes ball up on the horse's feet, and the manure is unsalable, making it necessary for you to pay someone to haul it away.

Peat Moss makes a soft bed, is easy to handle, is absorbent, has a tendency to lessen odors. The manure it makes is a good fertilizer and usually has a ready market. Horses won't eat it. But it is somewhat dusty and it will clog up drains, and it is expensive.

With all the numerous things that are coming on the market to cater to the rapidly enlarging horse world, perhaps the perfect bedding is just around the corner. But if horses get much more pampered it will be what some of us suspect—Beautyrest mattresses and percale sheets.

Insect and Pest Control

Fly sprays should be used in moderation. There is grave danger from the excessive use of insecticides. These compounds—many with an oil base—can build up on a horse's coat and skin and clog the pores and attract dirt. I strongly advise washing away the residue of old chemicals before applying a fresh coat.

To control insects—and they have to be controlled or your horse will suffer, lose weight, and become jittery—there are many repellents in spray and lotion and salve form on the market. In stick form, it is to be put around the horse's eyes, ears, nose, and mouth. One repellent comes in the form of premoist pads with which to wipe the horse all over. Whichever one is tried should be used sparingly until you are convinced it has no ill effect on the horse. Some horses have more sensitive skins than others, and some may be allergic to certain compounds. If in doubt, apply on one leg and check the results before putting it on larger areas of the horse's body. If the repellent irritates your own skin, it could have the same effect on your horse's skin. Some owners with the best intentions have applied repellents that took the hair off and caused the skin to flake. The poor animal was left not only more vulnerable to flies, but also to sunburn.

There has been much controversy over the chemicals used in pest control, and the search for the ideal one continues. In the meantime the overwhelming majority of stockmen follow the advice given by the Agricultural Extension Service of the Universities sponsored by the U. S. Department of Agriculture. In a brochure dated April 1969, and not amended since, the Maricopa County Agricultural Extension Service and the 4-H Club made the following information available to Southwestern horsemen.

FLIES AROUND STABLES AND FEEDLOTS

By J. N. Roney, Extension Entomologist—University of Arizona

Control of flies around the corral and feedlots and in the backyard is very important! For controlling flies around the corral, stable or backyard, one *must practice cleanliness!* All manure must be spread once a week during the summer months, or else treated weekly with an insecticide. In most instances, the house fly and stable fly are two fly pests with which you have to contend. The house fly breeds very rapidly during the summer and the stable fly also breeds rather fast. The stable fly sucks blood from the horses, thus really hurting them. The common house fly does not bite but annoys the animal to such an extent that it will not eat or go into the pasture for exercise.

There are several insecticides that may be used in the stable, corrals, on fences and trees:

(1) *Diazinon*—Use 0.5 pint of 25% emulsion concentrate or 0.5 of 25% wettable powder. To this add one cup of sugar or white karo syrup to 3 gallons of water.
(2) *Ronnell* (Korlan)—Use 1.0 pint of 24% emulsion concentrate or 1 pound of 25% wettable powder for 3 gallons of water.
(3) *Malathion*—Use 0.5 pint of 57% emulsion concentrate or 0.25 pound of wettable powder. You may use one cup of sugar or white karo syrup for 3 gallons of water.
(4) *Dimethoate* (Cygon)—Use 0.5 pint of 43% emulsion concentrate to 3 gallons of water.
(5) *Ciodrin*—For control around buildings. Mix 1.0 quart of emulsion concentrate (2 pounds per gallon) per 6 gallons of water. A 1% concentrate—spray at least twice per month.
(6) *Fly Baits*—There are several prepared baits of Dipterex (Dylox), Diazinon, Korlan, Malathion, Vapona, Dibrom and Dimethoate. You may purchase these materials in feed stores.
(7) *Vapona* (DDVP)—Spray in barns, or on fences, but DO NOT spray the animals. Vapona is in several strengths. Use according to directions on label. Use 1 pint of 20% Vapona in 3 gallons of water plus 3 pounds of sugar.
(8) *Fly Cords & Strips*—Several impregnated cords are prepared. When using them, be sure to keep them out of the reach of animals. Vapona resin strips may be used at the rate of a single 10 inch strip for 1000 cubic feet of space. There are also several other materials as cords, such as Ciodrin, Korlan, etc.
(9) Use strips of cloth dipped in any of above solutions for small areas. Place where flies congregate. Replenish daily.

CONTROL ON ANIMALS

Pyrethrins—0.5% plus Pipernoyl butoxide 0.5% in 3 gallons of water or a mixture of 1% pyrethrins and 1% pipernoyl butoxide as a mist spray.

Malathion—0.5%. Mix 1.5 quarts of 57% emulsion concentrate or 8.0 pounds of 25% wettable powder in 50 gallons of water; or mix 6 tablespoons of 57% emulsion concentrate or 2 cups of 25% wettable powder in 3 gallons of water. No time limit between applications.

CONTROL ON MANURE PILES

The mixture of Diazinon, Korlan, Malathion, Ciodrin and Vapona may be used to spray manure piles at least twice a week to kill any maggots that may be found in these piles.

In controlling flies, REMEMBER . . .

1. Keep corrals and barns clear of manure by spreading or treating the manure with an insecticide.
2. Control adult flies with sprays—in barns, on fences, in corrals and on trees.
3. You may spray horses with a Pyrethrum or Malathion oil spray.

FOLLOW DIRECTIONS AND BE SURE TO READ THE LABEL AND USE CORRECTLY!

The foregoing is obviously intended to serve the medium to large operators. The one- and two-horse owners will no doubt continue to depend on the proprietary brands of pest controls advertised in the horse journals or recommended by the stores they patronize. These products are subject to the controls and requirements of the Food and Drug Administration, not the Department of Agriculture.

In any region the county agents of the U. S. Department of Agriculture can supply only the recommendations the Agricultural Extension Services their Land Grant Universities have prepared for them. The research in this field and the resulting recommendations made originate with the universities, not the Department of Agriculture. For example, in New York State the county agents are dependent on Cornell State University for their information on the subject of insecticides and their use.

Brands and Silks

Even one-horse owners may like to emulate the mighty barons of the racing and ranch world by having their own brands and silks. Many find it satisfying to show ownership by stenciling an emblem of their own design and colors of their choice on their car, trailer, stable, and stable equipment.

At shows, a brand in combination with certain colors (silks) serves as an introduction, identifying the owner and his rig when he pulls into the grounds. Some indulge the fancy of using their stable colors and their brand on their shirts, scarves, chaps, horse blankets, and on specially made spurs, belt buckles, boleros, rings, cuff links, and tie clips. And on their table service and linens.

The King Ranch brands their breeding stock on the rump near the dock of the tail. On the left cheek of the rump is the initial of the horse's sire. And on the right cheek is the initial of the dam.

The barn dog is a good companion and guard. *Photo by Irene Laune.*

Barn Dogs and Cats

He may be a nonessential, but a dog or cat that makes his home in the barn can be a great comfort for the owner and his horses. Horses—at least all I have known—like dogs that are part of the ménage, and feel secure with them about. Dogs kill rats, serve well as sentries—barking when strangers come on the property—and they break the monotony of stable life and enliven the atmosphere by their presence.

One man I know has taught a big smiling shepherd dog to take the looped halter rope in his mouth and lead the horses down to a little stream for water. The horses go along with the stunt. Horses stabled away from home in a strange place are much less restive if their own dog companion is there acting as their guard.

Cats about the barn keep the place free of scorpions, and I have been told by ranchers that rattlesnakes will not come around where cats are. Cats also keep the mouse and rat population down, and horses seem to be comfortable with cats in the stable.

6

The Nature of the Beast

When you purchased your horse, he was of course already named by his former owner. But if you want to give him a name of your choosing (in addition to his registered name, if he has one), it is suggested the name be short and easily pronounced because you will be using it often and sometimes with a quick command.

Let's assume you are now on your own with a new horse you really know little about except for the rides you took on him when trying him out. We will also assume, because you are reading this chapter, that, whatever your age, you are a beginner at horsemanship.

Your horse no doubt is gentle and, if a Quarter Horse, is likely to have been Western-trained. You might already know some of the things mentioned here, but a step-by-step reminder may be of help. You might also find some different ways of doing things. The amateur should do some reading on the subject even if he is under the tutelage of an expert horseman. Often the experienced instructor lacks time or credits his pupil with more general knowledge of a horse than he should, thereby failing to explain the finer nuances of the horse nature.

To begin with, something should be known about the temperament and mental properties of horses in general, and their ways of expressing their feelings, in order to gauge what they are capable of understanding and doing. Remember they are bigger than you, and to control them you have to outsmart them.

Like people, horses are individuals. No two are exactly alike. They have varying degrees of intelligence, and while some are willing, cheerful, curious, and quick to learn, others are phlegmatic and dull. Some, as a result of mistreatment, ill health, lack of use, or loneliness, are sullen and quick to take offense. In rare instances, horses become aggressive, almost untamable outlaws. Others are spiteful, both with their own kind and with people.

Still rarer are those that are manic-depressive with suicidal tendencies. As a rule, horses lack a strong concern for their own safety when in a frenzy of action. Even when injured or sick they cling to life with less tenacity than do many other animals. Seemingly they show a disturbing resignation to their fate. In runaways and various kinds of accidents, particularly when in harness, horses are frequently badly hurt or killed, whereas mules who have an exaggerated sense of self-preservation might run away and tear up the harness, wagon, fences, or whatever else got in the way, and come out of it with hardly a scratch. Mules are also careful about overeating. Should they be left where there are unlimited amounts of grain, they will not founder themselves as will a horse. As an experiment, I once gave six ears of corn to a span of mules that were in the habit of being fed five ears of corn at each meal. Both mules left the extra ear of corn uneaten.

Wild range horses and the old mustang leaders were known to fight for freedom with utter disregard for their own lives. Starface, a fiery stallion who headed up a mustang *manada*—his band of mares—in the Black Mesa country in the far corner of Oklahoma's Panhandle, leaped to his death from a high canyon ledge rather than be captured by the whirring loops of the four cowboys who had him cornered. This action might have been one of unthinking fear, yet it is so easy for us to assume human motivation in horses, to see Starface as a horse patriot who saw eye-to-eye with Patrick Henry.

To carry the comparison of humans and horses a little further, it is true that horses even become dope addicts. Most of us who knew the West of an earlier day knew horses who had become users of the locoweed. This small plant with its gray-green furry leaves and purple blossoms is more of a rarity today. Horses that ate loco lost their appetite for other food, lost weight, and appeared dazed and unco-operative. An uncle of mine foolishly riding a locoed horse too near a coulee rim suddenly found himself in mid-air. The moody, discouraged horse had made a spur-of-the-moment decision to end it all and had leaped over the embankment. The horse had to be destroyed. My uncle was badly, but not permanently, hurt.

Old-time horse traders were known deliberately to make dope fiends of horses. Aged horses that had lost their appetite, becoming gaunt with dull eyes and coats, were given a little arsenic on the tip of a knife blade, mixed with their grain. The dose was increased until as much arsenic as could be held on the entire blade was given daily. The animals would puff up with fatty weight and their coats and eyes would brighten, but even moderate exertion would pull them down quickly, and if the dope ration was stopped, they would die.

Temperament

Most horses are social beings; that is, they are herd animals and live around other horses and other animals, including people, without undue friction. They are agreeable with their young and mildly protective— more so among the wild ones—and are quick to correct bad behavior with a squeal, snort, kick, or bite. They have been known to single out dogs, cats, roosters, and other barnyard denizens as inseparable companions and stall mates.

Some horses never grow up and take responsibility—a fault more in their training than in the horse. In Dutchess County, New York, where I once lived, I brought home a bright sorrel filly from an auction sale. She was only a year old and so pretty, with her waving flaxen mane and tail, that we named her Glory. And she had such an appealing good nature we made a pet of her. The emotional disruption of coming to a new place caused her to stay close to a grade Quarter Horse mare we called Dixie—because she resembled my mother's Dixie. Here let me say that, since Dixie was not registered, it would be improper to call her a Quarter Horse. Too often people speak of their horses as Quarter Horses, Thoroughbreds, Morgans, American Saddlebreds and what-have-you when the animal mentioned is not registered—the breeding not certified—and is therefore not a member of a breed but merely related to horses that are registered in a breed.

Glory's attachment to Dixie grew until she would hardly leave her side—sometimes to the annoyance of Dixie. She was like a high-school girl who worshiped a college girl, thinking her so much surer of herself and so much smarter, etc. Of course Dixie could outshine Glory in every way, being faster, experienced, and well trained. If Dixie was hard to catch in pasture, so was Glory. If Dixie decided to come quickly and nuzzle me, so did Glory. The fact became evident that Glory would never grow up. She was easy to break but always uneasy and slow to learn when separated from Dixie. Before we realized it, we had allowed a good filly to become a perpetual juvenile, always dependent on another horse. This problem with Glory could have been avoided if we had separated her from Dixie and trained and ridden her alone or with other horses.

Horses say what they are thinking or feeling with gestures and movements and occasionally with their voices, and it is necessary for the horseman to learn this sign language.

Riding up over a ridge and looking at a bunch of horses in pasture before they are aware of his presence, a good horseman can tell at a glance how it is with every one of them. Postures, manner of moving about, the set of head and ears say many things, such as: I am bored—I am cold—I am hungry—I am sick—I am in heat—I have a toothache—I wish that foal of mine would get weaned and quit bothering me—my feet or legs hurt—I have colic—or I have foundered myself. Postures and attitudes that indicate ailments or malfunction are discussed later on in this chapter.

When subtle body postures or action or ear twitching cannot be seen or when those forms of communication are much too mild for keyed-up emotions, the horse uses his voice. When feeling alone and forsaken by his kind, a horse may neigh or whinny—loudly and a little frantically—hoping for a reassuring whinny in return. (I never understood the use of the word whistle, which so many writers use instead of whinny or neigh.)

When coming upon other horses, particularly strangers, a whinny can be an expression of friendly greeting and pleasurable excitement. As they draw closer, the whinny becomes a more intimate nicker. In expectant moments, the soft throaty nicker is like an eager mumbling of greeting as another horse enters a barn, or like an "oh boy—oh boy—oh boy" sort of chatter as he is approached with his measure of grain.

When violently angry, a whinny is more like a scream of rage. Wild horses quite unaccustomed to the ways of men show fight and fear with guttural snorts—old hands call it "rollers in the nose." And the snorts can change to convulsive sobs, like human crying, when their struggles are of no avail as the ropes snake them down in the corral.

Intelligence and Reasoning

Almost all of us like to attribute to horses some human characteristics such as love and reasoning. At times it seems perfectly evident that our old pony is trying to express his affection, but the scientists say it is a matter of conditioning. The horse may be at ease with us, they say. He may feel secure when we are around and he may associate us with food and therefore be glad to see us. He does not reason like a human, however, and we would all do well to remember it. But although weak in the power of deduction, the horse has an almost infallible memory—long remembering places, scents, sounds, and ill-treatment. While with man, ever since he got up on his hind legs and left the animal world, instincts have been weakened by lack of use. While he gained in abstract mental life, reasoning, and so on, the horse's instincts continue to serve him as they always have since he evolved from the eohippus. To teach a horse, we must adjust to his instincts, his horse nature, and not expect him to adjust to ours.

In terms of intelligence the horse is not at the top of the list. Rutherford Platt, my good friend of many years, states in his book *The River of Life* that the chimpanzee with a cerebral cortex closest in size to man's is the most intelligent animal, with the Indian elephant, dog, horse, bear, beaver, and lion following in that order. Others have put the horse a notch or two down the list. Experiments now going on may bring porpoises, seals, and white whales toward the top of the list.

We know that the horse has a good memory and that he learns by repetition and rather quickly. The Arabian horse is credited with being the smartest. He has been the least affected by outbreeding and has had the longest association with man. Whatever mental grooves a horse makes by doing things over and over again are likely to stay with him. Horses that count up to certain numbers and stop, perform complicated routines without direction, do things like taking short cuts to an objective, opening door latches, etc., that seem to indicate reasoning capabilities, are for the most part repeating what they learned by rote or following aids given them. Sometimes their instincts or a memory of the result of some accidental happening cause them to do amazing things, things that make us wonder about their reasoning. But I leave it there and go on to the physical equipment of horses, a subject on which scientists do have most of the answers.

The Eye

Have you ever held a horse's head close to yours and gazed deeply into his eye? Such a loving gaze might be interpreted as adoration by an onlooker, but I recall that it furnished moments of fascination for me when I was a boy. The longer I peered inside, the deeper a fantastic jungle appeared with strange iridescent flower shapes, like pistils and stamens laden with a brown pollen that looks so soft and sootlike it seemed it would shatter at the slightest movement. Bluish rays filtered down through this eerie rain forest revealing even more hidden vistas.

From this I learned absolutely nothing, beyond what the inside of a horse's eye looks like. To learn about his vision, I turned to books. As with humans, horses have both day and night eyes that change back and forth. The horse does it better because his wider shutter opening gives him marvelous night vision. But even so it does not explain how horses—also other animals—can return to their homes on pitch dark nights over unfamiliar trails. Bats set out supersonic squeaks pitched at fifty thousand per second—much too high a frequency for human ears—that hit objects and bounce back, perfect sonar equipment that enables them to fly through a maze of threads in the dark without running into them. A sonar pattern perhaps leads them home—but where a horse gets his directional aids is unknown.

The horse, like the rabbit—because of the nose obstruction between the eyes—sees separate scenes with each eye without getting the two scenes scrambled. But unlike the rabbit and the squirrel, say the scientists, the horse can see forward with two-eyed vision like a human. It is supposed, however, that humans whose eyes are closer together and almost on a level, have a sharper focus and get more of a stereoptical effect than do horses. The horse is also dependent on moving his head or eyes to get the slanting rays to strike just right on the retina. Close to his face the horse may have an actual blind spot, but nothing as large as the blind spot of a bull, which extends in the form of a V directly in front for several feet due to the extreme width of the face and the heavy brow. It is this defect of vision that helps the matador control the "current of death" that flows past him.

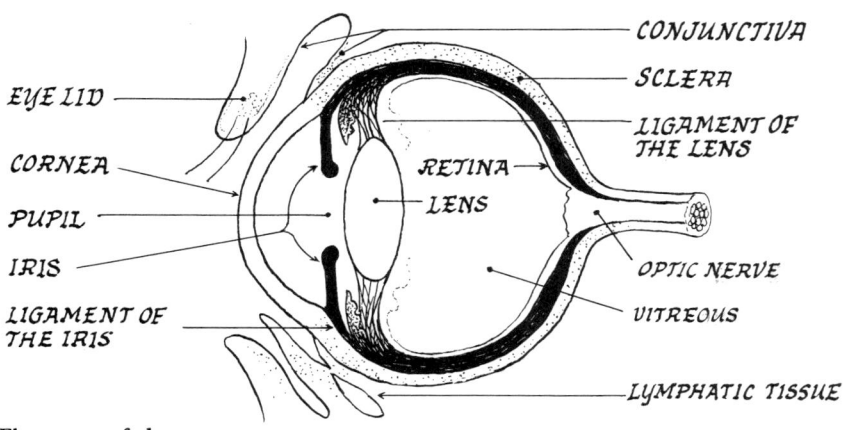

The parts of the eye.

If a horse held his head as high as a deer he would have full-circle vision, but since he doesn't, his rump blocks off the rear view. The only way one can come at a horse unobserved is from the rear. And a very poor practice it is, because, even if he can't see, the horse can hear and his protective instinct may trigger his hind feet.

Like the Arab-Barb horse from whom many of his good qualities come, the Quarter Horse has eyes set well apart and protected above the socket by rather prominent canopy bones. Soft, kindly brown eyes are favored in the breed. Any radical deviation such as wall-eyes, albino-eyes, watch-eyes, or moon-eyes (all such expressions mean eyes that are cloudy or opaque or are lacking in pigmentation) are inherited and will disqualify horses from being registered, no matter how good the animal is otherwise. Blindness from injury and unrelated to heredity does not exclude a horse from showing. Sparkling bright eyes usually denote a healthy, vigorous horse. Dull, cloudy, listless, or running eyes can be a warning of something troubling the horse. Constant ear twitching can indicate bad eyesight. The animal is making a great effort to detect with his ears what his eyes can't see.

Head-shy horses that suddenly jump sideways or rear back are in most cases reacting protectively—or in memory of an eye injury or blow to that side of the head. Suggestions for correcting this habit can be found in Chapter 13.

Ears and Hearing

Horses have good hearing, but perhaps not exceptional, as in the case of dogs and bears, whose acute hearing and sense of smell compensate for relatively poor eyesight.

You can always depend on your horse to hear the whir of a rattlesnake before you do, and he will smell the bad cucumber odor before you detect it, and will have taken evasive action or at least show restiveness. If one sleeps on the prairie at night with one's horse hobbled or staked nearby, the horse is most likely to first hear or scent—I don't know which—an approaching man or animal.

The ears of a horse turn forward, sideways, and back to catch sounds from those directions, and the ears serve as a sort of semaphore, signaling what goes on in his mind. When accompanied by body postures the meaning is even more precise. If a horse is angry, his ears go back as far as they can and his body tenses for action. If he is uncomfortable, tired, or dozing, his ears are only partly back and drooping slightly sideways, leaving it to his body stance and half-closed eyes to say whether he is dejected, weary, or just relaxing.

Fear brings the ears rigidly forward with the head thrust out toward the danger and the eyes glaring. If puzzled, wondering what to do, the ears move about seeking a clue. If blind, the ears keep moving to detect what the sight can't perceive. Curiosity, eagerness, and well-being cause the ears to prick forward while the body is relaxed and the eyes wide open and at ease.

It is not easy to get a good photo of the reining horse with his ears nicely forward when his owner-trainer is sitting in the saddle. This is because the horse is used to keeping at least one ear cocked back in order to listen to his rider. Ears back don't always mean anger or boredom. Study your horse's ears and you will learn his subtleties.

In describing the head of the Quarter Horse, it is obvious that, because of breeding trends in which Thoroughbred crosses play a big part, the two breeds are looking more and more alike. Many Quarter Horses look like muscled Thoroughbreds. The trend works both ways. Some Thoroughbred breeders are going more and more for the Quarter Horse conformation in the chest (wider) and in the quarters and gaskins (more muscled). At least three-quarters of the Quarter Horse breeders I have talked to, mostly breeders of Quarter Horse racing horses, welcome this trend, but they always add that by careful selection of individuals they try to perpetuate the workability, great emotional control, and comparatively trouble-free sturdy legs of the Quarter Horse.

The Heart

The added number of heartbeats caused by great exertion apparently has little to do with shortening a horse's life. It is the tension that causes heart strain. The human heartbeat is almost twice as rapid as that of a horse, and yet on the average the human lives almost twice as long.

Heart failure in horses is not uncommon, although the more frequent reports of it today seem to indicate more and better coverage of the news in the horse world, rather than that heart failure is an increasing cause of death in horses.

Muscles and Skin

The muscles and tissues generate energy. When they are oxidized— burned—they are reduced to carbon dioxide, and when muscles are fatigued they suffer a poisonous action from the buildup of lactic acid and other waste products. The Quarter Horse has a large heart to supply the muscles with blood. After violent exercise ceases, accelerated breathing must continue in order to replace the expended oxygen. Cooling out by slow but continued action, walking, keeps breathing at a higher rate than if the horse were allowed to stand still.

The skin of the Quarter Horse is comparatively thin with large veins close to the surface which aid in the cooling process. A thick-skinned cold blood has poorer circulation and with veins farther from the surface cannot rid himself of excessive heat quickly. Consequently his lactic-acid-filled muscles are unable to maintain a comparable expenditure of violent energy.

The tactile sense in thin-skinned horses is acute. They respond quickly when touched, generally moving to avoid the pressure. Training is accomplished by touch communication. As he is touched in various places, the horse learns what reaction is expected of him.

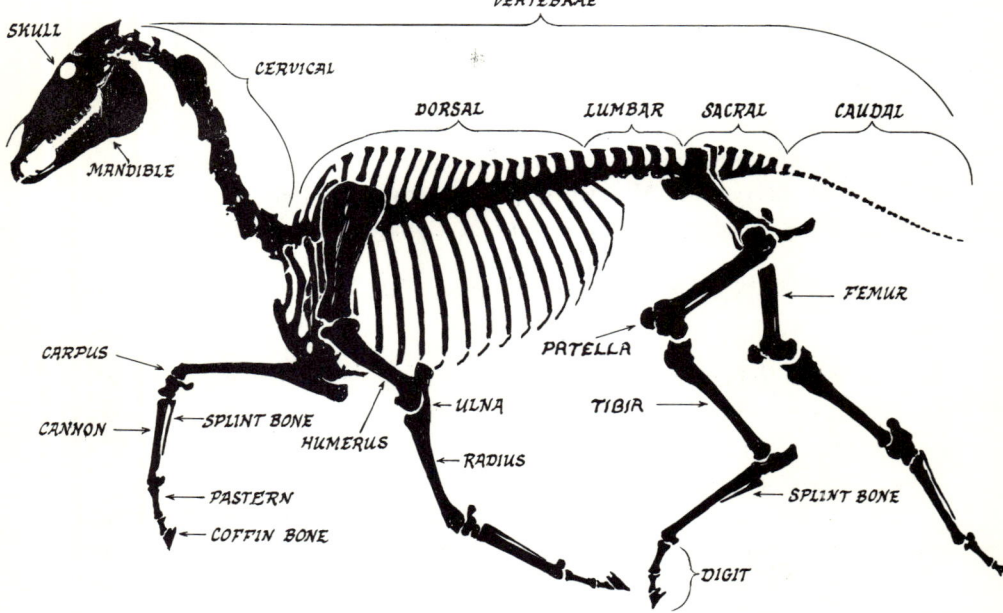

The skeleton or framework of the horse shows where the articulation of bones, cartilage, muscles, and sinews takes place. Knowing the areas helps in diagnosing any malfunction. To prevent confusion, the ribs on the off-side of the horse are not shown in this drawing.

Sense of Smell

As with humans, it is presumed that horses associate pleasant or unpleasant memories with odors. They are restive when odor memories are bad, and at ease when the odor memories are good. It is almost certain that a horse, like a dog, identifies places and people and other animals as much by scent as by sight. We know the horse nose is a keen selector of food. It leads him to the best barn offers and to the better grazing patches. And certainly the stallion's sense of smell plays an important part in his sexual drive, taking him unerringly to mares in heat.

Horses and other animals seem to have an uncanny ability to sense fear if it exists in those who approach them or try to handle them. How they do this is a mystery. The most common explanation of it—although to my knowledge never scientifically proved—is that the adrenal glands when stimulated by fear exude an odor which is far too subtle for human noses but easily detected by animals, and which instantly causes them to be on guard or to become fearful themselves. One might ask, "If one is afraid of an animal, why should it not feel dominant and remain unafraid?" The simplest answer is that fearful beings are potentially dangerous. For instance, those of us who have killed rattlesnakes may be desperately afraid of them. Everything about them repels us: their looks, odor, frightful sudden whirring, and of course the thought of what could happen if bitten by one. It follows that our fear makes us dangerous. If someone, even a friend, threatened to throw a rattlesnake, dead or alive, on us, as I have seen rough, uncurried ranch hands attempt to do with one of their crowd just for the hell of it, any one of us, I am sure, would use any weapon at hand to prevent it. Fearful people (and fearful nations too for that matter) are dangerous. They lose judgment and may do unpredictable things. Animals, however they detect it, know that fear creates danger. If you are afraid of a horse, he is afraid of you. He forgets his manners and gets concerned with what you might have up your sleeve, how you might be going to hurt him.

Horses are at ease with people who are at ease with them, who handle them forthrightly and without fear. Give commands positively and handle the horse—even punishing him if he deserves it—with assurance, and you will always be in good odor with him.

Stomach and Digestive System

The digestive process begins in the mouth of the horse, where the salivary glands produce almost ten gallons of saliva every twenty-four hours to be mixed with the feed during the chewing action. To supply this and other bodily liquids, the active horse will drink ten to twelve gallons of water a day.

The stomach of the horse lies close to the diaphragm, and the capacity of two to four gallons is comparatively small for such a large animal. In it the digestion of proteins begins and is continued in the small intestine, which is about seventy feet long with a capacity of about twelve gallons. Intestinal glands, the pancreas and the liver supply the digestive juices. The partly digested food passes to the large intestine, where the greater part of digestion takes place and where bile is continually produced to emulsify fats. A horse has no gall bladder. The large intestine holds about twenty gallons and consists of the caecum, a pouch high up on the right side, connected to the large colon, which in turn connects with the small colon and the rectum.

It is essential that all horse food be good and untainted. Whatever enters his mouth must pass through the horse's body. A horse cannot breathe through his mouth as can a man, nor can a horse regurgitate or vomit. Since material cannot be rejected through the mouth the horse might rupture his stomach in an attempt to sneeze or snort it through his nostrils. If rejected food can be forced through the pharynx region into the windpipe and lungs, the damage done may result in pneumonia.

The horse is a slow eater requiring a quarter of an hour to eat a pound of hay and five or ten minutes to eat a pound of grain. The hay portion of his diet is usually given him in the evening when he has plenty of time to chew.

A horse's digestive system is so productive it produces blood in such quantities that it accounts for about one fourth of his weight. In cases of overeating his powerful heart will pump blood with such force that the pressure on the membranes of the forefeet, the laminae, will distend and injure them. This condition is called foundering or laminitis. The reason the forefeet and not the hind feet are so affected is because they are closer to the heart and the arteries have fewer diversionary branches than do those that carry the blood to the hind legs and feet.

Feet

Although the hoof walls look rigid, there is however a "give" to them that allows some expansion at the heel whenever a horse puts his weight on his foot. And at each step the pressure on the frog of the foot causes a pumping action which ensures a strong flow of blood.

Diagrams with detailed discussion of the foot can be found in the chapter on "Feet and Shoeing."

Teeth

One of the distinguishing features of the Quarter Horse is his rather blunt muzzle and shallow mouth. There was a time when English sportsmen equated a small, slender muzzle—"One that could eat out of a teacup"—with speed and general excellence. This conceit persisted until Hambletonian, the founding father of the Standardbreds, came along. He had such a broad, blunt muzzle he could hardly eat out of a bucket, let alone a teacup, and no one ever questioned his speed or excellence. A blunt muzzle often indicates a good set of teeth. In any case, from the side of his family that had roughed it for many generations in the West the Quarter Horse inherited good hard teeth.

The age of horses can be told by their teeth with considerable accuracy until they have passed their eighth year. Beyond that time even those who are experienced may not be able to determine the exact age.

The mature male horse has forty teeth. Of them four are pointed teeth called tushes or, more commonly, bridle teeth. The two central incisors are called nippers; the ones on either side are called intermediates and the outer pair are called corners. The bridle teeth are located between the incisors and the molars. They are seldom present in the mare, therefore mares are considered to have a total of thirty-six teeth. The spaces on the lower jaws between the incisors and molars (on males, between the bridle teeth and molars) are called the bars. It is on them that the bit rests.

Foals have twenty-four temporary teeth—called milk teeth—that are much whiter than permanent teeth. There are twelve incisors and twelve molars; three molars are on each side and in both upper and lower jaws. The temporary nippers may be present at birth but certainly

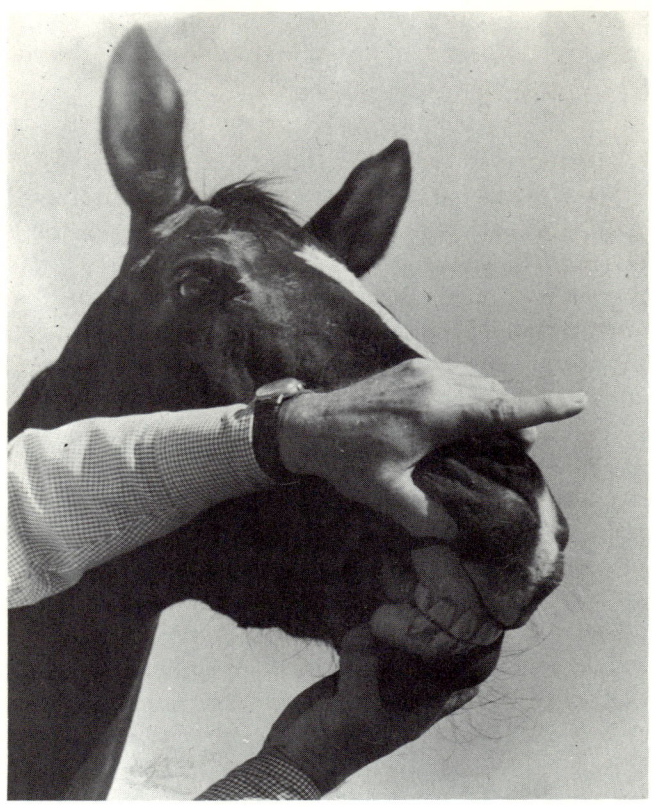

The author shows the usual way of opening a horse's mouth so his age can be determined by his teeth. This mare was not yet five years old. *Photo by Irene Laune.*

appear within ten days. There are two in each jaw. At the age of four to six weeks the intermediate milk teeth appear. When six to ten months old the upper and lower corner (milk) teeth come in. This gives the colt a full set of temporary front teeth. By the time the colt reaches the age of one year the crowns of the nippers show wear. In another six months the intermediates become worn and at two years all the teeth are worn. During the following six months there are no noticeable changes. At about two and one-half years the shedding of the milk teeth begins. At three the permanent nippers, above and below, replace the milk teeth. At four the permanent intermediates replace the milk teeth, and at about four and one-half years old the four corner milk teeth begin to shed, and at five the permanent teeth that replace them are well developed but not yet in contact. The horse now has what is called a *full mouth*. A horse's teeth continue to grow throughout his life.

In a six-year-old horse the corner incisors are on a level with the adjoining teeth, with a well-marked dental cavity or "cup" showing practically no wear. The nippers show wear over the entire surface; the cup, though visible, shows indications of gradual disappearance and is no longer concave. If the animal grazes in sandy pastures the wear is greater, making it more difficult to tell the exact age.

When seven years old the intermediates as well as the nippers show wear. The upper corner incisors are worn by the lower incisor corners, but because the lower ones are slightly forward a *hook* or *dovetail* is left unworn at the back of the upper corners. For the amateur this is the easiest of all ages to determine.

The eight-year-old horse shows all incisors worn. Cups have disappeared from the nippers, still show slightly in intermediates, and are well marked in the corners. At this age a transverse line called a *dental*

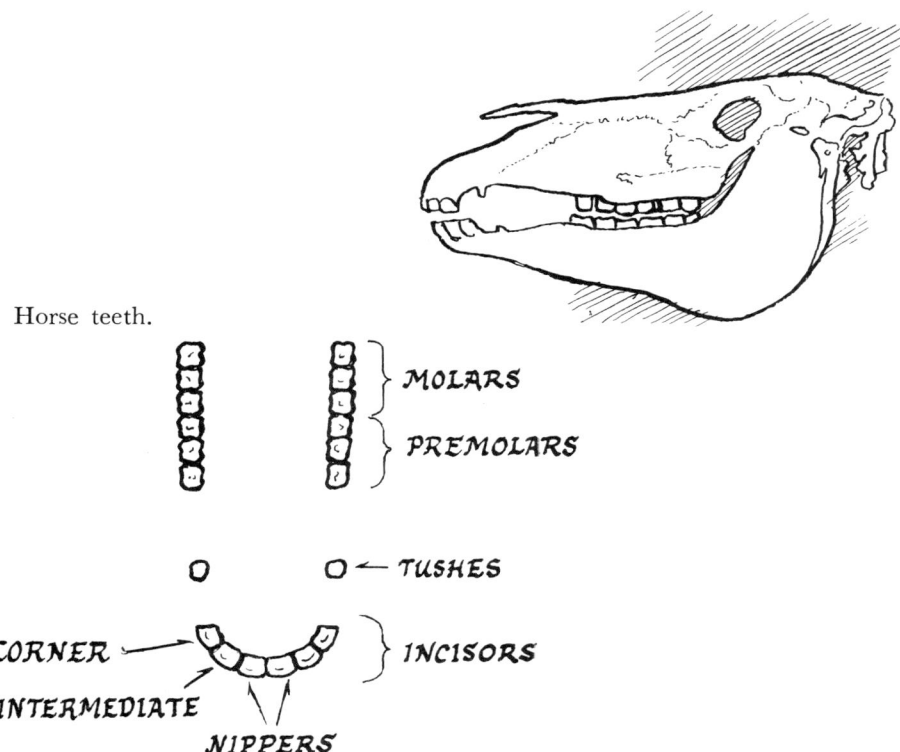

Horse teeth.

star appears back of the front edge of the table or flat surface of the nippers and intermediates.

In a nine-year-old animal the nippers take on a more rounded contour, the cup has disappeared from all but the corners, the dental star has moved toward the center of the nipper tables.

At ten years old the intermediates become rounded. Between this and age eleven or thereabouts, the horse is said to be a *smooth mouth*.

At eleven or twelve years of age the corners have become rounded. At thirteen all the lower incisors are definitely rounded, the dental star shows in the center of all the incisors, and the enamel rings which had surrounded the cups have disappeared.

At fourteen years of age the tables—contact surfaces—of the nipper incisors change from a round shape to a triangular one; this change occurs in the intermediates at fifteen and in the corners at sixteen or seventeen years of age.

A groove near the gums of the upper incisors called *Galwayne's Groove* appears and lengthens with age. At the age of fifteen it is about halfway down the tooth, at twenty it is all the way down, and thereafter it becomes less noticeable until it disappears at the age of thirty. The colt's teeth come together at only a slight angle, but with age the teeth protrude at a greater angle; to meet, they must be longer.

A horse with a toothache will usually carry his head twisted from a vertical position. The veterinarian will put a speculum—a metal clamp —in the horse's mouth to keep it open, and will diagnose the trouble. An abscess can be treated, but there are cases where a tooth will have to be extracted. *Floating* the teeth means filing them smoother along the grinding surface so that they make better contact. This is done sometimes even to young horses whose teeth need a little leveling off, to keep them from biting the inside of their mouths. When, and if, they should be floated should be discussed with your veterinarian.

Although I have never seen it, I have heard that valuable horses have had their teeth capped with stainless steel. And I am told this is true of high-priced dairy cattle, thereby prolonging their lives. Even with all the new methods that are known to veterinarians, the old saying that "a horse will last as long as his teeth" is still generally valid.

Life-span

I remember reading about a family buggy horse in a small town in upper New York State who lived to be forty-five years old, and of a mustang that lived almost that long in California. And Guinness's *Book of World Records* tells of an Italian Army horse named Topolino who was foaled in Libya in 1909 and died in Brescia, Italy, in 1960 at the age of fifty-one. I never saw a horse that attained such great age, but recently I saw one that was getting close to it. She is a mare named Lady and she is between forty and forty-two years old. She is owned by Fay Anderson of Shumway, Arizona, who recalled riding her in horseback square dances when she was a girl. Fay's family got Lady from Juan Tellez of southern Arizona.

Her knees are somewhat sprung but not as much as one would expect in an animal her age, and I was told she still whirls and rears when frightened. She was raced as a filly and is thought to be by a Thoroughbred sire and out of a Spanish dam. To me she looked more Spanish

This photo of Lady was taken just two weeks before her death. She was said to be forty-two years old. *Photo by the author.*

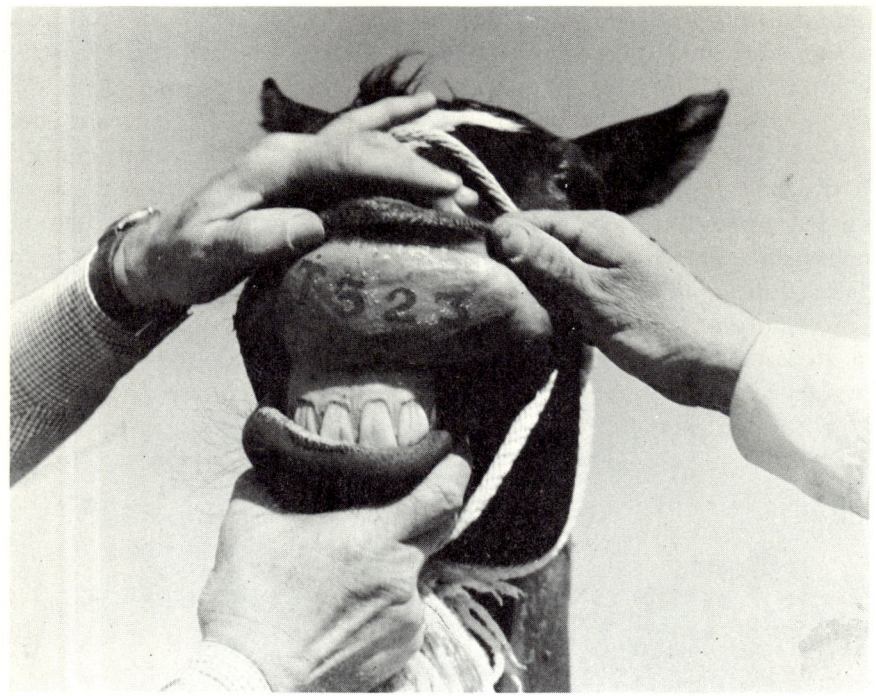

All Thoroughbred race horses and some Quarter Running Horses have a letter indicating the year of birth and the last three of their registration numbers tattooed inside their upper lips. The system started in 1946 with the letter A. *Photo by Irene Laune.*

than Thoroughbred. Perhaps I was overly influenced by the ornate Spanish brand that decorates her near hind leg, low down almost on the gaskin. And if I am not mistaken it is the famous old Tarrazas brand that was burned into more hides in Chihuahua a generation or so ago than any other brand before or since. I took a look at Lady's teeth and they were the most ancient I've ever seen. Not only were they loose, rounded, and worn, but also of different lengths. Brown and snaggled, they protrude extremely far forward.

The average life-span of a horse is not much over twenty years, though conclusive statistics on the subject seem to be unavailable. Age depends a lot on what a horse does, eats, and how he is cared for and whether his teeth hold out. To generalize: at fifteen a horse is middle-aged; at eighteen to twenty he is entering old age; at twenty-five he is definitely old; and at thirty or more he is a remarkable individual comparable to a man ninety years old or older.

Janus, the founding father of Colonial times, lived from 1746 to 1780, and his prepotency as a sire lasted for all of his thirty-four years. Diomed, who was brought from England to Virginia at the age of twenty-two in 1798, lived to the age of thirty-two. He sired his greatest son, Sir Archy, at the age of twenty-nine. Both he and Janus were exceptional animals in every way, including their longevity.

Race horses and polo ponies who experience great exertion and who generally stay keyed up and nervous long after strenuous action do not, as a rule, live as long as other horses. But there are always exceptions such as the magnificent and calmly regal Man O' War, who lived happily into his thirties.

An old cowpony, experienced and wise, who was pushing twenty-five, showed me plenty of action when cutting Chihuahua long-horn steers out of a herd in the shin-oak country of western Oklahoma. But as soon as each burst of speed was over, he resumed his easygoing calmness. Being of Quarter Horse type, he had the secret of throwing the switch that unstrung his nerves, and no doubt it added years to his life.

7
Feeding and Grooming

If you lavished all the attentions on your horse that are advised by instructors, friends, and horse books—including this one—your costs would be excessive and you wouldn't have any time left in which to ride the horse. From all the good advice, each horse owner must choose what will be workable for his own kind of time and money and way of using the horse. It stands to reason that a horse used for casual pleasure riding in one's home neighborhood is not going to be groomed and trained with the same time-consuming precision that would be given to a show or performance horse.

Only after you decide what kind of horse you want and how he will be used can you fit him into your life and daily schedule with any sort of realistic planning. For good average attention, a horse will require at least one hour a day, plus a half day spent at the weekends catching up on barn work, grooming, and care of tack and equipment. If the horse is entered in shows, much more time will be required.

As for costs, the national average cost of keeping a horse has been estimated at $735 to $800 annually. Half of this amount goes for feed and the other half for tack, shoes, health, trailers, and entry fees.

Feeding

Native grasses of many varieties that grew on many kinds of pasture land were the only food horses ever had until they were domesticated. Grasses, water, and salt still constitute the bulk of a horse's diet, but the grasses have been refined and cultivated so that they contain more nutrition.

Hay. Aside from pasture grazing, the most common form of grass for feed is hay. After grass has been cut and dried, it is called cured hay.

Timothy Hay, which is difficult to come by and expensive in some districts, is still looked upon as the best of the hays. Sometimes it is a mixture of timothy with prairie hay and a small amount of clover. Clover, generally avoided by horsemen because of its tendency to cause colic or to bloat horses, is now recommended in very small amounts in dehydrated alfalfa pellets where the amount used can be rigidly controlled. It is considered good for keeping the bowels loose.

Prairie Hay is simply native grass that has been cut and cured. Its nutritive value depends upon where it was grown, when cut, how well it was dried out and cured. The best of it, grown on soils that are not depleted and do not require nitrogen fertilizer for an abundant yield, is close to being nutritionally perfect horse feed. The fabulous endurance attributed to the Western horses of a hundred years or more ago was due to the good native grass. Few of those horses ever tasted grain. Indian horses, always gaunt after wintering on scant pickings of cured grass that often lay buried under the snow, and sometimes with nothing to eat but cottonwood bark, would fatten quickly on spring grass. Indeed, the month of June was known to the horse Indians of the plains as *the month when horses get fat.* The blue stem grass of Oklahoma's Osage Hills has been judged one of the most nutritious grasses known. Ever since the old cattle drive days it has been considered almost as capable of fattening cattle and horses as grain. Prairie hay of poor quality has little food value and if it is dusty, weedy, or slightly moldy it can be injurious.

Oat Hay in districts where it is plentiful and economical is a good feed but has less protein than good timothy hay.

Sudan Grass Hay is good when cut before it blooms, afterward it lacks sufficient protein.

Alfalfa Hay, which is called Lucerne in Europe, is now considered the most nutritious of all hays. It is rich in protein, calcium (lime), and Vitamin A. In the horse diet it is thought of as a supplement because it is somewhat too rich and too laxative to constitute the complete diet.

Buying hay in bulk is almost a thing of the past, and buying good baled hay is getting more difficult and expensive in some urban areas. Some stables in the metropolitan district of New York have for several years had to truck timothy and prairie hay all the way from Canada.

Alfalfa Pellets (dehydrated) with additives are as good as any horse feed on the market. Each manufacturer lists the contents of its pellets—always stressing the vitamins and minerals they contain. This type of feed has an immediate appeal to the horse handler. It is clean and convenient to store, handle, and ration out. And the biggest payoff of all is that the time-consuming job of cleaning out horse stalls is reduced with pellet feeding to a matter of a few minutes. It is claimed that pellet-fed horses leave about one pound of droppings a day. The fact that eating pellets consumes less time than munching on hay may mean the horse will have more time in which to be bored, and this should be countered by more use, association with other horses, or keeping a pet about the stable and corral.

Horses vary considerably in their individual likes and dislikes of various foods as well as in their nutritional needs. In recent years there has been a great deal of research on the subject. Now any serious horseman can get advice and can find innumerable food additives with which to experiment until he finds the one his horse will eat with zest and thrive on.

The AQHA has instituted elaborate projects on nutrition. Various manufacturers of vitamins and minerals maintain continuous and extensive experimental feeding programs with horses of all sizes and ages.

The kind and amount of feed necessary for a horse depends on the kind and the amount of work required of him. For example, a gelding that is used only three or four times a week for an hour or so each time needs only an occasional feeding of grain, if any at all, if he is on good pasture on good soil and gets plenty of good water and salt. He will also be easy to groom and keep because the sun and the open air will keep his hide smelling cleaner than if he is kept mostly in a stable.

The principal advantage of keeping a horse on pasture aside from the saving on grain is that when the owner is away the horse can take care of himself. The disadvantage is that his coat will get rough-looking when cool weather comes along, and of course he will have to be caught up from pasture every time one wants to ride him. If a gelding is still growing and the pasture is not on rich soil, he will need a supplement of manganese, zinc, iron, copper, iodine, cobalt, calcium, and phosphorus. All of which you will be glad to know can be purchased in the form of a salt mineral block at any feed store. And it is something that he can ration out for himself.

When green grass turns brown due to a dry spell or to freezing weather, it loses much of its mineral and protein content. Horses on such pasture, whether or not they are being used, will need additional vitamins. This can be supplied by a daily feeding of one or two pounds of dehydrated alfalfa pellets or five to eight pounds of leafy alfalfa hay. These added vitamins help horses convert the large amounts of dry grass or hay they eat, which is basically cellulose or a low grade carbohydrate.

Grain. If horses are ridden every day, a ration of grain should be added. And when cold weather comes larger rations of grain given morning and night will supply heat energy.

Corn is the most heat producing of all grains. Most horsemen who feed corn in some mixed form during the winter months start reducing the amount of corn in the diet in the spring and eliminate it entirely, concentrating on oats and barley, during the summer and warm fall days. A handful of bran mixed with the food ration will give bulk and will keep the bowels loose, although some depend on alfalfa pellets to do the same thing.

More horses have been ruined by too much grain than by too little and by too few vitamins than by too many. It is of course the quality of feed that counts rather than the quantity. A horse can get logy with fat from too much grain if he is deprived of sufficient vitamins and minerals that are present in green grasses or in alfalfa or dehydrated alfalfa in the form of pellets.

Heavily grained horses that are given a rest from their usual active work should have their grain ration reduced and the feeding of the vitamin- and mineral-bearing grass, or its substitute in the form of pellets, increased.

Old-time brewery and dray horses were grained as heavily on their Sundays of rest as they were on week days. Come Monday morning they were unable to stand up to heavy work and sometimes were known to collapse. The veterinarians of the day, not realizing the cause, called the condition "Monday morning sickness."

For more work and more weight, feed more grain and less hay. For less work, feed more hay and less grain. Grain supplies heat and energy. If a horse is not fed sufficient grain to supply the energy he must use for muscular work, his body fat must supply it. And when the fat is used up the other protein tissues must supply it, so that the horse becomes a gaunt, used-up animal.

There are many vitamin supplements on the market which contain every needed vitamin and mineral. However, very little of these additives is needed if the basic ration is well balanced between grain and grass.

Here is a diet recommended for a thousand-pound Quarter Horse that is ridden daily in active sessions, in moderate weather. One half to be fed in the morning and one half in the evening.

5 pounds of oats, ½ whole or crimped
3 pounds of cracked corn
1 pound of alfalfa pellets or 15 pounds of alfalfa hay and just to be doubly sure there is plenty of protein in the diet add:
½ pint of soy bean meal, or one of the concentrates on the market that contain it and other vitamins and minerals.
Salt and plenty of fresh water

If the weather is cold, more corn and less oats should be fed. A Quarter Horse that is used in the arena or in polo or wherever his muscles are being drained by bursts of action needs a very high level of protein in his diet.

In districts where barley is grown and priced reasonably it can replace the corn and part of the oats, especially in mature horses. For growing horses oats are considered preferable, at least by the veterinary nutritionists whose articles I have read. Bran is a good horse feed to supply phosphorus, but considering its only moderate nutritional value it is expensive. As a bulk food it is little better than hay, and as for keeping the horse's bowels loose, bran is no better than alfalfa hay or pellets, and it costs more.

Cane Molasses, when added to cracked corn and other feed, seldom in quantities of more than 10 per cent, gives zest to the horse's appetite and supplies energy.

Creep Feeding is the term used when high protein, vitamins, and minerals—in the form of oats, alfalfa, pellets and concentrated additives—are added to the diet of the nursing colt (or calf). When a foal is eating two or three pounds of creep feed a day, he is relieving his mother of producing his entire diet and he goes through the weaning stage almost before he knows it.

Feeding for Trophies. In preparing your horse for show, the important thing to remember is to start in plenty of time. Even with a natural winner on your hands you will want to add a little extra vigor, alertness, and glossy coat.

As you step up the work schedule, increase the grain ration and reduce the hay ration. This will shrink the belly somewhat. Since you are lowering the bulk protein, add concentrated protein in forms and amounts recommended by the manufacturer. It will give the extra vitamins and minerals for a silky coat.

After the show season ends, gradually over a period of a month or two bring your horse back to his usual ration and routine of work.

Carrots, Apples, and Turnips appeal to horses and can be fed as an occasional treat. Carrots, if plentiful, can be fed in fairly generous amounts, but they may put a horse off of less interesting food for a day or so. It is better to feed these things whole; the horse will chop them to the size he likes best. Horses share a taste with humans for many things, particularly sweets. One of our horses once devoured a whole apple pie that had been left a little too close to an open kitchen window. Arabian horses relish dates, and I have heard that in some places they practically subsist on them. I never knew a horse that didn't like sugar, but I have known plenty of horsemen who discouraged the practice of giving it to them. For one thing it teaches the horse to be hankering for something when you are around him instead of paying attention to what is expected of him. Then, too, it can get the horse in the habit of snapping at your hand.

Feeding linseed meal (flaxseed) is an old custom that has given way to the use of ready-prepared foods and additives, many of which utilize the amino acids of linseed that make up protein. It should be remembered that linseed oil—for paint—is quite another thing. It is a deadly concentrate that would kill a horse—and quickly.

Manufacturers are simplifying things for the horseman. Now if they would go one step farther and print the labels, contents, etc., in type large enough to be read—all horsemen do not wear glasses in the barn, you know—the air would be less turquoise at times.

Water should be where a horse can get at it at all times except when he is being used. Most people don't think of it that way, but it is a very important part of a horse's diet. It should be cool and clean and fresh.

Feed Bags are handy at all times, but remember, never put one on a horse that can get to water. It doesn't take much water to drown a horse and a feed bag can hold enough to do it.

Poisonous Plants

If you live in any of the Western states and have occasion to put your horse out in pasture, it is advisable to make inquiries or to check out the pasture to see if it has any plants that are poisonous. The Department of Agriculture has published Bulletin No. 327, called "22 Plants Poisonous to Livestock in the Western States," which pictures and describes the offending plants. They are:

Arrow grass	Greasewood	Locoweed	St. Johnswort
Bracken fern	Halogeton	Lupine	Sneezeweed
Chokecherry	Horsebrush	Milkweed	Spring parsley
Copperweed	Indian hemp	Oak	Timber milk vetch
Death camas	Larkspur	Poison hemlock	Veratrum
		Rubberweed	Water hemlock

It is pointed out that, unless horses are unusually hungry or thirsty or lacking in salt, they will generally avoid poisonous plants. And some plants that are toxic for cattle and sheep are less so for horses. Symptoms of affected animals and known methods of treatment are given in the bulletin.

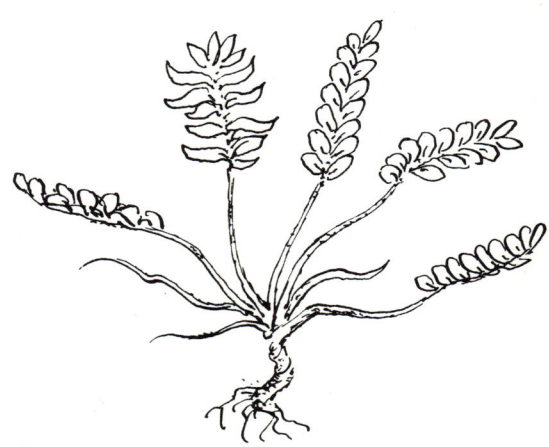

Locoweed. There are many poisonous species of this plant, which grows in the western half of the United States. The most common variety, and the one stock raisers are concerned with, has a purple blossom that resembles a garden pea but is much smaller, with velvety gray-green leaves.

To obtain this bulletin, write to Animal Disease and Parasite Research Division, U. S. Department of Agriculture, Beltsville, Maryland 20705.

No such bulletin is available at present for other districts in the United States, according to the county agents I spoke to about it. However, one can obtain bulletins dealing with individual poisonous plants such as poison oak, poison ivy, etc.

Starving Horses

Hidden away in grazed-out pastures or in the gloom of uncared-for barns are hundreds of horses slowly starving. This shocking statement is verified by national authorities and discussed seriously in horse journals. Unbelievable as it may seem, this condition has been discovered in seemingly prosperous districts. Each year a few people—thankfully a small percentage—who acquire a horse or two lose interest for one reason or another and neglect them. Some will go away on trips and days will elapse between feedings. Realizing their neglect, some owners rush out and dump a lot of feed, which, if normally rationed, would last a long time. Then they don't return for days. Shortage of money causes some people to cut the feed ration below good subsistence levels. In some instances, neighbors or riding acquaintances who suspect the conditions are bad hesitate to interfere in someone else's business, hoping some other person will bring it to the attention of the local ASPCA.

Horses out on their own are pretty good foragers and manage to stay alive. But those in captivity are dependent on their owners. One reason for mentioning this sad condition is to call attention to the fact that many good horsemen have purchased—at understandably low prices—thin, uncared-for horses and helped them to make dramatic comebacks to good flesh and spirit and usefulness. Here is a challenge for those who may be short on money but long on sympathy and patience and love of horses.

Grooming

Good horse handling calls for consistency and regularity. Get yourself and your horse into a daily routine of good habits as quickly as possible. Good habits once acquired are as hard to break as bad habits. They will make everything you do around a stable and with your horse easier and safer.

When taking your horse out for a ride, bring him from his stall directly

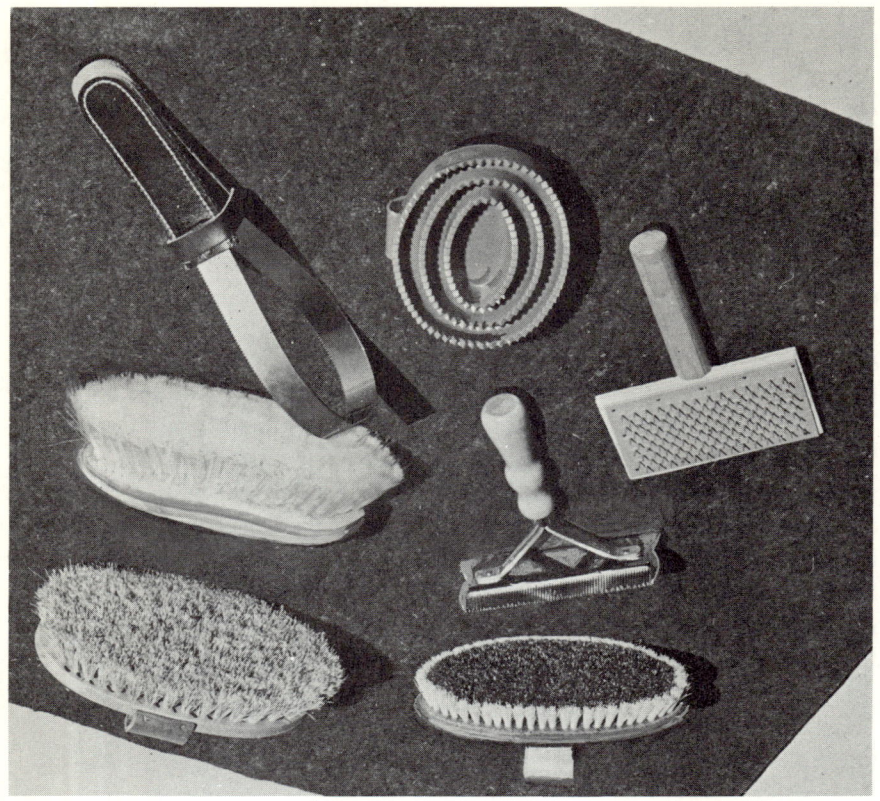

Grooming tools. *Photo by Irene Laune.*

to where he will be cross-tied in the passageway. Never snap the cross-ties into a bridle bit ring or shank. It might hurt the horse's mouth or break the bit or both if he is frightened and lunges or pulls back. Next make the horse presentable for your ride by wiping off his face with a cloth. Handle the horse gently around the head, eyes, and ears, but firmly over the rest of his body. Comb out his forelock, mane, and tail, and give him a brisk brushing with a stiff brush. Then a lighter going over with a soft brush to smooth his coat down. How briskly you brush him and how much hair is rubbed off depends on whether or not the horse is blanketed —and clipped—or allowed to keep his winter coat.

Pick up his feet and clean them with a hoof pick around the frogs and check to see if the shoes are tight. Take care that the pick does not dig under a shoe. Also be careful around the sensitive frog. The cleaner a horse's feet are kept, the less likely they are to get the damaging and odoriferous thrush.

When you lift his feet, lean against the horse and push his weight off the foot you want. It is a good practice to run your hands down his hind legs, beginning as high as the gaskins, so that he will become accustomed to your handling him. Don't dawdle when you grasp the fetlock joint. Simply lean against him, ask for his foot and lift it up. When it is off the ground, hold the hoof and bend the toe upwards. After a week of following this routine, your horse will be as familiar with it as you are.

After you ride, and your horse has cooled out, is the best time to give him a thorough grooming. But first, if he finds a sandy or dusty place to roll, let him do it. It relaxes his insides, and is his way of cleaning himself and drying his coat. It is certainly nothing that you can make him do, but give him the opportunity if the dust or sand is there.

If the weather is cold, clean him off with a brush and blanket him. Then roll the blanket back a little at a time and rub him dry. If the weather is mild, his back can be washed, scraped off, and rubbed dry. If the weather is hot, he can be hosed off or washed and scraped and the sun can dry him. The race-horse establishment people were disdainful when Rex Ellsworth of Arizona and California—whose horse Swaps won the Kentucky Derby in 1955 and was sold to stud for two million dollars —had his horses washed down with a hose. It just wasn't done, they said. But now most of them use a hose if weather is moderate.

When your horse is dry, go over him with a hard rubber curry comb or stiff brush and get the hair and skin scurf loose. Then brush him smooth and clean with a body brush. If the scurf is excessive—scurvy— it can indicate a lack of vitamin C in the diet.

Vacuum cleaners are on the market for horse grooming, and people I have talked with who have used them say they are pleased with the results and with being saved the workout.

With a rag or soft brush the coat can be rubbed smooth and shiny. Some hair tonic on the rag will give elegance for the show ring and is not likely to collect dust as does Vaseline or any oily substance.

Check the feet, and if there are any scratches or indications of chapping at the heels, wash them clean and when dry paint them with a medication or spray them with a wound spray. To keep the hoofs in good condition, use a hoof dressing three or four times a week.

A few times a year—oftener in warm weather—the well-kept horse is bathed all over in warm soapy water. Wash his face and nostrils and around the eyes—and avoid getting soap in his eyes and water in his ears.

Mildly scrub him all over. Wash under his tail and between his legs where he sweats the most and wash the sheath of a gelding and the teats and udder of a mare. Always rinse well with clear water. Scrape him off and if there is no sun to do it rub him dry. A soft brush will smooth his hair and hair tonic on a rag will give the final touch—and he should feel like a pampered aristocrat.

When it comes to grooming the mane and tail, a metal long-toothed comb is used to pull down through the hair. Try not to break or pull out hair haphazardly because, for show grooming, you may be pulling the wrong hairs. To thin the mane and make it look airy and flowing, the longer underhairs are pulled out. Manes and tails are never whacked off with scissors. They are pulled, a few hairs at a time, to give a soft blended edge. Wrap a few hairs around the comb and give a quick jerk, or pull them out with the thumb and fingers. A glove rubbed with rosin gives a better grip. The mane is usually about six to eight inches long and thinned so that it never looks bunchy. Ropers train the mane to hang on the near side to have it out of the way of the rope, or else they roach it. The English used the word "hogged" for the mane that was clipped close, and the word "roached" once meant a mane that stood up two or three inches. Now the terms are interchangeable. Westerners generally use the word "roached" as meaning a very close-clipped mane.

The majority of Western riders still prefer flowing manes to roaching. In one large Senior Reining Class at the Arizona National Horse Show, only a few horses were without their manes. In the Junior Western Pleasure Class about half the horses were roached, while out of twenty-eight horses in a Senior Western Pleasure Class, only five were roached. Strangely, in a halter class of yearling fillies, a quarter of them were roached. Only in English Pleasure Class did any Quarter Horses have their tails and manes braided.

When roaching, it is the custom with Quarter Horses to leave the forelock unclipped and to leave a small tuft of mane at the withers. This tuft keeps the clippers away from the short hair on the withers and makes a place for the saddle blanket so it will not be rubbing on bristles. Even on a horse whose mane is unclipped, a place in the mane, back of the ears where the bridle headstall rests, is clipped to give a neater appearance.

Pulling hairs from the mane and tail should be done in sessions that last only five or ten minutes, and only a few hairs should be pulled at a time. One owner who was watching from the sidelines while a mare of his was showing restlessness in a halter class, turned to say that he thought the mare's neck and tail were irritating her. He explained that his chil-

Mane with buttons. *Photo by the author.*

This photo of the famous Jole Blon, who traces to Peter McCue, shows the tuft of hair at the withers that is left when the rest of the mane is clipped. *Courtesy* Quarter Horse Journal.

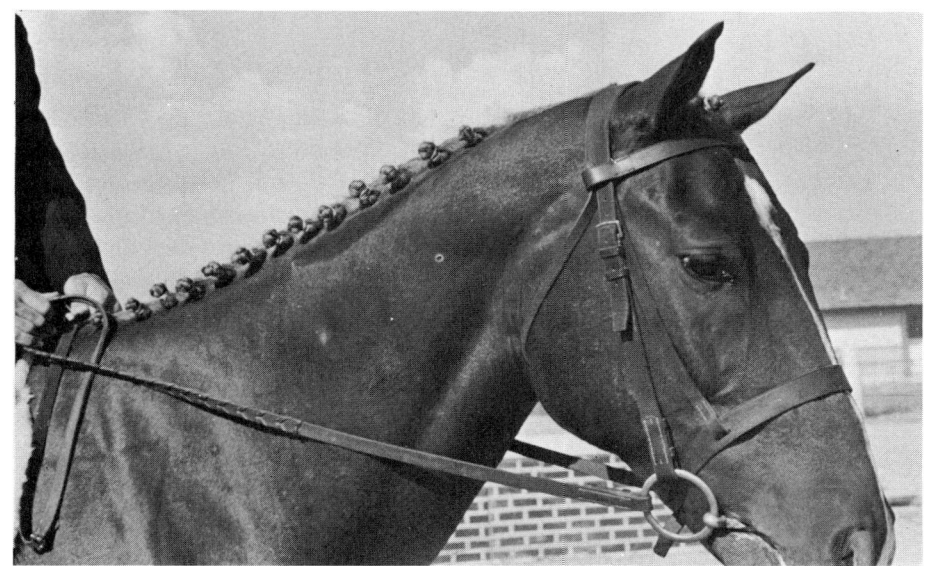

dren had done the hair pulling in one session the night before the show.

The hairs are pulled from the tail to slenderize it and minimize any bushiness near the dock. In Quarter Horses a feature to be proud of and displayed is the muscular development on both inside and outside of the gaskins. No exhibitor wants his horse to carry a tail long enough to conceal this feature. So Quarter Horses are groomed so that their tails never hang lower than their hocks. Being thinned out near the tip, the tail never appears clubbed.

Of all show horses, the Quarter Horses are usually presented with less artificiality in grooming. It is a point of pride with most owners and exhibitors to keep them natural-looking, believing them to be beautiful as they are.

Blankets and Clipping

In the spring, horses shed their heavy winter coats and by summertime, even without grooming if they are allowed outdoors, their new short-haired coat will be sleek. In the late fall, new winter coats grow in. The hairs are long and stand out from the body, and the horse is all set for cold weather—unless the owner arranges otherwise.

In the Southwest—and this is true of even colder areas—we let nature manage things whenever we could, and this meant that we never blanketed our horses in the wintertime. It is true that when used they sweat rather profusely, due to their heavy coats and the heat-producing diet they were on. Sweating, if not excessive, is beneficial for horses because it washes out waste matter through the sweat pores. But it means more time has to be taken to cool the horses out and to dry them—this last stage with blankets—because of the heavy coats. The natural coat, on the other hand, allows horses to spend more time in pasture.

In New York State up along the Hudson River, the severe winter weather seemed to require blanketing. So the first winter there I saw to it that the horses had warm woolen blankets—and they had colds and runny noses all too frequently. The compromise of not clipping off the winter coat but simply currying out part of it so they would look somewhat more presentable when ridden, and to keep them from getting too warm, simply did not work out.

A horse cannot wear two coats—his own and a winter blanket—even in freezing weather. So if he is to be kept closely groomed and covered with a blanket for warmth, his own coat must be clipped off. Of the two, his own coat is the more flexible. Nature's thermostat regulates the warmth of the winter coat. For more heat, the hairs stand out farther from the skin; for less heat, the hairs lie closer to the skin. There are long and short hairs. The long ones stand out more, to support the shorter ones, and from them rain drips off before soaking the coat to the skin.

The following winters along the Hudson, I did not blanket the horses at all, except when drying them out after they were ridden. And they stayed in fine shape.

The choice between nature's way and man's way is, as always, dependent on how the horse is used. If ridden frequently in cold weather, trailered about, used for hunts, shows, and performance events, the winter coat is clipped off when it comes in, in the late fall, and replaced with a blanket. A second clipping is necessary in midwinter. Clipping reduces the time it takes to groom a horse. In the days before clippers—and no shortage of grooms—horses were made sleek by long and careful currying and brushing. Excess winter hair was combed out and the weight of the blanket used depended on how much hair was taken off. In the West, many owners of show and performance horses still prefer the slower daily currying to clipping.

If you are going to clip your own horse, invest in a good electric clipper and try to get an "old hand" to help out the first time, because clipping a horse does require some skill.

The horse should be securely held by a helper, rather than tied up. Tying him might get him in the habit of pulling back on his halter rope if he is frightened the first time or two he feels the noisy thing on his hide. The hair must be dry. The horse can be clipped all over, legs and all. Or if he is a hunter, the legs can be left with the longer hair on for warmth and protection from brush. The custom of each locality and the type of use will dictate how the horse is clipped.

8

Feet and Shoeing

Since horses got along very well for a good many centuries without shoes it seems that most foot trouble is largely the result of the ways domesticated horses are used. The footing is often too hard and the weight of a rider puts an unnatural strain on the feet. Too much work starts irritations that lame the most vulnerable parts and may cause deposits of calcium that will aggravate the condition. Lack of exercise will allow tendons and tissues to weaken. Being forced to stand in his own manure and urine or on a dank ground contributes to foot ailments. A free horse on pasture never has to endure any of these damaging conditions. Grass and cured hay are the natural diet of a horse, so even the rich heavier diet of grains—fed to keep up strength for extra work—tends to interfere with nature's plan, causing extra pressure on the foot membranes due to excessive surges of blood.

A faulty structural conformation of the hoof, whether hereditary, from an injury, or man-made, can put painful strain on foot tendons. Horses whose hoofs have been purposely allowed to grow out to extreme lengths for show appearances are, in effect, cripples that would soon go lame if ridden—even moderately—for pleasure outside the show ring. Normally the hoof grows out about half an inch every month. Horses that run free in pasture without shoes wear the hoof off about as fast as it grows. But horses that are ridden must have shoes to reduce excessive wear on the horse's hoofs.

Shoes and Shoeing

Since ancient times, shoes of one kind or another have been nailed to horse's feet. Bronze, iron, steel, even silver for a few potentates, have all been used. Leather boots with bronze soles were used by postriders on the ancient stone-surfaced Roman roads. The Plains Indians sometimes laced leather boots on their horse's feet to protect them on long rides. But whatever kind they are, horseshoes are unnatural and they require muscle and body adjustments on the part of the horse.

Shoeing cavalry mounts was always given much serious attention in an effort to keep them ready for action at all times. General George Custer of Seventh Cavalry fame obtained a patent on a horseshoe improvement during the Civil War. The new feature was a corrugation in the bottom of the shoe whose edges would batter down and hold the nailhead more firmly. In 1870 he also got a patent on a toe calk. It is supposed that his father, Emmanuel Custer, who was a blacksmith, contributed a large part in these shoe improvements.

Every phase of horse foot care and shoeing requires much study and experience. Unless one has had competent instruction, even the trimming of the hoofs—which can affect the stance and balance—should be left to a skilled farrier. All mention of doctoring and horseshoeing in this book is of a general nature, aimed at giving the tyro horseman an understanding of the basic principles involved but with no intention of making a veterinarian or a farrier out of him in one easy lesson.

Should the pleasure rider wish to learn to diagnose foot trouble and trim and shoe his own horse, he should take a complete course to gain professional knowledge and skill. For years there has been a shortage of highly trained farriers, and although there are many horseshoeing schools springing up over the country, there are still not enough professionals in the business to keep ahead of the rapidly increasing horse population. In the new schools that are being established, girls and women along with ranchers, doctors, lawyers, schoolteachers, and about every variety of businessmen, have enrolled for horseshoeing courses so that they can assess the needs of their own horses. Even a few women have exchanged the housewife's pretty apron for the leather apron of the farrier and have entered the profession. To anyone who has ever started from scratch and put shoes on a horse, it is difficult to imagine a woman able to stand up to the heavy physical demands of the job. A horse is heavy, and he doesn't mind how hard he leans on you when his foot is in your lap. As for the scientific aspects involved in diagnosing and shaping shoes, there's no reason women couldn't be as effective in the profession as men.

In addition to the horseshoeing courses available in veterinary colleges and horse science schools, many of the state universities now offer them. There are also many privately owned farrier colleges. The tuition fees range from three hundred to six hundred dollars for short summer courses. In one six-week course in Oklahoma, the student works under expert

The farriers of the nation were never so busy or as well schooled. New schools are being established in every state.

supervision, Mondays through Saturdays, during which time he can expect to shoe as many as a hundred horses.

The word farrier, by the way, comes from Monsieur Farrier, the blacksmith who was in charge of shoeing horses for Louis II of France, a great-grandson of Charlemagne. An iron-working blacksmith and a farrier are synonymous terms for shoers of horses.

Horseshoes come from the manufacturers in many weights and sizes. The fit is sometimes so accurate, after the hoof has been rasped, that the shoe can be nailed on cold. But the preferred practice is to forge the shoe until cherry red and make precise adjustment by hammering the shoe and then setting it while hot—but not red hot—by placing it against the hoof and allowing it to burn itself into a snug fit. In fitting, the frog must not be impaired.

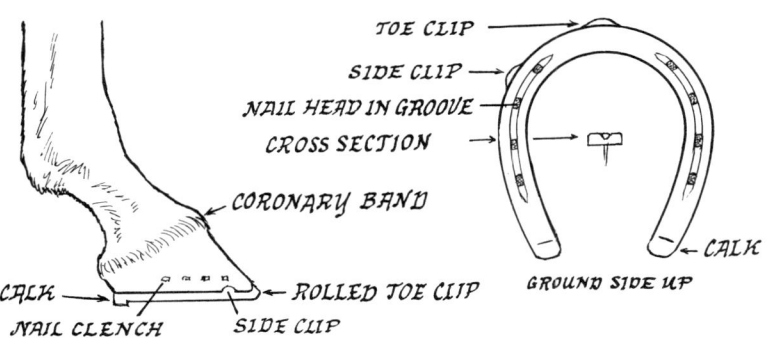

The parts of the foot and shoe.

Good care of a horse's feet begins with keeping them clean. Use a hoof pick before and after riding. This checkup will disclose any loose shoe nails, cracks, thrush, wounds on heels or fetlock joints, or dryness of the hoof walls. Don't ever rasp or scrape the outer wall of the hoof. The periople, its dense outer layer, is like a coat of varnish and is there to prevent the hoof from drying out. If dryness is pronounced, let the horse stand in some clean mud or even wrap his feet with moist burlap. Then apply a hoof dressing that will keep them from ever getting into that dried-out condition. Some horsemen use sweet oil or neat's-foot oil; others prefer patented formulas; and still others mix up their own formulas.

Veterinarians have hoof testers that give readings which can be helpful to the farrier. But more often the horse owner looks to the farrier rather than the veterinarian to deal with foot problems. Only he can produce, shape, and fit the metal that is needed for proper balance or to correct certain ailments or malfunctions, a discussion of some of the more common of which follows.

Navicular Disease and Shoeing

Two main tendons give articulation to the horse's foot: the extensor tendons run down the front of the cannon bone and attach to the front

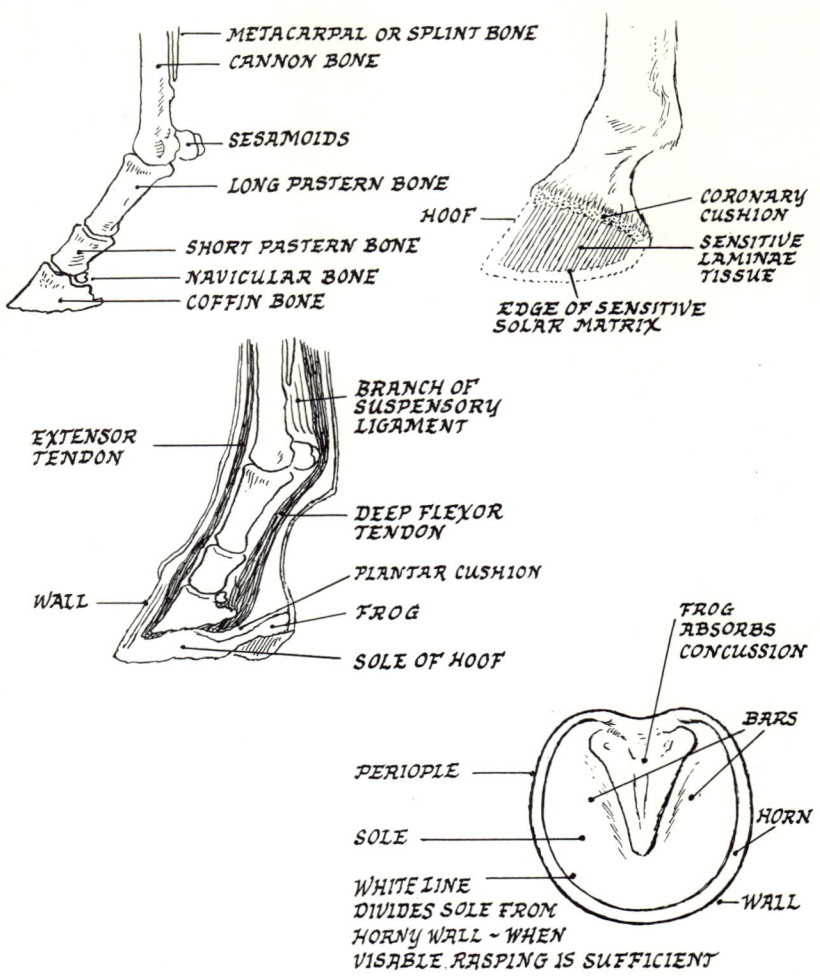

The structure of the horse's foot and ankle.

of the coffin bone, and the deep flexor tendons run down the back of the cannon bone and attach to the rear underside of the coffin bone. Just above the coffin bone at the rear of the short pastern bone is the small navicular bone. Over this slight bone—like an idler wheel for a pulley belt—the deep flexor tendon passes and slides. When it puts too much pressure on the navicular bone, the bone and its tissue become bruised, roughened, and inflamed. With the natural lubrication gone—as in bursitis—it is painful when the tendon moves over it. The condition is called navicular disease. The pain is increased when the frog of the foot pushes up and adds more pressure. To avoid the pain, the horse tries to get the weight off his heel and will try not to do things that require heel pressure, such as fast stopping. He will point the toe of his lame foot when standing and he may stumble often.

The causes of navicular disease can be prolonged concussion on hard roads, or great flexing of foot tendons while cutting, roping, or barrel racing, etc. Horses prone to the disease are those with feet that are small in proportion to their size, and horses that have steep pasterns.

The farrier, when convinced the lameness is caused by navicular disease, can bring relief to the horse by changing the angle of the hoof. He will shoe the horse so that he will stand up more on his toes, which will lessen the pressure of the deep flexor tendon on the navicular bone. To do this, he will prepare a shoe with a high wedge heel—a slipper heel—that is beveled and has a bar that joins the shoe heels at the back to protect the frog without touching it. The toe of the shoe is rolled so that it will not dig into the ground and cause stumbling. It also keeps a forward pressure off the nails. Shoes do not cure navicular disease, but they relieve the pain by relieving the pressure on the navicular bone, thus restoring better foot action.

Contracted Heels

Shoes that are too narrow at the heel or are left on too long can cause the heels to take the weight and prevent the frog from its normal blood-pumping action. The frog gets dry from lack of circulation. This condition can be alleviated by standing in water or mud or clay. Use hoof dressing frequently and have the horse fitted with proper shoes.

Corns

Pressure from a shoe that is too tight—as with people—can cause a corn to form, usually on the heels of the forefeet. Sometimes the growing hoof is impinged by a shoe that has been worn too long. The farrier pares away the corn and puts a shoe on that will relieve that part of the hoof of pressure. The lameness then disappears.

Founder and Laminitis

These terms are slightly confusing. It is foundering that brings on laminitis, which is an injury to the laminae tissue which laminates the outer layer, that is, the horny hoof, to the inner layer on whose nerves and circulation it is dependent. Underneath the laminae are the tissues that bind all to the coffin bone.

Grain founder is caused, some veterinarians say, by overeating high protein foods, such as soybeans and cottonseed cake, or concentrated carbohydrates in the form of corn or sweet feed. Another opinion (no doubt based on experience) is that it will occur more quickly if the horse has overeaten on wheat or barley. It is quite possible that what will founder one horse will leave another unaffected. Whatever the specific cause, the condition, digestively speaking, is called gastroenteritis. As previously mentioned, unlike the mule who always knows when he has had enough, a horse if given the opportunity will eat until he has foundered himself.

The overproduction of blood is pumped to the front feet in quantities that the veins are unable to carry back to the heart and lungs fast enough to keep the pressure of it from swelling and inflaming the laminae tissue. The hoof, unlike some other parts of the body, cannot expand to allow for the swelling. The sole is pushed down. The pain is intense. The horse tries to get the weight off the front feet, especially off the toe area. That is why he leans back on his halter rope with his feet far ahead and with weight on the heels, and with his hind feet as far forward under him as he can get them so they will take most of the weight. The feet will be hot to the touch (you can compare with hind feet), and the horse may frequently lie down, get up, and then lie down again.

Water founder has similar symptoms, but it is caused when a hot horse drinks a large amount of cold water. When a horse is overheated, the blood vessels expand to allow oxygen-purified blood to flow freely in order to carry off the waste of burned-up cells. The more violent the exercise, the more oxygen is needed to keep the tissue alive. When cold water suddenly cools the body, the blood vessels quickly contract, constricting the blood flow. The sensitive laminae tissue is deprived of oxygen

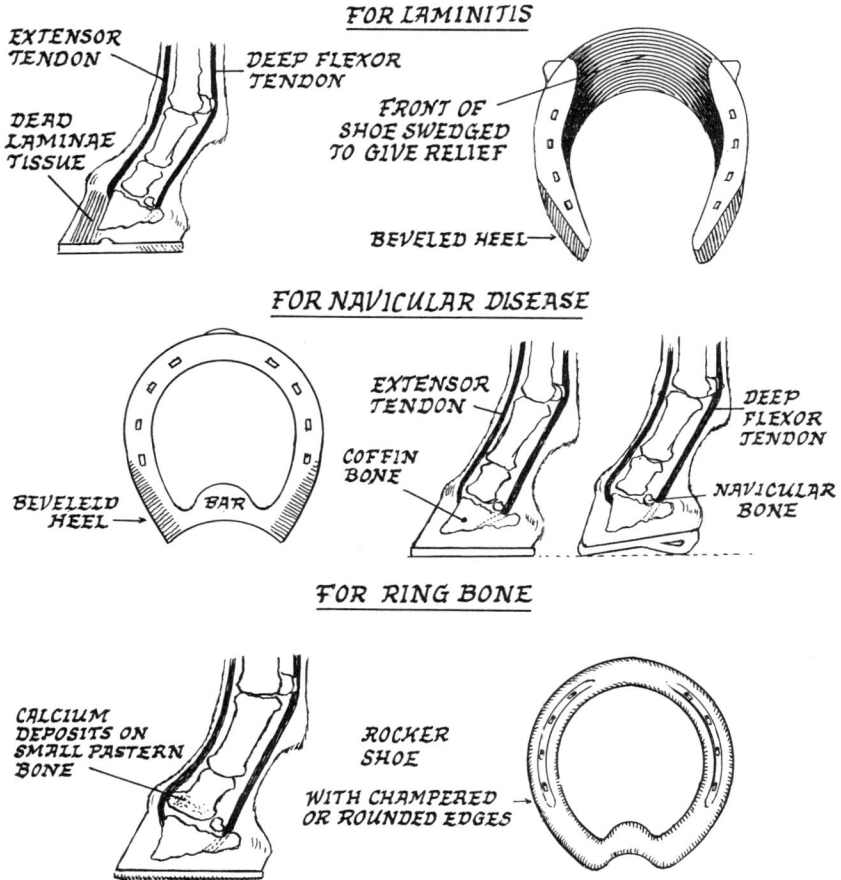

Three examples of special shoes used to correct or alleviate the discomfort of malfunction.

For *laminitis*, the reduced bearing surface of the shoe puts the weight farther back on the lowered heel. Large side clips are needed to hold shoe firmly, since the nails are farther back on the hoof away from the injured laminae tissue.

Shoes for the horses with *navicular disease* set the foot more on the toe. This change of angle reduces the pressure of the deep flexor on the navicular bone. The bar keeps the shoe from spreading.

The calcium deposits of *ringbone*—on the small pastern bone—lacerate the extensor tendon and its sheath with each movement of the coffin bone. A rocker shoe allows the foot to rock from heel to toe in a somewhat normal manner without the need of pronounced movement between the coffin bone and the small pastern bone.

and cells die, blocking the veins. This condition causes inflammation and swelling, and the pain builds up.

Road founder causes inflammation of the laminae from working the horse too many miles at too fast a gait, and perhaps on a road that is too hard. It differs greatly from the two other kinds of founder and may not be founder at all but rather a severe soreness in the feet and legs and shoulders. The laminae of course will be sore and inflamed. It is not necessarily a case for the farrier. Rest will usually clear it up in a week or so.

For laminitis caused by grain and water founder, the farrier can be of great help. The problem is to relieve the pressure where it affects the laminae tissue, in the front of the foot. To do this, a shoe is made that takes most of the weight on the side of the hoof and the heels. Side clips tie the shoe to the side of the hoof, the nails are farther back than usual, and the heels are beveled. The shoe is wedged down (see drawing) and the toe is sloped off so that little weight is put on it.

There are degrees of injury to the laminae tissue. If it is a mild case the recovery can be complete. Even moderately severe cases if treated within twenty-four to thirty-six hours have a good chance of recovery. If severe, the horse may never again move in a free manner due to the soles of the feet having dropped.

First Aid. If you happen to know that the horse has had too much feed or too much water when hot, though lameness has not yet appeared, the horse should be kept moving. This exercise may keep the capillaries and veins functioning so that the excessive blood is kept circulating. You may have noticed that on guest ranches, where horses are often given a pretty good workout, there is a tank or stream a half mile or so away from the barn where the horses are allowed to drink on the way in. This arrangement keeps them moving for a while after drinking before they can stand still in a barn.

Treatment nearly always includes cold packs or mud packs or standing the horse in cold water. But not all veterinarians agree on what is the most effective. Some give antihistamines to combat the allergy, cortisones to reduce inflammation, and purgatives to remove toxins in the digestive tract. One treatment recommended by a veterinarian is to withdraw a half pint of blood from the horse's jugular vein, add to it a solution to prevent clotting, and inject this blood slowly in both sides of the neck and in the chest muscles and massage vigorously for three or four minutes. The best procedure is to have your veterinarian estimate the extent of the injury and decide what to administer.

Seedy Toe

Old blood clots from injured laminae may grow down and separate the sole from the outside wall. This may also be caused by shoes that put too much weight on the wall of the hoof or by toe clips that have been hammered back too tightly. It is seen as a white line, or even a cavity, when the shoe is removed. When tapped with the hammer, the hoof gives out a hollow sound. Dirt forced into the separation puts pressure on the sensitive laminae matrix.

To induce healthy hoof growth, some farriers cut two grooves in the center of the hoof about an inch apart and running up to within an inch of the coronary band. These grooves are about one fourth of an inch wide and are shallow so as not to reinjure the laminae. Underneath the foot the grooves continue and converge at the point of the frog. The theory is that the grooves weaken the wall and allow for expansion and better circulation which, along with frequent trimming, will induce a healthy hoof growth.

Ringbone

There are several kinds of ringbone—high, low, incomplete, and the complete ringbone that circles the low pastern bone. It is a bony or osseous deposit about three-quarters of an inch above the coronary band and about the size of one's little finger. It is a nonmalignant tumor of the bone.

Concussions on hard roads, feet that are allowed to get out of balance, improper rasping and shoeing, blows or wounds, faulty nutrition, and, some say, a hereditary tendency are the causes. Calcium builds up and if it continues to collect until it circles the bone it is true ringbone. Lameness is evident. Your veterinarian may advise using the firing iron on an incomplete case, but if the ankle has become ossified and rigid, firing is too dangerous in that tendons and veins might be damaged. When in this advanced condition, the horse will stand with a forefoot on the heel and the ankle rigid. If the ringbone is on a hind foot, the toe will rest on the ground with the ankle rigid.

If the deposit is in front of the pastern, a shoe that puts the weight on the heel can relieve the condition. If the ringbone is affecting the rear and sides of the pastern, a shoe that puts the weight more on the toe is advised. If the ringbone is complete and stiffens the ankle, some farriers will try and give the foot some of the rocking motion it has lost, by making the bottom surface of the shoe rock from front to back. The shoe is thicker across the center and lower at the toe and heels.

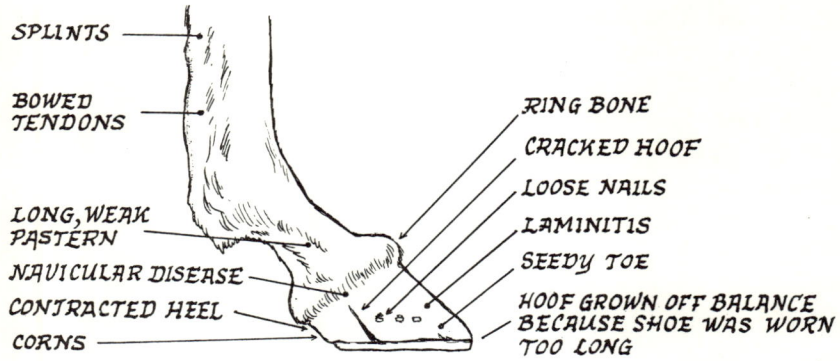

If a horse had a leg and foot like this one, he'd have about everything wrong. The point of the diagram is to show the location of each critical area.

Faults of Movement

Forging. After becoming the owner of a horse you will find a good many odd words getting into your vocabulary. Words like forging, interfering, scalping, clacking, crossfiring, overreaching, paddling, winging, speed cutting, and brushing. All of these terms have to do with the foot action of the horse and mean that the feet move asymmetrically or unrhythmically and even strike each other during movement.

Forging, the word used by most farriers (clacking and overreaching are synonymous), is caused when the front foot leaves the ground a trifle too late and gets hit by the oncoming rear foot. The reasons for it can be many, but among them are: improper shoeing, too much weight on the horse, fatigue due to poor condition, and hoofs that are grown out too long (for high action).

To correct it by shoeing presents the problem of speeding up the front feet and slowing down the hind feet. This is done by changing the angle

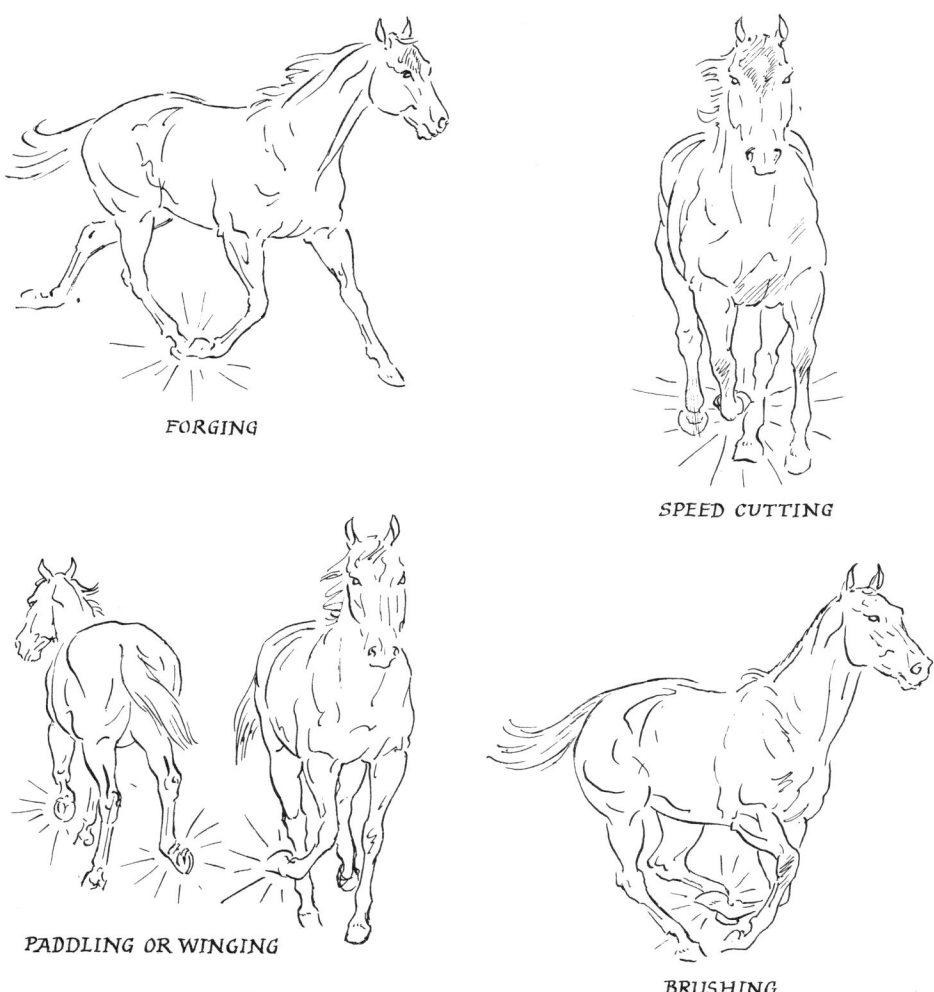

FORGING

SPEED CUTTING

PADDLING OR WINGING

BRUSHING

of the hoofs. A hoof protractor will determine just what the angle should be. The angle that stands the horse more on his toes speeds the breakover, that is, the moment the hoof leaves the ground. The angle that stands the horse more on the heels slows the breakover. Forging boots are sometimes used to protect the horse until proper shoes can correct the tendency.

Speed Cutting, Scalping, and Crossfiring are most often seen in fast trotters when the diagonal feet bruise or cut the pasterns. It calls for boots for protection and reshoeing for correction.

Brushing and interfering occur when a leg or fetlock joint gets hit by the opposite foot. Here again boots can be used until the condition is corrected by shoeing.

Paddling or winging is generally the result of pigeon toes, or toeing-in.

Toeing-In causes the foot to break over and leave the ground on the outside of the foot, describing an outward arc instead of moving as it should in line with the forward movement of the body. This paddling or winging action can be a fault on one or all four feet and is more noticeable at a trot or rack. A competent farrier can do much to correct this deficient way of traveling. Each horse presents his own problem, but in many cases a lateral extension on the outside of the shoe with a low calk on the outside heel, and no calk on the inside heel, will be beneficial. When the foot hits the ground the heel hits first. The calk will tend to turn the foot to the outside. And the extension will cause the foot to break over in the center. Shoes of this kind may get the leg muscles and the foot accustomed to a normal action and in time make extreme or even special shoes unnecessary.

Cracked Hoof

Although a hoof looks unyielding it really expands when weight is put on it and, of course, contracts when relieved of the weight. This action, together with the pumping action of the frog, draws and expels an abundant supply of blood to and from the foot. If a crack develops in a hoof, the expansion will take place where there is the least resistance, at the crack, and tend to make it wider. If not attended to, the crack may split on up to the coronary band where the hoof meets the hairline.

One of the ways to prevent the split from getting wider is to have a shoe put on that has a bar across the back. This prevents most of the expansion when weight is put on the foot. If the crack is a bad one—up to one fourth of an inch wide—a fitted iron cleat can be screwed to both sides of the break to hold it until new growth heals it. The crack is packed with cotton saturated with iodine and a hole in the cleat near the top will allow for more iodine to be squirted in. Clips on both sides of the crack will add extra strength to keep the crack from widening.

Shoes for Performance Horses

Not only reining horses but all horses that are called upon to perform abrupt footwork should have shoes that assist them. Most farriers will agree that quick, fast, muscular horses—and that describes so many Quarter Horses—need more help from shoes than do lighter, slower-moving ones. A reining horse or cutting horse or barrel-racing horse is shod quite differently than a less active horse while still using what would be called standard horseshoes. The proper shoes for your horse are something to be discussed with your farrier. There are many kinds of shoes of different weights, each for the purpose of giving a specific aid. Polo shoes are full swedged. That is, they are slanted on both sides, leaving only a sharp bearing edge. They give good traction no matter what the direction of take-off. Some shoes have rolled toes and some have toe grabs. Sliding plates which cover the underside of the rear feet and many kinds of sliding shoes with extended heel calks are not allowed

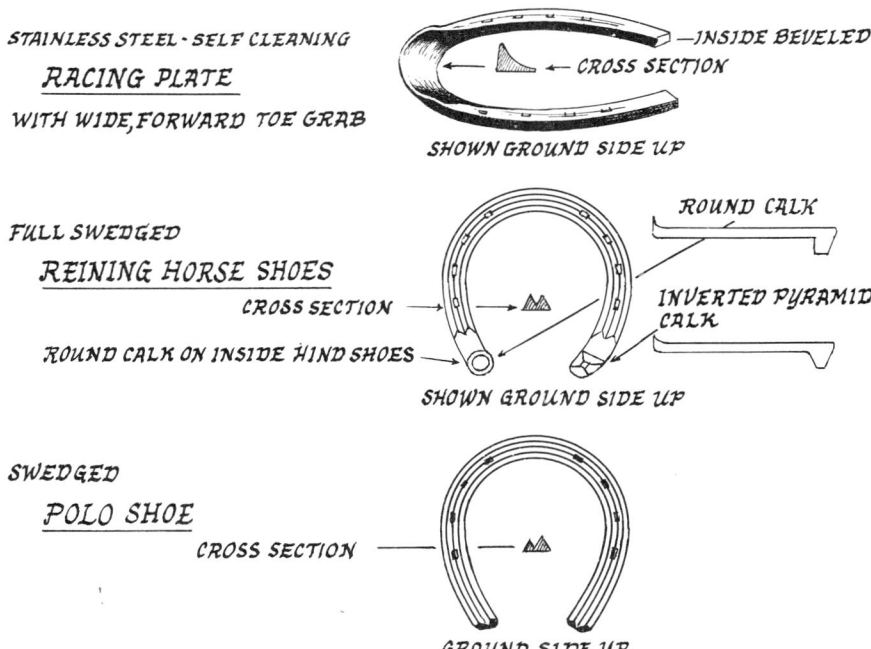

Three examples of special shoes in use for performance horses.

in most shows. For sliding stops, the long heels with calks once used put extreme strain on the ankles when the calks hung in the ground and especially when the horse rolled over his hocks. Some shoes made for rolling back over the hocks and permitted by judges have a round calk on the outside heel to serve as a pivot while an inverted pyramid calk on the inside heel slides easily. For racing there are training plates made of thin aluminum. Some have no calks or toe grabs. And there are racing shoes that have toe grabs set far forward. Self-cleaning shoes are slanted inward with no perpendicular surface to which mud can cling. Experiments in shoeing continue and what is popular today may give way to an entirely different development tomorrow.

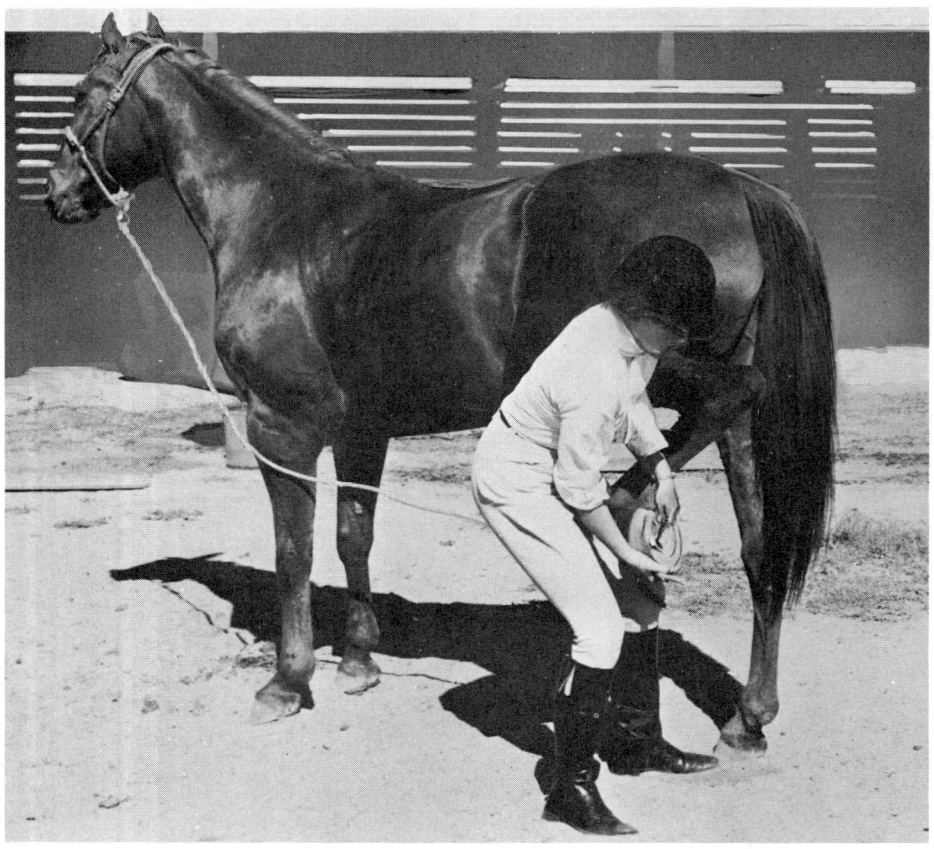

A few minutes of attention to your horse's feet before and after riding is a very worth-while habit to establish. *Photo by the author.*

While it is true most of the horse's foot problems will have to be put, literally, into the lap of the farrier, there are still many things you can do to keep your horse's feet in good condition even if you're a novice:

Clean out soles and cleft between frog and bars frequently.
Exercise whenever possible on dry ground.
Begin foot care in colthood. It will make shoeing and handling later much easier.
Trim only the ragged excess from the frog.
Do not pare out the sole, just clean it.
Never rasp the outside wall of the hoof.

For the horseman who has had some instruction in hoof care:

Use nippers to trim off the horn of unshod horses.
Keep feet well rounded if unshod.
Always rasp in such a manner that the heel is included in each stroke.

Hoofs grow out about a half inch every month, depending on age and conditions, so shoes should be changed every four to six weeks. Even if the horse is going barefooted the hoofs should be trimmed every four weeks, since normal growth will cause the walls to wear off unevenly or break off, making a later shoeing job more difficult. If a shoe is left on too long, the horse's base, where he naturally distributes his weight, grows out from under him, putting a strain on tendons and muscles. Shoes that are worn too long also invite casting, and worn, thin shoes may bend out of shape and be damaging. The friction of nails on slightly loose shoes can enlarge the holes in the hoof wall and become pockets for infection.

Some horses may be easily shod on three feet and yet be unmanageable with the fourth. Lift and handle all four feet each time the horse is groomed. He must be taught to be at ease all over.

9

Ailments, Their Symptoms, Causes, and Treatment

The novice should know something about the more obvious things that can affect the horse's health and bodily well being. As mentioned elsewhere in these pages, there is no intention to encourage the amateur horseman to go beyond his knowledge or ability when it comes to doctoring his horse. But first-aid is another thing. Everyone who handles horses should have some general knowledge that will enable him to do some good in an emergency and to recognize certain symptoms that are warnings of some kind of malfunction or disease. Moreover there are times when it will be impossible to get a veterinarian. Those are the times a horse owner wishes he knew how to do something. It is the custom to poke fun at and ridicule the do-it-yourselfers. But they are the ones who go right on making automatic horse feeders out of old corn planters, and the ones who usually know how and what to do until the veterinarian gets there. On the other hand, we've all seen people who couldn't pour sand out of a boot, even with the directions printed on the heel. They are the ones a Eugene Manlove Rhodes character was addressing when he said: "Keep away from that wheelbarrow, what the hell do you know about machinery?"

The following pages deal with some of the common ailments and injuries the horseman might have to cope with in some way, if only to keep the horse quiet until the veterinarian arrives. But try not to think of horses as being as delicate and illness-prone as they may seem to appear when reading about their ailments. Many people who have been around horses all their lives have had to contend with only a very few of the many things that can happen to a horse.

After learning something about the physical characteristics of horses

When a horse is sick, he should be covered and kept warm until the veterinarian arrives.

generally and getting to know your own horse and his mannerisms and habits, you will be the logical one to notice any deviation from the norm, any hint of injury, sickness, or malfunction. Don't panic and call the veterinarian for inconsequential things.

Veterinarian schools have made great advances in the past twenty or thirty years. The basic sciences and extensive research they have furthered are comparable with that of other medical schools. The men in this field are very capable, and the ones I have met are genuinely interested in and fond of animals. Unfortunately, there are not enough of them to go around in some districts where horses have greatly increased in numbers. In a real emergency when the veterinarian cannot be reached, the chances are your family doctor will honor your appeal with helpful advice, if not with an actual house call.

While waiting for a veterinarian, do the things that will help him get right to work as soon as he arrives. Have the horse in a clean box stall, or at least in a convenient sheltered place, and have soap and warm water and towels ready. Tell the veterinarian what you have observed and give him all the facts you can.

The normal healthy horse has a resting pulse of:

70–90 beats per minute from birth to 4 weeks.
60–71 beats per minute when 6 months old.
50–68 beats per minute when a yearling.
36–57 beats per minute when mature.

The pulse is easily checked on the side of the neck by the throat or on the artery that comes over the jawbone and is prominent on the side of the face.

The average respiration rate, easily checked by holding the hand on the flank or just watching it, is twelve to thirteen per minute. Exercise, excitement, hot weather, and poor ventilation will of course increase it.

The bowels move four to eight times a day and should be neither too loose nor too dry and hard and should be free from mucus and pronounced odor. Eyes are moist, brilliant, and alertly open. The appetite is good. The mucous membranes in eyes, mouth, and nostrils are a healthy pink color. The coat is sleek and lies smooth and the stance is a balanced one on all four feet. The skin is supple and neither dry nor excessively moist. The urine is light yellow in color and is eliminated five or more times a day in quantities of five to seven quarts a day, depending of course on the size of the horse. The average normal temperature is 99.5 to 101 degrees F., and anything over 103 is considered fever. The only accurate way of taking the temperature is with an equine rectal thermometer. It should be lubricated and inserted full length. There is a place to attach a string to keep it from getting lost in the rectum.

When to Call the Veterinarian

When body temperature is over 103 degrees F., fever is present, and a reading of 105 or 106 means there is serious infection.

When there are indications of worms, colic, impaction, founder, or where there are deep punctures or wounds that require suturing. If wounds are sutured soon enough and pressure packs applied over the stitches, they will usually heal without leaving unsightly scars. If treatment is delayed, the wounds may form proud flesh and may result in lameness.

When any symptom of serious disease or abnormality appears, call a veterinarian.

First Aid for Injuries

If possible get the horse in a comfortable place sheltered from sun or weather. Clean and medicate minor wounds.

To staunch bleeding of a wound, first get the horse in the best position to control him with the least excitement. Flood water on the wound to

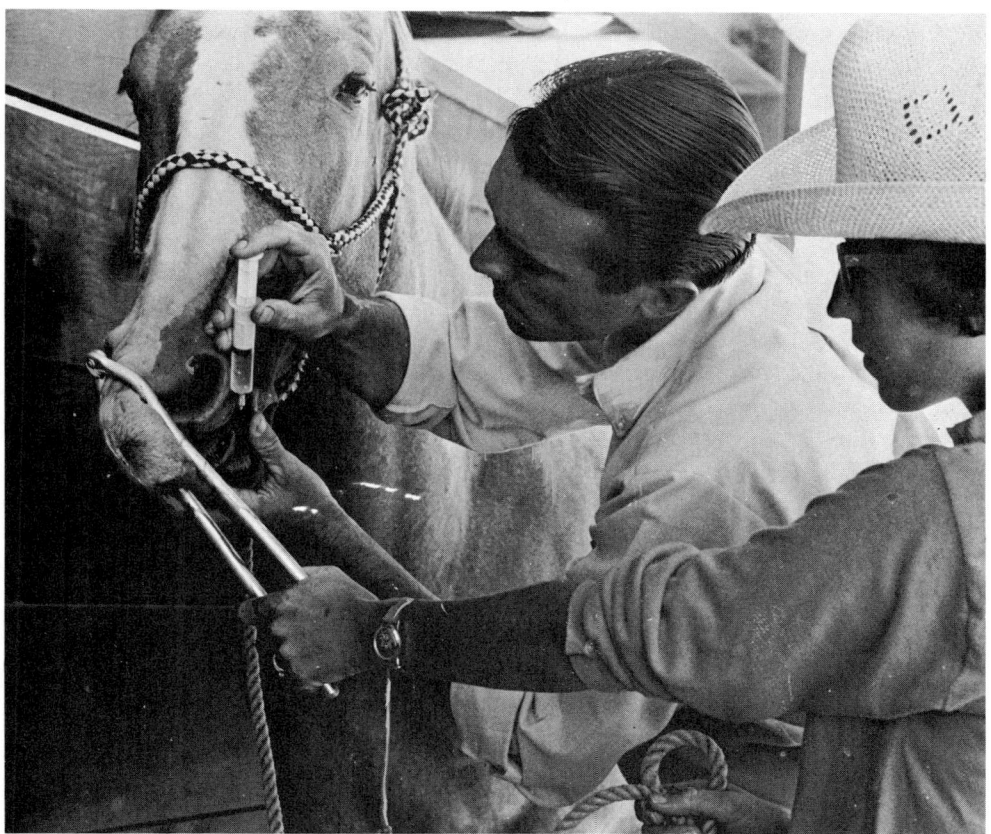

Clay M. Posey, D.V.M., preparing lip of young mare for suturing. Marcia Paxson of the Don-Mar Ranch, Paradise Valley, Arizona, is shown holding the nose clamp. *Photo by Irene Laune.*

get the dirt off and press the cleanest cloth you have at hand firmly over the wound. If the dressing becomes saturated with blood, lay more dressing over it and continue pressure. If direct pressure does not stop the bleeding and blood comes in spurts, an artery is indicated. Try shutting off circulation in the artery by pressing with the hand. If this is successful, apply a tourniquet above the wound. Cloth or something soft and strong and a little bulky tied around and then twisted with a stick will serve. A necktie will do, but if stockings are used they should be padded underneath to keep them from cutting into the skin. To avoid gangrene, the tourniquet must be released every fifteen minutes. Arterial bleeding calls for professional help—the sooner the better.

If a wound is gaping open it should be sewed up. If a veterinarian cannot be reached, and you feel up to it, do it yourself. If you can give a muscular injection of a tranquilizer, do so. Sparine in quantities of 5 to 10 cc. is still much in use. Acepromazine, a newer drug also injected into the muscle in the amount of 2 to 5 cc., is now preferred by many veterinarians. Veinous injections should never be attempted by anyone except a veterinarian. If time allows, the safest of all tranquilizers are granules given orally in the feed. There are several sold under proprietary brand names on the market. The quieting effect is noticeable in about an hour.

Before suturing, sterilize needle and thread, wash hands thoroughly, and, if available, wear sterilized gloves. Leave about one-half to three-quarters of an inch between the edges of the wound and the place the needle enters, so that the stitches will not pull out. Do not pull stitches very tight. Allowance must be made for swelling.

Once when we were unable to get a veterinarian my father and I sewed up a cut about eight inches long and an inch deep on the chest of a good saddle horse. Using what we had at hand—darning needles and heavy cotton thread dipped in an antiseptic—we did the job after throwing the horse with soft ropes in deep bedding in a box stall. The wound healed up rather quickly, but the scar was much more noticeable than it might have been had a veterinarian performed the operation.

Digestive Ailments

>Azoturia
>Colic
>Founder (see Chapter 8)
>Impaction

Azoturia (myohemoglobinuria, if you want to try and pronounce it and startle your veterinarian) is a sudden temporary paralysis of a horse's hind legs during exercise. It is caused, say authorities, by an excessive buildup of lactic acid, necessary for the chemical change of food into body energy, in the muscles. It has been commonly called "Monday morning sickness" and occurs because the horse has had too much grain proteins, not enough vitamins and minerals, and not enough—or consistent—exercise. It seldom attacks horses under four years of age and never horses out at pasture.

Besides restricted movements of the hind legs, stiffness, and trembling, heavy sweating will usually be noticed. The urine is often dark and thick. In fact an old name for the ailment was "black water." Although it is more of a chemical change than a digestive disorder, the symptoms are very much like those of colic.

Stop the horse immediately. Sweating is desired, but if under a hot sun, move him slowly to a shady place if he can walk. If the horse does not sweat profusely, put blankets drenched in warm water over him and cover with a dry blanket to induce it. In cold weather use the dry blanket only to bring on sweating. Keep the horse as quiet as you can. Call a veterinarian. Mild cases clear up in a few days if aided with a reduced diet of grain and a more laxative food such as alfalfa hay. After a few days of rest the amount of exercise should be gradually increased.

Colic. Colic is a form of indigestion, a disorder of the intestines often accompanied by impaction, and there are several variations of it. Because the horse shows great distress it is sometimes hard to diagnose correctly. Twisted gut has been mistaken for it. Colic can be caused by eating bedding or moldy hay, wind sucking, bad molar teeth that fail to masticate food properly, lack of exercise, or overeating or overdrinking, especially when tired. Remember, a horse can't vomit. Symptoms are a sudden lack of appetite, restlessness, an expression of anxiety, and general discomfort. The horse will lie down and then get up stretching and yawning as though trying to gag. As pressure builds up in the intestines, the pain increases. Then he may groan and stomp, paw, swing his head around and look at his side. He may even cow-kick at his belly or throw himself down abruptly, then get up and do it again.

Treatment must be prompt. Until the veterinarian arrives, keep the horse on his feet, leading him about slowly; do not ride him. Blanket his back and loins. Blood has rushed to the abdomen, leaving circulation in other areas insufficient. Do not drench a colicky horse. Do not feed or water. An enema will relieve the pain, if there is someone sufficiently experienced to administer it (see methods of treatment).

A well-bedded box stall should be prepared for the horse that can't be kept on his feet. Stay with him. Try and keep him quiet. Rub him all over with a cloth, talk to him to soothe him mentally.

Founder. See Chapter 8.

Impaction in the large colon means that food or feces have been tightly packed there and, owing to the absence of muscular function in the intestinal wall, cannot be dislodged. It occurs in most cases of colic. It can also be accompanied by gas from fermentation which inflates the stomach.

It can be caused by green apples, overripe grass, overeating, frosted hay, or violent exercise on a full stomach. In general the symptoms are the same as with colic, with perhaps more lassitude and head-drooping resignation. An enema is helpful. Call a veterinarian.

Eye Injuries and Disease

An injury to the eye should be cleaned by flooding it with a solution of boric acid or one of the many eyewash preparations. Afterward cover with a warm moist towel.

The way to put the liquid in the eye is to saturate a small piece of cotton wool with the solution and hold it above the eye touching the lid. A slight squeeze and the liquid will run down into the eye. An eyedropper is not used because it might jab the eye if the horse made a sudden jerk.

Eye injuries can be from cactus, thistles, wheat beard, or lacerations in the region of the eye. If the eyeball is punctured and the water runs out, the sight is gone forever. Put the horse in a darkened stall, call a veterinarian who will administer a local anesthetic, and then try and locate the cause.

Moon Blindness, or periodic ophthalmia, is a forewarning of an infection called leptospirosis and is an inflammation of the inner eye. Its cause is only vaguely known but is thought to be a deficiency of riboflavin.

The eyes become inflamed and tearful. Sometimes pus can be detected in the fluid inside the eyeball. The veterinarian may inject antibiotics and later use ointments to dilate and constrict the pupil of the eye. Because it is periodic, getting better then worse, the ancients thought the ailment was affected by various phases of the moon, hence the name.

Injuries—Abrasions, Cuts, Lacerations, Punctures, and Bruises

Clean and wash the wound with water, dry it, and apply a wound spray, blue ointment, sulfa or other healing powder. If the wound is a deep puncture, the danger of tetanus is increased and a tetanus booster shot may be advised.

Once when my Old Red cut his head badly while trying to get under a fence that crossed a gully, I found him with blood all over his face and dripping from his nose. After washing the wound I saw it was not quite as bad as I had feared. Using what was at hand in the barn cabinet, I poured an envelope of sulfa powder in the wound. The speed with which it healed amazed me.

If the injury is in the foot from a horseshoe nail that was driven too deep or too close to the laminae tissue, the horse will go lame a day or two after being shod. So if lameness develops a few days after being shod look in that area to find the cause. If caused by a horseshoe nail, the shoe and nail must be removed and the wound treated. The horse must be given a rest and then fitted with a special shoe that relieves pressure from the sore spot.

Wounds below the knee and hock, which were once generally bandaged to keep them clean and to keep off the flies, are now treated mostly with wound sprays and left open to the air. If bleeding is excessive apply a pressure bandage directly to the wound. Use clean bandage and enough cotton padding under it to allow for circulation (see first-aid). Oily greasy preparations for cuts, lacerations, abrasions, rope burns, etc., are avoided because they collect dirt, can induce the growth of proud flesh, and may delay scabbing and healing.

A bruise that does not break the skin is usually noticed by the swelling that results. Cold water from a hose or cold packs will reduce the swelling (see methods of treatment). A day later, if the swelling is down, a hot poultice will speed healing. If the bruising blow is noticed at the time it happens, massaging, if done instantly and vigorously, is helpful. It works well for humans also. The next time you hit your finger with a hammer or get your hand pinched in a door, regardless of how much it may hurt to do it, massage it energetically right after it happens and the chances are the finger will not even turn blue.

Capped Elbows, Fistulas, Galls, Setfast, And Tumors

Capped Elbow or Shoe Boil is a blemishing swelling caused by the horse's foot—or the shoe that is on it—repeatedly bruising the point of the elbow when the horse is lying down. The swelling gets large and firm and contains a watery serum. It is not pus and should not be lanced. It is like a sweat blister on the palm of the hand.

A veterinarian may inject a solution that will dissolve the fibrous tissue. Afterwards a daily rub with liniment will keep the tissue healthy.

Galls are the type of abrasions from repeated rubbing that should never have been allowed to develop into real skin sores in the first place. They are caused by lack of grooming, cinches that are dirty, dried out and rough, or cinched too tightly, or all of these things combined. A horse with a sensitive skin should be washed after every ride with a solution of salt water or an astringent to toughen the skin and keep it clean and healthy.

Setfast is a gall or sore over the loins caused by the pounding of the saddle seat. It can become as persistent and painful as a boil. The very fact that it developed at all indicates an indifferent rider and a heartless one for riding the horse after the back was first galled. A horse should not be ridden until a cinch or back gall is completely healed.

Mutilation of horses by cutting the strong flexor muscles on each side of the tail and setting the tail in stocks until the wound heals is a practice that so arouses the ire of most horse lovers that they got legislation against it passed in many of the United States in the early 1930s and in England in 1949. According to Francis H. Rowley, president of the Massachusetts Society for the Prevention of Cruelty to Animals, the English have respected the law and since it was passed no "set-tail" horses have been exhibited. In this country, on the other hand, certain exhibitors continue to flout public opinion, abetted by show officials, by showing set-tail horses. Under pressure from this group the courts ruled that a tail-set horse may be shown in a state where tail setting is illegal as long as the operation was performed in a state where it wasn't illegal. The tail-set operation so restricts the horse's use of his tail that he is made quite vulnerable to flies and the raw underarea of the tail being exposed is more likely to chap in cold weather or blister under a hot sun. Some tail wounds are slow to heal properly and some leave unsightly scars. Quarter Horses are never subjected to tail setting.

Fistulas And Tumors

Fistulas are deep-seated abscesses that are caused by an accidental blow or by repeated bruises, and usually occur on the poll, withers,

AILMENTS, SYMPTOMS, TREATMENT

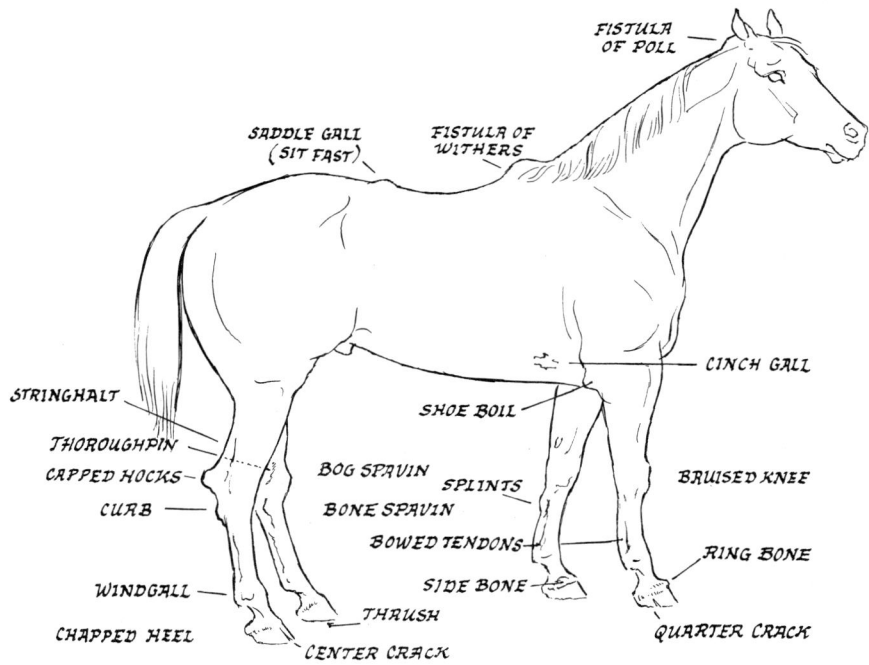

The horse that has everything! These are the well-known ailments some horses suffer—but, thankfully, seldom simultaneously.

or shoulders. After soreness and swelling a fistula may come to a head and discharge pus. Lancing, injections, and surgery are sometimes resorted to. Vaccines, blood toxins, and free drainage of the pus are the accepted treatments. A grease should be put on the skin below the wound where the pus drains to keep the hair from coming out.

Tumors are of many different kinds ranging from small harmless warts to large growths. A tumor can be benign (curable) or malignant (cancerous and generally incurable). The cause of tumors is unknown. Any abnormal growth should be called to the attention of a veterinarian. Appearance can be deceptive. I have seen large, ugly, tumorlike growths that developed on the hind legs of horses that had been wire cut, which healed quickly after surgery and treatment by a veterinarian.

Contagious and Infectious Diseases

Strangles (Distemper) and Glanders
Encephalomyelitis (Sleeping Sickness)
Swamp Fever (Malaria)
Tetanus
Equine Influenza—see Lungs

Strangles (Distemper) and Glanders were once dread diseases, but, thanks to rigid government control and modern medicines, have been practically stamped out. Should either be encountered the veterinarian will report it immediately to the local U.S. agricultural agent.

Strangles inflames the mucous membranes of the nose and causes abscesses to form in the lymph glands. Some even break through the skin to ooze a yellow serum. The nasal discharge is profuse. Temperature may rise to 106° F.

Glanders is mentioned because it is a disease of horses that became well set in the minds of the public, although it last reached epidemic proportions in the British cavalry during the Boer War. It is a disease that generally attacked horses that were confined in large numbers to a limited area.

The symptoms are somewhat the same as in strangles, with the exception that the glands under the lower jaw are the ones most affected. Penicillin, terramycin, and aureomycin are most effective in controlling these two diseases.

Encephalomyelitis (Sleeping Sickness) is an inflammation of the nerve tissue in both the brain and spinal cord. The dominant symptoms are disturbance of consciousness, uncontrolled movements, and paralysis. It is transmitted by mosquito bites. Horses themselves do not carry the disease.

Although this disease is still prevalent, it is well controlled by the injection of vaccines. Several medical companies sell disposable syringes containing 2 cc. of vaccine for the horse owner to inject; however, most owners rely on the expertise of a veterinarian. The injection is intradermal and repeated at a different site a week or ten days later. Equine encephalomyelitis has long been known in Europe and was first identified in this country in Kansas in 1919. By 1929 it was in California and shortly after in the Eastern United States and Canada. Two strains were identified as Eastern and Western.

Then in 1969 a third most virulent strain spread rapidly in South America and was called Venezuela equine encephalomyelitis, or VEE. Moving into Central America, the disease then invaded Mexico in epidemic proportions in 1970. In October 1970 the American Horse Council of Washington, D.C., warned the general public about VEE, and in February 1971 the Texas Agriculture Extension Service warned all county agents that VEE was moving relentlessly toward the Rio Grande. Congress approved a one-million-dollar expenditure to control the disease. By the end of June there were reports of horses having been attacked by VEE north of the Rio Grande in southeast Texas. On June 25 VEE vaccine was released by the U. S. Department of Agriculture for use in the Rio Grande Valley. By August most horses in the Southwest—an estimated million and one half—had been vaccinated. In most cases it was free of cost to the owners. It is estimated that about 1500 horses died of VEE in Texas and that Mexico suffered a loss of 10,000 horses from the disease in 1970 and 1971.

Swamp Fever (Malaria) is an infectious equine anemia (septicemia). It is a summer disease associated with the drinking of water from pools where vegetation is rank. It is also transmitted by the mosquito. As difficult as it is to diagnose, the symptoms being so similar to those of other disorders—stiffness, weakness, lameness, high fever, and loss of appetite—the antibiotics now available to the veterinarian are generally successful in combatting it. And insect-killing sprays and spray paints in stables have greatly diminished the chances of the rare mosquito that carries the disease ever landing on a horse.

Tetanus is caused by the puncture of a rusty nail or other object only when the nail or object happens to bring with it the specific microbe called the tetanus bacillus *(Clostridium tetani)*. The deeper into the body the microbe gets, the more serious, because the bacilli grow better without oxygen. It can bring on lockjaw with symptoms something like those of rabies and is often fatal. The tetanus bacillus produces a toxin that is the most powerful of known poisons. What it causes is a continuous spasm of the muscles. Unfortunately a wound may heal before the onset of an attack warns of its existence, which is the reason for systematic immunization with tetanus toxoid and annual booster shots.

Internal Parasites

Some pessimists estimate that nine out of ten horses have had or do have worms. The condition is sufficiently prevalent to cause hundreds of laboratories to seek formulas for killing and controlling the estimated fifty different kinds of worm parasites.

The symptoms of worms are a dull coat, poor condition, lassitude, and loss of flesh. Horses that are subject to repeated attacks of colic are almost certainly being debilitated by bloodworms.

The most deadly of worms are the *strongyles,* which vary from one half to one and a half inches long and of which there are about forty varieties. The worst of the lot is *strongylus vulgaris,* called the bloodworm. They develop in the blood vessels and when mature live in the digestive tract. Eggs by the milions can be passed by a single horse in a day, making it possible for horses to infect and reinfect themselves on contaminated pasture land.

Bots are really flies instead of worms. They look like sluggish bees, and they are just as busy when they go about depositing their eggs on the hairs of horse's forelegs, and occasionally on the hairs of flanks and hind legs. A horse will stamp and paw and try to keep the pests off, but it is when he nips or licks his legs that the larvae get in his mouth and hence to his stomach. There they attach themselves and live on the poor horse until the following late spring, when they release their hold and pass out with the droppings. In the manure they are metamorphosed into bot flies to start the vicious cycle all over again.

To keep the infection to a minimum, scrape the eggs off the hair with a knife blade or wash off with hot water or even kerosene. The latter will serve to keep the horse from licking his legs. But to destroy the eggs inside the animal, the veterinarian will have to administer medicine of his choosing. Carbon disulfide is sometimes used. The most frightening of the worms are the ascarids, which live in the small intestines and can be numerous. The eggs are deposited on the ground with the manure and are picked up by a grazing horse. They are more usual in a young horse. The largest ascarids may reach a length of twelve inches, but the majority of them are about one-half inch long. Strangely, even with the large worms, they are less destructive to the horse's health than the much harder to detect smaller strongyles. It is the oxyurid worm that so irritates the anus of the horse, causing him frantically to rub his tail.

Some preparations are effective only against one or two types of worms. Some manufacturers claim their preparations will get rid of all five of the most common types; bots, ascarids, and both large and small strongyles. Some are effective with all but bots. It is advisable to read labels carefully if you are going to attempt the medication yourself. There are worm pellets on the market that are recommended for twice-a-year feeding. The control of worms is something you should discuss with your veterinarian.

Screwworms, although a killer of cattle rather than of horses, created a problem strangely related to horses. In fact, the control of the screwworm larvae almost put the old cowhorse out of business. It once took a lot of good cowhorses to help the cowboys rope and throw cattle in order to doctor them for screwworms. Then the eradication program changed things. Federal and state agencies, with half the money being put up by the livestock raisers, eradicated the screwworms in the states of Alabama, Mississippi, and Louisiana and are rapidly finishing the job in Texas and the West. On April 16, 1970, the United States Department of Agriculture announced that the nation had set a record by going 121 days without a single case of screwworms being reported, the last having been in Comal County, Texas, in December 1969.

It means that roping horses on big ranches are seldom needed. Jeeps and helicopters can serve for the inspection of cattle when there is no need of doctoring them on the spot.

Those whose tongues are good at rounding up syllables no doubt speak of the screwworm as *Cochliomyia americana* of the family Melopiidae of the order of Diptera, but none I know of attempt it. The eradication center is in an old airplane hangar at Moore Field west of Brownsville, Texas. Here screwworm flies are sterilized at the rate of one hundred million—whose count I don't know—per week by the use of cobalt rays. Both sexes of the flies get the treatment because nobody has yet been able to tell which is which. The eggs from these treated flies incubate and hatch into sterile worms which are distributed by dropping them from airplanes. The sterile male screwworms are very active sexually—dominating untreated female worms found in the locality where the treated ones are dropped. The results are negative. This method of control is terminating the species.

Now, with the carcasses of victims of the screwworm no longer dotting the big pastures and furnishing food for the blowflies, that pest too is being eradicated.

For insect and pest control see Chapter 5, on "Stables and Corrals."

Environmental Ailments

Heatstroke or Sunstroke results when a horse is overworked under a blazing sun, and is more likely to happen if his body is deficient in water and salt or if in generally poor condition.

The horse plays out. He has to be urged to go on. Sweating stops and the horse starts panting, and at this stage you had better get someone else to call a veterinarian because you will be too busy taking care—belatedly—of your horse. As his temperature rises the eyes will water and become bloodshot. In severe cases the pulse will get more rapid and weaker, and in the final stage the animal will fall unconscious and will usually die.

If shade is nearby get him to it, or, if not, shield him with coats or shirts—anything—from the direct sun. Sponge his head with water and rub up and down the spine. *Don't throw water on him or hose water on him.* Dash a little water in his mouth, but don't give him water to drink until he is quieter and cooler. Massage his legs, with liniment if it is handy. Complete rest is what he needs. Later when he can be moved see that he gets plenty of salt and water. Forever after watch him carefully when you ride him in hot weather. He will be more vulnerable to sunstroke. Horses out in pasture or corrals should have shade and plenty of salt in hot weather.

Shipping Fever was once equated with influenza. They certainly are a related virus, although enough of the former have been isolated to establish differences. All horses seem to be susceptible, whereas it was once thought only young horses were. It is contagious.

Being thrown with other horses, change of water, food, and environment seem to be the things that turn on this particular virus. Symptoms are loss of appetite and the appearance of a bad cold with high fever. It is a very serious condition if allowed to develop; however, the almost routine use of antitoxin serums has this disease well under control.

AILMENTS, SYMPTOMS, TREATMENT

Legs, Feet, and Lameness

Bog spavin	Curb	Thoroughpin
Bone spavin	Fractures	Thrush
Bowed tendons	Sidebone	Windgall
Bursitis	Splints	Wounds
Chapped heels	Stringhalt	

Ailments and injuries that affect the feet and can be helped by special shoeing are dealt with in Chapter 8.

Ninety per cent of all leg trouble and foot trouble is in the forelegs and forefeet, but the hind feet and legs present a special problem because lameness in them is harder to detect and diagnose.

Because of his well-muscled legs and rather large joints due to his working horse heritage, the Quarter Horse (if not strictly of the racing strains) is comparatively free from leg and foot trouble. Of course he is as susceptible to damaging founder and laminitis as any other horse.

Bog Spavin is the distension of the capsule of the hock joint. It is a puffy or "boggy" swelling on the front of the hock one-third of the way down and toward the outside. It may get large enough to impede the free flexion of the joint. It may come on so gradually as to go undetected until it has reached considerable size and the horse has reached considerable age. Horses with pronounced upright hocks are more likely to have it. Wrong feed or lack of exercise or poor feet can also cause it.

Treatment consists mainly of rest. It is not a very serious condition except as a blemish. Liniments massaged on may be helpful.

Bone Spavin is a bony enlargement on the inside of the hock joint, the result of a calcium buildup. The lameness it causes when forming may disappear, but the disfigurement will remain to bar a horse from a conformation class. It is considered a serious defect.

Rest, special shoeing, blistering and firing, and sometimes surgery are the treatments used.

Bowed tendons are the result of a sprain of the deep flexor tendons behind the foreleg cannon bones. The tendons thicken and bow out at the back. The condition is frequent in race horses that are put on the track at too early an age. The lameness may not be permanent but the unsoundness remains, and the tendon may never be as strong as it should be. Leg bandages are a common sight on horses that are prone to this weakness or to give added support to prevent it. They are seldom seen on any type of Quarter Horse except the racers.

Bursitis in horses results from overuse or from an injury to the bursa, which secretes a small quantity of lubricating fluid in the joints. When inflamed the bursa exudes excess amounts of fluid, the walls of the bursa increase in thickness, and a soft, almost painless swelling results when the fluid becomes dense and hardens. Both capped hock and capped elbow are forms of chronic bursitis.

Allow rest and paint with a counterirritant. Removal of the affected mass by surgery has been done with good results.

Chapped Heels are unlikely to occur if the horse's feet are examined and painted with a dressing after rides, especially if the rides were on icy or rocky trails. It is the same as chapped hands in a human. But because they are often wet and in the muck, a horse's heels, the fleshy part, may crack open and bleed and become infected.

Curb results when the tendons and ligaments on the back of the hock are strained and bulge out. The bulge appears about four inches below the point of the hock and is easily seen from the side because the line from the back of the hock to the fetlock joint should be straight. Narrow, weak, or sickle hocks are most likely to be strained in this manner. Jumpers, race horses, and reining horses performing spectacular sliding stops are subjected to great strain in the hock area. There is temporary lameness with heat and swelling. The horse must be given a rest for several days. Some people resort to blistering and firing. Others just use a mild liniment. The blemish remains but will seldom cause permanent lameness. It is hardly an unsoundness, yet the advice is: never buy a curby horse.

Fractures, unless quite evident, will sometimes show no strong signs of trouble at the time they happen, because a fractured bone has little pain the first fifteen or twenty minutes. So if an injury is suspected, it is well to dismount and keep the horse quiet. All fractures should be X-rayed, and unless you are lucky enough to be in a district where a well-equipped veterinarian has a portable X-ray, it means transporting the horse if he can be loaded into a trailer. A temporary splint, well padded, should be put well above and below the break for support. Slings under the horse's belly anchored to the sides of the truck or trailer are helpful in keeping the horse from swaying and putting undue strain on the injured leg.

Sidebone is an inflammation of the cartilage under the coronary band where it joins the hoof. It is on the side of the foot and usually on the forefeet. As with so many other injuries it is the result of too much strain at an early age. Consequently the usual sufferers are race horses. Quarter Horses not used for racing are comparatively free of this trouble because they seldom have great demands made of them at an early age.

Calcium forms in the irritated places and lameness is pronounced but disappears when the calcium has become set and ossified. Until this happens the horse should not be ridden. The hardening process in the tissue can be hastened by blistering and firing.

Splints. The splint bone is a long, narrow bone on the inside of the cannon bone and is bound to it by ligaments. When the ligaments are torn, calcium or bone substance fills the space between splint and cannon. Most horses by the age of four years have these little knotty growths. Each time a ligament is torn the knots get bigger. They seldom cause permanent lameness. When they form, a blister should be applied to harden up the ligaments. Do not use cold packs. If severe, a veterinarian may suggest further treatments. If low on the leg where it is likely to be hit by the other foot, protect it with a leather boot. Stay off the horse and give the leg a chance to heal. When you do start using the horse, take it slow and easy for a while. If lameness returns, have the leg X-rayed. Splints are caused by too much hammering on hard roads and working too hard and fast when out of condition. Splints are rare in horses over six years old because by this age the cannon bones and the splint bones have fused.

Stringhalt is indicated when a horse suddenly snatches up a hind foot when walking or, less often, when trotting. It is caused by a spasmodic contraction of the flexor muscles of the hock, which brings the foot up higher than normally. It is commonest in horses five or six years old and when they have been seldom used.

Check to see if the shoes are fitting well. See that the horse gets more but mild exercise and work on soft ground.

Thoroughpin is an inflammation of the deep flexor tendon. It does not cause lameness, although it looks as though it would. It is a swelling on the sides and in front of the point of the hock. Rest, blistering and firing will reduce the swelling.

Thrush is a very common foot disease and it is contagious. It comes and goes with no apparent reason, but dirty stall floors are blamed. The odor is so foul and pervasive that one usually detects it before further effects, such as lameness, a softening of the frog of the foot, and a watery discharge from it, are advanced.

Treatment for it is readily available in several proprietary brands of medicines which will often bring recovery after one or two applications. Keep the stall floor clean and dry. Wash the floor with creolin solution or other antiseptic, let dry, and then put down new clean bedding.

Windgall is also a blemish that does not cause lameness. It is a swelling around the fetlock joint somewhat similar to bog spavin but not as serious. Astringent lotions are used as a preventive. Rest the horse until the swelling goes down.

Lungs, Throat and Respiratory Ailments

Broken Wind is a chronic alveolar emphysema and is sometimes called heaves, which it resembles. It is a breakdown of the air cells in the lungs in which the tissue, spongelike, fills the air cavities, reducing the area in which oxygen can purify blood. It can be caused by injury to the lungs when a horse is run to the point of exhaustion, by pneumonia, acute bronchitis, chronic cough, and influenza. If exercised at all vigorously, short coughs and heaves will be noticed; the horse is trying to get more air than his lungs have capacity for, and he heaves to expel what is in the clogged cells.

There is little that can be done to alleviate the condition. The horse might earn his keep as a slow-gaited pet for a youngster who loves horses.

Choke is indicated by a horse that tries, rather frantically, to wretch or cough up something. There is profuse salivation.

Tie the horse up. Do not let him eat or drink and do not try to pour medicine down his throat. The primary cause is due to a spasm in the gullet muscles (like the cramp in a swimmer's leg), which holds some object tightly so that the animal cannot swallow it or cough it up. The spasm may end quickly and the object be swallowed, but call a veterinarian immediately. He can inject an antispasmodic which works rapidly.

AILMENTS, SYMPTOMS, TREATMENT

Coughs and Colds are usually associated with drafts and cold or changing weather. At the first sign of coughs, running nose, tearful eyes, fever, and lassitude, something must be done to avoid more serious disease such as pneumonia, bronchitis, and influenza. If a cough is simply from a throat irritation caused by dirt or dusty feed or hay, the other symptoms will be lacking. In this case change to cleaner, more moist food and give a cough remedy that will soothe the throat. If a horse shows the other symptoms mentioned above, give a cough remedy, feed warm mashes, get the horse away from other horses and where he will be out of drafts and comfortably bedded. Many believe the horse should continue very mild outdoor exercise daily, but be super careful in cooling him out. If the condition continues, call a veterinarian.

Equine Influenza quickly brings on high fever, up to 106 degrees F., with a dry cough, and if severe the horse loses appetite and moves as though in pain. The virus for this disease was not isolated until 1957. One type of the disease known in the United States was not isolated in Britain until 1963.

With plenty of rest and the proper vaccine administered by your veterinarian, the horse usually makes a rapid recovery.

Pneumonia, if not treated quickly, can result in broken wind or heaves. The symptoms are sudden; fever shoots the thermometer up to 105° or 106° F., breathing is fast, the pulse is rapid, and the horse has a dry hacking cough. It is imperative that you get a veterinarian as soon as possible.

With modern drugs, expert doctoring, and good care, your convalescent horse may be carrying his nurse about in two or three weeks. But the nurse shouldn't rush him. If he gets too tired he could have a relapse that could damage his lungs and heart.

Heaves is a condition closely related to broken wind in that the air cavities of the lungs have been filled up with swollen tissue and the horse heaves, trying to empty these cavities and to get enough air. As with broken wind, heaves can be an aftereffect of pneumonia, influenza or bronchitis. The difference is that a cough, almost a gasp, is present in heaves that can be caused by an allergy to which some horses are predisposed by heredity, as with people who have asthma, which it resembles. Hay is blamed for the allergy and some horses are cured when hay is replaced by pellets that supply the vitamins and minerals of hay.

A horse with well-developed heaves is a sick horse and cannot be used for any active riding. Veterinarians with modern drugs have been very successful with cases caught in the early stages, and they have managed to make the disorder much less prevalent than it once was.

Skin Eruptions

Good care and careful grooming do much to prevent most skin trouble. Horses have rather sensitive skin and some are allergic to certain insecticides, so be sparing in their use until you can judge the reaction.

Zinc oxide and some other ointments in the household medicine cabinet clear up skin irritations quite effectively.

Hives are due to bodily chemistry being put off balance by food that is too rich, a sudden change in diet, or even by a change in the weather. Little swellings appear under the skin and spread rapidly. With smaller rations and a mild laxative the hives may disappear as suddenly as they came. If the condition doesn't clear up within a few days, ask the veterinarian about it. He may advise giving an antihistamine.

Teeth

Routine dental examinations are a part of horse care. When a horse carries his head tipped sideways instead of vertical, it can indicate he has some tooth trouble. And unless you have become an experienced horseman, practically all tooth correction and treatment will have to be done by a veterinarian.

Floating is necessary about once every year. This term means filing the teeth down level so that the molars grind evenly.

Young horses may have teeth that are too sharp on the edges or that protrude sideways enough to cut the inside of the mouth or tongue. Floating the teeth is not especially discomforting and some veterinarians can simply grasp the animal's tongue with one hand, keep the mouth wide open, and go to work with a dental file or rasp in the other hand. If the horse makes it too difficult to do it that way, a metal device called a speculum is put into the mouth to hold it open.

Wolf Teeth grow out in front of the molars in some young horses. They are little extra teeth that can cut the membranes and tongue. If they do no damage, some veterinarians allow them to remain, but others, knowing that they are practically rootless and easily removed, do so.

Methods of Treatment and the Medicine Cabinet

How well your medicine cabinet is stocked depends on how capable you think you are as a nurse. Many people prefer to have only the basic items, assuming the veterinarian will bring along the drugs and equipment to deal with each specific ailment. Here are the basic items. A balling gun is included because even a beginner can quickly learn how to shoot a pill (ball) far back into a horse's mouth.

Balling gun—pills are oval but they are called balls.
Blister ointment
Colic remedy
Cough remedy
Disinfectant
Equine thermometer—a human rectal type can be used
Foot dressing
Liniment
Mild laxative
Powder—sulfa, iodoform, or other to dust over wounds
Rolls of bandage, cotton wool, adhesive tape
Rubbing alcohol
Scissors
Towels
Vaseline
Wound spray
Worm pellets

Some of the things you will have to do for an ailing horse will require the help of an assistant. Some may even require the use of a twitch, which is explained later. But mostly the things you will do to hasten the recovery of your horse are simple and can be done without help if your horse is reasonably well mannered and trusts you.

Bandaging is seldom done except for bowed tendons because they are so difficult to keep in place and because most wounds, having been cleaned and treated with some medication, heal better if left open.

For tendons wrap cotton wool smoothly around the leg in sufficient quantities to give good padding and to allow for circulation—maybe swelling—and over this wrap a Derby bandage, which is muslinlike cloth about two inches wide, to hold it in place. With practice you will be able to wrap the ends in so it is neat and secure.

Blistering is simply applying an irritant, a caustic ointment, that draws the blood to the affected area and hastens healing. The ointment mixtures range from mild to severe. Iodine is severe, but a Spanish fly blister is even more severe. When a blister is applied, tie the horse so that he cannot get his head or mouth to the area. There are blister sprays on the market called muscle and tendon stimulants, and they are handy and clean to use.

Cold Packs and Cold Water are something that any horseman can apply to reduce pain and swelling. Packs wrapped around the legs and feet are hard to maintain in place, but they will serve to keep the area moist and cool if water is doused on them occasionally. If a cool stream is handy, stand the horse in it. The most usual method is to hose the affected area. Start at the foot and work up, the same principle as massaging toward the heart. Twenty minutes is long enough at a time, but treatment can be repeated several times a day. Rub dry, especially heels and pasterns, to prevent chapping and cracking.

Drenching is not as old-fashioned as it sounds. It means pouring liquid medicine down a horse's throat, but the day of holding the animal's head up high and putting a leather bottle in his mouth (a glass bottle might have broken in the struggle) and forcing him to drink the contents is a thing of the past.

Now it is done with less struggle. The last time I assisted in the operation, I held my sick mare's head against my chest and poured soothing words into her ear while the veterinarian pumped about a gallon of medication directly into her stomach. She couldn't even taste the odoriferous stuff. The veterinarian had slipped a lubricated rubber hose about one half inch in diameter through her nostril, past her gullet, which he carefully felt with his fingers to be sure it was slipping into the stomach and not into the bronchial tube, which would have been fatal. I have noticed that horses are not greatly concerned when the tube is run into their nostril and seldom oppose it.

AILMENTS, SYMPTOMS, TREATMENT

Here veterinarian Posey is shown tubing a horse. The author is at halter.
Photo by Irene Laune.

Enemas are recommended for colic and impaction. Two to four pailfuls of soapy water at body heat (a little glycerin added is beneficial) is slowly poured through a piece of small garden hose by means of a funnel on the outside end. Lubricate the end that is inserted. It should be done slowly in order to give the bowel wall time to expand. If the horse is able to walk around, stand him downhill. Walk him around a bit before evacuation if you can. If the horse is down in his stall proceed the best you can but don't make the mistake a man at my place did when he trapped himself with the horse between him and the door. Things happen fast.

Liniments are rubbed on strained tendons, windgall, bog spavin, ringbone, stiffness, bruises, and saddle galls, and a few drops in water make a good cooling-out wash. Used in the standard strength, it does not cause loss of hair or blistering. There are some that can be sprayed on so that one's hands can be kept clean.

Pills are usually large and oval and called balls. They are given with a balling gun that sends the ball so far back in the horse's throat that he has little choice but to swallow it.

Pinfiring does the same thing that blistering does, except that it pinpoints the spot to which the blood is drawn to hasten the healing. It is done with a heated iron. Many polo ponies, race horses, and performance horses show the telltale marks of the firing iron.

Massage, usually with rubbing alcohol, can relieve soreness and stiffness and tone up the muscles. Rub toward the heart.

Treating Wounds is simplified by wound sprays, which are applied after the wound has been cleaned and the blood flow stopped. There are two types. One is an antiseptic, antifungus spray for fresh wounds. It fights bacteria in infected areas. The other is used for noninfected wounds. It serves as a coating and protection from flies. Both are quick and easy to use. Greasy salves are avoided because they collect dirt, are messier to apply, and are inclined to keep the wound open and delay formation of a natural scab. Sometimes the wound, instead of scabbing over, develops proud flesh.

After medication is applied, most horse wounds are left unbandaged.

Twitch is the term for a simple device that will hold a horse immobile while being treated. It is a wooden handle—a small boy's bat is just

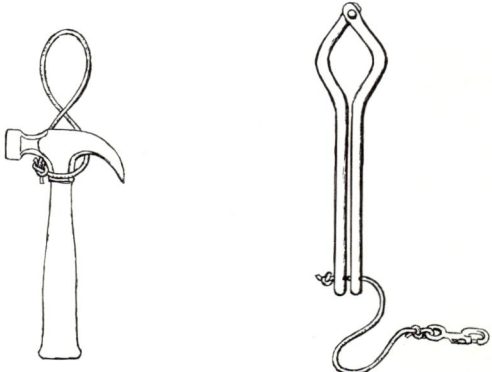

A quick way of improvising a twitch is to loop a thong or cotton clothesline over a hammerhead. *Right.* Equine nose clamp—a more humane type of twitch that has come into use in recent years. The cord can be wrapped around the clamp.

right—with a loop of stout cord or braided leather about five inches in diameter running through a hole in the end of the handle. When this loop is put over a horse's upper lip and the loop twisted until it holds the lip in a vicelike grip, the intense pain or the deadening of a nerve seems to paralyze the horse. It is said that one can feel only one pain at a time. As long as the pain on the lip exceeds whatever else is being done to the horse, he will stand still. Be sure the lip's outer skin is being gripped, otherwise the mucous membrane will be injured. Cowboys seldom had a twitch handy when they wanted to saddle and ride a wild-eyed bronc with rollers in his nose, so, in lieu of it, the horse's ear was pulled down by a cowboy helper who put the tip of the ear between his molar teeth and clamped down. The effect was exactly the same as a twitch, really less hurtful to the horse, and the bronc stood like a statue while being saddled and cinched.

The best remedies are preventive: good care, feeding, grooming and exercise.

The horse is not a delicate animal. But neither is he free to cope with drafts, barn conditions, and cleanliness. All that is up to the owner.

10

Horse and Riding Equipment

Xenophon had a few suggestions about horse equipment, an old subject even then (c. 430–c. 355 B.C.), mostly concerning bits and bridles. Since his time, experiments in horse tack (tackle) have never ceased. One might suppose that a new device for a horse could not conceivably be dreamed up. Yet in the past twenty years or so more styles and types of tack have come on the market than in the preceding hundred years.

Many items are so original they have been patented. To mention a few: for easy mounting there are let-down stirrups that spring up into proper position; electrified reins, with buttons to push, to speed up neck-reining training; electrical exercisers; electrified breast straps to speed up backing, so necessary in reining and roping horses; and even motorized cows for the training of cutting horses. Horse swimming pools will condition race horses in days instead of weeks. Many of the new things for horse use, however, are simply refinements in design of traditional equipment, such as rubber colt bits, or the adaptation of synthetics such as nylon ropes and reins and nylon bar bits.

The two distinct styles of riding, Eastern and Western, call for quite different tack. European riding masters and their followers in this country who teach equitation have heretofore had very little understanding of Western methods or equipment, and proponents of the Western style of riding have been slow to see merit in some of the Eastern methods. Now more riders travel and ride in all parts of the country, losing provincialism and prejudice along the way, and the two types of horsemen are showing more tolerance for each other's methods, tack, horses, dress, and horsemanship. Many riders are quite at home riding both Eastern and Western.

Much credit for a better understanding between the two schools of riding is due to the Quarter Horse, whose versatility has allowed him to enter the best of all possible horse worlds in which he works well in more events and in more kinds of gear than any other breed of horse. His habiliments range from the trick-riding saddle and roping saddle to the forward seat jumping saddle, and from the hackamore to the Weymouth (full) bridle.

Equipment for Training

Halter—made of cotton rope—with lead rope and snap
Halter—made of leather with chain shank—rope or leather lead
Hackamore for breaking and training
Colt bit—straight bit of nylon, leather, or rubber
Hobbles—for forelegs above fetlock joint
Pastern cuffs—sheepskin lined for casting
Soft rope—for casting or drawing up one leg
Martingale or tie-down (standing martingale or running martingale)
Bat—a short whip or stick for training or racing
Long whip—for use in conjunction with a long rein or slender rope if horse is to be lunged

Clothing for the Horse

2 cotton summer sheets for cooling out
2 blankets—wool-lined canvas—for stable wear if needed
Boots—for protection in trailer, for sliding, for interference
Leg bandages
Elastic bandages for tendons
Saddle pads or saddle blankets
Jowl sweat wrap
Sweat hood—to sweat away unwanted fat

Saddles—English

For Eastern riding there are three basic types of saddles: the English show saddle, the hacking saddle, and the Forward Seat or jumping saddle. In addition there are the postage stamp saddles that weigh but ounces that are used on both Thoroughbred and Quarter Horse racers, and the deep-seated and knee-rolled polo saddles.

The English show saddle has a cut-back pommel, or head, and straight flaps. It puts the rider far back on the cantle—practically over the horse's kidneys—and the stirrups are ridden long so that the legs are almost straight.

The English or hacking or simply flat saddle, as it is so often called, has long been popular for pleasure and general riding. The best known is the type that follows the Whippy pattern, in which the seat is moderately deep with flaps somewhat forward. It has slightly padded knee rolls concealed under the flaps, and comes with two- or three-buckle girths.

The Forward Seat or jumping saddle is favored by more riders for hunting and jumping and trail riding today than any other type. It was designed and introduced by the Italians with the purpose of throwing the weight toward the withers by tipping the deep seat forward. The flaps are angled far forward and have padded knee rolls, some on the flaps and some concealed beneath. The billets are for two- or three-buckle girths. In the children's version of this saddle the seat is even deeper.

Robertson jump saddle with thinly padded flaps. Made in England. *Photo by the author.*

All saddles have a reinforced tree so that the gullets can withstand great pressure without breaking. The racing saddles have a flexible steel wire tree that won't break even if a horse falls on it.

All English or flat saddles have safety stirrup bars. These are metal bars under the fender that open or close at the rear end so that the stirrup leather which hangs from the bar will slip out if a rider is thrown and gets hung up in a stirrup.

Stirrup Irons for the English saddle should be chosen with some care because they come in different sizes; a tread or footrest that is a little over an inch wider than the rider's boot sole is about right. They are rustproof and come in standard straight styles with the leather opening centered over the tread, and in an offset style in which the tread is at an angle to allow for the downward slope of the boot sole and with the leather opening offset to be farther away from the horse, thus causing the ankle to flex inward. There are safety stirrup irons that will open outward to release a boot in case the rider goes out of the saddle.

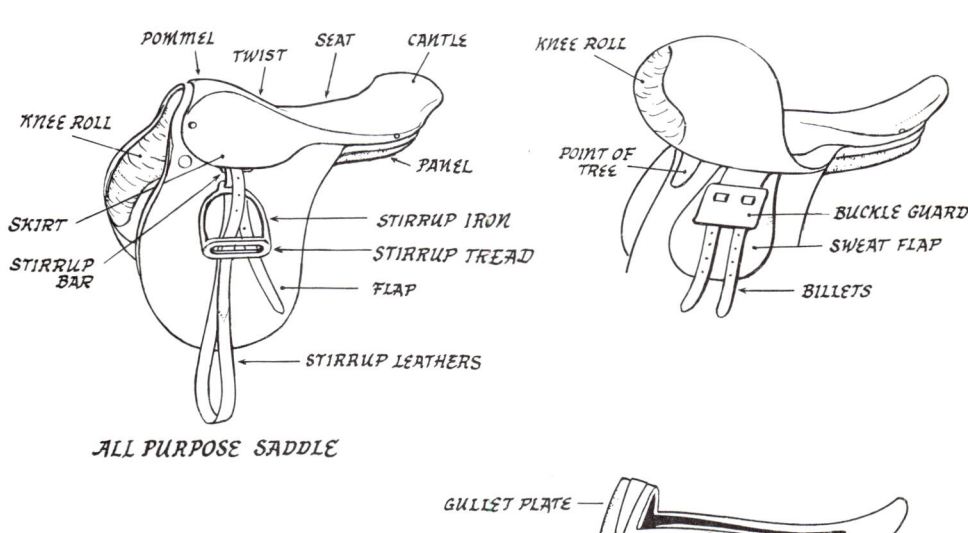

Parts of the flat saddle.

Saddles—Western

The western saddle is simply a modification of the saddle used by the conquistadors. And theirs was a version of a saddle that had been in use since the time of Theodosius (346–95), when even then saddles had a pronounced bow in front and a cantle at the back. The term "saddle" comes from the Latin word *sella,* meaning "chair." Spanish riding was influenced by the invading Moors, and more particularly by the tribe of Zinettes from whom they borrowed the style of riding called *"à la jinette."* With padded saddles set high above the horse's back and riding with short stirrups, they gained an advantageous reach with sword, mace, or lance. The high pommel and wrap-around chair-back cantles provided the security of seat and protection a fighter on horseback needed.

North of the Pyrenees riding with long stirrups prevailed. It was called *"à la brida"* and was certainly the custom at the time of William the Conqueror as shown in the Bayeux Tapestry.

In the New World the knight's saddle was soon modified for stock handling. The high cantle which made mounting difficult was lowered, and the pommel was given a tie post. These very large soup-plate or poker-table cabezas or apples (horns) became the distinguishing features of Mexican saddles. Stirrups were let out for ease of mounting and for better circulation in the legs that had to be astraddle a horse for long hours.

In the late 1700's a fitted *mochilla,* a leather cover, was thrown over the pommel and cantle, which kept it in place. This leather was large enough to serve as fenders, skirts, and leg guards.

When roping stock, the forward tipping was solved by rigging the cinches farther back on the saddle frame. It became known as the center-fire rig. Horns were made somewhat smaller in California, which made it easier to *dar la vuelta* (take a turn with a rope) around the horn. The word was Americanized to "dally."

Later, when Texas became the center of the cattle industry, the Texas ropers held their saddles in place by adding a rear, or flank, girth. Texas saddles had to be stouter than any heretofore made because when roping the Texans did not dally, which can ease off a sudden jerk. They tied the lariat solid to the horn and when a big Chihuahua longhorn hit the end of the line, something had to give—the steer, the rope, or the saddle. It was so difficult to get at the wild cattle for a throw of the loop when they hid in the brush that the Texans took no chance of losing them with an unsuccessful dally hold. Moreover, even with the long lariats they used, some as long as fifty feet, they might be so far away from the steer that there was no slack rope to dally with. To strengthen their saddles, the Texans covered the hardwood trees and metal horns with bullhide that was sewed on when wet. To give more comfort to the horse, the skirts were lined with sheepskin, even though blankets, often Navajo woven, were also used under them.

The double-rigged saddle continues to be used today for roping. There have been many modifications but only slight basic changes have been made.

When Cheyenne, Wyoming, was a booming cow town, the saddle makers changed the rounded bead edge of the cantle by widening it and giving it a flat top—a sort of ledge that extended back. It was named the Cheyenne roll.

Once when I was riding with a cowboy named Lawrence Beach, a horse he was breaking suddenly got his head down and then started swapping ends up off the ground. Lawrence's seat must have been three feet out of the saddle when a remarkable thing happened. He caught his spur under the Cheyenne roll and sort of hung there in the air until the horse brought the saddle back to him on the next bound and Lawrence was in business again. He rode the horse out.

Whatever its reason for being, the Cheyenne roll lost favor when I was a youth and none of us would have been caught dead in that kind of saddle. Then to my surprise it popularity returned in the late 1930s, and now practically all Western saddles are made with Cheyenne roll cantles with strange-to-behold shapes. In 1937 only two out of the six saddles awarded to the World Champions at Madison Square Garden had Cheyenne rolls. In 1940 all of the six saddles had them. Now, however, the trail riders who want more room to tie lunches, slickers, canteens, etc., may start a trend back to the trimmer bead roll cantle.

The endless varieties of Western saddles are beautiful examples of the saddler's art. The stirrup fender doubles for a stirrup leather, which reduces weight. In many saddles the flank girth attaches to the skirt, which eliminates the weight and lumpiness of an extra D ring. Thinner leather is used where there is little wear. Some pleasure saddles now weigh under twenty-five pounds, whereas a good roping saddle still weighs about thirty-five pounds.

On good saddles, stirrup leathers and rigging are skived, that is, they

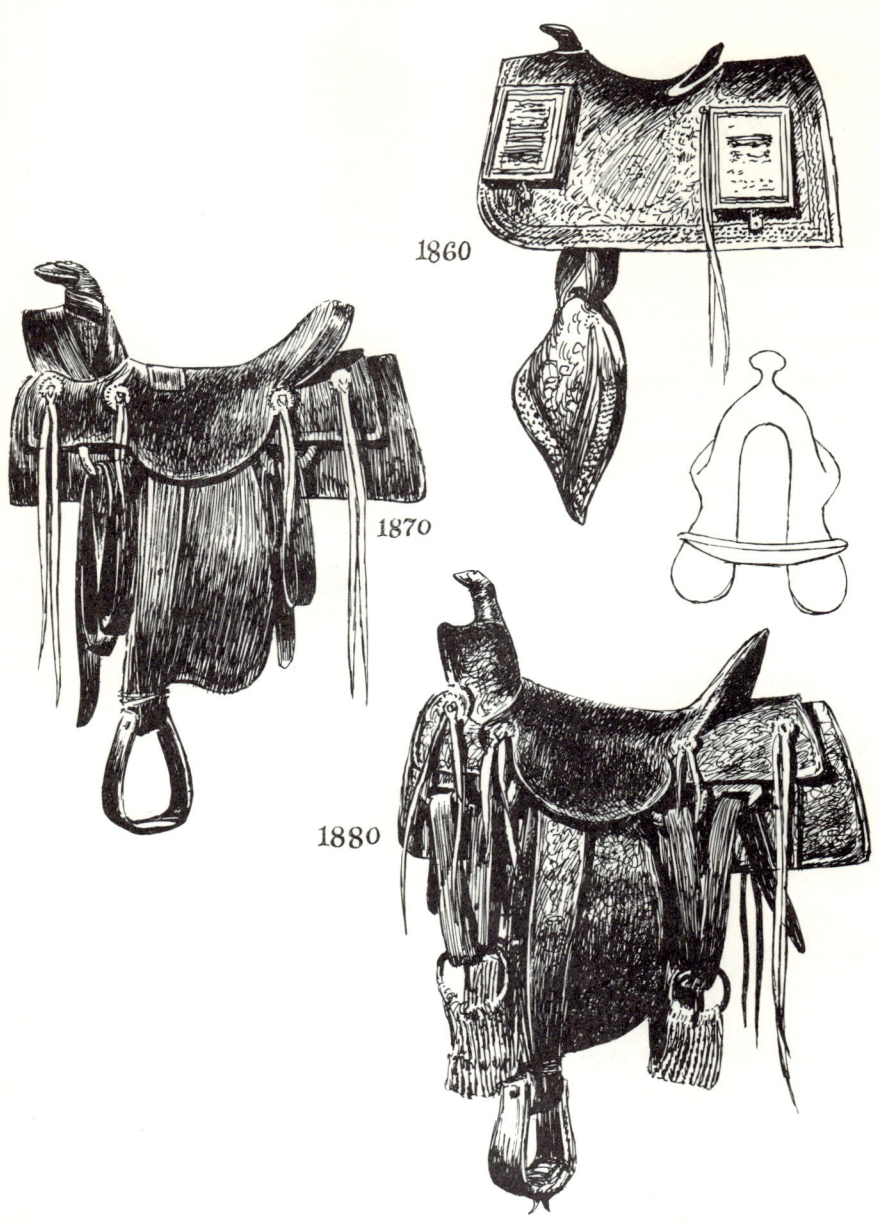

(Top) The riders of the pony express used a *mochilla* with mail pouches attached. It could be removed quickly and thrown over the saddle frame on a fresh horse without changing saddles.

(Center) This saddle was first called the Denver, then it was called the Cheyenne saddle when the makers there added the wide roll to the cantle.

(Bottom) The early Texas saddle met the needs of the ranchers and cowboys so well that its basic design has undergone only slight changes.

All three saddles shown here had "A" forks or slick forks. Now nearly all stock saddles have varying degrees of swells on the forks. And cantles are much lower.

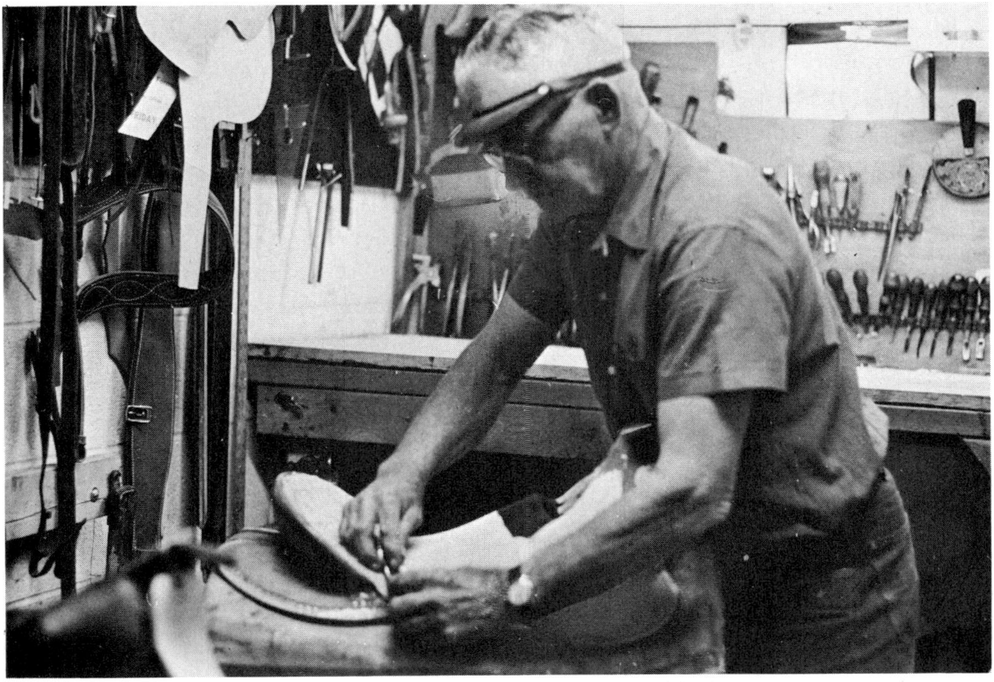

Long-time saddlemaker "Pick" Pickering in his workshop at the Thurston Saddlery, Paradise Valley, Arizona, and an example of his craftsmanship, priced at $850. *Photos by Irene Laune.*

are beveled and tapered to reduce lumpiness. A sharp tooling, carving, and stamping job means good leather, because on inferior leather it won't stay sharp. Such decorative work is done with a purpose beyond ornamentation. Without it, highly polished smooth leather will show every scratch and mar. Padded surfaces, stitching, and roughed-out leather also gets around that problem. Many saddles have foam-cushioned suede seats.

As in the English saddles, the Western saddles are made to meet the needs of specialized performance events. The roping saddle, for instance, has a gullet as low as the horse's withers will permit in order to reduce the leverage of the taut lariat. It also has large, deep stirrups and a low cantle for ease in both mounting and speedy exit from the saddle.

Many saddles have the stirrups set forward to put more weight toward the withers, and the cutting saddle not only has this feature but it also has front swells that are as much as sixteen inches wide.

The early models of saddles in our West followed the Mexican tree and had what were called "slick forks" or "A forks," with practically no swells. To get a better grab with the legs, old-time bucking horse riders used bucking straps under which they could slip their knees, or strapped their slickers across the front of their saddles which gave the effect of swells. Then the manufacturers, spurred by the growing popularity of bronc riding in rodeos, started making saddles with bucking rolls or swells. Within a few years all kinds of odd saddles with wrap-around swells and steep cantles came on the market. They locked a rider in so well that his big worry was whether he could get out of the contraption if he had to in a hurry. All sorts of innovations were tried, for all kinds of saddles: small horns, polished steel or silver-plated horns, tall horns, steep and sloping cantles, cushion seats, and pointed swells. Once I thought it would be a good idea for the swells to contain thermos canteens so that I could turn a little faucet and get a cold drink on those long stretches between windmills. To my knowledge it has never been done, though, all kidding aside, it might work.

Because the square skirts of saddles often curled at the corners due to lack of care and proper racks to hold them, they were discontinued along in the 1940's, except for parade saddles, and the rounded skirts of the California saddle became popular. Now styles have orbited us back to a fuller-skirted saddle. Without the use of blankets made with a roll to fit snugly around the edge of the rounded skirt saddles, the square saddle skirts seem to go better with the square Navajo blankets, which are still the favored Western saddle blanket.

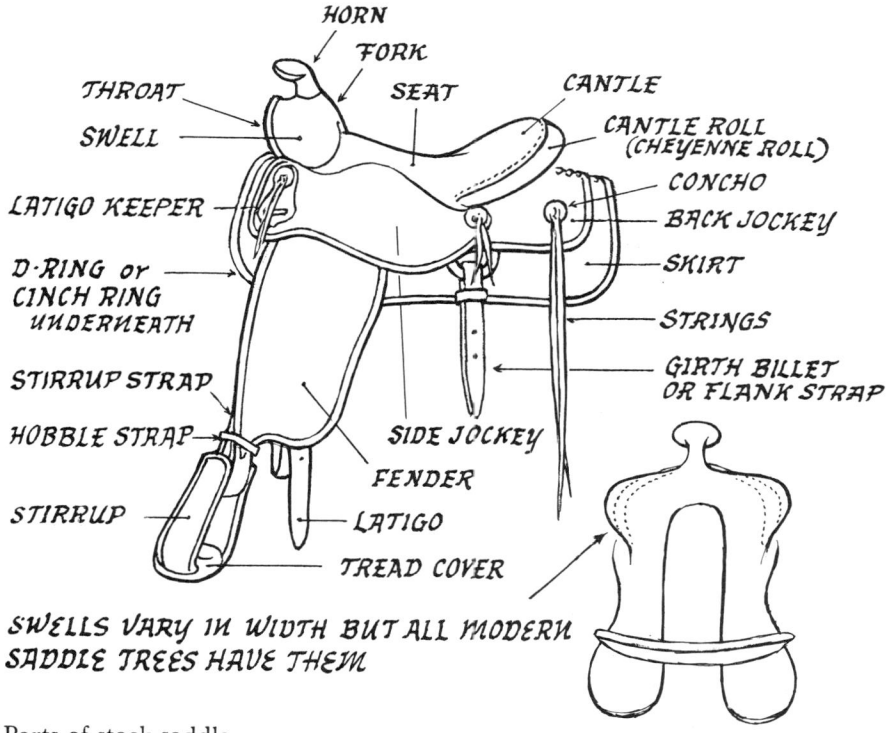

Parts of stock saddle.

The criticism in the present trends in design most often heard is that the cantle rolls—basically the Cheyenne rolls—have become ungainly in exaggerated width and irregularly flared shapes. And that the foam-cushioned suede-covered seat, the result of catering to the new generation of strictly pleasure riders, has been raised so high near the pommel that, instead of favoring the forward seat, the steep slant backward throws the weight too much on the cantle. Realizing this, there are now several makers of Western saddles that are returning to some of the virtues of the stock saddle seats of a former era.

In many of the Western saddleries, the owners are men who have had years of riding and stock-handling or rodeo experience, and know exactly what is needed and where the strains and stresses affect the saddle and tack. Moreover many makers of Western saddles are now producing flat saddles and the tack that goes with them.

If practical, each horse should have his own saddle. Like gloves and shoes, a saddle will subtly adjust with use, will get set to the shape of the withers and the back of the horse, if it is suitable to begin with. A saddle must fit two ways. Underside it must fit the horse. Top side it must fit the rider. The rider will quickly make changes if he doesn't like the fit, but a horse is not much of a complainer and so it is up to the owner to see that the saddle fits and is sufficiently padded so that the horse's back does not get galled.

The Horn and Western Riding

"The horn, although essential for roping, is of no use at all in ordinary pleasure riding." And "western riding . . . is just a rough and ready means of transportation." These are quotes from a recent book by an Eastern writer for the flat saddle establishment. The derision intended only brings smiles to the faces of Western riders who realize that it is only lack of knowledge that prompts such statements.

First let's list a few uses of the horn. Some of the best riders in the world "cuff" the horn to spare their horse in sudden action. Steer wrestlers often do it when coming out of the box. Riders of cutting horses often rest a hand on the horn for better balance when the horse is making his lightning-quick sideway leaps. Because it gives a positive grip allowing the rider to quickly take a forward position, the horn makes mounting and dismounting the Western saddle an easy, fluid motion while in full control of the horse. It is a much easier and more sightly action than that required in mounting or dismounting from the flat saddle. In dismounting from the flat saddle the rider is momentarily out of control when he must kick his feet from the irons and use his hands for support while he comes down in an ungainly sideways position. In moments of rest when the horse is standing and the rider is relaxed, the rider with a horn to rest his hands on is more at ease. There are moments when a rider needs to secure the reins while putting on a glove, adjusting a tie or hat, or zipping or unzipping a jacket. In these moments a horn is handy and the reins much more secure than resting on a low pommel. And with split reins a horn is even more necessary.

In the open, where there are no trees or fences, the safest way to tether two horses is to tie the reins of each to the horns of the saddles of the other. The horses facing in opposite directions may move in a tight circle, but they can't go anyplace. Horses normally stand head-to-tail so they can fight the flies off each other's faces.

There are times one has to lead another animal from horseback. If there is any pullback at all, one is thankful for a horn to dally on.

As for balance in the saddle, the horn on a Western saddle does nothing to affect it. People who have learned to ride both types of saddle find that they are as much in balance in a jumping saddle as they ever were, even after days in a Western saddle.

Stirrups

On the western saddle stirrups have gone through many changes, from the decorative Mexican styles carved from one piece of solid wood to the early Texas box stirrup, the oxbow, the galvanized ironbound oak stirrup, and many leather-covered types. And now they are back to the old Texas box stirrups, the only difference being that they are handsomely leather covered.

When I was a small boy, my father insisted that I ride with wide wooden stirrups for protection in case the horse fell and rolled on my leg. On several occasions horses did just that and the wide stirrups no doubt propped up the horse and saved me from getting a leg crushed or broken. So that is one good reason for their use. Other reasons are that they are large and heavy enough to stay in place, never requiring a rider to place them with his hand. They are so easy to step into that men who are on and off horses frequently, such as ropers, would use no other kind. The large area of tread in them gives support for the foot, making them much less tiring to ride than the narrow kinds which cowboys rode with their foot "clear home."

Tapaderos

Tapaderos are thick leather stirrup covers, another item of Mexican gear that was adopted by the early *Americanos* of the Southwest. They serve several purposes. Mainly they are used by working cowboys to keep spiny chaparral (brush), cactus, manzanita, catclaw, and wild plum from ripping the toes out of good boots. As used on cavalry and police and children's saddles, they prevent the foot from going through the stirrup.

The bull-nosed tapadero was often sheepskin-lined for warmth, and the monkey-nosed tapadero was a little larger and sported more conchos and tie thongs and hand-tooled decorations. The eagle-bill tapadero is the largest of all and has long decorative leathers that hang down as much as a foot or more below the stirrup. They are theatrical trappings, beautifully tooled, often decorated with silver, but they are heavy and are seldom seen except in parades.

Cinches and Girths

Cinches are made of cotton cords, horsehair, mohair, and leather lined with sheepskin. The cotton cinches are by far the most generally used. The others are strong and long-wearing but much more expensive.

On double-rigged saddles the rear girth is most often made of leather. Since it is never pulled up tight and sweated, it is long wearing.

A device once used a great deal for saddle cinches is now seldom seen and I don't know why. It is a tackaberry buckle. It laces into the latigo and firmly hooks on the cinch ring. Ranch workers found it very convenient. A slight tug on the tackaberry buckle released the cinch without the trouble of unlacing the latigo.

Breast Straps

Breast straps are used with both English and Western saddles to prevent the saddle from slipping back from the withers and as supports for martingales. They are most needed in active events or on the steep grades of mountain trails. They come in a wide variety of styles from the slender stitched breastplates for use with the English saddle or the workaday cotton cord cinches used with Western saddles to the highly ornamented silver-studded creations that enhance the trappings of parade horses. Leather ones, usually tooled and stitched, are most generally used by Western riders. Some are contoured to assure a snug fit on the horse's shoulders. Most have slender adjustable straps that pass over the withers to support them, but many riders dispense with these, finding the breast strap stays in place without their use. The breast strap should be adjusted so that it is directly over the point of the shoulder. If too high it interferes with the horse's breathing. If too low it will chafe against the muscles directly above the forearms. To get the best placement, many horsemen prefer the type of breast strap that has a ring in each end to which two straps can be attached, one going to the D-ring and

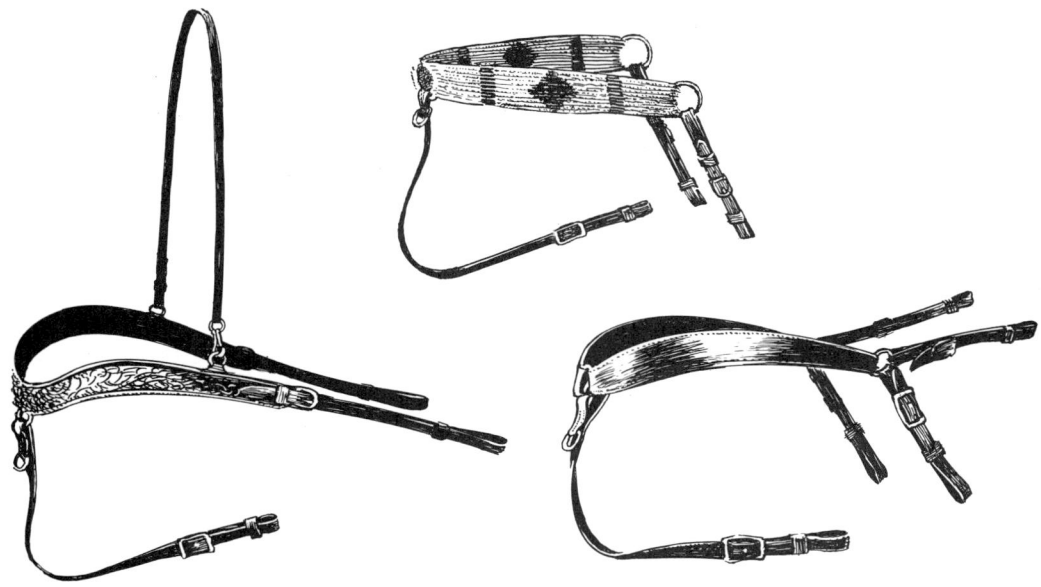

Breast straps.

the other to the cinch ring. By adjusting these straps the breast strap can be raised or lowered to the proper position.

Spurs

Spurs are for the experienced rider. They furnish a quick and positive communication with the horse. As previously stated the horse has an acute tactile sense. When touched his instinct is to move away from whatever is touching him. When he responds to each kind and location of touch and the reaction is consistent and habitual, the horse has learned your tactile language. Those touches are called "aids" or "cues," or, as some say, they are "pushing the right buttons."

Spurs, being of metal, are a quicker, more positive touch aid than leather, and so are used as an accentuation of leg aids. Most well-trained horses are spur-trained. It is the quickness of response that gives perfection to their performance. All expert riders use spurs to emphasize leg aids.

Spurs should be dull with no edges that can cut, scratch, or gouge. When properly used, simply a light touch of metal, the horse responds without feeling pain whatever. Spurs are preferable in every way to boot heels that thud into a horse's belly—a really obnoxious practice.

A spur shank that is curved turns downward. And like the straight-shanked English spur, whether roweled or blunt, is simply laid against the horse's side. It is not hooked into the horse. The only place I know of where spurs are worn with the shank slanting up is in the Spanish Riding School of Vienna. There, because the Lipizzaner horses they ride are relatively small and the men who ride them are often long-legged, the spur shanks are turned upward so the horse can be touched without raising the heel.

English and Eastern riders often wear their spurs as high up on their boots as their own anklebones for the same reason. When wearing English boots I had to wear spurs as low as Western spurs are worn, because I found that the spurs up around my ankles were very uncomfortable if not outright painful. Today one sees many spurs attached low down at the heel of English boots without the use of straps.

Some Western spurs have the shank set at an inward angle to reduce the leg and heel movement when the spur is applied.

Spurs got a bad name during the period in our West when in handling wild half-broken horses and wild longhorn cattle men used brutal means to force a mount quickly into or out of a dangerous situation. There is the old saying that the cowboys of the trail-drive days used spurs that could drive a horse into hell and used bits that could stop a locomotive. But many riders, including myself, have worn long-shanked roweled spurs on even young horses in training without undue excitement. A spur, no matter how extreme, never hurts a horse unless the rider wants it to, or by accident when used by an inexperienced rider.

Indians were the exception among great horsemen. They did not fancy the idea of encumbering spurs on their soft-heeled moccasins. For them the quirt was a sufficient horse goad. The Gauchos of Argentina on the other hand, even if barefooted, strap spurs to their feet, and their horsemanship and their horses are highly regarded.

What is often erroneously called "buck hooks," the blunt curved piece that extends upward on the top of the shank near the heel, is simply a chap guard. Its purpose is to keep the chaps or long trousers clear of the rowels.

Western spurs have gone through many styles, and after a period of light frames the trend is again toward rather heavy ornamented frames. With them the strap or chain tie-down under the instep is considered superfluous, although many old hands still like the firmness they give.

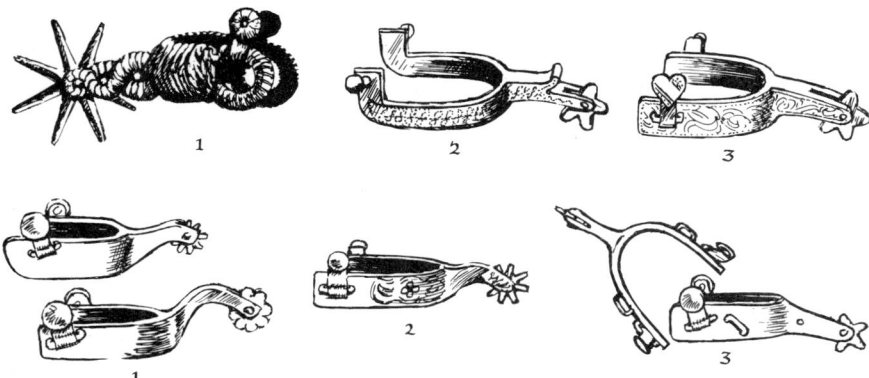

(Top) 1. Pancho Villa's iron spurs are said to weigh five pounds each. 2. Mexican spur with chap guard. Decorated brass is on the outside of the heel band. 3. Spur favored by many Western riders. This one has ornamented silver heel band and silver button.

(Bottom) 1. Cutting horse spur. 2. Toots Manfield roping spurs. 3. Jim Shoulders' bronc and bull riding spurs. The shank is set off center so the foot does not have to turn out. On the sides of the bands are loops for tie-downs or hobble straps.

The real meaning of a tie-down for a spur is the lacing of the shank with a leather thong that is wrapped under the heel. Bronc busters sometimes do this to keep the spur shank from flopping up.

Spurs are for riders who have passed the beginner's stage and have a well-balanced seat. Flat saddle riders who, because of shorter stirrups, have their heels closer to the horse's body should postpone using spurs until balance is perfected to the point where legs and heels can take on the added management of spurs. Spurs are, to repeat, simply to accentuate leg aids. Balance should be in the body, seat, and stirrups, with the heels away from the horse except when deliberately used as an aid.

Bits

The ideal mouthpiece is the one that controls the horse and transmits subtle signals and still leaves the horse's head, his balancer, free. Bits have been used ever since the domestication of horses. There have been and still are hundreds of shapes and sizes, and all are variations of two basic bits; the snaffle and the curb.

The variety of bits and hackamores and shank hackamore bridles to choose from seems unlimited, and new ones are appearing all the time. *Photo by Irene Laune.*

The mouthpiece of a bit is called the cannon. The snaffle, being jointed in the center, has two cannons. The simple bar bit, sometimes used in place of the snaffle as in the hunting bridle, has a single cannon. Aside from the rings at the end of the cannon where reins are attached, some bits have cheek pieces to prevent them from sliding sideways through the horse's mouth. Neither snaffle nor bar bit has any jaw leverage. The pull on the reins is directly toward the hands that control them.

Snaffle. The snaffle bit, also called a jointed bit or a broken bit, gives a scissor action. Being jointed in the center, it forms a V when pulled, causing the two cannons to ride on the outer edge of the bars of the horse's mouth. Because of the upward direct pull the snaffle is inclined to slide up into the corners of the mouth. A bridle with a snaffle mouthpiece is correctly called a bridoon. The "full bridle," called a Weymouth, consists of a bridoon plus another headstall with a curb bit plus a cavesson or noseband; with of course two reins for the snaffle and two reins for the curb. Flat saddle riding calls for the reins to the snaffle to be kept just tight enough to be in contact with the horse's mouth at all times. With light hands that move with the horse the pressure is constant but very light.

Curb. The curb bit is dependent upon a curb strap or chain that goes under the chin or lower jaw to give leverage. The cannon has a curved shape that juts up in the center, called a port. Cheekpieces, more accurately called shanks, are on the ends of the cannon. The reins attach to the shanks. When the reins are pulled the bit turns forward, causing the port to thrust toward the roof of the mouth. The ring above the bit where the headstall and the curb strap are attached also goes forward, causing a leverage action against the jaw which brings the cannon against the bars of the mouth. This action, which tightens the curb strap, tends to keep the bit from riding up to the corners of the mouth. The greater the distance between the cannon and the rings above it where the headstall and the curb strap attaches, the greater is the leverage and severity of the bit. Longer shanks also add to the leverage and higher ports add to the severity. The curb bit with two reins is the bit associated with Western riding.

With all its potential severity the curb bit can and should be the least severe of all bits because it is used with a slack rein, which means it is used much less. The slight weight of the reins suspended from the shanks can with a slight movement, without a pull, get the response from the horse that is wanted whether it be for a turn, change of lead or gait, or for rating speed.

Pelham. The Pelham is a mild curb bit with rings at the end of the cannon for reins in addition to the reins at the ends of the shanks. Thus with four reins a rider can keep in contact with the mouth while allowing the curb reins to be slack until needed for more control.

The Hackamore

The hackamore consists of a rawhide braided noseband or bosal kept in place by a soft leather headstall and a rope throat latch. The bosal joins under the jaw in a heavy heel knot to which is tied the mecate, a

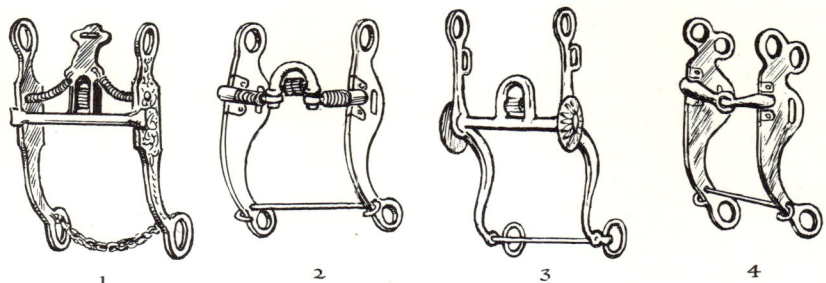

Here are four examples from among many correction bits or bits designed for special training.

1. Spade bit. Most spade bits in use today are patterned after the Santa Barbara or Salinas bits used in early California. The spade or spoon presses against the roof of the mouth when pulled forward by the leverage of the cheek pieces or shanks. The curved arms wrapped with copper wire prevent the straight bit from riding up to the corner of the mouth, where it is no longer effective on the bars of the mouth. The copper roller or cricket quiets the horse by giving his tongue something to play with.

2. This loose-jawed, swivel port bit is somewhat similar to the English Eldonian correction bit. The difference is that it has copper-wire-wrapped bars and a cricket in the port.

3. A bit with the port rising from a straight mouthpiece has for years been called a half-breed bit. This one has a cricket, conchos on the cheek pieces, and a curb strap placed very high to give a gagging action.

4. This loose-jawed curb with snaffle can be used with two or four reins and can be had with a choice of mouthpieces—low or high port curb—plated in copper or chrome or with a rubber training bit.

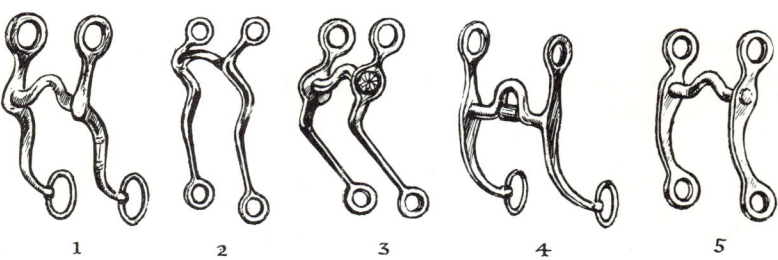

1. Cutting-horse bit. 2. Roping bit. 3. Grazing bit. The shanks are swept back out of the way when the horse's muzzle is close to the ground. 4. High port curb with cricket. 5. Low port curb, the most commonly used of all Western bits.

HORSE AND RIDING EQUIPMENT

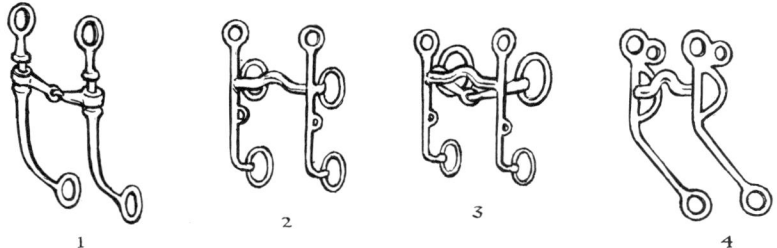

1. Loose-jawed sliding snaffle, used with curb strap or chain.

2. Pelham bit for four reins. Used with curb chain.

3. Pelham and snaffle. With both bits in the horse's mouth, each with its own reins and head stall, it forms the Weymouth or full bridle.

4. The Western version of the Pelham bit. The cheek pieces are swept back in the manner of a grazing bit, but the purpose is to keep the pull on the reins from lifting the bit up into the corner of the mouth.

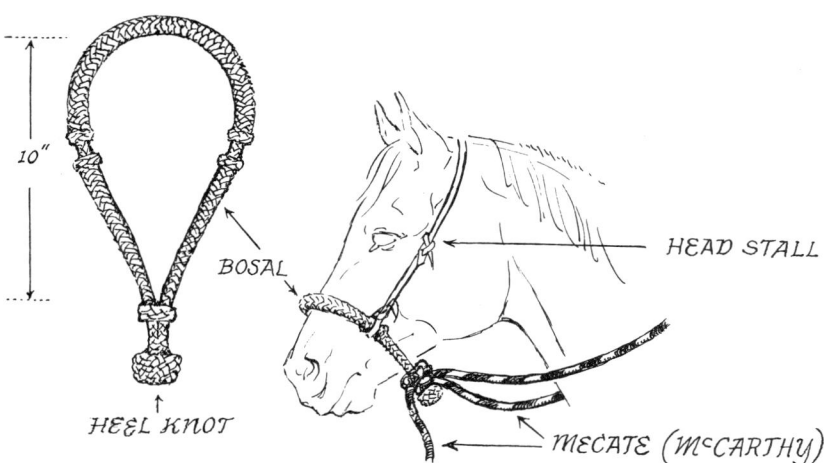

The word hackamore—from the Spanish *jaquima*—is a braided noseband. So is a bosal—from the Spanish *bozal,* meaning muzzle. The only difference between the two is that the hackamore is heavier—over a half inch in diameter—while the bosal is less than that. Traditionally the lead and reins of a hackamore—called the mecate—are of braided horsehair. The word became "McCarty" in cowboyese.

rope long enough to loop over the horse's neck for reins with enough left to tie again to the knot to serve as a lead. Old-time cowboys would tie the lead rope around their waists so the horse couldn't get away from them even if they were thrown. Today's trainers of green stock tuck the mecate in their belts or tie it on the near side of the saddle so it can be snatched quickly if they have to come out of the saddle. Extra knots of the mecate above the heel knot tighten the bosal, making it more punishing to the nose and underside of jaw.

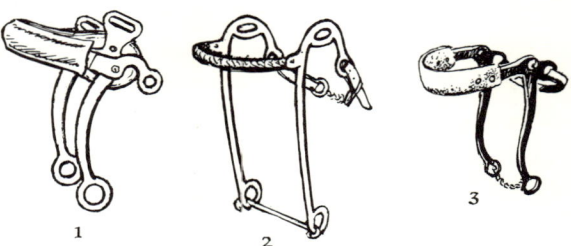

1. Hackamore with leather-covered bosal and leather cheek guards came into use in the early 1950's and has been used extensively ever since. 2. Extremely long shanks give this hackamore of braided leather over metal a strong leverage. 3. Hackamore bridle with sheepskin-covered bosal with only moderate leverage.

The hackamore is favored by many trainers during the breaking period because it gives them plenty of control without a mouthpiece that might be harmful to a green horse. The rawhide braided bosal can with pressure be somewhat punishing to the nose, and the heel knot under the jaw can rap a horse smartly if he misbehaves. By plow reining the horse's head can be pulled around while weight shifts make the signal to turn very evident. When neck reining is taught, the horse responds to it because it is easier on his nose than plow reining.

Some ranch, trail, and pleasure riders continue with a light bosal and find the horse responds so well they never resort to headgear that has a mouthpiece.

Hackamore bridles are available in many styles. All have some shank arrangement that puts leverage on the bosal, by using conventional reins. Some have leather bosals padded with sheepskin; some have cables covered with leather.

The use of various kinds of bits and headgear is further discussed in the following chapter on riding.

The throat latch of the hackamore—not always used—is called the fiador. It is made with intricately knotted rope. Cowboys call it the "theadore." Extra knots of the mecate above the heel knot reduce the size of the bosal, making it more punishing to the nose and underside of the jaw. *Photo by Irene Laune.*

Martingales

The Standing Martingale is a tie-down attached to the cinch or girth at the lower end and to a cavesson or bosal at the upper end. At mid-point the martingale is kept in place by a breast strap or a light supporting strap that hangs from the withers. The purpose of a martingale or tie-down is to prevent the horse from carrying his head too high, to prevent head tossing and rearing, and to flex the neck, which keeps the horse from thrusting his head forward in order to slip the bit off the bars of the mouth and into the corners. The cavesson or bosal to which the tie-down is attached can be set tight enough to limit the width the horse can open his mouth, further preventing him from getting behind the bit or cheating on the bit, as it is termed by some horsemen. A horse that becomes accustomed to a standing martingale may develop the bad habit of leaning into it.

The Running Martingale has a tie-down attached to the girth that comes up between the forelegs to be supported by a breastplate or a lightweight collar strap that goes over the withers. Above this point, the upper part of the tie-down is split to form two rein lead-up straps with a ring in the end of each one through which the reins pass. This section is called a racing fork. The main function of the running martingale is to put a downward pull on the reins to keep the bit on the bars instead of in the corners of the mouth, and to keep the head down, causing more flexion in the head and neck. Unlike the standing martingale, the restriction is not rigid and constant, but varies with the amount of pull on the reins, which makes it a very helpful training device. With a full bridle only the snaffle reins are used in conjunction with the running martingale, but many trainers who use only a curb bit will train with the running martingale to achieve the aims mentioned.

Draw Reins

Draw reins, running reins, sliding reins are names given to reins that are anchored to the D-rings of a saddle or to the rings of a running martingale at one end and then passed through the bit rings and on to the rider's hands. By sliding through the bit rings they give the rider great leverage and are so severe they should be used only by experienced horsemen. Reins attached to running martingale rings are preferred by many trainers to the ones fixed solidly to the saddle, because they give a more downward pull while giving the horse more lateral movement of the head. The purpose of draw reins is to train the horse to travel with his head lower, to flex head and neck, to control head tossing, and to keep the bit down on the bars of the mouth.

The three devices just mentioned should be considered as training gear. *The well-trained horse does not require any of them,* and they are not allowed in reining and stock seat classes in approved AQHA shows.

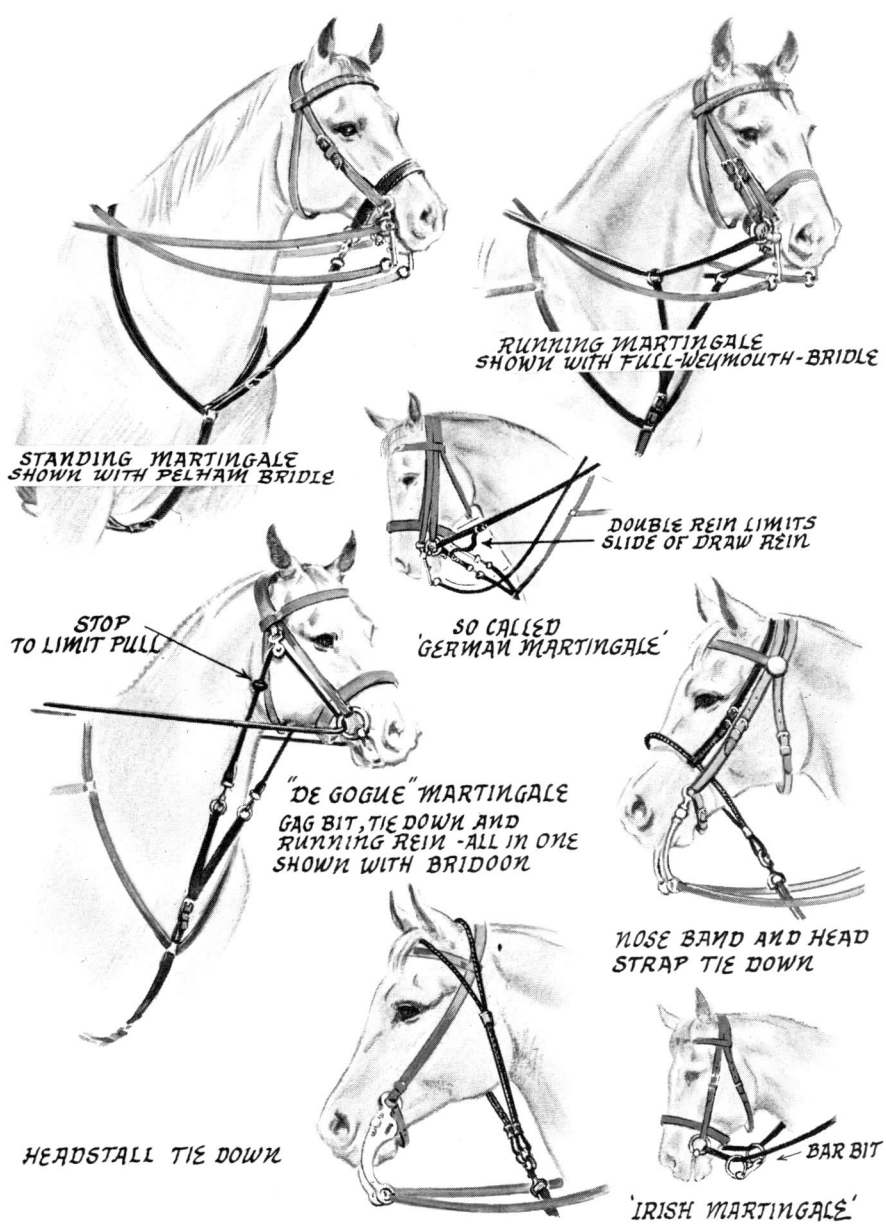

Martingales

In hard-riding events and competitions where winning is more important than gentle methods, tight cavesson and dropped nosebands to keep the horse from getting behind the bit, and standing martingales to keep his head out of the rider's face are frequently used. Ropers and barrel racers often use them, and I have never seen a polo pony or a photo of one without a standing martingale.

Whips, Bats, Quirts, Romals

Although some of these names sound cruel, they are not used to torture a horse. The long whip is used like a spur, to reach out and touch the horse, or to indicate without touching him what is expected of him. It is used largely when training a horse on a lunge line or when hitched to a breaking cart. If the horse is circling to the left on the lunge, the whip is held in the right hand so as to be somewhat behind the horse. It is used to keep the horse going and to keep him out at the end of the lunge. When direction is reversed and the horse is moving to the right, shift the whip to the left hand.

Short whips or crops are something few Western riders will be bothered with. Horses well trained in the Western style do not require them. They are seldom seen except for special occasions such as hazing a steer in a bull-wrestling contest where a whip sometimes comes in handy to move a horse in closer or to reach out and haze the steer closer to the bulldogger.

If you ride a Quarter Horse working hunter, you will no doubt follow the custom of your group and carry the whip or crop. In addition, there are four types of "sticks" the Eastern rider accustoms himself to handling: the flexible riding whip used on gaited horses; the more rigid walk-trot stick; the feathered jumping bat; and the traditional hunting crop whose crook handle is handy for opening gates, and whose long lash is for controlling hounds.

The *Western bat* is used for training: to tap the horse on the chest to back him up, on the neck or shoulder to turn him, and, until he is spur-trained, on the haunch to speed him up.

A *romal*, which is an extended lash on the rein ends, was devised by California rancheros for use as a quirt and will do for speeding up one's horse, but for tapping the horse just where you want to during training, the bat is more effective and controlled than a lash that is flying through the air.

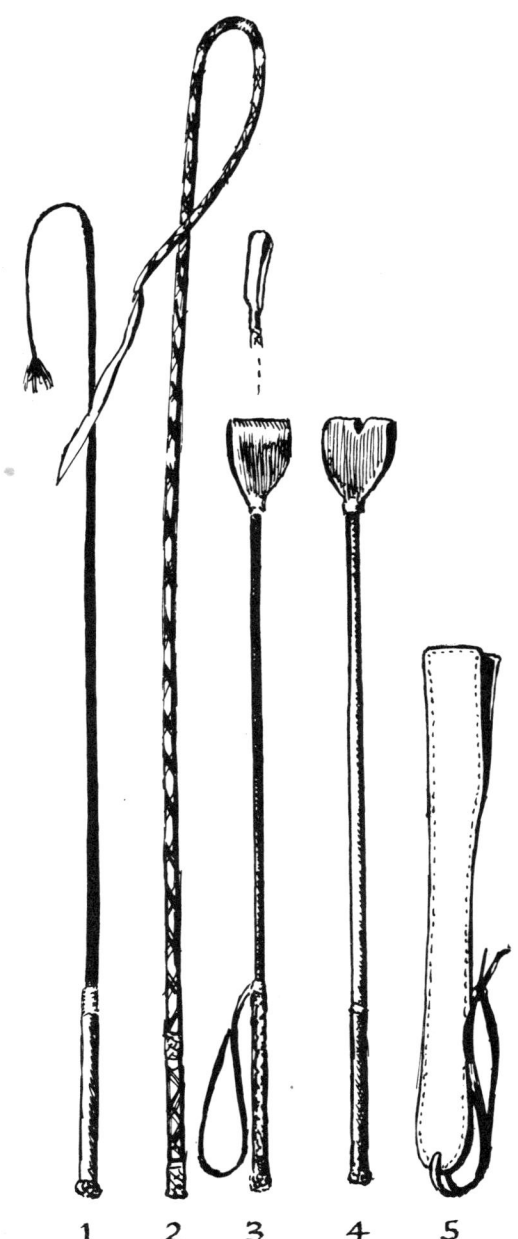

Whips are made in a variety of weights, lengths, and materials. Some are of fiber glass covered with nylon or leather. The whips shown are the types most generally used.

1. Riding whip. 2. Training whip. 3. Riding crop. 4. Racing bat. 5. Dogging bat.

Hobbles

Hobbles were once required equipment in Western riding classes when closed reins were used, or for the horse that hasn't been taught to ground-tie even if ridden with split reins. They are optional but are generally carried.

The most popular are the braided California type hobbles that are often sold as part of a set to match the braided leather riata that is carried on the saddle in Western classes.

The Utah hobble is simply a strong, soft leather strap that goes around one leg and passes through a keeper and then is buckled around the other leg.

Hobbles are placed above the fetlock joint. After the horse gets used to hobbles he can lift both front legs simultaneously or take little mincing steps and move about slowly to graze, but he can never wander very far. In my opinion a horse is less likely to get in trouble with them than on a picket rope.

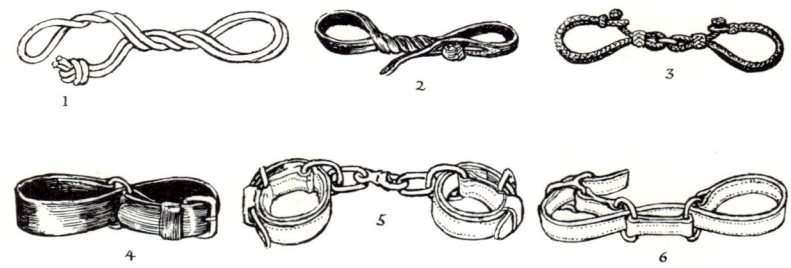

1. Hobble made of soft rope. 2. Twisted latigo hobble with leather button held in slot. Strong but easy on horse's legs. 3. Braided leather hobble popular with show riders. 4. Figure-eight heavy duty hobble lined with soft leather. 5. Heavy duty hobble. The soft-leather-lined cuffs are attached with chain links and a swivel. 6. Utah type hobble. Stitched nylon lined with soft leather.

Hobbles can be improvised by using a twisted gunny sack. Wrap it around one leg, then twist it two or three times before wrapping and tieing it around the other leg. Soft rope can be used in the same manner. For casting horses, or for holding up legs for shoeing or doctoring, or for antikicking rigs, a heavy leather cuff type hobble is advised. Some of this type have a ring stitched in for a rope to pass through. And some are sheepskin-lined to prevent possible hurt to the underside of the pastern. Sometimes the word hobble is confused with hopple. The latter is a restricting device, credited to John Browning of Indiana, that goes around the lateral legs to keep a pacing horse from breaking gait. The encircling straps are suspended from the withers and from the crupper strap. They are sometimes called "Indian pants." The Irish custom of hobbling at the hocks is called "spanceling."

Ropes

The use of the rope—*la reata*—with noose—*lazo*—later to be Americanized to lariat and lasso, was brought to a fine art that bugged the eyes of American stockmen who traveled in early day California. The Mexican vaqueros and a goodly number of old Southwestern cowboys made their own strong lariats from the fibers of mescal, the century plant, from which fiery tequila is also made. Others braided stout lariats from rawhide. These leather ropes had the weight to be thrown against a stiff wind, and they were not prone to figure-eight in the loop, but they were slick and too stretchable when wet. Mexicans and Indians, but very few Anglo cowboys, had the patience to weave horsehair ropes which were excellent but understandably rare and hard to come by. Linen was sometimes made into stock ropes and soaked in various wax and oil preparations to give weight and to resist moisture. But the main source of the lariat most used through the years was, and still is, a manila fiber fabricated by the Plymouth Rope and Cordage Company of Massachusetts.

For ranch roping when split-second timing was not important, ropes were long, sometimes as much as fifty feet. Now most roping is done in rodeo competition against time, and no cowboy, after roping a calf, wants to run any farther down on a rope to entwine its feet than necessary, so ropes average about twenty-five feet long.

In 1950 the Plymouth Rope and Cordage Company came out with a hard twist rope made of a manila silk fiber from the abaca plant. Ever since that time this slender rope, about the diameter of a man's little finger and of a cream color with a bright sheen, has been the favored lariat both for ranch work and for competitive roping.

For use against the rather persistent Oklahoma winds of my youth, we would sometimes dunk our ropes in pitch and then drag them through the buffalo grass for hours until they were dry and smooth. The extra

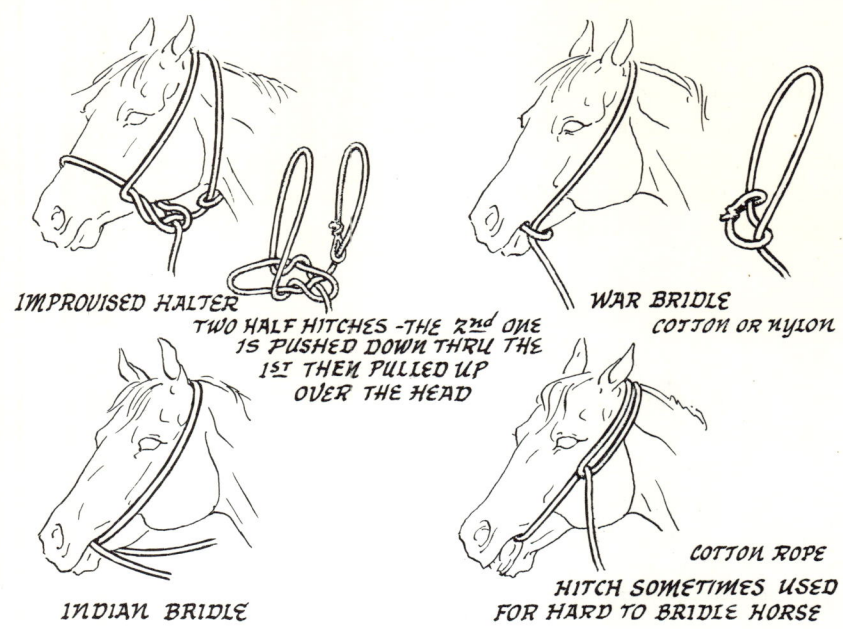

Various ways ropes have been used as halters and bridles.

weight they got from the pitch treatment was helpful when we had to throw against the wind. It also took the rattling snarl out of the rope as it ran through the honda when a loop was being built. Some spooky horses, especially those who had experienced the whirring rattle of a rattlesnake, didn't like the sound of the rope as it whirred through the hard twist rope honda.

In much smaller numbers, but increasing, are the ropers who favor nylon ropes, which are stout for their size and heft and whose strands are so melded there is slight twisting or unraveling.

There was a time when metal hondas were used with the rope woven in to hold them secure. And cowboys who ran out of reading material during bunkhouse evenings sometimes plaited in the strands of the rope to make a neat honda. Mostly a simple knot honda is used, with a leather reinforcement called a burner stitched in to reduce wear and give an easy slide to the rope.

Ropers take good care of their ropes. Metal or plastic cases like hatboxes are to be seen in their tack rooms and in the tack compartments of their horse trailers.

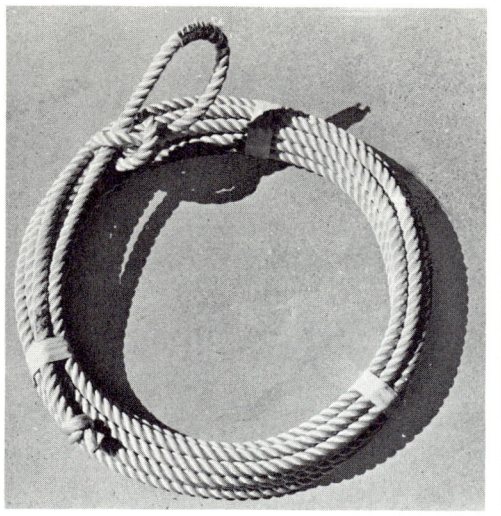

Left. Nylon lariat with tied honda and burner. *Photo by Irene Laune.*
Right. Braided leather riata—for show riding. *Photo by Irene Laune.*

In Western classes at shows, don't irritate a sharp-eyed judge by having your riata laced on your saddle backwards. It should have the honda facing forward. The riata carried in shows is short and small so that it makes a neat set of loops no more than eight or nine inches across. Most are of braided leather. The bitter end, the knot end of a hard twist manila lariat, should be finished off with a button knot by plaiting the strands and trimming them flush.

1. A honda tied into the end of the lariat with a leather burner sewed on is the most used type. 2. Copper hondas around which the rope is fitted and braided have been in use since the days of the great cattle drives. They are not often used today. 3. Jerkaway honda is quickly attached to the knot type honda. It releases the calf when pressure comes on the loop. 4. Aluminum horn loop holder.

Two other rope items are part of the roper's gear. The piggin' string is a short riata, manila rope or nylon, with a loop in one end. The roper carries it tucked in his belt, or even between his teeth so he can get at it quickly. When the calf is thrown, the piggin' string loop is slipped on a front leg, and then the hind legs are brought forward and secured with several wraps of the rope, and then a half-hitch is drawn around them.

A rope about the horse's neck is for the purpose of causing the horse to face the calf. The lariat is run through it before being tied to the saddle horn, and when the pull on the rope comes, the horse's head is swung in line with it.

Care of Tack

Everybody has a preference in methods of tack care, but until you've been at it long enough to develop one, you can do a good job of keeping your leather goods clean and supple by washing them every week or so with saddle soap. And when the leather shows signs of drying out, go over it with some proprietary brand of leather conditioner or neat's-foot oil. Be sure to give boots the same attention other leather items get, and keep them in shoe trees so they will maintain their shape.

To set and keep the stirrups of a Western saddle in position, facing forward, run a pole through them whenever the saddle is put on its rack.

On your workbench, the things you will need for making repairs and cleaning are: a leather punch; rivets; an awl; some waxed thread and leather needles; a sponge and rags; and some extra leather, whang leather, strap leather, and thongs.

Riding Clothes and Accessories

English Style. Riding clothes—boots, hats, and accessories—have such a wide range of prices, weights, and quality, with a wide variety of stores and catalogues to choose from, that it would not be feasible to deal in detail with the subject in this book.

The concern here is with the functions of riding attire and the items helpful for the rider. Answers to questions about the niceties of what is worn and when and where—the Kentucky jodhpurs, the top hat, the soft or wing collar, the brass or bone buttons, and the boots with colored tops, for example—will be found in books more particularly devoted to

English riding and in the establishments that cater to the needs of riders engaged in hunting, jumping, or flat saddle seat activities.

Fine English boots were once often called "Peels" for the London bootmaker of that name, just as the brass-buttoned scarlet coats for fox hunting are called "hunting pinks" for Mr. Pink, the London tailor who excelled in making them back in the 1800's.

The scarlet coats, by the way, are to distinguish masters and gentlemen members of the hunt. Junior or inexperienced members and women wear the black split-tailed jacket in summer or winter weight, with buff, canary, or brown breeches, and if eighteen years or under the regulation hunt cap is prescribed. The cap is also worn by the field master and whippers-in. A silk hunting hat or bowler derby is worn by gentlemen and lady members. In 1963 the AHSA abolished all requirements for formal hunting attire in any Junior Classes.

The hard hunting caps are worn for the same reason motorcycle helmets are, for protection during spills. They stay on well in a wind and are less likely to be brushed off by tree limbs than are brimmed hats. Granted that the derby's formality is noticeable today because it has not, for a generation or so, been an article of general wear, it does add dignity and fits almost as snugly as the hunting cap. Even so, formal riding requires that a hat guard be attached to it.

Much of riding attire has a dual purpose. The coats are long enough to serve as covering for an injured rider. The neck stock and lady's veil can double as a bandage. The cap bows, if placed vertically, indicate an amateur rider. Sandwich cases carried on the off side near the cantle and flasks attached on the near side close to the pommel are obviously useful accessories.

Many of the conventions as well as the ritualized language of hunting clubs is maintained in order to promote safety through recognized rules and quick response to hazards.

Ratcatcher clothing (attire for informal riding as opposed to formal hunting attire) usually consists of a tweed coat, tan breeches, felt hat, and brown boots.

Most beginners wear jodhpurs and jodhpur shoes. Even though the peg in the jodhpur breeches is less accented than it used to be, the bulkiness around the thighs lacks trimness unless the jodhpurs are expertly tailored. Both jodhpurs and riding breeches are reinforced on the inside of the knees where the wear is greatest for flat saddle riders, and suede leather gives a better grip.

Even though they may be snug fitting, jodhpurs and the shoes that are worn with them are much easier to get into than breeches and boots. For this reason, some experienced riders prefer them. However, the majority of seasoned and consistent riders still wear boots. With daily flexing of the arch of the foot, until it is almost in line with the leg, it is possible to get into boots with high tops that fit as snugly as gloves. In formal hunting attire boots are of black calf with brown tops. The tops originated with the purpose of keeping white breeches from being soiled by boot polish.

Leather jackets, suede, deer, elkskin, sheepskin-lined, and quilted nylon windbreakers are worn for comfort on chilly casual rides in both East and West. And blue jeans and work shirts are universally worn around the stable or for training, regardless of whether the horses wear flat or stock saddles. Some Easterners have succumbed to the cowboy boots for such work because of the comfort and the fact that the boot tops keep out dirt, gravel, grain, and straws. Tommy Smith, Jr., attracted attention by wearing a cowboy hat when training Jay Trump in England for the Grand National Steeplechase at Aintree, which they won in 1965 to become the first American pair ever to do so. The Easterner also occasionally dons the Western straw hat for protection during training under a hot summer sun.

Western Style. Because of the increasing number of people who enjoy the really exhilarating sport of riding and horsemanship and are enjoying both styles of riding—Eastern and Western—tack and riding attire are less limited than formerly to one camp or the other. Whatever serves best will be chosen. Jumping saddles are naturally for jumping and hunting, and for some kinds of pleasure riding. Some use them on trail rides to cut down weight. Stock saddles are for Western performance and training and for long rides into rough terrain. I trained my own horses to work well under either rig, although I don't recommend switching bits if your horse is working at ease with a bit he is used to. One of my horses didn't mind the change from a Western low port long shank curb bit to the full four-rein Weymouth bridle. Indeed, Quarter Horses may be more adaptable than their riders who, if accustomed to cowboy boots, may find it difficult to struggle into high-top English boots.

Certainly more people are learning the reasons for differences in tack and dress just as some differences are blurring. As mentioned before, blue jeans and waist-length windbreakers are found to be practical for both Eastern and Western riders. It wouldn't be surprising if more split-tail riding coats and jackets gave way to the very handsome waist-length Spanish type of jacket.

Boots worn by Western riders (and for daily wear by many businessmen in the West) came by their shape and structure to serve a definite purpose. The pointed toes make it easy to spear a stirrup and slip into it easily. The high heels keep the foot from going on through the stirrup, especially the old "oxbow" stirrups. High heels, by digging into the ground, are also helpful to corral ropers and bulldoggers. The high heel that slants under is in fact today called the "bulldogger heel." With the wide-tread stirrups now so much in vogue on Western saddles, the foot can hardly slip through them, so a good many Western riders who ride less, and walk more, wear boots with flat heels. For winter riding, flat-heeled fleece-lined boots are popular.

The steel arch support that is built into cowboy boots assists ropers, cutting horse riders, and riders in rough country who, often on green half-broken stock, ride with their weight on the arches of their feet or "clear home" as they say. They can't take the chance of a foot slipping out of a stirrup.

The Western boot is easy to get on and off even without a boot jack, which can't be said for a really nice-fitting English boot. And surprising to those who wear them for the first time, the Western boot is about the most comfortable shoe one can wear. The arch support and the soft ankle leather have a lot to do with it. The pointed toe is well forward so it does not impinge.

The cowboy hat, with a wide price range from felt to beaver, is designed for shade and protection from rain and hail. And oh yes, you can drink out of it too, but dip a little water on top of the brim and don't use it like a bucket, although that too has been done where there was no other way of getting water for a horse. The general rule is that the hotter the country, the wider the brim. The cattleman's dress hat of Oklahoma and Texas and other places has a brim that is only two and one-half inches wide. Brims almost double that width can be seen on ranch workers. Even the modest cowboy dress hat has occasioned stares in New York, just as the almost brimless New York hat, reminiscent of the headgear of carnival clowns, draws stares in the smaller Western towns.

Inexpensive Western straw hats, formed into wide-brimmed flaring shapes, are perhaps the most worn of all Western hats. For one thing, warm weather lasts longer than cold weather in much of the West's horse and cattle country.

Pleasure riding has changed some of the styles. Today riders who are seldom out in the sun or weather for many hours will wear short-sleeve shirts, whereas working stockmen had to have more protection from sunburn, so they always did, and still do, wear long sleeves. When riding in hot weather for long hours at a time, we used to wear wool shirts. It sounds like an odd thing to do with a blazing sun overhead, but they served two purposes. They kept the sun from burning us, as would happen if we wore thin cotton shirts. And the wool, saturated with perspiration, quickly dried in the hot wind and served as a cooler.

Windbreakers of quilted nylon are very popular with both pleasure riders and working cowboys. For more bitter weather, leather jackets lined with sheepskin are used, and for the in-between weather, leather vests are practical and have pockets and room for a good many odds and ends. Pockets with flaps are favored in both vests and jackets so that things won't bounce out when riding gets active. Western riders avoid, if they can, putting anything that is at all bulky in their pants pockets, especially the hip pockets. That accounts for the vests that have been standard riding wear since the West was settled.

Men and women, boys and girls dress somewhat similarly except for the more formal riding coats, more delicate and brightly colored boots and shirts, scarves, gloves, etc.

As with the shirts, the riding pants fit snugly. The more faded and washed-out the blue jeans are, the better they seem to be liked. If you happen to have a nice clean sandy-bottomed stream running through your place, you can do what the cowboys did to soften and condition their jeans. They would toss them, when brand new, into the stream, put a rock on them to keep the current from washing them away, and leave them there for a day or two. When they took them out, the jeans would be just right, or so they said. I never tried it.

Blue jeans and frontier pants are rather tight-fitting. They have no cuffs and because Western riders do not grip the saddle with their knees they seldom have leather knee patches. The pants are worn outside the boots to give a less rumpled appearance. Some men of the older generation still fancy the idea of tucking their trouser legs inside, figuring what's the use of having boots with exquisite stitching on the legs if it doesn't show. Generally warm-weather riding breeches, jeans, or riding pants are made of fairly light washable material; the heavier garments for cooler weather are sent to the cleaners.

Chaps were originally worn by vaqueros as a protection from chaparral (brush thickets), which gave them their name of *chaparajos,* to be shortened to "chaps." They are close-fitting like seatless leather trousers or leggins, and fringed more often than not. Later, to have their protection but to be able to get out of them easily in hot weather, the

Chaps: Shotgun and, right, batwing.

cowboys devised the batwing chaps. Large and flaring, they are held at the back of the leg with only three or four snap and ring fasteners.

In the cold Northwest, Angora goat and bearhide chaps with the hair left on were once used for warmth. Today soft leather, trim fitting, fringed chaps, shotgun or shorter soft ones, called chinks, are an accepted item of Western costume in reining, Western pleasure, working cowhorse, stock seat, and cutting events. Many types of chaps fit snugly with zipper fasteners. Chaps are dispensed with in roping, barrel racing, and pole bending. Bronc and bull riders wear them not only for display but, I am told, also because they save many a knee or leg from getting scraped as riders come rocketing out of the chutes.

The bola tie consists of a plaited leather thong with silver-tipped ends, and a sliding decorative brooch, often of silver and turquoise made by the Indians. Or the brooch can be of native stone or ornamented wood. It gives an elegant touch to the cowboy costume and is much less restricting than a knotted tie. It is now so accepted by Western men that many of them wear it daily with business or dress-up clothes. The state legislature recently made the bola the official tie of Arizona.

11

Riding and Horsemanship

Let us remember that a horse learns by rote, which makes it necessary for his handler and rider to have certain basic ways of doing things so that they will become habitual and recognized routines the horse learns, and to which he responds. A horseman who schools himself in proven and accepted ways that are effective about the stable, around horses, and on them can manage not only his own but almost any horse.

Saddling and Bridling

Place the blanket forward on the withers and move it back into place. If it is dragged forward, it roughs the hair against the grain. If an English saddle is used, the stirrups should be up in the leathers and the girth lying across the seat. Place the saddle so that the throat of the saddle fits snugly against the withers, then walk around to see that everything is in place on the off side. Return to the near side and buckle the girth to the billets but not tight. Later when the horse is bridled and led from the stable and is no longer tensed against it, you can take up the final notch, but never so tight that you can't slip two fingers under the girth. If a shaped pad is used, be sure the leather straps on it are looped around the billets to keep it in place.

If using a stock saddle, again place the blanket well forward, as with the English saddle, and then back slightly so as not to rough the hair against the grain, and see that the withers are well covered. Unless you are an expert, it is a good idea before saddling to hook the off stirrup over the horn and lay the cinch over the seat of the saddle. A flopping stirrup may hit the horse and startle him and get him in the habit of dancing around when being saddled, and a cinch ring if it strikes sharply can hurt a knee or cannon bone. Set the saddle throat over the withers and rock it sideways to see that it is snugly set, and to take the tautness out of the blanket over the wither bone. Check on the off side to see that tie thongs, cinch billet, and blanket are in place before setting up the cinch. Some horses swell up to prevent tight cinching. Some even have pains comparable to arthritic pains until they can move around and limber up. Instead of a sharp slap on the saddle seat, a practice of the old cowboys to make the horse unswell, it is better to wait until after putting on the bridle and leading the horse from the stable before setting the cinch to the proper tightness.

When outside, and before setting the cinch up tight, it is a good practice, for either type of saddle, to pick up the horse's forelegs one after the other and pull out toward you as far as you can. This action will pull any wrinkles of the hide out from under the cinch, making it much less likely to cause cinch galls. Pull latigos up on the cinch until getting more than two fingers under it is difficult.

Connie Tupper's good riding form and training methods have made her a consistent trophy winner. *Photo by Paul A. Quinn.*

If you use a double rig, one with a rear girth, the latter should be just tight enough to touch the horse's belly. Many riders prefer to see daylight between it and the belly. Be sure the short strap that links the girth to the cinch is in place. Without it the girth can ride back until it gets too close to the horse's flank.

To *bridle* the horse, remove the halter but draw the halter throat latch or the lead up over his neck so he can still be controlled.

With right hand over his head to keep it down, slip the bridle headstall up so your right hand can hold it out ahead of the ears. This will keep the bridle in place while your left hand opens the horse's mouth. Force the thumb on one side and the fingers on the other side into the mouth at the bars. There is no danger of being bitten because the fingers are in the space between the incisors and the molars. With a gentle pressure the teeth will open and allow the bit to slip into the mouth. Try never to bump his lips with the bit. If the bit is extra cold, warm it with your hands.

The chin strap should be loose enough so the bridle will slip on without a struggle. Adjust the headstall behind the ears, smooth out the hairs of mane and forelock, and see that the forelock hangs out over the brow band. If using a bridle that is new to the horse, check the fit of the headstall. It should not pull the bit too tight against the corner of the mouth or allow the bit to hang too far down from the corner. With the headstall in place, buckle the throat latch, leaving plenty of room for the horse to pull in his chin and draw his jaws close to his windpipe without being restricted.

Mounting the English Saddle

The easiest way is to have someone give you a leg up, but of course it is not always feasible. Obviously the horse must be taught to stand still while being mounted. Teaching this sometimes requires patience and determination. (See Chapter 13, "Bad Habits and Vices and Their Correction.")

After the horse has been led from the stable and the girth set securely, place the rein in position. While your right hand steadies the stirrup, your left hand, holding the reins, controls the horse. The left hand, with the reins, grasps the mane at the withers or the pommel of the saddle. With the left foot in the stirrup, the knee against the horse's shoulder keeps the boot toe from punching into his side. From a position almost

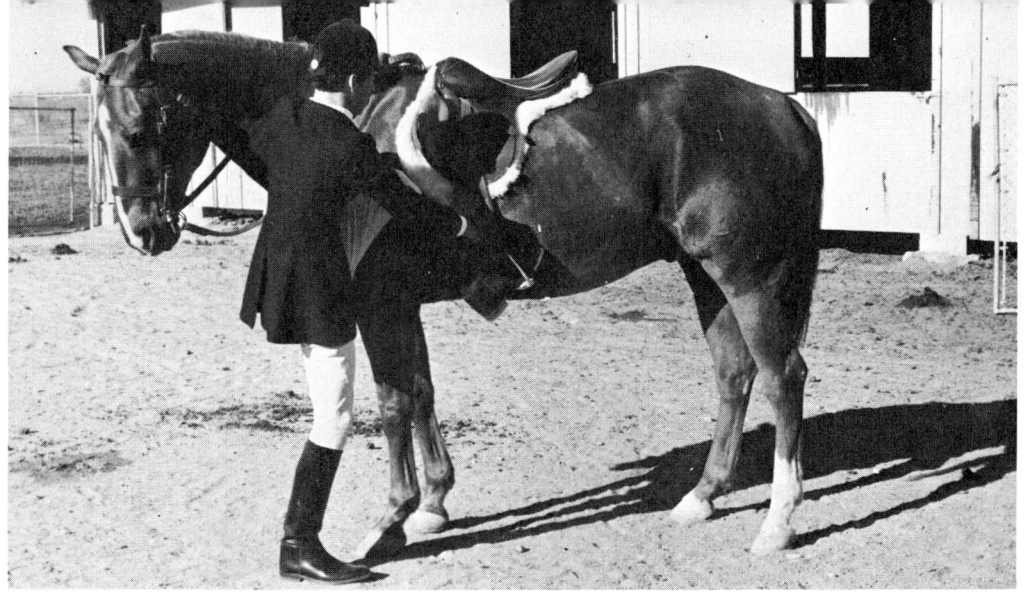

Mounting the English saddle. Larry Dunford of Paradise Valley, Arizona, demonstrates good mounting form.

When the toe of the right foot makes the turn forward, care must be given to avoid gouging the horse. *Photo by the author.*

facing the side of the horse, the right hand grasps the cantle and a spring from the right leg sends you up. The left leg balances the weight over the horse momentarily, as the toe turns forward, before swinging the right leg over and sitting in the saddle. This last movement should be done easily to avoid a hard plop into the saddle that jars the horse. Reins are equal in length and held short enough for control.

Mounting the Stock Saddle

There are several ways of mounting the stock saddle. The Old Montana style has the rider face the rear, with the left hand holding the reins on withers or pommel. The right hand places the stirrup. Then with the foot in the stirrup and the left knee against the horse's shoulder, both hands go to the horn and the rider pivots on his knee and swings half-circle into the saddle. Forward movement of the horse, should it occur, gives momentum to the swing up.

The Texas or Oklahoma hop is showy and fast and rather rough on the horse's withers. Here the rider faces about three-fourths forward and with reins in the left hand and both hands on the horn springs from the ground with both feet. On the way up, the left foot spears the stirrup in time to give the thrust that sends the right leg over and the seat into the saddle. Some riders do this so expertly that there is no undue jerk on the withers. Some show-offs swing into the saddle without using the stirrup.

With good rein control and large stirrups that require no placing, most Western riders face about three-fourths forward, and as they step into the stirrup the right leg springs them up and over. The left hand with the reins is on the neck or just ahead of the horn, and the right hand grasps the horn. The weight is kept in the left stirrup until the rider can ease into the saddle. Since Western riders use stirrups that are let down more than those of riders of English saddles, they reach them easier, which makes mounting more of a fluid motion.

To lower the stirrups for even easier mounting, there is a stainless steel and aluminum device called Easy Mount that can be attached to the near stirrup of any Western saddle. It is a boon to short riders with tall horses or those with skin-tight breeches. After mounting with this low stirrup, the toe touches a button at the top of the stirrup that causes the stirrup to spring up and lock in a position level with the off stirrup.

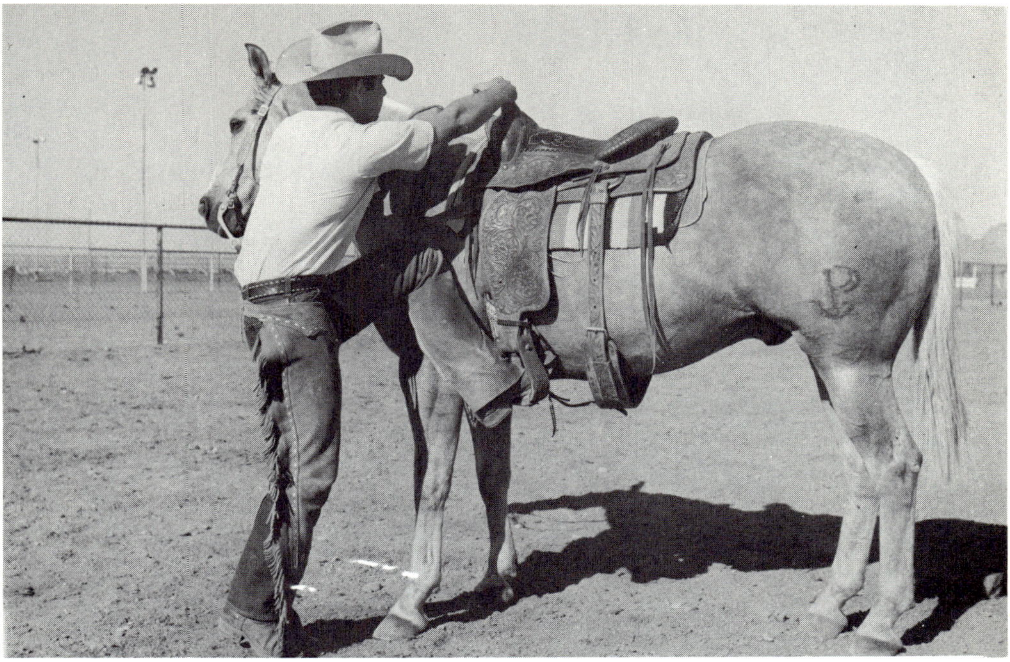

The Montana style of mounting. *Photo by Irene Laune.*

After the right leg is thrown over the saddle, pause for a fraction of a second so your weight can be let down in the saddle without a jarring plop. *Photo by Irene Laune.*

The Hop—also called the Western Hop, the Oklahoma Hop, and the Texas Hop. Notice both feet of the rider are off the ground while the left foot has not yet put weight in the stirrup. *Photo by Irene Laune.*

The foregoing descriptions of mounting may seem unnecessarily elementary, but it is in the observation of small details of procedure that riders become horsemen.

Now, mounted up and ready to go, swing your horse's head away from the stable and move out at a walk. (If he refuses to leave the stable, see "Bad Habits and Vices and Their Correction.")

Riding the Forward Seat

For both Eastern and Western riding, much attention is given to the forward or the balanced seat, also called the hunt seat or jumping seat in Eastern riding, as distinct from the saddle seat, which is farther back toward the cantle. If you ride well bareback, you have achieved both a forward and a balanced seat without bothering to put a name to them. The forward seat, like bareback riding, keeps the weight close to the withers where, because it is the horse's point of balance, he can best handle weight. Even some of the new stock saddles are coming back to a design used almost a hundred years ago which slides the weight closer to the saddle swells.

You will have good posture in the saddle and a balanced seat if, when viewed from the side, a vertical line from your chin is in line with your heel, and if your kneecap is almost directly over the stirrup. The pelvis is slightly tucked under and riding is more on the crotch and inside of the upper thighs than on the buttocks. Heels are down lower than the ball of the foot. With good position your weight will go down toward the pommel into the horse's withers if he makes a sudden stop, whereas with the feet forward, the pivoting action on the stirrups might send you over the horse's head. About half the weight should be in the stirrups and the seat should not be rubbing the cantle. Center your weight by equalizing the stirrup pressure. When the horse leans in a turn, lean with him and stay centered in the saddle. Feel for the rhythm of your horse's gait and try and get with it. Usually beginners will jounce around for a week or so and then suddenly shout, "I've got it!"

Although the same good saddle seat that places weight and keeps balance in a way that aids the horse and makes riding comfortable and secure is common to both flat saddle and Western saddle riding, there are distinct differences in the two styles.

Riding Western Style

If you ever learn to sit a Western saddle at all gaits, you will never forget how to do it.

I have taught children to sit a saddle well by asking them to try to imagine they have a heavy knapsack strapped on their shoulders. The downward thrust automatically puts the pelvis in a good position. Beginners also did well when told to imagine their bodies were jello and that their skeletons were moving up and down while their bodies sat in the saddles. The jar of the hoofbeats is absorbed, beginning with the little spring in the foot where the heel rocks down from the instep, and it gets less as it goes on up through the body where the waist absorbs

The Western seat—the weight in the stirrups puts the weight on the withers. *Photo by Irene Laune.*

much of it. There is no obvious posting in the Western saddle. The Western rider sits the saddle at all gaits, greatly assisted by stirrup pressure. Extended trotting is seldom indulged in, but should a judge call for the extended trot in a stock seat class, posting is allowed but scored on how much in rhythm the rider is with the horse and how little up and down movement he shows in the saddle. Cowboys and some trail riders who sometimes use the extended trot to cover ground stand in their stirrups to relieve themselves and their horses of the jar of the trot beat.

Because of the necessity of sitting the stock saddle at all times, it takes a little longer to learn this way of riding than in the flat saddle, where posting by taking the jolt off the seat can delay the need to find the rhythm of the horse's gait. Riding without using the stirrups or riding

RIDING AND HORSEMANSHIP

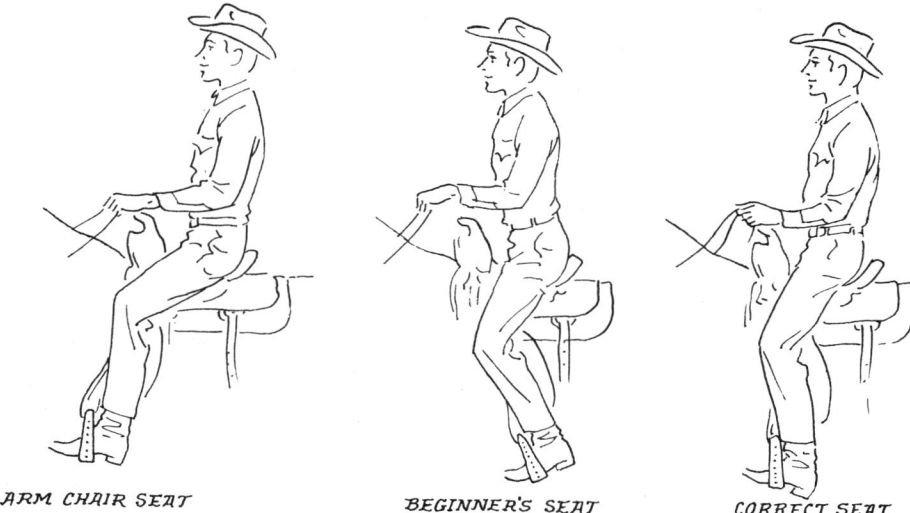

ARM CHAIR SEAT   BEGINNER'S SEAT   CORRECT SEAT

Armchair seat. Beginner's seat. Correct seat.

bareback at a jog trot will induce the proper seat. Keep shoulders back and relaxed.

The stock saddle is ridden with longer stirrup leathers than the flat saddle. The old saying, "the shorter the stirrups, the shorter the ride," makes sense to those who spend long hours in the saddle. Longer stirrups cause knees to be less bent and tense, allowing for better circulation, and they center the weight so that less weight is on the buttocks.

Reins and Bits and Ways of Using Them

In the chapter on tack, the better-known bridles and bits and hackamores are shown, and their reasons for being explained. The manner in which one rides is largely influenced by the kind of bit he uses and how the reins are handled.

Since the beginning of horse mastery, control and communication with the horse has been centered on the mouth with a deliberate intent of causing pain. Literally hundreds of variations of the basic snaffle and curb bits have been stuffed into horses' mouths. And as long as the horse's mouth is ridden on and used as the focus of communication and balance for the rider, the experiments with bits and their subtle—and not so subtle—punishment will go on.

The truth is that the well-trained horse will respond and be controlled even in bursts of action if a style of riding that is not dependent on riding on the horse's mouth is perfected.

Even the torture instruments used by horse warriors and stock handlers, from the ancient Greeks to the California spade and ring bit users, indicate a style of riding that stayed off the horse's mouth. Xenophon, a soldier whose right hand must have been occupied with a sword rather than with reins and who therefore must have been a neck reiner, said, in effect, that if a horse responds, give him his head, refrain from pulling at the mouth with the bit. The point he tried to make has long been understood by one-handed riders, which includes the stock-seat riders.

That the East and West have much that would be of mutual benefit to share, there is no doubt. Training and riding methods that seemed only a few years ago to be worlds (the Old World and the New World) apart are being discussed and experimented with in both camps. Even horsemen devoted to traditional old-school methods are adopting some that are associated with the Western style—specifically, to minimize bit use. California bosals and training hackamores are no longer an uncommon sight in the Eastern U.S. and in England. And in turn, nearly all Western horsemen have learned much from the Eastern schools.

In an article titled "All Done by Kindness—The Bosal vs. the Drop Noseband," in the June 1967 issue of *Horse and Hound* (Vol. LXXXIII), published in London and reprinted in the *Quarter Horse Journal*, John Paget, a British horseman, wrote: "Change even at the cost of disregarding the German Cavalry Manual of 1912, is not necessarily wrong." He further states that "adopting the forward seat for roping was an undreamt of departure from western tradition—but it paid off at the rodeo. Once upon a time the cowboy shared our opinion that the best horseman made the least effective use of his stirrups. Now he knows better." Again referring to the California bosal, he says: "The degree of gentleness and patience called for by their hackamore and bosal technique only seem strange to us because the idea that kindness might also be the best policy is not endemic on our side of the Rockies."

An Englishwoman, Moyra Williams, also conceived the idea that getting off the horse's mouth would be a revolutionary method of horsemanship. Her experimentation had led to no positive results when on a visit to the United States she saw cutting horses in action at a rodeo.

It came as a revelation to her when she saw these lightning-quick Quarter Horses demonstrating the head freedom she had hoped to perfect. Back home in England she proceeded to train her horses in what amounted to hackamore training, and soon had them well-controlled and responding with precision, which included neck reining, while wearing a bitless bridle with a dropped noseband or cavesson and a chin strap. She wrote a book about her methods, called *Adventures Unbridled.*

Vladimir S. Littauer, who had instructed several generations of New Yorkers in equitation methods, frankly revised his former opinions in his book *Common Sense Horsemanship*. In it he states: "Dressage teaches a horse to do things unnaturally by emotionally stimulated movements. The idea is to have a horse carry one across fields and over fences in exactly the way he would do it himself when free and unrestrained. The horse in motion uses his head and neck as a balancer in a similar manner to the way we humans use our arms. The horse, deprived of his balancer, finds himself in the situation of a man who runs with his hands in his pockets. It stands to reason that more freedom of the head encourages more initiation in the horse."

William Steinkraus, longtime captain of the United States Equestrian Team, stated in his book *Riding and Jumping:* "The riding master's constant cry is 'contact, contact, contact,' but there are also circumstances under which, as a practical matter, I think it is quite permissible and even desirable to lose contact with the horse's mouth altogether."

As precise and lovely as the performances of circus and dressage horses appear, they bear as little relationship to the initiative required in a cutting horse or any free-headed horse as does playing patty-cake to boxing.

Wallace Stegner, one of America's highly regarded writers, who has scrutinized the West with more than a passing glance, wrote: "Most education trains us for the past, as most preparation for war readies us for the war just over . . . just as education planned by the eastern establishment has for too long taken westerners . . . and tried unsuccessfully to make Europeans out of them."

Western horsemen have formed their own distinctive brand of horsemanship, and they now constitute the largest body of all horsemen.

Riding with Slack Reins is an essential part of Western riding and requires that the horse be trained for it. Reins are held in the left hand with slack enough so that there is no pull whatever on the bit. They pass through the hand from either direction with the thumb pressing

Marcia Paxson starting a green horse in training. The second set of reins can be looped over the horn to draw chin in slightly for head setting. *Photo by the author.*

them against the forefinger. In AQHA shows it is permitted, if one prefers, to have a finger between the reins, except in Youth Western Equitation. Reins wrapped across or around the hand or held with more than a finger between them gives judges the impression that a tight grip is needed by the rider to control his horse and is often penalized. The right hand holds the reins about ten inches below the rein hand in order to shorten reins by sliding them when necessary. The ends of split reins should hang down on the near side. Closed reins terminating in a romal hang down on the off side.

To be able to ride with swinging reins that give the horse complete freedom of the head is the result of teaching the horse to anticipate the pressure on the mouth. Reins hanging pendant from the bit shank can, by slight movements, send signals that are understood by the horse before leverage on the bit is necessary. Where pressure is applied that part of the horse tries to go away from it. In neck reining when the right rein is drawn against the horse's neck it causes him to turn away from its touch and go to the left. When weight is shifted the horse tries to get under it for balance.

During training the horse learned how a bosal, when used, hurt his nose and how a bit can hurt his mouth. The ideal in a trained horse is for him to respond to the *memory* of a bit or a bosal. The truth is that only accomplished horsemen ever approach this ideal of expert handling. The most punishing bits, and the Santa Barbara and the Salinas Spade bits will serve as examples, can be the gentlest of bits in the mouth of a well-trained horse if the reins are in the hands of a true horseman. The amount of pressure needed to transmit the cues for stops, change of gaits, and lead changes, turns, and even backups would not break a thread if used to attach the reins to the shank of the bit. As generally taught, cues call for too much bit manipulation. Use of the bit can be reduced by perfecting subtle body and leg aids to the point where the mouth can go practically untouched.

Flat Saddle Riding and Reining differ from the Western method in many ways. One of the most serious problems that riding stables, dude ranches, etc., have to contend with is the Eastern rider who, when mounted for the first time on a Western-trained horse, pulls back on the reins. Too often the horse rears or plunges and throws the rider; and if he is seriously injured a lawsuit for damages follows.

The most marked difference between the two styles of riding is in the handling of the reins. The fact that English pleasure riders hold the reins in both hands calls for a different posture and balance. The reins are used somewhat in the manner used in driving an active harness horse. The horse is signaled to turn by a direct pull on the side of the mouth on which the turn is to be made. It is often called plow reining. The rein used for the turn is the pressure rein. You may have noticed that harness horses step out against a very firmly held rein. It is as though they are trying to pull the rein away from the driver to get free. In a lesser degree this is true of the riding horse trained in the English manner. He is accustomed to having a constant pressure on his mouth no matter how light it is. Good hands, or light hands, move with the horse's movement to avoid any sudden or increased pressure, but contact with the mouth is always there. The horse that tucks his chin in or stops or rears to avoid this contact of the bit on the bars of his mouth is said to "get behind the bit." If the horse needs more control than the snaffle, the reining bit that is kept in contact, a full bridle is used that has a curb bit (Weymouth bridle) as well as the snaffle. The snaffle reins are used for cues for turns and the various actions desired, such as when the mouth is touched more firmly and then let off accompanied by a slight seat shift forward with leg pressure to signal a change from trot to canter. The curb bit with a curb chain under the chin and with shanks to which a second pair of reins are attached is used for rating speed or when more control is necessary. The curb reins can also be "milked" with a hardly noticeable on and off movement to keep the horse collected. Snaffle reins wrap through each hand, going to the bit outside the little finger. Curb reins pass between the second and third fingers (some separate the reins with two fingers), which leaves the thumb and first two fingers to give a good grip. The bight (end of reins) falls to the off side. When the wrist is flexed inward and downward, the pressure shifts from the snaffle to the curb reins. When turning the horse, in addition to the direct pull, leg pressure or spur is given on the side the turn is being made, so as to turn the body and not just twist the neck. No one aid or cue is ever given without being accompanied by seat and leg movements, even though they may be too subtle to be observed.

The reins are always closed, but the snaffle reins can be unbuckled if they are to be used with a running martingale, whereas the curb reins are sewn together.

The Gaits

The Walk has a certain rhythm, particularly a brisk walk of four miles an hour or a little better, and the rider who synchronizes with it, keeping some of his weight in the stirrups, does his horse a big favor. Walking is a definite gait and the horse should be schooled to improve it so that he always walks briskly and holds the gait when asked to.

The Jog Trot is a very slow trot, a two-beat gait not much faster than a brisk walk. It is a favored gait with many riders of Quarter Horses who sit their saddles comfortably while the miles—about four and a half or five an hour—are shuffled by.

The Fox Trot is an artificial slow gait similar to the running walk, or amble, capable of five to eight miles an hour. In the booklet, "History and Rules of the Missouri Fox Trotting Horse Breed Association, Inc.," it is described as "a broken gait, the animal walking with the front feet and trotting with the back feet. . . . The head and tail are slightly elevated giving the animal a graceful carriage and the rhythmic beat of the hooves, along with the nodding action of the head give an appearance of relaxation and poise."

The slow gait or single-foot and the rack are the gaits added to the walk, trot, and canter that distinguish the performance of the Five-Gaited Saddle Horse.

The Single-foot is an artificial four-beat gait in which the side legs move together but not quite in unison. The hind feet hit the ground before the front feet do. Each foot hits the ground separately, making four distinct beats. Having a single foot on the ground gave the gait its name. It is a very comfortable gait to ride.

The Rack is the showiest of all artificial gaits and can attain speeds comparable to a very fast trot. Although the lateral legs move together somewhat as they do in the pace, they are not in unison. The hind foot precedes the front foot in hitting the ground, thereby making four distinct beats. The gait has been perfected in the American Saddle Horse ever since its development as a breed in 1891, and since the 1940s by the Tennessee Walking Horse, who racks remarkably fast and with an exaggerated action. Unfortunately its spectacular performance is too often dependent on grown-out hoofs and the deplorable practice of "soreing" the front feet to induce extremely high action.

The Trot is for those riders who like to post. It is a natural two-beat gait in which the diagonal legs move in unison as in the walk but faster. The diagonal feet hit the ground at the same time, making the first beat, then as they leave the ground there is a moment called suspension, when all the feet are off the ground. Then the other diagonal feet hit the ground to make the second beat. The trot has a wide range from a moderate trot of eight to twelve miles per hour to an extended trot, which can reach a speed comparable to the gallop. Most instructors of English riding put emphasis on training at the trot and the posting in the saddle that is necessary to ride it with any comfort. If you feel in rhythm and are comfortable when riding the trot, the chances are that you are posting on the correct beat. In the ring one should post, that is, rise from the saddle on the outside diagonal. For instance, when moving toward the right in the ring one should post on the left diagonal. When the left forefoot and the right hind foot leave the ground, one should rise in the stirrups, then sit when those same feet hit the ground and are better able to take the weight. When moving to the left in the ring, post on the right diagonal by rising when the right forefoot leaves the ground.

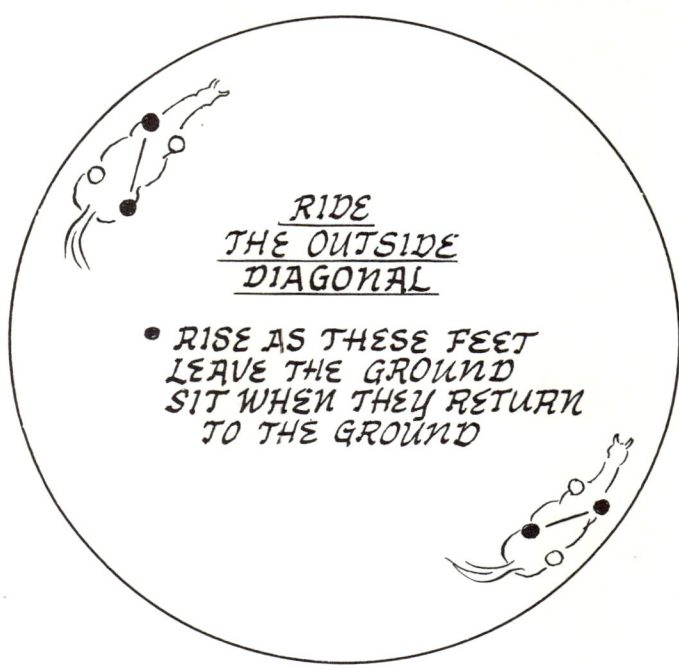

Posting the diagonals.

One should always equalize the amount of right and left posting to avoid tiring the set of muscles on just one side of the horse. It takes experience to recognize the proper beat when the horse steps into the trot. If not with it, just sit the jar of an extra beat and rise on the next. The knee acts as the pivot from which the rider moves up and down. From the knee down the leg should feel free to move with the stirrup.

The Canter is a three-beat gait, a slower version of the gallop in which the hind legs drive the horse with a series of plunges so that the forward movement rolls over the front legs, which give direction and support but little if any propulsion. One of the front legs is always in the lead of the other. On a *right lead,* for instance, the right forefoot reaches out ahead of the left forefoot and after it hits and then leaves the ground there is a moment of suspension when all the feet are off the ground. Then the left hind foot, which has shifted to the right to be in line with the body, hits the ground and is followed by the beat of the right hind and left fore, which hit the ground simultaneously. When a horse changes direction his leading foreleg should be the one on the inside of the curve to give support and balance. When front legs change leads the hind legs must also change leads, otherwise the gait is disunited or out of "sync."

Much attention is given by judges to lead changes and the aids with which the rider calls for them. But whether for show or not, horses must be trained to make fluent changes to the proper leads. Most well-formed active horses do this naturally when free in pasture, but a green horse in training, in an effort to keep unaccustomed weight on his back in balance, and particularly if his head is restricted, may lose his instinctive grace of movement and have to be reminded of it.

Changing Leads at the Canter or Lope is achieved by *the Western rider* by neck reining, say, to the *left,* then letting off rein pressure so the horse can get his head balance. With slightly more weight in the left stirrup out ahead of the cinch, the right leg presses back of the cinch with perhaps a touch of spur, which gives impulsion to the horse's motive power and causes it to move to the left in line with the new lead. Now lined up with the forward thrust, there is no noticeable bending of the body or twisting of the neck. The action of the reins started the lead change, but the rider's seat and legs, or rather his weight and legs, gave the aids that controlled the power of the rear of the horse and caused it to move to the left to follow the lead.

The Western lope is a free canter, and if well trained the horse should lope quite slowly without any contact with the mouth or any head restraint other than what the weight of the reins on the bit shanks and their slight swinging movement give.

The Flat Saddle Rider in changing leads often moves the horse's head slightly to the right for an instant to "open the shoulder" just before the strike-off into the *left lead.* (Neck reining does this automatically since the right rein is the bearing rein on the bit when turning

The author, with left foot ahead of cinch, steps horse into a left lead. *Photo by Irene Laune.*

left.) Then the flat saddle rider pulls on the left rein, but using both hands in unison as though the reins were rigid shafts, so as to turn the horse's whole body instead of just twisting the neck. With more weight in the left stirrup ahead of the girth, the right leg presses with perhaps a touch of spur back of the girth to move the motive power in line with the thrust to the left so that it will be in rhythm with the changed lead. From the collected canter, in which the horse is held in some restraint, he may be extended to a faster but still restrained hand gallop.

Quarter Horses are naturally good lead changers, as are most nontrotting horses, because they are called upon to canter more and trot less, and the canter or lope is the gait that calls for changing leads. Their wide chests and their collected way of moving give them sure balance. If you can train your horse to change leads smoothly at a slow lope, using positive but not obvious leg and stirrup pressure, and can step him into a lope from a walk, you will have a horse that is a pleasure to ride.

And just because I thought you'd like to know—if you don't already —some scholar or other credited the pilgrims to Canterbury with traveling at a canter to avoid being jounced around at the trot, thereby earning the gait the name canter.

Collection

This is the term used to describe the action the rider causes when he gets the motive power, the rear of the horse and his hind legs, under his body, while by cues or restraint keeping the forelegs back, thus making the legs available for higher action, change of gait, or change of direction.

The cues or aids for collection are: a gentle contact with the horse's mouth (not a steady pull but one of contact and release) repeated on and off if necessary, to restrain the forehand, while at the same time pressing with the legs with perhaps a touch of spur and an almost unobservable movement of the seat to increase the drive of the hind legs, which keeps all four legs well under the horse.

Being collected causes the horse to give and flex his neck and draw in his chin. The horse can be kept in collection by slight movement of the reins (milking them, as some say) so that the movement of the bit shanks is sufficient without constant contact with the mouth. A collected horse is a wound-up spring. He can be collected while stand-

Collection is demonstrated superbly by cutting horses. Here Shorty Freeman is schooling a young horse. *Photo by Irene Laune.*

ing, trotting, or cantering. His hind quarter power is cocked like a trigger and a cue for impulsion can shoot him in any direction.

Cold Weather Riding

If you intend to ride your horse during cold and wintry weather, there are several things to consider.

First you must see that your horse gets the kind of food that will keep him warm. Whether it is sacked mixed grain or in pellet form, it should have a high percentage of corn, which is the most warming of rations, and should contain the other additives the horse usually gets. The decision whether or not to clip the horse's winter coat and blanket him will be resolved by the way the horse is to be used on trail rides, in shows, heated or unheated stable, time allowed for cooling out, etc. (see Chapter 7, "Feeding and Grooming.")

Trail riding can continue throughout the year in many parts of the country. The crisp air gives special zest to both horse and rider. Wear warm clothes and gloves. Carry a hoof pick. This photo was taken in Arizona's McDowell Mountains during a late December trail ride sponsored by Maricopa County Parks and Recreation Department. *Photo by Irene Laune.*

For riding in snow or on icy trails, see your farrier about special shoes. He may advise rubber and fiber pads to protect the soles of the horse's feet. Some pads have a rubber protuberance in the center which prevents the buildup of balls of snow. Pads should not be kept on the feet too long, since they deny the feet the ventilation and natural contact with the earth they need.

It may seem to you when riding in bitter weather that your horse can't possibly overheat, but he can, and what is worse, you can tire him out or injure his wind. Remember, he is expending a great deal of energy in breaking trails through snow and in keeping warm.

As for the rider, earmuffs will allow the use of the broad-brimmed hat, but a deer hunter's cap is more practical. The stores are full of warm clothing—chaps, long underwear, quilted nylon or sheepskin-lined leather jackets, fleece-lined boots and gloves. If dressed for it, cold weather riding can be great fun.

Safe Ways of Handling Your Horse

Accidents are usually caused by carelessness or from lack of knowledge of the safe and proven ways of doing things with a horse. To list all the ways you and your horse can invite accidents and mishaps would be impossible, but a few examples of the more common causes of them may be helpful.

Old and worn tack, cinches, girths, reins, bridle headstalls, and stirrup leathers should be discarded or thoroughly repaired.

Footwear is important. Heels on boots serve a purpose in a stirrup. They keep one's foot from slipping on through it. Heelless shoes are tempting fate. Feet should slip out of stirrups as easily as they slip in, which means that rubber-soled shoes should not be worn.

Spurs are for spur-trained horses, and for riders who know how to use them. A sudden gig with a spur may orbit the novice in a neat parabola.

When riding with a group, stay away from the heels of other horses. One might be a kicker. If your horse kicks at others, punish him instantly. (See Chapter 13 on bad habits and their correction.)

On unknown trails be alert for holes and obstacles. Around old fences watch out for wire hidden in the weeds or tall grass.

Horses that get loose cannot only cause damage to gardens and flower beds, but they can also get entangled and hurt themselves or go on a highway and cause accidents. A free-roaming horse means someone was careless in tying reins or halter lead, or failing to secure a stall door or corral gate. There are also horses that escape by rearing back and breaking the reins, halter, bridle, or tie rope. Those that have this habit must be broken of it or sold to an experienced horseman who can correct the problem.

Group riding can be fun, but carelessness and the wrong kind of horseplay can turn fun into an accident. Horses don't like unexpected actions or loud noises. With true horsemen, fun never gets so distracting as to cause neglect of common-sense horsemanship, such as checking cinches, tying up properly at hitch rails, avoiding jam-ups at gates, barn doors, and narrow trails. Or using caution in crossing streets and highways.

Falling off horses (few people are actually thrown off) is not the only way people get hurt around horses. A horse outweighs a person by an average of eight hundred pounds or more, so it stands to reason that he can't be managed by strength alone. He must be outsmarted.

Never be brutal with a horse. He has a long memory and won't soon forget it. Make a trusting friend of him. But always insist on obedience no matter how gentle he is so that he will keep his good manners.

Even sound tack can sometimes cause accidents if it isn't kept in good condition. I was once riding a horse I had never seen before and was on a saddle that had not been used for some time. I carefully checked the cinch before starting out. We had not traveled more than fifteen minutes or so when I leaned far to the left to assist a young inexperienced rider. The next instant, to my consternation and embarrassment, I was sitting on the ground with a startled and frightened horse on the end of the reins. His saddle was under his belly. By some quick soft-talking, the horse was kept from bolting, and no damage was done except to my pride. The cause of the accident was a dried-out latigo. It was perfectly strong but I noticed on the rest of the ride that the dry leather—it was not the buckle type—would quickly loosen. It had to be lashed with a tie thong to make it safe.

Until you are well acquainted with your horse, keep him at the slow gaits. If he is in good condition it is beneficial to work him until he sweats up, although this is not advised if one is riding rented hacks.

Jump some small ditches. Put him around some figure-eights in both directions, striving for steadiness of the gaits and for smooth lead changes at the slow canter. The rider must always feel that he and the horse are dancing to the same music.

With more action—galloping, rotating on the forehand, barrel racing etc.—the rider's body leans farther forward with much of the weight pressing in the stirrups in rhythm with the horse's movements.

When riding up steep hills, lean forward and get most of your weight in the stirrups. If your horse is not wearing a breast strap to keep the saddle from slipping back, grasp the mane, rather than the horn or pommel. It will help hold you and the saddle forward. In going down steep hills sit in the saddle but keep most of your weight in the stirrups.

End your ride by quieting your horse down and walking him the last quarter mile or so toward the stable. When you dismount lead him about for a while with the saddle on so his back won't get chilled. In warm weather wash his back when you take the saddle off, scrape off the water, and rub him with a rag. In cool and cold weather dispense with

Cooling out and relaxing are an important part of every ride. *Photo by the author.*

the water, but rub his back with a rag or gunny sack—the rubbing gets the circulation going where a saddle pad, blanket, or cinch may have pressed. Then blanket him until he is dry.

In the midst of a ride it is all right to let your horse have a drink of water—not too much—since he will continue to be active. But when you stop using him, let him cool out thirty minutes or so before giving him water or feed.

On *entering a straight stall* speak to your horse—call his name—put your hand on his rump or back and enter on the near side (left side). Untie and hold the gathered lead close to the halter shank and as you pull him back say "back" and push him over with your right hand. Maybe slap his side so his rear will be moving out sideways instead of straight back into the passageway. The quicker and more matter-of-fact your manner, the less time the horse has to decide to oppose you. If he is the kind that acts slightly frightened and comes rushing back out of

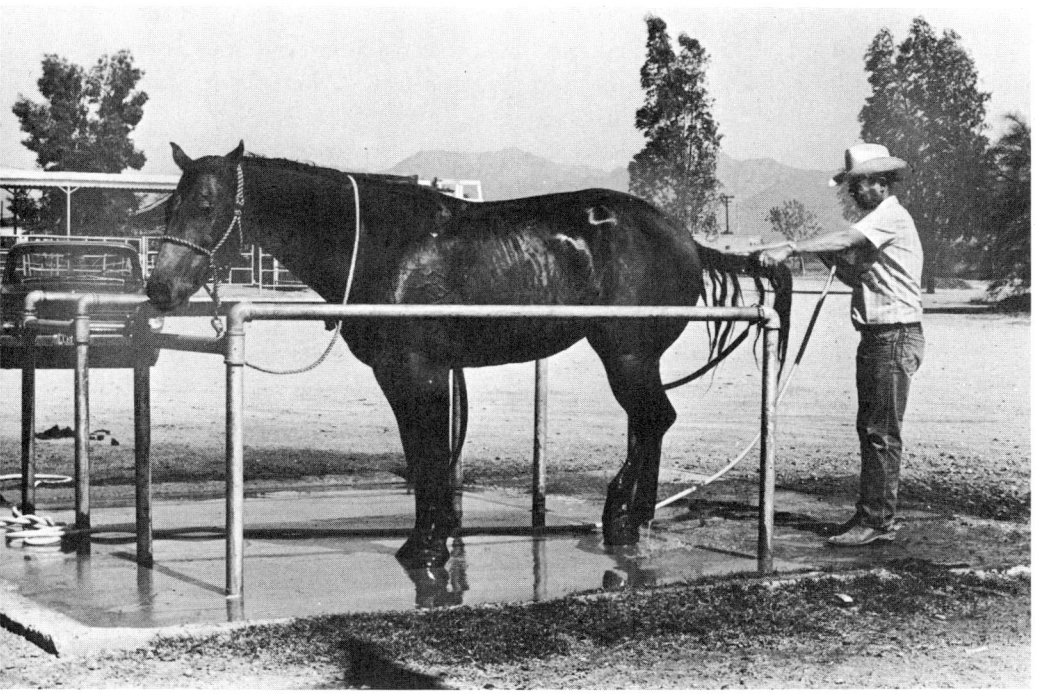

Earl Brock, foreman of Adrian Berryhill's Bend Inn cutting horse establishment, Scottsdale, Arizona, is shown hosing down Can Can Miss. *Photo by Irene Laune.*

a tie stall before you have time to control him, you may have to hook a chain across the back of his stall to teach him that he can't come back until you say the word. If you have a helper who can stand aside and give him a smart smack with a paddle when he comes rushing back, it may stop him from doing it. Two or three such lessons are usually enough and it is better to stop the habit than have to bother with a chain barrier.

On *entering a box stall* the horse is usually so curious or hungry or glad to see you he will come to you. When he does, push his head sideways so he cannot brush you aside and get out the door. Have the halter ready to slip on if he is without one, or have the lead shank ready to snap on if he is wearing a halter. Force him to stay behind you so you are well ahead when you lead him from the stall. If he tries to forge through the door with you, one of you is going to get crushed—and you can guess who.

In returning a horse to his stall when he may be eager to get his feed, this business of making him stay behind and letting you lead is equally important because he might trample your feet. If he tries it, stop him, turn him, lead him past his stall; outstubborn him.

In stables or out-of-doors, always let your horse know where and who you are. Place your hand on him when you walk behind him. Speak to him. Your voice will tell him who you are and your hand will tell him where you are. The more you touch and handle your horse, the better he will trust you not to hurt him and the more you will know about his whims, touchy spots, and sudden moves. If he is not your horse, don't get too familiar with him at first. Make friends gradually. Being alert and careful around all horses can save you from being bitten, kicked, or stepped on.

Riding on slippery footing may bring a horse down on top of you. Riding up to the rear of a strange horse may get you or your horse kicked. Riding too close to a fence or a half-opened gate may get your legs cut or bumped badly. Many people have had their heads banged when riding through a barn door. Many have been hit or dragged out of the saddle by limbs of trees.

It isn't good to go around nagging your horse all the time, but your judgment should be, in any kind of chancy situation, better than his, so tell him, "This time let's do it my way." But it is another thing when you are lost on a strange trail especially at night. That's a time when you had better defer to his judgment. His sense of direction is more than likely to be better than yours.

When working around a horse, stay close to him. Then if he kicks you won't get the full impact.

If the lead shank is held firmly, a horse that whirls and kicks will, with the movement, pull you out of harm's way.

And if you will allow a finger to be wagged at you a few more times, here are more suggestions:

Don't ever tease a horse.

Don't leave a halter on a horse that is turned out to pasture; he can catch it on something or even put his foot in it.

Don't tie a horse to a board of a fence on the side it is nailed to the post. It might be pulled away and a flopping board with nails in it can spell real trouble.

Don't wrap a lead strap or rope around your hand. Always be able to let loose if necessary.

Tie your horse far enough away from strange horses so they can't kick each other.

Before carrying a lariat on your saddle learn to handle it and see that your horse has no fear of it.

Always fasten the front cinch first, the rear girth last.

After riding for fifteen minutes, check the cinch for tightness; it nearly always needs to be taken up a notch.

When passing other riders, always slow down and avoid shouts or actions that might spook their horses.

Cross a winding road at a spot where approaching traffic can be seen from both directions.

On slippery, rocky, or treacherous footing of any kind, give your horse plenty of rein so he can look down and see where he is stepping.

Never mount a horse in a barn under eaves or outside too near trees or overhanging branches.

When the trail is wide enough, ride abreast with another rider rather than trail behind. The gentleman rides on the left, the lady on the right.

On steep tricky descents or climbs on rough trails, stay well back from the horse ahead.

Most state laws require horseback riders to face oncoming traffic when riding on the verges of roads and highways.

For night riding, wear light-colored clothing. Some riders carry flashlights; some have reflectors on the brow bands of their horse's bridle.

Actually the percentage of horse accidents is not high, and people who love horses will go on riding just as skiers will go on skiing and mountain climbers will go on climbing, while always trying to reduce the risks.

How to Say "No"

"Can I ride your horse?" How many times have we heard it? And how difficult at times to answer with a "No." But unless you are absolutely sure of the person's horsemanship the answer "No," softened in any way you think of, should be given to all comers.

This may sound ungenerous and selfish, but there is simply too much at stake to do otherwise. If your horse is in some phase of training, and most horses are, an indifferent rider can so confuse a horse that he will fail to respond to aids you have patiently taught him. It may be unnoticeable to the non-horseman, but the direction and slight difference in the pull of the reins, the weight shifts in the saddle, the leg pressure on turns and lead changes, the lift and touch of the bit to indicate a change of gait are set signals to the horse that should be always the same.

If the horse is still fractious and does not react quickly to controls, there is even more reason for not putting a strange rider on him; he could get excited and before you know it, you could have an accident on your hands.

When the request comes from a rider who assures you he "knows all about horses," and you happen to know his experience is limited to a few lessons at a riding stable or astraddle a chunk following in single file at a dude ranch, be even more on your guard. A little knowledge is a dangerous thing. Some horse owners explain that it is feeding time or cooling-out time, with the suggestion, "You may lead him around for a while," an invitation that is welcomed by most young horse lovers. And some find it a treat to sit on the horse while a competent person leads him about to cool him out. I know of no better way to solve this touchy problem than to have a very gentle old horse about the place who can keep his cool no matter how inexperienced the rider.

With the using strains of Quarter Horses, one is relieved of much worry about jittery horses. I have seen them brought in from fast work dancing with excitement, and then almost immediately calm down when a youngster was tossed into the saddle and given the reins to walk them until they cooled out. This was done, of course, under safe conditions in an enclosed area.

12
Training Methods

This is an era of the one- and two-horse ranch—ranch often being a euphemism for a back lot with a converted garage. The owner is usually pressed for time, being quite often occupied by other activities. Where people were once upset if they missed the last wagon train of the season headed for the West, they are now impatient if they miss an open section in a revolving door. About the first problem all this rushing and lack of time creates for the horse owner, especially if he has but one horse, is that his horse will suffer from loneliness and boredom. Horses are gregarious. They like companionship and they want and need action. Remember their natural state is to roam in herds like big families. So if you are your horse's only companion it is up to you to be companionable. Practice the three Ts—touch, talk, and teach. Spend some time with your horse when he gets his grain. Look him over, feel his legs. Give him an occasional carrot or apple but go slow on the sugar—it can get him in the habit of snapping at your hand.

If you don't give your horse the companionship he needs, he might replace you with a rooster, goat, or dog—and wouldn't that be flattering? The Godolphin Arabian is said to have had a cat that became his inseparable companion. Even sheep have been cronies and that is scraping the bottom of the barrel for a cowhorse breed which normally dislikes the sheep, no doubt sharing in the cowman's and sheepman's feud. But even this rare barn mate is more acceptable to a Quarter Horse than a calf who is classed in his feudal mind as a menial to be put strictly in his place.

If another horse becomes the object of your horse's affection to the point of whinnying their heads off every time they are separated, you have a problem on your hands. It may seem heartless, but they must be separated or each will be ruined as a pleasurable riding horse.

Like the dog, the horse has always lived on terms of feudal relationship with his master. But unlike the dog he is not fawning and servile.

This friend and companion of Judy Webb's horse got to go to the 4-H Fair. *Courtesy Robert Gilliland.*

He is spared that too close relationship that the dog frequently endures —that of being always in sight and at his master's beck and call. His size alone gives him poise and a certain dignity that discourages careless and flippant treatment.

The horse is not by nature an aggressor. Thus he does not, as dogs sometimes do, attack other animals merely to win praise from his master —or simply to draw attention to himself.

The horse is usually, when with people, doing something useful or at least displaying his athletic prowess. The close bodily contact between himself and his rider is required by purposeful teamwork. The contact therefore is more matter-of-fact and less in the nature of fondling and idle companionship that is so often the case with dogs.

It is assumed that the novice will get a well-trained horse. But regardless of who trained the horse in the first place, the owner-rider must see to it that the horse does not forget his good manners and training. A good rider is always a trainer in that sense.

A horse with basic training is one that stands still while being mounted, responds to reins and body movements for turning, slowing down, and stopping without tugging at the bit, and is not difficult to control in a trot, canter, or gallop. It is assumed the horse is gentle and has no vicious habits such as kicking and biting.

Beyond basic training is a whole repertoire of specialized training for racing, hunting, cutting, jumping, polo, bulldogging, barrel racing, pole bending, and other activities. Any one of these can involve the owner-rider in very active competition along with considerable traveling and trailering.

A horse highly trained for any specialty field is generally unsuitable for pleasure riding in the hands of a novice, because the horse would soon lose his sophisticated training. However, a young rider of moderate ability would be fortunate to get a horse that has been retired from competition and showing if the horse is still sound. The rider could learn a great deal from an experienced horse.

Quarter Horses that have specialized in racing, like all race horses, generally require some retraining by an experienced trainer before they can be suitable for relaxed pleasure riding. Many have made the transition. Enhanced, one of the first eight AQHA Supreme Champions, was retrained by John Hoyt of Phoenix, Arizona, a recent president of the Arizona Professional Horsemen's Association. John told me that Enhanced was easy to handle and soon learned to turn speed off as quickly as he turned it on.

It is assumed that an owner-trainer-rider of limited experience is not going to start from scratch and take on the job of breaking a green horse, or an obstreperous or undisciplined one. But he should know the methods of training in order to maintain good training in a horse. Knowing how the horse was trained in the first place will help the rider understand the horse's reactions, what he reacts to kindly, and what bugs him. The routines in which he was drilled should be understood by the one who rides him.

Breaking is the Western term for training and gentling. It sounds rather turbulent and it does sometimes imply direct and forceful methods.

Many ranch-bred horses become wild by running free in pasture, and they get much less handling than farm-raised animals. They are also a little older as a rule when broken, unless they are race horses or cutters. A rancher might say a "broke horse" when a show or rodeo man or a polo player would say a "trained horse," and a trainer of jumpers and dressage horses would say a "schooled horse."

Training the Colt

Training the colt starts, ideally, when a foal is only days old. His own haltered mother may help you squeeze him into a corner of a box stall. When up close to him, let him make the advances, and when he sticks his muzzle out, let him touch your hand. In a short time you can rub and scratch his neck. When he is no longer afraid of your touch, slip a rope over his head without tying it. If he gets excited and wants loose, let the rope slip off. Lay the rope on his back whenever you handle him so he will lose any fear of it. He should be given a name while very young and you should use it often. If he is to be registered, his name can have no more than sixteen letters in it, including spaces and hyphens and punctuation marks. When he is no longer rope-shy, slip a soft web halter or a rope hackamore with a soft rope bosal on him. You had better be out in the corral away from fences or anything the foal can hurt himself on should he struggle. A lead rope about twenty feet long will give him room to move about. Pull him from side to side gently instead of a straight pull and try and get him to step out. Don't look at him—you'll make him self-conscious—but look where you are going and act as though you expected him to follow you. Don't pull too hard on the shank, just try and get him to walk along with you, or a little ahead of you. If he needs urging, some trainers toss a large nonslip noose (made with a bowline knot) over his hind quarters. When he hesitates, a slight tug on the rope brings him forward to get away from the rope. I prefer to toss the rope like a large half-hitch over the back and quarters. Not being tied, it can easily be removed when the colt steps along nicely.

Each time you stop, say "Whoa" and let him feel the pressure of the bosal on his nose. Repetition of the word and action will begin to mean *"Stop."* Don't be heavy-handed. Let him play a little. A hard jerk could bow a young tendon, or at least make him wary of you. When he does well, stop him and pat him and praise him and call him

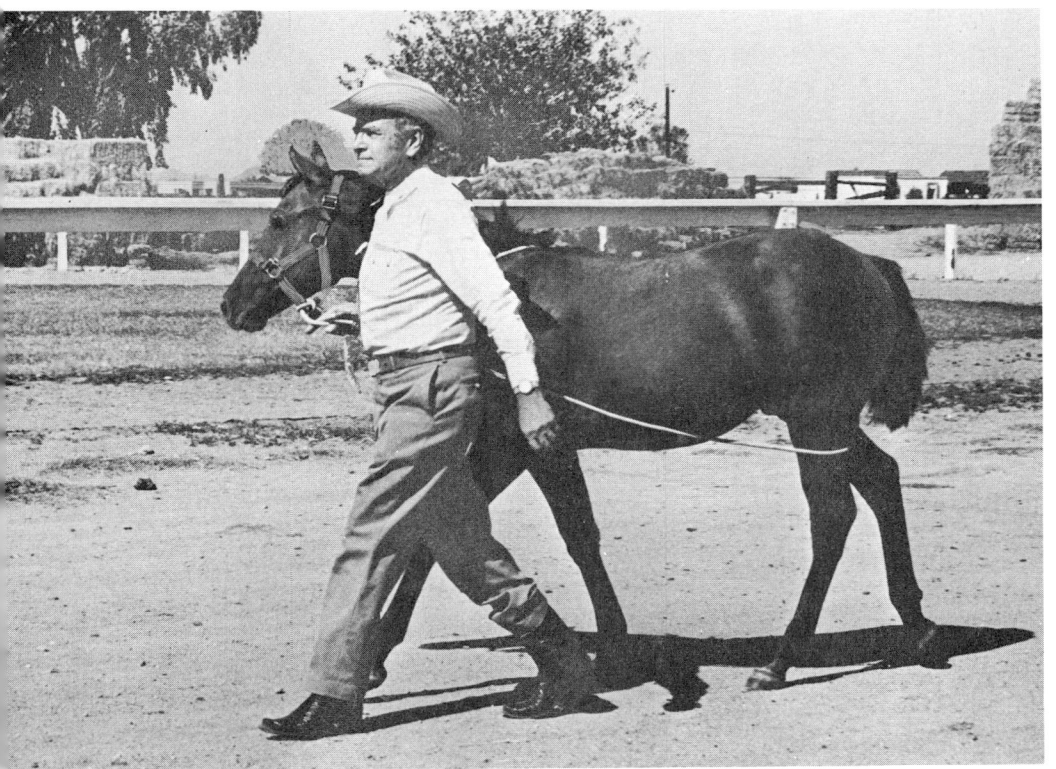

The author leading a son of Poco Speedy, still unnamed, at the Bend Inn Stables in Scottsdale, Arizona. *Photo by Irene Laune.*

by his name. Even horses, it seems, love the sound of their own name. A foal should lead well at least by the time he is three months old.

On ranches throughout the West and Mexico where colts outnumber the people who have time to teach them to lead, the job is turned over to fellow animals. The colt's halter rope is tied short up to a rope or heavy strap about a jenny's or female burro's neck. Jacks and male burros are not used because they are inclined to kick the foals. The two animals can be linked together in a corral, but if more direct action is wanted, the foal is tied to the jenny out in a pasture some distance from the barn where the jenny knows her feed awaits her. This is the way it is done on the Johnny Ferguson Ranch, southwest of Wharton, Texas, whose Bar JF racing Quarter Horses are known on the best of the nation's quarter-mile tracks. The jenny makes a beeline for the barn—at a patient walk—and after a few moments of confusion while deciding who is going where and with whom, the foal marches along resignedly and by the time the barn is reached, he is practically halter trained.

Handling the Feet. Feet should be handled at every opportunity during the period the foal is being taught to lead. Run your hand down his shoulder and forelegs, keeping a firm grip on the halter shank, until you can reach down and pick up a forefoot. Don't be too quick to put it down. When picking up the hind feet, lean against the foal's side to take the weight off the foot you want. Don't shove, just lean. Begin as high as the stifle and run your hand down the leg. Go through the foot routine often, and each time pick up all four feet—one at a time, of course! It is possible for a horse to be gentle with three feet and remain fearful and touchy with the fourth.

Grooming is another good excuse to accustom the foal to being touched all over.

Tying. Tie him first in the box stall with his mother. Do this several times. Run the soft rope around his barrel and tie with a nonslip knot. Then bring the rope between his forelegs and through the ring on his halter. Tie up the rope as high as he normally carries his head. If he is tied too low, he might get a foot over it. If he pulls back, the pressure will be on his withers, not his head and neck. If tied too high, the foal will tire and become tense. After a few such lessons, the foal is given his liberty until he is weaned at about seven months, when more halter training and foot handling are resumed. Also at this time, during the early part of his training, the foal should be led into a trailer, maybe fed in it, every day. His mother can be put in first if he is at all frightened. Early trailer training will make him easy to load during the rest of his life.

When the foal is outside, tie to a rail fence or a ring on the side of the barn, or someplace where he can turn only in a half circle. If tied to a rail or board instead of the post of a fence, do not tie the foal on the nailed side, as it might be pulled off and cause damage. *Continue gentling* the foal. Twirl a rope near him. Let him nose your hat. Put a blanket on him. Rub him with a sack. All this will teach him to tolerate handling and will make saddling and later training much easier. Get him used to the sight of cars and trailers and people and the noise they make. Play some rock records—that will do it—but please, not too loud!

Foals and weanlings are fed some grain and hay through their first winter and as yearlings the following fall. At about eighteen months old they are well-muscled youngsters ready to take on more training.

Lunge Training

Lunge training (it is pronounced "lunge," even if you prefer to spell it longe) is dear to the hearts of many horse handlers, and there are as many who dispense with it entirely. The reasoning of the former is that training at the walk, trot, and canter can be started at an early age. By reversing the direction, they avoid one-sided training and the foal gets more active training, they believe, than he would get if driven with lines in a corral. While being lunged he can be wearing a saddle and bridle and getting used to the rig he will eventually have.

The reasoning of those who dispense with it is that lunging sets up an unreal situation between rider and horse. Training, they say, should be more like it will be when the horse is ridden, with the aids and control coming from behind the eyes and ears. To their way of thinking, driving from behind with reins is preferable. They also feel that working at slower gaits until the horse can be ridden is no disadvantage.

For lunge training, a web strap or cotton rope twenty or twenty-five feet long is fastened to a lunge cavesson, halter, or hackamore with a swivel snap. (See Bridles and Hackamores.) Then with a long whip— a buggy whip or stockman's whip—with a small lash that pops and makes a noise, walk the colt around in a circle, and by letting out rope and keeping him away from you with the whip pointed, get him out twenty feet or so on the line. The whip is in your right hand when the horse is moving toward the left, and in your left hand when he is moving toward the right. The whip is always behind the horse when he is moving forward. To stop the colt, shift the whip to the other hand and hold it out toward and ahead of him, order "Whoa" and at the same time give the line a jerk. Should the colt start to come to you, hold out the whip and flip the line to halt him. To reverse, motion with the whip or snap it and give the line a reverse jerk. Practice until the colt reverses without your having to go up to him to turn him. The whip, the voice, and the line are the cues. The whip accents the meaning by pointing, blocking the way, or popping to excite action. The jerk on the line identifies with the commands to "walk," "trot," "canter," "reverse," and "whoa."

Even Westerners who use the word "lope" say canter when training, because lope sounds too much like whoa.

When cantering, should the colt get on the wrong lead, stop him and start him over again. Reverse him often. Keep sessions under twenty minutes. A tired colt can't learn. The extended trot is not encouraged in Western-trained pleasure horses.

Driving with Long Reins

This procedure is often advised for colts whether or not they have had lunge training. Hobble the stirrups—that is, tie them together under the colt's belly so they won't flop—and run the driving reins through them.

Driving with long lines is good training for all green horses during the head-setting period, except cutting horses whose heads should remain natural and somewhat low. Here the training is in a "bullpen." The high board fence cuts off outside distractions so the young horse can concentrate. *Photo by Irene Laune.*

With long lines the colt realizes the pull and voice commands come from directly behind, not from the side. The reins keep him lined up somewhat like shafts. In addition to the driving reins, other reins from the hackamore or colt bit can be attached to the saddle to position the head. Some trainers go from this stage of training to the breaking cart so they can work at a faster gait.

Hackamore Training

This method is considered by many to be the safest and most satisfactory. There is danger, they think, of hurting the nerves in the bars of the mouth with any bit, even a colt bit, in the early stages of training, since some force has to be used on green colts, and the lightest and best-intentioned hands can have accidents. The hackamore postpones the time until the colt is schooled in the basic aids or cues of the bit.

Hackamores vary in severity. For mature range horses, a heavy bosal of braided rawhide is used for preliminary training. It can be quite punishing and the horse soon learns that his nose and underside of his jaw won't get hurt if he does not resist. With gentler horses, smaller, lighter, and softer bosals are used.

Before a green horse understands neck reining or turning aids, the hackamore is excellent because turning him is done with a direct sideways pull on the head, not the mouth. To a horse, punishment of the mouth should mean (if it makes sense at all) restraint for slowing down or stopping, whereas turning is a forward movement that should be unrestricted. Turning, jumping, any outgoing action of the horse—even collection—should be free and have no association with mouth punishment.

Head Setting

Achievement of correct head position is helped along further by tying the reins to the saddle and allowing the colt to wander around in the corral on his own. The reins of the hackamore or breaking bit bridle should not be severely tight but just taut enough to tuck the chin in a little and to put an arch in the neck. Should the horse hurt his mouth or nose a little, he associates it with his own movement, not with a rider.

Hugh Bennett, ex-World Champion Cowboy and ex-President of the AQHA, used a device he calls a Dumb Cowboy to help set the heads and teach some of his champion Quarter Horses to neck-rein. Before

The Quarter Horse will set his own head and neck if allowed to move about in the corral for periods of an hour or so with reins attached to the cinch rings or looped over the saddle horn. They should be just tight enough to maintain good position. If they are used with rubber rings, the horse can turn his head slightly and will be less likely to become excited or irritated as he might with rigid reins that have no give.

The neck of the Quarter Horse is seldom set with an extreme arch. Ideally, the area between the crest and the poll should be horizontal.

they are three years old, but after having been ridden three or four times, the horse with saddle and hackamore on is put in a box stall that has a swivel device suspended from the ceiling. With the hackamore reins attached, it mildly maneuvers the horse about in the stall.

Saddling and Riding the Green Horse

The first time he is saddled and ridden is a test of how gentle and trusting your eighteen-month-old colt has become. Take him into the corral and put the blanket on, saddle him, and cinch him up only moderately tight. Then lead him about for a few minutes with whatever you intend to train him with—a straight, leather, or rubber-covered colt bit, a snaffle bit, or a hackamore. By this time he should be a pretty gentle animal. But lead him around a little and quietly set up the cinch so the saddle will not turn. While you hold him, have a light, good rider, get in the saddle. Continue to lead the colt while the rider plow-reins him this way and that. Then if he seems quiet and well behaved, turn him over to the rider. If he remains quiet at a walk, the rider might press him into a slow trot. He should be stopped often while the rider dismounts and mounts. Ten minutes is long enough for this lesson.

After a few such lessons, a ranch colt, unless he is to be a race horse, would be turned out to pasture and not ridden again until he was two and one-half or three or even four years old. When caught up and saddled, he would remember much of his preliminary training. But understandably he would be strong and willful, jumpy and excitable.

The kind of colt the two- or three-horse owner is likely to have would be around people all the time and would get occasional training, such as lunging or driving with reins, as well as leading and foot handling. So there would be no reason for him to be difficult to manage when at the age of two and one-half or three or a little over he is put into full training. And even before this time, a lightweight person might have sat bareback on him occasionally. And he might have worn a saddle at times while free in the corral.

When you ride the young horse for the first few times, take him to the center of the corral for mounting. Have someone on horseback stand out in front of the colt three or four feet or so to keep him from going forward when you mount. It is better not to have anyone hold him; his attention should be on you, and restraint might excite him. Hold the near rein tighter so you can swing him sharply to the left if he starts to jump. Then with left hand on his neck and your right hand on the horn, come up into the stirrup, and if he is quiet, bring your leg over and settle easy in the saddle. Don't be too quick to move the young horse out. Usually when the rider who is assisting you starts his horse away, your horse will step out without much urging. Keep him moving and if he wants to slow trot, allow it, but try to keep it slow by giving gentle tugs on the reins. Plow-rein to turn. Dismount and mount several times while facing the fence.

Even a three-year-old is not mentally or physically mature and should not be soured by too much training. Twenty or thirty minutes at a time is plenty. Stop often and give him a rest. Give him a carrot or an apple if he has done well (whole, never in small chunks, as he might suck a piece down his windpipe). But constant pampering and feeding as a reward does not work as well with horses as it apparently does with sea lions and dolphins. In relaxed moments, go along with some of his little whims. But if he shows bad manners, put him on his Sunday behavior, pronto.

After the first ride, the training schedule should be daily. Thirty-minute lessons morning and evening five or six days a week are better than one-hour lessons once a day. As the horse increases in strength, the riding time can increase, but for later soundness in legs, heart, and wind, it is better to bring the young horse along slowly. When he does things well pat him and praise him. Try to end each lesson on a happy note, when things are going well. If you or the horse are disturbed, rest a moment. Try once more, and if it comes off moderately well, let that be it for the day. If the colt becomes confused during a lesson and balks, quickly say "whoa" and let him rest a moment. He will think he minded you.

During training, weight shifts in the saddle, along with pulling for turns, will have prepared the colt for neck reining and a manner of traveling with loose rein and free head.

Ways of giving aids for collection, lead changes, etc., are discussed under the subject of riding. The only difference in training the green horse is that it is necessary to be more obvious and deliberate in giving aids.

Walk, then jog, and later canter over and around obstacles on the ground—old tires, poles, etc. Slow canter in figure-eights in both directions at a steady rate of speed. When the horse is changing leads smoothly, let up on routine drills before he gets bored and does things by rote before being asked to. Get him out of the monotonous home lot. Uneven and strange footing makes a horse come alive. See that he walks briskly. Ride up and down trails. Jump ditches. Let him try out his brakes on some steep slopes. All this will develop muscles and bone to help him in the many actions he'll be called on to perform. When well along in training—and only then—let him open up and sprint for two or three hundred yards. Do this only about every third time you have him out. Don't make a daily practice of it or he will always want to run. If he gets excited, circle him, walk a while, and then stop and rest. Workouts that overtire him may make him dislike his outings. Always turn back in plenty of time to give him a slow cooling out.

Backing Up

This is another requirement of the well-trained horse, and is featured in reining classes and others. The horse should come back in a straight line without any head tossing or tail wringing, or squatting too low on his haunches. Backing is an unnatural move for a horse because he likes to know where he is going.

Whatever is used, hackamore, snaffle bit, straight bar bit, or regular curb, the pull back with the command "back" should be an on-and-off pull, never a sustained pull that becomes punishing. When he is well trained, jiggling the bit shanks will suffice. Press with both legs at the cinch or forward of it. Reach out and tap the horse on the chest with a bat. A bat in each hand will bring him back straighter. (See "Training the Cutting Horse," below.)

If he resists, or gets excitable with you in the saddle, dismount and try training him from the ground, pushing back on the reins, giving the order and tapping with the bat. Hang something that jingles on his breast strap, it may distract him. Horses can't think of two things at a time. He might forget what he was being stubborn about. Perhaps you would do better by training from the ground with long lines. Place two long poles on the ground about two and one-half feet apart to act as guides to keep him in a straight line. When he backs up pretty well with you on the ground, try him again from the saddle.

If he will tolerate a rope tossed in front of him, try dragging something with it such as a sack or a log. Have someone in front of him haze him back with a switch. Anything is better than sitting on him sawing at his mouth, which can make rearers of horses. Don't work him too long, and end happily whether it was really good or not.

The Sliding Stop, Pivot, Spin, and Roll Over the Hocks

When training your horse to make abrupt or sliding stops and to pivot and roll over the hocks and to spin, hold your reins close to the withers. When hauled up with a high rein, the horse is likely to throw his head up and become a star gazer. If he does that he will have to be worked on until he quits it. Aside from being bad form, it destroys his balance and, if the habit persists, he will have to wear a tie-down or a martingale of either the standing or running type.

If being trained with a snaffle or breaking bit, running reins can be used if the person in the saddle has enough experience and judgment to use them. The drawing in the chapter on tack shows the various ways of rigging them. The low pull they give keeps the horse's head down, but remember, they have great leverage and must be used gently.

The use of the hackamore makes running reins unnecessary. Its hard pull is on the nose, not the mouth, and it brings his head in, not up. All punishment should be utilized during training, not later. Later the schooled horse should respond to the *memory* of severe lessons without the need to have them repeated.

The horse must be trained to stop on his hind feet and legs. Special shoes are sometimes needed, so speak to your farrier before you start training your horse. But in shows, the use of any but standard horseshoes is now discouraged and may be penalized by judges. When perfected, the sliding stop and doubling back is easy to ride. It is the horse who bounces to a stop on his forelegs who is hard to ride. Forelegs are for giving direction to the turn and should leave stopping to the hind legs.

A good way to train for the sliding stop is to ride along a high board fence about four or five feet out from it. Put your horse into a stiff canter and then plow-rein him in toward the fence. The fence forces him to make a tight turn with his hind legs well under. Then as he momentarily stops, the only way he can jump is back where he came from. The horse has been "doubled," as they say. He has been rolled over his hocks—if he did it right. A good roll back consists of: a stop on the hind legs; a turn that pivots on them; and a change of lead and direction, performed by the front legs, all in one fluid motion.

Later, at the instant the horse comes around to the one-half circle, catch him as his front feet hit the ground and whirl him away from the fence to complete a full circle. Now he has rolled over his hocks twice, but the last time without the fence to force it.

This circling is the basis of the pivot and spin. The spin is accelerated until the horse whirls rapidly in place.

A hackamore is good for this training because it allows for a strong pull that brings the head around. Neck reining comes later when the horse knows what's wanted. Be sure to work the horse in both directions. Take a look at the diagram that shows what is required of a reining horse in the show ring, and you will see the importance of this training.

Doubling back, rolling over the hocks, whatever you prefer to call

Teaka Cee, 1966 Honor Roll Reining Horse, in a sliding stop with only moderate pressure on the reins. Owned by Bob McClure, Grove City, Ohio, and ridden by Clayton Woosley. *Courtesy AQHA.*

it, is very wearing on a horse and should be limited to short lessons. Remember that recalcitrant horses are punished by circling, doubling, or spinning them.

When you pull for a stop, the horse must have something to stop with. That is, his hind feet must be coming forward under his body to act as a brake. Until you can sense this moment, ride in the early morning or late afternoon so that you can see the shadow cast by you and your horse. When his hind legs start the swing forward is the instant to pull for the stop. And when you pull for the stop, sit fairly straight in the saddle, not reared back on the cantle as so many do, but as a rider does on a cutting horse. Come forward, if anything, and keep the hands low with weight in the stirrups to keep it off the horse's loins and kidneys. Give him his head as soon as he starts the stopping squat,

Monte Foreman, Western trainer, shows his horse with a relaxed head down, slack rein sliding stop. *Courtesy Dorothy Gilbert.*

otherwise his head will go skyward. And for doubling back, as his front legs touch ground, press for the about-face take-off, as in a change of leads.

The long slide is featured by some and played down by others. A roping horse is a stopper that wrote the book, yet he does not do much long sliding. A cutting horse stops and rolls over his hocks with stunning perfection and can take off in any direction, but he does not slide much. Some judges, without regard to whether or not the footing is suitable, want to see the long slides in reining classes. The ones that do are being unfair to many good reining horses that stop and double back beautifully without the exaggerated slides.

To aid the spectacular slides, special shoes—some with sliding plates that cover the sole of the foot, and trailer shoes with extensions at the

With a well-balanced head (not too high), Stormy Pink's front feet are giving the impetus for a rollback after a sliding stop. Trained and ridden by John Hoyt of Scottsdale, Arizona.

back instead of calks—have been used. But now the AQHA rules allow judges to penalize the users of unusual shoes in performance classes. Skid boots to protect against scuffs and bruises on the heels and fetlock joints on both reining and roping horses are permissible. Trainers have been known to remove the shoes from the front feet and work the horse until the front feet were so sore and tender the horse would slide to a stop on his rear feet. This method, though effective, is frowned on and considered a sort of last resort type of training.

Training the Quarter Horse Jumper

Jumpers, authorities agree, should be endowed by nature with well-developed quarters, sound feet and legs, good shoulders, a deep heart girth, a closely coupled body with muscular loins, and a bold nature. All this is a good description of a Quarter Horse. Yet it is only in recent years that he has won recognition in this field which has long been

Champion Alfred Riker, with Mrs. Jon Riker up. *Courtesy Westenhook Farm, Inc., Southbury, Conn.*

dominated by Thoroughbreds or grade horses of three-quarters or more Thoroughbred breeding.

Mr. John Riker, owner of the Westenhook Farms, Inc., of Southbury, Connecticut, and West Palm Beach, Florida, whose Quarter Horse Alfred Riker (traces to Wimpy P-1) was ridden to victory in many shows by Mrs. Riker to become the AQHA Champion Jumper of 1967, commented in a letter to the author in December 1969: "It has only been in the last couple of years that the words Quarter Horse were mentioned in Hunt-Jump circles. They were always referred to as half-breed and three-quarters breed, or other than Thoroughbreds. [Now] at all American Hunt-Jump shows, the Quarter Horse is very well represented, and always holds his own—wins some, loses some. However more and more people are leaning toward and learning more and more about the Quarter Horse because of his wonderful temperament all the time!—in the stall, during training at shows, and etc. The greatest Quarter Horse our U.S. team has ever used was Fire One. He was by Firebrand Reed who is a full brother to Leo P-13335. I now own Firebrand Reed and it is my aim—in horse breeding—to breed another Fire One."

Fire One, foaled in 1954, was a brown horse bred at Littleton, Colorado, by the Leo Dales. He was bred for speed—top and bottom—and they raced him as a colt, as did his next owner. He won now and then, but it was certain that he would never be a world beater. So he passed to other owners and for several years worked on a ranch as a cowhorse, and then as a pickup horse in the rodeo arena for Hoss Inman.

Courtney Meyers, who carefully researched his career, wrote that Royce Cates, on his annual foray into the West to buy carloads of horses to resell back East as jumpers, bought Fire One. At his headquarters in Tennessee, he sold him to J. Arthur Reynolds, a trainer of jumpers. When tried out, Fire One, who had never jumped a fence, toppled the first one he was run at. But on the second try he got the idea and cleared it with a foot or so to spare. The Reynolds children, Betty and Bucky, started him over low fences and were delighted with his quick thinking and good nature—what they called "his Quarter Horse disposition."

Then came owner O. C. Carmichaels of Michigan, followed by Mr. and Mrs. Patrick Butler of Minnesota. All the time Fire One was gaining in experience and athletic ability. Jumping was a new job, but he worked at it just as deliberately as he had gone about his fast ranch chores or arena work. And in 1961 he proved he could hold his own against—and beat—many of the finest in the national field of Open Jumpers. All the time the fences were going higher. Later, Kathy Kusner was to put Fire One over 6'9" fences.

When the Butlers were asked, in 1961, by Bert de Nemethy, the coach of the United States Equestrian Team, to lend Fire One to the team, they generously did so. Two top riders of the team, William Steinkraus, captain of the USET, and Kathy Kusner alternated in riding him in this country and in England, Canada, Ireland, Italy, and Mexico. A big day of glory for Fire One was at Harrisburg, Pennsylvania, when William Steinkraus rode him in four sensational clear rounds to win over the European Jumping Champions.

In 1965, Fire One earned the Reserve International Championship at Washington, D.C. And with Kathy Kusner aboard, he won the $12,000 Florida Concentrate Open Jump Sweepstake, in the rain, with sloppy footing. His last fence was jumped in 1966.

Another cowpony who made good as a jumper was Nautical, a Palomino-colored Quarter Horse, made even more famous by a Walt Disney movie based on his career and called "The Horse with the Flying Tail." Nautical, who was an outstanding performer with the USET in international competition, was by Muchacho de Oro by Billy Van, a horse raised and owned by Billy Van Vactor, a steer wrestler and roper who once lived in Woodward, Oklahoma.

Nearly all horses like to jump, and with training most will get moderately good at it. But to become good enough to win in shows, the horse you decide to train should have special qualifications. If he is to jump over four feet, a horse fifteen hands high or over is recommended. One with moderately sloped shoulders and pasterns—they are sloped at the same pitch—is best. If too steep, the jar of landing may make the horse go lame. If too sloped, great strain is put on the pasterns. The horse that lacks zest in moving out is a poor prospect. A jumper must be eager to go when asked to, but, like all good saddle horses, should be easily controlled. Jumping is strenuous and calls for a strong, vigorous horse. Unlike the race horse, his bones and muscular development are given time to mature before he is pushed into very active service. In fact, his training as a smooth, steady-gaited saddle horse should be well along before serious jumping training begins. Good wind, strong legs, shoulders, and quarters, balance and sure-footedness should have been developed on rides over rough country, uphill and down, and such rides should continue.

The Saddle recommended for jumping is the forward seat jumping saddle. Its advantages are mentioned in the chapter on tack. If your horse has been accustomed to a Western saddle, he may find the flaps on the jumping saddle something to get used to because they are farther forward than the skirts of the Western saddle and will brush his shoulders.

The Bridle used most of all is the bridoon or snaffle. The snaffle bit is sometimes replaced with a bar bit, and less frequently with the Pelham bit. The double bridle is also sometimes used.

Don't be surprised if you find that some generally accepted hard and

Cabot, a large Quarter Horse, ridden by Kathy Kramer of Rillito Farm, Tucson, Arizona. *Photo by Louise L. Serpa.*

fast rules for training and equipment are here disregarded or modified as not necessarily representing the best or only way of getting results. Frankly, methods of training should be flexible enough to allow for initiative and imagination on the part of the trainer. No two horses or their handlers are identical. It may be flying in the face of convention to say it, but there is no valid reason why a horse that neck-reins and works well with a low port curb bit, or a light bitless hackamore bridle, should not be jumped that way instead of switching him to the hunt bridle which the AQHA and the AHSA rules now require except for some open jumping classes where the tack used is optional.

Kathy Kusner of the USET successfully rode a horse called Aberali in a bitless bridle.

With a snaffle bit there is certainly more likelihood of riding the horse's mouth. Jump photos show far too many riders pulling on the reins to benefit their own balance, it appears, rather than to assist the horse. Even with light hands, a steady contact puts some pressure on the bars of the mouth, which so irritates some horses they will throw their heads up to get the bit in the corner of the mouth and off the bars. This is an action that calls for the use of a martingale—a pity, because a free-headed horse looks so much better. Horses that open their mouths to cheat on the bit have their mouths shut with tight cavessons.

Switching to the snaffle bit usually entails retraining a neck-reining horse until he responds readily to plow-reining. However, some jump riders who use the Pelham bit continue to neck-rein. When retraining the neck-reining horse to plow-reining it is assumed he will no longer be ridden in the Western style. Retraining can be helped along by driving with long lines from behind, which gives the direct pull.

All prospective jumpers should be ridden over obstacles (as should any saddle horse) first at a walk and then later at a slow trot or slow canter. The obstacles can be old truck or car tires or poles or timbers or all three placed here and there in the training field. The object is to teach the horse to lift his feet and fold his legs to avoid striking the obstacles but to have no fear of them. This exercise is continued daily until the horse can go over the obstacles at a steady gait.

The cavalletti, a series of logs or crossties six to eight inches high placed railroad fashion at intervals to fit the horse's stride (which should be measured), gives the novice jumper a more prolonged and precise exercise in lifting feet and folding legs at a steady trot. Allow the horse to examine the logs and set his own rate of travel at first, then the tempo can be increased as the horse gets more sure of himself.

In preliminary training the more that is done outside the jump field or training ring the better. Jumping ditches and logs while out riding is one of the best ways of getting a horse to make quick lead changes, which he must do before being ridden at fences. When training fences and obstacles of various kinds are set up, they should be on fairly level turf that is soft and free of stones, and not muddy. During training it is a good precaution to have another person on hand, just in case.

Regardless of the animal's previous experience many people favor lunge training. After the horse is familiar with the lunge line and the

Larry Dunford training Easter Jim over the cavalletti. *Photo by the author.*

whip signals, changing and controlling gaits, reversing easily, etc., he is trotted between the fence posts or standards with the rails lying on the ground, so that he must pass over them in stride.

Next, two rails are set with one end of each up on the standard and the other end on the ground. This forms a low V in the center. A rail lying on the ground out about eighteen inches—one on either side of the jump—gives a ground line to prevent the horse from getting too close and hopping over. Naturally he will go over the rails at the lowest part of the V—about fifteen inches—which sets up the good habit of taking his fences midway between the posts. Rails are set to fall either way so the horse can be reversed and jumped in either direction.

The training starts at the trot and progresses to the canter, at which gait the trainer must do some fast footwork himself to ensure plenty of lunge line as the horse jumps and then canters a short way beyond the fence. Lunge training continues until the horse is adjusting his stride for an unhesitating take-off, folding his legs, spreading sufficiently for a jump of moderate width, and clearing a three-foot rail easily.

Those who do not use lunge training for their horses for other purposes can be expected to dispense with it for jump training. To encourage freedom and initiative, many trainers prefer to start their beginners (after general saddle training) in an enclosed jumping runway or lane, called by some a "Hitchcock pen." It is long enough for an adequate approach canter and wide enough for a standard post and rail jump. After being warmed up on a preliminary ride the horse is turned into the runway without saddle or bridle. After he has trotted or cantered without breaking stride over the rails which are left lying on the ground, the rails are set up at the height and manner described for lunge training. Outside the enclosure the trainer is in a good position to study the jumping form of his student and with the long whip can touch up legs if they dangle without sufficient fold. With jumps centered in the runway various types can be used—a sloping chicken coop, post and rails, baled hay, evergreen boughs, or just a neat pile of brush, and they can be jumped from either direction. Steadiness and consistency of good jumping form are more the goal at this stage than height of jumps. In pastures horses may freely, with an economy of effort and rating their own approach canters, jump ditches or creeks they are familiar with. They perform somewhat similarly in the jumping lane. Left alone for a while, they may even jump on their own volition just for the fun of it, or, as I have noticed, to get nearer to other horses.

When the horse is started on his first rail jumps while being ridden, he is warmed up and then shown the rails he is to go over. The rails may be lying on the ground or up about fifteen inches if he is familiar with small jumps. Walk or jog him back thirty or forty feet and without stopping circle him toward the jump, keeping him still at a slow gait until when about twenty feet from the obstacle he is stepped into a canter to give impulsion for the leap.

If the horse tries to rush the fence, circle him away from it and continue to circle him until he is back in a steady slow trot or jog. Throughout training the horse should be turned away from the jump if his approach is faulty. Should the horse renege, refuse to take a jump, don't get excited or let your horse get excited. Circle back and try again. If he again refuses, ride him about for a while, lower the rail, and keep at it until he clears it. If he runs out to the side to avoid jumping the fence, rails may have to be placed on the ground or propped against the posts to form wings which will funnel him into the jump.

To increase the horse's reach, I have found that a canvas rolled out ahead of a brush blind is very helpful. The horse will not see the canvas, which is hidden by the brush and the rail that tops it, until he is in the air. Then when he does see it he will stretch with his forelegs to avoid landing on it. It is more noticeable than a ground bar. As the rail is raised the canvas can be rolled out further to increase the stretch. Poles on the ground beyond the fence will serve the same purpose but may injure a foot or pastern if the horse lands on them.

Raise the rails as practice continues, a few inches every week, depending on the clearance the horse leaves himself as he goes over or the frequency with which he brushes or touches rails. Try and end each session on a satisfactory jump even if rails have to be lowered.

Several kinds of fences, post-and-rails, and post-and-rail combinations set thirty-six feet apart or more, chicken coop, brush and rail, hogback, gate, etc., placed about the field will be helpful. After clearing one, canter on and take another. By the time the horse is entered in a Maiden Jumping Class at least eight 3'6" to 4' with spreads of 3' to 4' must be cleared in a matter of minutes, and in a Green Working Hunter Class your jumper must take 3'6" to 3'9" fences. A seasoned jumper should be able to clear fifteen or twenty fences in less than that many minutes without tiring, but when the beginner is jumping three-foot fences see that the workouts are limited to half that number. End on a good clean jump and go for a leisurely fun ride.

Some horses hit their stride and take off better on either a right or left lead, but approaches from different directions should be made to condition the horse so that he jumps equally well on either lead. I learned something about the limitations of a one-lead horse. He was a monster of an old gray horse at least seventeen hands high who had spent his life doing nothing but specialty jumping acts in a circus. Soaring over automobiles and through blazing hoops had become the breath of life for this old trouper. He was about to be retired to pasture when my friend Vern Walter, the founder of Cimarron Ranch in Putnam County, New York, bought the old horse thinking he could be used in Sunday afternoon arena shows to entertain his dude ranch guests. The men who brought the horse knew little about him except that he jumped from the left lead only, or was it the right? Vern didn't take the matter too seriously and come Sunday afternoon he tossed a light stock saddle on the big gray (there wasn't a flat saddle on the place), and after a few warm-up jumps, paying no attention to which lead the horse jumped from he swung him on a left lead toward a convertible car with the top down and with a tarpaulin flung over it. The jump was a fiasco. Both Vern and the horse piled up on the far side of the car with the horse on top. Vern went to the hospital and the big gray went lame. A few weeks later when I happened to stop by to see how Vern was doing, he remarked, "Now I remember, the man I got him from said to jump the gray on the right lead only." And then he asked if I would try the old horse out and see if he still wanted to jump now that his shoulder seemed well again.

I wasn't about to jump in a stock saddle, so I rode him bareback. The old horse was as cold-jawed as any horse I ever rode, but I brought him to a birch rail about four feet up and let him look at it, and I was careful to turn right away from it and to turn him into a right lead for the approach. As he turned, his off eye caught a glimpse of the rail and his head snaked out and he swung like a cutting horse toward it. I realized I was on a fanatical jumper. I couldn't have checked him if I tried. Anyway his frantic lunge forward had sent me back along his spine and I had just wriggled to his withers when he took off, stretched and soared with plenty of clearance, I was told, and landed as softly as a cat. I went on to jump him several times—always on the right lead to be sure—and each jump seemed better than the last. Not very long afterward this old one-lead perfectionist sustained an injury in the pasture that was to put him down.

A jumper soaring into the air can be a lovely sight, brilliant, judges say, if he jumps with confidence, zest, and supple grace. A feature of good form is a well-extended head and forward look. Both horse and rider while clearing one fence should have their eyes up and to the fore, sighted on the fence ahead. The downward-looking horse loses balance and spread, and the rider who looks down is marring his own performance. In both cases the impression is given that there is too much concern over whether the rail will be cleared. The old saying, "Throw your heart over the fence and jump after it," pretty well sums up the spirit to be shown. After many safe jumps both horse and rider should have gained head-up confidence.

Higher fences and familiarity with various kinds of obstacles, a powerful thrust at take-off, legs well drawn up, the neck extended and the back first rounded and then straightened out in a stretch—all will come along with more training. But remember, it is the controlled and steady approach and unhesitating leap that will make all other aspects of jumping easy and will reward the trainer with an unexcitable, willing jumper.

Linda Dunford jumping her mare Per Leo. *Photo by the author.*

There are many training methods advocated. It is up to the owner of a Quarter Horse to follow methods that are especially suited to his horse. He might have had previous training that minimized contact with the mouth because of neck reining, or he might be able to start over low jumps without preliminary lunge training. With a very capable student there is the risk that too much routine and repetition of things already learned can bring boredom and lack of initiative.

Riding the Jumper

Jumping calls for the same forward seat as in general riding. The only marked difference is made just before the take-off when the rider's body hinges forward from the hips with the seat three to ten inches out of the saddle. The weight is in the stirrups, which, for good balance, are almost directly below the kneecaps. Constant, balanced weight in the stirrups is an aid to the horse, since he needs to know where the weight is that he must lift. Any weight in the seat of the saddle as he leaps may cause him to drag his feet.

The hands with a rein in each are down and touching the horse's neck forward of the withers. At the moment just preceding take-off the rider presses with his legs for impulsion and gives a little nudge with his hands as he turns them down to signal a slight lift on the horse's mouth for collection. It should be a touch, not a pull, and as the horse leaves the ground, his head and neck must be free to extend for balance. When a horse is jumping three feet or higher, he is likely to need less if any touch on the mouth for collection. As the rail is cleared the rider's arms come up and go forward to give even more rein so that the horse's head is completely free when he lands. Being on the mouth when he lands will seem to the horse that he has been punished for having jumped. On landing shorten reins and resume a forward seat in the saddle.

Crop and Spurs are used only after a month or so of training and then only when they are needed. The crop is used on the horse that tries to run out and the spurs on the horse that gets sloppy in action.

One of the advantages of riding with the leg from the knee down close to vertical (seen sideways) or at least with the stirrup far enough forward to be under the kneecap, is that in case a horse stops cold at the barrier, the pressure in the stirrups will brake the forward movement and allow the weight of the body to go into the pommel. When stirrups are further back the weight is less well supported and the rider will more likely go forward out of the saddle. Stirrup leathers should be fixed at a length that gives the rider a good posture and allows for a forward inclination. If too long, the rider cannot clear his saddle seat with ease, and if too short, his weight is likely to be too much on the seat and not enough in the stirrups when the horse lands.

Heels, as in all riding, should be below the ball of the foot level. Ankles are bent inward so that the soles of the boots face outward slightly. Knees do not grip for balance. Legs are used for giving aids.

Movies and photos of jumpers here and in other countries show how varied are jumping techniques. One ungainly form of jump riding seen occasionally is that in which the rider seems to jump simultaneously with his horse. He floats with his seat far above the saddle with his body down on the horse's neck. His weight is no longer in the stirrups and the leathers are loose while the irons hang from his boots. In this position a rider can seldom shift quickly enough to catch his weight in the stirrups on landing. The theory seems to be that the rider relieves the horse of his weight as he goes up and over. But the fact is, just so much weight has to be lifted no matter how. And a shifting weight is no help to the horse who tries to adjust to it as he exerts himself to leave the ground.

Some riders like to speak softly to their horse as he approaches the jump and then just before take-off, saying, "Now!" or "Over!" in a pronounced tone. Others think speaking at such a moment is distracting. Certainly in order to listen, one or both of the horse's ears are likely to come back, marring the look of eagerness and pleasure that forward ears give.

The Show or Open Jumper

Even more than the working hunter or steeplechaser, the open jumper must demonstrate in the show ring a highly perfected athletic skill. He must exhibit control, faultless timing in his strides, good judgment, yet boldness and lack of hesitation as he attempts ever higher and wider jumps.

Fences are on level ground but are set in combinations and at challenging angles. They usually start at 3'9" to 4'. Hopefully more open-jumping classes will give Quarter Horses the opportunity for competition against all comers whether registered horses or not. The ultimate of horse jumping is to be found in International Puissance—or simply Puissance Jumping, in which fences are the most difficult of all in both height and width—often 7' high with a 6' spread. And they go higher and wider as each new world record is set.

A jump of 8'3.3", made in 1949 by Captain Laraguibel on Huaso at Santiago, Chile, is still listed as the world's high-jump record. The official world's record for the broad jump is 27'1½", made by Amado Mio ridden by Lieutenant Colonel Lopez de Hierro of Spain at Barcelona in 1951. But it was reported that Tiberetta's hoofprints from take-off to landing, made in clearing the "chair" jump in the 1959 Grand National at Aintree, England, measured an incredible 45 feet.

In scoring, AQHA and AHSA are quite similar. Both penalize faults and make eliminations for the same reasons.

Extreme speed is a fault that is generally penalized by AQHA, but not AHSA rules.

The AQHA rules and regulations can be obtained by writing for their official handbook (P.O. Box 200, Amarillo, Texas 78105). It should be studied as training progresses. Here are some of the more salient points on jumping taken from the handbook:

392. No horse shall be allowed to show in more than one approved AQHA registered jumping class per show. (This would not prevent a horse from being exhibited in both one approved Jumping class and one approved Working Hunter class.)

393. Arena arrangement:

   a. There will be a minimum of four (4) obstacles; horses are to make a minimum of eight (8) jumps.

   b. Type of obstacles which may be used:
     1. Post and Rail (at least two).
     2. Chicken coop.
     3. Stone Wall
     4. Triple Bar.
     5. Brush Jump.

   c. Obstacles should be located about 36 feet apart.

   d. Height of obstacles must be at least three feet. In case of ties, rails will be raised four inches on each go-round.

394. Scoring:

   a. Touch of obstacle with any portion of horse's body behind stifle: ½ fault.

   b. Touch of obstacle with any portion of horse's body in front of stifle or with any part of rider or equipment: 1 fault.

   c. Touch of standard or wing in jumping obstacle with any part of horse, rider, or equipment: 1 fault.

   d. Knockdown of obstacle, standard, or wing with any portion of horse, rider, or equipment: 4 faults.

   e. First disobedience (anywhere on course): 3 faults.

   f. Second disobedience (anywhere on course): 6 faults.

   g. Third disobedience (anywhere on course): Elimination.

   h. Fall of horse and/or rider: Elimination.

   i. Jumping obstacle before it is reset or without waiting for signal to proceed: Elimination.

   j. Starting before starting signal; jumping obstacle before start whether forming part of course or not; jumping obstacle out of order; off course: Elimination.

   k. Failure to enter ring within one minute of being called: Elimination.

   l. Failure to cross the starting line within one minute after judge's signal to proceed: Elimination.

m. Jumping any obstacle before crossing starting line unless said obstacle is designated as a practice jump: Elimination.

n. At a brush element, the touch of the brush only, without touching the framework or pole on top thereof, is not scored as a fault.

395. Equipment:

a. Bridle: May be either double, Pelham, or plain snaffle. Chain curb may be used, but must be at least one-half inch in width, can not be twisted, must be the standard flat variety used with Pelham bit, and must meet the approval of the judge.

b. Breastplate: Optional.

c. Martingales: Optional.

d. Saddles: Flat saddles.

The Working Hunter

After the hunter has mastered good jumping form his training centers on endurance, quick adjustment to uneven terrain, good manners, and boldness in clearing natural obstacles like stone walls, rail fences (timber), ditches, gates, etc. Training for height above four to four and one-half feet and spreads of more than five feet is not considered needed or advisable. Even jumps that high should be made only a few times each session at the peak of training. A hunter that jumps his fences with extravagant clearance tires himself unnecessarily.

Even if your hunter is to be used mostly in shows, his training should have endurance in mind. Remember, during the course of a hunt a hunter has to fly over a lot of obstacles. However, until he is a seasoned hunter it is well to by-pass some of the jumps to keep from tiring him. Always at the first sign of fatigue call it a day and start cooling him out.

If you have or expect to have a membership in a hunt club, your hunter should be ridden to hounds as soon as can be arranged. If he is well mannered and does not make a nuisance of himself, you may be welcome to ride out with a small group when the young hounds are being trained. During these cubbing outings, before the season opens, you and your horse can learn much about hunting etiquette, where to ride to avoid interfering with the hounds, and also get acquainted with the terrain, obstacles, sights, and sounds, etc. And it is wise to go to as many shows as you can to see what you will encounter if and when you enter them.

An ideal course arrangement for country or some fairground shows is for the hunter to enter and make his initial jump inside the show ring and then jump from it to an outside course which affords room enough for some brisk gallops between challenging obstacles that can show up the sureness and responsiveness of the working hunter before he returns to the ring with his final jump. The following is from the AQHA rules on Working Hunters:

396. No horse shall be allowed to show in more than one approved AQHA registered working hunter class per show. (This would not prevent a horse from being exhibited in both one approved Jumping class and one approved Working Hunter class.)

397. The Working Hunter class may be divided into two sections: Senior Working Hunter and Junior Working Hunter, based on the age of the horse. In Junior Working Hunter, the same rules shall apply as in the all-ages or Senior Working Hunter, except that the minimum of obstacles should be three (3) feet.

398. A hunter course shall be any course which management deems a fair test of a hunter.

399. Arena arrangement:
   a. Minimum of four obstacles to be jumped.
   b. Types of obstacles which may be used:
     1. Fences shall simulate obstacles found in the hunting field—such as post and rail, brush, stone wall, chicken coop, aiken, hedge, etc. A pole over brush, and jumps such as triple bar and hog backs are prohibited.
     2. The top element of all fences must be securely placed so that a slight rub will not cause a knockdown.
     3. Obstacles should be located at least fifty (50) feet apart; farther, if room permits.
     4. Height of obstacles must be a minimum of three (3) feet and three (3) inches.
     5. The use of wings on obstacles in hunter classes is recommended.

400. Scoring:
   a. Performance: An even hunting pace, manners, and style of jumping, together with way of moving over the course as well as being jogged for soundness.
   b. In all classes, judges shall line up horses on merit of performance before considering soundness. Horses may be required to show at a walk, trot, and canter.
   c. Soundness: All horses must be serviceably sound. Any horse showing lameness, broken wind, or impairment of vision shall be refused an award.

401. Faults:
   a. Light touches are not to be considered. Judges shall penalize unsafe jumping and bad form over fences, whether touched or untouched.

b. Faults for knockdowns, disobediences, and falls shall be the same as in the jumping class.

402. Equipment: Same as in jumping class.

Training the Cutting Horse

The Spanish horse's instinct to charge and dominate cattle dates, in the opinion of many horsemen, to the time when his forebears charged fighting bulls in the rings of old Spain, which served as training grounds for them and the lance-carrying knights who rode them. And it is postulated that from the Spanish horse the cowhorses of the Southwest passed on some of this inbred cow sense and combat instinct to their descendants, the Quarter Horses.

The Cutting Horse indulges in a form of combat. Like all rodeo exhibitions—except bulldogging—cutting was, and still is, on a few of the larger spreads a necessary ranch chore. It requires initiative, quick thinking, cow sense, and spectacular athletic prowess on the part of the horse.

From the moment he quietly enters the herd and singles out the cow or steer he must cut from it, the cutting horse is on his own. The action is too rapid for the rider to give cues, and in competition he must not give any noticeable ones. As the cow-critter darts this way and that, trying to return to the herd, the cutting horse must outguess and outmaneuver it with blocking sideway leaps, quick back-ups, and split-second direction changes until he can put it with the cut or (cut-out) herd. The amazing thing about the performance is the startling contrast in action from a quiet catlike tread to explosive action.

Training the cutting horse is more expensive than other forms of training because cattle are needed to practice on, and the same cattle, about ten in a herd, can't be used many times before they become too stale and disinterested to give the horse much opposition. They aren't so dumb but that they catch onto the fact that they can't win. Some trainers have solved the problem by using tireless fiberglass cows on wheels, electrically driven, and with a radio control system that has a range of nearly a half mile. The effectiveness, I am told, depends a lot on the operator. But that, too, is being solved by a programed magnetic tape that may be able to take over the job in some way quite beyond my understanding. The mechanical cows, I am also told, are still in rather short supply. Before giving up on the idea of using real cattle you might inquire about some of the training arenas to be found in all parts of the country, such as Rex Cauble's Cutter Bill Arena at Crockett, Texas; Hurst's Palace in Spanish Fork, Utah; E. J. Freeman's Training Center at Clyde, Texas; Woodland Hills Estate's luxurious facilities in the Ventura area of California; and the Pony Palace, Dr. Stanley E. Deal's elaborate setup at Polson, Montana—to mention only a few at random. Most training centers carry on an active cattle sales business which ensures a steady supply of fresh cattle for cutting horse and roping horse training. All contain facilities for boarding horses and are welcome havens for weary travelers who are pulling loaded horse trailers. Most have arenas with spectators' seats where shows, contests, and events take place several nights a week and where training can continue throughout the winter months.

Some owners who train their own cutting horses buy cattle and fatten them and, if lucky, sell at a profit that helps defray expenses. The larger the pen used for training, the fresher the cattle will remain. However, there is a use for stale stock and that is for the beginner. He must be allowed to win so as not to get discouraged at the start. Five minutes of rigorous cutting action is enough without a rest. The beginner is seldom fast enough and determined enough. But as he gets imbued with the spirit of the contest, his speed and pantherlike pounces will increase and call for the use of fresher cattle.

An owner who hopes to develop a cutting horse has the choice of: training and showing his own horse, which presupposes he is a horseman of ability and has plenty of working space or easy access to ranch facilities; sending the colt at considerable expense to a professional for cutting training and then getting him into contests in which he rides the horse himself; or sending the colt to a professional who not only trains him but takes him to the important shows and rides him in contests until the horse becomes a champion. The last route is the one taken by breeders who want to enhance the value of their stock and by others who can afford an expensive hobby that just might pay off.

The colt to be trained for cutting gets all the usual preliminary training. Then in the fall of his third year, his training starts in earnest. He was probably selected for cutting horse training because his breeding strongly indicated it. Not all colts chosen will live up to their promise, any more than all Quarter Horse and Thoroughbred racers are destined for turf glory.

Training, from the moment it starts, concentrates on what will benefit a cutting horse. Reining is kept to a minimum. Later the horse will work almost entirely with a free head. He must, of course, be gentled, carefully spur-trained, and made familiar with cattle by working with them in pastures, with ropes—but not generally as a roper—and in other ways that will widen his experience. Some men take their young cutters to rodeos and horse shows before they have a hope of winning for the purpose of teaching them to load and haul well in trailers, and to accustom them to the hubbub of crowds, cars, and blaring loudspeakers.

Hackamore training is perhaps the fastest way to prepare the horse for the swinging rein bridle. When working, the only times a cutting horse feels the reins is when he is pulled up or stopped. He must be a quick and straight backer. A bat is used to teach this. And to keep him backing straight, two bats are helpful. One may cause a horse to back diagonally away from the bat. With two, one in each hand, this is corrected, and he comes straight back. Backing with only the slightest use of reins further teaches him to work with a free head. Backing is important to a cutting horse because if a cow gets too close he hasn't sufficient room for maneuvering. Often to get this necessary room, he will have to back up—and fast.

The cutting horse works with his head rather low in order to be eyeball-to-eyeball with his opponent. His ears are mostly back—not in this case to listen to his rider, who is too busy just staying in the saddle to talk—but because he is in combat with another animal and to him it is serious business. When a cow sees those ears back and the piercing eyes and the fighting look, she is likely to be cowed—the pun just happened. At this moment, the cow is the enemy, and if encouraged to—as were some old ranch cutters I rode—the horse will reach out and bite the animal at the root of the tail and give it the "bum's rush" right out of the herd. In competition, such action would be penalized, as would deliberately striking a cow with a hoof.

When on the ground and leading your horse, and you have occasion to drive cattle into corners, through gates, etc., yell at them, make fighting gestures, make them go where you want them to. They are the enemy and you and your horse are a team that opposes them. The horse will sense your attitude and want to emulate it.

In early training when a less active animal is cut out, it should be followed some ways out from the herd, but not too close. Leave room to work if it suddenly tries to return. As your helper, the turn-back man, starts it back to the herd, let your colt go into action, with plenty of aids given, to block the cow from doing so. When the cow stays

Senor George—World Champion Cutting Horse in 1961—owned by Rusty Belt's Bar James Ranch, Fort Smith, Arkansas. Sonny Perry is riding. *Photo by James Cathey.*

put for a moment, the act has been successful, so let the turn-back man take over and put the cow with the herd. Dismount, praise and pat your colt. Let him know he's the star of the act. While training him, at any lack of attention wake up the colt with spur or bat but stay off his mouth.

When the horse is working fast and really feels his oats, the edge may have to be taken off by a good workout before cutting on him. He must be at a quiet walk when he enters the herd. Near-stealth is required, and he must stay at a quiet walk until the victim is selected and started from the herd. Slight leg aids are all the horse needs to suggest, "This one is in good location, let's take him." With that he starts easing the critter out. Working too fast inside the herd and scattering them draws a big penalty, as does losing a cow. When he goes by a cow too fast, the advantage goes to the cow. To regain it, he must turn and jump violently. Judges are critical of such action.

Early training on uneven pasture is good, but for final fast-action training, try and work on footing not too dissimilar to the harrowed or disked or sanded arenas.

Always during training, after a cow has been cut out, stop and quiet your horse. Let him know that each cutout is a separate job and that you are not there to chouse cows around all day. When he will stand quietly with you after hot and furious work, he's well on his way to being a cutting horse.

It can be said in a thousand ways, but the gist is always this: what the cowhorse training taught the Quarter Horse and what his training should continue to be is to work hard and fast when working and turn it off and rest when resting.

Training the Roping Horse

The best way to start training your roping horse is to make a quick, well-mannered reining horse of him first. After perfecting the quick stop, not necessarily the long sliding stop, you should practice coming out of the saddle so that the horse will associate the two actions. At first the reins will signal for the stop. Later the action of leaving the saddle will serve as the signal. All this is done preferably in a corral or arena, but don't do it in the same spot. The horse must not be given the idea that a certain spot is the place to stop. Nearly all Western-trained horses, except bulldogging horses, will stop when the rider leaves the saddle—something that brings pleased comment from most flat saddle riders who ride Western for the first time. It is obvious that bulldogging horses must be trained to do the very opposite. When a steer wrestler leaves the saddle, he wants his horse to keep on running in order to give him the necessary time to get a good hold on the steer and to keep the steer from making a quick left turn. To perfect the stopping action, some trainers use a jerk line. It is a strong, slender cord that passes through a pulley attached to the throat of the saddle and is tied to the bit. With this cord in his hand the trainer can be out in front of the horse and still pull him back if he requires it.

Some of the rope training for your horse, such as getting him used to having it on the saddle and having it swung over his head and past his head, can come along simultaneously with other training. He must get used to having the rope touch him. Drag it over his rump and gently tap his legs with it until he loses all fear of the rope. When

336   AMERICA'S QUARTER HORSES

you first drag the lariat on the ground, don't tie on fast to the horn, you may have to drop the rope to grab your horse. As you drag it, increase speed, until the day comes when your pony will run with it flapping and dragging behind without being spooked by it.

Whenever possible, work him in a closed area with small calves he won't have much trouble catching up with. Show him how to outguess the calves by cutting corners and reaching them quicker. All this teaches him to watch and follow cattle and to move deliberately into position behind them. Rounding up cattle in pasture also sharpens his cow sense, and the variety of uneven ground will make him come alive.

After he is at ease with a rope, you can start teaching your horse to pull on things, logs or a sack of sand, with the rope dallied on the horn at first, then later tied fast. The weight should not be more than fifty

Donna Wooden, a Quarter Horse mare owned by Elbert and Dorothy Gilbert of Phoenix, Arizona, being rope-trained by Roy Patten. *Courtesy Dorothy Gilbert.*

pounds to begin with, as the exercise is intended to muscle up the withers gradually. Strong withers are a prime requirement in a roping horse. Increase the weight of the object dragged until the horse will pull against and keep the rope taut on a weight of about 150 pounds. Practice must continue until the horse is not frightened when he hits the end of the line and feels the sudden jerk and pressure on his withers. When you drag from the rear and pull back from the front, it is well to do it on both sides. Also teach your horse to let you get in and out of your saddle from either side.

No doubt you have been whirling the loop at every opportunity and casting it at bushes, dogs, chickens, and imaginary calves, so your horse is prepared for more unexpected moves when you start his chute training. Enter the chute quietly, turn right so your loop will not get caught on the fence, back into the corner, and then start revving your horse up. Pivot him a time or two, but do not spur. When a helper slams a gate and the excitement triggers the horse, try and hold him back for a split second until the barrier is released; the time it takes the calf to reach the scoring line. Then let him go. To keep him from breaking the barrier requires patient training. Trying to speed up the lesson by electrifying the barrier, as some do, may ruin him as a quick starter, by making him fear to leave the chute. The horse should think of you and the barrier as his release, not the sound of a gate rattling, a calf lunging. The ideal is for him to dance in place until the barrier zips past and your legs close in and your rein arm goes out.

Even a quiet horse should become so eager to spring out that spurring is unnecessary. I once made the mistake of allowing a horse I had never ridden before to quiet down too much in the chute while adjusting my rope. So, to bring him out fast, I spurred him. He was so shocked it brought him out all right, but he came out pitching instead of running and he sold me some real estate!

After racing from the chute, cast your loop, stop fast, and leave the saddle as the rope hits the ground and run and grab the noose end. A flourish of the rope may give your stopped horse the idea of backing up and pulling a little against you. A neck rope through which the lariat runs before tying to the horn, causes the horse to face you to get the pressure off his neck. The next lesson when coming out of the chute is to cast your loop near a sandbag that weighs as much as a calf. And when you run to it slip the noose over the sack and encourage your horse to pull back on it. If he pulls back too fast, step on it to slow him down.

Whatever is done to train him he must overcome any fear of the rope

Roping can be fun for riders of all ages. Here a father and son are team-roping at a Saturday rodeo at the Western Riding Club in Phoenix, Arizona. *Photo by Roger Buchanan.*

and the pull on his withers, and be steady in holding it taut when you are out of the saddle after casting a loop on an animal. Horses can, and have, run off with a calf on the end of the rope. There is a lot of excitement of running and throwing a calf and arm waving to signal that it has been tied. Lessons in actual roping should be done for accuracy and good action on the part of the horse, rather than for speed at first. Speed comes later. Try and have a helper on hand during practice. And have him release the roped calf after you have mounted your horse.

Heeling in team roping is good early-stage training for the roping horse. The head roper comes out of the box fast, ropes the steer about the horns, and brings him around into good position for the heel roper, who at a much slower gait moves in behind the steer to cast a slanting loop under the animal's belly. The try is for two hind legs, but one is better than none. When a catch is made the heeler swings his horse off at an angle stretching the steer on the ground between the two horses and toward the running head roper, who has leaped from his horse to

A team event in which the boy ropes and holds the calf while the girl rides into position, leaps off, and snatches a ribbon off the calf's tail. *Photos by Roger Buchanan.*

tie the steer. Left alone, the head roper's horse must head away from the steer and keep a steady pull on the rope. The heel roping horse still has his man in the saddle to make suggestions, such as: don't pull so hard, or lean into the rope a little more.

There are five categories of AQHA roping. Two are against the clock: Calf Roping and Steer Roping. And three are scored events. They are: Team Tying (in which steers are roped by a header and a heeler with ropes tied hard and fast to the horns of their saddles); Dally Team Roping (in which both header and heeler dally their ropes on the horn of the saddle); and Dally Steer Stopping (in which the steer is roped but not thrown and tied). In all events it is only the performance of the horses that count. Scoring is done on the basis of 60–80 with 70 denoting an average performance. For the header and the Dally Steer roper legal catches are: both horns; half head; and around neck. Any front leg in the catch is not legal.

Horses are judged on manners behind the barrier, rate of speed to steer, ability of horse to rate, check, stop straight, and to stop and turn the steer to face the horse.

In Team Roping the heeling horse is judged on ease of manner in which he turns and puts his man into position for the throw of the loop, and the jerk he puts on the steer to make him accessible for the header to tie. Each horse in team roping is judged separately. All roping requires speed, plus expertise and quick thinking.

The horse must come out with a racing-gate start, then at an all-out stretch of speed he must dodge and turn and follow the animal while maneuvering for position. The roper must be able to depend on his horse to rate his own speed and to do his stuff while he decides which instant is best for a sure throw. When the horse plows to a stop when the catch is made in Calf Roping, the roles are reversed: the man leaps from the saddle and does the running. If the horse comes back on the rope a few feet, he can shorten his rider's run by bringing the calf closer.

Competitive ropers use a short rope—about twenty-five feet—to shorten their race to the calf or steer. There is an old saying that sums it up: "Long rope, slow horse—short rope, Quarter Horse." Speed is essential in roping steers that must be thrown and tied, as in rodeo contests, because there must be enough slack in the rope left after it tightens on the horns or neck to be flipped over the steer's right side before the horse races off obliquely to the left to make the throw.

Today's horses are perhaps as strong and as enduring as were the old working ranch horses, but few are put to such rigorous tests. King Merritt,

Keeping that line taut. *Photo by Roger Buchanan.*

a great man with a rope a few years back, said his horse Gangster could throw seven or eight steers in a row, and do it on all kinds of rough ground. And Gangster, he stressed, never made a lame step in his life, never had any leg or foot trouble. It was his opinion that all good using horses should be like that.

Yours may not be quite such an iron horse, so watch for fatigue when working him and at the first sign that he is tiring or favoring a leg or a foot give him plenty of rest.

Because of the temperament of both the horse and the man who trains him, and the degree of confidence and directness in the latter, it is pointless to lay down hard and fast rules of training. One cowboy I knew in the Texas Panhandle, who was fearless and direct in handling horses, brought a wild four-year-old in from pasture, broke him to the saddle, and was roping steers on him six weeks later. The horse, he told me, was as good a roper as he ever rode. Once out on the high plains of the Texas Panhandle, east of the old settlement of Ochiltree, when the buffalo grass still stretched away in all directions like the open sea, I saw a lone horseman approaching. I waited for him to ride up. The horse he rode was magnificent, and I asked about him. I learned his horse was a five-year-old. "I've been taking my time with this one," the rancher remarked, "been schoolin' him since he was a little over three. Another year and I'll have me a real good ropin' horse."

There, within the same ranching area, were two men with very diverse methods of training. Neither, I am sure, would tolerate any roping horse that wasn't mighty good at his job.

After general roping training, you and your horse can sharpen up on whatever specialty—calf and steer roping, or heading or heeling—you prefer. (You can prevent some rope burns on your steers by putting heavy elastic webbing bands around their horns.) Beyond this basic knowledge of what roping requires of the horse and roper, superior skill in the sport can come only through much practice, observation of competitors, and perhaps by attending roping classes conducted by top rodeo ropers.

Riding and Training the Barrel Horse

In barrel racing the rider should be forward over the withers and leaning inward with the horse on turns. Be there consistently—don't make the horse guess where your weight is going to be.

A short rein—not on the horse's mouth, understand—but for quick reining and control, clips a fraction of a second from the time. On a too close turn, a corrective rein-hand movement of a few inches is better than a wave with a long rein. The arm gives the slack for the horse's head. All this applies whether riding with curb or hackamore. And better not use split reins. If one dropped—well, you can picture what could happen.

The more experienced the horse the quicker he responds to a slack rein. An old barrel-circling pro wants lots of headroom. Just see that he doesn't get so much that an inside rein flies over his head. This could really tangle things up—as it has done on more than one occasion. An easily breakable string joining the reins under the neck will prevent it.

For a sure grip, some contestants use nylon reins. There are a variety of types and sizes.

Training for Pole Bending and Stake Racing

As in barrel racing, what is called for is a demonstration of the quick start, abrupt turns, and lead changes for which the Quarter Horse is

Young rider and her horse leaning into a turn. *Photo by Guy Kassal.*

distinguished. These events come closer to the sprint races of the quarter tracks than any other. What they require is the speed of a sprinter but the control of the reining horse.

Start the patterns slowly and increase speed as training proceeds. For diagrams of the patterns for each event and the basic rules, see Chapter 15.

Training for the Reining and Working Cowhorse Contest

This training calls for bringing your horse to a high degree of perfection in the basic requirement of the Western-trained horse—in sliding to a stop, rolling over hocks, changing leads, backing up, pivoting, etc., all done with reasonably slack reins and without undue use of aids. For patterns see Chapter 15.

Vicky La Piccolo preparing her horse Brite Cord for the trail horse event. *Photo by John Dutson.*

Training for the Western Pleasure Contest and the Trail Horse Class

The same basic manners and responses in the horse as for the reining and other events are required. But all is done with much less accent on speed. In these events, the rider and horse must be relaxed and at ease as they perform gaits, lead changes, and all that is required of them with no show of excitement. And with no need of obvious restraint of the horse. This training calls for many wet saddle blankets to perfect such quiet and confident appearances! See Chapter 15 for patterns to be ridden and other details of these events.

Sue Schecter putting Bar Cita over some tricky obstacles. *Photo by John Dutson.*

If you want to win consistently in show classes, strict attention will have to be given—whenever and wherever you ride—to your horse's manners, fluency of lead changes, quick response to aids for changes of gait, direction, etc., as well as to your own posture in the saddle and the ease with which you give aids. In other words, even when you are alone, you are onstage, as though an invisible judge has his eye on you.

Attending the type of shows you want to enter and studying the event or events in which you are most interested will enable you to judge the competition you will have to face. You will learn ways to improve your own and your horse's performance. Your instructor and riding associates will give advice. Then when you think you are ready and you do enter show events be satisfied with the decision of the judges and, win or lose, consider it part of your schooling.

To Show or Not to Show—A Summary of Training

In training horses for the various show classes and contests, there are clever ways and cruel ways, and devices and gimmicks that help to get quick results. Electric breast collars will back the horse up or stop him. Electrified reins will neck-rein him. Cavessons or dropped nosebands can be buckled so tight he can't get his mouth open to cheat on the bit. Tie-downs will keep his head in place. Rubber bands an inch and a half wide tied around the tail near the dock will stop him from switching it. Soreing up the front feet will make him hard-stop on the rear feet. Stinging irritants (scooting juice) and grown-out hoofs can cause high action. Tranquilizing drugs can quiet him down. And this is only a partial list of the things that can be done and are being done in the course of training horses, though such practices are prohibited at recognized shows. Just think it over. Wouldn't you rather take the necessary time to do the training job well and develop a natural horse that is a joy to ride? Or even stay out of shows entirely?

A true horseman never hurts a horse with whip, spur, lead rope, or a bit, except in moments of punishment. The mark of a gentleman, it is said, is that he never insults anyone unintentionally. The mark of a good horseman is that he never hurts a horse unintentionally. When he hurts a horse he does it deliberately to correct a bad habit or implant a lesson.

There are no patents issued to trainers. No one trainer has the magic secret. All borrow ideas and methods from others. Regardless of all the pronouncements and admonitions of trainers and self-titled "riding masters" to do it "my way," there are a hundred ways horses can be trained. And surprisingly, horses being the nice creatures they are will perform reasonably well even when trained and ridden in the most eccentric manner. The end result of all training, whether the horse is to be used for jumping, roping, cutting, working cowhorse, or for some young person's pleasure horse, should be to make a horse with good manners, with trust in the rider, and with confidence enough left to move and act like a cheerful horse instead of a captive.

Traveling with Your Horse

If your horse was taught as a foal to enter and sometimes eat his grain in a trailer, he is almost sure to be an easy loader and a good traveler. If he gets his first lessons on entering a trailer as a mature horse, or if some accident or fright associated with a trailer makes him wary about entering it, you must expect to spend some time in training him. Practically all horses are transported from place to place these days. Even ranch horses are taken in trailers or trucks to the far pastures where cattle are to be worked.

A livestock inspector I recently met carries his saddle horse, a handsome young stallion, with him in a pickup truck everywhere he goes. It was interesting to see how nonchalantly the young horse peered about from his high perch as he rode about the country. The ease with which he got up on the truck was demonstrated when his owner backed up to a sloping bank at the side of the road. Although the bed of the truck was a foot and a half or so from the ground, the horse turned around and jumped out and as nimbly jumped in when his owner was ready to go.

In dealing with a horse that balks or hesitates to enter the trailer, you may have to put a rope over his rump and lead him as you would a foal being taught to lead. Be sure that the tail-gate ramp is steady so that his footing feels secure when he steps on it.

Luring in with feed, or with another horse, can be helpful. Wings may have to be placed at the sides of the tail-gate ramp to keep a horse from dodging or accidentally stepping off sideways. If *you* walk in the trailer, the horse is more likely to follow you. This means loading him at first in a two-horse trailer so that you have a way to get out.

If your trailer has an escape hatch forward, the most natural way to get him in is for you to go ahead, with the horse following you. If the trailer has no forward escape hatch, start your horse up the ramp and stand aside as he enters. Pass the lead rope up to where you can grasp it through the front window. Keep the window partly closed so the horse can't get his head through it. Do not snap or tie the horse until after the chain has been hooked across at the back and the tail gate closed. If tied fast before this is done, the horse, if frightened, might come back, and with nothing to stop him but his halter lead, one or the other is almost bound to break during the struggle. Even if he does not break anything or hurt himself, the commotion and fright will prejudice him against trailers.

It is best not to water your horse before traveling. Some horses will not urinate in a trailer. If the trip is a long one, stop a few times and walk the horse about. Hay in the manger will help to keep him from fretting.

Stall partitions are generally made so that they are not solid to the floor. This is done so horses will have room to spread their legs for better balance.

It can be assumed there will be times when a horse will have to struggle somewhat for balance, so to keep him from hurting his legs, a good precaution is to strap hauling boots on his legs or wrap them with cotton padded track bandages. In cold weather, horses should be blanketed if the trailer is open at the rear.

The floor of the trailer should not be slick. Rubber mats give good footing and do not hold moisture which can rot the flooring. Remove mats and examine flooring periodically, to make sure the floor is sound.

After the horse or horses are in the trailer, it is wise to run through a ritual before you start—something like what an airline pilot does before take-off. If done in sequence, it can become a good habit.

In this order:

Hook chain at the back of the horses.

Secure tail gate.

Snap manger tie chain to halter.

Close and latch side windows and door to tack compartment.

Check all four tires.

Check to see if trailer hitch is securely latched, and the electrical connection for brakes and lights plugged in.

While someone puts on brakes, brake lights, and directional signals, stand back and see that all are functioning.

Take it easy on any rough road and on turns so your horse will not get frightened. Allow for much more distance in passing other cars, and for braking to a stop. Until you learn to back a trailer expertly—something that should be practiced until mastered—stop only in places at filling stations, restaurants, or showgrounds, etc., where you can get out by going forward and without having to make any tight turns.

As an added measure of safety, you should ride in the trailer, without your horse, and see if it has any rattles or bangs, and how it performs on turns, abrupt stops, etc. Your good or bad driving will measurably affect your horse's attitude to trailer riding. So drive caefully and you'll both get wherever you want to go in good shape.

R. A. Phillips of Arlington, Texas, has traveled thousands of miles and carried on a voluminous correspondence in order to produce his *Horsemen's Travel Guide*. It has a listing of places across the country that can furnish accommodations for horses and is very helpful when planning a long trip to shows, races, or trail rides.

13

Bad Habits and Vices and Their Correction

Horses aren't born with bad habits. They don't know good habits from bad habits until a trainer sets them straight. Most horses—and it is certainly true of the sensible Quarter Horses—can be raised from colthood without any disciplinary problems. If trained with consistency and never hurt beyond mild correction, they will learn and remember the way they are expected to do things. If handled mostly by a single owner, they become so responsive that one wonders if they understand human language. Gently and carefully trained horses are very trustful of those who handle them well, and will do what they are asked quite willingly. They will climb up and go down canyon walls that seem impossibly steep, crawl over stone fences, jump over ditches and obstacles of all descriptions, and face and outmaneuver angry bulls.

Unfortunately all horses are not well trained or raised in happy homes. New owners may find they have to deal with blocks and traumas resulting from bad handling or overpermissiveness of a former owner.

The one-horse owner with limited time has to be very much on guard against bad habits caused by idleness. Because he isn't called upon to demonstrate the things he does well, the idle horse will gradually replace his good manners and eagerness to please with a lot of annoying habits.

It is a temptation, when you can spend only short periods with your horse, to be too permissive with him. You will do your horse and yourself a favor by steeling yourself and correcting every bad habit before it becomes set. To keep your horse a well-mannered, pleasant companion, the following are some faults to be on the lookout for, with suggestions of how to cope with them.

Barn Sour

A horse that is pampered and petted, used little, and well fed can easily become lazy and reach the point where he hates to leave his comfortable stable. It is the place for him. It is where the feed is and where he doesn't have to mind any one or exert himself. After being saddled and mounted he may refuse to leave the stable area. If badly spoiled he may, when switched or spurred, throw his weight around and whirl and rear. Such a stubborn, sulky, rebellious horse is worthless unless his faults are corrected.

An experienced horseman would never allow a horse to lose his manners and training to such an extent. But should an experienced horseman be faced with such a problem, he wouldn't let the horse get away with it. He should stay with him, outstubborn him, spur him away from the barn area, and give him a good workout.

A less experienced rider might have to dismount and lead the horse away from the barn. If the horse refuses to move out when mounted, he should be circled, using whip or spurs, until he is slightly confused and doesn't know which way to refuse to go. It should be said here that kicking a horse's belly with blunt heels is a very bad practice. Spurs are more effective and much less painful. All horsemen should learn how to use them early in their own training as riders.

If all fails and the horse refuses to move on out and becomes excited and angry, dismount, put a halter on him, and lead him some distance from the barn and tie him up. Leave the saddle on. Later in the day try him again. Give him a good workout so he will forget his troubles and come in relaxed. If the next day he refuses to leave the barn area, don't fight with him, just tie him up someplace clear away from the barn. When feeding time comes remove the saddle, water and feed him, but leave him tied up overnight if the weather is not rainy or too cold. When you ride him take his halter and some feed tied on your saddle, and when you are the farthest you are going from the barn, feed him and let him graze a bit. After a time or two of this novel experience your old pal will begin to realize that feed is not always in a stable. And when he learns this he is on the road to recovery. Whenever you return from rides after this, leave him tied up for a while outside and then jump on him and take another five-minute ride. And about the most important thing of all is to use him oftener.

Biting

Biting is not just an annoying habit, it is dangerous. I know of two women who were scarred for life by horses biting them. And the left deltoid of a good many men show marks that prove the horse's head is sometimes quicker than the eye. Whatever is done to stop the vice must be done quickly and effectively or the horse is ruined.

The biting problem calls for ingenuity. One man told how he heated a part of a ham and strapped it to his well-padded shoulder, and when his horse bit at him its teeth sank into the fiery hot ham—and he learned his lesson. Others I know of have tried rattraps, spiked sprinting shoes, and red-pepper-saturated sponges tied on their upper arms for the animal to snap at. All these methods are too complicated for my taste. Even to make such preparations is an indication that the biting habit has been tolerated for some time.

Here is the way I have stopped it quickly in more than one horse, but I realize a young inexperienced person might need a heavy glove with rivets or some rough surface over the knuckles to be effective. Mr. Muller, a kindly old gentleman who used to care for our horses and who so loved animals he was entirely too permissive with them, reported that a beloved gelding had become a biter. I was disbelieving as I had saddled and ridden the horse but a few days before and had seen no such action. To prove his point, Mr. Muller threw a blanket on the gelding while I stood in the background to watch. Sure enough the head whirled around, the teeth snapped, and although he missed, Harvey, the gelding, seemed to smile at his new power over human beings. When I stepped over and spoke to Harvey, I dropped the halter lead to the floor as I always did, since he was gentle, took the blanket off, and then tossed it back on him. His ears came back and his head moved slightly and that is all that happened when I threw the saddle on him. But when I started to draw the cinch tight, Harvey decided to try on me what had given him such dominance a minute or so before. As his head snaked around with teeth showing, I hit him a hard blow right in the lip above his teeth. Harvey was startled, to say the least, and Mr. Muller was shocked. He said, "I didn't think I would live to see the day when you would strike that horse in anger."

"Well, I wasn't angry—I was just determined that he wouldn't bite again," I answered.

This may sound as though I got out of that difficulty too easily. But the truth is, that gelding never attempted to bite again in the five years that I owned him after that time.

Just remember when you punish a horse, it must be done instantly, at the moment of the bad action if possible.

Of course, cross-tying will prevent the horse from getting his head around very far. But there are times when it can't be done. If no cross-tie is available, bridle the horse before saddling and when the saddle is on, before tightening the cinch tie the off rein to the girth billet or cinch ring to prevent him from swinging his head around.

Some biters have been shown the error of their ways by being jabbed in the muzzle when they attempted to bite someone who had had the foresight to strap a colt weaner around his upper arm. A colt weaner has a leather muzzle piece that bristles with small sharp spikes.

Until the bad habit is corrected, a good precaution is to bridle the horse and hold the reins close to the bit as the saddle is tossed on. Then, before setting up the cinch, tie the off rein to the D ring of the saddle so the horse's head can't swing around toward you.

Bolting or Running Away

The fact is that bolting is almost never experienced on Western-trained using horses. The hackamore training with which most of them are started, followed by curb bit training, gives such a positive control that from the very beginning the horse knows that he cannot get away. With such firm control, if needed, the rider uses it less and less until the horse works on a swinging rein. His mouth, never *ridden on,* as with the so-called milder snaffle bit, remains sensitive and responsive (see Refusing the Bit). Then, too, except for bulldogging horses, most Western-trained horses stop when their riders come out of the saddle. For instance, if both reins were broken, leaving no head control, all the rider would have to do would be to start leaving the saddle and a well-trained Western horse would slide to a stop. Or if both reins were dropped, the horse would stop because the long unattached reins would drag on the ground and the horse would step on them. Dragging reins are used to teach a horse to stand ground-tied, that is, to stand whenever the reins are dropped to the ground.

Bolting is much more usual in Eastern-trained horses that are ridden with flat saddles, because with that style of riding the horse is in hand at all times and the mouth bars become accustomed to pressure which makes them less sensitive. It follows that the horse that is used to a bit always against the bars will take a little more mouth punishment in order to have his own way. Attached reins used with flat saddle riding cannot, of course, be used to ground-tie a horse.

If your horse does bolt, do *not* haul back on both reins evenly and keep up the pressure. Pull up and let off, more on one rein than the other in order to circle your horse. Tighten the circle until you are in control. A horse cannot run very fast with his head pulled sideways.

Stay with him—don't try to leap off. A running horse is easy to ride —actually there is not as much rhythmic balance required as in a fast trot or even a canter—so continue to try to circle him. Strong rail or board fences—if he is not a jumper—may stop him. A clump of trees might do it, but there is the danger of being hit or raked off by limbs. Circling your horse in the clear is the best bet.

If you are in a group of riders when a friend's horse bolts, do not chase after him. The pounding hoofs behind will only increase the excitement of the runner. You might, if he is coming toward you, try to block his path. But be sure you do it at an angle with room to move so you and your horse can avoid a collision. If the horse slows a bit, you might get near enough to help circle him until he stops.

At the Vermont State Fair at Rutland in 1965 I watched a bolting horse that had thrown his rider from an English saddle come tearing down the track headed for a mixed pleasure horse class assembled there. A rider in a Western saddle, either trying to block the path of the oncoming horse or to get out of his way, was sideways when the runaway hit him. He and his horse went down like a struck bowling pin. Fortunately, man and horse got up, apparently not badly hurt.

A good rider tries never to let his horse reach the bolting stage. He will be aware of mounting excitement in his horse and will hold him down and do what he can to calm him. This can be done by riding away from other riders, by stopping and dismounting and distracting the horse, by checking the cinch and rigging, slapping at horseflies, etc. It's fun to ride a running horse, but only when you are in control.

Carrying Head Too High

This tendency is more than likely caused by improper training, an unsuitable bit, or heavy hands, or all three (see also Head Tossing).

To correct it, if the horse is still young enough to learn, put a straight or bar bit, sometimes called a training bit, in the horse's mouth and tie the reins to the D rings on the saddle. They should be tight enough only to tuck his chin in a little and cause him to flex his neck. Then turn him into the corral for an hour or so at a time and let him set his own head. If he doesn't move about enough to benefit from this kind of head control, run some lines through the stirrups (hobble them) and drive him from the rear as if he were hitched to a cart. The horse soon learns that as long as his head is down and his neck arched, there is nothing to bother his mouth. As in all training, be as gentle on the mouth as possible. Later when riding, keep the rein hand close to the withers. Try different bits, or if you suspect he resents all bits work him for a while with a hackamore bridle. Some trainers use a Pelham bit and anchor the top reins on the horn to keep the horse's chin in while the other set of reins is used to rate the horse's speed and to neck-rein with. Using a running martingale will achieve the same results, while a standing martingale, although it keeps the horse from carrying his head high and from throwing his head up, seldom assists in setting the horse's head correctly.

Cribbing

Cribbing can be just a bad habit of gnawing on manger, fence boards, partitions, and the like. Sometimes it is merely a weanling's teething solace. But it can also be a serious ailment which causes the horse to clamp his teeth on board, stump, or post—some say on metal as well if no wood is handy, although I have never seen it—and suck air and grunt. The muscles expand at the bottom of the throat. He may be trying to expel gas. In his effort he sucks air into his stomach, which can result in colic. He can cause his gums to bleed and he can wear down or injure his chopper teeth. Opinions vary, but it is generally thought to be the result of some lack in the diet or from boredom. Horses left for too many hours a day in a stall are the ones most likely to start it, say some horsemen. It can also be picked up from a cribbing stall mate.

At the very first signs of cribbing, get busy. Try a change in feed. See that your horse is getting plenty of salt, and you could switch to a different salt block that has more or other mineral additives. Spend more time with him and ride him oftener. Maybe a dog, cat, goat, chicken—you never can tell what, but something—will ease his restlessness.

Some owners replace wood wherever they can with some form of metal to eliminate places for the cribber to clamp his teeth. A more effective way is to string an electrified fence wire—the charge is very slight—on insulators over the places that could be gnawed and sucked.

The most commonly used preventive is the old-time practice of buckling a one-and-a-half or two-inch strap around the horse's neck like a big throat latch. It shouldn't be choking tight, but it should leave no room for the throat muscles to expand, which they do when the horse cribs. There is plenty of room, however, when he thrusts his head down to eat and drink. The strap is removed, of course, when the horse is used. The vice, habit, or ailment seems to be one that cannot be cured if not caught and arrested in the early stages.

Gulping Down Feed

This habit is sometimes evidence of faulty teeth. If the teeth are sound, it can simply be the action of a greedy and barn-soured horse.

The grain can be mixed with coarse-chopped hay to force the horse to masticate his food. Stones as big as your fist can be put in with the grain to slow him up while he sorts out the grain from the stones. Whatever the cause, the habit, if not stopped, can cause indigestion.

Jiggling, Head Tossing, and Tail Wringing

These three bad habits often go together. They are so aggravating that they must not be tolerated. The causes are: inadequate training, lack of use, permissiveness, unsuitable bits, riding on the mouth until irritated, headstalls or throat latches that are too tight, something irritating about the saddle, wanting always to be in the lead (as with ex-racers and ex-polo ponies, and even horses often used to lead trail rides). Some horses are alone so much they become overexcited when with other horses. None of these habits is generally associated with Quarter Horses because of their inbred tractability. But any horse may get into bad habits if riders and handlers are careless.

There is a big difference between jiggling and jog-trotting or any controlled slow gait. The first is a nervous annoying habit, while the latter is a comfortable gait that can be ridden for hours without tiring the rider. To begin correcting the jiggling habit, the horse should be given daily workouts, and if he is in good condition, they should be strenuous, followed by long cooling-out walks back to the stable. A good walk is a good gait and should be practiced like any other gait. Owners who have horse trailers and who find their horse is fretful and anxious to get back to the stable should take the horse in the trailer to more

Walking is a good gait and should be taught just as any other gait. Few horses that are good walkers are head tossers. Here Chuckie, five-year-old son of Don and Marcia Paxson, happens to be in a brisk walk, although he rides McElroy News at a brisk canter if he so desires. This gelding was an Arizona State Champion in Western Pleasure, Working Stock Horse, and Trail Horse Class. *Photo by the author.*

open country to do their riding. Returning to a trailer is less exciting to the horse than returning to his stable, and he will more readily calm down, walk, and cool out.

Keep off the mouth when possible, milk the reins—fiddle them with your fingers—rather than putting constant pressure on the bars of the mouth. Try a change of bits. Maybe go back to hackamore training for a few days. Try a bit with a cricket in the port—a rowel that makes a little cricket noise—and the horse may be quieted by his absorption with the sound it makes when he plays with it with his tongue. Some horsemen, in using a low port curb bit following hackamore training, put a rather heavy noseband or cavesson on the bridle to remind the horse of the hackamore bosal.

A tie-down may control the head-tossing somewhat, but it does nothing to correct the nervousness that causes it, and the jiggling and the tail wringing. Tie-downs and standing martingales are restrictive devices that should be thought of as training equipment rather than perpetually used riding gear. Well-trained horses seldom require their use, and they are not allowed in certain AQHA sponsored classes. A tie-down habitually used sets up another bad habit—that of leaning into the noseband, which limits the freedom of the forehand.

A little jingling trinket on a breast strap will sometimes so fascinate a horse he will forget his nervousness. He can think of only one thing at a time.

If other horses overly excite your horse, turn him away from them and take a side trail. Stop him often and make him stand quietly. Dismount, talk to him, check equipment. When in the saddle, every time the horse walks quietly give him his head instantly so he can walk with a swinging rein and feel how nice it is to have the freedom of his head.

If all else fails, give him a few sessions in the corral with his reins tied to the cinch rings of the saddle, as suggested for horses that carry their heads too high. For tail wringing some riders tie rubber bands around the root of the tail. It may stop the wringing and switching for a while, but it is no answer to the problem. If one can find the answer to the horse's nervousness and uneasiness, then the problem may be solved.

Kicking

A horse that kicks must be broken of the habit or disposed of. He is too dangerous to have around. The pleasure of riding with friends can end abruptly if your horse gets known as a kicker. Among hunt club riders a known kicker is required to wear a red ribbon on his tail and to stay in the rear of the field. It is a precaution all thoughtful riders should take when riding with groups.

The fact that a horse has become a kicker means that he was allowed to do so. All horses do some kicking in pasture or corral to emphasize some point of disagreement with an equine acquaintance. But with the beginning of training this natural defense or attack mechanism is not to be tolerated. Kindness and considerate handling—and quick decisive correction when needed—show the horse that he does not have to defend himself while in your care.

At the first instance of kicking, the horse should be punished instantly if you are on him or near enough. If on a halter lead, jerk him back into a corner so he cannot swing sideways. Whip him once or twice on the shoulder or thighs—never on the head—with the doubled-up lead and scold him in no uncertain tones. Let him know you are fighting mad. Make an act of it. Justice Holmes, after returning from the army camps of the Civil War, once said, "The full potential of the English language cannot be appreciated until one has heard a teamster search the soul of a mule." Your anger, unlike your usual kindliness with him, will be a punishment to him.

If he kicks at another horse when you are riding him, come back instantly on the bit and try and set him on his haunches, turning him if you can over his hocks. That in itself is punishing to a horse and it gets him away from the other horse. If you have a bat, whip him with it. One or two lessons like this will cure all but the most determined.

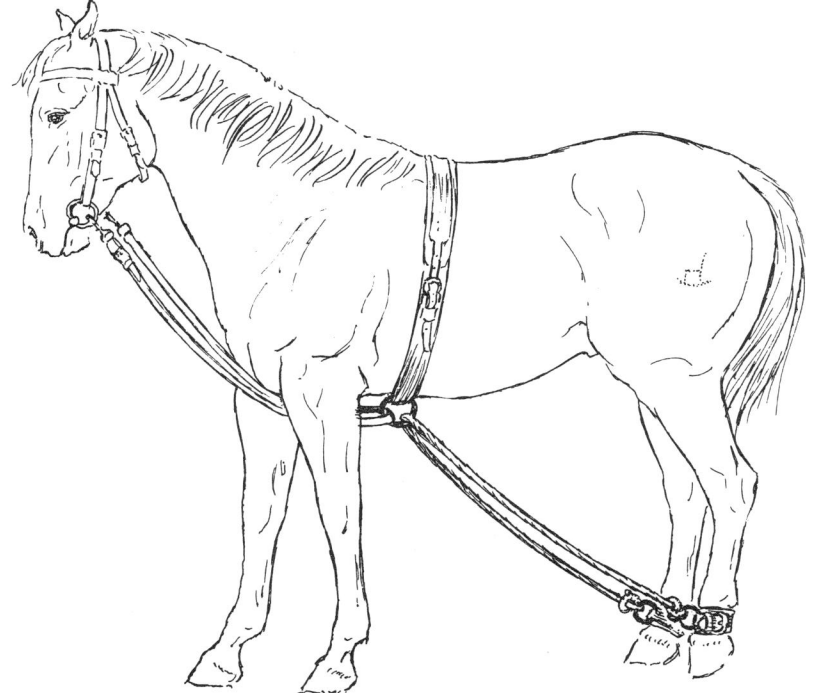

With the hitch pictured here for reforming a kicker, the horse can walk, but should he kick with even one hind foot, his mouth gets punished. A less severe method is to run a rope from the surcingle, between the front legs and up around the neck near the withers where the horse will receive the punishment, instead of on the mouth.

kickers. If the kicking persists, however, take no more chances. Give him a treatment that will stop it once and for all. Put a running-W rig on him and sack him out. Even the amateur horseman can do this if he has moderate control over the horse. The diagram shows how the ropes from the cuffs on the hind pasterns run up through a ring in the surcingle and how a rope from a straight heavy bit or a bosal runs between the front legs to the surcingle ring. This rig can be arranged to punish the withers rather than the mouth or nose if thought preferable, as many do.

The rope from the rear pasterns sliding through the surcingle ring allows the horse to walk, but there is not enough slack for the horse to kick without punishing himself. After a kick or two he will associate the kick with the punishment. While in this rig a thorough sacking out is advisable. Rub him all over his body with a sack or rag. The only thing that will hurt him while this is going on is a kick. Tempt him to kick by throwing a sack or paper at his heels. Let him get a thorough lesson. Pick up his feet, rub his heels.

If your horse is a cow kicker, one that kicks out sideways when being saddled or cinched up, he might be broken of it by whipping his leg, but if not, give him the treatment.

We once had a gelding that had been put in a running-W rig to stop his kicking. Sometime later I was riding out in a big pasture and saw this same gelding dash after another horse and whirl to deliver a vicious kick, but as he whirled he threw his head in the air and instead of kicking he almost sat down on his heels. He had been Pavloved. Just as a bell meant food to Pavlov's dogs, a kick meant punishment to that gelding. He was cured for good.

Moving When Mounting

The horse that refuses to stand still makes mounting an English saddle difficult if not impossible and is annoying to say the least for the one who mounts a stock saddle. If the horse is really green and undisciplined and needs firm control, the rider of a stock saddle can hold the headstall of the bridle with his left hand and pull the horse's head around toward him, forcing the horse to stand still while he mounts by grasping the horn and reins in his right hand. Obviously such control is impossible when mounting an English saddle. In either case the horse must be trained to stand or he will forever be a nuisance.

It is essential that your horse be well-trained, as this one is, to stand still while being mounted. *Photo by the author.*

You may have to try many things before you break this habit. Have someone stand in front of the horse but not hold him when you mount, or have another rider bring his horse in front of him to block any forward movement. If no one is handy, face the horse close to a fence, preferably in a corner, so he is blocked. Be kindly with him until he moves, then scold him.

If you have been in the habit of moving right out the second your seat hits the saddle, your horse may be trying to anticipate your wish by starting before you are in the saddle. Here both of you are at fault. When you mount a horse you should keep him from moving while you get set in the saddle, adjust your reins, hat, gloves, etc., before giving the signal to move out. Your own deliberation and quietness with horses will in time be accepted by them as the right way to do things.

Pulling Back on the Lead

To have a horse pull back when being led is aggravating. No one is strong enough to drag a grown horse. The habit probably started in colthood when someone did try to drag him about instead of teaching him to lead. Even a horse that was taught good leading habits can, by careless and indecisive handling, forget them and get the idea he can always have his own way.

The habit of pulling back when tied in order to get free is much more serious. It can be destructive of ropes, halters, reins, bridle headstalls, tie-rings, and hitch rails, and lead to all the untold problems a loose horse can create.

Remind your horse of his good leading habits by leading him briskly, so that he knows he is going someplace. Don't dawdle along and let him decide where you're going. If you really want to mosey around in the pasture with him, use a longer rope and let him know he is at liberty to graze if he wants to. He will learn the difference between the long and short lead. If he requires it, start all over and teach him to lead just as you would a colt.

In leading, hold the lead shank up close to the halter. Don't look at the horse but look where you are going. Insist on his staying away from you so he won't trample on your feet or try and drag you.

The horse that jerks back when hitched in an effort to get free has usually had some fright or other and fears getting trapped. So the thoughtful horseman forestalls such reactions by using a little psychology. Whenever he puts the horse in a strange place, he does not hitch him to anything until the horse is at ease. Some riders simply give the reins or tie rope a turn around a hitch rail and the horse thinks he is tied. But should he come charging back he finds he is free and nothing has been broken. If he pulls back in a tie-stall a chain should be hooked across the back to stop him. The chain doesn't bother him much; his phobia is having his head anchored when he is frightened; perhaps it is somewhat similar to human claustrophobia. All this should be remembered when loading a horse in a trailer. Always hook the chain across the rear after he is in place; some even close the tail gate before snapping the horse to a tie rope or chain. If before the rear chain can be hooked in place the horse becomes frightened, it is better for him to be free to come on back unrestrained. A frightened horse thrashing

A method of hitching to break a horse of the bad habit of pulling back when tied. The horse comes forward to relieve the pressure on his withers. The knot in the loop that circles the body should be a bowline, not a slipknot.

around fighting to be free usually breaks something and is momentarily free, and a bad habit is started or aggravated. A horse that succeeds in breaking free once is almost certain to try it again. If handled carefully and gently as a colt, this habit of pulling back in fright is one that is not likely to get started.

The sketch for this text shows a method of breaking a horse of the habit of pulling back on his tie rope. If used it is suggested that the horse be tied to something unbreakable and solid such as a tree or a deeply set heavy post. The punishment is not too severe but it is enough (and where the horse least expects it) to make him quit fighting the rope.

If he has a box stall instead of a tie stall, the problem is obviated at least when the horse is in the stable. There are other ways of correcting this habit, but basically they all try to make the horse identify his pulling back with some form of punishment. The disadvantage of corrective punishment that hurts the withers is that it may start another bad habit. The horse might go forward when being cinched or when the rope pulls on the horn if he is a roping horse.

Always tie high enough so the horse can't get a foot up over the tie rope or reins. Pull the end of the rope down through the loop. A smart horse might untie himself if he happened to pull on the loose end with his teeth.

When tying with the bridle reins it is a good idea to tie to something that has a give to it. If the horse should come back he is less likely to panic if he finds he is not anchored hard and fast. Stout rubber bands such as sections of an inner tube serve the purpose well. On trail rides when it is necessary to tie up with reins it is preferable to tie to a branch that is small enough to have some spring in it.

Rearing

Many showmen have taught their horses to rear prettily. But rearing is a bad habit and dangerous when the horse does it unbidden as a gesture of fright or rebellion, as for instance when asked to leave the barn or to back up properly.

To make a horse stop throwing his head up violently or rearing, the "warm water in the paper bag trick" has worked for some people, I have been told. When the horse rears up, the prepared rider smashes the paper bag over the horse's head. The horse thinks he is bleeding and is so shocked and concerned he learns his lesson and stops rearing. Even if it was efficacious for some, I would not go to all that trouble. Nor would I recommend hitting a rearing horse over the head with a hat, fist, or rope end as some riders do to correct the bad habit. If for no other reason there is the risk of making the horse head shy.

The first time the horse rears slap him over the neck and shoulders with the rein ends. Don't ever haul back on the reins of a rearing horse. He might come clear on back and fall on you. When his forefeet are back on the ground, circle the horse, keeping your hands low, close to the withers, or even below them if you have a rein in each hand. Very expert horsemen who quickly punish bad actions before they become habits can take chances on rigorous methods that the less experienced horseman must avoid in favor of slower and gentler correction.

BAD HABITS, VICES AND CORRECTION

A few lessons with a draw rein or running rein are usually effective in correcting the bad habits of rearing, head tossing, etc. A snaffle or bar bit is customarily used. If a curb bit is used, a lighter hand on the reins is required. Strong rubber bands or rubber rings connecting the reins to the saddle are advised in order to assure a little extra give to the reins.

If the horse persists in rearing and you are beyond the amateur stage, ride the horse with a running rein for a fifteen- or twenty-minute workout each day for a week or so, always completing the ride with the regular bridle. The running rein pulls the horse's head down and back, making it difficult for him to rear. It gives the rider great leverage and should be used with judgment, applying only sufficient pressure to keep control.

A tie-down does somewhat the same thing as the running rein, but in giving the horse something for his head to lean into all the time, it sets up another bad habit.

Refusing the Bit, Hard to Bridle

This habit or reaction is the result of rough treatment or memory of some unpleasantness. A young horse that has never been hurt by his handler and has been taught good manners has no reason to refuse any normal handling.

A thoughtful horseman will warm a bit on a frosty morning rather than jam the freezing metal against the animal's lips. He will open the lips so that they won't be crushed against the teeth by the bit. With the slightest pressure of the thumb and fingers at the bars of the mouth the trusting horse will open his teeth wide enough for the bit to be slipped in.

With the horse that is difficult to bridle the problem is accentuated if a full English bridle (Weymouth) is used. Not only does the horse's mouth have to be stuffed with metal—two complete bits—but two headstalls must be draped over his head while a third set of leathers hangs down to support a cavesson. If the horse requires all this he will probably also require a martingale. My disapproval of the full bridle is evident. If a rider is incapable of training and controlling his horse with one bit and two reins—or no bit at all as with the hackamore bridle—he will be incapable of training and handling him with two bits and four reins.

To correct the problem, first check the headstall for size and see that it is not too tight. The memory of a hurting bridle may be the cause of the head-fighting when being bridled. Also check the bit to see if it is too narrow or unsuitable in any way. Try another type of bit on the horse and see if he performs better with it or is more at ease with it.

If the bit is cold, warm it for a minute or so in your hand. Handle your horse's head often and get him used to having it pulled down with your arm over it and your hand rubbing about his ears. Be matter-of-fact and businesslike when you bridle him. Give him as little time as possible to think about opposing you. If the curb strap (chains are used only with Eastern tack) is tight, there may be a moment of struggling and pulling to get the strap past his chin and the bit all the way in. This, if a problem, can be solved by having the chin strap fixed with a hook or snap that allows it to hang loose while the bridle is being put on. Then it can be snapped in place later.

If the horse is really hard to manage, fighting and rearing back, you will patiently have to retrain him, provided he is still young enough to learn anything. Back him into the corner of his box stall or the corner of the corral, where his movements are limited. A halter gives more control, so you may have to bridle him over a halter a few times. Some have calmed the habit down by putting a handful of feed in the feed box and bridling the horse while he is distracted by eating. Whatever you do, be patient; don't hurt him, just outstubborn him.

Shying and Head Shyness

Nearly all green horses will spook or shy at unfamiliar things. Head shyness is another thing, the result of having banged his head on something or having been hit on the head or near the eye, or it could be the memory of a bad fright—a snake striking, a tumbleweed whizzing past, or a blown paper. Even if he sustained no injury the horse may remember the evasive action he took. It is this sudden movement to avoid harm that becomes a habit.

Be very understanding with the young horse that shys at things. Don't scold him—he wants you to defend him from this frightful whatever—so josh him out of his fear, show great confidence, laugh at him, force him up close to the thing and stay off his mouth as much as possible. If you see that he is really frightened and getting in a panic, dismount and lead him up to the object and touch it, slap it or kick it. Let your horse know that his big brave owner is not going to let anything hurt his horse. Sometimes one feels that a colt or filly puts on this act just to get attention. Even so it is a time to let your horse know that you are a team and will stick up for each other.

Head shyness takes more time and patience to overcome. Start off easy. Be very careful in handling the side of the head the horse so favors, but do handle it often and rub it gently when bridling and currying. Make no sudden movement on that side. When riding lift your hand on the shy side and as he goes sideways talk to him calmly and let him know all is well. Increase the activity on the shy side each day. Raise your hat, lean out in that direction, ride up to things that frighten him, and show him that they are harmless. Let him see and smell them at close range. As he loses some of his shyness, play with the free end of your lariat. Swing it past his touchy eye, be well set in your saddle the first time you do it, and be patient and kindly and stay off his mouth. The day will come when you can swing a rope over his head on either side and he will take it in stride as steady as a rock and you will feel like a real horseman.

A note of warning: if there is any question of blindness, have him examined by a veterinarian. Even if he is blind in one eye, you can by careful handling get him to work calmly with you, trusting you to protect him on his blind side.

Tail Rubbing

This is usually an attempt to assuage an irritation or itching rather than a bad habit. A skin abrasion under the tail may cause it, or it may be an indication that the animal has worms. Sometimes when the condition that caused it is cured, the habit of rubbing continues. Horses whose tails have been cut and set understandably are prone to rub and scratch at the irritation caused them. Stables for them still have tailboards which stand out from the walls of the stalls and which are too low on which to rub but prevent the horse from rubbing against the walls. Any horse that does it will make his tail unsightly, marring his looks for the show ring.

First look to see if there is any rawness or irritation under the tail. If not, have his droppings examined for worms. Bandage his tail to preserve its appearance for any forthcoming show. If all apparent causes have been attended to, and the rubbing remains as a bad habit, string an electrified fence wire on insulators around his stall or corral fence at the right height. The slight electric shock the horse gets when he touches it is certain to stop the practice.

Weaving

Weaving or swaying from side to side while standing in a stall is a nervous habit reminiscent of the same motions made by animals kept caged in a zoo. If you ever notice your horse doing it, get busy and take action that will arrest the habit.

The chances are that the horse is confined to the stable too many hours a day. Get him out of doors more often. Even in chilly weather let him spend more time in a pasture or corral. Ride him oftener. Give him strenuous workouts. If he is the only horse on the place, let him see other horses by riding with a group. A pet of some kind is almost certain to be welcomed by such a horse.

Orneriness in General

Old Red was a handsome deep sorrel gelding, easygoing and past the skittishness of youth. I had bought him at an auction and we were soon delighted with him as a well-mannered pleasure horse. Unfortunately he was turned into pasture with three other horses who felt very much at home together. When Old Red tried to join their little clique and make friends, they gave him a good letting alone. They even chased him away if he came too close. Being lonely and unhappy, he started to mope and then to show irritation by kicking at them. He made several attempts to get away, once cutting his head severely while trying to get under a fence wire. In this unhappy state he looked a little mean and some boys told of running from him in the pasture. One day in the corral he charged the man who looked after the horses. The man scurried away through a gate. After being away a few days, I found on my return that I had a vicious horse to contend with. I could hardly believe my eyes when I walked out in the pasture and saw him coming for me, ears back and mouth open. I dodged sideways, yelling at him and waving my hat, and was barely beyond his reach when he whirled and kicked. That did it. I declared war. Old Red saw me pick up a tree branch and was slightly cowed as I waved it and drove him into the area way of the big barn. When I closed all doors, Old Red knew he was faced with some sort of confrontation. I called to him and started toward him— my gestures with a stout tree branch and the tone of my voice told him he was in for the licking of his life if he didn't behave.

Twice he started for me, ears back, but was stopped by the threat of being hit. He was very startled. He had never been punished by me before. Within a minute or so his head came down, the ears twitched and he stepped a pace toward me. He realized his bluff hadn't worked and he seemed to be saying, "Let's be friends again."

Still talking to him but less severely, I walked up to him and took hold of his forelock, and with the branch held to the side from which I might expect a kick, I led him over to where a halter hung and slipped it on him. In the corral I felt him all over and handled his feet, including his hind feet, all the while keeping a tight grip on the halter shank—and I did it with directness and pressure, no babying or petting. Then in a very matter-of-fact way I saddled him up, warmed him up slowly, and then gave him a real workout, figure-eights at a sustained canter, some ditch jumping, and an all-out run, and then a long jog and walk back to the barn. When I unsaddled and washed him down he was my old pal again.

Whatever had made him go berserk—loneliness or neglect—I don't know, but whatever the cause it was cured, and without actually striking or hurting him physically. After that we did show him more attention and used him oftener. Two years later he was purchased by a dude ranch, and later they reported he was one of the most dependable in their string.

Any horse that comes at you in a fighting manner or strikes out at you with his forefeet is badly spoiled, a real outlaw, or loco, and until he is retrained by a very experienced horseman the amateur should leave him alone.

14

Racing Quarter Horses

No spectator sport, whether it be baseball, basketball, or football, has ever begun or can begin today, to equal horse racing as a drawing card. In 1970 almost sixty million people attended the 170 flat racing tracks which include the seventy-five recognized Quarter racing tracks in the U.S. and Canada. Since almost half of the tracks have both Thoroughbred and Quarter Horse racing, the number of people who came solely to see Quarter racing cannot be determined. But ever since 1945, when the AQHA sanctioned its first races, the sport of racing Quarter Horses has grown, let's say, by leaps and bounds. From a mere twenty-five Quarter races in 1949, in which the awards to winners amounted to about $150,000, the number has increased to 7,438 sprint races in 1970, with a pari-mutuel handle of $102,858,245 and with a total gross purse to winners of $9,427,886.

In the 1940s, William Kyne, then president of the Bay Meadows Track at San Mateo, California, started using a 330- or 440-yard race as a curtain raiser. Soon other tracks were adding a sprint race or two to their daily racing cards. All were for small purses, seldom over four hundred dollars. So it is obvious that the men who entered their horses did so for the love of the game rather than for the money.

By 1950, Quarter racing had reached such proportions that it was evident it needed a governing body to regulate the sport. So in that year, the Board of Directors of the AQHA created the Racing Committee of the AQHA. Its function has been to formulate rules and regulations to govern racing and race meetings held on tracks recognized by the Association. Since then, the Racing Committee has maintained co-operation between recognized tracks in the U.S., Canada, and Mexico, who abide by the rules and foster clean, well-regulated racing and assure close competition. It accumulates and distributes information useful to racing secretaries and stewards in order to establish positive identification of competing horses, and to keep accurate records of the performance of all

GRADING AND QUALIFICATON STANDARD

NOTE—In order to qualify for the Register of Merit at the bottom of Grade AA, horses must carry the STANDARD weight for age or more after time has been corrected by use of the WEIGHT ALLOWANCE table.

	220	250	300	330	350	400	440	GRADE
			:15.5	:16.9	:17.8	:20.1	:22.0	"AAA"
		:13.4	:15.6	:17.0	:17.9	:20.2	:22.1	
		:13.5	:15.7	:17.1	:18.0	:20.3	:22.2	
REGISTER	:12.1	:13.6	:15.8	:17.2	:18.1	:20.4	:22.3	
OF MERIT	:12.2		:15.9	:17.3	:18.2	:20.5	:22.4	
					:18.3	:20.6	:22.5	
	:12.3	:13.7	:16.0	:17.4	:18.4	:20.7	:22.6	"AA"
	:12.4	:13.8	:16.1	:17.5	:18.5	:20.8	:22.7	
			:16.2	:17.6	:18.6	:20.9	:22.8	
						:21.0	:22.9	
	:12.5	:13.9	:16.3	:17.7	:18.7	:21.7	:23.0	"A"
	:12.6	:14.0	:16.4	:17.8	:18.8	:21.2	:23.1	
			:16.5	:17.9	:18.9	:21.3	:23.2	
							:23.3	
	:12.7	:14.1	:16.6	:18.0	:19.0	:21.4	:23.4	"B"
	:12.8	:14.2	:16.7	:18.1	:19.1	:21.5	:23.5	
			:16.8	:18.2	:19.2	:21.6	:23.6	
						:21.7	:23.7	
	:12.9	:14.3	:16.9	:18.3	:19.3	:21.8	:23.8	"C"
	:13.0	:14.4	:17.0	:18.4	:-9.4	:21.9	:23.9	
			:17.1	:18.5	:19.5	:22.0	:24.0	
							:24.1	
	:13.1	:14.5	:17.2	:18.6	:19.6	:22.1	:24.2	"D"

WEIGHT ALLOWANCE

AGE	220	250	300	330	350	400	440	ALLOWANCE
4-year-olds							140	minus .3
	132	131	129	140	138	134	132	minus .2
				128	127	125	124	minus .1
	116	116	116	116	116	116	116	STANDARD
	100	101	103	104	105	107	108	plus .1
							108	plus .2
3-year-olds							136	minus .3
	128	127	125	136	134	130	128	minus .2
				124	123	121	120	minus .1
	112	112	112	112	112	112	112	STANDARD
				100	101	103	104	plus .1
2-year-olds								minus .3
	116	115	126	124	122	118	116	minus .2
			113	112	111	109	108	minus .1
	100	100	100	100	100	100	100	STANDARD

SCALE OF WEIGHTS FOR AGE

AGE	DISTANCE 440 Yards	January February March	April May June	July August September	October November December
2-Year-Olds		104	108	112	116
3-Year-Olds		120	122	124	126
4 and older		128	128	128	128

TRACK CONDITION

No table can be prepared to show exact corrections for track conditions since the amount the track is "off" must be estimated by the handicapper. In general, however, about .2 should be subtracted from time at 440 when made on a "good" track, .3 for "heavy," .4 for "slow" and .5 or more for "mud."

horses on recognized tracks, so that those qualifying for Register of Merit may be reported to the AQHA.

The AQHA publishes a booklet of Rules and Regulations, bringing out new editions when necessary to include rule changes. Definitions for all terms for Added Money, and Age, to Scratch Time and Subscription, are precisely stated so that every rule is clearly understood. The age, for instance, of a Quarter Running Horse is reckoned, as with the Thoroughbred racing horse, as beginning on the first day of January in the year in which the horse is foaled.

For the Register of Merit a Qualification Standard was adopted. It is a rating that has been followed generally since the mid-forties. Here it is as it appears in the AQHA book of rules and regulations for Quarter racing.

It will be noticed that, to qualify for the Register of Merit with a rating of AAA, the time for the 440 must be between 22.0 seconds and 22.5 seconds. The standard weight a four-year-old must carry is 116 pounds, but should the horse carry as much, say, as 140 pounds, a weight allowance of .3 of a second is deducted from his time. If on a *slow* track, another .4 of a second is deducted. In such an instance, if a horse runs the 440 in 23.2 seconds, he is given .7 of a second allowance, which brings his time to 22.5 seconds—just under the wire for AAA rating. If the figured time is 22.0 seconds the horse gets top rating, designated by AAAT.

Standard distances for qualification for Register of Merit are those traditional with short racing—220, 250, 300, 330, 350, 400, and 440 yards.

A "Regulation Quarter Track" is a straightaway course of 440 yards in length. All races must be started from a closed starting gate in which the horses' heads are exactly at the starting line. Timing is done electrically and is taken the instant the gates are open until the winner's nose reaches the finish line. The electric eye, as it is so often called, is also frequently used in barrel racing, pole bending, and other speed events. The superiority of electric timing is evident. The horse breaks the beam with much more accuracy than can be recorded by a hand reflex action, and the time is read in one-one-hundredth-of-a-second fractions rather than the one-tenth fraction of the stop watch.

A wind gauge is required at every regulation track, and if it shows a tail wind of more than eight miles per hour, the time is not accepted for a record. In case of a dead heat, the first and second money is divided between the two winners. There is no second place.

The regulations for jockeys in Quarter racing are practically the same as for those in Thoroughbred racing. The jockey must unsaddle his own horse after the race and with his equipment in his hands must never touch any person or any thing before being weighed out. A jockey may bet only on the horse he rides and he must place the bet through the owner. In order to foster confidence in racing, the public is kept well informed about the safeguards with which the jockeys are hedged. All the rules that apply to the men apply also the the women who have scaled the barriers of this traditionally men's preserve. Jockeys cannot have a personal attendant, except for one limited to two days' service who is appointed by the track management. The attendant is not allowed to touch the horse—only the bridle—and he is prohibited from placing a bet for himself or for anyone else. Jockeys must be sixteen years old or over.

By 1967 there were close to seven thousand Quarter Horse races run with $6,984,557 being distributed in winners' purses. The pari-mutuel handle exceeded seventy million dollars. Since then the interest in Quarter racing has steadily grown and the 1970's seem propitious for continued popularity. With an eye on the revenue from the pari-mutuel take, more states are considering legalizing Quarter Horse racing. Such a bill has been brought up each year for several years in New York State's legislature, but to date has been defeated by the strong lobbies of the Thoroughbred and harness tracks.

There is no estimating the amount of the side bets made at the tracks where pari-mutuel betting is not permitted. Much wagering is done through "Calcutta pools," in which the "opportunities" of each horse in a race are auctioned to the highest bidder. The bids go into a pool from which the track takes a small percentage and the top bidder on the winning horse gets the rest. Walter Merrick, owner and trainer of many of the greatest sprint horses, told me that the pools at even lesser known tracks would frequently build up to several thousand dollars.

Like poker playing, the horse-racing game would be almost pointless without wagers being made on the outcome. Unfortunately this means that horse-racing news and stories are too often about money rather than about the horses that carried it home.

Among the Winners

For the great masses who push their money past the pari-mutuel wickets, the love of horseflesh has very little to do with it. Most of the stuff written about the track habitués who dream of picking winners, stories that picture them as horse-lovers smitten with exquisite feelings for the animals, is pure baloney. The crowds may thrill to the spectacle of racing, but the hope of winning is what got them there. Wagers are known to have reached fabulous proportions. Prospector George Warren is reputed to have lost his share of the Copper Queen Mine on a horse race at Bisbee, Arizona, on July 4, 1880. The share he lost later became worth twenty million dollars.

Except for the comparatively few breeders, trainers, handlers, and jockeys, not many who attend the tracks have much concern or understanding of the horses. But to listen to the men who recall short racing some years back, one gathers that it was then still a true horseman's sport, largely attended by knowledgeable horsemen. That does not imply that it was innocent of wily tricks of the sport, high wagers, and vicious rivalry. Uncontrolled by the strict track regulations of today, the race horse man faced many kinds of risks.

Brownie Tiffin, an old-timer whom I met in Gage, Oklahoma, recalled some of the race horses he had known in his youth when he worked for Mr. W. L. Allen, his wife's father. Mr. Allen raised race horses in the Oklahoma Panhandle near Laverne, not far from where old Tommy Moore's mare, Cutthroat, gave birth to Oklahoma Star. He later bought Cutthroat's mother, Big Em. Among the Allen horses were Duck Hunter by Peter McCue and Golddigger by Lock's Rondo. Both were extremely fast horses, and Golddigger bequeathed his speed to a son named Henry Star, who, before he was gelded at the age of three, sired a filly christened Barbara Allen. This filly once outran Cutthroat, Brownie recalled. This positive statement by a man who had handled him that Henry Star was gelded before he ever left northwest Oklahoma puts a question mark on a good many pedigrees that claim him as a sire, including the claim often made that he was the sire of Old Dedier (D. J.).

Brownie told of the fate of Duck Hunter and Henry Star. It was a strange one and still a mystery. Both horses were sold by Mr. Allen to a Mr. Burke, who took them to Juárez, Mexico, to be raced. There Burke and his two horses disappeared, simply dropped out of sight. Mr. Allen and others who tried to solve the mystery were baffled at every turn. No clues, no trace ever came to light. It was the period when the Mexican border was stirred to violence and turmoil by the marauding bands of Pancho Villa and other factional leaders. One can easily imagine some such mustachioed, sombreroed chieftain, crisscrossed with bandoleers, spurring Duck Hunter or Henry Star to the head of his mounted column. Conjuring up such a picture is aided by the most famous photograph of Pancho Villa, which shows him in a comfortable vaquero slouch astride his favorite horse, Brown Jug, a horse also of impeccable breeding, being a grandson of Old Billy and Paisana.

The early entrepreneurs had a tough speed mark to shoot at because a bay gelding, Bob Wade, had set a record of 21.25 seconds for the quarter mile at Butte, Montana, in 1890. He was owned by W. H. Chambers of Scottsbluff, Nebraska, and it was rumored that he also traced to Old Billy and Paisana. His record was somewhat less disheartening since it is generally believed it was made from a scored or running start. Later, when quarter-mile races were timed from a standing start, the time was understandably a fraction slower. And with the required use of electric timers, no horse gets favored by imperfect reflex action on a stop watch.

Mr. Garard A. Harrison, whom I met at the King Ranch, said that he thinks the interest in preserving the best blood of the Quarter Running Horses was given a big boost when ranchers in the 1930s got proud enough of their speedy cowhorses to match them in public, where the fun and rivalry had much more to do with horses than with money. He was living in Wharton County, Texas, at the time Bob Denhardt, Johnny Ferguson, Jack Hutchins, Tootie Davidson, Clay Myers, Dink Bishop, young Allen Wright, and others in the vicinity were fired with the idea of ending the anonymity in which the Quarter Horse existed by establishing it as a breed. Garard Harrison told how he and Jack Hutchins decided to match the speed of their working cowhorses. The race was to be run in front of the old Wharten Grandstand, which stood on stilts out at the fairgrounds. The distance was to be 440 yards, the date thirty days hence, and the wager was set at twenty-five dollars. Both were prosperous men. Hutchins was manager of the old Shanghai Pierce Ranching Estate, and Harrison was a young cowman who had ridden well-bred horses most of his life and was destined to become one of the nation's better known cattle raisers.

Both men got busy putting a sharp edge on their horses' training. Each took pains to shroud their methods and morning workouts in secrecy, which only increased the frequency of sudden visits at each other's stables. Each sought every trick of professionalism that might give an advantage. Harrison said he was fortunate in getting the services of an old Negro named Will Hysaw, an ex-jockey and trainer, who had known his way around in the race horse world of Louisiana at the time Old

D.J. (Dedier), the sire of Della Moore, was reigning turf horse there. In an ancient trunk of tack he managed to cling to, Will found an old moth-eaten blinder hood, which he decided to use on Harrison's horse, who had flown the track a time or two, and besides it gave a real professional touch. Hutchins' horse apparently didn't want to go past those blinkers, because Harrison's horse won. In telling about this race, which cost him several hundred dollars to win twenty-five dollars, Harrison thought it was typical of the time when ranchers got the racing bug and began to reevaluate the potential of their speedy cowponies.

A whole crop of working cowhorses that came along about this time streaked down the brush tracks with such Western flair that the aura of legend grows with each retelling of their exploits by the old short-horse aficionados.

One such horse was Rusty Jiggs, who was foaled in 1935 on an Arizona ranch. Pastures were dry, life was austere. Gelded as a yearling and broken at the age of three, he learned his trade working as a cowhorse. The chance that he would ever break the pattern of his routine was slim indeed. However, when he was five years old he was sent along with a half brother to California to balance the two-horse trailer. The half brother was supposed to be the racer of the family and was to be given an opportunity to prove himself. Rusty was to be sold as a cowhorse if a fair offer for him was made. As it turned out, the half brother wasn't so fast after all, but Stanley Gomez, the prominent San Mateo horseman who bought Rusty for two hundred dollars, found out the sorrel cowpony could really turn on the speed. Another race horse in the district was named Rusty, so Jiggs was added to his name to avoid confusion. Rusty Jiggs was almost six years old when he started his racing career. Like the steady cowhorse that he was, he would walk into the starting gate with deceptive calm, seemingly relaxed while his keyed-up rivals were lunging and dancing. But when the gates flew open it was Rusty Jiggs who was out first and leading the pack within a few strides.

After seven years of winning more than his share of 200- to 400-yard sprints, he was matched against a young Oklahoma horse named Fire Wagon in a 220-yard dash. Each owner put up five thousand dollars. Both horses were ridden by lightweight jockeys. The result? Jack Widner, who told about this race in his book of a decade ago called *The American Quarter Horse,* quoted Claude Powers, who had trained Rusty Jiggs, as saying: "Old Rusty just ran away and hid from that horse. . . . I was sorry for the boys who had driven hundreds of miles to watch the race."

The stunned backers of Fire Wagon refused Stan Gomez's challenge to another race the following day. But when big John Bowman, onetime World's Champion cowboy, offered to ride Rusty Jiggs with his heavy roping saddle, making a total load of 240 pounds, and put up one thousand dollars that said he'd win, they couldn't resist the odds. The race was scheduled for the next afternoon at the Stockton, California, race track. A large enthusiastic crowd showed up to see and lay money judgments on how a thirteen-year-old horse carrying a mighty big load would fare against a young race horse carrying 110 pounds. Well, again Rusty Jiggs won! And, said Claude Powers: "I thought John Bowman would die laughing . . . when he came back to the finish line to pick up the marbles."

After winning a few more races that same year, Rusty Jiggs was retired to become a well-known and privileged character around the San Mateo, California, track. Here he was often ridden by Claude

My Texas Dandy. *Courtesy AQHA.*

Powers as well as the children—as many as four at a time—of the trainers and jockeys. If kept away from the sight of the starting gate and the excitement it induced, he was a wise and gentle saddle horse who stood calmly as the children scrambled on and off his back. Unfortunately Rusty Jiggs had been gelded, so his rare heritage of speed died with him.

Perhaps the most noted cowhorse of the time that became a top race horse was Clabber, who was often called the "Iron Horse." Foaled in 1937 on the Clyde Smith ranch at Big Foot, Texas, he became the most famous son of My Texas Dandy, and if, as Bob Denhardt believes, he was out of Golden Girl, he traced to Traveler through her grandad King Possum. The *AQHA Stud Book* lists his dam as being Blondie S by Lone Star. Either way, there was plenty of Thoroughbred blood in him. With a big plain head he lacked beauty, but he proved he had everything else.

A. A. Nichols of Gilbert, Arizona, who had other My Texas Dandy horses that he liked, bought Clabber when he was a yearling. Later when Nichols' sons started roping on him, Clabber proved to be a fast learner. He broke from the box with such speed his racing ability seemed evident. Soon he was a regular contender on the Tucson tracks and in matched races. All this time he remained a hard-working ranch horse. Bandages, liniments, blankets, all such pampering were simply unknown to him. His routine included putting his riders in top money in both steer- and calf-roping in rodeos within hauling distance, servicing an average of two mares a week, and taking time out from ranch work to run at the regular meets at Tucson and in any match race that could be arranged. It is easy to see how the sobriquet of the "Iron Horse" was pinned on him.

In 1941, Clabber ran and won three 440-yard races in one day—all in 23 seconds or better—with only an hour to rest up between the second and third races. Open starting chutes were used, and on the last race he was so eager to jump the "go" signal that a rope was run through his bridle bit and held by a man on either side. When the flag was dropped his lunge forward was so much faster than the reflexes of the men holding him that he jerked them off their feet and he himself went to his knees. Then, with the rope flapping behind him, and his jockey desperately squirming back off his neck into the saddle, Clabber took up the slack to catch the field, and then stormed past them to win. His best time, made from a running start, was 22.4 seconds. His best time from a standing start from a regulation gate was 22.8 seconds, good enough to

Clabber, the "Iron Horse."

make him the World's Champion Quarter Running Horse, a record that stood until Shue Fly came along.

On February 18, 1942, every short horse man in the Southwest who could possibly make it to Tucson, Arizona, was on hand at the old Hacienda Moltacqua Track to see the World's Champion Quarter Horse Race. A purse of one thousand dollars was to go to the winner. On this day Clabber was entered against Shue Fly, Joe Tom, and Nobody's Friend, the great Running Quarter Horse from the King Ranch.

Shue Fly had been trained carefully and she was tuned to a high pitch for this race. Sleek and expertly groomed, she made a marked contrast to the Iron Horse, who, although about the same age, showed the wear of his rodeo contests, racing, and frequent breeding, and who had been brought from pasture without special preparation and hauled to the starting gate.

Shue Fly, a sorrel with a white sock on her off hind foot, traced directly to Lock's Rondo through Cowboy P-12 and his dad Yellow Jacket. Like so many others, this pedigree has been questioned, but all the horsemen I have discussed it with accept it as true. She was bred

Shue Fly. *Courtesy Robert M. Denhardt.*

by Lloyd Miller of Chamita, New Mexico, passed into the hands of J. M. Baca of Santa Fe, and then into those of Bob Burris, who made her famous on the tracks before her final owners, the Hepler brothers of Carlsbad, New Mexico, bought her.

In her race that day in Tucson, Shue Fly had an accident which was somewhat similar to the one that befell Clabber the year before and which put her to the supreme test. At the start of the race, Bob Burris, her owner, was standing back of the starting gate. When the doors flew open, knowing his horse was faced with the world's best Quarter Horse, he snatched off his hat, and in an excess of eagerness to get her going, gave her a wallop with it. The mare was so startled she went to her knees. One big simultaneous groan came from the spectators. Jockey Hank Laswell would have been forgiven if he had sailed over her head. He didn't, however, and was back in the saddle as the astonished and screaming crowd watched Shue Fly streak through the dust to shorten the seven-length gap between her and the field. And when she caught it and passed it to win by a nose, pandemonium broke loose. Within minutes afterwards, Elmer Hepler was signing his name to a three-thousand-dollar check for her. She never lost a race for the Heplers and in 1946 she won the World's Championship Race at Albuquerque, New Mexico.

The offspring she produced after retirement from the track were not numerous because several foals died at birth or at an early age. La Mosquito, by the Thoroughbred Little Request, and Royal Charge by Depth Charge, also a Thoroughbred, had the best track records of Shue Fly's foals. She died in 1963.

Had it been left to the owners and breeders of the early Quarter Horse racers, the public today would know little about their bloodlines and turf careers. Much is still hearsay, but fortunately a few dedicated writers were on the scene to get the essential data into print. The most noted of all is Nelson Nye. He was closely associated with the National Quarter Horse Breeders Association and the American Quarter Horse Racing Association at the time they were jockeying for control of the new breed. At his home in Tucson he recently told of those contentious days before they pooled their interests and rejoined the AQHA. All who do independent research on Quarter Horses, particularly the racing strains, invariably find themselves crossing the tracks of Nelson Nye.

Reverting to Clabber for a moment, it can be pointed out that the defeat by Shue Fly didn't wash him up by any means. He went on to lower the Tucson track record for 350 yards to 18.4 seconds. He was purchased by Frank Vessels, among the nation's top breeders of race horses and widely known as the founder of the famous Los Alamitos Race Track in California. Clabber died at Frank Vessels' stud farm in 1946. This great stallion's life had been concentrated into ten tempestuous years. His half brother, Colonel Clyde, John Bowman's rodeo horse, has been ranked among the all-time greats. Among Clabber's numerous get, many were daughters. One named Clabber Girl, owned by the Finley Ranches of Gilbert, Arizona, became a champion halter mare who produced three Register of Merit runners. Another of Clabber's half brothers, Texas Dandy, founded a whole dynasty of superior horses for the Finleys.

Tom Finley's success with Quarter Horses is attested to by hundreds of Grand Champion trophies earned by his Quarter Horses, whose genesis dates to a trip made by the Finley brothers to Wharton, Texas, in 1946, where they purchased Texas Dandy. This half brother of Clabber was bred by R. C. Tatum of Junction, Texas, and was by My Texas Dandy and out of Streak by Lone Star, a Thoroughbred. In the first two years, Texas Dandy's service fees repaid his purchase price. And twenty years later he was still going strong. The Finleys never saw any need to purchase another stud. Texas Dandy had it all: speed, cow sense, easygoing disposition, conformation, and the prepotency to transmit his good qualities. His daughter, Little Egypt, was the first AAA AQHA Champion. Two of her records were standing sixteen years after she made them.

Another daughter of Clabber, Tonta Gal, bred by Chester Cooper of Roosevelt, Arizona, set a world record of 12.1 seconds for the 220 yards. After being retired from the track by her owner, Roy Gill of Arizona, she produced six Register of Merit runners, including the great AAA runner Tonto Bars Bill by Three Bars. One of Tonto's notable sons is Tonto Bars Hank, also a famous AAA race horse. He had been bred in Oklahoma by C. G. Whitcomb and his son Milo, and when he was a colt, Milo's eleven-year-old daughter rode Tonto Bars Hank and, as reported to Nelson Nye, she found him so gentle and unexcitable she used a bat on him to get him out of a walk. His amiable disposition continues to this day, but it can be said that on the track a bat was seldom needed. In 1961, he was a co-holder of the world's record of 19.9 for the 400-yard sprint and was listed on top because he carried more weight, 122 pounds. In 1962, Tonto Bars Hank was called the top money-winning Quarter Horse of all time, and his stud fee rose to $1500. He was under the management of Walter Merrick, whose 14 Ranch lies in a big bend of the South Canadian River just east of the Antelope Hills in western Oklahoma. A few miles to the south is Cheyenne, Oklahoma, where Peter McCue once held court, presided over by his owner and ex-jockey, Milo Burlingame.

It was on Walter Merrick's ranch that I saw Tonto Bars Hank when he was five years old. Those who know Walter, a tall, muscular but trim man (he could kill a bear with a stick, as the saying goes), can better understand his liking for big horses. As I stood close to Tonto Bars Hank in his small paddock, it came as a surprise to learn that the horse weighed 1430 pounds, because he is such a beautifully built bundle of action.

Texas Dandy. *Courtesy* Quarter Horse Journal.

In the hospitable home of Walter and Christine Merrick, Walter spread hundreds of horse and race finish photos on the floor of the living room, and as we crawled about to look at them, he pointed out horses he had bred, trained, raced, or managed—or all four. The collection before us represented some of America's most influential Quarter Horses: Gray Badger, Hot Heels, Midnight Jr., Steel Bars, Three Bars, and many others too numerous to mention. He had run Midnight Jr. sixteen times without losing a race. Steel Bars became a celebrity stallion

Tonto Bars Hank. *Photo by the author.*

on the B. F. Phillips ranch at Frisco, Texas, where many of his progeny were shown to me by trainer John Payne.

Bob's Folly by Three Bars, another Merrick headliner, ran the quarter mile five times under 22 seconds. Three Bars, a Thoroughbred who was destined to become the greatest sire of running quarter horses of all time, was at the 14 Ranch.

I have often wondered how big those piles of photos have become in the intervening years. They must now include Bar Money, a Supreme

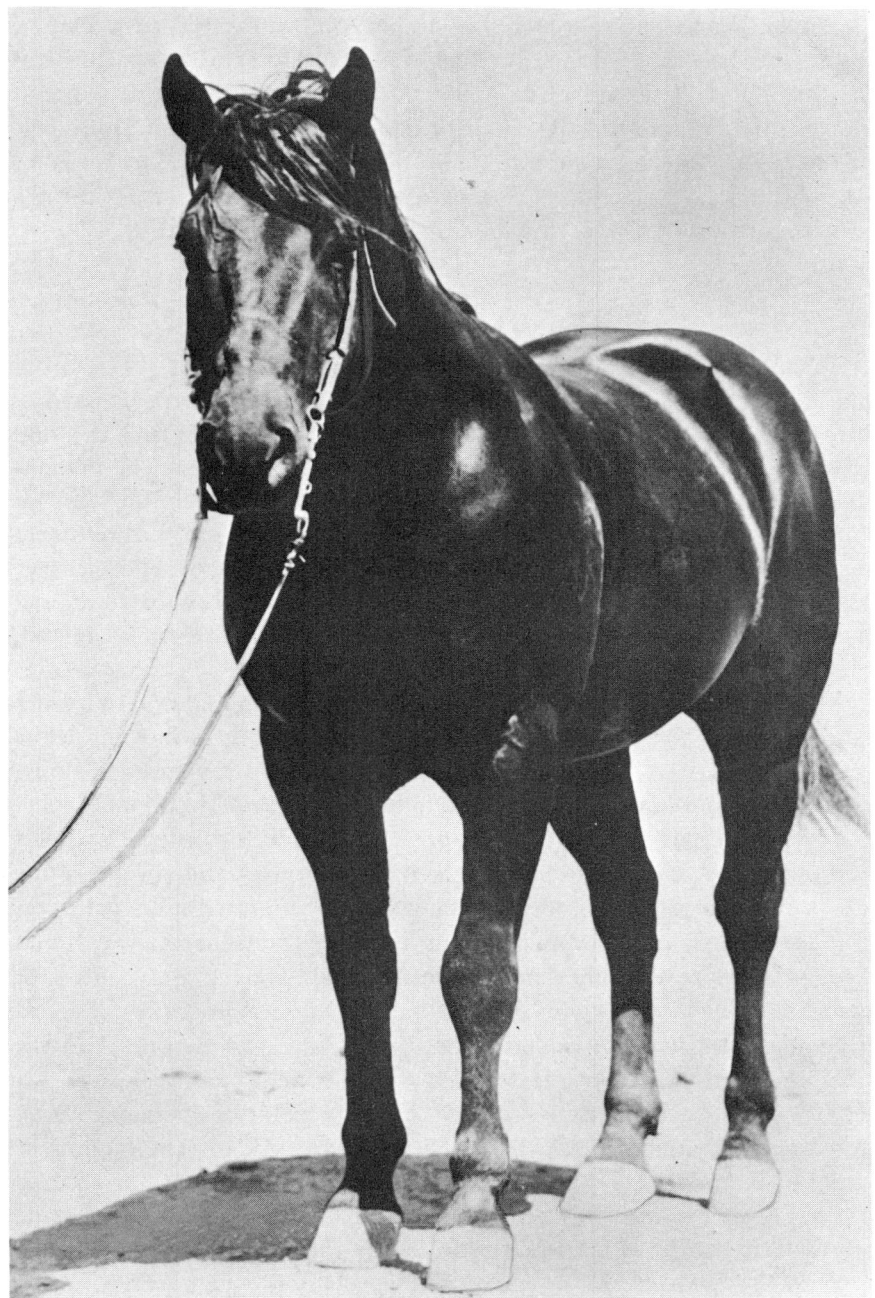

Midnight Jr. *Courtesy* Quarter Horse Journal.

Champion, and Easy Jet, who won the Kansas Futurity, equaling a track record of eleven years' standing (a race Walter Merrick also won in 1968). Easy Jet also won the 1969 All-American Futurity at Ruidoso Downs, making him the all-time high money earning Quarter Horse colt ($384,347). And near the top of the pile must be Good Bird by Papa Red Bird, who presently heads up the dramatis personae at the 14 Ranch, commanding a fee of $2000 for a guaranteed live foal.

Breeding for Speed

Speed is a relative thing. What with mechanics culminating in spaceships, speed is an abstraction. With flesh and blood speeders, it isn't the rate of speed, but rather the potential of it that thrills, whether it be demonstrated by one's own sprinting effort or the ability to develop it in an animal. Garford Wilkinson, who has written voluminously on the subject of animals for newspapers and magazines, once wrote: "The Quarter Horse is the darling of those who were determined to produce an animal that could run a quarter mile faster than any other large, solid footed, man-carrying animal."

Man's fastest sprinting time is at the rate of about thirty miles per hour. When a horse runs the quarter in 22 seconds he is moving at the rate of almost forty-one miles per hour. This is a bit faster than a greyhound, rabbit, or red fox, but considerably slower than a cheetah, which can cover ground at seventy miles per hour, while the winged speeders like the golden eagle glides at eighty miles per hour and the peregrine falcon has been rated at between ninety and one hundred miles per hour.

Whether he is more dramatic about it and more thrilling to watch and ride, or because the other fast-moving animals are hard to control or are seldom kept in captivity, it has been the horse whose trials of speed have most fascinated mankind since the beginning of history. And the efforts to get him to move faster have never ceased.

The greatest advance in breeding speed in horses was made during and since the founding of the English and American Thoroughbreds and the Running Quarter Horse. Yet the actual increase of speed in the horse as a species has been very gradual. Records that were made many years ago have been bettered only by the merest fractions.

With the Quarter Horse, whether his specialty is racing or not, speed, and especially early speed or "early foot," as some horsemen like to call it, is what makes him a Quarter Horse. Other qualities such as good disposition, good conformation, and sturdy legs are developed as a bonus.

Breeders of race horses have always searched the bloodlines and the speed records of possible mates for their stock. This search includes the records of the dams as well as the sires. All agree with the motto that decorated the gate of R. L. Underwood's ranch near Wichita Falls, Texas: "Good horses like good men had good mothers."

Even when used exclusively, registered horses can produce slow horses unless the individuals chosen have proven records of speed or proven records as sires and dams of speed. The saying "Quality without pedigree can often be a better risk than pedigree without quality" would seem apt.

Many Quarter Horse breeders think the show ring has been detrimental in the breeding of Quarter Horses, as it has proved to be with other show breeds. All ask, "What can the horse do besides look pretty?" To old Ott Adams, the breeder of Zantanon, the Man O' War of the Quarter Horses, and a herd of other top quality sprinters, looks did not necessarily mean quality. Quality in his book meant speed.

Although some fortunate breeders seem to have the magic set of genes to work with for a few generations, the frustration as well as the fascination of raising race horses is that no one has yet found an absolutely sure-fire combination. I have been told by breeders that they consider themselves lucky if one out of twenty promising colts can succeed against the tough competition at the track.

One race horse owner, an Oklahoma Indian named Hoot, hit the exact combination by rather unorthodox methods. Instead of arduously studying pedigrees, he had a dream. He dreamed that if his race mare Useeit was mated with Colonel Bradley's great stallion Black Tony (TB) she would produce a Derby winner. He knew about Black Tony's son Beggar Boy, who was at the time adding fame to Ronald Mason's Nowata, Oklahoma, ranch by fathering a notable stock of race horses, Quarter Horse performance horses, and polo mounts. Before he could bring to fruition his dreamed-up plan, Mr. Hoot died. But his widow had such a firm belief in her husband's dream that she allowed nothing to deter her. Colonel Bradley, an important magnate and race horse breeder in the East, was not an easy man to meet or deal with. However, Mrs. Hoot managed to face him with her proposal and by persistence and determination surprisingly got an acceptance to it. The resulting colt, named Black Gold (Oklahoma Oil), *did* win the Kentucky Derby in 1924. When he was nine years old, he won another, a tragic, distinction. After breaking a leg in a race in New Orleans, he finished the race on three legs. He is buried within the race track oval.

Reunion of Runners

The long and the short of it, where speed is concerned, lies within the Thoroughbred family of horses—the English and American Thoroughbreds and their Western cousin, the Quarter Horse.

During the latter's development outbreeding was employed at times to gain harder bones, more muscle for stock work or for weight carrying. But for speed, and specifically early speed, the only crosses ever considered were those with the Thoroughbred.

With the great resurgence of interest in short racing, breeders made a concerted effort to breed back to the short-horse branch of the Thoroughbred from which all notable Quarter Running Horses sprang. Not that these equine Ishmaelites were trying to return to the fold—they now had a larger family of their own—but rather it was a reunion in their own pastures to which Thoroughbreds, with the family trait of early speed, were welcomed.

Although the pedigrees of Peter McCue and other great sires have been questioned, there are plenty of others where there is no room for controversy because they are straight out of the American Stud Book with unquestioned pedigrees as Thoroughbreds. Custom Jet, Bud Warren's Quarter Horse turf star, traces through Jet Deck to Man O' War. Oklahoma Star's sire was Dennis Reed, a Thoroughbred, and his mother, Cutthroat, was by Bonnie Joe, also a Thoroughbred. Ronald Mason's Thoroughbred, Beggar Boy (TB) by Black Tony, sired a whole herd of Quarter Horse celebrities. Leo traces directly to Joe Blair (TB), and on to the breed's noted Faustus. Clabber and Tom Finley's Texas Dandy carry the blood of two Thoroughbreds, Porte Drapeau, the French Thoroughbred who sired their father, My Texas Dandy, and Panmure, their maternal grandsire. With all these examples, and there could be many more, it comes as no surprise to those familiar with Quarter Horse bloodlines to read that the largest family of all Quarter Horse runners of today was sired by the incomparable Three Bars, a Thoroughbred.

THREE BARS (1940–68)

As with so many individuals who make good in a big way, there were obstacles to overcome with Three Bars. Lameness was the bête noire in his youth. His owners, a partnership made up of Jack Goode, Bill Talbert,

Three Bars. *Courtesy AQHA.*

and Ned Brent, bought Three Bars before he was born. That is, they bought his mother, Myrtle Dee by Luke McLuke, when she was already in foal by Percentage. This was in 1939. When Three Bars was ready for the track, he showed amazing speed, but he always came in with a gimp in his stride caused by a restricted muscle in his rear leg. After unsuccessfully trying everything they could think of to cure the trouble, the owners sold Three Bars for three hundred dollars. Even that was to be paid only on condition that the new owner, Beckham Stivers, could win a race with him. Stivers tried without results and finally gave the aristocratic but ailing Thoroughbred colt to Vernon Cloud as on outright gift.

Whether Cloud treated the ailment in some unknown way or whether the colt simply outgrew his leg trouble is not known. But in 1944, at the age of four, nothing much was slowing him down, because he won three out of four starts. This proof of speed drew the attention of prominent racing stable owners, among them Sidney H. Vail of Nacoma, Texas, who bought the onetime gift horse for $10,000 and sent him to his stud farm at Victorville, California. In 1946 Three Bars quickly repaid his purchase price by winning $16,940. This was from eight firsts and three seconds out of seventeen starts. At the age of seven, Three Bars' track record was not so good, so he was retired from the track.

In the early 1950s, some of his colts running in Arizona, although out of ordinary mares, showed speed enough (all favored the sprints) to catch the attention of Walter Merrick, whose sagacious ability to judge unproven horses caused him to lease Three Bars and take him home to Oklahoma, where he stood him for a three-hundred-dollar fee. He also bred him to his own Hot Heels, a granddaughter of Midnight, who produced Bob's Folly. The report of Three Bars' get was so glowing that Sid Vail could hardly wait for the lease to expire so he could get his horse back for his Victorville, California, stud. It was there that Three Bars sired a large proportion of his stock, which included 358 starters. Among them were 185 AAA, 88 AA, and 15 A racers. Ten of his sons are listed among the top 22 sires of AAA Quarter Horses. They are: Rocket Bar, Sugar Bars, Tonto Bars Gill, Mr. Bar None, Lightning Bar, Triple Chick, Bob's Folly, Royal Bar, Clabber Bar, and Barred. Three Bars was second leading sire of brood mares and he fathered the first three AQHA Supreme Champions and a herd of winners at halter and performance events—a list much too long to deal with here.

At the peak of his stud career, his stud fee is rumored to have reached (in private treaty) more than ten thousand dollars. When Three Bars was twenty-six years old, Walter Merrick again leased him and in his own trailer got him to his Southwestern Stallion Station, and then later to his 14 Ranch in Oklahoma. It was here, on April 5, 1968, just two days before the old sire's twenty-eighth birthday, that Three Bars' great heart stopped beating. His body was taken to the Sidney Vail ranch in Texas for burial.

Now, with so many proven sires of speed available, it is doubtful if any sire in the foreseeable future will have the opportunity to equal or even approach the accomplishment of Three Bars in procreating Quarter Horse runners.

The stallion that preceded Three Bars as the leading sire of Quarter Running Horses was Leo. The following lists show how prominently his

No Butt. *Courtesy Valley View Ranch.*

stock featured, and it should be remembered that a large proportion of the mares that produced the Register of Merit qualifiers by Three Bars were daughters and granddaughters of Leo.

There are, of course, many famed Running Quarter Horses who traced to the old founding families without recent relationship with the Thoroughbreds. No Butt is a good example. She was foaled in 1955. Her sire was Joe Less of Traveler breeding, and her dam Red Bottom traced through four generations to Peter McCue. No Butt was foaled on Guy Purinton's Rafter P. Ranch near Tipton, California, and when she was three years old, she ran in AAA+ time. In 1962 she was loaded with honors: World's Champion Quarter Running Horse; Champion Quarter Running Mare; Champion Quarter Running Aged Mare. She had run forty-four times in AAA time, and still this racing pro was so gentle Guy

Purinton's ten-year-old daughter, Jo Anne, could ride her as she would any family riding horse.

In 1962 Charles W. Mickle of the Valley View Ranch in Scottsdale, Arizona, purchased her for thirty-five thousand dollars. Wes Mickle, his son, told me that in the seven years they had her before she died she produced five speedy foals.

The Valley View Ranch is the present home of Rebel Cause by Top Deck (TB), and Vanny Bar by Three Bars (TB). Rebel Cause was once owned by Chet and Dale Robertson of Yukon, Oklahoma. He was Co-Champion Quarter Running Three-Year-Old for 1961 and Champion Quarter Running Aged Stallion for 1962. Vanny Bar was also an AAA Champion.

Miss Bank, another sprinter, was bred on the Ross Perner Ranch near Sierra Blanca, Texas. At one time or another she held every world record open to Quarter Horses. Over a period of eleven years she ran three hundred official races, winning more than three-fourths of them. She was the dam of Bankette, who was the dam of Rebel Cause. C. W. Mickle wanted her enough to pay forty-one thousand dollars for her.

When Miss Bank set her record in 1940, there were three other horses that came along to equal it. They were Lightfoot (1943), Barbara B (1943), and Stella Moore (1945).

Queenie by Flying Bob had her record duplicated by six other horses, including Leota by Leo, and Pelican by Joe Hancock Jr.

Blondie L by Jimmy Allred also had her time equaled by six other horses, including Liberty Girl by Little Joe Jr. and Hardtwist by Cowboy.

Nobodies Friend by Boojum had his time equaled by six other horses, including Piggin String and the notable Miss Panama by Ace of Diamonds.

No Butt winning at centennial in 1962. *Courtesy Valley View Ranch.*

Joe Reed II by Joe Reed P-3 and Clabber by My Texas Dandy were the first to run the 440 yards in 22.8. But they were followed by sixteen other racers who matched their time, with perhaps the best remembered being Squaw H by King, Tonta Gal by Clabber, Vandy by Going Light, and Dee Dee by Flying Bob.

LEO (1940–67)

On a blistering hot day I drove up and parked in the shade of the big cottonwood trees that border the Courthouse Square in Perry, Oklahoma. Across the street I spied the Palace Club and got to its refrigerated interior just one jump ahead of sunstroke. I soon learned that the genial proprietor who slid a cold beer into my hand was Harold Meeks, a former resident of my home town of Woodward, Oklahoma. Mutual acquaintances were recalled. Men sauntered over from where they had been watching the card, dominoes, and checker games.

Such a meeting place is not only friendly and comfortable, but is also a combination stock exchange and town-meeting-hall where the nuances of politics, promising studs and bulls, dispersal sales, and horse races get talked over. And where, if one listens attentively, he can learn the time and whereabouts of the next "chicken fight." Yes, cockfighting with its nocturnal, clandestine old frontier appeal still has its enthusiastic aficionados.

When they learned I was an Oklahoman, although I had lived in the environs of New York City for many years, any reticence where pride in Oklahoma was concerned vanished like the froth on beer. The greats of the state were mentioned with a wealth of personal knowledge of each individual's beginnings. Truly the list of Oklahomans who have found fame in baseball, ballet, television, show business, movies, publishing, literature, finance, architecture, rodeo, and many other fields is a long one. Then, having extolled the two-legged celebrities, they went on to the names of the four-legged ones. It was only natural that this list started off with the famous Leo, a patriarch of the Quarter Horse breed, whose days of glory were drawing to a close on the breeding farm of Bud and Reba Warren, only ten minutes' drive away from where we stood. Later, at the Warren home, which stands amid rolling pastures where many of America's fastest Quarter Horses have grazed, I learned much about the part Leo played in the phenomenal success of the Warrens and their Running Quarter Horses.

Leo P-1335, a bright sorrel stallion with a generous blaze in the face and with socks on his front feet and stockings on his hind legs, was

Leo P-1335. *Courtesy Nelson Nye.*

of Joe Reed breeding on both sides. His sire was Joe Reed II by Joe Reed P-3 by Bonnie Joe (TB) by Faustus (TB). His dam was Little Fanny by Joe Reed II. His third dam was Della Moore, the dam of Joe Reed P-3, one of the nineteen founding fathers.

Leo was foaled in 1940 near Cameron, Texas, a product of J. W. House's fast mare Little Fanny. Lester Manning, who bought him, broke him out and ran him a few times on local brush tracks, which brought him to the attention of John W. Tillman, who bought him and took him to Pawhuska, Oklahoma, when the promising colt was still a two-year-old.

With trainer Bill Morgan, Leo was trailered a lot of miles and burst from a lot of starting gates like a sorrel blur. It is said that he won over twenty matched races. At Pawhuska he set a track record of sixteen seconds for three hundred yards. He was bought by Gene Moore

Joe Reed II P-985. *Courtesy AQHA.*

of the Rocking M Ranch at Fairfax, Oklahoma, where he sired his first notable sprinter, Leota W, who was to enter the list of the greats. But before this foal was on the ground, Bud Warren's clairvoyance where horses are concerned caused him to buy Leo in his fourth year and bring him to his Perry, Oklahoma, stud farm, where the grand speedster and sire spent the remainder of his life, procreating a good share of the racing inhabitants of the world of the Quarter Horse.

Leo stayed with racing longer than most noted sires and might have continued even longer had he not suffered a serious accident which damaged both his front legs. He was seven years old when he ran his last race.

Leo came along when the AQHA was in its infancy, and he soon headed the list of sires of Running Quarter Horses. To mention but a few of his best-known sons, they include Croton Oil, Palleo Pete, Leo

San, Leo Bob, Tiger Leo, Mr. 89er, Dynamo Leo, Hygro Leo.

The Warrens were especially fortunate with their mother stock. From their good Joe Hancock mare, Julie W, they got Lena Horn by Dock by Zantanon. Before she died in 1967, this mare of Peter McCue and Traveler breeding produced seven Register of Merit qualifiers. Her daughter, Lena Leo, by Leo, was the dam of Sugar Bars, an AAA runner by Three Bars. Sugar Bars is passing on the Leo and Three Bars heritage of speed.

There is no place in the United States where one has to drive very far to see champion Quarter Horses. But near Purcell, Oklahoma, there seems to be a concentration of them.

In the parklike pastures of Melvin Hatley's Briarwood Farm, Monita, the top-money-winning Quarter Horse of 1955, roams and grazes at leisure with other track celebrities such as Josie's Bar, Gold Angel, and Paula Laico, the dam of Laico Bird, an All-American Futurity winner.

Nearby is Green Pastures, a stud farm owned by A. B. Green, where the first AQHA Supreme Champion Kid Meyers, by Three Bars, makes his home. Go-Man-Go, who traces to Man O' War through his sire Top Deck, was also once a resident. Go-Man-Go's odyssey started out on the Johnny Ferguson Stud Farm near Wharton, Texas. For eight years he scorched the Quarter tracks. Then A. B. Green, who is president of Ruidoso Downs Race Course, bought him for $40,000. Green sold him profitably for $125,000 to Frank Vessels of Los Alamitos, California, and William Peckham of Richmond, Texas. Then Go-Man-Go returned to the Purcell area when Marvin Hatley paid $300,000 for a one-half interest in him.

When one reads of this or that stallion selling for a fabulous amount of money, one cannot help but wonder how such an investment can be profitable. Although the rules of the AQHA prohibit artificial insemination which involves the use of semen at any time except immediately following its collection and at the place of collection—in other words, no frozen or transported semen is to be used—the artificial procedure still enables a stallion to serve up to ten times more mares than would be possible by natural service. Thus, for example, a normal breeding schedule of sixty mares a year is, theoretically, increased to six hundred mares. Several Quarter Horse stallion owners today advertise stud fees that range from one thousand to two thousand dollars for a live foal. So even supposing the insurance premiums and other costs amount to two hundred dollars per day, or seventy-three thousand dollars per year, the potential profit is huge.

Joe Sherry, the fastest Quarter Horse, has held the record for the 440 yards since 1965. Billy Powell is the jockey. *Courtesy La Mesa Park,* Raton, New Mexico.

Joe Sherry winning the 400-yard race at La Mesa Park in 1965. Time: 19.97. *Courtesy La Mesa Park,* Raton, New Mexico.

AQHA World Record Holders

(data furnished by AQHA)

440 yards

Year	Name of Horse	Time
1965	Joe Sherry	21.5
1962	Pokey Bar	21.6
1962	She Kitty	21.7
1962	No Butt	21.7
1961	Manor Man	22.1
1957	Mr. Bar None	22.1
1955	Arizonan	22.1

The following records were made before the use of electric timers and regulation starting gates.

1943	Woven Web (Miss Princess)	22.0
1937	Shue Fly	22.3
1940	Miss Bank	22.4
1939	Queeny	22.5
1941	Blondie L	22.6
1939	Nobodies Friend	22.7
1937	Clabber	22.8
1936	Joe Reed II	22.8

The Racing Commission of the AQHA no longer classifies times made with regard to whether the animal is a mare, stallion, or gelding, but it can be stated that Joe Sherry was a four-year-old gelding when he set his record in 1965 at La Mesa Park, Raton, New Mexico.

400 yards

Year	Name of Horse	Time
1968	Lady Yolanda	19.54
1965	Decketta	19.69
1963	Super Chick	19.88
1963	Dariman	19.94
1962	Jet Deck	20.00

350 yards

1968	Linda Charge	17.33
1960	Vandy's Flash	17.50
1960	Tonto Bars Hank	17.60

330 yards

1968	Ralph's Lady Bug	16.51
1964	Pasamonte Paul	16.69
1962	Kimaleta	16.70
1962	Uncle Van	16.80

300 yards

1968	Go Josie Go	15.38
1968	Bar None Doll	15.38
1965	Deckette	15.47
1951	Clabbertown	15.50

250 yards

1969	Suwanee Bars	13.07
1965	Sir Vixen	13.33
1965	Mighty Bert	13.38
1949	Monita	13.40
1948	Clabber II	13.60

220 yards

1969	Junior Meyers	11.62
1965	Joe Sherry	11.82
1965	Flying Cobre	11.98
1965	Music Note	12.08
1949	Shubalee	12.20

15

Shows and Contests

Because of the shameful record of the people who have owned and shown artificially gaited, high-action, and cut-tail horses—horses that have been tortured and mutilated—all artificiality in horses is suspect.

The first National Horse Show was held at Gilmore's Garden in New York City in 1883 and was not a high society affair. However, the exhibitors had one thing in common with the social arbiters: they loved good breeding and had living proof that it showed up better in horses than in people. By 1890, society had seized on the National Horse Show opening as an occasion for ostentatious display of jewels, furs, and formal costumes that distinguished the wealthy and thus put it somewhat on a par with the annual opening of the Metropolitan Opera. And so began an urge to win trophies and ribbons for further ostentation that transcended any love of horses. The domination of horse shows by society was on the wane by the 1950s, but as it shifted to other types of horse owners, the standards of humane treatment were not noticeably improved.

Shows are the same today as they were fifty years ago. When Britain prohibited the cutting of horses' tails, the British respected the law, if not the horses, and the practice stopped. When some states in the United States passed laws prohibiting tail cutting, the practice continued through the connivance of the show entrepreneurs, who allowed, and still allow, such mutilated horses to be shown if the tails have been cut in a state where it is not illegal.

As recently as 1970 I saw two cut-tail horses, the only ones in a class of natural horses, including several Quarter Horses, awarded first and second place in an Open English Pleasure Horse, Saddle Type Class. Both the AHSA and the AQHA, along with APHA (Arizona Professional Horsemen's Association) and others, sponsored the show. So one can only assume the award met with their approval. In the gaited Harness Pony Class and the Tennessee Walking Horse Class, every horse was tail-fixed and obviously gingered.

For years, those who were standing close enough when Tennessee walking horses left the show ring saw the blood oozing down over the hoofs, and they also saw the handlers kick dust over the feet as fast as they could to prevent the public from seeing the blood.

I sat by a man and his wife whose horse was being shown in the gaited class at the 1970 A to Z (Aid to Zoo) National Horse Show at Phoenix, one of the ten top shows, with horses brought in from all over the country. When asked about the tail-cutting, feet soring, and irritants, the owner laughed and said, "We leave all that and the training to the people we hire." When the beautiful, quiet-mannered, natural Arabians and Quarter Horses under stock saddles went through their paces in the ring, the man turned to me and asked, "Where are the good horses I heard they had in Arizona?"

The show promoters and owners have been given more than enough time to adopt and enforce humane rules. But rather than do so, they are waiting for the lawmakers to point the finger at them. Senator Tydings' (of Maryland) bill designed to stop the "soring of horse's feet" and to prohibit the interstate shipment of "sored" horses for showing or exhibition, will be, we hope, a law that is respected. It will be interesting to see what the American Horse Council, established in 1969, which represents the horse owners of America, will be able to do about unifying state and federal laws that deal with the humane treatment of horses.

The plea here is for exhibitors to speak up and insist on only the show practices they approve of before entering any show. Pertinent questions should be asked. And one of them could well be, "Will my horse be competing against any mutilated horses?" If gingering horses—or the use of irritants—is allowed, it should be known. Some families have quit trailering their horses around to shows and tell me they are enjoying their horses more than they did when they attended shows. Trail riding, hunting, gymkhana games and contests, where the owner-rider-trainer and horse relationship is at its best, seem to have a greater appeal for them.

The AHSA publishes suggestions for horseback games without stating precise rules. Usually the more popular games are very informal, allowing bareback riding and either stock or flat saddles. Games and contests often include musical chairs (in which sacks are used for the bases on which riders dismount and stand when the music stops), relay races, potato races, egg-and-spoon races, balloon races, etc., plus new ones which each district seems to develop.

Those who show horses consistently (in 1970 there were over 250,000 entries in 1476 AQHA-sponsored shows, of which 277 were "A," 573 "B," 550 "C," and 76 "D" shows, and in addition 1290 Approved Youth Activities Shows) do so for definite reasons. And the horse owner should understand those reasons before going all out on a ribbon-winning campaign.

A breeder is dependent on horse shows. They are his display cases where he shows his product. Ribbons and trophies attest to the superiority of his stock and provide the publicity that increases the value. It is also necessary to show in order to get distinguished horses in the various categories noted in the books of their breed.

The AQHA, for instance, awards three major degrees with coveted titles that distinguish the peers in the realm of the Quarter Horse. Lowest ranking, somewhat as an equine duke or marquis, is the horse with an ROM after his name—a Register of Merit horse. Next in rank is the equine earl or viscount, the AQHA Champion (with a Reserve Champion also designated). And far above—comparable to a baron, and in such exclusive society that even today less than one in ten thousand win such distinction, and the odds were far greater when the first eight horses won this highest of awards—is the AQHA Supreme Champion. They are shown with some biographical data on the following pages.

Register of Merit

The purpose of the Register of Merit is to establish a record of performance. There are actually two Registers of Merit: one for working events and one for racing. Halter points are not applicable. To earn the Register of Merit, a horse must have won at least ten points in two or more of the following categories, in which only registered horses compete.

1. Racing
2. Reining—Working Cowhorse—Western Riding
3. Barrel Racing—Pole Bending
4. Jumping—Working Hunter—Polo
5. Western Pleasure—Trail Horse—English Pleasure
6. Calf Roping—Steer Roping—Cutting (both Registered and Open)

If both Registered and Open Cutting are held at the same show, points will be awarded only in registered classes.

AQHA Supreme Champion Kid Meyers, a sorrel horse foaled in 1963, was the first to pass the rigid requirements to win the coveted award. Owned by A. B. Green of Purcell, Oklahoma, and trained by Jerry Wells, this big horse came from the tracks to performance events. His sire was Three Bars and his dam was Miss Meyers, World Champion Quarter Running Horse of 1953, whose sire was Leo and whose dam was Star's Lu by Oklahoma Star. Building up points at halter, in Western Pleasure and Roping, Kid Meyer managed in eighteen months after his last race to win the highest honor the breed association could bestow. *Courtesy Orren Mixer, Circle M Ranch Studio and AQHA.*

Until 1968, 50 percent of the ROM horses were made by their owners. Now that points for the award must be made in two categories, it is likely more professional training will be required to make winners.

AQHA Champions

To gain the title of AQHA Champion, a horse must have won a total of thirty-five points or more in five or more official shows and contests, and under five or more judges. At least fifteen of the points must be earned in halter classes, with at least eight of these points being earned in A or B shows. A minimum of fifteen points must be earned in per-

AQHA Supreme Champion Fairbars was bred on the Quincy Farms near Denver, Colorado, owned by Ed Honnen, ex-president of the AQHA, who became head of the National Horse Council. Although Fairbars was an AAA racer, Roy Savage, manager and trainer for Grafton Moore, who bought the horse, found him quiet and sensible. The AQHA Supreme Champion award came in February 1968. *Darol Dickinson photo. Courtesy AQHA.*

formance events, with at least eight points achieved in Class A or B shows, and with at least five points gained in each of at least two categories of performance events. The Grand Champion stallion or Grand Champion Mare must have received one point more than any other competitor. The runner up is called Reserve Grand Champion.

Bar Money, who also became an AQHA Supreme Champion in February 1968, was the third son of Three Bars to win the top honor. He was foaled in 1960 on Walter Merrick's 14 Ranch near the Antelope Hills in Western Oklahoma. His dam was an AAA race mare called Miss Ruby. It was his fourth owner, J. Thomas Heckel of Pacific, Missouri, who had him campaigned for the Supreme Championship. Lanam Riley trained him for roping, and Phil Hatcher, Tommy Manion, and Laura Cotter (in the saddle here) added more refinements to his training to give the great horse a chance to prove himself. *Courtesy AQHA.*

AQHA Supreme Champions

To quote from the official handbook of the American Quarter Horse Association:

"The title 'AQHA Supreme Champion' will be awarded to any stallion, mare, or gelding which has been issued a numbered registration certificate by the American Quarter Horse Association or has been listed in either the Appendix or New Appendix by the Association, provided said horse meets the following requirements:

(a) Has earned two official grades of AAA;
(b) Has been named Grand Champion at a minimum of two approved A shows under two different judges; and
(c) Has won a total of forty (40) or more points in recognized halter and performance classes at A Shows approved by the Association; and that
  (1) At least fifteen (15) of those points have been won in halter classes, and
  (2) At least twenty (20) of those points have been won in performance events at A shows or in races recognized by the Association; with at least eight (8) of the twenty (20) performance points earned in one or more of the following events: Reining, Working Cowhorse, Western Pleasure, Western Riding, and Jumping; and with at least eight (8) of the twenty (20) performance points earned in one or more of the following events: Calf Roping, Steer Roping, and Registered Cutting."

From these rigid requirements, it is easy to see that this highest plateau in the world of the Quarter Horse will not become crowded.

The Point System

Scoring is based on the amount of competition in which horses in all approved classes can win full points.

No. of Horses in Class	1st	2nd	3rd	4th	5th	6th
5-9	1					
10-14	2	1				
15-19	3	2	1			
20-24	4	3	2	1		
25-29	5	4	3	2	1	
30 and over	6	5	4	3	2	1

For example, should your horse win first place in a class of thirty or more, he earns six points. If he should win sixth place in such a large class, he earns one point. Points are not awarded in classes of less than five horses, although the class is judged.

AQHA shows are classified as A, B, C, D, according to the number of entries. Class A—225 or more entries
B—150 to 224 entries
C—75 to 149 entries
D—29 to 74 entries

In Quarter Horse Racing, one point is awarded for each race run in AA time, three points for each race run in AAA time, and five points for each race run in Top AAA time.

The AHSA has a much more complicated system of rating their shows, which requires many pages of explanation in their rule book. Basically the difference between A, B, and C shows depends on the number of specified classes offered and the amounts awarded as prizes. The points gained in an A show are quadruple and in a B show double those in a C show.

As mentioned before, the American Quarter Horse Association, P.O. Box 200, Amarillo, Texas 79105, will supply their Official Handbook to prospective Quarter Horse exhibitors. The American Horse Shows Association, 527 Madison Avenue, New York, N.Y. 10022, will send their Official Rule Book only to members. Membership dues are: Life $250; Contributing $25; Senior $15; and Junior (under eighteen) $7.50. Both handbooks set forth show and contest rules and regulations and are recommended as important additions to any horse-book library.

For those, other than breeders and professional trainers and rodeo contestants, who seek financial gain from horse shows and contests, the ones who campaign cutting horses seem to be the most successful.

Winning stakes in various classes and in barrel racing can be sizable at times, but except for a few outstanding examples, they seldom amount to enough to pay expenses. The costs of showing can mount up. Besides entry fees, stable fees, trainer and groom costs (if their services are used), there are the usual costs of traveling, in which motels and restaurants, car and truck maintenance, and the investment in a good horse trailer all represent a considerable outlay.

The horse show circuit can also be—and here's where you will run into much of your tough competition in performance events—a trophy safari for wealthy patrons whose horses, trainers, and riders are expected to bring down the finest specimens and win publicity to reflect glory

AQHA Supreme Champion Jetaway Reed, a grandson of Three Bars, was foaled in 1964. His dam was Jo Van Reed. After he had earned thirty-one points racing under the management of Walter Merrick, Art Holiday of Hominy, Oklahoma, his owner, turned him over to trainers George Tyler and Matlock Rose. The top award came in June 1968, and in the same year D. J. Cooper of Stillwater, Oklahoma, bought him for $41,000. *Photo by James Cathey, Fort Worth. Courtesy AQHA.*

on the owner. But horse shows viewed from the nonprofessional side of the fence, and with less accent on the prestige angle, present an entirely different picture, especially in the Junior division.

Entering shows can be an experience in facing up to top competition. It offers an opportunity to learn about riding techniques, horses, tack, attire, etc., and to gain confidence by performing before an audience. At shows one can find new friends and share with them an exhilarating

Miss Roy Deck was the first mare to become an AQHA Supreme Champion. She was bred by the Driggers Land and Cattle Company of Santa Rosa, New Mexico, and was foaled in 1963. At the tracks she raced AAA four times. After being purchased by John O'Brien and James Brennan of Lake Forest, Illinois, the owners of her sire Roy Deck by Top Deck, she was taken from the track to be trained for Western Pleasure by Helmuth Lekschas. Ken Ecker, in the saddle in this photo, carried on for other phases of her training. *Photo by Bobbie, Milwaukee.*

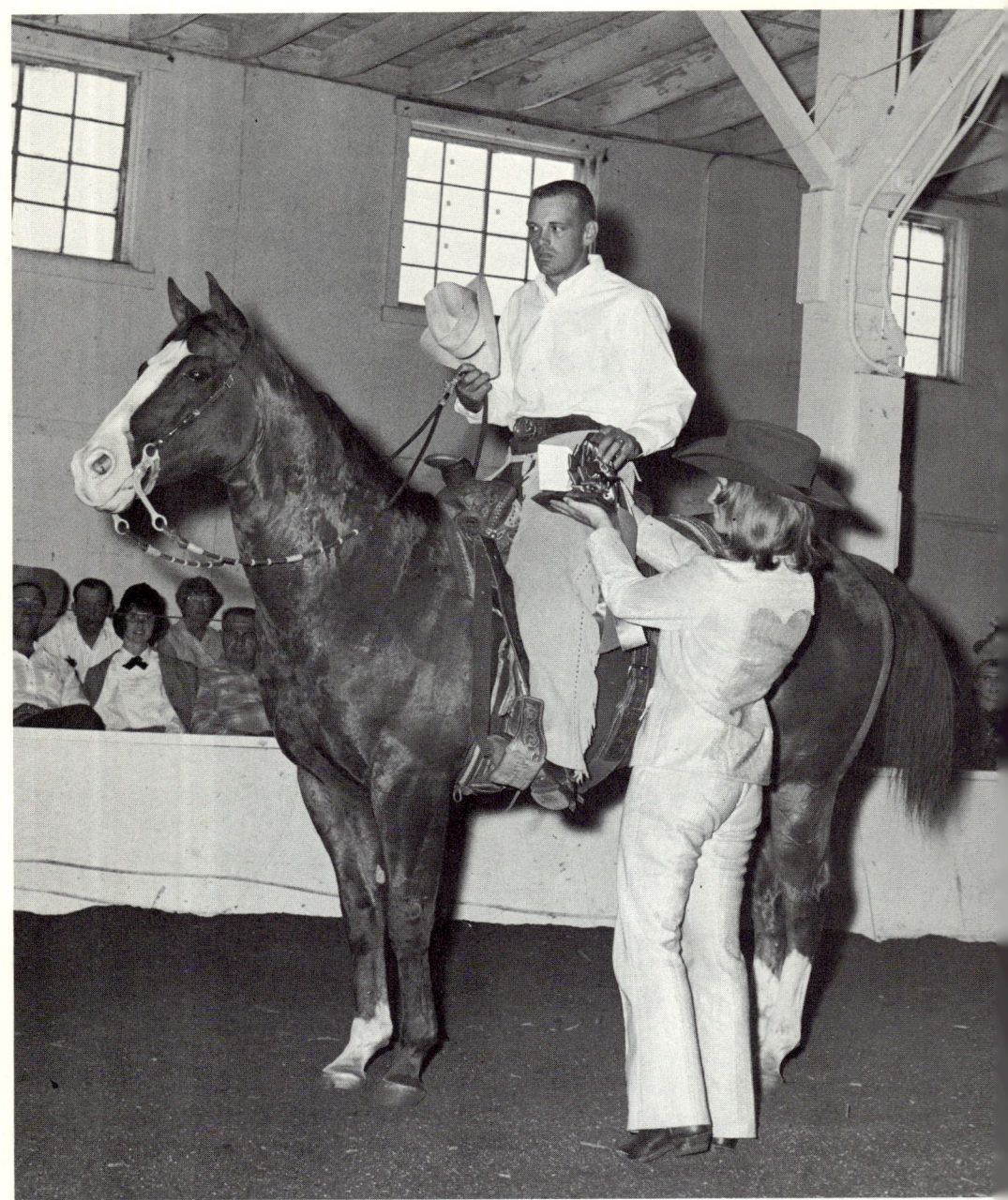

Cat's Cue Bar became an AQHA Supreme Champion in November 1968, the first gelding to win such honor. He was bred by Homer D. Sims of Lebanon, Oregon, and later became the property of Le Roy McCay of Eugene, Oregon. After earning ten points in racing, he went on to win fifty halter points and thirty-nine performance points. *Photo by Miss Jimi Rabinsky.*

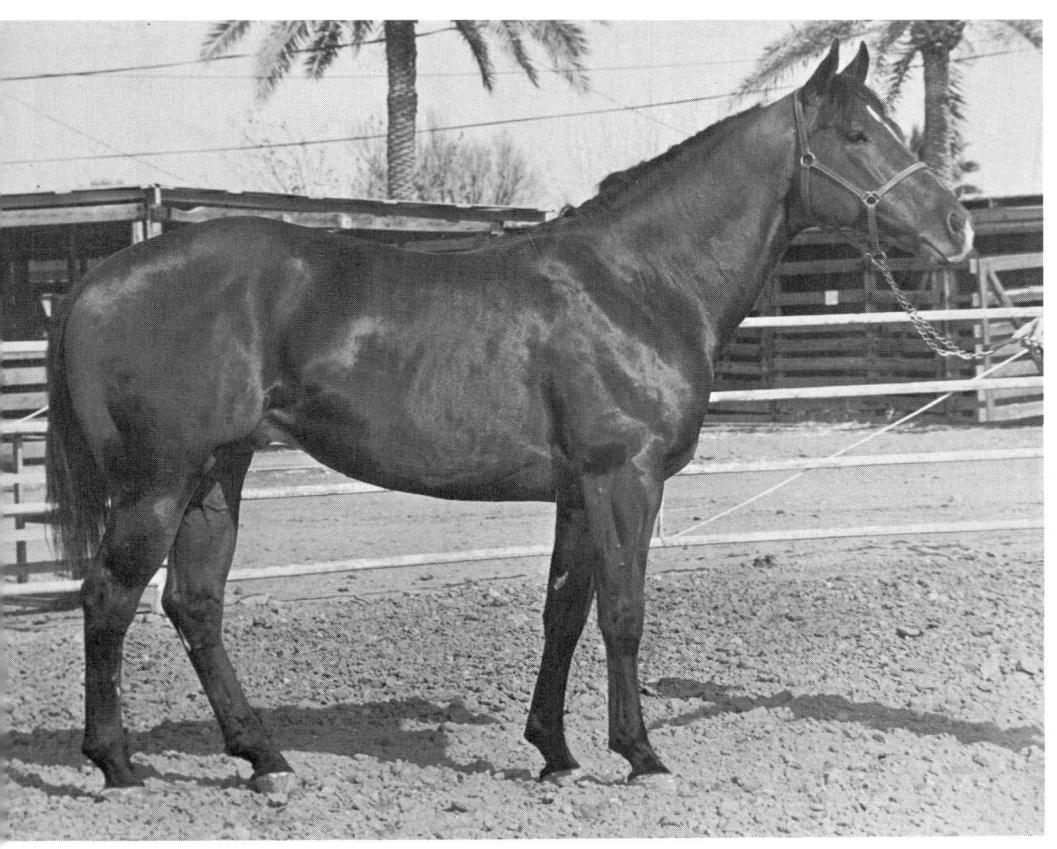

Enhanced, a bay stallion foaled in 1962, became an AQHA Supreme Champion in November 1968. Through his sire he traced to Peter McCue, and through his dam Nancy Hance to My Texas Dandy and Yellow Jacket. Enhanced had earned thirteen racing points and two AAA racing credits when Jay Parsons of Cody, Wyoming, who bred and owned him, headed him toward the Supreme Championship.

John Hoyt, a well-known trainer in Arizona, made him into a steer roping and performance horse. Enhanced was sold in June 1969 to the American Breeders Service in De Forest, Wisconsin. *Photo by Johnny Johnston. Courtesy AQHA.*

The rise of Mach I to the AQHA Supreme Championship is particularly notable for two reasons: he is the only Palomino to be so honored; and he was ten years old at the time, making him the oldest champion. His sire was Junior Reed and his dam was Spanish Joy. Bred by Leonard Milligan of Granada, Colorado, he was sold to the late Denver Davis of Colony, Oklahoma. Under the management of R. D. Davis, Mach I did well as an AAA runner until he was six. Then, at an auction at Oklahoma City, Mr. and Mrs. L. L. Prichett bid him in for fifteen thousand dollars. Becoming an expert roping horse did much to build up points for Mach I. *Photo by Dalco Film Company, Inc., Irving, Texas. Courtesy L. L. and Linda Prichett.*

sport. It is the best of all training grounds for those who want to make a career in the world of horses.

Horse Show Judges

Nobody likes to lose, but generally exhibitors take defeat gracefully. There are, however, some determined souls who squawk to high heaven when they think they have "been robbed" by a judge. It is true there have been instances where it appeared that favoritism, politics, or money influenced a judge. There were so many complaints, in fact, that by 1964 the list of approved judges was closed until better methods of selecting them could be worked out.

In 1965 new rules required a prospective judge to give his qualifications on an official application to the AQHA which is reviewed by three members of a regional group for their acceptance or rejection. If accepted, a judging committee and executive committee of the AQHA reviews the report. An approved judge is then permitted to judge two AQHA approved shows per year. He must not appear at a show ground more than fifteen minutes prior to the judging, nor will he talk with any of the contestants. From the time he arrives in the town where he will officiate until he departs, he must maintain the dignity and integrity of a qualified judge.

Now, with such high standards set, true sportsmen will accept with good grace the rulings of such a judge. Remember, you and your horse are also being judged by the spectators. All contestants should be properly dressed and present their horses with pride. If one disapproves of certain requirements or demands made of the exhibitor, or of competitors in a show, it is better to stay out of it.

Classes and Contests

Halter Classes. Before demonstrating how to train a mule, the old mule-breaker stepped over and hit the animal over the head with a ball bat, explaining, "Before trying to teach him anything, you must first get his attention." So goes the old story.

In training and showing your horse, his attention is gained in a milder manner, we trust, and, once gotten, is held. You must get him alert and in a halter class keep his eyes on you by such slight gestures and sounds that they are not noticeable to the judge. This means practice sessions for many days before show time. Hold the lead shank up to his nose. Slap your own chest with it. Draw his head back to attention every time he tries to gaze around at other horses or people. When approaching the judge, hold the neatly coiled lead shank in the left hand. The right hand should be close up to the halter. Walk on the near side and turn right after stopping in front of the judge. Keep a good safe distance from the horse ahead. Step aside to allow the judge to walk around to get a good look at your horse.

If the ground is at all uneven, while walking toward the judge look for a level spot on which to place your horse. If it is slightly uphill, that is better. If he stands with his front feet downhill, they well be too far forward for a good stance.

Lead him forward for positioning and stop him when he has a good square stance, with his legs well under. If backed into position, he might

Lady Line Rider at the State Fair of Texas in 1967 shown with owner Nancy Cunningham of Beloit, Wisconsin, J. L. (Dusty) Rhoades, then president of the AQHA, and Don Dodge, well-known trainer and owner of champion cutting horses, who served as judge. Lady Line Rider had been named Grand or Reserve Champion in every major show in the nation. *Photo by Dalco Film Company, Inc., Irving, Texas.*

get his rear legs so far under that he might look sickle-hocked. But if only one leg is out of position, backing up may square him.

The old exaggerated stretch stance is not for the Quarter Horse. For show, the legs of the Quarter Horse should come straight down in a natural four-square stance. If the front feet are too close together, he may look narrow-chested. Look from the side as well as from the front to see if he is well positioned. Kicking his foot with yours to get him to move it is not a good practice unless it is a mild nudge. I have seen exhibitors, including girls and women, stoop down and place a foot with their hands, which, aside from being a bit noticeable, is one way of doing it.

In preparing your horse for showing, proper feed and additives will give gloss to his coat, but you will have to add plenty of elbow grease to bring it out by daily brushing. There are sprays that can be used shortly before showing that add to the sheen. Your horse should have

Sugar Bars, a son of Three Bars, has sired a large family of individuals that are well known in the arenas as well as on the tracks. *Courtesy AQHA.*

been used enough so that he is fit and solid instead of fat and flabby. Some judges want to see the structure of the horse, and too much fat can conceal it. Hoofs should be clean and polished-looking, but the use of a steel brush is not advised as it can injure the outer wall covering. Petroleum jelly put on and then rubbed off will keep the hoof soft and in good condition. But if it is used just before showing, it may collect too much dust and give the hoof a dull look.

Teach your horse to move out and follow readily at the trot, so that when the judge wants to size up the action of your horse, there will be no appearance of tugging at the lead rope. Manners are of prime importance. A horse that shows lack of discipline will be dismissed from the ring.

You can show your horse in only one halter class at each show. The classes have a wide range in age and sex, so there is room for one and all—if registered. There are separate classes for colts and fillies; as weanlings and yearlings if they are *eligible* to be listed in the Registry's new appendix; and as two-year-olds and three-year-olds if they *are* listed in the new appendix. Other classes are for four-year-old and older stallions and four-year-old and older mares with Registry Certificates. Gelding classes, in which horses must have similar registry proof, are for two-year-olds, three-year-olds, four-year-olds, and older.

To mention but one recent Halter Class Champion, I can do no better than to name Aledolita by Aledo Bar by Three Bars and out of Red Aunt, who is the first horse in history to earn 276 halter points in one year. She is owned by Mary Anne Parris of Lubbock, Texas. There will not be too many relatives to compete with her, because her dad, the remarkable Aledo Bar, met an untimely death at the age of ten in 1969, when he reared while exercising in his paddock at the stock farm of his owner, Joe Kirk Fulton of Lubbock, Texas, fell over backward and broke his neck.

Working Cowhorse Contest. *First half:* The class enters the ring at a walk and moves at a jog trot and slow lope upon request of the judge. After a line-up, if the judge so requests, the class retires, and then each contestant returns to ring work individually.

First ride a figure-eight at the slow lope—two times around—during which your horse's change of leads, both front and back, and fluency and evenness of gait are critically judged.

Next ride to the end of the arena, turn and run its full length, making a straight sliding stop. Turn away from the rail, and run to the other end, making a sliding stop. Turn away from the rail and run to the center of the arena for the third sliding stop. Allow your horse to gather himself, then back up for ten or fifteen feet. Ride up to the judge, stop, then with weight on his hind quarters swing your horse a quarter turn to the right, half a turn to the left, half a turn to the right. Then retire from the arena.

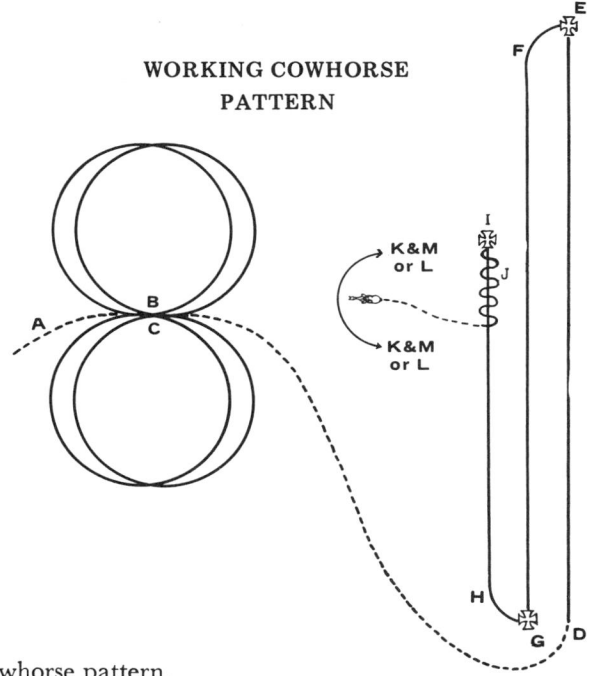

Working Cowhorse pattern.

Second half: Following this comes the cattle working part of this event, which is mandatory.

One cow is turned into the arena and held at the far end to demonstrate that your horse is watching it alertly. Allow the cow to run down the side of the arena, turning it twice each way against the fence. Next take the cow to the center of the arena and circle it once to the right and once to the left. Scoring is from sixty to eighty, with seventy considered average. A fall of the horse or the rider does not eliminate the entry.

Faults are: tail switching—exaggerated opening of the mouth—hard mouth—throwing of head—lugging on bridle—halting or hesitation when being run out—anticipating signals—losing a cow.

Easter Cody, Honor Roll Reining Horse in 1965, and Honor Roll Working Cowhorse in 1966 and 1967. Owned by C. T. Fuller, Catasauqua, Pennsylvania. *Courtesy* The Western Horseman.

The winning qualities you must train for are those to be found in the best of Western-trained horses: good manners; well collected, with feet well under at all times and with hind feet well under when stopping; responsive to a light rein, with head in natural position. Speed should be sufficient but well under control of the rider. A stock saddle is used and the rider wears chaps and carries a rope or riata. Spurs are optional.

The classes in the larger shows are:

(a) Senior Working Cowhorse (five years old or older—all horses shown with bit).
(b) Junior Bit Working Cowhorse (four years old and younger).
(c) Hackamore Working Cowhorse (four years old and younger, with hackamore or snaffle bit. Two hands may be used).

Reining Contest. This contest is quite similar to the first half of the Working Cowhorse contest, but more attention is given to the precision displayed in following the pattern, the use of aids, the expertness of rein hands, responsiveness of the horse, and his fluency in lead changes, straight backing, etc.

Faults against the rider include: changing hands on the reins, losing a stirrup, and giving excessive or exaggerated aids (spurring, quirting, talking, petting, etc.).

The following patterns are recommended by the AQHA, or the pattern for the Working Cowhorse may be used by the show management if there is *no* Working Cowhorse contest.

AQHA
REINING PATTERN
NUMBER 1

Upright Marker Mandatory at Point Marked X

Upright Marker Mandatory at Point Marked X

JUDGE

START

Reining patterns.

AQHA REINING PATTERN NUMBER 2

♣ Mandatory marker on arena fence or wall.

AQHA REINING PATTERN NUMBER 3

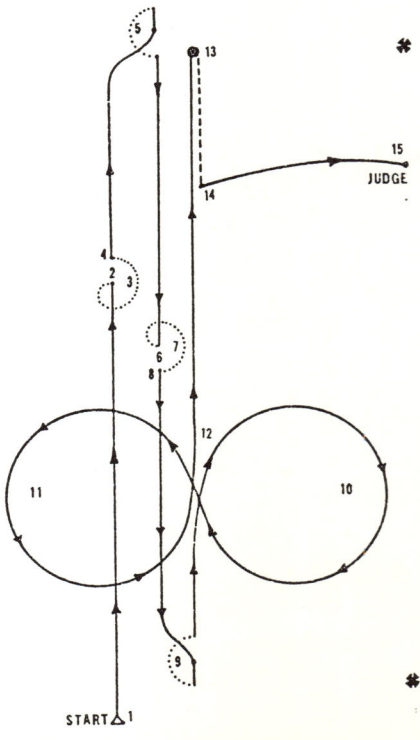

♣ Mandatory marker on arena fence or wall

AQHA REINING PATTERN NUMBER 4

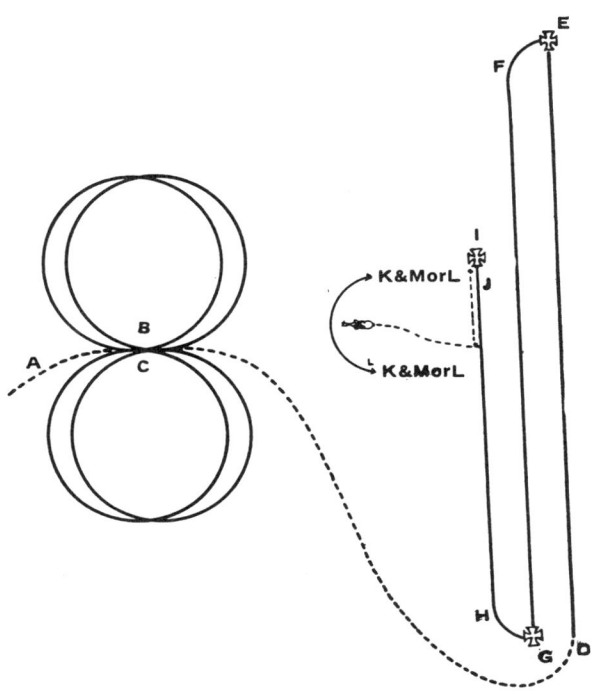

Trail Horse Class. In this event the emphasis is on the ease and accuracy of gait changes, walk, trot, or lope—with a minimum of restraint and on a reasonably loose rein. It is a test of the relaxed teamwork that can exist between horse and rider. The horse must show intelligence and be aware of what he is doing when moving over and around obstacles, and passing through and allowing the rider to open and close a gate. These movements are done slowly and deliberately—a contrast to the quick movements the horse is called on to make in leaping over rails or ditches.

Conformation rates	10 percent
Rail work	30 percent
And the confidence and sureness with which the horse works around obstacles	60 percent

Patsy Lee of Bethel Park, Pennsylvania, Youth Honor Roll Trail Class Champion for 1967. *Courtesy AQHA.*

Elaborate equipment rates no higher than a simple good working outfit. The rider wears Western hat and boots, and suitable dress, without tapaderos. A hackamore, or a curb, snaffle, half-breed or spade bit is permissible, but a martingale or tie-down is not. The use of spurs and chaps and the carrying of a rope or riata are optional.

The AQHA handbook lists all the mandatory and optional obstacles to be encountered in sponsored shows.

Western Riding Horse Contest. This is neither a stunt nor a race. It is a competition to determine which horse in the class displays: the most well-mannered, willing disposition, the best sensible, free, and easy-moving characteristics. The least use of obvious aids helps one's rating. No extra credit is given for expensive, fancy, or parade equipment of the horse or the costume of the rider. Nor is the conformation of the horse judged, only his ability.

One hand only is used on the reins and hands must not be changed. The hand is to be around the reins, but one finger between them is permitted. Romal or spurs must never be used forward of the cinch. No nosebands or tie-downs or severe chin straps or curb chains are permitted.

The pattern shown in the chart is similar to most show requirements. The distances indicated are not obligatory. They vary somewhat depend-

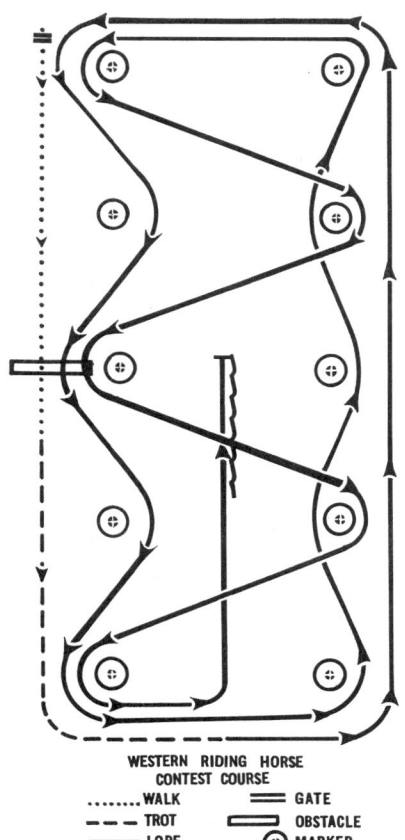

Western Riding Horse Contest course.

Toppereno, Honor Roll Western Riding Horse in 1963, '64, and '67, owned by Mrs. A. S. Kelly, Chester, Vermont. *Courtesy* Quarter Horse Journal.

ing on the size of the arena. The horse must quickly put his rider in position, without dismounting, to open the gate and to close it after passing. Following that, the gaits and action of the horse and easy control shown by the rider are of prime importance.

AQHA English Pleasure Class. Horses are shown at a flat-footed walk, square trot with the rider posting, and at the canter. Reversing is called for frequently by judges, but not asked for at the canter, and it must be done easily without excessive use of aids. The rider should be on a reasonably light rein. As in Western Pleasure, keep a horse's length fore and aft from other horses and observe the other suggestions for class riding. When reversed, horses must turn away from the rail toward the inside. Extended hoofs and the use of other than standard shoes are discouraged and may be penalized by the judge. Martingales, tie-downs, hackamores, or draw reins are prohibited. Excessive speed is penalized. English tack is required, with a choice of full bridle, Pelham, snaffle, or curb bit.

Riders wear the hard cap covered with black velvet, riding coats of black or various colors, and breeches that are generally white, cream, or buff, and boots. Girls wearing pony tails should club them so that they will not cover the rider's number attached to the back of her collar.

Western Pleasure Class. Horses are shown on a slack rein at a walk, jog trot, and lope, and if some judges call for an extended trot, the riders must sit the gait without posting. When reversed the horses must turn away from the rail toward the inside of the ring. Horses must work both ways in the ring at all three gaits and demonstrate their ability with different leads. Horses are not asked to reverse at the lope or to extend the lope into a gallop. Riders are not asked to dismount. Horses are always asked to back. Horses are shown with stock saddle. Extra elaborate equipment has no advantage over a good working outfit. A hackamore, or curb, snaffle, half-breed, or spade bit is permissible, but a martingale or tie-down is prohibited. Other than standard horseshoes are prohibited. This is a brief summary, and as with all classes mentioned in these pages, the more detailed regulations should be studied in the AQHA and AHSA Official Handbooks.

Riders shall wear Western hats and cowboy boots. The use of spurs, chaps, or similar gear and the carrying of a rope or riata is optional.

AQHA Jumping Class. If you wish, your registered jumper can be entered in one approved AQHA Registered Jumping Class per show, plus one open Jumping Class and one approved Working Hunter Class.

There will be a minimum of four obstacles, and your horse must make a minimum of eight jumps.

Jumps may be: post-and-rail (at least two jumps), chicken coop, stone wall, triple bar, brush jump, and should be located fifty feet apart or farther if room permits. Height must be at least three feet. In case of ties, rails will be raised four inches on each go-around.

Obedience, lack of hesitation before the leaps, and willingness of the horse to respond to the rider's aids are more important in this event, at the present time, than the difficulty of the jumps. Although the knockdown of an obstacle, standard, or wing with any part of the horse, rider,

Honor Roll Champion Pleasure Horse Lady Barbie Sox ridden by Dave Page, who showed her to her championship, and owned by Salt Meadow Farm, South Dennis, Massachusetts. *Photo by Tom Esler.*

or equipment draws a penalty of faults, it is in the area of manners and control that the highest fault count or even elimination is encountered.

In shows co-sponsored by the AQHA and AHSA, to conform with the latter's rules, martingales are optional, as are breastplates. Bridles may be either double, Pelham, or bridoon. Curb chains must conform to AQHA standards (flat ends at least one-half inch in width). The forward seat or hunt saddle is used.

Candisugar Riker, owned by the Westenhook Farm, Inc., of Southbury, Connecticut. Sandy Vaughn is riding. *Photo by Hank Cohen,* Florida Horse Journal.

Working Hunter Class. As in the Jumping Class, your registered Quarter Horse is eligible for showing in an approved AQHA Working Hunter Class, and an approved Open Working Hunter Class. Classes may be divided into Senior and Junior Working Hunters.

A minimum of four obstacles must be jumped, and the fences may be post and rail, brush, stone wall, chicken coop, aiken, and hedge. Jumps such as pole over brush, triple bar, and hogbacks are prohibited in AQHA Registered Working Hunter Classes. They must be a minimum of three feet three inches.

Horses are judged for their even hunting pace, good manners and style of jumping, grace of movement over the course, and soundness. Lack of any hesitation at the obstacles adds much toward a brilliant performance.

Hunting requires horses of unusual bottom (stayers) who can keep up a grueling pace. Only the exceptional Quarter Horse meets this test.

Bob's Bay King, ridden by owner Mrs. B. F. Allday of Huntington, Maryland. *Photo by Peter Winants.*

But there are plenty of exceptions. Within the breed are some taller, slightly lighter-muscled horses that are chosen as prospective hunters. Quarter Horses, except for those that are three-quarters Thoroughbred with the distance running ability of Thoroughbreds, are best suited to cross-country hunting where continued speed is not called for but where they can be depended on for durability and burst of power that will get them over the fences.

Calf Roping. In all roping contests in AQHA approved shows, it is the performance of the horse that counts. He is judged on his manners behind the barrier, scoring speed to calf, rating calf, the stop, working

Larry Dunford riding Easter Jim in a practice session. In a Junior Working Class of a hundred jumpers at the 1970 Del Mar, California show, Easter Jim and Larry were in sixth place. *Photo by the author.*

Jess Goodspeed roping from Pistol's Hornet. This nationally known roping horse is owned by Roland Stacey of Mississippi. *Photo by Guy Kassal.*

the rope, and his manners while the roper returns to him and mounts after the tie has been made.

If the roper carries two ropes tied to the saddle, he may throw a second loop. If he carries only one rope and misses on the throw, he must retire from the arena.

Breaking the barrier or any unnecessary whipping, jerking of reins, talking or any noisemaking, slapping, jerking rope, or any exaggerated action to make the horse perform better will certainly be judged unfavorably.

For Calf and Steer Roping in rodeo contests, where ropers and their horses are racing against the clock, see Chapter 16.

Team Tying and Dally Team Roping. These are the only steer roping contests acceptable as AQHA-approved events. In both events the header and heeler leave the chutes or boxes the split second the steer crosses the scoring line. The header races after the steer and ropes him about the horns and swings him about as the heeler comes in to rope the hind legs. If a catch has been made on one or two hind legs, the heeler moves his horse out to take up the slack and to stretch the steer out in the direction of the header, who, as soon as he sees a catch has been made, leaps from his horse and runs to tie the steer's hind legs.

In Team Tying, both header and heeler can carry two ropes, both tied hard and fast to the horn, ready in case a second loop has to be thrown.

In Dally Roping, the rope must not be tied to the horn and only one rope can be carried. When either roper makes a catch he must dally the rope on the horn for a solid hold. If either misses a throw, the single rope carried must be recoiled and a loop run out, for a second attempt, if it can be done within a two-minute limit.

More about Team Roping can be found in the chapter on rodeos, called "Partners in Big Business."

Barrel Racing Contest. This race against time naturally calls for standard courses that are accurately measured. The dimensions and directions in which it is to be run are shown in the chart.

Other than standard horseshoes are discouraged and may be penalized by the judge. Riders—a high proportion of them are women and girls—dress in Western clothes but never wear chaps.

A running start is allowed. Timing starts as the horse's nose reaches the starting line, and stops when the horse's nose reaches the finish line.

SHOWS AND CONTESTS 433

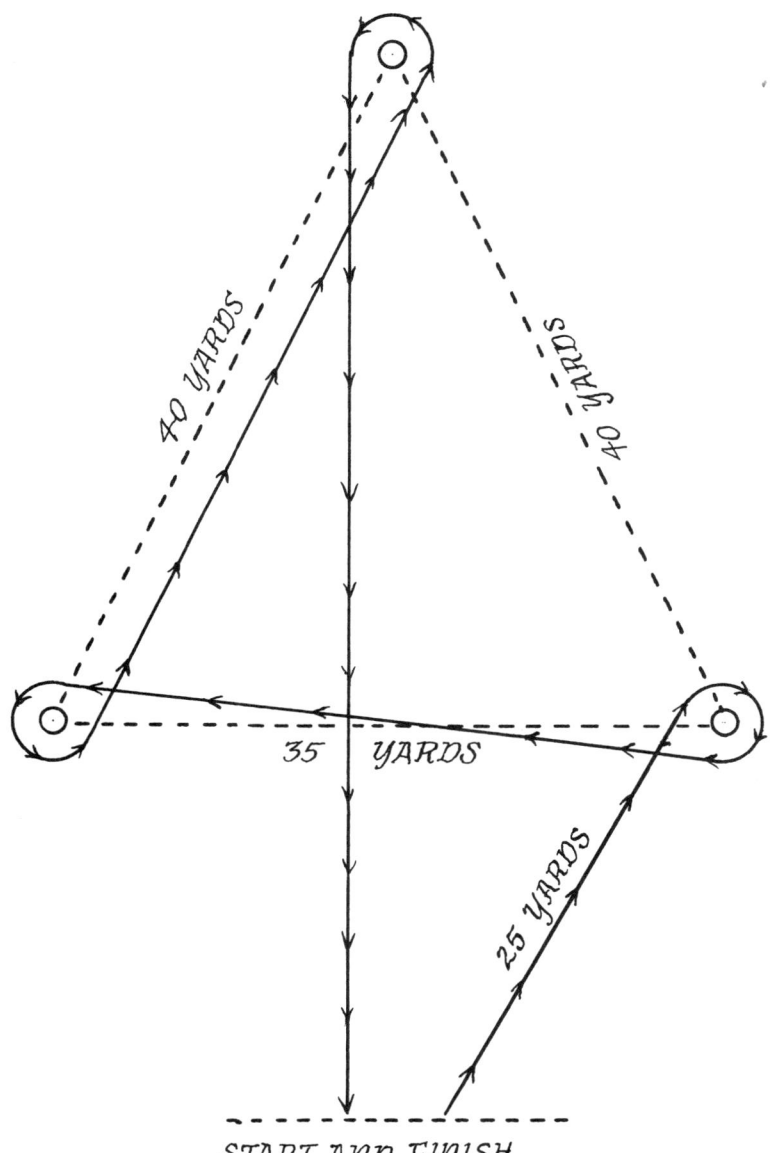

Barrel racing pattern.

After going round the third and last barrel, the horse has a straight sprint home of almost sixty yards.

The contestant has the privilege of reversing the pattern and starting with barrel No. 2, then No. 1 and No. 3.

The Appaloosa Club makes the contest more of a horse race, where space permits, by having two courses laid out on either side of the start-finish line, so that two contestants start simultaneously. Horse against horse is always more exciting than horse against clock, judging by the shrieks and pandemonium of the spectators as they root their favorite home.

AHSA rules and regulations require a much smaller barrel pattern to be run, and whereas a five-second penalty is imposed for each barrel knocked down, the AQHA rules require that the contestant be eliminated if a barrel is knocked down. The AHSA puts no restriction on the type or severity of bridle used, while the AQHA prescribes Western equipment be used with optional use of hackamore or other type of bridle, but gives judges the authority to disqualify any who use bits or equipment considered too severe.

Pole Bending originated in the State of Washington. It is a race against the clock that calls for a good fast running horse, because the horse must weave between and around six stakes or poles set twenty-one feet apart. The race starts with a sprint of 136 feet to the first pole, and after weaving around the poles and back, the horse makes a final sprint of 136 feet to the finish line. Like the barrel race, the timing starts after a running start, and ends when the horse's nose reaches the finish line.

The contestant has the option of running to the right or left of the poles. In other words, reversing the pattern shown in the chart.

Hackamore or other type of bridle is optional, but the judge may prohibit the use of bits or other equipment he may consider severe. Knocking over a pole, touching the pole with a rider's hand, or failure to follow the course will cause disqualification. Two stop watches or an electric timer is used, as in other clocked events. Other than standard horseshoes are discouraged and may be penalized by the judge.

AQHA Polo Pony Class. The Polo Pony Class is first shown collectively at a walk, trot, and canter, then individually, with special emphasis on handiness, way of going, manners, and balance while going through a figure-eight, first at a slow and then at an extreme pace. The horse must stop quickly and straight, reverse direction in tracks,

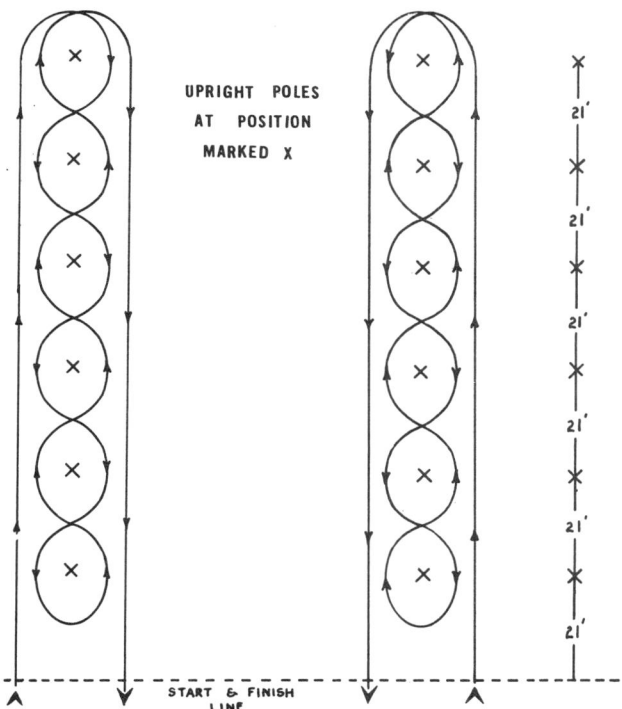

Pole bending pattern.

gallop back, stop, and back quickly. 25 percent of judging points are for way of reversing and responsiveness of the horse's mouth to the bit; 20 percent are for handiness at slow gaits (reining response to aids and light reining); 30 percent are for handiness and light rein response during fast work; 25 percent go to conformation.

The rider must, while at the canter, make the basic polo strokes on both near and off sides: (1) neck shot, (2) forehand, (3) back hand, (4) tail shot. The rider must also ride off another contestant in a race to a given mark and return.

To play along with the polo fraternity, no device, no matter how punishing to the mouth, is prohibited. The rule (No. 446, AQHA Handbook) merely states that preference is given to ponies shown in a straight-mouthed Pelham or short cheek smooth bridoon or double bridle and standing martingale, over the use of hackamores, draw reins, Indian martingale, figure-eight, tongue tie, high ports, sharp snaffles, etc., and presumably such other devices as gag bits and tightly buckled dropped nosebands.

Quarter Horse Polo Ponies

At the present time, Thoroughbreds or horses with a high percentage of Thoroughbred blood dominate the game. They have the courage and the heart for it, and the height and speed and endurance, but they tend to lack the disposition that makes them easily controlled. Quarter Horses have marvelous dispositions and are easily controlled, and have the quick take-off and blazing speed and the competitive courage, but they often lack the height and the endurance for the amount of racing that is required during the seven-and-a-half-minute periods. A Quarter Horse has great endurance, but not for long stretches at top speed. If rested in between, he can put on bursts of speed all day long. Likened to human athletes, the Quarter Horse is a hundred-yard sprinter, while the Thoroughbred is a half-miler.

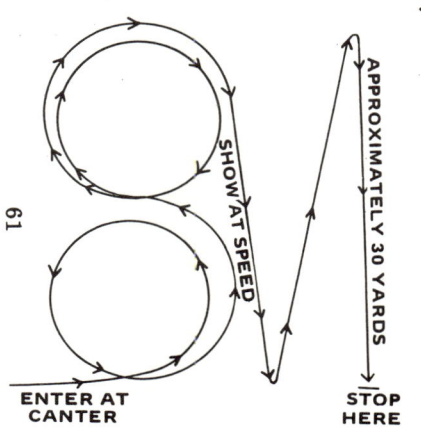

AQHA polo pony pattern.

There was a time when the quarter running Texas horses dominated the game. William Anson of the San Angelo district (the Concho country) and Q. W. Cardwell of Junction, Texas, the great one-armed polo player, along with Dan Casement of Colorado and Kansas and Donald Mason of Oklahoma and other Western horse breeders, developed many outstanding polo ponies. But it was Jim Minnick, so influential later in founding the Quarter Horse breed, who managed to raise, train, and sell more polo ponies between 1906 and 1925 than any other breeder in the United States.

In 1905, Jim Minnick and Will Rogers, Tom Mix, and a number of other cowboys destined to become famous, performed in the first rodeo ever held in Madison Square Garden in New York City. Colonel Zack Mulhall of Ohlahoma was the promoter of the show, which may account for so many Oklahomans, then and later, becoming cowboy showmen.

Jim Minnick and Will Rogers decided New York was a good place to sell horses. But before they sold any, they were so flat broke they couldn't buy food for themselves, and Jim's horse was working on his last quart of oats.

It was then that Will Rogers, hungry but his usual ebullient self, sold the manager of the old Union Square Theatre into letting them put on an act in his evening show. The pay was twenty-five dollars and a sack of oats and a bale of hay. Jim rode his horse onstage and dodged him about while Will roped the horse, then did some rope spinning, and talked some Oklahoma at the audience—to cover up mistakes and gaps in the action.

Their small and sudden success helped break the ice for both cowboys. Will, of course, went on to make his fame in the theater and in movies, and Jim returned to New York the next year with a carload of polo ponies. From his training lots at Red Bank, New Jersey, he got a horse business going that became immense. At one time he had a thousand brood mares and over forty stallions on his ranches in Texas and New Mexico. Jim knew everybody. Among the Long Islanders who admired him and his horses was ex-President Theodore Roosevelt. Jim himself became a superb polo player. He captained the Wichita, Kansas, team in 1923 when it won the Oklahoma Championship. He taught Will Rogers and Fred Stone and many others to play the game well. Jim's daughter Peggy was among the first girl riders to be nationally known. She and her prized mare, Fanny, were known in arenas from coast to coast as a champion barrel racing team.

Red Angel was Jim Minnick's favorite polo pony. He was a half brother of Concho Colonel, who traced to Old Billy and Paisana. Others of his were Little Mike, Rainy Day, Dude Minnick, and Bill Thomas.

In 1913, when the Big Four won the International Polo Championship, eight of the fourteen American-bred ponies on the team were raised in the Concho country of Texas.

Jacobs was said by some to have been the greatest polo pony America ever produced. He was raised on the Jacobs farm near San Antonio,

Texas, and was Harry Payne Whitney's top horse. He was ridden by Devereux Millburn in four international polo events. Three were winning years.

Others give as their horseback opinion that top honors should go to Fireball, foaled in 1914 by Concho Colonel, the grandson of Old Billy and Paisana, bred by William Anson and sold to Dan Casement, who made him famous as a sire of great polo and performance horses.

Polo probably reached its most dramatic heights in 1928 in the games between the United States, represented by the Meadowbrook Team of Long Island, and the Argentine Team under the leadership of Lewis Lacey, whose mastering of a powerful and accurate backhand drive was reminiscent of Meadowbrook's great Devereaux Millburn, who had recently retired. Besides Lacey, the Argentine team had on it the Cavanaugh brothers, Roberto and Juan, and Manuel Andrada.

The Meadowbrook quartet that rode onto the field for the third and crucial game—each team had won a game—was made up of Averell Harriman and Earl Hopping as forwards at positions No. 1 and No. 2, with Tommy Hitchcock playing the pivot position at No. 3, and Winston Guest as defensive back at No. 4.

The North Americans won after a fiercely fought contest. I was one of the more than forty thousand spectators at Meadowbrook that day, and I vividly remember the furious ranging of the entire field by the spectacular Manuel Andrada, and the neck-and-neck races he made for the ball. Tommy Hitchcock's most famous horse was Roxanna, a quarter-type mare from San Angelo, Texas.

When the rule that limited polo ponies to 14.2 hands high was abolished, the way was opened for the taller Thoroughbreds, which quickly changed the character of the game from quick maneuvering, in which the ball was passed on to teammates, into one of long races between opposing players.

The Quarter Horse, I frequently hear, is now making a comeback as a polo pony. The high percentage of Thoroughbred blood in so many of them gives them the height wanted, with the ones chosen being more like half-milers than quarter-milers.

Perhaps the main reason why Quarter Horses are back in the game is that the game is returning to what it was more than fifty years ago, low-goal polo, in which the players and horses concentrate on precision teamwork rather than riding hell-for-leather after the ball as the international players do.

The rules are the same, but more consideration is shown to other riders and their horses. If the game is played in this manner, the chances of injuries are also reduced. With women riders greatly outnumbering men riders today, it is not surprising that women are key players on many polo teams.

In some places the game is simplified by playing fewer chukkers (six instead of the regulation eight seven-and-a-half minute periods) and, where space is limited, by using playing fields that are only one-half the regulation size of 900 by 450 feet, while official arena polo is only one-third the size, being 300 by 150 feet. The smaller fields put more scramble and close action into the game and particularly eliminate the extended horse races, which in turn reduces the number of horses needed. This reduces expense all down the line, from feed and veterinarian bills to trailering or trucking to out-of-town matches.

If the regulation sized field is used, it normally takes twenty-four horses to mount up a team. Ten would normally be held in reserve in pasture, and fourteen trucked to the game. This would mean that each horse plays an average of about two chukkers a game.

The equipment required for each player consists of: a helmet, knee guards, and a mallet (made of bamboo with a cane shaft that weighs a little over a pound). For the horses, polo saddles are used (deep seat hunting saddles), leg wraps for protection against mallet blows, and traveling boots. The official polo ball is a little over three inches in diameter and weighs four and one half ounces. It is made of bamboo root, or willow. There are four players on a team—two forwards or offensive players who move out to set up plays, and two defensive players or backs. The game is similar to and has the general rules of hockey, with the object of putting the ball between two goal posts set twenty-four feet apart. Simple traffic regulations are followed to avoid collision. Based on goals made in games sponsored by the United States Polo Association, players are rated from zero to a ten-goal player, and the total of the rating of the players on each team represents the rating of the team. To give beginners a fair break, the sum of the rating of the weaker team is subtracted from the total sum of the stronger team. This resulting number is divided by three-fourths and is the starting score of the weaker team.

Many teams that enjoy the sport of low-goal polo keep the sophistication of polo playing and its costs down by dispensing with such extra grooming touches as braided manes and tails, etc. The Tyler brothers, Ronny, Lyle, and Larry, of Pierce, South Dakota, whose family interest in polo has continued for close to fifty years, find that even horseshoeing is not necessary or helpful for their Quarter Horses and cross-bred Thoroughbred polo ponies. Without shoes, they sustain fewer injuries while being trucked to matches. Others in the low-goal circuit have adopted the no-shoes practice. The Tyler Team once traveled three thousand miles and played eleven games in twenty days.

Another team of polo-playing brothers is composed of Bill, Harold, Claude, and Roy Barry. Bill Barry, who was rated from 1941 to 1961 as a seven-goaler by the United States Polo Association, has been a top player since his youth, when he learned the nuances of the game and the horse training that went with it from his neighbor and mentor Jim Minnick of Crowell, Texas. Bill still plays and trains horses, turning out some of the best polo mounts in the nation. He prefers to start with mature horses that have been used for general ranch and cow work. He favors the less muscular type and believes mares make the best polo ponies.

Broom Polo is a fun game in which the players generally ride stock saddles. With brooms for mallets to stroke a volley ball, each team can have from four to twelve players. Such games can turn into quite a jolly hassle.

Training the Polo Pony. The horse selected for a polo mount must be fast and aggressive enough to ride off another horse, but the accent in the fun game is to minimize bumping and to develop nimble maneuverability. The qualities wanted are those to be found in a good, bold reining horse. The easier he is controlled, the better. As for the expertise required, it can only be taught to the horse by playing on him. If he is a natural, he will start watching the ball and following it with the same intentness a roping horse follows a calf.

Small Shows

The club or group that decides to put on a horse show has well-set precedents to follow. One might say that the precedents are so well set that they are often followed blindly. Too few innovations are allowed that will assure better attendance. More spectators can be encouraged to come if: temporary road signs are set up to make the location easier to find; there is adequate room for parking; and if boys are delegated to see that traffic is directed and parking orderly. Simple programs with events listed in consecutive order can be sold for modest fees.

Places for the public to stand or sit or to picnic should be fenced off to separate them from horses and contestants. A site that offers trees for shade or other shelter will attract more people. Dusty grounds should be sprinkled down. A refreshment stand is always welcomed.

Horseback games and contests for youthful riders are always of interest to spectators, whereas seeing pleasure horses dutifully make their rounds can become boring, except, of course, to their owners.

A parade in smaller towns can nearly always be arranged, and it is a sure way to stir up interest. Stable area or trailer area should be in a well-defined spot, and off limits to the public to reduce the likelihood of accidents to horses or people.

16

Partners in Big Business

The rodeo and the horse sports it popularized was the outgrowth of an immense cattle industry that expanded through the Western part of the United States and put a large body of expert riders in the saddle.

The rodeos of the Californian Spaniards, the *charreda* of the Mexicans, the roundups and cowboy reunions of our Western cattlemen, and the stampedes of the Canadians headed the contests down the road to big business. For exciting entertainment it is hard to beat a bucking horse or a roping act.

In Deer Trail, Colorado, on July 4, 1869, before a roaring crowd of well-oiled miners, an Englishman with the elegant name of Emilnie Gardenshire rode a rank bucker to a standstill. His ride lasted fifteen minutes, and he had the bronc practically broken to ride when he stepped down. By the 1880s, roping contests added to the excitement of small-town shows. Judged by modern standards, scoring times were slow. One minute and forty-five seconds at Peco, Texas, in 1883 was good enough to win the three-hundred-dollar silver-mounted saddle. I can imagine the big longhorn steers they were throwing presented a tougher problem than the stock used today. However, I am sure the men of that day, like the Mexican *charros* in their *charreados* of today, put more accent on artistry and skill than on speed.

Interest in Western horsemanship and the hazardous skills of the ranch riders was greatly publicized by the Wild West Shows of Buffalo Bill, and the Oklahomans Pawnee Bill, Zack and Lucille Mulhall, and the Miller Brothers of 101 Ranch fame, when they started out to give the circuses some competition.

Following the Mulhalls' Wild West Show at the Fat Stock Exhibition at Fort Worth, Texas, in 1917, it was decided by the planners of the next year's show that the events would be contests instead of exhibitions of skill. In dispensing with the acts of professional showmen it was evident some monetary incentive would be necessary to get men to leave their ranch work and raise, train, transport, and perform with their horses.

The 1918 performance at Fort Worth set a successful pattern for such contests which soon replaced the wild west shows. It also gave the name "rodeo" to them. When the California Spanish word *rodeo* (ro-daý-o) was suggested, it was adopted, but it was generally pronounced by the Anglos the way it looked to them—ró-de-o. It took the Easterners to pronounce the word properly, something that is not yet done uniformly across the country.

By the mid-1930s, cowboys and ranchmen who competed in rodeos more or less as a sport or hobby were largely replaced by riders and ropers who followed the rodeo circuit as year-round professionals. By 1929 they were loosely organized into what they called the Turtle Association, with the Rodeo Association of America naming the champions. In 1945 the Rodeo Cowboys' Association was formed and has since been the official organization that keeps records and announces championship standings based on the amounts won in contests.

The horses used in all rodeo events, except the bucking horses, are, with very few exceptions, Quarter Horses.

Rodeo is really big business. Aside from thousands of small rodeos, in 1970 there were 547 professional rodeos in 42 states and 4 Canadian provinces that were sanctioned by the Rodeo Cowboys' Association. They drew an attendance of eleven million fans, and the contestants won over four million dollars.

It is difficult to classify rodeo. At least it is for newspapermen. They seem to treat it as local news rather than as a national sport. Is it a sport or not? The RCA thinks it is. They even think it has ceased being a regional Western sport, and point out, in addition to their own outfit, the Junior Rodeo for competitors from eight to eighteen years of age, the National High School Rodeo Association, and the National Intercollegiate Rodeo Association. They think the celebrities from these associations should appear on the sports pages along with golfers, boxers, football and basketball players. Even professional wrestling gets in the sports pages—and who really accepts it, except newpapers, as a sport?

Sports Illustrated, with the largest circulation of any sports magazine, has always recognized rodeo as a sport. So why not newspapers? the RCA asks.

Whether or not it is a sport that rodeo cowboys pursue, a lot of men risk life, limb, and money. What they do is as tricky to rationalize as auto road racing—or getting shot out of a cannon. And for the competitors who follow the rodeo circuit and put up entry fees, it is a risky business financially, too. There are relatively few big money winners— perhaps 5 percent—but with fourth- to sixth-place winners now sharing in the purses, some contestants who are never headliners can make more than they could in workaday ranch jobs. And enjoy it a good deal more to boot! Some of them are persistent and dedicated athletes who have managed to break into rodeo professionalism without much, if any, outside backing. Far from being paid, they put up their entry fees to help create a show for which the public pays to see.

Since 1957, the rules have given new members in the RCA a better break. Now the permit system adopted by many rodeos allows a beginner to work until he has won a thousand dollars. This opens the sport to young men who may never have had ranch experience and have no other opportunity of learning on rodeo-quality livestock.

Although rodeo contestants are frequently injured, they minimize it. The biggest danger, and a big expense, they say, is getting there. I have been told the ones who make 40 or 50 percent of the top rodeos wear out an automobile every year, in addition to flying fifty to seventy-five thousand miles. Casey Tibbs and Gerald Roberts started flying to meet rodeo dates, but because neither of them could fly a tenth as well as they rode horses, they were in one emergency after another. Then they got another cowboy to do the piloting for them in return for his entry fees. However, he couldn't fly very well either, so, as Casey said, they were "In wrecks or lost most of the time."

All-Time Rodeo Greats

The Rodeo Reference Book lists the all-time greats of rodeo through the year 1970:

Most Consecutive All Around Championships .... Larry Mahan, 5
Most All Around Championships .... Jim Shoulders and Larry Mahan, 5
Most World Championships .... Jim Shoulders, 16
Most Total Money Won .... Bill Linderman, $443,013
Most Money Won One Year .... Larry Mahan, $57,726, 1969
Most Money Won One Rodeo .... Todd Whatley, $8,898, N. Y. Garden, 1947
Most Won in Single Event, One Year .... Dean Oliver, $38,118, CR, 1969
Most BB Championships .... tied—Eddy Akridge, Jim Shoulders, 4

Most CR Championships .... Dean Oliver, 8
Most SB Championships .... Casey Tibbs, 6
Most SW Championships .... Homer Pettigrew, 6
Most BR Championships .... Jim Shoulders, 7
Most TR Championships .... Jim Rodriguez, Jr., 4
Most SR Championships .... Everett Shaw, 6
Youngest World Champion .... Jim Rodriguez, Jr., at age 18, TR, 1959
Oldest World Champion .... Ike Rude, at age 59, SR, 1953

From 1929 through 1944, three men were All-Around Cowboy Champions for two years each: Everett Bowman, Clay Carr, and Louis Brooks. Since founding of the RCA those that have been All-Around Cowboy Champions for two years or more are: Jim Shoulders, Bill Linderman, Casey Tibbs, Harry Tompkins, Dean Oliver, and Larry Mahan. The last has held the title from 1966 through 1970.

The bill of fare at the best rodeos is now quite standardized. All have: bareback bronc riding, saddle bronc riding, steer wrestling, bull riding, calf roping, team roping, barrel racing, and clowns for entertainment who take great risks to divert the bulls and protect the bull riders.

Some rodeos have steer roping, wild horse races, and cutting horse contests, and all feature trick riders, cowboy bands, and popular movie or TV singers. And of course all have pickup men to gather in the bronc riders and clear the arena of loose stock. Aside from bull riding, all contests, including the daring riding required of the steer wrestler and his hazer, are based on ranch work skills. Perhaps the ranch skill that requires the closest of teamwork between the cowboy and his horse is roping.

Roping

Compared to AQHA registered roping, rodeo roping is simply more professional. The horse's performance is not judged by a man but by a clock. The roper is in a business partnership with a horse. Both have to do their job at the peak of their skill, or the partnership fails.

Ropers have been teamed up with Quarter Horses more than any other breed or type of horse, and if one is good at remembering names, it soon becomes evident that the great roping horses are rather closely related. Nearly all trace to the great Quarter Horse families. Long before the breed was founded, ranchers were on the lookout for the most efficient horses they could get for the necessary roping work that the cattle business required. Pride in their horses, as much as in their own skill with a rope, led to roping contests.

Steer Roping. Two ranches near Canadian, Texas, had worked up such rivalry that their best ropers were matched at a Cowboy Reunion in 1883. J. Ellison Carroll was the winner. His best time was one minute and two seconds, a time that was not so slow when one learns that the steer was given a head start of a hundred yards.

Twenty-four years later, in 1907, Carroll competed at San Antonio, Texas, against Clay McGonigal, whose skill with a rope and in training roping horses had made "McGonigal horses" of Old Billy breeding famous.

The steers were given a twenty-yard start, and Carroll roped, threw, and tied a steer in sixteen seconds and made an average of 22.5 seconds on ten steers. This record was to stand for a quarter of a century. It was not beaten until ropers who followed the rodeo circuit and kept in practice the year round came along. At a Cowboy Reunion at Stamford, Texas, when Carroll was seventy-two years old, he bettered the time of some cowboys who were less than half his age.

During the past forty years, Oklahomans have been outstanding in steer roping. Everett Shaw stands out as the most consistent winner of all steer ropers. He was Champion for six years—1945, 1946, 1948, 1951, 1959, 1962—and runner-up four times. For twenty years—a long span for an athlete—he was at the top or among the top five ropers.

Shoat Webster, also from Oklahoma, was Champion for four years—1949–50 and 1954–55—and was runner-up three times plus being among the top five for nine additional years.

Clark McEntire of Oklahoma was three times Champion, 1957, 1958, 1961, and was among the top five four other times.

Ike Rude of Oklahoma, also a Champion for three years—1941, 1947, 1953—was among the top five for three other years. John Bowman of Arizona was Champion in 1933, 1936; Tom Rhodes of Arizona in 1943, 1944; Don McLaughlin of Colorado in 1960, 1964. Many great ropers who won the championship for a single year made no attempt to travel to all the bigger rodeos.

Calf Roping. The fastest official time for roping and tying a calf was made in 1967 by Junior Garrison of Oklahoma (1970 Champion) in a rodeo at Evergreen, Colorado. His time was 7.5 seconds. Even with a few more seconds to work with each one is crowded with expert moves and decisions that must be made by both the roper and his horse from the moment they enter the box or chute to the moment the roper's arms are flung upward to signal the tie has been made.

Mr. Nimble Toes, owned by D. W. Graham of Saratoga, California, is an Honor Roll Steer Roping Horse, shown here an instant before bedding down a calf. *Courtesy* The Western Horseman.

When entering the box the rider turns his horse around to the right to face forward, to avoid snagging his ropes on anything. Two lariats are tied to the saddle horn in case the first throw misses and a second rope is used. The coils of the second rope are tucked into the support straps of the breast strap to keep them out of the way. Held between his teeth or tucked in his belt is the roper's piggin' string or tie rope. The horse is keyed up with slight rein and leg movements and well in hand in case he tries to hit the ribbon barrier before it flies open. The roper gives the signal that he is ready. The calf is released and the horse with a free head comes out after it with the speed of a racer leaving a starting gate. As the loop whirls over the roper's head, the horse dodges after the calf to put his man in good throwing position, and he does not check his speed when the loop is thrown, only doing so when he feels his rider going out of the saddle, the signal that the throw was successful. For a split second the perfect performance depends entirely on the horse. As the roper leaves the saddle to run to throw the calf, the horse plows to a stop and even steps back a step or two to tighten the rope, which has the good effect of shortening his man's run. Then he holds steady while the calf is wrapped up, and continues to stand quiet as his man returns to him and mounts and then waits to recoil his rope after it has been removed from the calf.

Calf roping was dominated by Oklahomans and Texans for twenty years. Although Everett Bowman of Arizona was Champion in 1929, 1935, and 1937, Clyde Burk of Oklahoma, who was killed while hazing a steer at Denver in 1944, took over as Champion in 1936, 1938, 1942, and 1944, and Toots Mansfield of Texas, who appeared to have wrapped up the top calf roping honors for all time, was Champion in 1939, 1940, 1941, 1943, 1945, 1948, and 1950. However, the boys with hungry loops were coming in from a wider range.

Royce Sewalt of Texas, a roper with a pullback pulley rigged to the horn of his saddle, to pull the reins back to stop his horse fast when he left the saddle, took the honors in 1946. Troy Fort of New Mexico snagged it twice—1947 and 1949. Then Don McLaughlin of Colorado took over top place for the longest consecutive winning streak up to that time—1951, 1952, 1953, 1954, and won another in 1957. Dean Oliver of Idaho had broken the sequence by winning the Championship in 1955. Ray Wharton took it in 1956. Then Dean Oliver won his second Championship in 1958, dropped out in 1959, when Jim Bob Altizer of Texas was Champion, but in 1960 he was back again swinging an accurate loop. And for five straight years Oliver was Champion. So the excitement in the Oliver camp was understandable when in 1969, after a lapse of four years, he wrapped up his eighth Championship. A remarkable record for any athlete.

Dean is not a ranch boy. He was born in Dodge City, Kansas, and his father was a pilot. Not until his late teens when the family was living in Nampa, Idaho, where he saw some fast calf roping in a rodeo, did he get interested in the sport. Then while working on a local farm he started practicing. The fact that he was quite outclassed in the first rodeos he entered didn't keep him from entering others and improving all the time. Dean Oliver is a credit to the Rodeo Cowboys' Association and the sport it represents. He neither smokes nor drinks, being a dedicated athlete. He is expert in many sports, particularly in skiing, and when confined to towns and cities he is a difficult man to beat at bowling. Wherever he is he tries to run at least a mile a day.

Dean Oliver. *Courtesy Rodeo Cowboys' Association.*

RIGHT:
Jerold Camarello of Oakdale, California, started roping when he was seven years old. He and his brother Leo—both still in their twenties—have forged to the top in both calf roping and team roping. *Courtesy Rodeo Cowboys' Association.*

Team Roping. This sport, also called team tying, is popular in the West and particularly in the Southwest, where men who can afford a hobby or can make a hobby pay its way take it up for relaxation and exercise in much the same way other, less active men take up golf. They do their practicing at jackpot roping sessions in the evenings and over weekends. Some teams are made up of executives and professional men of all kinds. At some big-time rodeos it may seem incongruous to the spectators to learn that the winning team ropers are not professional cowboys at all but some odd combinations like a banker and an architect or a doctor and an artist or a lawyer and a dentist.

The head roper is the number-one man on the team. He must come out fast and try for a quick catch so he can swing the steer around in good position for the heel roper. The instant the head roper is assured the heeler's loop has snagged a hind leg or two, he must leap from his saddle and run to tie the hind legs. The heeler tightens his line, stretches and throws the steer, and tries to sled him toward his running teammate, who slides in for the tie-up somewhat like a football tackle.

The stretching and holding of the steer is theoretically done by the heeler's horse. However, the head roper's horse, after being left riderless, too often does some pulling on his own instead of just keeping his rope taut. One of the most difficult things to teach a steer horse is to pull on his rope without overdoing it and dragging the steer. It is asking a lot of a race horse—and remember a roping horse comes out at top speed—to stop and hold quietly with no one on his back to remind him. Roping horses are overwhelmingly Quarter Horses.

Famous Roping Quarter Horses. Some roping horses are equally good at calf roping and steer roping, although the technique is different. After a calf has been downed the horse faces him and pulls back on the rope. When a steer is down there is more weight to pull against, so the horse faces away from him and pulls with the rope going back past his hind quarters.

Rodeo men, I have found, are pretty reliable when they tell about horses they admire. They are realists who would soon be out of business if they let their judgment of performing horses go soft. It is outside of tough competition that there are those who, when telling about their favorite steeds, get carried away. Fences somehow get higher and higher, speed accelerates, and the old pony shows such wisdom one wonders why he hasn't been elected to office. Of course we all know that the only way of stopping anybody—cowboy or park rider—from talking about his equine pride and joy is to decapitate him. However, in the horse world that is considered cruel, and besides they like to hear about good horses.

To mention only a few of the great roping horses that come to mind necessarily means leaving unmentioned hundreds of great or near-great ones. But here are some of the generally recognized stars.

BALDY tops most lists and he heads the one at the Cowboy's Hall of Fame in Oklahoma City. This bald-faced sorrel was foaled in 1932 on the ranch of John Dawson at Talala, Oklahoma. He traced to Cold Deck through his sire Red Buck by Red Man by Tubal Cain. Tubal Cain, it will be remembered, headed up the Blake Family of horses in eastern Oklahoma.

Baldy's dam was Babe Dawson by Little Earl, who traced to Printer I. Ronald Mason bought Baldy as a colt, had him gelded, and sold him as a three-year-old to Ike Rude, who had him working well as a steer roping horse before he was four years old.

William H. Porter, a horseman and roper of Tucson, Arizona, who has a wide acquaintance in rodeo circles and who rounded up a lot about ropers in his book called *13 Flat*, said that it was on the way from Winnipeg, Canada, to Burwell, Nebraska, that Baldy suffered a near-fatal accident. Either Ike or Junior Caldwell, who was with him, threw a cigarette butt out of the car window which landed in the loose hay in the trailer and started a fire. Before they could get Baldy out he was badly burned from his left foot up his leg and chest and the side of his neck and head. Only hope against hope that he wasn't as critically burned as he appeared to be kept Ike from shooting him to end his suffering. Hurrying on to Burwell, Ike found veterinarian Darell S. Trump, who had come from Utica, Nebraska, to see the rodeo and who after preliminary treatment agreed to undertake the job of saving Baldy. Only after weeks of intensive care was it certain that Baldy would make a satisfactory recovery, but when Ike came for him nine months later he found not only a well horse but one who seemed more full of energy than ever before. Although he was scarred for life, he was soon the most used, fastest, and brainiest horse on the rodeo circuit. Clyde Burk, who had twice been World Champion Calf Roper in the 1930s, became obsessed with becoming Baldy's owner, and he never saw Ike Rude without offering to buy the great performer. The ante kept going higher until in 1941 he offered $2500, a real tempting price, and Ike took it—and kicked himself ever afterward for doing it. Clyde made out all right with Baldy by winning two more World Championships on him. After Clyde's tragic death—as previously mentioned, he was killed while hazing a steer in a rodeo in Denver in 1944—Troy Fort of New Mexico purchased Baldy from his good friend's widow. Baldy by this time was used to being ridden by only the very best ropers. If they weren't champions he'd teach them a thing or two, speed them up and make champions of them, or so some of the contestants said. At any rate Troy Fort was carried to two Calf Roping World Championships on Baldy, and at San Angelo he helped Troy wrap up a calf in 10.6 seconds. Baldy was such a fast stopper he threw several riders as hard as he did the calves. He was a good-natured horse but in the arena he was all business, and says William Porter, if a roper missed a throw and had to go for his second rope, Baldy would show his annoyance by putting on twice the speed and stopping twice as hard to make up for lost time. He died of a heart attack at Troy Fort's place and is buried at the Jake McClure Rodeo Arena at Lovington, New Mexico.

BARTENDER, who carried many noted ropers to the pay window, was another of Clyde Burk's roping horses.

OLD TOM, a little dun Quarter Horse gelding only thirteen hands high, was ridden to five consecutive American Junior Rodeo Association All-

Around World titles by Barry Burk, a nephew of Clyde's. The horse was given to Barry when he was ten years old by Phil Williams of Texas, who gained fame with his champion cutting horse Skeeter.

POPCORN, a big bay gelding, was the favorite roping horse of Shoat Webster of Oklahoma, who was Champion Steer Roper four times.

PAT was made famous by John Rhodes (Mr. Heeler of Arizona), the Champion Team Roper. Many noted ropers, including Jiggs Burk, a brother of Clyde Burk, Cliff Whatley of Arizona, and Zeano Farris of New Mexico, rode him.

NICKELS, a blaze-faced sorrel, was foaled at Ronald Mason's famous Cross J Ranch at Nowata, Oklahoma. His sire was Oklahoma Star P-6, and his dam was Pretty Lady by Red Buck by Buck Thomas. He became the roping horse of Chalk Dyers, whose rodeo career spanned thirty years. Nickels' self-control is mentioned in the chapter on training.

BULLET was one of the greats in the early days of rodeo. He was trained by Bob Crosby and ridden by such notables as Ike Rude, Everett Shaw, John Bowman, and King Merritt. He was by Jack McCue.

NIGGER was one of Don McLauglin's favorite rope horses. He was bred by Hal Cooper of Woodward, Oklahoma. In 1959 he assisted Don in making the incredible record of tying down eleven steers in an average time of seventeen seconds each.

COLONEL CLYDE was a half brother of Clabber. He was a beautiful horse from the throat latch back, but his head was big and plain, typical of his sire's—My Texas Dandy—stock. Bred by Ab Nichols of Arizona, he was sold in 1938 to John Bowman, who made him famous in rodeo. He was a quadruple threat horse, being one of the rare ones who were equally good at calf roping, steer roping, team roping, and still more surprising bulldogging, because in the latter the horse must keep running after his rider leaves the saddle, whereas a roping horse must stop. He was so good that Homer Pettigrew, the cowboy who won more World Championships in steer wrestling than any other, often rode him in the event.

DECORATION was another arena horse made famous by John Bowman. He was by Bowman's horse Colonel Clyde, just mentioned. He was versatile like his dad and even added another event to his repertoire by becoming a cutting horse. In 1945 John Bowman won All-Around Cowboy title on him at the Pendleton Roundup.

HAZEL EYES carried Hugh Bennett to his first calf roping Championship.

SILVER and LEGS were the two horses that put Jake McClure so often in the money.

HONEY BOY was by Cotton Eyed Joe, and raised by George Clegg. He carried Toots Mansfield, next to the greatest calf roper to date, to many of his World Championships. Jake McClure won his 1930 Calf Roping Championship on him. His last owner was Juan Salinas of New Mexico.

ROAMER was one of the horses ridden by the early-day roper J. Ellison Carroll.

ROWDY was a Billy horse and was ridden by Clay McGonigal in many roping contests in the period before World War I.

MARK, by Red Cloud by Possum by Traveler, was foaled on the Burns Blanton Ranch in Arizona. Carl Arnold, a well-known Southwestern steer roper, got him to many rodeos, but he is known as well for having sired:

CARROT, a heavily muscled horse that was foaled in 1938. First he was raced, then trained as a roper. He was only fourteen hands high but was so fast, yet easily controlled, that he was a favorite with many of the best ropers in the Southwest.

DRIFTWOOD deserves to be on any list of rope horses no matter how brief. Anyone who rides in California or Arizona not only hears his name often but also has many horses of Driftwood breeding pointed out to him. Several I have seen are a beautiful seal color with faint dapples showing through the coat. Driftwood was made famous by Channing and Katy Peake of Rancho Jabali of Lompic, California. In 1940 they set out to breed rope horses that were second to none, and their search for the ideal sire ended two years later when at a rodeo in Payson, Arizona, they saw Driftwood in action. He had previously been raced and was known by the name of Speedy. In the arena he would do whatever he was asked to do and do it well—calf roping, steer roping, dogging, and when he was entered in a stock saddle cowhorse race down the length of the arena, he won it. For the Peakes he sired many exceptional arena horses.

One of them was:

POKER CHIP PEAKE, who was foaled in 1950. His dam was Sage Hen, whose dam was by Harmon Baker by Peter McCue. Poker Chip Peake, a beautiful dappled gray, has dark points. He was a favorite with the roping fraternity of Southern California and southern Arizona. Dale Smith, his last owner, got him to many of the top rodeos before retiring him.

SARGE (Sergeant Gill) is a big stout roping horse by My Texas Dandy Jr. by My Texas Dandy. Foaled on the Gill Cattle Ranch in Arizona in 1950, he was trained and roped on by Herb Doenz of Big Horn, Wyoming. When Bob Lytle of Santa Rita, Montana, rode him at Fort Worth in 1958, he started dickering for him. Bob got him in 1959 and ever since he and Sarge, one of the best stoppers in the business, have been a well-known roping team in the Northwestern states and Canada.

ROANIE is the smooth-working roping horse of Lee Farris of California, who has been among the nation's top ropers since 1963. Roanie traces to Possum, the famous son of Traveler, who was brought to Willcox, Arizona, in the 1920s by Jim Kennedy for matched quarter racing.

MICKEY and VERNON were good enough to be the rope horses of the all-time World's Champion Calf Roper, Dean Oliver. Friends of Dean say they are probably the best-cared-for horses that ever lived. Mickey had previously belonged to top contender Lee Cockrell and before that to Jack Saunders. The last I heard, Vernon had been sold to Herb Doenz.

Steer Wrestling

The steer wrestler has a helper, another mounted cowboy called a hazer. While they wait in separate but adjoining chutes their horses, like roping horses, must be all aquiver and rarin' to go. When the steer is released it must cross a designated score line before the flag is dropped. Then the elastic barrier before the horses is released and they come bursting out at top speed. Breaking a barrier adds a ten-second penalty.

The hazer tries to keep the steer running as straight as possible. The owner of each horse gets one-eighth of whatever is won in the contest and the hazer gets one-eighth.

A good steer wrestling horse, or dogging horse as it is sometimes called because the sport was originally called bulldogging, gets to the steer fast, and as his rider leaps from the saddle, he sweeps on by leaving the cowboy's feet swinging into the steer's path to slow him down. The horse continues to run to be out of the way. The steer wrestler reaches for the right horn while using his left hand and arm for additional leverage under the steer's jaw. The off-balance momentum plus the upturned head throws the steer. Running falls do not count. The steer must be on his feet before being wrestled down, and he must be flat on his side with all four legs extended before the flag comes down to signal official time.

In Canada the steer is not wrestled to the ground. The contestant leaps from his running horse onto the steer and places an elastic band on the animal's horn. The sport is called "steer decorating."

Bill Pickett, a part Negro and part Indian cowboy of great courage and skill, was the originator of the dangerous stunt. Zack Miller of the

Roy Duvall, with Jim Smith hazing, about ready to put the brakes on. *Courtesy Rodeo Cowboys' Association.*

101 Ranch Wild West Show of Oklahoma had seen Bill Pickett perform the act once and hired him on the spot for his forthcoming show scheduled for June 11, 1905, in Ponca City, Oklahoma. The show was attended by an immense crowd, including many people from all over the country who had come to nearby Guthrie, Oklahoma, for the National Editorial Association convention. Bill's daredevil exhibition was the talk of the show. He leaped from the saddle at breakneck speed, throwing his weight over the running steer's neck. Instantly he fastened his teeth in the side of the steer's mouth which drew his head down and had his horns plowing the ground before he halted and flipped over. The fact that he used his teeth as much as his arms was the source of the term bulldogging.

Pickett got a standing ovation. The 101 Ranch Wild West Show gained invaluable publicity—with a bunch of editors on hand it was a natural—and was launched on a world tour with Bill Pickett a headlined star.

In 1908 in Mexico, Zack Miller's show was playing to meager crowds and losing about a thousand dollars a day when, to create publicity, Miller bet five thousand dollars plus the gate receipts, which came to forty-eight thousand dollars that day, that Bill could hang on to Chiquito Frijole, a particularly vicious fighting bull, for five minutes.

Bill hung on for six and a half minutes, but he got his favorite horse Spradley gored and himself battered against the barrier. Several ribs were broken, and Bill had to be rescued by Miller and show friends from the enraged ruffians who had bet on the bull.

Bill Burchardt, who has done exhaustive research on many Oklahoma characters, including Bill Pickett, told in an article in *Oklahoma Today's* 1967 autumn issue how an old Mexican assisted the weeping Bill Pickett, who was kneeling by his downed horse Spradley. The horse seemed on the point of expiring from shock and loss of blood from the horn wounds in his haunches. The old Mexican started peeling red bananas—not yellow—and thrust them deep in the gore wounds. Within minutes the horse stopped quivering with pain, and it is said that the wounds healed without swelling.

Bill Pickett went on bulldogging for years. He was past seventy when, in 1932, he corral-roped a snorty bronc and was knocked down by a fighting forefoot as he walked up the rope to fix a war bridle on the animal. He is buried on the 101 Ranch. Zack Miller, who spoke at his funeral, said he was the best cowboy the ranch ever had. And he recited a poem he had composed in Bill Pickett's honor.

Bill Pickett. This drawing was made from an old photo supplied by Bill Burchardt, editor of *Oklahoma Today* magazine.

To place him above all the 101 cowboys was a large tribute when one recalls that among them was Milt Hinkle, the irrepressible cowboy who was a daredevil at whatever he tried, including a movie stunt leaping out of a low-flying airplane onto a big running bull. It killed the bull, and put Hinkle on crutches for life. But it didn't dampen his spirits. He was pushing ninety and promoting small-time rodeos when I last heard of him. And then there was Guy Shultz, three times World Champion Rodeo contestant in the early 1920s, and the only cowboy to bulldog a buffalo. After his rodeoing days he raised and trained race horses.

The all-time record holder in steer wrestling is Homer Pettigrew of Texas. He was World Champion six times in the 1940s. He was All-Around Cowboy Champion in 1941, earning extra points in calf and steer roping. James Bynum of Texas was Champion four times—1954, 1958, 1961, 1963. Harley May of California is notable in that he was Champion in 1952 and after a lapse of thirteen years came back to become Champion in 1965. Since then, the top place has alternated between Jack Roddy of California, 1966, 1968, and Roy Duvall of Oklahoma, 1967, 1969. Both are big men. Jack Roddy is 6'5" and Roy Duvall is 6'2". Close behind for the Championship—breathing down their necks, so to speak—are Billy Hale of Oklahoma, John Jones of California, and Jim Houston of Nebraska.

My friend the late Mike Hastings, World's Champion Steer Wrestler in 1928, was the owner of a roan gelding out of a Joe Bailey (of Weatherford, Texas) mare who became as well known as his owner.

In his book *The Quarter Horse* published in 1950, Robert Denhardt wrote: "Speaking of dogging horses, Stranger, Mike Hastings' red roan is generally considered the greatest that ever lived." This opinion was strengthened in 1969 when a poll of ex-rodeo contestants voted, via the Cowboy Hall of Fame, that Baldy, Ike Rude's roping horse, and Stranger, Mike's bulldogging horse, were the greatest rodeo horses they ever rode. In one year in the 1930s, ninety-two contestants rode Stranger in steer wrestling contests. Ninety of them won first place, and the other two were in second place. With all his fire and eagerness to go, Stranger had the Quarter Horse levelheadness to a marked degree. Seldom did he break a barrier. Mike was a perfectionist in training horses—and people. Many young riders who got beyond the initial barrier of his laconic, brusk directness became, under his coaching, excellent riders. Harry Tompkins is a good example. With some pointers from Mike, Harry, who was learning to ride at a dude ranch, developed so rapidly that within

Mike Hastings and his famous horse Stranger, bulldogging in 1930. The hazer is unidentified. Photo by R. R. Doubleday. *Courtesy Estelle Gilbert.*

two years he was on his way to becoming the second ranking bull rider in rodeo.

Estelle Gilbert, a city girl whom Mike put on a horse for the first time, became an excellent rider. After Mike's death in 1966 she cared for his last arena horse, Domino, a Quarter Horse with whom she won many barrel races in the New York area before old age put him down. My daughter Sidney had the opportunity occasionally to ride Mike's second-best horse Dog, a blood bay Quarter Horse who, although he was a winner of several quarter-mile races, was beautifully mannered and worked quietly on a slack rein.

No attempt is being made to mention all the great bulldogging horses by any means, but Coon Dog, a horse raised by George Clegg of Texas, comes to mind as being one of the good ones in the 1930s.

Lightfoot was Hugh Bennett's best. But the one that ranks along with Stranger is Baby Doll, raised by H. M. Bostick of Otaka, Oklahoma.

She was by Oklahoma Star Jr. P-598 by Oklahoma Star P-6. First sold to Bill Odom, who trained her, she was then sold to Willard Combs in 1955. Willard was a seasoned rodeo hand who, with Baby Doll's help, won the 1957 Steer Wrestling Championship. Every steer wrestler down to fifth place also rode her that year. And that same year in thirty-eight rodeos, Baby Doll carried twenty-seven riders to first place. In one night at Madison Square Garden, contestants won $8,112 with her professional assistance. From 1955 to the time of her untimely death of a ruptured intestine in 1960, she placed her riders in just the right position to drop on their steers to win $360,000.

Cutting Horse Contests

It is generally agreed that the first cutting horse contest with a record of money having been posted took place in 1898 when Sam Graves rode Old Hub, a twenty-two-year-old gelding, about to be retired, at a Cowboy Reunion at Haskell, Texas, and won first money of $150.

Cutting cattle from one herd and segregating them in another called the cut is still, despite modern pens, chutes, and gates, a necessary ranch chore that requires a top hand and a well-schooled horse if the job is to be done without running the fat off the stock. But by far the greater number of highly trained cutting horses today see their action in training arenas and in NCHA (National Cutting Horse Association) contests rather than on cattle ranches. (For training and performance of the cutting horse see Chapter 12.)

Aside from race horses, cutting horses earn more money for their owners than any other horse specialist. At present one of the most important and lucrative events is the NCHA Futurity. It is limited to three-year-olds who are making their debut performance. A talented young cutter can win as much as five thousand dollars for two and one half minutes of fast footwork. The 1969 NCHA Futurity was held in the Will Rogers Memorial Coliseum at Fort Worth, Texas, where 257 entries competed for $106,737, the highest purse to that date. The winner Cee Bars Joan, ridden by Matlock Rose, won $15,723 for the Burnett Estates, her owners.

The nonprofessional futurity attracted twenty-nine entries who had a $4,000 purse to shoot at. Chickasha Bingo, owned and ridden by Dr. Allen Hamilton, took the top money. Carol Rose, the wife of trainer-rider Matlock Rose, won title of World's Champion Nonprofessional Cutting Horse rider for two years in a row.

Another show of national importance is the NCHA World's Champion Cutting Horse Finals, which has been held since 1949 and is now held each November in Las Vegas, Nevada. The location indicates what appeal this top event has for the sporting world. The NCHA Tournament of Champions, started in 1958, is held in conjunction with the AQHA annual convention in a different city each year.

In a show with both AQHA registered Cutting and Open Cutting contests, only the points won in the registered Cutting will be awarded. But if a Quarter Horse wins points in an open Cutting contest or a National Cutting Horse Association or Canadian Cutting Horse Association contest, in a show that is approved by the AQHA in which no Registered Cutting class is held, the points will be awarded.

For the quality of the Cutting performance see Chapter 12 on Training the Cutting Horse.

For rules and regulations write:

National Cutting Horse Association
P.O. Box 12155, Fort Worth, Texas 76116
or
Canadian Cutting Horse Association
10123 112th Street,
Edmonton, Alberta, Canada

The National Cutting Horse Association was founded in 1946 and was a hundred percent Texas sport when in the beginning Ray Smith, Volney Hildreth, George Glasscock, Hughie Long, Robert M. Corbett, Alex Fambro, Lloyd Jinkens, Tom B. Saunders, Phillip Williams, Ray and A. D. Edsall, and one or two other Texans I may have missed organized the NCHA and stuck with it until it was well on its feet.

In the early 1950s Marion Flynt began attending some local cutting contests near his home town of Midland, Texas, with his horse Tumbler, who, he admitted, was a devil to ride. Then when his filly by Silver Wimpy, whom he named Marion's Girl, began to show great promise under the tutelage of Buster Welch, Flynt's enthusiasm grew and he became such an active member that he was handed the reins in 1956 and ever since then has been president of the association. His devoted work in furthering the interests and building up the strength of the NCHA has earned him the sobriquet of "Mr. Cutting Horse." Marion's Girl had lots of "cow" in her and loved to tell cattle where to go, and, said Buster Welch, she could read a cow's mind and tell long before the rider could what the next move was going to be.

In 1954–56 Marion's Girl was NCHA World's Champion Cutting Horse, the only mare to win the distinction twice.

Today there are many regional Cutting Horse Associations which work closely with the NCHA and the CCHA (the Canadian Cutting Horse Association).

There are over seven hundred NCHA-sponsored Open Cutting Horse events each year, in addition to which the NCHA now sponsors Youth Cutting Horse Contests. Girls score in these events, as they do in so many other horse events, about as high as do boys. From the ranks of these youth riders will come the arbiters of shows and horsemanship that will prevail in the 1970s and 1980s. Hopefully it will be an era of naturalism to offset the artificiality that seems to be endemic in every kind of show business.

Sad to relate, its evils also reach out and touch the cutting horse. In a brochure sent out by the NCHA, the opinions of many prominent owners, riders, and judges of cutting horses were well summarized in a letter which states, ". . . we have lost sight of the true cutting horse. Judges who are not able to recognize one have been officiating at many different shows. Contestants have developed imitation cutting horses [that are] marked better than . . . true cow horses with natural ability, who move with their heads low, and never make unnecessary steps to cut a cow or block her return to the herd. A horse that thinks for himself, and rates cattle, and makes the move on his own, and not because he has been spurred to such an extent that a slight movement of the rider causes him to jump sideways, whether the cow moves or not. Then comes the crowning blow to our event. Some riders even train their horse in the dance or act (to be performed) in front of thousands of people [by] spurring and jerking, dancing and spinning the horse, prior to the beginning of his work. Consequently, when the horse gets in and cuts a cow out, he is still dancing and jumping to get away from the previous punishment he has just received from the rider. Let's go back to marking our cow horses and not circus horses."

Some years ago when I stopped by the Bill Gaynier Ranch east of Denton, Texas, I met J. D. Tadlock, who was then managing it and training some cutting horses. He made the point that only those who have worked cattle on a ranch realize the big difference between a ranch cutting horse and the contest cutting horse. In actual ranch cutting, neither the rider nor the horse could stand up for very long to the choppy, bouncy, extremely showy action required of the contest-winning cutting horse by so many of today's judges. A man-made horse, in his opinion, can seldom be ridden successfully by more than one or two riders. Whereas the horse with cow sense will perform well with most any expert rider.

On a swiftly dodging, showy horse, it is mighty difficult for the spectators or even the judges to see whether the flick of a finger on the reins rated the horse or not. Obviously the rider can't take hold of the horse, but if done subtly, the message can reach the bit shank with definite meaning, causing a horse to appear to be doing his own thinking. Recently I was pleased to read that J.D's Hanky Pinky, which is co-owned by Tadlock and Phil Williams, took second money in the semifinals jackpot at the NCHA finals in 1969.

Cutting horse contests are no longer a Texas or even an exclusively Western sport. Contests and exhibitions are now to be seen not only all over this country but also in Canada and Mexico and even in Arabia. England, too, has a sprinkling of cutting horses. In 1964, sixteen members of the Canadian Cutting Horse Association toured England with seven cutting horses for three months. While there, they gave sixty performances. At Stoneleigh, England, seventy thousand spectators passed through the turnstiles. On the polo field just below Windsor Castle, the Queen, Prince Philip, dukes and duchesses, and the Queen Mother expressed pleasure with a horse performance which was so novel to them. The Queen Mother was photographed with the riders, and the young fry, raised on U.S. Westerns, never failed to ask the riders, "Where are your guns?"

In 1968, seven of the top twenty cutting horses in the United States were owned east of the Mississippi River, the farthest east being Hollywood Ollie, owned by Mrs. A. S. Kelly of Chester, Vermont. In 1969, the World Champion, Jose Uno, was owned by John Bradford of Alabama, who has since moved to Tucson, Arizona.

Great Cutting Horses. Among the other all-time great cutting horses of the past twenty years, the names of Poco Lena, Skeeter, Snipper W, Booger Red (Hall of Fame Certificate No. 3), Snooky, Trinket Bennett, Senior George, Holey Sox, Peppy San, Royal Chess, Cutter Bill, and Chicasha Dan are bound to be long remembered.

Poco Lena by Poco Bueno won more cutting horse awards than any other horse, and was the only mare ever to be NCHA World's Champion twice. She was Reserve World's Champion four times.

Poco Lena was bred on the Waggoner Three D Ranch in Texas

Poco Lena with B. A. Skipper, Jr., riding. *Photo by Charlie Ray. Courtesy NCHA.*

and given to Glen Turpin, who started her training. Don Dodge, who has owned, trained, and ridden as many top cutting horses as any man in the business, bought her when she was three years old. He then had her on the circuit for eleven years, where she placed in 395 contests and won $99,782. She holds the Hall of Fame Certificate No. 1.

HOLEY SOX by Leo, an AA runner, was among the top ten NCHA and Registered Cutting Horses in 1963 and would most certainly have gone on to more fame had not a cataract caused him to lose the sight in his left eye. He is a horse of keen intelligence who loved to work cattle. Owned by Woody Searle of Vernal, Utah, and trained for cutting by Jim Lee, he was then leased to B. A. (Barney) Skipper, Jr., who campaigned him and Poco Lena in the nation's top cutting contests.

While piloting his plane back to Texas, the plane crashed and Barney was killed. During the confusion of hunting for the plane wreck—it had gone down in isolated country—Holey Sox and Poco Lena, who had been trailered back home, were left standing in the trailer for four days. Luckily there were no lasting ill effects.

Once Holey Sox demonstrated the true Quarter Horse agility in cutting by making such a fast sideways move during training that his rider-trainer Jim Lee had his hip thrown out of joint. Lee could not move without intense pain and could not get off the horse. Then Holey Sox demonstrated another Quarter Horse quality by doing something that no other type of hot-blood stallion would be likely to do; although he was excited and in a corral near which five other stallions and a mare were tied, he stood perfectly still and waited for over a half hour before someone came along to help Lee out of the saddle.

A somewhat similar accident gave a stallion belonging to the Burk family—friends of mine who raise Quarter Horses near Brandon, Vermont—a chance to show his remarkable self-control and good sense. Janice Burk was riding him through a gate into pasture when one of

Holey Sox, ridden by Rhett Searle, son of the owner, Woodey B. Searle, of Vernal, Utah. In the summer of 1970 a son of Holey Sox, called Mr. Holey Sox, was number two in the nation in cutting. *Photo by Charlie Ray. Courtesy Woodey Searle.*

the mares in the pasture kicked out at the stallion but missed him and hit her, breaking her leg above the knee. The young stallion remained quiet when she fell from the saddle with a bleeding compound fracture, and by doing so most certainly saved her life. The horse was still standing close in a protective posture when her husband found her lying unconscious on the ground. This story has a happy ending. Months later, shortly after the cast was removed, Janice was back in the saddle.

PEPPY SAN by Leo San by Leo, the nation's top cutting horse of 1967, is like the majority of horses of Leo breeding. He has a willing and amiable disposition. At the time of his championship he was owned by G. B. Howell and ridden by Matlock Rose, who was also his trainer.

MARION'S GIRL, also of Leo breeding, showed her dependability in the Cow Palace in San Francisco when her trainer and rider Buster Welch received an eye injury just before entering the ring for the finals in a cutting contest. He said, "It was too late to do anything about it . . . I could scarcely tell light from dark when we moved into the herd. Marion's Girl selected a cow from the herd—a rank one as it turned out—and worked by herself and did an outstanding job."

CUTTER BILL is the only horse I know of who ever got the kids out of school. After he won the World's Champion Cutting title in 1962, the Mayor of Crockett, Texas, his home town, proclaimed "Cutter Bill Day." School was closed and the longest parade the town had ever seen was led down Main Street by none other than Cutter Bill himself, with his owner Rex Cauble aboard. He was trained by Willis Burnett. His first important win came in 1959 when he became Champion Junior Registered Cutting Horse. Through his sire Buddy Dexter, this golden Palomino stallion traced to Peter McCue, and through his dam to both Traveler and Lock's Rondo. He was bred on the ranch of R. L. Underwood near Wichita Falls, Texas.

Since Wimpy, the number-one foundation sire of the breed, has been mentioned so many times, it may be of interest to know that his final home was at Rex Cauble's luxurious horse establishment, along with Cutter Bill and other horses of note.

Bronc Riding

Bronc riding is an event that calls for extremely precise timing that can only be learned by doing it. Amazingly rapid reflex actions and

Cutter Bill with owner Rex Cauble up. *Photo by Dalco Film Company, Inc., Irving, Texas.*

Major King, one of the great cutting horse sires. *Courtesy Millie Leonard.*

Dirt-plowing action photos seldom show the beautiful conformation and natural stance of the cutting horse. This quiet pose shows the handsome King Skeet with onetime owner and trainer Carrol Lemons, of Mesa, Arizona. He was National Cutting Horse Champion in 1970. *Courtesy Carrol Lemons.*

coolheadedness are more of a requirement than unusual strength. If one loses the rhythm of the pitching action and cannot sense the direction or tempo of the next jump, as I know from experience, something snaps off like a broken current in the brain, and one knows he's a goner. A good rider is an astute observer of bucking stock, judging what he will try with this or that horse and what he will try to avoid. Saddle bronc riding is an actual ranch skill that most riders of ranch horses have performed more or less successfully at one time or another. Whereas bareback bronc riding and bull riding are strictly for arena contests and have very little tie-in with ranch skills. In the early-day bronc riding exhibitions, the idea was to ride the horse until he gave up and quit bucking. It was a direct way of breaking a range horse. As a small boy I saw a great-grandson of Kit Carson ride a bucking horse to a standstill at Alamosa, Colorado. I cannot remember how long it took or other details, but I do remember Carson's fancy beaded buckskin vest being whipped through the air by the violent motion.

I have heard some riders who have competed in both bareback and saddle bronc riding say that the hand grip on the rigging in bareback riding makes a big difference and that they would rate it somewhat below saddle riding in the skill required. But I'm sure opinions vary.

In both events the names of the bucking horses for each go-around are put in a hat and drawn by the riders. The best riders want the hardest bucking horses—or at least the ones that appear to be frantic buckers—so that they can put on a good performance that will score high.

Saddle Bronc Riding. The saddle used for this event must be an Association-approved bronc tree with swells fourteen inches wide and no more than nine inches high. The gullet is five and three-quarter inches wide and the cantle five inches high with a maximum width of fourteen inches. Saddles are center fire with low D-rings, and the stirrup leathers come down almost in line with the swells of the saddle. Many of these saddles have no horn or have had the horn cut off. The stirrups are rounded—the oxbow type—in which the rider's boot is all the way home against the heel.

Spurs are short shanked with dull rowels and have tie-down straps to keep them in place. Chaps are snug around the thighs. They are worn for protection from bumps and scrapes in the chute as well as for show.

The bronc in the chute wears a halter with a braided lead rope called a buck rein with which the handlers control him as he is being saddled. The bronc rider climbs to the top of the chute and eases himself down into the saddle on which the stirrups have already been adjusted to the length he wants. Sometimes the rank horse rears and fights in the chute, forcing the rider to scramble back up on the chute until the horse quiets down. When he does get set in the saddle he is handed the buck rein, which he holds about as high as his shoulder, knowing that it will be pulled down lower when the horse gets his head down to buck. A rein held too short might jerk him forward out of the saddle. Just before he calls for the chute to be opened, the flank or bucking strap is pulled up snug. When the horse leaps from the chute, the rider must have his spurs over the shoulder points. It is called starting the horse. On the next few jumps the rider's legs, if the ride is going to be successful, must get in rhythm, going forward of the shoulders as the horse kicks high behind and going back when the bronc jumps ahead. The free

Badger Mountain, an old-time noted bucker.

hand and arm act as a balancer and must keep fanning and never touch the horse or saddle.

The length of the ride is the choice of the stock contractor, who can make it either eight or ten seconds, based on the size of the arena. Following the buzzer sound which signals that the required number of seconds has passed, the rider can pull leather, that is, grasp the saddle or steady himself in any way he wants to, to put himself in good position to scramble off the horse and be helped by the pickup man.

Each year brings in a new crop of mettlesome bronc riders, but the business is one of close comradeships and enduring loyalties. And the names of the puissant twisters of yesteryear are often heard behind the chutes, in the contestant sections, and wherever cowboys gather.

Midnight.

During the period prior to 1945 and the founding of RCA, the great rider Pete Knight of Canada held the Saddle Bronc Riding Championship for four years, and Fritz Truan, Burel Mulkey, Earl Thode, Doff Aber, and Louis Brooks held it for two years each. In addition, Louis Brooks rode bulls. He was also Bareback Riding Champion for two years.

When I spent a day with Louis Brooks and his family in their gracious ranch home, the Bar-O-One, south of Sweetwater, Texas, several years ago, he showed me his fine Quarter Horse breeding stock—he then owned over a hundred—in well-planned stables and behind welded metal fences. But the successes and accomplishments of this soft-spoken and modest man I learned mostly from others.

Now a rancher with sixty-two thousand acres in Texas and Colorado

Larry Mahan on Hi Hopes. This remarkable rodeo rider of bulls as well as of horses has won the All-Around Cowboy Championship five times. *Courtesy Rodeo Cowboys' Association.*

to manage and a prominent Quarter Horse breeder as well as a bank director, Louis Brooks has come a long way from the time when, as a sixteen-year-old orphan in Oklahoma, he took a job driving feed wagons for a ranch outfit near Pawhuska, Oklahoma, for fifty cents a day. In addition, he milked cows—so early in the morning or late at night that he said it was two months before he knew what color they were. But somehow he found time to "cowboy" on Sunday and learn to ride broncs. He got so good at it that he was employed to break horses for Ronald Mason, the owner of Oklahoma Star, Beggar Boy, and other famous horses. By a fine quirk of fate, these same horses, along with Leo, another Oklahoma horse, were to father the foundation stock for the Brooks Quarter Horses, which in 1960 won more firsts in arena performances than any others. On his cutting horse Vandal, Louis won many trophies.

Louis's wife Nita (nee Boyd) was one of the sponsored "Ranch Girls" at the 1943 Rodeo in Madison Square Garden in New York, where Louis met her. An excellent rider, she once taught equitation at college. And it follows that the Brooks daughter Leigh and son Louis, Jr., are very much at home in the saddle. Louis, Jr.'s room, in fact, had in it several of his father's trophy saddles, arranged to sit on in place of chairs.

Regardless of the many spills Louis took when riding bucking stock, he said he never had a broken bone in his body. But his knees, he said, had been banged up many times in the chutes. He quit riding bulls, he explained, when an older rider convinced him that the different timing required wasn't helping his bronc riding.

Louis Brooks on Amos, a famous bucking horse of the 1940s. Photo by J. Homer Venters, Sun City, Kansas. *Courtesy Louis Brooks, Jr.*

Bill Smith on Faraway. *Courtesy Rodeo Cowboys' Association.*

Casey Tibbs, of South Dakota, World Champion Saddle Bronc Rider for six years, 1949, 1951, 1952, 1953, 1954, and 1959, must be rated the best and most consistent Saddle Bronc Rider the arena has known. He was also bareback Champion in 1951.

Bill Linderman of Montana and Deb Copenhaver of Idaho were Champion Saddle Bronc Riders for two years each. Marty Wood of Canada (now Missouri) and Shawn Davis of Montana each held the World's Championship for Saddle Bronc Riding for three years, although neither held it consecutively. Bill Smith of Wyoming was Champion in 1969, and Dennis Reiners of Clara City, Minnesota, took the honors in this sport in 1970.

Bareback Bronc Riding is subject to the same rules and scoring as saddle bronc riding, except the ride is for eight seconds, and in place

Gary Tucker on Cannonball. *Courtesy Rodeo Cowboys' Association.*

of a saddle the bareback ride is made with a surcingle rigging with a leather handhold to which the rider clings with one hand while the other hand and arm swing free for balance. Spurs are short shanked with dull rowels. Chaps are optional. Scoring ranges from one to twenty-five on the rider's action and one to twenty-five on the horse's action with four judges turning in score cards. The four cards are totaled for the score.

In the 1950s Jim Shoulders, the great bull rider, was also a Champion Bareback Rider, holding the top place for four years. Eddy Akridge was Champion for three years and Casey Tibbs, Harry Thompkins, and Jack Buschbon rounded out the decade by holding the championship one year each. Akridge and Buschbon started off the 1970s by each gaining another Championship. Ralph Buell, John Hawkins, and Paul Mayo each held the Championship for a year, and Jim Houston and

Clyde Vamvoras each held it for two years with Larry Mahan winning the Championship in 1969 and 1970.

The Broncs. Strangely, the meanest, most cantankerous of horses, the rodeo buckers, get the best care and live *la doce vita,* being worked about ten minutes a year. Contrary to the often expressed opinion of people who have never been closer to a bucking horse than the first-row arena seats, the bucking straps used on the horses do not hurt them. The strap induces bucking, yes, but only because the horse does not like to have anything strapped close to his flanks. The blunt spur rowels roll over the hide but do not dig in to hurt the bucker. Nor does his mouth get jerked and hurt as happens to so many horses. The only head restraint is a loose halter. The life the bucking horses lead must be a satisfactory one, because many of them stay at the peak of their performance until they are twenty-five to thirty years old.

As mentioned in Chapter 2 it is from the Northwestern horses, so often chunks, that the short-fused obstreperous broncs are recruited. They are the product of cross-breeding horses that carry Thoroughbred, Morgan, Quarter Horse, Percheron, and mustang blood. This wild mixture of genes has made the top performers in one of the world's roughest sports. Only a few of the headliners can be singled out for mention.

MIDNIGHT was bred and broken to the saddle by Jim McNab, a Canadian range rider and mange inspector. The first few times he was ridden, McNab related, he was easy to handle and didn't try to buck, but one day when a friend cranked up an old Ford car it spooked Midnight and he pitched like a fiend. After that McNab never knew when he started out on the big black gelding whether he'd get where he was headed for or get bucked off. The horse had become absolutely unpredictable. When Jim McNab finally sold him as a rodeo bronco, Midnight quickly made a name for himself by tossing some of the most famous riders in the rodeo world. Midnight died in 1937. A marble monument marks his grave at the Cowboy Hall of Fame in Oklahoma City.

FIVE MINUTES TO MIDNIGHT, his popular successor, is mentioned in a newspaper clipping datelined Cheyenne, Wyoming, August 1, 1937. "The twisting, sunfishing, Five Minutes to Midnight dumped Burrel Mulkey right in front of the grandstand in just 8 seconds last night, to the cheers of 15,000 spectators, and emerged unridden in Cheyenne's

Annual Frontier Days Festival." It is pretty tough going when the horse instead of the rider gets the cheers.

BADGER MOUNTAIN, another Northwestern bronc that made good, is well remembered by men who were catapulted by his tremendous lunging take-offs that pointed him like an arrow toward the sky. At the Pendleton, Oregon, Roundup in 1944 he threw his three hundredth bronc rider. Only five men had ever stayed with him for the full ten seconds.

MISS KLAMATH was the first mare to join the rodeo bucking stock. Previously only geldings had been used. From 1951 to 1955 she was ridden but once and that was by Bill Ward, who was raised in Miss Klamath's own home range in Oregon.

It was Casey Tibbs, six times Saddle Bronc Riding Champion between 1949 and 1959, who I believe ramrodded the idea of awarding the title Bucking Horse of the Year through the policy-making bunch at the RCA.

WAR PAINT, a bay and white gelding from the Klamath Indian Reservation, owned by Christensen Brothers, was the first to receive the title in 1956. He earned it again in 1957 and shared the honors in 1958 with:

JOKER, a rampageous package owned by Harry Knight of Fowler, Colorado.

TRAIL'S END, at first called Dexter, was the next bronc to hold the title, which he did for three years running. I heard or read someplace that Dexter threw a ranch hand so high his Montana owner got tired waiting for the fellow to come down and gave Dexter away. For a while it seems Dexter allowed a five-year-old Indian boy to ride him, but no one else. When he became a pro with the Oral Zumwalt bucking stock, he was not a difficult horse to ride, but after a winter in pasture, he came on strong in 1959 with new determination and zest for the game. At Denver he threw Casey Tibbs in four seconds flat. Tibbs called his bucking "sensational."

BIG JOHN and JAKE are two great buckers that have won the top honors since that time. They are owned by Harry Knight of Fowler, Colorado.

WANDA DEE, a big 1300-pound Palomino, was another mare to come along to hold the spotlight.

DESCENT, who is going strong in the seventies, is another explosive Palomino who weighs close to 1300 pounds. This big gelding is owned by Beutler Brothers, Vald, and Cervi, a rodeo stock-owning combine. Descent is a Thoroughbred-Morgan cross, who traces, it is claimed, to Man O' War.

The very names of the bucking stock, when blared out of the loudspeakers, carried excitement, and I've corraled some of them in the following verses:

THE BUCKING STOCK

There's a folk-song surge to the bucker's names
From Midnight down to Dangerous Dan
And blinding falls in the toughest of games
Hammer home memories of Ole Flight Plan,
Bear Cat, Trail's End and Alacran

Ten seconds aged 'em on Turpentined Cat
Raking with spurs hobbled down on the boots
Stirring for busters more names in the hat—
Badger Mountain and other kings of the brutes
That jarred 'em loose as they lunged from the chutes

Satan's Pard, Jake, and Screaming Eight
Still more names in the old go-around
War Paint pounds at the white chute gate
Hell's Angel and Steamboat shake the ground
While nerves hang on till the buzzer's sound

Round in the buster's head they go
China Doll, High Boy, Golden Lock,
Widow Maker, Rattler, Copper Joe,
Bottoms Up, Eight Ball, old White Sock
The show-bill names of the buckin' stock.

Bull Riding

Tightly strapped spurs, a glove, and chaps—the last are optional—and a lot of experience are the only equipment needed to put a bull rider in business. Riding bareback on a cross-bred Brahma bull that might weigh close to a ton, he grasps the end of the flat braided manila rope surcingle rigging and wraps it about his hand clockwise to give a firm grip. If wrapped counterclockwise he could get so hung up he couldn't let loose.

Doug Brown on Snuffy. *Courtesy Rodeo Cowboys' Association.*

Getting set on the bull's back in the chutes is tricky business where the bulls sometimes throw their weight around, particularly when the bucking strap, often with a bell on it, is pulled tight. And when they come bounding out of the chute, only riders with precision reflexes and a lot of bull savvy can ride out the animal's savage plunges and gyrations and still be aboard when the eight-second buzzer sounds. Touching the bull with the free hand draws a penalty. Spurring does not rate so high in bull riding as in bronc riding because the beasts twist and spin more than horses, making any uniform leg movements completely unpredictable.

Even after a successful ride there is still the problem of getting off and away before the bull can attack. Few can keep their feet when they let loose of the surcingle and hit the ground, although I have seen exceptional athletes swing a leg over and land on their feet and walk away with all the nonchalance of one who had just stepped off a lunch counter stool.

Bull riding is a sheer, desperate sport—or business if you prefer. It has nothing to do with necessary ranch work. It is as pointless to rationalize as mountain climbing. "Why do you ride them?" Jim Shoulders, the most successful bull rider to date, was asked. "How else could a green old country boy with just a high-school education get his hands on this sort of money?" was Jim's frank counterquestion. From the age of nineteen to thirty-two Jim averaged thirty thousand dollars per year with fifty thousand dollars being his peak year. What his expenses amounted to is anybody's guess. Certainly his doctor and hospital bills were a big item. My friend Bill Burchardt, well-known author and editor of *Oklahoma Today* magazine, asked Jim if he was ever seriously injured. Jim said, "Well, not seriously, but . . ." and Bill learned that he had only had two arms, two legs, two ankles, and two collarbones broken. Then Jim added, "But I do have to strap down a thigh muscle before I ride. It gets pulled pretty often." Bill remarked that the ASPCA looks after the rodeo stock mighty well, but nobody is around to prevent cruelty to cowboys.

Jim Shoulders was Bull Riding Champion seven times and runner-up three times. He is not the product of ranch training. His older brother Marvin, who started rodeoing as a young man, put Jim on his first bull at an amateur rodeo when Jim was thirteen years old. At the first lunge of the Brahma monster in the chute, Jim was scrambling to safety when Marvin shoved him back on the bull, saying, "All right, kid, if you want to rodeo, it's now or never." Jim's main interest today is a school for bull riders he and his wife Sharon conduct, and raising Brahma bulls for the arena at their place near Henryetta, Oklahoma. Big Bad John and Mighty Tornado, a 1725-pounder, are two of Jim's bulls that were seldom burdened when the eight-second buzzer sounded.

Harry Thompkins, another nonranch boy who was from New York State and now lives in Dublin, Texas, racked up five Championships between 1948 and 1960. Twice he was runner-up when Jim Shoulders took first place, and four times he came in third. His phenomenal balance and body control, it is said, enable him to walk a tightwire or ride a bull with equal grace.

The decade of the sixties has seen the unsinkable Freckles Brown, who at the age of forty-eight is still contending for the Bull Riding crown, and another Oklahoman, Bob Wegner, and George Paul and Bill Kornell of Texas, and Doug Brown of Oregon, became Champions for one year each.

Ronnie Rossen was Champion in 1961 and 1966 and runner-up in 1965. Larry Mahan, who was Champion in 1965 and 1967, moved into top place again in 1970.

Ronnie Rossen, raised in Colorado, rode his first bull at a high-school rodeo in Glover, Colorado. Then following a two-year hitch in the Marine Corps, he headed for rodeos with a gleam in his eye. The money he won during the next ten years helped him and his wife Wanda get started in business in Montana, where they raise Quarter Horses and Hereford cattle and are in the theater business as well.

Larry Mahan of Oregon has rapidly climbed to the top to take his place along with the rodeo greats. Besides being Champion Bull Rider and Champion Bareback Rider three times, he earned enough in the great number of rodeos he attended to make him All-Around Cowboy Champion for five years in a row, averaging over fifty thousand dollars per year—all before his twenty-seventh birthday.

The bulls used in the bull-riding event are cross-bred Brahmas capable of savage and sustained bucking. These large, powerful, loose-hided animals are the kind that have been used since the 1920s. Although many of them weigh more than 1500 pounds, they are amazingly fast on their feet. When a rider is thrown these belligerent bovines deliberately try to gore him with their thick blunt horns, and were it not for the quick and fearless action of the bull-baiting clowns, they would do so.

The Clowns deserve a great deal of credit for their assistance to the bull riders. I recall talking to George Mills and Jasbo Fulkerson, a great pair of clowns featured in many rodeos in the 1940s, about the risks they took. Jasbo was a "barrel man" and although his hard rubber barrel with him inside it was sent spinning by the horns and head of a charging bull innumerable times, he received few injuries. Both made light of their close calls in drawing off the bulls, but the riders say that when they part company, willingly or otherwise, from a raging bull they feel a whole lot safer knowing that a fearless bull deflector will be there at the critical moment.

After a lapse of almost thirty years, I was startled to see George Mills back in the arena in the 1970 Phoenix Rodeo, where he was injured, but fortunately not seriously, by a bull he drew away from a thrown rider.

J. D. Gaudin, the "Kajun Kid," and Buck Le Grand were noted rodeo clowns in the 1950s.

Three of the best-known clowns working today are William Plaugher, Wick Peth, and Jimmy Schumacher. Plaugher, a six-foot-three red-hatted clown who introduces a dozen animals, including several sizes of dogs, along with ducks, in his entr'acts, was a top competing cowboy who still holds the record for lap and tap dogging of 2.6 seconds. In this event the time starts when the horse laps the steer. That is, when, looking from the side, the horse's head passes the steer's rump. Many people recall seeing Plaugher in a featured role in Disney's movie *Run, Appaloosa, Run*.

Wick Peth is more strictly a bull-baiter and lifeguard for bull riders. He makes little attempt to be funny, although he dresses like a clown. He thrills the crowd by his hairbreadth escapes from the charging bulls during which he often reaches out and touches their horns as they flash past.

Jimmy Schumacher, a barrel man, is an Arizonan who has been in rodeo for over thirty years, either on or off bulls and broncs or out in front of the bulls giving them that come-hither look that distracts them from attacking downed riders with hoofs and horns. As with the others, it is surprising that Jim has had so few injuries.

Girls Rodeo Association

The GRA was formed in 1948 for the protection and benefit of professional contestants. There is no age limit. Little Ann Lewis was nine years old when she won the World's Barrel Racing title in 1968. Annual dues are twenty-five dollars. A nonmember may ride in a rodeo by paying ten dollars for a permit. She will be covered by GRA insurance the same as a member.

Members are not allowed to participate in amateur rodeos, but may enter RCA, college, and high-school rodeos, horse shows, and National Cutting Horse contests. After a permit holder wins two hundred dollars, she is obliged to join the GRA. There are now about three hundred girls throughout the United States who are active members.

Each year the fifteen members who have won the most money are eligible for the GRA National Finals. The events are the same as in RCA rodeos with the exception of steer wrestling. In this event, the Canadian custom of decorating the steer's horn with an elastic band is reversed, and called "steer undecorating." It takes the place of wrestling the steer to the ground. Barrel racing, which became popular in Texas in the early twenties, is now the favorite event of the majority of GRA riders.

One of the best-known all-around performers in All Girl Rodeo is Wanda Harper Bush of Texas, whose father, Alvin Harper, kept her well supplied with superb well-trained Quarter Horses from the time she was a child. Among them was the well-known Dee Gee, a mare that won 166 halter points, 52 reining points, and 8 roping points in the 1950s, in addition to being named the World Champion Barrel Racer for two years. Wanda's brilliant performances on her smooth-working Palomino Eagle H won her the World Calf Roping Championship seven times and Ribbon Roping—breakaway roping—four times. For over twenty years she has been a top roper and barrel racer. Another horse she brought to high performance was Royal Chess, on whom she won many Cutting Horse contests. He became World Champion Cutting Horse gelding for 1968. Today Wanda and her husband Stanley are in business raising performance Quarter Horses, with her father and her brother, A. C. Harper.

Other associations for girls are the National Barrel Racing Association and the Canadian Girl Rodeo Association. Members compete in local rodeos as well as in RCA and GRA rodeos.

Some of the champion girl riders of the 1960s who come to mind are: Jane Mayo of Oklahoma; Mildred Farris of Texas, who rode a grandson of Oklahoma Star P-6; Sherry Combs, Jo Poarch; Sammy Thurman, who with her friend Nelda Carmichael now conducts a Barrel Racing Clinic at Chatsworth, California. Ardith Bruce is a consistent contender from Colorado; Joyce Burk is a sister of top roper Barry Burk; Connie Stinson of South Dakota is a keen competitor, whose inside foot almost brushes the ground when her fourteen-hands-high Quarter Horse filly Sizzler leans into the turns around the barrels.

Florence Youree of Oklahoma was All-Around Champion of the GRA in addition to being a Champion Barrel Racer. Janice Brown was Barrel Racing Champion of Wisconsin, and Faye Faullin of Alabama was the first entrant east of the Mississippi River to be among the top fifteen barrel racers. Riding her Quarter Horse Flynt Bar Best, she won $1,200 in Houston, Texas, the largest single win ever made in GRA. Kay Whittaker of Texas was runner-up in 1968 and Missy Long of Oklahoma was Champion Barrel Racer of 1969.

17

Youth in the Saddle

Youth Activities Program

The idea conceived by Garford Wilkinson, director of Public Information for the AQHA, that grew into the Youth Activities Program is among the most important steps ever taken by the American Quarter Horse Association.

During his years of writing for newspapers and magazines, and later for the United States Department of Agriculture, Garford became greatly impressed by the 4-H Club and Future Farmers of America projects. Believing in the need to draw more of the youth of the nation into activities where their inherent love of animals could find expression, and also furnish a healthy outdoor outlet for their energies, he reasoned that a useful, obedient, companionable, sturdy, and active horse was the most satisfying and logical choice. The ownership, care, training, and riding of a horse furnishes an object lesson in sportsmanship, discipline, and the responsibility for the health and welfare of a valued dependent. With the horse also comes the most natural instruction in breeding and the fascinating study of performance in relation to bloodlines. In addition, such a youth and horse project offers the possibility of developing into a profitable venture in producing and selling registered horses either as colts of marketable age or as trained and fully developed individuals ready for competition in shows and performance contests. It is logical that anything that encourages the horse interests of the youth of today who are the horsemen of tomorrow will be beneficial to the breed the organization represents. The youth movement was given impetus when 4-H Club leaders and vocational agricultural teachers offered assistance. Another boost came when a field day held at the Lee Berwick ranch at St. Joseph, Louisiana, for adults and children, with horse games, contests, and a clinic, was so successful it served as a pattern for similar outings and horse clinics in other states. Lee Berwick, a breeder of fine

Kathy Gunson on Fire Biscuit. Kathy was active in the Colorado State High School Rodeo Club and then continued her interest in horses and riding at Colorado State University. There she became the leading exhibitor in the gelding division of the Youth Activities program. *Darol Dickinson Photo. Courtesy AQHA.*

Quarter Horses, a former president of the AQHA, and onetime member of the University of Louisiana faculty, encouraged other teachers to join in the youth and horse movement.

Orville Burtis of Kansas, a former president of the AQHA, and Orville Kalsem of Iowa, both veteran 4-H Club leaders, along with most of the ex-presidents of the AQHA, worked to bring the Youth Activities Committee into being at the annual convention of the Association in 1960. With Dallas Poteet of Oklahoma as chairman, the project was off to a good start. In 1961 an American Junior Quarter Horse Association was launched. Since that time its growth has been phenomenal.

Tim Walker of Canton, Kansas, started showing his mare Frosty Money in 4-H events when he was eight years old. Three years later, in 1966, he emerged victorious among the nation's exhibitors of mares in Youth Activities shows sponsored by the AQHA.

Annual sponsored shows in the U.S. and Canada now number around 1400, with approximately 15,000 boys and girls competing.

Any boy or girl eighteen years of age or under who owns a registered Quarter Horse can participate in AQHA-sponsored Youth Shows. And those who are members of a recognized State Junior Quarter Horse Association are eligible for membership in the American Junior Quarter Horse Association.

The latter association awards several trophies in the Youth Activities Division, with points computed on the same basis as used in the adult division.

The events are:

Halter Mare	Western Riding
Halter Gelding	Trail Class
Showmanship at Halter	Stake Race
Western Pleasure	Pole Bending
Cutting	Western Horsemanship
Reining	Jumping
Barrel Racing	Working Cowhorse
Calf Roping	Working Hunter
Breakaway Roping	English Pleasure

Write to the American Quarter Horse Association, P.O. Box 200, Amarillo, Texas, 79105, for their official handbook. It explains all events and the points required for the All-Around Performance Trophy, which is awarded to the highest scoring contestant of either sex in approved Youth Activities Performance events. The contestant does not have to use the same horse in each event.

Fletcher Deerman, El Paso, Texas, a Youth Honor Roll Pole Bending Champion. *Courtesy* The Western Horseman.

Youth AQHA Champion is a title awarded with a proper certificate to those who own their own horse with which they have earned thirty points on two or more shows, and in two or more classes. Of the thirty points, twelve must be won in Youth Halter Classes, of which four points must be won in A or B class shows. And twelve points must be won in Youth Performance Classes. The Halter Classes for Youth are limited to mares and geldings.

Dema Thorton, Salinas, California, a Youth Working Cowhorse Champion. *Courtesy* The Western Horseman.

Showmanship at Halter is a class that judges the ability of the youth to prepare his horse—grooming, trimming, hoof appearance, etc.—and the expert manner in which he handles and presents his horse in the show ring. (See "Halter Classes" in Chapter 15.)

These three awards and the Stake Race are the only categories that are not included in the adult division.

Rick Skelly of Milton Junction, Wisconsin, an outstanding horseman in the Youth Activities program, has won many classes and events, including the All-Around High Point Youth Award. *Courtesy* The Western Horseman.

The Stake Race. This race calls for a good fast horse that reins well, though the turns are not as tight as in the barrel race. The pattern can be run in either of the ways shown. The only difference is that the first turn and lead change is on a left lead in one, and a right lead in the other.

The word *stake* is used in several ways. In this **AQHA** Youth event, it is a race around two stakes. In the gymkhana games, a stake race has a row of stakes ten feet apart driven into the ground four inches to

STAKE RACE PATTERN

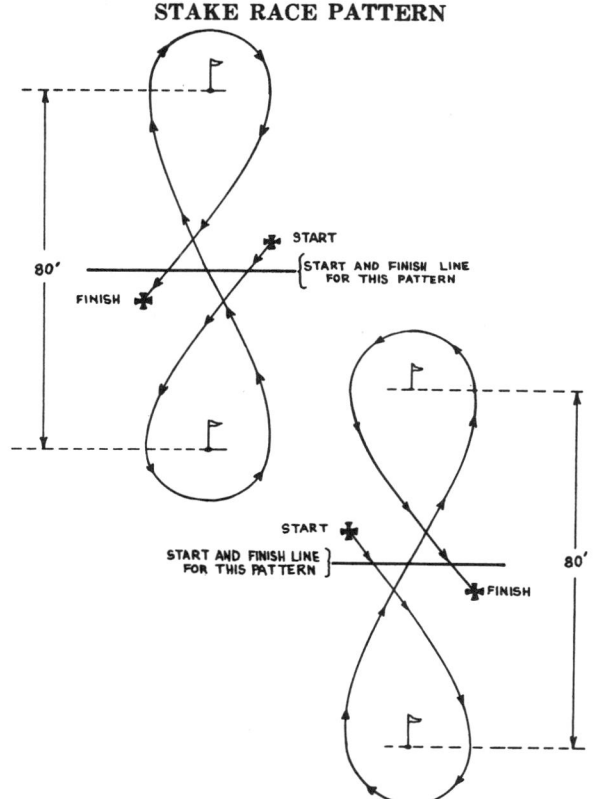

six inches. The contestant rides to the farthest stake, pulls it up, and races back to deposit it in a box, and then races to get the others, one at a time.

Generally a stake race or event means that a money prize—or stake—has been put up for the winner.

4-H Clubs and Other Riding Clubs

Aside from AQHA-sponsored Youth Activity Shows, the 4-H Clubs and other riding clubs for young people offer additional opportunity for participating in group activities. In districts where there is no 4-H Club, one can be organized with a moderate amount of assistance from the community leaders. The county agent will most likely know someone in the adjoining county who has worked with 4-H Clubs and who will come over and help in the preliminaries of setting up the organization. Local businessmen, newspapers, and radio stations may assist to publicize it. Each club must have a leader twenty-one years old or older and a co-leader. Interest in young people and a flair for organization are more of a requisite than extensive knowledge of horses. Some of the members can be as young as ten years old. Required also are a president, vice president, treasurer, secretary, and a news reporter. Since only five members are required, everyone in the minimum-sized club could be an officeholder. Five business meetings must be held every year. Every member must keep a barn record that lists the cost of feed, horseshoes, veterinarian fees, equipment and riding clothes, etc. The activities can include horseback picnics, trail rides, small horse shows, riding with other horse clubs, and participation in town events such as parades and county fairs. Horsemen can be invited to give instruction and talks. A library of horse books and magazines and horse pictures can be shared by members and will add interest to the club's meeting room.

The experience of being associated with a 4-H Club can be a very rewarding one, not only in learning about horses and riding but also in meeting new people and developing lasting friendships. Many who have become junior leaders have grown in knowledge and in horsemanship and have later served their communities as leaders in other character-building activities.

Pretty, blond Martha Mayberry of Washington, New Jersey, is a good example of how helpful membership in a 4-H Club can be. She became a member of the Little Derby 4-H Club, which had about twenty-five members, when she was ten years old. Since then she has held every club office. Her first horse was a strawberry roan which she trained so well she could compete in almost any division of a horse show, whether in English or Western classes. In 1967, when she was sixteen years old, she won a state-wide 4-H Club essay and record book contest in which 130 members of 4-H Clubs competed. The prize was a Quarter Horse yearling filly named Cass's Vickie, given by Anthony Ferrante and Sons, who own the Tall Oak Quarter Horse Farm at Whitehouse Station, New Jersey. Later Martha arranged to award Cass's Vickie each year —on a loan basis—to a worthy 4-H Club member while she herself was away at college. She hopes to study ways of using horseback therapy for crippled children. As for Cathy's own pleasure with her mare, she finds it in training and showing in Quarter Horse Pleasure, Reining, Hunting, and Halter classes.

In addition to the 4-H Clubs and other riding clubs, there are train-

Happy arrival at the end of the 4-H road. *Courtesy Robert Gilliland.*

A livestock specialist of the Agricultural Extension Service of the University of Arizona gives instruction to a group of 4-H members. Similar clinics are held in all parts of the country. *Courtesy Robert Gilliland.*

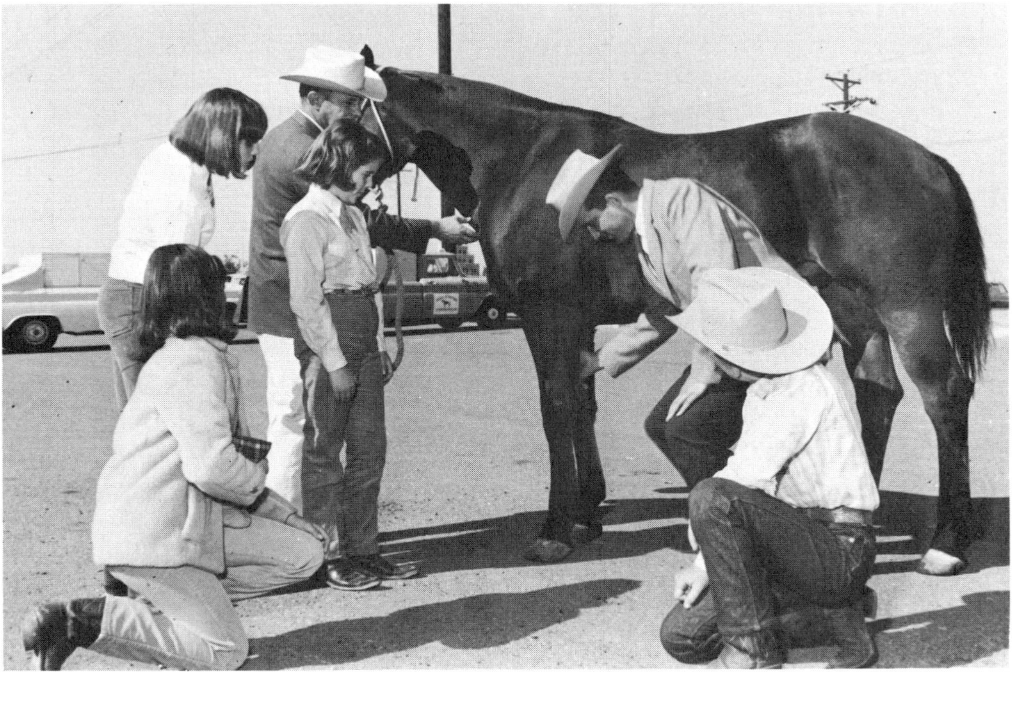

ing centers, clinics, and rating centers sponsored by the American Association for Health, Physical Education and Recreation, a Department of the National Education Association, through two divisions, DGWS (Division of Girl's and Women's Sports) and the DMA (Division of Men's Athletics), which are held in many parts of the country.

The training centers offer six- to eight-week sessions, with the purpose of training teachers, camp counselors, and leaders of Youth Activities, riding groups, etc., in basic horsemanship and horse care.

Clinics may hold sessions that vary from one to seven days which afford novices and beginning horse owners the opportunity to add to their knowledge of horse care and riding.

Rating centers hold one- and two-day sessions at which the more advanced rider's skill is evaluated.

National High School Rodeo Association

Among the contestants in Junior Quarter Horse Association-sponsored shows are many who become active in the NHSRA. High schools in twenty-two states now sponsor rodeos in which contestants strive for points that will qualify them to represent their school and then their state in the NHSRA finals, which are held in a different city each summer. In 1969 the finals were held in San Antonio, Texas, and in 1970 at Fargo, North Dakota.

As in other school athletics, team members must maintain certain scholastic standards.

Understandably the Western states in which ranching is an important industry send top contenders to the finals. But states as far removed as Florida, which entered high-school rodeo for the first time in 1969, and Minnesota and Mississippi have made a good showing. The sons and grandsons and the daughters and granddaughters of famous rodeo performers and ranchers are often among the group of trophy winners. However, the horse world is changing so rapidly that many among the four hundred to five hundred contestants who assemble each year represent a new cowboy and cowgirl elite—young people who never before were associated with ranches or rodeo.

The barrel racing, roping, and dogging horses owned and ridden by the contestants are nearly all Quarter Horses. The partnership between rider and horse is a close one, and, as I say, not all started back on a ranch. Some began in a 4-H Club. The love of horses and riding is not terminated for the lucky few who are able to take their horses with them when they go to college. It goes without saying that the college of their choice is one in which rodeo is part of the regular and extracurricular athletic programs.

National Intercollegiate Rodeo Association

From Wisconsin to California there were in 1970 an estimated 1500 campus cowboys and cowgirls in 100 colleges who were members of NIRA. These arena performers, until recently largely from ranch or farm, are conscientious, individualistic, conservative, and a marked contrast in every way but dress to those of the hippy cult. Infiltrating their ranks are an increasing number of nonranch-bred young men and women who cling to the love of horses and riding that may have started in a pony club or in their own backyards.

Intercollegiate rodeo is very popular in Arizona. The University of Arizona, Arizona State University, Northern Arizona University, and Mesa Community College all have hard-to-beat rodeo teams.

Cal Poly (California State Polytechnic College) in San Luis Obispo has sponsored a county fair on the college campus for thirty-two years in which the Poly Royal Rodeo is the main event. Others that rank high in the sport are the University of Nevada, City College at Long Beach, California, and Pierce College at Woodland Hills, California, and many small colleges throughout the Southwest.

Some school staffs oppose rodeo activity on the ground that some of it is too hazardous and that it is carried to such a point of semiprofessionalism that it is bound to distract students from their class work. Others take the attitude that since it is a healthy outdoor sport, they had better go along with it and give it some supervision and demand creditable scholastic rating of the team members.

College football, basketball, track, tennis, etc., are open to any aspirant whose grades are up to a specified standard who is good enough to make the team. With horse sports there's another factor. In the West as in the East, horse sports are not the most democratic of games to play, because the fact is that they are fairly expensive. Those who go in for shows and rodeos must maintain their own horses and the trailers in which to transport them, and the cars or pickup trucks to pull the trailers, and buy the gas to keep the cars going. Good riding clothes are rather costly and of course saddles and ropes and shoeing and vets and quite a number of other things add up. Like polo and horse shows, college rodeo or even high-school rodeo can be indulged in only by at least moderately well-heeled students, unless they are good enough to ride horses belonging to someone else. Riders whose parents own ranches where horses and equipment are at their beck and call do certainly have an advantage. Many prosperous ranchers go along with college rodeo because they feel it is a good release for youthful exuberance and because they are pleased to see their sons and daughters carry on the old traditions. Indeed, some leathery souls are happy to pay the price to assuage their own nostalgia.

In the best of the college rodeos the student contestants rope calves or ride broncs and bulls and wrestle steers with an expertness close to that seen on the professional rodeo circuit. But not by any means does all horse activity center in the arena. More and more attention in educational institutions is being given to general horsemanship, breeding, genetics, and care of horses. These studies require very little extra expense. The horse stock is maintained by the school. The University of Minnesota, the University of Wisconsin, the University of California, and Arizona State University are among the more recent ones to set up or expand courses to be in line with other schools that have long had them. Eastern New Mexico University gives a noncredit course in horsemanship. The highlight of the course is a field trip to Guy Troutman's ranch near Tucumcari, New Mexico, where his Quarter Horses have brought credit to the breed since its founding. The class also welcomes a visit, as I have on several occasions, with Roy Davis, the knowledgeable editor of the *Quarter Horse Journal*.

The Animal Science Department of the College of Agriculture at Colorado State now gives college credits in horsemanship, although not a degree. The course is on three levels: beginning, intermediate, and advanced horsemanship. Each class meets for four hours each week. Instruction includes lectures on diseases, feeding, breeds, age determination, etc. And B students who go on to assist instructors for two quarters are awarded certificates of merit which qualify them to teach basic Western riding. Colorado State University also maintains a Quarter Horse breeding program that concentrates on mares and fillies.

There are forty Quarter Horses and fifteen Saddlebreds now at Iowa State University under the supervision of James J. Kiser, professor of animal science. From Colorado breeder Ed Honnen, former president of the AQHA, and currently president of the National Horse Council in Washington, D.C., Professor Kiser obtained Bar Keep by Three Bars and Ida Red F. by Texas Dandy to add further distinction to the institution's breeding program. As at other universities, the object is to breed better horses for class use and for teaching of Western and English equitation.

Vaulting and Drill Teams

Vaulting is a team sport involving the performance of gymnastic exercises on the back of a horse while it is circled on a lunge line. Quarter Horses are ideal for this activity. Well established in Germany, the land of circus training, it is considered helpful in developing in young people confidence and suppleness and a real feeling for the movements of the horse as a preliminary to riding.

While the horse moves at a slow gait, circling the instructor, a young performer lightly runs from the inside and grasps the hand grip on the surcingle rig and vaults to the back of the horse. Once up, various positions are taken, such as shoulder stand, kneeling, stand with arms outstretched, hanging from leg, and many others. Kneeling on one knee, with one leg stretched back and one arm forward, is called the "flag." In some performances, two or even three riders are on the horse at once.

In 1970, Miss Bonnie Bither, of Scottsdale, Arizona, an attractive student at Arizona State University who had gone to California for instruction in the sport, conducted a performance of her team, the Canyon State Vaulting Team, at the Arizona Horse Show. Mrs. D. W. Beall, also of Scottsdale and an enthusiastic supporter of the sport whose daughter performs with the team, told me there are only twelve vaulting teams at present in the United States. Two of them are in Scottsdale. The Valley of the Sun Pony Club Vaulting Team has for its instructor Mrs. Gail D. Newbury.

Both teams use Quarter Horses. Nick, the amiable Quarter Horse that works on the end of the line for Bonnie Bither, is a working hunter who came from Virginia. And the Quarter Horse who has endeared himself to the young people who train with Mrs. Newbury is Arizona Fred, an ex-roping horse. The good manners and steadiness of both horses while the young riders clamber all over them would do credit to the rosin-backs of the Big-Time Circus.

Many equestrian organizations, riding camps, sheriff posses, and groups that follow the tradition in dress and tack of the old cavalry troops engage in mounted drills. They are good training for both horses and riders. But a more advanced spectacular variation has been developed by twin sisters Mrs. JoAnn Postel and Miss Nancy Turrill, who own the Foxfield School of Equitation at Westlake Village, California. Their Foxfield Drill Team is composed of riders eleven to eighteen years of age and their own horses, which are ridden without the aid of saddles or bridles, but with simple neck wires. The riders demonstrate jumping, dressage, and precise drill maneuvers. The group rehearses weekly and each individual practices as much as possible without neglecting schoolwork. The team performs without charge in shows that will pay their traveling expense, and in 1970 was the intermission feature at the National Horse Show at Madison Square Garden in New York. Sharon Byford, who wrote about the team in the March 1970 issue of *Western Horseman* magazine, said it took from six months to a year for the average previously trained saddle horse to be safely ridden with just the neck wire. Some horses were quick to learn and some horses, she said, would never learn. Nancy Turrill found that horses that have had stock horse or dressage training respond most readily to the voice commands, weight shifts, and leg pressure that serve as the only aids. The neck wire is used mainly in rating (slowing the horse down) during action.

At the present time the team has five registered Thoroughbreds, one registered Quarter Horse, and one registered Arabian. The others are grade horses of various breeding. It appears that certain individuals of any breed can be developed for this kind of performance with the minimum of control if schooled properly and with patience.

Several years ago while riding with a group into the Superstition Mountains in Arizona, we were delighted at the lovely sight of a young woman whose smart Western dress and Western horse gear complemented in every way the handsome sorrel on which she loped up to join us. A few eyes bugged when it was noticed that her horse's head was naked, without hackamore or bridle. His head was as free as that of a ranging dog that flushed the mourning doves beside the trail. Throughout the ride, her horse walked, jog-trotted, slow-loped, stopped, pivoted, and in fact played with perfect freedom and seemed to be having as much fun as the rider. Her only control of the horse depended on a tack collar which rested much of the time on the horse's neck like the support for a breast strap. Inside a tack collar are some rivet heads which, when used, punch the underside of the horse's neck to let him know there is something there to control him.

Riding with a tack collar or neck wire is not a new thing. Many years ago I saw cowboys use twisted baling wire for the same purpose. Like a bit that is there but seldom used, the horse learns that if he responds to body and leg signals, the tack collar will not be used. It is a horseman's dream come true to see brideless horses perform with precision, such as a cutting horse or roping horse without even the aid of a neck wire.

18

Trail Rides

Trail riding has become one of the most popular horse sports in this era of more leisure time. More national and state parks with good roads and horse trails that penetrate remote areas have lured many riders from their confining urban districts. Owners of good horses who care for their own horses have greatly increased and are widening the range of horse activities. Another factor that contributes to the trend toward trail riding, one often hears, is the confidence to be out on one's own with one's horse that has resulted from updated methods of teaching horsemanship, and the helpful books and magazine articles they have engendered.

It is heartening to see that a large body of riders are finding enjoyment with their horses amid the beauties of nature with its seasonal color changes—not only far removed from the competitive life in the cities and towns, but also far removed from competitive trail rides and shows. A whole new generation is finding that competition against the horses or horsemanship of others is not the only reason for owning and riding horses.

From the days of the early Californians who rode in a body to call on some of the old Spanish ranch families—later organized as the Rancheros Visitadores—riding groups have been sponsored in almost every district from California to Maine and from Canada to Mexico. Nor are they unknown in Europe and other countries. England has trail rides in addition to her many hunt clubs. One group, the Remuda Western Club, is composed of fifty-eight Londoners who ride with Western tack.

Many trail rides are sponsored by the NATRC (North American Trail Ride Conference), an organization that promotes high standards of humane horsemanship and better trail ride planning. In 1968 NATRC's highest trophy was awarded to Quarter Horse Dandy Bar Four, ridden by owner Dave Nicholson, at a presentation at the Cow Palace in San Francisco.

Zora's Lady Jo, owned and ridden by Walter B. Lee, Bethel Park, Pennsylvania, became an Honor Roll Trail Horse in 1967. It will be noted that a light hackamore is all the control this mare requires. *Courtesy AQHA.*

The American Forestry Association sponsors twenty-five annual Trail Rides within the wilderness areas of the United States and Canada. Arizona and California have more trail rides—many that are competitive—than any other states, with the Rocky Mountain regions and other Western states close behind.

In the Eastern United States, the Vermont hundred-mile Trail Ride has long been well known. It is a real pleasure to ride, not a grueling test, since there are two overnight stops allowed for rest and physical checkups.

Virginia has two endurance rides, one of fifty miles and one of a hundred miles that start from Hot Springs, Virginia, each summer. More vigorous is the Speed and Endurance Test of the Three Day Event sanctioned by the U.S. Combined Training Associations.

New York's Governor Rockefeller, who has ridden horses since his boyhood and who at last report counted a Quarter Horse among his favorites, sponsored the Adirondack Trails to preserve for present and future riders paths through an area of rare scenic beauty.

In Wisconsin, the Plymouth Trail Riders sponsor an annual Endurance Ride of a hundred miles in the Kettle Moraine State Forest. It is called the Kettle Moraine Colorama.

A popular and much-heralded trail ride that tests the stayers, both equine and human, is the Tevis Cup 100 Miles One Day Ride held each year under the direction of Western States Trail Ride, Inc., whose headquarters are in Auburn, California. The Tevis Cup is awarded by William, Gordon, and Lloyd Tevis in memory of their grandfather, Lloyd Tevis, who, as president of the Wells Fargo Company in 1861, reorganized the pony express after its costs of operation had forced its founders, Russell, Majors, and Waddell, into bankruptcy. The Tevis Cup is presented to the winner of this endurance ride. The rider whose horse finishes in the best condition receives the James B. Haggin Cup.

Contenders in this competition, like entrants in all rugged competitive endurance rides, start several months before to build up legs, wind, and stamina in their horses on daily rides of twelve to fifteen miles with an occasional long ride of forty to fifty miles. Since the ride starts at Tahoe City, California, at an altitude of six thousand feet in the rugged Sierras and winds down through rough breath-takingly beautiful country in the Sacramento Valley and to the town of Auburn, which lies at an altitude of one thousand feet, it is considered best to train in somewhat similar altitudes. Just how important this acclimatizing is, however, has not yet been determined, says Richard B. Barsaleau, D.V.M., one of the vets who give each horse a thorough inspection the day before the ride to judge whether or not he is in condition to enter.

Horses must carry a minimum of 150 pounds. Since its beginning in 1954, the average weight has been 184 pounds. Along the ride are three checkpoints where the horses get a thorough examination. In addition there are several other unannounced checkpoints where riders must register on a tally sheet. A horse may be disqualified if he shows excessive fatigue. The field of starters is also gradually reduced in numbers as horses go lame, or cast shoes, or riders become too exhausted to continue. At each of the three stops there is an hour of enforced rest. Saddles are removed, horses rubbed down, watered, and fed. Riders eat and get the kinks out of their legs and rest as much as the time allows. In 1962 four women made the ride—six had started in a total field of thirty-one. In 1967 thirty-one women, among the hundred and nine riders, started, and nineteen completed the ride.

Ride officials lead out at a moderate pace for the first six miles from Tahoe City in the chilly air of predawn darkness. Just as the first streaks of sunlight break over the high Sierras, riders are sent ahead in small groups, each to set the pace he thinks best. Riders travel at the walk, jog trot, more extended trot, and the lope, depending on the nature of the terrain. Riders favor their horses as much as possible by keeping their weight forward toward the withers, particularly when the horse is climbing. The mountainous nature of the trail can be judged by the fact that it climbs a total of 9,500 feet and descends a total of 15,250 feet. Riders are still in the high rugged country when night falls. With a full moon the trail is easy to follow. Without moonlight, riders are more dependent on the good night eyes of their horses, or on riders from the Sierra Ranger Club of Auburn, who may helpfully appear out of the darkness at some obscure branching of the trail.

Nick Mansfield on his TB-Cross gelding Buffalo Bill has completed the ride ten times. He won it once and was among the first ten three other times. Wendell Robie, president of Western Trail Ride, Inc., has won four years and placed near the top in four others. He rides his home-raised Arabian horses. In 1960, a wiry mustang, ridden by Ernie Sanchez, an ex-jockey, darted through the gate a few tenths of a second ahead of Wendell Robie's Arabian. "But listen to this," wrote Randy Steffen, artist, writer, and horseman, who helped organize the 1959 and 1960 rides: "Ernie had gotten lost, rode 18 miles out of his way and when his horse cast a shoe he tacked an old mule shoe on his horse with shingle nails flattened with a rock, and made the last stretch in a dead run."

The mustang traveled 118 miles in an incredible 14 hours and 35 minutes—an average pace of over 8 miles per hour on one of the most rugged trails in the West. And the vets found him in good condition.

In 1961 Drucilla Barner set a record of 13 hours, 2 minutes, and 55 seconds on her three-quarters bred Arabian Chagita, a 10-year-old gelding that weighed 828 pounds and stood 14.2 hands high. He carried the regulation 150 pounds.

Alexander Mackay-Smith, editor of *The Chronicle of the Horse,* which features Eastern horsemanship and breeds, completed the ride and wrote: "The ride requires a degree of courage and fitness and an effort on the part of both horse and rider which is fully comparable to the Speed and Endurance Test of the Olympic Three-Day Event." He also commented that the toughness of the feet of Western-raised horses was considered "extraordinary to the easterner."

So far the Arabians and their distant relatives the mustangs, both notable through the centuries for their endurance, have shown up better on the long rides than other breeds of horses. One Arabian that weighed only 700 pounds and stood but 14 hands carried 166 pounds and came in in sixth place. A mustang 14 hands high and weighing but 850 pounds brought in a load of 184 pounds in under-average time. A grade Quarter Horse mare of only 14 hands but weighing 1050 pounds completed the ride with a load of 234 pounds!

Australia's Tom Quilty Gold Cup is a 100 Mile One Day Endurance Ride. Four Americans entered it in 1969, and one of them was Marian Robie, the young granddaughter of Wendell Robie. The long ride was won by Australian John Coyle on a Waler—Australia's own breed of horse—with Mrs. Lorraine Robbins in second place and Marian Robie in third place. Of the thirty-five riders who started, fifteen finished, among them the four Americans.

Although Quarter Horses have occasionally distinguished themselves on long competitive rides, comparatively few have been entered. Being built and trained for quick bursts of speed, as a rule they carry too much muscle for great distances of sustained travel at a gait of six to eight miles per hour. The old cowponies could jog-trot with some cantering here and there for a hundred miles or more, but seldom in record-breaking time. Moreover, because today's Quarter Horses are so often top performers that can make money for their owners, they are spared the long trail rides where the only payoff is in the form of a trophy cup or buckle.

It is on the rides of moderate length, whether mountainous and rugged or not, that Quarter Horses are very popular. Their good manners on the trail, easy gaits, and willingness to attempt all kinds of terrain add pleasure to any ride.

One of the newer noncompetitive trail rides is in the Palo Duro Canyon State Park, sponsored by the Chamber of Commerce and the Will Rogers Ranger Riders Association of Amarillo, Texas. Planned as an annual August event, it got its first group of riders together in 1967. The ride is limited to the first three hundred riders who make applications. Although most riders haul their own horses in for the two days of entertainment and rides, horses are available for rental. The rides vary in distances and ruggedness to meet the preferences of beginners and experienced riders. Camping sites, rest rooms with showers, state-approved water supply, outdoor grills and tables are an extra inducement for families to vacation there before, during, and after the trail ride event. Deer, coyote, fox, antelope, and jack rabbits can still be seen in the 120-mile-long and 20-mile-wide canyon park area. In a large outdoor theater, Paul Green's historical musical drama *Texas* can be enjoyed by those who are foresighted enough to have made reservations.

Although only a few have been mentioned, there are many competitive trail rides of varying distances in various parts of the country. Many clubs and riding groups have annual rides of from one to six days that are open to members and guests only. For a fee, some organizations will furnish horses and everything necessary for pack trips into scenic country. For trail ride information, chambers of commerce in the cities in the areas where rides are planned will most certainly be able to supply the addresses of horsemen's associations which can give detailed information on the rides they sponsor.

Some families load their horses in a trailer and camp and ride in various national and state parks. Before such a venture, inquiries should be made through the Park Service so that all requirements and conditions are thoroughly understood and complied with. To cross state lines, one must have health certificates for the horses signed by a veterinarian. Proper feed is generally available in most sections of the country, but water, particularly city water containing chlorine, may taste funny to your horses. A spoonful of vinegar in a bucket of water will change the taste or odor so that most horses will drink it. Ropes can be used for improvised corrals if there are trees to tie them to. Where there are

The Verde Vaqueros crossing Sycamore Creek. Most of the members of this long-established group of trail riders are mounted on Quarter Horses. But there are exceptions: two individuals appear to prefer to ride mules. *Photo by Slim Brown. Courtesy Dorothy Gilbert.*

no trees, some horsemen travelers carry a few metal posts with the wire, insulators, and battery for an electrified fence. A manure fork and a rake are absolutely essential. Campsites must be left meticulously clean or other campers and the ranger will be furious and may start moves to bar horses from the area.

To preserve old trails and open new ones call for the concerted efforts on the part of organized horsemen. Some districts, even though the home of great numbers of horses, often lack good or even adequate public places to ride them. A great stride in correcting such a situation was made by the Horse Owners Association, Inc., of Long Island. With a membership of over 2500, composed of both Eastern and Western style riders, it made a strenuous effort to preserve for themselves and future riders some places to ride safe from encroaching highways, industrial developments, and urban sprawl. While federal and state money was plushing up every other known kind of recreation facilities, with the interests of golfers, tennis players, swimmers, boaters, and bird watchers catered to by the planning engineers, the horse owners and riders were being thwarted at every turn. Within two years after going to work, many benefits for horsemen were gained. New York State's General Obligation Law was amended. Now private landowners can permit access to their property without being liable, with the result that landowners are in many cases willing to have riding paths cross their property. The State Park Commission changed policy and opened five parks on Long Island to riders. Eight parks in Suffolk County, Long Island, are scheduled to have bridle trails, trailer parking areas, and show and exhibition rings. A bridle path along the outer border of the Long Island Expressway for a certain stretch has been approved. The Long Island Lighting Company has granted an easement for forty miles of trail on its right-of-way. A model zoning ordinance was developed that ensures the rights of both horse owners and their neighbors. Four horse clinics in connection with the Suffolk County Extension Service have been established. And it has sponsored the Island Wide Celebrity Trail Ride in Montauk at the eastern end of the island. Through their efforts an amendment to the National Scenic Trails bill now in Congress was added, which provides for the establishment of riding trails along the edge of federally supported highways wherever feasible, a bill that has yet to get sufficient votes and funds from the lawmakers.

While looking to the National Horse Council of Washington, D.C., for help on the federal level, horsemen's organizations over the country continue in their efforts to improve the riding conditions in their own areas. Some have found that many trails can be widened at comparatively small cost to serve both hikers and riders. The Appalachian Trail, mostly a hiker's trail, could be made useful to riders, at least in segments throughout its full length. Farmers and ranchers, if presented with the idea, relieved of liability, and shown that strips of their nonproductive land could serve a local need, might be won over. There isn't a county that couldn't set aside some ground for good trails, safe from traffic, and at very little if any cost to the taxpayer if riders would pool their interests and show there is a need for them. Old abandoned railway right-of-ways, aqueduct right-of-ways, state- and county-owned lands, easements to verges adjacent to private property—there are many possibilities. It is something that has to be solved locally, district by district.

What it takes to make pleasure riding a national sport is for the flat saddle and the stock saddle people to ride together toward a common aim. When they do, they find that the enjoyment in horsemanship really has very little to do with the way one dresses himself *or* his horse.

19

Roundup

In drawing a book of this nature to a close, one is tempted to be clairvoyant and try and peer into the future of this breed of horse whose acceptance in such staggering numbers has been a phenomenon of the past thirty years.

In talking to hundreds of horsemen—breeders, exhibitors, trainers, pleasure riders, cowboys, ropers, and cutting horse owners and riders, etc.—and discussing major trends, a number of predictions were garnered to add to my own. The consensus seemed to be that there is a bright future for the Quarter Horse and the other good saddle breeds as long as the owners who love to ride and use their horses overwhelmingly outnumber those who own horses purely for show.

It was the owner-trainer relationship and teamwork that brought the Quarter Horse to such a peak of perfection. And this is true even of his early racing days. The show and performance Quarter Horse of today is still mainly a using horse. A horse that can stand up to work. A horse that can do something. But already the question is being asked: will the Quarter Horse, now that he is valuable as a show horse, go the way of all breeds that become strictly show horses to be turned over to trainers and grooms to be handled a few minutes a day? Will the Quarter Horse follow in the path of the saddlebred, Morgan, and Tennessee Walking Horse, who became the nation's most popular show horses—and status symbols—only to lose their hardiness and usefulness, to be left unused as real pleasure horses by their owners?

For the breeds just mentioned a heartening trend seems to be developing. Irene Zane, executive secretary of the American Saddlebred Pleasure Horse Association, stated in a letter to the author that she believes that at least 50 percent of saddlebred horses are now being used for pleasure without being shown. Mr. Charles J. Cronan, Jr., secretary of the American Saddle Horse Breeders Association, thinks the figure might be as high as 75 percent, which is about the percentage of Quarter Horses that never see the inside of a show ring.

Recalling the artificialities and cruelties practiced on show breeds of the past, one can only hope that such practices are dying out. The trainers who once worked for the wealthy had a job to do and the job was to make winning horses whether or not they could train the owners to win on them. That era is ending. Now trainers are more knowledgeable and are better organized, many being members of local or state professional organizations that have set high humane and ethical standards. Training is frequently undertaken on a contract basis, and many professionals maintain their own independent establishments.

With increasing frequency one hears this advice from seasoned horsemen: unless you are a breeder or a trainer who depends on showing for a living, enjoy your horse and show only if showing is instructive and satisfying. But if some shows bring you into an unpleasant atmosphere created by people to whom money counts more than horses, stay away from them. People with warped egos will ruin human associations as readily as they will mutilate horses to win.

After learning to ride well, and if one has a horse of outstanding quality, it is natural that one will find great satisfaction in showing him in classes or events where he shines. But one should try and pick congenial shows. After winning a number of ribbons and trophies in smaller shows one can better judge whether or not to buck up against the big-time, really prestige events.

Showing a gelding, who is at the end of the line genetically speaking, brings only trophies as a reward unless he wins in competitive arena events. A mare may make a name for herself in shows, and a colt of hers, if by a worthy sire, may become valuable. But remember your financial interest in showing can't be compared to that of the breeder who must show to publicize his stock. The owner-trainer with several good brood mares may build up a supplementary income, and if fortune smiles and his foals are fast, he may tie into big money. Generally, however, even with risk capital to invest, it takes years before a breeding farm can pay its way.

Some predict that the trend will be toward dressage training, because the population explosion of both humans and horses will so limit riding space that horse owners will devote more time to precise training in their own backyard paddocks. My own opinion is that precision training in gait changes, subtle aids, and a minimum of head control will become more universally practiced. However, since dressage training presupposes that the performance the horse has been taught will be exhibited in shows and since owner-trainers are well aware they are overmatched by the wealthy and the professionals they can employ, I think it unlikely that competition in dressage will increase in any great proportion. Only a comparatively few owner-trainers in America have the patience or the time for so-called classical training, which has always been more prevalent in Europe. As for other kinds of precise training, only a comparatively few riders can or want to rope a calf or a goat or cut out a cow. But the euphoria that comes with being on a good horse, the invigorating tempo change in the daily routine, and the open trail ahead will continue to be as beckoning as the sound of the huntsman's horn.

In predicting trends it is more than likely that jumping, because of its strong appeal to most good riders, will become increasingly popular. And the Quarter Horse will find an ever-increasing acceptance in this field. More facilities for jumping in public areas will probably be developed. More and better boarding stables with arenas and better training areas will no doubt be established on the periphery of almost every urban center. It seems the trend will bring better riding trails with more opportunities for enjoying group riding, games, and training fostered by the growing number of horsemen's associations aided by the National Horse Council, which will also be of great help in swaying public opinion in the use of federal, state, and county lands.

Again in our history, horses are heading West. In 1959 the Southeastern region of the United States accounted for 33 percent of the horses in the entire country. By 1970 the percentage had dropped to 28 percent. Texas with its vast area has for many years had the largest horse population, but California has now taken second place, which until 1959 was held by North Carolina.

The shift West in the United States extends all the way to Hawaii. Jackpot roping held at night under lights can be seen near Honolulu. And on the famous quarter-million-acre Parker Ranch at Kamuela, Quarter Horses feature in their breeding program. On the island of Maui several ranches raise Quarter Horses exclusively, with the Hamilton McCaughey's Kipahula Ranch specializing in a strain that traces to Oklahoma Star P-6.

The foothold the Quarter Horse has gained in thirty-eight countries around the world—an estimated ten thousand in 1970—is so secure that he is already considered the most cosmopolitan of all performance horses. Even China has eight registered Quarter Horses and Cuba at last count had 257. Quarter Horse cutting contests have been held in such diverse places as the burning sands of Arabia and the high plateaus of the Andes in Colombia. Canada and Mexico have large populations of Quarter Horses, and England and Australia are rapidly developing the breed. In 1969 the Double A Ranch of Bloomington, Indiana, shipped twenty-four Quarter Horses via a chartered TWA cargo jet to the Lower Woodend Farm near Henley on Thames in Oxfordshire, England, to be crossbred with English jumpers and hunters.

The Australian Quarter Horse Association has made rapid growth in the past four years and is keeping standards for the breed high. Regardless of the papers that arrive with imported horses, they must pass a rigid inspection to get into the Australian Stud Book. *The Horse World,* a British publication, has reported the activities of Greg Lowther, a former rancher of Clements, California, who runs the lush Clover Leaf Quarter Horse Stud near Murrurundi, 220 miles northwest of Sydney, Australia. Lowther first came to Australia as a serviceman during World War II. After another, later visit, he returned in 1967, to establish the stud. With him he brought nine Quarter Horse stallions that represent some of the well-known bloodlines including the Peaks' famed Driftwood line. Now Australians are becoming familiar with the many uses to which the Quarter Horse can be put, including cutting cattle, which the Australians call "camp drafting."

From many sources one hears expansive predictions about the growth of the saddle horse breeds—with estimates of twelve to fifteen million head in the United States before the end of this decade. It is rather amazing that horses continue to be so wanted when so much they are called on to do today is nonessential. An association that has lasted through the ages is not terminated easily. It may be better understood when one realizes that, next to man, horses have played the most important flesh-and-blood part on the stage of history. Every conquest, every migration of mankind since history has been recorded, and continuing to within the memory of living men, has depended on the motive power or the spirited charges of horses. In our own age, Winston Churchill shared his great moment in battle with a horse, riding in a cavalry charge at the Battle of Omdurman during Kitchener's campaign for the reconquest of the Sudan. It is surely significant that nothing on earth, aside from man himself, has been painted, engraved, or sculptured as much as horses. Nothing has served so persistently and eloquently as a symbol of beauty, spirit, and power.

APPENDIX A

Genealogical Charts

Space allows for only a comparatively few individuals to be listed in the two bloodline charts on the following pages, but with these few it is possible for the student of Quarter Horse bloodlines to find the source of the majority of all present-day Quarter Horses.

Some have been included because they distinguished themselves at stud, on the turf, or in the arena, while others are present because they were the link between noted families. Following each name in the alphabetical listing is the number of the line on which it appears in the chart.

Chart 1 (*overleaf*)

Chart 1 shows the origin and relationship of the predominant Quarter Horse families from which came the original pedigree holders, with special attention given to the first nineteen, who were later designated as founding sires of the American Quarter Horse breed. Bloodlines are based on the Sanders D. Bruce *American Stud Book* and its appendix and on the stud book of the AQHA. The chart was prepared by the author.

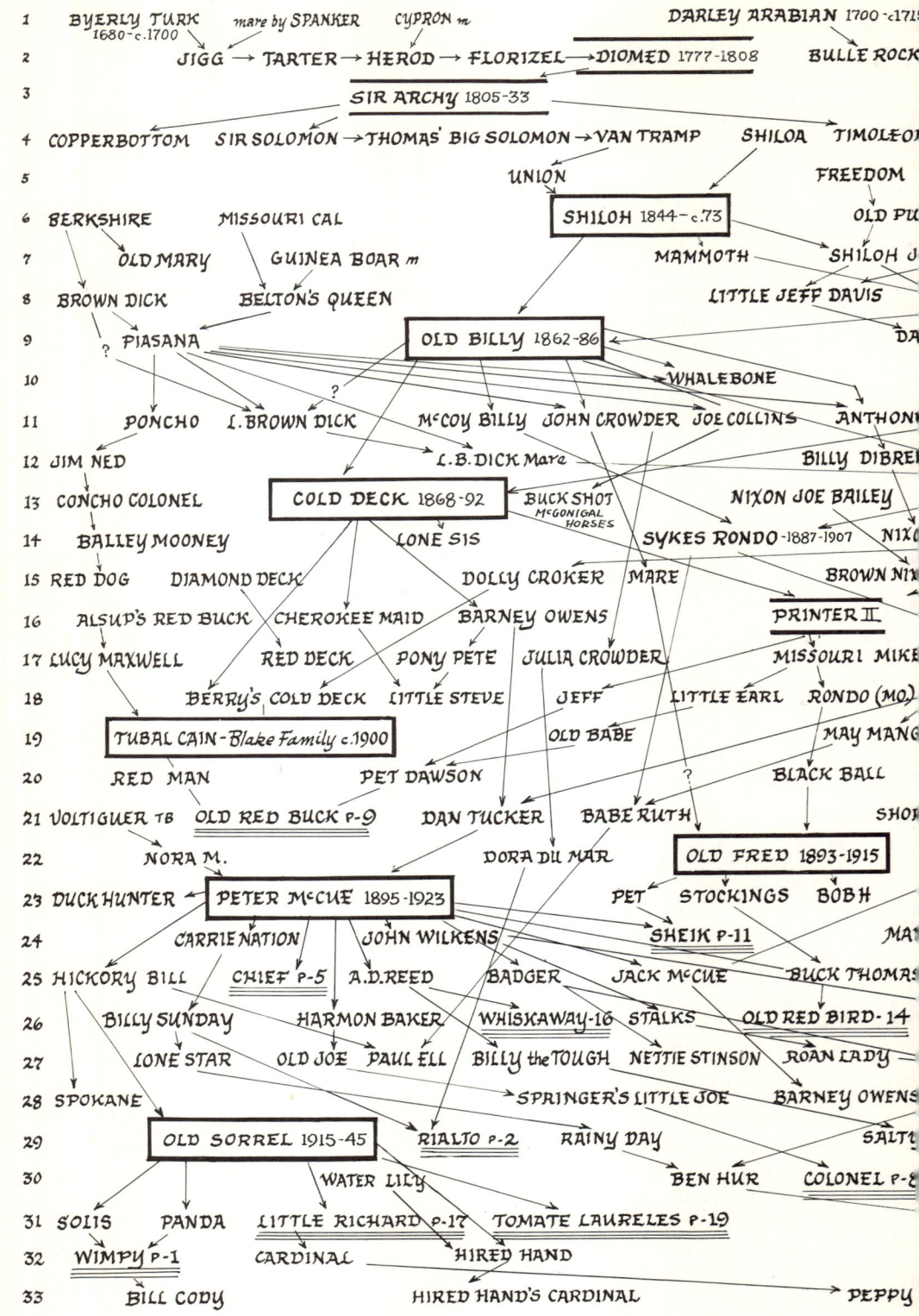

HORSES LISTED IN CHART 1

	line		line
A. D. Reed	25	Bulger	22
Aguinaldo	17	Bulle Rock	2
Alsups Red Buck	16	Butt Cut	11
Anthony	11	Byerly Turk	1
Aury	13		
		Cardinal	32
Babe Ruth	21	Carrie Nation	24
Baby King	24	Cherokee Maid	16
Badger	25	Chickasha Bob	17
Balley Mooney	14	Chief p-5	25
Barbee Dun	16	Chubby	29
Barlow	15	Chule Munde	23
Barney	15	Cold Deck	13
Barney Owens	16	Colonel p-8	30
Barney Owens II	28	Columbus p-7	22
Bay Cold Deck	6	Concho Colonel	13
Bay Puss	11	Copperbottom	4
Beetche's Yellow Jacket	24	Cowboy p-12	28
Belle	29	Cutthroat	20
Belton's Queen	8		
Ben Bolt	20	Dan	20
Ben Hur	30	Dan Secres	7
Berkshire	6	Dan Tucker	21
Berry's Cold Deck	18	Darley Arabian	1
Big Em	19	Dash	9
Big Nance	5	Dedier	29
Bill Cody	33	Della Moore	30
Bill Garner	8	Dennis Reed TB	19
Billy Dibrell	12	Diamond Deck	15
Billy Sunday	26	Diomed	2
Billy the Tough	27	Dolly Croker	15
Black Ball	20	Dora du Mar	22
Blackburn's Whip	4	Duck Hunter	23
Black Dick	13		
Blue Dick	12	Ed Echols	31
Boanerges	7	Eureka	13
Boanerges (Greenfields)	6		
Boanerges (Owens)	5	Fanny Wolf	7
Bobby Leach	17	Florizel	2
Bobby Lowe	18	Fourth of July	25
Bob H	23	Freedom	5
Bob Wade	16		
Bonnie Wilkens	26	Godolphin Barb	1
Booger Red	23	Grey Badger	31
Brown Dick	8	Guinea Boar	7
Brown Nixon mare	15	Guinea Pig	24
Brown Possu p-15	23	Hamburg Dick	5
Buck Shot	13	Hampton's Paragon	4
Buck Thomas II	25	Harry Bluff	6

APPENDIX A 519

	line		line
Henry Texas	28	Mammoth	7
Herod	2	Marguerite	21
Hickory Bill	25	Mary	18
Hired Hand	32	Mary Cook	5
Hired Hand's Cardinal	33	Maude	24
		Maude	10
Jabalena	25	May Mangum	19
Jack Traveler	8	Mexican Dun mare	13
Jane Hunt	5	Midnight	28
Janus	2	Midnight Jr.	30
Janus II	3	Missouri Cal	6
Jenny	18	Missouri Mike	17
Jenny Capps	12	Mittie Stephens	10
Jigg	2	Mollie	9
Jim Miller	15	Monkey	8
Jim Ned	12	Mount's Steel Dust	9
Jim Wells	27	Munch Meg	9
Joe Bailey (Old)	19		
Joe Bailey p-4	25	Nellie Trammel	25
Joe Blair TB	30	Nelly Grey	9
Joe Chalmers	6	Nettie Jacket	24
Joe Collins	11	Nettie Stinson	27
Joe Moore	31	Nixon Joe Bailey	13
Joe Reed p-3	31	Nora M	22
Joe Reed II	32		
John Crowder	11	Oklahoma Star p-6	21
John Wilkens	24	Old Babe	19
Jole Blon	30	Old Billy	9
Julia Crowder	17	Old Cade	2
June Bug	10	Old Fred	22
		Old Janus	1
		Old Jim	26
King p-234	30	Old Joe	27
		Old Joe Bailey	19
Lady Gladys	11	Old Mary	7
Lady Luck	26	Old Puss	6
Lath	2	Old Red Bird p-14	26
Leo	33	Old Red Buck p-9	21
Little Ben	16	Old Sorrel	29
Little Brown Dick	11		
Little Earl	18	Paisana	9
Little Joe	26	Panda	31
Little Joe Jr.	28	Paul Ell	27
Little King	24	Peppy	33
Little Richard	31	Pet	23
Little Rondo	16	Pet Dawson	20
Little Texas Chief	23	Pid Hart	13
Lock's Rondo	14	Poco Bueno	33
Lone Man	16	Poncho	11
Lone Star	27	Poncho Villa	27
Lucy Maxwell	17	Pony Pete	17

Possum (King)	22
Printer	4
Printer II	16
Rainy Day	29
Ram Cat	8
Rebel	8
Red Deck	17
Red Dog	15
Red Man	20
Rialto p-2	29
Roan Dick	14
Roan Lady	27
Rocky Mountain Tom	17
Rondo (Lock's)	14
Rondo (Missouri)	18
Rondo (Syke's)	14
Royal King	33
Sam King	19
San Siemon	31
Sheik p-11	24
Shelby	11
Shiloa	4
Shiloh	6
Shiloh Jr.	7
Short's Whip	5
Shorty	21
Shue Fly	30
Sir Archy	3
Sir Solomon	4

Solis	31
Spokane	28
Springer's Little Joe	28
Stalks	26
Steel Dust	7
Stockings	23
Stranger	21
Susy McQuirter	17
Syke's Rondo	14
Tartar	2
Texas Chief	15
Thomas' Big Solomon	4
Tiger	7
Timoleon	4
Tomate Laureles p-19	31
Tom Driver	9
Tony	25
Traveler	21
Tubal Cain	19
Waggoner's Rainy Day p-13	32
Whalebone	10
Whip	3
Whiskaway p-16	26
Wimpy p-1	32
Yellow Boy p-18	27
Yellow Jacket	19
Yellow Wolf	20

Chart 2 (*overleaf*)

Chart 2 shows the continuity of the old Quarter Horse families, their continuing alliances with the Thoroughbred, and the dominant families that have emerged since the founding of the American Quarter Horse breed.

#							
1	BILLY McCUE		POSSUM (KING)		HARMON BAKER'S STAR		JOHN WILKENS
2		WILL STEAD	DOC	PANITA	MAN-O-WAR	PANMURE TB	JOE HANCOCK
3		COTTON EYED JOE	PEPPY		PRETTY LADY	LITTLE JOE the WRANGLER	JOAN
4	SARGEANT	BILLY VAN	WIMPY P-1	PEGGY COOPER		CAPTAINS COURAGEOUS TB	
5	GRANO de ORO	BILL CODY	SAN SIEMON	PAUL ELL	PORTE DRAPEAU TB	QUARTER LADY	
6	MARE	COWBOY H	FRILLETTE TB	EQUIPOISE TB	NELLY	MISS BANKS	WIMPY II
7	ACE of DIAMONDS	PEACE PIPE TB	JOE BARRET		BILLY CLEGG	SADIE MAY	ED ECHOLS
8	MUCHACHO de ORO	EQUESTRIAN TB	RIVER BOAT TB		BANKETTE		MIKE ECHOLS
9	NAUTICAL	TOP DECK TB	MOONLIGHT NIGHT	STREAK		MY TEXAS DANDY	
10		OLD POCO BUENO		CHICKASHA MIKE	CLABBER		COLONEL CLYDE
11	JOE CODY	REBEL CAUSE		CHICKASHA ANN	CLABBER II	TEXAS DANDY	
12	KING P-234	YEAGER'S LADY JA.		VERY WISE TB	TONTO GAL		LITTLE EGYPT
13		MOON DECK		LIGHT FOOT SIS TB	ELMENDORF TB		RUBY
14	89er.			GO-MAN-GO		ONE EYED WAGGONER	
15	SQUAW H	MISS TAYLOR		F.L.LADY BUG	GO-JOSIE-GO	BILLY the KID	ROAN ALICE
16		POCO BUENO	TOP MOON	HANK H.	GO-BUG-GO	MOON HARRIS	NANCY HANCE
17	EASTER CODY		ROY DECK		ROYAL KING	TONTO BARS GILL	
18	POCO LINE RIDER		TOP LADY BUG	GOETTA		MAJOR KING	
19	CHICLE TB	LADY LINE RIDER	GOING LIGHT TB	LITTLE JOE JR.			SAM KING
20	CHICARO TB	JEAN ANN BLAIR		LADY BUG'S MOON		TONTO BARS HANK	
21	CHICARO BILL	RED BUD L.	VANDY	ARIEL LADY	GOLDEN CHIEF	MARE	
22	CHICADO V. m	CODALENA	VANDY'S FLASH	POKEY VANDY		TOM SCOOTER	
	LOCK'S RONDO						
23	DRIFTWOOD	FLYING BOB	LIGHTNING BAR			MISS TOMMY	J.B. KING
24	DRIFTWOOD IKE	QUEENY	POCO PINE	SILVERTONE	DEXTER		
25	VANETTA DEE	POKER CHIP PEAKE	POCO SHOCK		THREE CHICKS		JET DECK
26	CHICABAR DOLL	SILVER CASH	TEXAS PINE	LIGHT BAR			OLD RED BUCK P-9
			ACE of DIAMONDS - line 7				
27	SILVER WIMPY	BAR Y FANCY	MISS PANAMA	BILLY SILVERTONE	BUDDY DEXTER		BABE DAWSON
28		POCO POCO	PANA BAR	KING GLO		BALDY	HIRED HAND
		FLIT - line 11	JOE REED P-3			LITTLE NELLIE BARS	
29	KING'S PISTOL	JOE'S LAST	KING SKEET		CUTTER BILL		HIRED GIRL
					SPOTTED BULL TB		
30	MARION'S GIRL	POCO LENA	JOSE UNO	ROYAL CHESS	CHICKASHA DAN		SKIPPER W.
		BATTLE GROUND - TB	AWE g.d. of THREE BARS	SHERRY'S DAY - TB	JOE QUEEN	JOE REED P-3	
31		LADY YOLANDA		JOE SHERRY		MANOR MAN	CATECHU
32	FIRST 8 AQHA SUPREME CHAMPIONS ▶		MISS ROY DECK		CAT'S CUE BAR		ENHANCED

Horse Pedigree Chart

BEETCH'S YELLOWJACKET DAN	OKLAHOMA STAR p-6	JOE REED p-3	JOE MOORE	
JIMMY ALLRED	OKLAHOMA STAR JR.	MISS BOSTICK	JOE REED II	
	BARNEY OWENS II	BABY DOLL FANNY ASHWELL	CANOVA HOBO	
JANE HUNT	STAR DECK	STAR'S LU	LITTLE FANNY	STELLA MOORE
FLAPPER HUNT		JULIE W. DOCK HORN TB	JOE LESS	FIREBRAND REED
LITTLE BLACK JOE	KING PLAUDIT TB	LENA HORN COWBOY P-12	NAVIE GIRL	SUE REED
JO-JO m	PLAUDIT	JENNY DEE IDA RED	OSAGE STAR	JOAK
DIXIE BEACH (MARE)	SUNKIST		OSAGE STAR LADY	LEO FIRE ONE
PAUL A	RED BOTTOM	RANDIE'S LADY LENA LEO		ROBIN REED
MIDNIGHT	MARE SHUE FLY	CROTON OIL PALLEO PETE		ROSA LEO
MIDNIGHT JR.	HARDTWIST MISS PAWHUSKA	ZEFF'S LEO FLIT		LEO LENA
CLINT HIGGINS	CHUBBY	FRONTERA SUGAR		JULEO
BELLE of MIDNIGHT	MYRTLE DEE TB	NO BUTT	LEOLA LEOTA W.	
PERCENTAGE TB		MISS CHUBBY	MISS MEYERS	PRIORITY TB
HOT HEELS	THREE BARS TB STREAKY JANE			GOODWINS JUANITA
STEEL BARS		JOSIES BAR JOLE BLON	BOLD VENTURE TB	
BARRED		BOB FOLLY	DEPTH CHARGE	MONITA
CASBAR	SUGAR BARS	BY THUNDER	DEPTH BARS	BOB WELLS
BAR HEELS		LEO BAR SAN SIEMON = chart 1		BEA VAN
MISS NIGHT BAR	MR. STREAKY BAR	VIRGIE LEE ALEDO BAR		
LADY COOLIDGE	TRIPLE CHICK	LEE BAR SAN SUE DARKS		JO-VAN REED
MISS RUBY	SCOOPER CHICK	LEO SAN BLACK ANNIE		RED DOG
RUBY TOO	ALAMITOS BAR	PEPPY SAN JOHNNY DIAL	LADY FAIRFAX	
LOYAL WIMPY		WIMPY LEO		TADPOLE
ALFRED RIKER		LENA'S BAR SUWANNEE BARS		LITTLE MEOW
MR. MEYERS	CUSTOM JET	DOC BAR BARTENDER PRETTY BUCK	PETER McCUE	SHE KITTY
NICK SHOEMAKER	MURL L.	CLAUDE MISS BARTENDER		RED JOE of ARIZ.
SIDE CAR			SUPER CHICK SNIPETTE Y. JACKET KING p-234	TOPSY
POKEY BAR	EASY JET JET SMOOTH	LINDA CHARGE WARDLO		NELLY BLY
SKEETER	MR. BAR NONE	SENIOR GEORGE FIZZABAR TERESA TIVIO	SNIPPER W.	BOOGER RED
	BAR NONE DOLL	JUNIOR REED	SPANISH JOY	HOLEY SOX
BAR MONEY	KID MEYERS MACH I	FAIR BARS		JETAWAY REED

HORSES LISTED IN CHART 2

	line		line
Alamitos Bar	23	Cowboy H	6
Aledo Bar	20	Cowboy p-12	6
Alfred Riker	25	Croton Oil	10
Ariel Lady	21	Custom Jet	26
		Cutter Bill	29
Babe Dawson	27		
Baby Doll	3	Dan	1
Baldy	28	Depth Bars	18
Bankette	8	Depth Charge TB	17
Bar Heels	19	Dexter	24
Barney Owens II	3	Dixie Beach	8
Bar None Dall	31	Doc	2
Bartender	26	Dock Horn TB	5
Bar Y Fancy	27	Driftwood	23
Bea Van	19	Driftwood Ike	24
Beetch's Yellow Jacket	1		
Belle of Midnight	13	Easter Cody	17
Bill Cody	5	Easy Jet	29
Billy McCue	1	Ed Echols	7
Billy Silvertone	27	Eighty Niner (89er)	14
Billy the Kid	15	Elmendorf TB	13
Black Annie	22	Enhanced	32
Bob's Folly	17	Equestrian TB	8
Bob Wells	18	Equipoise TB	6
Bold Venture TB	16		
Booger Red	30	Fair Bars	32
Buddy Dexter	27	Fanny Ashwell	3
By Thunder	18	Firebrand Reed	5
		Fire One	8
Captains Courageous TB	4	Fizzabar	30
Casbar	18	Flapper Hunt	5
Catechu	31	Flit	11
Cat's Cue Bar	32	F.L. Lady Bug	15
Chicado V	22	Flying Bob	23
Chicaro Bill	21	Frillette TB	6
Chicaro TB	20	Frontera Sugar	12
Chickabar Doll	26		
Chickasha Ann	11	Go-Bug Go	16
Chickasha Dan	30	Goetta	18
Chickasha Mike	10	Going Light TB	19
Chicle	19	Go-Josie Go	15
Chubby	12	Golden Chief	21
Clabber	10	Go-Man Go	14
Clabber II	11	Goodwins Juanita	15
Claude	27	Grano de Oro	5
Clint Higgins	12		
Codalena	22	Hank H	16
Colonel Clyde	10	Hard Twist	11
Cotton Eyed Joe	3	Harmon Baker's Star	1

APPENDIX A 525

	line		line
Hired Girl	29	Leo San	22
Hired Hand	28	Leota W	13
Holey Sox	31	Light Foot Sis TB	13
Hot Heels	15	Lightning Bar	23
		Linda Charge	29
Ida Red	7	Little Black Joe	6
		Little Egypt	12
Jane Hunt	4	Little Fanny	4
J.B. King	23	Little Joe Jr.	19
Jean Ann Blair	20	Little Meow	25
Jetaway Reed	32	Loyal Wimpy	24
Jet Smooth	29		
Jimmy Allred	2	Mach I	32
Joak	7	Major King	18
Joan	3	Man O' War TB	2
Joe Barret	7	Marion's Girl	30
Joe Cody	11	Midnight	10
Joe Hancock	2	Midnight Jr.	11
Joe Less	5	Mike Echols	8
Joe Moore	1	Miss Banks	6
Joe Sherry	31	Miss Bartender	27
Joe's Last	29	Miss Bostick	2
Johnny Dial	23	Miss Chubby	14
Jo-Jo	7	Miss Meyers	14
Jole Blon	16	Miss Night Bar	20
Jose Uno	30	Miss Pawhuska	11
Josie's Bar	16	Miss Roy Deck	32
Jo Van Reed	21	Miss Ruby	22
Juleo	12	Miss Taylor	15
Julie W	5	Miss Tommy	23
Junior Reed	31	Monita	17
		Moon Deck	13
Kid Meyers	32	Moon Harris	16
King Glo	28	Moonlight Night	9
King Plaudit TB	6	Mr. Streaky Bars	20
King p-234	12	Muchacho de Oro	8
King Skeet	29	Murl L	27
King's Pistol	29	Myrtle Dee TB	13
		My Texas Dandy	9
Lady Bug's Moon	20		
Lady Coolidge	21	Nautical	9
Lady Fairfax	23	Nelly	6
Lady Line Rider	19	Nelly Bly	29
Lady Yolanda	31	Nick Shoemaker	27
Lena Horn	6	No Butt	13
Lena Leo	9		
Lena's Bar	25	Oklahoma Star Jr.	2
Leo	8	Oklahoma Star p-6	1
Leo Bar	19	Old Poco Bueno	10
Leola	13	Old Red Buck p-9	26
Leo Lena	11	One Eyed Waggoner	14

	line		line
Osage Star	7	Scooper Chick	22
Osage Star Lady	8	Senior George	30
		She Kitty	26
Palleo Pete	10	Side Car	28
Pana Bar	28	Silver Cash	26
Panita	2	Skeeter	30
Panmure TB	2	Skipper W	30
Paul A	9	Snipper W	30
Paul Ell	5	Spanish Joy	31
Peace Pipe TB	7	Star's Lu	4
Peppy	3	Steel Bars	16
Peppy Cooper	4	Stella Moore	4
Peppy San	23	Streak	9
Plaudit	7	Streaky Jane	15
Poco Bueno	16	Sue Reed	6
Poco Lena	30	Sugar Bars	18
Poco Line Rider	18	Sunkist	8
Poco Pine	26	Super Chick	28
Poco Shock	25	Suwannee Bars	25
Poker Chip Peake	25		
Pokey Bar	29	Tadpole	24
Pokey Vandy	22	Texas Dandy	11
Porte Drapeau TB	5	Texas Pine	26
Possum (King)	1	Three Bars TB	15
Priority TB	14	Three Chicks	25
		Tom Scooter	22
		Tonto Bars Gill	17
Queeny	24	Tonto Bars Hank	20
		Tonto Gal	12
Randle's Lady	9	Top Deck TB	9
Rebel Cause	11	Top Lady Bug	18
Red Bud Lady	21	Top Moon	16
Red Dog	22	Topsy	28
Red Joe of Arizona	27	Triple Chick	21
River Boat TB	8		
Robin Reed	9	Vandy	24
Rosa Leo	10	Vandy's Flash	27
Royal Chess	30	Vanetta Dee	25
Royal King	17	Vanny Bar	29
Roy Deck	17	Virgie Lee	20
Ruby	13		
Ruby Too	23	Wardlo	29
		Wimpy p-1	4
Sadie May	7	Wimpy Leo	24
San Siemon	5	Wimpy II	6
San Sue Darks	21		
Sergeant	4	Zeff's Leo	11

APPENDIX B

Early Western Studs

The following are some of the race horse sires whose get—only partially listed—were among the first important horse families in the trans-Appalachian West in the late eighteenth and early nineteenth centuries. A large proportion of them contributed to the Quarter Horse branch of the Thoroughbred.

In perusing Volume VII of Sanders D. Bruce's *American Stud Book,* one notices the numerous listings of "dam by Janus," dam by Diomed," "dam by Sir Archy," and "dam by Bertrand." These are the meager records of the origins of the Quarter Horses that went West.

Not until about 1840 were the distance runners of the Thoroughbreds well established in Kentucky and its bordering states. The trotters—descendants of Messenger and Hambletonian, and the resulting Standardbreds—remained in the East, centered mostly in New York State. Not until after the Civil War were harness racers bred in the Midwest.

Few Quarter Horses were given space in the *American Stud Book* after 1840, except in the Appendix, where clarification of relationships with other horses required it, or where horses with imperfect pedigrees were listed. Only there can references to Harry Bluff—sire of Steel Dust—Dan Tucker, and Steel Dust himself be found.

Preceding the general listing of sires and their get is this brief listing of some of the horse pioneers in the new states.

Ohio
    John Van Meter brought good horse stock to the Scioto Valley from Virginia. Among them was Spread Eagle by Volunteer, who traced to Morton's Traveler.
    Printer I fathered many good horses in Fairfield County. "He was a Quarter Horse," says the American Stud Book. So were his get.
1820–30 Kentucky Whip came to Scioto Valley to stand at stud as did Bertrands. And Old Baccus was well known in the state.
    Highland County had Eclipse horses—among them Governor Allen Trimble's racers.
1825—There were by this time many Cook and Blackburn Whip horses in the western part of the state.

    From the early 1800s race meets were held at Cincinnati, Chillicothe, Dayton, and Hamilton.

Michigan
    Many good horses came to this state from Vermont, New York, and Kentucky.
    Kippalo was owned by Governor Porter. He was by John Richards by Sir Archy.

John Baccus and his full brother Telegraph were popular sires. The latter was said to have run the quarter in twenty-seven seconds, probably from a standing start.

The best-known tracks were at Detroit, Adrian, Cold Water, Jackson, Kalamazoo, and Marshall.

In 1850 A. Y. Moore wrote that there were many good horses in the state of Baccus strain from Old Baccus of Ohio.

Illinois

Brimmers were well liked for their intelligence and for their Quarter Horse muscling.

Indiana

Tiger, who made a big name for himself in the state, was a grandson of Printer I.

Kentucky and Tennessee

In as much as most of the Virginia blood-horses that influenced the Western strains merged in these states, the districts, breeders, and prominent sires are too numerous to mention in detail. All six states mentioned in this appendix served as pioneer assembly stations from which came the stock that was to found the Southwestern Quarter Horse families.

To cite but a few; Alsup's Farm in Tennessee developed a strain called the White Lightnings. It traced to both Bertrand and Brimmer stock. There was a profusion, and confusion, of Brimmers. Here are seven Brimmers as listed in Bruce's *American Stud Book,* Volume VII.

Brimmer b.h. by Herod—bred and owned by John Goode Sr. Esq. of Powhatan County, Virginia.
   * 5th dam by Imp. Fearnought
   6th dam by Janus
   8th dam by Janus

Goode's Brimmer b.h. 1766–86 bred by Thomas Turpin of Powhatan County, Virginia. (Purchased by Colonel John Goode Sr.) by Harris' Eclipse
   1st dam Poll Flaxon by Imp. Jolly Rogers
   2nd dam Imp. Mary Grey by Roundhead

Brimmer by Imp. St. George bred and owned by John Goode Sr.

Brimmer by Imp. Valiant owned in Virginia and North Carolina

Brimmer by Harris' Eclipse owned in North Carolina

Brimmer by Stockholder—owned and bred by Eben Bess Brimmer in Kentucky (Scott County)

Brimmer by Blue Blood bred in South Carolina—owned in Kentucky.

* Numbered dams refer to number of generations back.

APPENDIX C

Contributors to the Quarter Horse Branch of the Thoroughbreds

Imp. **DIOMED** 1777–1808   To Virginia 1789 by Florizel by Herod by Tartar by Jigg by Byerly Turk

Some of his noted sons:
Accummulator   foaled 1803
Bonaparte
Eclipse
Ceder
Centinal
Chamberlain
Constitution
Crop
Cultivator
Curtius
Deception
Duroc   foaled 1806 died 1826 on Long Island
Sir Archy   foaled 1805 died 1833
Tartar

daughter:
Old Ledbetter Mare

In the following listings:

b. = bay	b.h. = chestnut horse	br.h. = brown horse
br. = brown	b.m. = gray horse	bl.h. = black horse
ch. = chestnut	ch.h. = bay horse	r.h. = roan horse
gr. = gray	gr.h. = bay mare	

Imp. **MEDLEY** named for Mr. Medley, owner of a famous London Coffee and Gambling House frequented by the Duke of Cumberland. Medley was imported to Hart and McDonald of Louisa, Va., in 1784.

Most noted sons: with date of birth and owner and his state—if recorded in stud book

Aleppo	1792		
Alfred		Craig's	Va.
Boxer	1790	Curd's	
Dionysus gr.	1787		

Dungannon gr.	1789	Bland's	
Fitz Medley		died in 1805	
		owned by Colonel Sharp	Tenn.
Gim Crack gr.			
Grey Childers gr.	1799		Va. & N.C.
Grey Diomed gr.	1786		
Grey Medley		to Tenn. between 1795–1800	
		owned by Colonel Sharp	
Halicarnassus	1792		
Hyder Ally gr.			
Medley br.h.		Jones	N.C.
Medley gr.		White's	
Medley gr.h.		owned in	Ky.
Medley		Thompson's—owned 1803 in	Ky.
Medley gr.		Ridgeley's—owned in	Md.
Melzar b.	1791		
Opemico b.	1787		
Pot-8-O's			
Quicksilver gr.		Tayloe's—owned by Ed Jordan in 1802	
Randolph's Roan	1789		
Republican ch.	1793		
Sheridan b.	1793		
Snap gr.		bred in Md.—owned in in 1797 (see George West)	Ky.
Trimmer gr.	1791		
Wild Medley			
Yarico	1796		

Imp. **JANUS** 1746–1780 to Virginia 1752 (by Old Janus by Godolphin Barb).

Most noted sons:

Arabian	1772–1777	there were four by this name	
Agustus	1791		Va.
Babram	1766–1789	Goode's—out of Janus mare	Va.
Bacchus	1776–	Scott's	
Ball	1774–	out of Janus mare	N.C.
Braddock gr.h.			Va.
Buie			Va.
Camillus		standing in 1777 in	Va.
Celer	1774–1802	Meade's—dam by Imp. Aristotle	Va.
Clubfoot	1778–		N.C.
Cripple gr.h.			
Crippled Janus ch.h.	1757–	owned by Geo. Floyd	N.C.

APPENDIX C

Dominica			N.C.
Fabricius ch.h.	1776–	1st & 2nd dam by Fearnought	Va.
Fabricius	1776–		N.C.
Firemane ch.h.		Williamsons	Va.
Fleetwood ch.h.	1770–	Tho. Turpin's—stood in	N.J.
Goldfinger ch.h.			Va.
Janus		Baylor's	Va.
Janus b.h.	1771–	Young Hayne's	
Jolly Roger b.h.	1774–	Jones's—Halifax country. There was a Jolly Rogers by Meade's Celer and another by Imported Jolly Rogers	Va.
Junius ch.h.			N.C.
Junius gr.h.		1st dam by Fearnought	Va.
Jupiter bl.h.			N.C.
Jupiter ch.h.		1st dam by Janus—owned by Augustus Willis	Va.
Jupiter ch.h.	1772–	owned by Captain Wm. Bell	Va.
Moggy gr.h.		owned in 1779 by J. H. Dancy	Va.
Nabob ch.h.		bred and owned by Col. Burwell	Va.
One-Eye bl.h.		owned in 1798 in Martin Co.	N.C.
Pandolpho lt.b.h.		owned in 1779 in	N.C.
Peacock	1760–1786	out of Spanish mare—bred by Joseph J. Alston—owned by Mr. Brinkley. The fastest racehorse of his day.	Va.
Peacock br.h.	1772–	Roland's	Va.
Peacock ch.h.		William's—owned in 1793 by Sam Glenn	N.C.
Protector br.h.	1774–	Hanley's	Va.
Protector		Buchannon's line bred	Va.
Purse Full ch.h.	1778–	Hayley's	Va.
Purse Full		owned in 1801 by Eaton Sr.	
Mercury			
Ranger		line bred—owned by Geo. Wilson	
Scott		bred and owned by John Dickson	Va.
Shad ch.h.	1761–		Va.
Silverheels		owned by Clifford in 1782	Va.
Sorrel ch.h.	1776–	owned by Leake's	N.C.
Spider	1774	full brother of Roland's Peacock	N.C.
Sporty		out of General Nelson's Spanish mare	Va.
Sprightly ch.h.		owned in 1770 by Alex G. Jones	N.C.
Sprightly gr.h.		owned by Willis in 1780	Va.
Starling	1766–	out of Spanish Dam—Halifax Co.	N.C.
Statesman		owned in 1775 in	Va.
Stern		Bennehan's	

Sterne gr.h.		owned in 1776 in	N.C.
Syphax			Va.
Terror		owned in 1779 by John Moore in	N.C.
Traveler ch.h.		owned in 1774 by Mr. McCrea	Va.
Tusk r.h.		owned in 1804 by Francis Ballard	Va.
Twickham b.h.	1778–		N.C.
Twigg b.h.	1778–1798	owned by John Goode of	Va.
Warning b.h.	1774–		Va.
Warren ch.h.	1778–		Va.
Why-Not		owned in 1795 by Capt. Arundell	N.C.
Wilkes b.h.	1774–	Goode's—1st dam Janus—2nd dam Janus	Va.

SIR ARCHY by Diomed-Florizel-King Herod-Tartar-Jigg Byerly Turk out of Imp. Castianira, out of Tabitha by Rockingham.

Most noted sons:

Arab	1820–		N.C.
Alabama			
Alexander (Peeble's)			
Archy b.h.	1819–		N.C.
Bacchus b.h.			Tenn.
Balsora	1819–		
Baron Trenck			Ga.
Bertrand	1821–38	James Lindsay Lexington, a family of Bertrands derived partly from Jenet Bertrand by Sir Archy, were called the *White Lightnings* raised on the Alsup Farm in	Ky.
			Tenn.
Bill the Batchelor	1827–		N.C.
Black Heath	1831–		Va.
Black Streak			N.C.
Blucher br.h.		ran in	Tenn. & Miss.
Bronze br.h.	1830–		Va.
Brutus b.h.	1829–		Va.
Cadmus			Ky.
Character	1824–		N.C.
Childers II	1818–	bred by Gen. Wynn—stood in	Ky.
Childers ch.	1817–	bred by John Goode Sr. out of Robin m. a full brother of Sumpter & Rattler	Va.
Cherokee ch.	c. 1824–	out of Roxana by Hephestion	Ky.
Cicero			

APPENDIX C 533

Copperbottom ch.	1828–	bred by Edward Parker of Lancaster, Penn. Owned 1839–60 by Sam Houston—Texas 1. dam by Imp. Buzzard 2. dam by Rattle by Imp. Shark 3. dam by Imp. Medley 4. dam by Symme's Wildair 5. dam by Nonpareil	Texas
Crusher		Owned 1840 by Henry Tayloe	Va.
Damper	1827–		
Democrat (The)	1834–		Ark.
Director	1811–27	Bertie Co.	N.C.
Don Pedro		Bertie Co.	N.C.
Eclat ch.	1827–	bred in N.C. owned in	Va.
Emperor ch.	1822–		Va.
Giant b.	1816–		N.J.
Golden Fleece	1831–		N.C.
Greasy Butcher		George Smith	Miss.
Gray Archy	1811–	Philips	Tenn.
Harwood b.h.		Davie's	N.C.
Henry ch.h.	1819–	bred by L. Long in N.C.— Wm. Johnson	Va.
Hobgoblin b.h.	1815–		N.C.
Hyacinth b.h.		Crump's	Va.
Istorm b.h.	1814–		Va.
John Richards			Va.
Jackson ch.h.		(blind)	Va.
Jenet Bertrand m.		Alsup Farm	Tenn.
Kosciusko	1815–		
Larry O'Gaff ch.h.	1827–	by Sir Archy Jr.	
Lawrence br.h.	1814–		Va. & Ky.
Long Waist	1828–		Ala.
Macbeth	1828–		Va.
Martha			
Mercury b.h.	1827–	J. M. Selden of Va. sold to	Tenn.
Mark Anthony b.h.	1821–	out of Roanoke by Ball's Florizel who was foaled in 1815—bred and owned by John Randolph of Roanoke, Va.	Va.
Merlin b.h.	1824–		Va.
Napoleon	1815–30	died of kick Colonel Elliot	Ky.
Norfolk r.h.	1828–	dam by Medley	Va.
Orange Boy ch.h.	1829–		
Pay Master ch.h.	1827–	Wm. Wilkins	Va.
Pacific		full brother of Bertrand	
Rattler ch.h.	1816–	out of Robin m. by Robin Redbreast full brother of Childers & Sumpter. There were 7 other Rattlers between 1825–32	

Riot b.h.	1829–		N.C.
Rockingham b.h.	1822–		N.C.
Saxe Weimer b.h.	1822–	out of Lottery by Imp. Bedford full brother of Young Lottery 1813 and Kosciusko 1815	
Roxana m.		There are 23 Roxanas in Stud books of this period—two were by Sir Archy—5 by his sons and one by Diomed	
Sir Archy Jr.			
Sir Archy (Young's)			
Sir Archy Horse b.h.	1830–		N.C.
Sir Charles ch.h.	1816–33	out of mare by Citizen by Imp. Citizen. He died the same day as his dad.	Va.
Sir Erin ch.h.	1829–	owned by James S. Garrison	Va.
Sir James b.h.	1819–		
Sir Sampson b.h.	1815–		
South Carolina br.h.		owned and bred by Jonathan Pope	
Standard b.h.	1827–		
Stockholder		owned in 1820 by Henry Cotten in	N.C.
Sumpter	1818–31	full brother of Rattler and Childers	Ky.
Sir Peter Teazle	1820–	dam Harriet Eaton by Bellair	
Sir Richard	c. 1820–	dam Lady Jane by Potomac	
Telemachus b.h.		owned in 1825 in	N.C.
Virginian b.h.	1815–	dam Meretrix by Magog	
Waxy			
Whalebone b.h.	1829–		Ala.
William ch.h.	1830–		
Yazoo	1824–		Va.
Young Henry ch.h.	1826–		Fla.
Young Sir Archy			Va.

BERTRAND b.h. foaled 1821– by Sir Archy—out of Eliza by Imp. Bedford out of Mambrina by Mambrino. He was a full brother of Pacific and founder of the Bertrand strain in Kentucky and Tennessee.

Most noted sons:

Alroy b.	1831–		Ky.
Balie Peyton b.	1833		Tenn.
Barton Red			Ky.
Bay Bill b.	1833	dam by Cherokee	Ky.
Bay Bolton b.	1834	dam by Cherokee Maj. W. R. Peyton	Tenn.

APPENDIX C

Bear Meat br.	1837		Ark.
Bedford b.	1831		Ky.
Bertrand	1829		Pa.
Bertrand Jr.			Ky.
Big John ch.	1834		Ky.
Bill Austin	1831		Ga.
Billy Medley gr.	1829		Ky.
Burgundy	1838		Tenn.
Buzzard b.	1837	J. C. Mason	Ky.
Canton	1839		N.C.
Cascade b.	1834		Ky.
Cavalier Serviente gr.	1835		Ga.
Chronometer	1832		Ga.
Conflict b.	1834		Ky.
Crichton ch.	1837		S.C.
Deceiver	1831		Va.
Director b.	1830		Ky.
Driver	1830		
Duff Green	1832	Wade's	Ky.
Franklin ch.	1834	Sold into Missouri	
Freedom ch.	1836	John Calvert's	Mo.
Factor b.	1834		S.C.
Gauglion Gangle b.	1837		Mo.
Granby b.	1828	M. & T. J. Well's	La.
Independence b.	1827		Ohio
James Crowell b.	1836	James J. Allen	Ky.
John B. Jones b.	1837	A. Webster	Ark.
Kavenaugh ch.	1834	James Shy	Ky.
Kentuckian (Kentuctian) b.	1833		Ky.
Leather Stocking b.	1830		Ind.
Little Barton	1833		Mo.
Little Red ch.	1832		Ala.
Long Measure b.	1830	full brother of Bill Austin dam by Sir Archy	
Lorenzo b.	1834		Ky.
Maltravers b.	1834	Col. R. H. Long	Ala.
Marcellus b.	1828		Ga.
McDonough b.	1828		
Mediterranean	1830	Buford	Ky.
Moreau b.	1831		Ky.
Nelson b.	1830		Ky.
Nonsuch b.	1830		Ky.
Oliver Cromwell b.	1831		
Orphan Boy b.	1831	dam by Whip	Ky.
Orphan Boy b.	1827	dam by Sir Archy	
Pacificator b.	1833		Ky.

Paul Clifford br.	1832			Ala.
Powhatan ch.	1830	N. G. Fitch		
Rich M. Johnson ch.	1830	dam by Cook's Whip		
Sir Clinton b.	1832			
Streamlet b.	1832	P. R. Hazel		Ind.
Tariff b.	1830	Col. Wm. Buford		Ky.
Tasso gr.	1838			Ohio

STOCKHOLDER   By Sir Archy—owned in 1820 by Henry Cotten   N.C.

Most noted sons:

Ben Franklin			
Brimmer	1830–	bred and owned by Eben Bess Brimmer, Scott Co. 1st Lamplighter 2nd Medley 3rd Fearnought	Ky.
Bucephalus b.	1832–	4th Janus	Ky.
Cashier	1829–		Tenn.
Cave Johnson b.	1832–		Ky.
Cup Bearer	1824–		Tenn.
Deception	1838–		
El Balero b.			Tenn.
Grey Hound gr.	1831–	Henry Smith	Tenn.
Hailstorm	1834–		Tenn.
Hardy M. Cryer br.	1833–	Later owned in Ky.	Tenn.
Jim Polk br.	1838–	Dam by Bertrand	Tenn.
Little John b.	1837–		Tenn.
Major Domo b.	1827–		Ala.
Marshall Ney b.	1827–		Tenn.
Metamora b.	1833–	Dam by Janus	Ohio
Mercury	1828–		
Murat b.c.	1827–		Tenn.
Narses gr.	1827–	Gelded	Tenn.
Paul Clfford b.	1828–		Tenn.
Polander b.	1827–		
Pumpkin Boy ch.	1835–		Tenn.
Robert Burns b.		Dam by Sir Archy owned in 1832 by Lewis Sherley	Ky.
Rattle the Cash gr.	1827–		
Rocky River ch.	1829–		
Sam Bell b.	1836–	Dam by Medley	La.
Sam Houston		Owned by Shelby in 1830	Tenn.
Smoloff ch.	1830–		Tenn.
Stockholder ch.	1828–	Young's—dam by Wilkes Wonder	Tenn.

Stockholder gr.	1829–		
Stockholder		Dunbar's—owned by him in 1829	Tenn.
Telegraph b.	1828–		Tenn.
Tom Fletcher ch.	1827–	Dam by Pacolet	Ill.
Uncas ch.	1827–		Tenn.
Walk in the Water, Jr.	1828–	Died of a fall in 1838	Tenn.
Warwick ch.	1841–		Tenn.
William Tell ch.	1832–		
Wing Wilson b.	1837–	Bred and owned by Judge Harding	Ill.
Young Stockholder ch.	1828–		

CHEROKEE by Sir Archy—thought to have been foaled about 1824 and to have been chestnut like his dam Roxana who was by Hephestion and out of Roxana by Imp. Marplot. Bruce edition of 1873 shows 23 Roxanas.

7 were chestnut	2 were by Sir Archy
13 were bay	2 by Timoleön
2 were brown	1 by Diomed
1 was black	1 by Stockholder
	1 by Sir Solomon
	1 by Sir Charles

Most noted sons:

Alamanzer b.h.			Ky.
Ben Duncan b.h.	1823–		Ky.
Ben Sutton ch.h.			Ky.
Big Davy b.h.	1831–		Ky.
Cooper b.h.	1829–		Ohio
Jim Crow ch.h.	1835–		Ky.
John Adair b.h.	1832–	Dam by Sir Archy	Ky.
Lighthouse ch.h.	1831–		Ky.
Little Davy br.h.	1836–		Ky.
Little Wonder b.h.	1837–		Ky.
Monticello b.h.	1832–		
Murat br.h.			Ky.
Oceo bl.h.	1835		Ohio
Othello bl.h.		Owned in 1830 in	Ky.
Othello br.h.		Owned in 1828 in Dam by Blackburn's Whip	Ky.
Sam Chifney	1837–		Ky.
Sir Charles ch.h.	1827		Ky.
Another Cherokee	1847–1872	—"a quarter horse"—died at Council Bluffs, Iowa.	

MEDOC

Most noted sons:

Charley Anderson	1839–		Ohio
Cow Boy	1837–		La.
Frenchman	1836–		Ky.
George Kenner gr.	1835–	Dam by Bertrand	
Gov. Wickliffe	1837–		Ky.
Hemlock ch.	1838–		Ky.
Irad ch.	1838–	Dam by Tiger	
Joe ch.	1839–	Dams Sir Archy line	
John C. Stevens b.	1840–		Ky.
Kanawha ch.	1836–	John Lewis	Ky.
Langham ch.	1838–	Bred and owned by C. F. Jackson	Mo.
Leg Treasurer ch.	1837–		Ky.
Mad Anthony b.	1836–		Ky.
Nick Biddle b.	1836–		Ky.
Nick-O-the-Woods ch.	1837–		Miss.
Nolachucky b.	1836–		La.
O'Hara b.	1840–	Dam by Tiger	Ky.
Partner ch.	1838–		
Pathfinder ch.	1838–		Mo.
Powell ch.	1836–	Buford	Ky.
Prentice b.	1838–	Saml. Davenport	Ky.
Red Hawk ch.	1835–		Ky.
Medoc Jr.		(–had a son Santa Anna 1846)	Ky.
Sharatack ch.	1840–		Mo.
Sir Halpin ch.	1835–		Ky.
Stevenson b.	1840–		Ky.
Stub Twist ch.	1836–	J. G. Perry	La.
St. Julien b.	1839–		Ky.
Tom Marshall b.	1838–	Buford	Ky.
Trap Ball b.	1838–	Dam by Bertrand	Ky.
Troy ch.	1837–	Dam by Tiger	Mo.
Whipster b.	1837–	Dam by B's Whip	Ky.
Wild Buck ch.	1838–	Born in Ky.—owned in	Ill.
Wisconsin Medoc		Out of Bertrand mare	

TIMOLEON ch. 1814– by Sir Archy out of Saltram mare by Imp. Saltram.

Most noted sons:

Andrew Jackson	
Bendigo gr.	1835–
Brunswick	1827–
Canova b.	

Cassawaga b.	1835–		
Centurion	1821–		
Citizen	1829–		Tenn.
Don Pedro			
Door Keeper	1831–		
Escape ch.			
Washington			
Gen. Jackson b.	1827–		
Hazard ch.	1829–	Sproul's	
Hero gr.	1829–		S.C.
Hot Spur ch.		Plummer's	
Jackson b.		Sproul's	Fla.
Marshall ch.	1832–		
Mazeppa ch.			Ga.
Miantonimoh ch.	1830–	Owned by Gen. McArthur	Ohio
Michigan		Owned in 1835 in	Mo.
Molo b.	1827–		
Monsier Tonson ch.	1829–	Bred and owned by W. Peebles	Tenn.
Nick Biddle b.	1832–		
Paragon ch.	1824–	Moore's	
Paragon ch.			Ala.
Washington	1819–1841		Ohio
Rattler ch.m.		Out of Constitution by imp. Diomed	
Rob Roy ch.	1829–		Tenn.
Sam Patch ch.	1830–		Tenn.
Sir John Falstaff b.	1822–		
Soap Stick	1824–	Bred and owned in Tenn.— dam by Pacolet	
Stafford ch.			
Tryo ch.	1832–		
Velox b.	1831–		
Timoleon	1829–	out of Pocontas by Pacolet	Tenn.
Timoleon		out of dam by Telemachus	Tenn.
Timoleon	1826–	out of Martha by Sir Archy	N.C.

Other noted sires (get not listed) whose stock contributed to the racing strains in the trans-Appalachian region:

American Eclipse	Pacific
Bellair	Pacolet
Eclipse	Rattler
Fearnought	Silvereye
Hedgeford	Trumpator
Jolly Rogers	Waxy
Mark Anthony	Wildair
Monkey	

Some of the better known race horse sires, most of whose stock was identified with the Quarter Horse branch of the Thoroughbreds in Kentucky and Tennessee and surrounding states:

Alasco	1812–28	By Tiger 1	Ky.
Alexander		By Tiger 1 Buford's	Ky.
Arabian Bagdad Imp.		His mares produced Vanity and Ariadne by Bertrand	
Cade		By Imp. Fearnought—died at age of 5 in	Ky.
Baccus (Old)		Shot during race—by a bad loser	Ohio
Bay Cold Deck		By Hamburg Dick by Printer 1	
Bertrand	1821–38	By Sir Archy. J. Lindsay's	Ky.
Boanerges		By Printer 1	Ky.
Boxer	1812–30	By Imp. Expedition—died in	Ohio
Brimmer		By Stockholder—owned by Eben Bess Brimmer. There were 8 Brimmers.	Ky.
Blackburn's Whip	1805–28	By Imp. Whip	Ky.
Cherokee	1824–	By Sir Archy out of Roxana	
Cherokee	1847–72	"a quarter horse"—died Council Bluffs	Iowa
Collector	1813–	By Mark Anthony by Sir Archy	Tenn.
Constitution	1805–27	By Diomed	Tenn.
Dare Devil	1792–	By Don Carlos—Johnson's	Ky.
Dragon Imp.	1787–1812	By Woodpecker—died in	Tenn.
Eclipse	1814–47	By Duroc by Diomed	Ky.
Gim Crack	1830–	By Pacolet out of Tiger mare	Ky.
Gim Crack	1835	By Am. Eclipse—Hunt's	Tenn.
Glencoe	1831–57	By Sultan—A. Keene Richards	Ky.
Grey Medley		Taken between 1795 and 1800 to	Ky.
Harry Bluff	1831–	By Boxer—owned by Ichabod Grummer	Ohio
Harry Bluff	1838–	By Imp. Autocrat—Willie Taylor's	Tenn.
Hephestian	1807–33	By Imp. Buzzard	Tenn.
Jefferson	1828	By Saxe Weimer by Sir Archy	Mich.
John Baccus		Out of Printer mare—Armstrong	Mich.
Kentucky Whip		—Scioto Valley	Ohio
Kippalo		By John Richards by Sir Archy	Ky.
Medley		By Imp. Medley—owned by Thompson in 1803 in	Ky.
Medley gr.		Ridgeley's—there were two other Medleys that went west	
Midas ch.	1778–	Bred and owned by Senator Goode—sons in	Ky.
Moses		By Bellair—founded early strain in	Mo.
Napoleon	1815–30	By Sir Archy—Col. Elliott	Ky.

Oscar	1814–25	By Wilkes Little Wonder—Sumner Co.	Tenn.
Peace Maker	1800–27	By Diomed	Tenn.
Pelion b.h.	1836–	By Imp. Luzborough out of Bertrand mare	Ky.
Printer l.	1800–28	—Scioto Valley	Ohio

Origin of Tennessee Harlequin family of horses—

Harlequin br.h.	1800	By Imp. Gabriel—bred and owned in	Md.
Harlequin br.h.		By Eclipse—stood in 1805 in	N.J.
Harlequin 11		By Harlequin—James Bramble in	Va.

APPENDIX D

Spanish and Mexican Color Terms for Horses

alazán—sorrel
alazán roan—light sorrel, golden-maned
alazán tostado—chestnut sorrel
andaluz—yellow with golden mane and tail
aplumado—bay, dun, sorrel, black with featherlike flecks
azeitunero—olive-colored (De Soto's horse)
azulejo—dark blue roan
barroso—smudgy dun
bayo—dun
bayo azafranado—light bright dun (saffron)
bayo coyote—dirty dun, black points
bayo tigre—line back leg striped dun—zebra dun
blanco—white
canelo—blue roan, cinnamon-hued
cebruno—dark brown, smoky-hued
champurrado—chocolate brown
colorado—bay (red)
coyote—dirty dun, black points
gateado—cat-colored
golondrino—dark brown, golden flecks
grullo—crane-colored—the word means sand-hill crane

güero—albino, pink eyes, skin
labuno—wolf-colored
manchado—soiled or splotched white
melado—white with age
mojino—dark brown, almost black
morzillo—black (Cortés's horse)
negro—black
obscuro—dark bay
palomino—golden dun, flaxen points
pangare—bay with tan muzzle
pardusco—mouse-colored
pinto—spotted (English—piebald if black and white; skewbald if varicolored)
prieto—black
retinto—bright bay
rocillo—roan
rocillo azul—blue roan
rocillo picado—white with roan flanks
rusbayo—light dun, dash of gold
sabino—piebald
tordillo—iron gray, thrush-colored
tostado—parched sorrel
trigueño—wheat-colored ($trigo =$ wheat)
zaino—bay with light markings
zarillo—polecat, black with white points

APPENDIX E

Spanish and Mexican Horse, Ranch and Southwestern Terms

alacrán—scorpion
albo—white as in combination
alto—high, upper
amarillo—yellow
bajo-a—lower, short, underneath
botas—leggings
bozal—noseband (English—cavesson), English spelling: bosal
brasada—brush country
caballada—herd of horses
caballo—horse
caballo con huevos—stallion
caballo de cría—stallion
caballo entero—stallion
cabestro—soft hair rope
cabeza—head
cansado—weary, tired
carablanca—white-faced
carreta—two-wheeled cart
casquinegro—black-hoofed
chaparral—brush
chaparajos—chaps, leather leg coverings to protect from brush
charqui—jerky, dried meat
charro—gentleman rider
cobre—copper
cola de pato—duck's tail, decoration behind saddle, covering rump
comanchero—traders with Comanches—later any trader with Indians
coraza—saddlebags (like mochila, had pockets)
corno—horn
cortar—cut back, as with cattle
corto—short
cría—breeding
cruzado—crossed, as horse with one white forefoot and one white hind foot
cuervo—crow (*el cuervo*—a name for black horse)
cuidado—take care
dar la vuelta—take a turn as with a rope. Corrupted to *davelta* and then to dally. A *vuelta* is a go-around in a bicycle race.
despecho—indignation
domador—horse breaker
dosalbo—two white feet
duro—hard, firm, durable (palo duro—hard wood)
encerrador—enclosure or pen
entrenador—horse trainer
estacado—stake
estribos—stirrups
fiador—throat latch on hackamore
goucho—the forsaken, vagabond
hacienda—estate, ranch
hondo—small loop at end of a rope through which the noose runs.
horno—oven made of mud
jaquima—hackamore
la babona—Bob Tail
lazo—lasso
llano—plain, prairie (*llano estacado* = staked plain
loco—crazy
lucero—morning star, star-faced
manada—band of mustang mares and colts kept in control by a single stallion, a herd, drove
manalbo—white forefeet
mañana—tomorrow
mangana—the roping throw that catches the forefeet (from *manga* = sleeve)
manso—gentle, tame (in hand)
martillo—hammerhead
mecate—braided rope on hackamore
mercedor—rocking chair (easy riding)
mesa—table, flat
mesteño—mustang
mestizo—person that is part white, part Indian (half-breed)
mochila—leather, with pockets, thrown over saddle (pony express)
monoblanca—one white forefoot
monte—wood, grove
moral—fiber nose bag

motilla—tuft, as remaining tuft on mane
palo—wood
partido—party of men
paseo—walk, ride, promenade
patablanco—white-footed
peale—throw of loop to catch hind feet (from *peal* = sock). It applies to horses rather than cattle, where the word "heeling" is used.
pelado—hairless
pico—muzzle
pilón—a special treat
pinole—corn meal sweetened
porto—unbroken horse
quatralbo—four white feet
quento—quint

reata—rope (*la riata* = lariat)
relámpago—lightning fast, off the mark
remanche—short-barreled
remuda—band of saddle horses
salvaje—savage
tapaderos—shields, covers, specifically stirrup coverings
tasajo—jerked beef
tecolote—owl
tintero—ink (a black)
tresalbo—three white feet
trosalbo—white hind feet
vaca—cow
vaquero—cowboy
yegua—mare

GLOSSARY

ACTION—manner of going: high knee; smooth; choppy; trappy; paddling, etc.
AGED—ten years and older.
AIDS—use of reins, leg pressure, weight shifts, voice, spurs, and whips, to communicate to the horse changes of gaits, leads, and tempo.
ALBINO—a horse lacking normal pigmentation in skin, eyes, and hair, generally with white coat and pink eyes. A breed of albino horse was developed in Nebraska and a registry was established in 1930.
AMATEUR—one who rides, trains, and works with horses for the love of it rather than for financial recompense; not necessarily a novice but not a professional.
AMBLE—a natural but cultivated four-beat swinging walk.
AHSA—American Horse Shows Association.
AMERICAN PAINT HORSE—a varicolored spotted horse long known in the Western United States. Often identified with "Indian Horses." Stud book opened in 1962.
AMERICAN SADDLEBRED (AMERICAN SADDLE HORSE)—a breed of horse of elegance and high action—a show breed—15 to 15.3 hands high, trained for three or five gaits. The foundation sire was Denmark, an imported Thoroughbred by Hedgeford and out of Betty Harrison (1839).
ANDALUSIAN—a breed of horse brought to perfection by the Moors and later the Spaniards of Southern Spain; Arab and Barb crossed on native stock, the horse that was brought to the Americas by the Spanish conquistadors. A few of the horse breeds that trace directly to them are: Mustangs; Criollo (of Argentina); Lipizzaner; Hanoverian; Trakenen; Percheron; Quarter Horses.
APPALOOSA—Horse breed originating in the Western United States with a registry founded in 1938; roan, brown, or gray, often sprinkled with white hairs and with a "blanket" of white extending from near the middle of the back over the rump and quarters, that is splattered with dark spots. Developed by the Palouse Indians, a branch of the Nez Percé, by careful selective breeding from Spanish horses that had been acquired as early as 1730.
AQHA—American Quarter Horse Association, founded in 1940; has a registry of more horses than any other breed.
AQHBA—American Quarter Horse Breeders Association.
AQHRA—American Quarter Horse Racing Association, organized in 1945.

ASK AND ANSWER—a race between two horses in which the start depends on one jockey asking the other if he is ready. If he answers "yes" or "go" the race is on. Since each wants an advantage this old-time method caused many false starts.

BALANCED SEAT—is achieved by consistent stirrup pressure, which puts rider's weight over the horse's withers, which aids the horse in balancing himself; it allows the horse more head freedom, as the rider does not depend on pulling on reins or gripping with knees to maintain balance. Riders who ride for a purpose with but one hand to manage the reins (which requires neck-reining), such as cavalrymen, stockmen, and polo players, have used this seat since the invention of stirrups.

BALD FACE or BLAZE FACE—a horse face marked with white from forehead to nose.

BALL—medicine pill for horses, administered with a balling gun.

BARREL—midsection of horse, which is said to be well ribbed up or churn-barreled if the body is well rounded.

BARREN MARE—one that cannot or does not produce a foal.

BARS—the part of a horse's hoof that turns inward at the heel.
—the metal pieces under the skirts of a flat saddle to which the stirrup leathers are attached.
—the braces across the back of some horseshoes.
—the toothless spaces of the lower jaw inside the mouth between the incisor and molar teeth, where the cannon of the bit rests.

BAT—a short racing or training whip or stick.

BAY—can range from bright orange to dark red, but as long as the mane and tail are black, the horse is called a bay.

BEHIND THE BIT—expresses the action of a horse that slows, halts, backs or rears, or flexes the neck excessively rather than accept any pressure on the bars of the mouth by the bit.

BELL MARE—one that wears a bell in a remuda so that the horses are easy to find in pasture.
—a Judas mare who leads the others into captivity.

BILLET—the straps on an English saddle to which the girth is buckled.
—the strap on the off side of a Western saddle to which the cinch is attached, and the straps on the rear D-rings to which the rear girth is buckled.

BITS—the metal mouthpieces in a bridle to which reins are attached.

BLINKERS, WINKERS, or BLINDERS—eye shields to prevent horses seeing distracting objects or movements.

BLISTER—to apply an irritant, such as mercury ointment, to draw blood to the area in order to relieve strained muscles or tendons.

BLOOD HORSE—highly bred race horses; predates the Thoroughbred but the expression is still used largely to indicate that breed.

BOLT—the horse runs away.

BOSAL—noseband, as on light hackamore—from Spanish *bozal,* meaning muzzle.

BOT FLY—lays eggs on leg hair of horses.

BOTTOM—endurance, stamina in a horse.

BREAK—gentling and training a horse to saddle or harness.

BREEZE—to give a horse a fast, short gallop.

BRIDLE—headpiece for horse, consisting of headstall, mouthpiece (bit), and reins.

BRIDLE HAND—the hand on the reins; the left hand in Western riding or polo or any riding that calls for some other use of the right hand.

BRIDLE WISE—when a horse becomes accustomed to and responsive to the bridle and bit.

BRIDOON—single headstall with snaffle bit.

BRIDOON HEAD—the separate headstall with the snaffle bit in a double bridle.

BROKEN WIND—indicated by heaving flanks; difficulty in breathing. Such horses are said to have the heaves and are called "windies." A horse run to the point of exhaustion can be ruined in this way.

BRONC—from broncho: a wild unbroken horse of the West; a bucking horse in a rodeo.

BROOMTAIL—mustangs or any feral horses after they deteriorated, so named because the heavy tails were matted with burrs.

BROW BAND—see TACK.

BRUSH TRACK—small-town local race tracks in the West. Sometimes called bush tracks.

BUCKEROO—the Western cowboy; the cowboy pronunciation of the Spanish word *vaquero,* meaning cowboy, since the Spanish-Mexican pronunciation of V is very close to that of B.

BUCKING STRAP (FLANK STRAP; POOP RIGGIN')—a leather strap fastened around the flank area of a horse in rodeo bronc-riding contests, to induce bucking. Often supposed a cruel device, but it is not painful to the horse. It is simply an unaccustomed thing in a touchy place. Many gentle horses will buck if touched in the flanks.

BULLDOGGING—the original name for the arena event in which the contestant, working against time, leaps from a running horse, grasps the steer (not bull) by the horns, and twists him down. It is now called steer wrestling.

BYERLY TURK—one of the famous trio of Oriental sires brought to England in the late seventeenth and early eighteenth centuries, to whom all race horses trace.

CALICO PONY—another name for a paint horse.

CALKS—the metal parts or lugs on the heels of horseshoes that project downward to prevent slipping.

CANNON BONES—tube-shaped bones that extend from the knee and the hock of a horse to the fetlock joint.

CANNONS (OF A BIT)—the mouthpiece of a bridle that rests on the bars of a horse's mouth. A jointed bit (snaffle) has two cannons.
CANTER—a natural three-beat gait, a slow gallop.
CANTLE—the rear part of the seat of a saddle that projects upward, opposite to the pommel.
CAPSULE (TO)—to impregnate a mare artificially.
CAQRH—Celebrated American Quarter Running Horse (for mare change last letter to M).
CAST—to cast a horse is to throw it down with ropes or hobbles. A horse who has gotten down, in a stall for instance, in such a way that he cannot get up is said to be cast.
CASTRATE—to remove the testicles of a horse by surgery; to geld.
CAT-HAMMED—a horse that is undeveloped in the quarters.
CAVESSON—the noseband with the English bridle; from Spanish word *cabezón,* meaning pigheaded, stubborn.
CAYUSE—Cayuse Indian pony; became widely used to designate any Western horse.
CHALLENGE CUP—one that must be competed for more than once.
CHAPS—pronounced "shaps"—contraction from Mexican word *chaparreras.*
CHESTNUT—the callosities or bony protuberances on the inside surfaces of horse's legs.
—see "COLOR" in Chapter 4.
CHIN (TO)—to place one's chin on a horse's withers to measure his height.
CHUKKER—one of the eight seven-and-a-half-minute periods in the game of polo.
CINCH—the band, leather or multistranded cotton, that goes under the horse's body to secure a Western saddle.
CLAIMING RACE—a race in which the losing horse can be claimed afterward for a previously stated price, while the winner must be auctioned off to the highest bidder.
CLEAN LEGS—those without long hairs from knees and hocks down to pasterns; without long fetlocks; without unsoundness or prominent blemishes.
COLD-BLOODS—horses of the draft horse strains (see HOT-BLOODS).
COLD JAW—a horse unresponsive to bit, one with a calloused or hard mouth.
COLLECTION—a state in which the horse with hind legs well under and neck flexed is influenced by the rider's aids to maintain gaits or change gaits, tempo, or direction with energetic but well controlled action.
COLT—male horse until four or five years old.
CONFORMATION—the general build of a horse; what is ideal for one breed may be unacceptable in another.
COOLER—light woolen or linen blanket used to cool out horse after strenuous exercise.
CORONET—the part of a horse's foot where the hair and flesh bulge out and join with the hoof wall.

CORRAL—a pen, usually round, for holding stock, breaking and training horses, branding calves, etc. A paddock differs in that it is usually smaller; any horse pen.

COUPLING—space between the last ribs and the loins of a horse; a short-coupled horse (most Quarter Horses are) is well muscled and rounded in this place.

COVER—when a stallion mounts and serves a mare, he is said to cover her.

COW KICK—a horse kicks forward and out like a cow.

COWPONY—a working cowhorse (has nothing to do with size).

COWPUNCHER—any cowboy, but the term came into use when cowboys traveled with trainloads of cattle and used long poles to punch up cattle that had gotten down in the stock cars.

CROP—short wooden whip stick for training, used by the English and Eastern U.S. riders for hunting, hacking, etc.; seldom used on spur-trained horses.

CROSS FIRE—when a hind foot overreaches and strikes the side of a forefoot; most common with pacers.

CROUP—rump of a horse from loins to root of tail; or the dock, as the bony root of the tail is called.

CROW HOP—to buck mildly in a direct line.

CUE—synonym for aid.

CURB—swelling at back of hock below the point.

CURB BIT—mouthpiece with extended cheek pieces or shanks and with a curb strap under the chin to give leverage.

CUT (TO)—to geld, to castrate.

CUTTING HORSE—horse that is trained to cut cattle out of a herd and to head them off so that they cannot return to it; and in ranch work to put them in a herd called the cut.

DALLY—to take a wrap of the rope around the horn.

DAM—mother parent of a foal (also used for dogs).

DARLEY ARABIAN—one of a famous trio of Oriental sires brought to England, to whom all race horses trace.

DERBY WEIGHT—126 pounds for colts, 121 pounds for fillies.

DOCK (TO)—to cut off the bone of a horse's tail several inches from the tip, a practice now outlawed. Also the bony part of a horse's tail.

DOGIE—a motherless calf (rhymes with bōgey).

DOUBLE BRIDLE—also called full bridle or Weymouth.

DRAFT BREEDS—horses bred for heavy work in harness. Cold bloods.

DRAG—riding drag is to bring up the rear of a herd.

DRAG HUNT—a strong-smelling lure, usually aniseed, is dragged across country as a substitute for a fox to be followed by hounds.

DRAW REIN—a running rein or sliding rein.

DRENCH—to give liquid medicine to a horse.

DRESSAGE—French term for classical high-school training of horses.

D-RINGS—the rings on the rigging of a stock saddle to which the latigo and the girth billets are attached.

DROP JUMP—a fence or other obstacle to be jumped which has the landing side lower than the take-off side.

DUMB JOCKEY—device used in training young horses and setting their heads.

DUN—tan coat color.

EARLY SPEED—to reach top speed quickly. Quick burn and early foot are other ways of saying it.

ENTIRE—an entire horse is one that is uncut, ungelded.

EQUITATION—the art of riding; horsemanship.

EXTENDED—increased tempo of gait, such as an extended trot.

FAN (TO)—swinging one's hat while riding a bucking horse. If the horse is actually hit with the hat, it is called dusting him.

FARRIER—a blacksmith who shoes horses; derives from the name of the Frenchman of the ninth century who shod the king's horses.

FAULT—to fault a horse—or anybody—is to point out his deficiencies.

FAULTS (IN JUMPING)—knockdowns, refusals, runouts, and, in some shows, ticks or touching of the rails, and in time classes, excessive delay.

FEATHER—long hair on fetlock—indication of cold blood.

FENDER—the shield on the stock saddle stirrup leather that protects pant legs from sweat and rubbing.

FILLY—female horse under four or five years of age.

FLEXION—arching the neck and drawing in the chin.

FLOAT (THE TEETH)—to file a horse's teeth.

FLY SHEET—summer horse blanket.

FOAL—colt or filly until weaned.

FOAL (IN)—mare that is pregnant.

FOAL (TO)—to give birth.

FOAL (WITH)—mare with foal at side.

FOREARM—the part of a horse's front leg from his elbow to knee.

FOREHAND—the part of the horse ahead of the rider.

FORWARD SEAT—originally called the Italian seat in England, where it has almost entirely superseded the traditional English seat. In America it had long been featured in cavalry training at Fort Riley, Kansas, and was given the name of the Fort Riley seat. With weight forward closer to the withers and with much of it in the stirrups, much strain is taken off the horse's back and kidney area.

FOX HUNTING—practiced in early Colonial America and later formalized in England, due in large part to the efforts of John Warde of Squerries, Kent, England (1752–1838).

FOX TROT—a broken gait in which the front feet walk while the back feet trot. With the rhythmic beat of the hoofs there is a slight nodding action of the head. A very comfortable gait to ride. Capable of five to eight miles per hour.

GLOSSARY 551

FURLONG—one-eighth of a mile—220 yards.
GAG BIT—bit with upward pull that draws the mouthpiece up into the corner of the horse's mouth. It is very severe.
GAITED HORSES—the field is dominated by the American Saddle Horse, although Tennessee Walking Horses are famous for their spectacular rack gait. Added to the walk, trot, and canter of the three-gaited horses are a slow gait (running walk or fox trot) and the rack, which distinguish the performance of the five-gaited horses. Three-gaited horses are shown with roached manes and tails clipped at top. Five-gaited horses are shown with full manes and tails.
GAITS—the paces of a horse. Natural gaits are those used by a horse at liberty. Artificial gaits are those cultivated by man.
GALICEÑO—(gal-i-ceen'-yo) a small, active, and enduring horse 12.2 to 13 hands high, that weighs 600 to 650 pounds. A direct descendant of the Spanish horse that was taken to Mexico in the sixteenth century. The Galiceño Horse Breeders Association was founded in 1962.
GALLOP—the natural running gait of a horse, in which the hind legs give the propusion as in a series of leaps. In effect the horse rolls over his front legs, which have little propulsive action except when in a climb.
GALWAYNE'S GROOVE—a groove near the gums of a horse's upper incisors which lengthens with age. It is about halfway down these teeth at the age of fifteen and reaches the bottom edge of them at age twenty. Thereafter the groove becomes less noticeable and at the age of thirty it disappears.
GELD (TO)—to castrate a horse, i.e., to remove the testicles by surgery.
GELDING—a castrated horse.
GET—the offspring of a stallion.
GIG—a two-wheeled, single-seated carriage; in Western slang means to spur, hook, or jab a horse.
GIRTH—the circumference of a horse's body just behind the elbows. Complementary expressions are: plenty of girth; deep through the heart, etc.
—the band of leather, webbing, or cord that goes under the horse's body to hold the saddle in place. The word girth generally applies to the flat saddle girth and the rear girth on a stock saddle, but not infrequently some Westerners and suppliers call the cinch a girth, whereas users of flat saddles never call a girth a cinch.
GLASS EYE—horse's eye that is lacking normal pigment, usually pale in color, often bluish instead of brown. Other terms used: walleye, cotton-eye, watch-eye, and mooneye.
GO-AROUND—in rodeo contests a go-around has been complete when all who have entered an event have performed.
GODOLPHIN ARABIAN or BARB—imported to England from Syria in 1728. One of the famous trio of Oriental sires to which all race horses trace.

GOOSE RUMP—horse rump that is narrow, steeply sloped, and with a low-sprung tail.

GRADE (HORSE)—unregistered horse.

GREEN HORSE—untrained horse.

GYMKHANA—horse games and contests (Anglo-East Indian).

HACK—riding stable horse. The word comes from the Spanish *jaca,* pronounced *haca,* or from the French word *hacquenée;* to hack is to ride moderate gaits, as in hunter hack.

HACKAMORE—a headstall with a rigid (woven rawhide) noseband or bosal. The word comes from the Spanish *jaquima.*

HACKAMORE BRIDLE—a refined hackamore with long side shanks to put leverage on the bosal; takes the place of a bitted bridle.

HAMS—the lower part of the rear quarters of a horse. Quarter Horses are consistently well muscled there.

HAND—a unit of measure, four inches, for the height of a horse. The measure is taken from the ground to the withers.

HANDS—good or light hands or heavy hands is a way of expressing how a rider handles the reins (thus the bit).

HAULING PAPER—official document provided to a horse owner by a livestock inspector which permits a horse to be moved from one state to another by motor vehicle.

HEADSTALL—the part of the bridle that fits over the horse's head, and to which the bit is attached.

HEAT (IN)—when a mare or bitch is biologically in condition to be bred. A mare is also said to be *horsing* when she is ready to be bred.

HEAT (OF A RACE)—a single course of a race that calls for more than one test of speed and endurance. The winner of such a race must win two out of three heats.

HIGH SCHOOL (*haute école*)—schooling that prepares horses for performing difficult movements called *airs*; which include *airs on the ground* such as double-tracking, Spanish walk, pirouettes, etc., seen in dressage and *airs above the ground,* such as the courbette, levade, croupade, ballotade, and capriole.

HINNEY—offspring of a horse and she-ass, whereas a mule is the offspring of a jack and a mare.

HOBBLES—straps or woven bands to be buckled or tied around a horse's forelegs to prevent him from straying.

HOBBLE (TO)—to tie so as to restrict, such as hobbling stirrups by tying them under a green horse's belly with a thong or cord to keep them from flopping when he is being trained with driving reins from the ground.

HOGGED MANE—clipped short—shorter than roached.

HOG-TIE—to tie a downed calf or steer—or even a hog—by three legs.

HONDA—the small loop at the end of a lariat through which the rope runs to form the noose.

HOODED STIRRUPS—see TAPADERO; leather guards to keep foot from going too far into stirrup; to protect boot from brush.

HOOLIHAN—a sudden overhead throw of the lariat loop, without preliminary swinging. Used in corrals to catch horses without overly exciting them.

HOPPLES—leg harness to prevent racing pacers from breaking from a lateral to a diagonal movement. Sometimes called Indiana pants.

HORSE—name of the species but specifically used for the stallion and generally used for geldings as well.

HOT-BLOODS (HORSES)—Arabs and Barbs (desert horses) and all horses that mainly derive from them, such as Thoroughbreds, Quarter Horses, Morgans, American Saddlebred, etc.

HUNTER—a horse able to jump obstacles while following hounds or in hunter show classes; sometimes registered Quarter Horses, and more often registered Thoroughbreds, but most at the present time are Thoroughbreds crossed on other stock.

HUNTING CROP—short whip with notched handle for opening gates; usually combined with long whip and lash for use with hounds.

INBREEDING—the breeding of closely related horses, i.e., father to daughter, mother to son, brother to sister.

INSEMINATE—to impregnate a mare artificially.

INTERNATIONAL ARABIAN HORSE—an association of owners and breeders of Arabian Horses, with a registry established in 1908.

JENNET—small riding horse of Spain.

JENNY—female ass.

JOG TROT—the Western term for a slow collected trot—not much faster than a walk, the more collected the more showy the gait.

JUMPER (OPEN)—any horse that can jump, as distinguished from a working or conformation hunter.

JUMPS—obstacles to be cleared; brush, timber (fences), rails, combinations, and banks.

LAP AND TAP—in early-day races between two horses, if they were lapped as they passed the starting line after a scored start, the starter tapped them off, perhaps with a cane on a fence rail, and shouted "go."

LAPPED—when one horse is less than a body length ahead of another in a race they are said to be lapped.

LATIGO—the strap that laces the cinch to the D-ring on the near side of a Western saddle.

LINE BREEDING—breeding of related horses, but not horses that are as closely related as in inbreeding.

LIPIZZANER—a breed of horses long used in the Spanish Riding School of Vienna. Born black, they turn white as they mature. They take their name from Lipizza, where the stud farm of Archduke Charles, son of Emperor Ferdinand I, was founded in 1580. They are descended, it is said, from the large horses developed at the stud farm of Kladrub in

Bohemia (the Kladruber) and a strain of smaller horses from the Trieste district, with infusions at various times of Arabian and Barb blood from Spain. Although all Lipizzaners were sold and dispersed in 1918, their breeding started afresh soon after, which resulted in horses of longer life and sounder legs and feet.

LIP TATTOO—identification letter and numbers tattooed inside the upper lips of all Thoroughbred race horses.

LONG HORSE or DISTANCE HORSE—one bred for racing distances of a mile or more (Thoroughbred) as distinct from SHORT HORSE, one bred for short races (Quarter Horse).

LOPE—a natural three-beat gait, the Western term for canter.

LUNGE LINE (or LONGE)—rope or rein twenty-five to thirty feet long attached to halter or training hackamore and used in conjunction with a long whip to exercise a horse by circling. Some use the derivative of the French word *allonge,* spelling it longe, and pronouncing it lunge.

MAIDEN CLASS—open to horses which have not won a blue (first place) ribbon at a recognized show in the division in which they are showing. This term also applies to riders in equitation classes who have not yet won a blue.

MANDIBLE—the lower jawbone.

MARE—female horse after the age of four or five, prior to which time she is called a filly.

MATCH RACE—a race matched between two horses.

MATURE—a horse with full mouth between five or six years old and ten years old.

MAVERICK—unbranded, unclaimed. In early-day Texas a rancher named Maverick had so many cattle on open range it was assumed if any calves were found unbranded they belonged to Maverick.

MILK TEETH—the two incisors in upper and lower jaw a colt is usually born with, and the other incisors that appear within a few weeks.

MORGAN—a light saddle horse breed whose stud book was established in 1894, that traces to one progenitor, "Justin Morgan, the Horse," who by ability, speed at the quarter mile, and endurance in harness, won fame in Vermont in the last years of the eighteenth century.

MUSTANG—feral horse of Spanish origin that roamed the Western plains. From Spanish word *mesteño,* meaning unclaimed.

NEAR SIDE—the left side of a horse, the side from which most riders mount a horse. Ropers mount from either side and Indians until recent years generally mounted from the off side or right side.

NICK—to nick well means that the blood genes of one parent join those of the other parent successfully to produce a promising foal.

NOVICE CLASS—open to horses or equitation riders who have not won three blues (firsts) in the class in which they are competing.

OFF SIDE—the right side of a horse.

OUTBREED or OUTCROSS—to breed horses to individuals from an unrelated or at least a distantly related family.

OVERO—a pinto with a dark primary color, with white or pale secondary colors.

PACE—a two-beat gait, natural with some horses, in which the lateral pair of legs moves in unison, causing the horse to be supported alternately on the right legs and then on the left legs. Developed in the U.S. first under saddle, later in harness.

PALOMINO—a golden tan or golden yellow horse with flaxen mane and tail, often used as a showy parade horse. Palomino breed Registry was founded in 1937.

PARROT MOUTH—badly formed horse mouth in which the upper lip droops noticeably below the lower lip.

PASO FINO—a small horse thirteen to fourteen hands high that weighs seven hundred to eight hundred pounds. This horse has a distinctive single-foot type of gait that is duplicated by no other breed of horses. Importations from Spanish America, its home of origin, began around 1960. There are now three active breed organizations in the U.S.

PELHAM BIT—a curb bit with ring attachments for a set of reins to be attached at the ends of the cannon and for another set of reins at the ends of the shanks.

PIEBALD—a black and white spotted horse.

PIGGIN' STRING—cowboy term for a small rope about five feet long with a noose in the end, used by ropers to tie the legs of a thrown calf or steer.

PINTO—a spotted varicolored horse, either overo or tobiano; general usage also includes piebald horses but never Appaloosa horses. There is a Pinto Horse Association of America, Inc., with headquarters in San Diego, California.

PIVOT—a movement in which the horse starts a spin but completes only about a fourth of a circle when he swings back to repeat the movement in the other direction. Before a judge in classes that call for it, the rider pivots his horse first to the left and then to the right.

POINTS—the leg, mane, and tail color of a horse when different from the body color, i.e., a bay with black points.

POLL—the top of a horse's head.

PONY OF THE AMERICAS—a breed of small horses founded in the early 1950s, resulting from the crossbreeding of Arabians, Quarter Horses, and Appaloosas, and more often than not resembling the latter. The maximum height is 13.2 hands, which is 2 inches less than the minimum height of the Appaloosa, which is 14 hands.

PRODUCE—the offspring of a mare.

RACING PLATE—a lightweight horseshoe, generally aluminum.

RACK—an artificial gait in which the side legs move together but not quite in unison since the hind feet hit the ground before the front feet do, making four distinct beats. It is the fast showy gait of the five-gaited American saddle horse.

REMUDA—the band of saddle horses on a ranch, specifically when they are taken in a herd on a roundup.

RIDGELING—male horse improperly castrated, in which one testicle never descended. One with malformed genitals. Usually such a horse has the horsing characteristics of a stallion but is impotent or sterile, or both. Called a rig in England.

ROACHED—mane clipped short—once meant mane long enough to stand erect.

ROAN—horse color—caused by intermingling of white and red hairs.

RODEO—ro-day'-o—a contest and performance show of ranch skills. From Spanish word meaning roundup.

ROLL BACK or ROLL OVER THE HOCKS—an action in which the horse stops suddenly and reverses direction. The propulsion for the spin is given with the forelegs as the weight rolls over the hocks, which are well under. If continued for the full circle it would be a spin.

ROMAL—California whip or lash attached to rein ends.

ROUNDUP—a gathering, a bringing together, as of horses and cattle.

RUNNING-WALK—a cultivated half walk, half trot, overstepping four cornered slow gait similar to a fox trot.

SCORED START—in which horses are given a running start up to the actual strating line and are clocked from the instant they cross over it.

SERVICE FEE—fee paid to owner of stallion by owner of mare being bred.

SETTLE (A MARE)—when a mare is definitely pregnant she is said to be settled.

SHORT HORSE—a horse bred for short races—a Quarter Horse.

SINGLE-FOOT—an artificial four-beat gait, a slow version of the rack, in which the lateral legs move together but with the hind foot hitting the ground soonest, thus each single foot hits the ground separately, accounting for the four beats and for its name. Very comfortable to ride.

SNAFFLE (BIT)—a jointed bit.

SORREL—reddish or copper red. Mane and tail usually same color as body, but may be flaxen.

SPANCELED—Irish word for hind legs that are hobbled.

SPECULUM—metal device to keep horse's mouth open while teeth are being floated (filed).

SPIN—term used by Western horsemen for the action in which the horse rapidly circles in place. The front feet give the whirling propulsion while the hind feet, well under to take the weight, move only enough to allow for the spin.

SPRINTER—a short horse, one bred for short races—a Quarter Horse.

STALE—to go sour; to be bored.

STALE (TO)—for a horse to urinate.

STAYER—a horse with endurance, a distance horse.

STALLION—male horse, a stud; an entire horse not castrated.

STEEPLECHASE—a race over country with various obstacles to jump. Originated with Irish and English race contestants in mid to latter part of eighteenth century. Races were run from steeple to steeple, that is, from one visible point to another, which accounts for its name and for point-to-point races. Though steeplechases are now set courses within a given area, the latter for hunters are run cross-country.

STONE—English measure of weight, equals fourteen pounds.

STONE HORSE—Old English term for stallion.

STRETCH—for a horse to stand with his forelegs forward and his hind legs far back. Called a pose or a spread. The English use the word camp. Now a formalized pose for show, but it originated with a practical purpose of putting a harness horse in such an uncollected position that he could not move out quickly while someone was entering or descending from a carriage.

STRING—a number of cowhorses assigned to one man. Or polo horses owned or assigned to one player.

SUNDAY HORSE—a comfortably gaited, well-mannered saddle horse.

SUNFISH—twisting, sideways contortion of a bucking horse, changing direction at each jump.

SURCINGLE—any band that goes around horse's girth.

TACK—saddles, bridles, and other horse equipment; includes the rider's equipment also.

TAPADERO—leather guard over front of stirrup to protect rider's boot from brush and weather; to prevent foot from going too far into stirrup, and for ornamentation.

TENNESSEE WALKING HORSE—originally called the plantation horse and noted for its comfortable single-foot gait, which was later perfected into a spectacular rack gait with which it can attain almost the speed of a pacer. The stud book was opened in 1935.

THOROUGHBRED—the name of a breed of horses, not to be confused with purebred. The Thoroughbred breed was established in England in 1823, and the first American Registry for the breed in 1827. The New York Jockey Club purchased the Sanders D. Bruce stud book and consolidated its data with other listings, becoming the proprietor of the official stud book of the Thoroughbreds in 1894. It is called the *American Stud Book*. Foundation sires were the *Byerly Turk,* imported to England in 1689; the *Darley Arabian,* imported to England in 1705 or 1706; the the *Godolphin Arabian or Barb,* imported to England in 1730. All recognized breeds of race horses in the world trace to these three stallions.

THROTTLE—the part of a horse's throat or gullet that is encircled by the throat latch of the bridle.

TOBIANO—a paint horse whose primary color is white with splotches of secondary color. All four legs have some white. The head is entirely dark but may be marked with a star, blaze, or stripe.

TOP LINE—contour of a horse's back; the top line of a genealogy bracket on which the sire's name appears. The dam's name is on the bottom line.

TOPS—black calf English boots with brown leather cuffs at top to keep white breeches from soiling.

TOUT—to gather crowds so betting could flourish, touts carried tin horns on which they tooted. First called "toots" then "touts." From them comes the expression of "tinhorn gambler."

TROT—a natural two-beat gait in which the legs move from one diagonal to the other. The left front foot and the right hind foot leave the ground just before the right front foot and the left hind foot hit the ground. The extended trot can attain speeds comparable to the gallop.

TWITCH—a device consisting of a handle with a cord loop in the end. The loop is put over the upper lip of a horse and twisted tight to keep the horse quiet and under control while being doctored. The pressure so affects the nerves of the lip or so distracts the horse that he stands quietly.

USING HORSE—a horse that is ridden for pleasure or for practical purposes, not solely for showing in the ring.

WALK—a natural four-beat gait in which each pair of diagonal feet alternate in leaving the ground. As with any gait it should be developed into a brisk smart action (see Chapter 11).

WALLEYE—see GLASS EYE.

WEANLING—a recently weaned foal.

WEYMOUTH—a double bridle; one with snaffle bit, the other with a low port curb bit. A third set of cheek leathers supports a cavesson (noseband).

WINDY—a windy is a wind-broken, roaring, wheezing, or whistling horse.

WINGS—wooden rails or hedges set at an angle on sides of jump to prevent horse from running out and by-passing a jump.

WRANGLER—horse herder—tender of the remuda—guest-ranch worker who looks after dude riders.

YEARLING—a colt or filly more than one year and less than two years old.

ZEBRA DUN—dun horse that is line-backed and with horizontal black stripes on forearms.

ZENATA—most prominent of the Moorish horsemen who invaded Spain in A.D. 711. From their name come: *jennet,* a small, well-trained saddle horse of Spain; *à la gineta,* which means to ride in the manner of the Zenata, with higher saddle and with shorter stirrups.